"An **absorbing** drama.... Keefe's narrative is an architectural feat."
—*The New York Times*

"**Fierce** reporting. ... An **exceptional** new book ... explores this brittle landscape [of Northern Ireland] to **devastating** effect."
—*The Wall Street Journal*

"Keefe is an **obsessive** reporter and researcher, a master of narrative nonfiction."
—*Rolling Stone*

Entertainment Weekly

"Extraordinary.... A **masterful** history of the Troubles."
—Maureen Corrigan, NPR

"*Say Nothing* **powerfully documents** a society benumbed by trauma attempting to reckon with the abyss that engulfed it."
—*Los Angeles Times*

NATIONAL BESTSELLER

Praise for Patrick Radden Keefe's

SAY NOTHING

One of Barack Obama's Favorite Books of the Year

"A fast-paced, gripping history that never leaves context behind.... This book is a harrowing but fascinating examination of history in Northern Ireland, revealing and accessible for novice and expert alike."

—*The Christian Science Monitor*

"A fresh accounting of the moral balance sheet not just for those killed but for those who did the killing.... As a cautionary tale, *Say Nothing* speaks volumes—about the zealotry of youth, the long-term consequences of violence and the politics of forgetting."

—*The Washington Post*

"A riveting account of the bombings and assassinations carried out by the Irish Republican Army, as told by those who planted the bombs and pulled the triggers."

—*Minneapolis Star Tribune*

"As the narrator of a whodunit... [Keefe] excels, exposing the past, layer by layer, like the slow peel of a rotten onion, as he works to answer a question that the British government, the Northern Irish police and the McConville family have been seeking the answer to for nearly fifty years.... Keefe draws the characters in this drama finely and colorfully." —Paddy Hirsch, NPR

"Patrick Radden Keefe's great achievement is to tell Northern Ireland's fifty years of conflict through personal stories—a gripping and profoundly human explanation for a past that still denies and defines the future.... I can't praise this book enough: it's erudite, accessible, compelling, enlightening."

—Melanie Reid, *The Times* (London)

"Vivid, sophisticated.... Keefe shows an exemplary fairness."   —*The Times Literary Supplement* (London)

"Keefe is forensic in his writing and research.... Narrative nonfiction journalism ... at its best."

—*The Irish Times*

"Gripping.... For those who care to know more about the Troubles, this is an enlightening read."

—*The Post and Courier* (Charleston, SC)

"Breathtaking in its scope and ambition.... Keefe has produced a searing examination of the nature of truth in war and the toll taken by violence and deceit.... Will take its place alongside the best of the books about the Troubles."   —Toby Harnden, *The Sunday Times*

"*Say Nothing* is a harrowing but absorbing account of the murder of Jean McConville by the IRA in 1972, and of its intricate aftermath.... Meticulously researched and finely written."   —John Banville, *Irish Independent*

"Keefe's sweeping, switchblade-sharp narrative explores the terror and abiding grief at the heart of sectarian violence. To his credit, Keefe doesn't attempt a traditional history of Ireland's woes. Instead, in *Say Nothing* he has produced a nonfiction masterpiece."

—*Los Angeles Review of Books*

"Keefe is accomplished at unraveling old crimes,... *Say Nothing* is about how conflicts end, and who can end them." —*The Atlantic*

"Assiduous journalism.... Northern Ireland remains a laboratory of protracted communal violence, relevant to conflicts on any scale.... Keefe's fine, searching book shows that a political agreement formally resolving a conflict marks only the beginning of a long, agonizing, and fitful process of reconciliation." —*Foreign Affairs*

"Meticulously reported, exquisitely written, and grippingly told, *Say Nothing* is a work of revelation. Keefe not only peels back, layer by layer, the truth behind one of the most important and mysterious crimes of a terrible conflict; he also excavates the history of the Troubles and illuminates its repercussions to this day."

—David Grann, *New York Times* bestselling author of *Killers of the Flower Moon*

"A shattering, intimate study of how young men and women consumed by radical political violence are transformed by the history they make and struggle to come to terms with the blood they have shed, *Say Nothing* is a powerful reckoning. Keefe has written an essential book." —Philip Gourevitch, author of the National Book Critics Circle Award winner *We Wish to Inform You That Tomorrow We Will Be Killed with Our Families* and *The Ballad of Abu Ghraib*

"Smart, searching, and utterly absorbing, *Say Nothing* sweeps us into the heart of one of the modern world's bitterest conflicts and, with unusual compassion, walks us back out again along the road to reconciliation. This is more than a powerful, superbly reported work of journalism. It is contemporary history at its finest."

—Maya Jasanoff, author of the
National Book Critics Circle Award winner
Liberty's Exiles and *The Dawn Watch*

"Patrick Radden Keefe uses the old Irish phrase 'Whatever you say, say nothing' to suggest and to say just about everything. Keefe's great accomplishment is to capture the tragedy of the Troubles on a human scale. By tracing the intersecting lives of a handful of unforgettable characters, he has created a deeply honest and intimate portrait of a society still haunted by its own violent past. *Say Nothing* is a bracing, empathetic, heart-rending work of storytelling."

—Colum McCann, *New York Times*
bestselling author of *TransAtlantic* and *Let the Great World Spin*, winner of the National Book Award

"Patrick Radden Keefe's gripping account of the Troubles is equal parts true crime, history, and tragedy. Keefe's incisive reporting reveals the hidden costs of the Troubles, illuminating both the terrible toll of the conflict and how it continues to reverberate today. A must-read." —Gillian Flynn, *New York Times*
bestselling author of *Gone Girl*

OTHER BOOKS BY PATRICK RADDEN KEEFE

Chatter: Dispatches from the Secret World of Global Eavesdropping

The Snakehead: An Epic Tale of the Chinatown Underworld and the American Dream

PATRICK RADDEN KEEFE

SAY NOTHING

Patrick Radden Keefe is a staff writer at *The New Yorker* and the author of *The Snakehead* and *Chatter*. His work has been recognized with a Guggenheim Fellowship, the National Magazine Award for Feature Writing, the Arthur Ross Book Award from the Council on Foreign Relations, and the Orwell Prize for Political Writing. He is also the creator and host of the eight-part podcast *Wind of Change*.

www.patrickraddenkeefe.com

SAY NOTHING

A TRUE STORY
OF MURDER AND MEMORY
IN NORTHERN IRELAND

PATRICK RADDEN KEEFE

ANCHOR BOOKS

A DIVISION OF PENGUIN RANDOM HOUSE LLC

NEW YORK

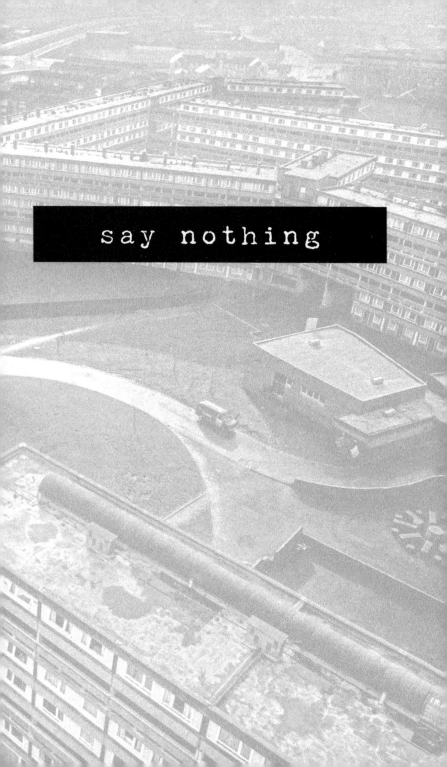

say nothing

FIRST ANCHOR BOOKS EDITION, FEBRUARY 2020

Copyright © 2019 by Patrick Radden Keefe

All rights reserved. Published in the United States by Anchor Books,
a division of Penguin Random House LLC, New York, and distributed
in Canada by Penguin Random House Canada Limited, Toronto.
Originally published in hardcover in the United States by Doubleday,
a division of Penguin Random House LLC, New York, in 2019.

Anchor Books and colophon are registered trademarks of Penguin Random
House LLC.

The Library of Congress has cataloged the Doubleday edition as follows:
Name: Keefe, Patrick Radden, 1976– author.
Title: Say nothing : a true story of murder and memory in Northern Ireland /
    Patrick Radden Keefe.
Description: New York : Doubleday, 2019.
Identifiers: LCCN 2018031745
Subjects: LCSH: McConville, Jean. | Irish Republican Army. | Abduction—
    Northern Ireland—History. | Murder—Northern Ireland—History. |
    BISAC: TRUE CRIME / Murder / General. | HISTORY / Europe /
    Ireland.
Classification: LCC HV6574.G7 K44 2019 | DDC 364.152/3092—dc23
LC record available at https://lccn.loc.gov/2018031745

Anchor Books Trade Paperback ISBN: 978-0-307-27928-6
eBook ISBN: 978-0-385-54337-8

Author photograph © Phillip Montgomery
Book design by Maria Carella

www.anchorbooks.com

Printed in the United States of America
20 19

TO LUCIAN AND FELIX

All wars are fought twice, the first time on the battlefield, the second time in memory.

—VIET THANH NGUYEN

CONTENTS

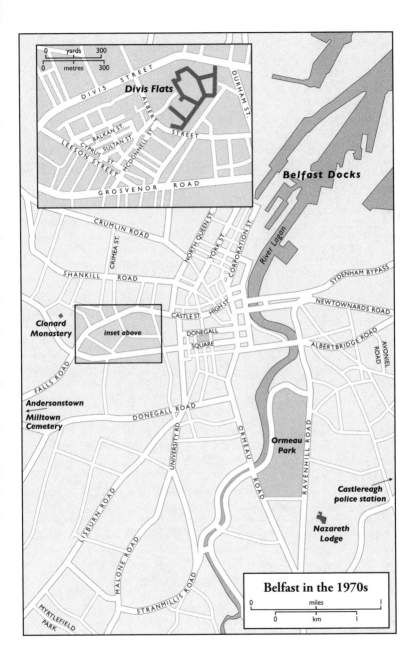

DIVIS STREET

Divis Flats

ALBERT STREET

DURHAM ST.

BALKAN ST.

CYPRUS ST.

SULTAN ST.

LEESON STREET

McDONNELL ST.

GROSVENOR ROAD

Belfast Docks

CRUMLIN ROAD

CRIMEA ST.

NORTH QUEEN ST.

YORK ST.

CORPORATION ST.

River Lagan

SYDENHAM BYPASS

SHANKILL ROAD

NEWTOWNARDS ROAD

Clonard Monastery

inset above

CASTLE ST.

HIGH ST.

DONEGALL SQUARE

ALBERTBRIDGE ROAD

AVONIEL ROAD

FALLS ROAD

Andersonstown

Milltown Cemetery

DONEGALL ROAD

UNIVERSITY RD.

ORMEAU ROAD

Ormeau Park

RAVENHILL ROAD

Castlereagh police station

LISBURN ROAD

MALONE ROAD

STRANMILLIS ROAD

Nazareth Lodge

Belfast in the 1970s

MYRTLEFIELD PARK

0 miles 1

0 km 1

SAY NOTHING

THE TREASURE ROOM

JULY 2013

THE JOHN J. BURNS LIBRARY occupies a grand neo-Gothic building on the leafy campus of Boston College. With its stone spires and stained glass, it looks very much like a church. The Jesuits who founded the university in 1863 did so to educate the children of poor immigrants who had fled the potato famine in Ireland. As Boston College grew and flourished over the next century and a half, it maintained close ties to the old country. With 250,000 volumes and some sixteen million manuscripts, the Burns Library holds the most comprehensive collection of Irish political and cultural artifacts in the United States. One of its librarians, years ago, was sent to prison after he was caught trying to sell to Sotheby's a tract by Saint Thomas Aquinas that was printed in 1480. The library developed such a reputation for purchasing valuable antiquities that a subsequent director once had to call the FBI himself, when an Irish grave robber tried to sell him looted tombstones bearing ancient Latin crosses and intricate rings and inscriptions.

The rarest and most valuable objects in the Burns Library are kept in a special enclosure known as the Treasure Room. It is a secure space, exactingly climate-controlled and outfitted with a state-of-the-art fire suppressant system. The room is monitored by surveillance cameras and can be accessed only by entering a code on an electronic pad and turning a special key.

The key must be signed out. Only a select handful of people can do so.

One summer day in 2013, two detectives strode into the Burns Library. They were not Boston detectives. In fact, they had just flown into the country from Belfast, where they worked for the Serious Crime Branch of the Police Service of Northern Ireland. Passing beneath colorful stained glass windows, they approached the Treasure Room.

The detectives had come to collect a series of secret files that for nearly a decade had been stored in the Treasure Room. There were MiniDiscs containing audio recordings, as well as a series of transcripts. The librarians at Boston College might have saved the detectives a trip by just sending the files to Belfast in the mail. But these recordings contained sensitive and dangerous secrets, and when they took possession of the material, the detectives handled it with the utmost care. The recordings were now officially evidence in a criminal proceeding. The detectives were investigating a murder.

book one

THE CLEAR, CLEAN, SHEER THING

AN ABDUCTION

JEAN McCONVILLE WAS THIRTY-EIGHT when she disappeared, and she had spent nearly half her life either pregnant or recovering from childbirth. She brought fourteen children to term and lost four of them, leaving her with ten kids who ranged in age from Anne, who was twenty, to Billy and Jim, the sweet-eyed twins, who were six. To bear ten children, much less care for them, would seem like an impossible feat of endurance. But this was Belfast in 1972, where immense, unruly families were the norm, so Jean McConville wasn't looking for any prizes, and she didn't get any.

Instead, life dealt her an additional test when her husband, Arthur, died. After a grueling illness, he was suddenly gone and she was left alone, a widow with a meager pension but no paying job of her own and all of those children to look after. Demoralized by the magnitude of her predicament, she struggled to maintain an even emotional keel. She stayed at home mostly, leaning on the older kids to wrangle the younger ones, steadying herself, as if from vertigo, with one cigarette after another. Jean reckoned with her misfortune and endeavored to make plans for the future. But the real tragedy of the McConville clan had just begun.

The family had recently moved out of the apartment where Arthur spent his final days and into a slightly larger dwelling in Divis Flats, a dank and hulking public housing complex in West Belfast. It was a cold December and the city was engulfed in darkness by the end of the afternoon. The stove in the new apartment was not hooked up yet, so Jean sent her daughter Helen, who was fifteen, to a local takeaway restaurant for a bag of fish and chips. While the rest of the family waited for Helen, Jean drew a hot bath. When you have young children, sometimes the only place you can find a moment of privacy is behind a locked bathroom door. Jean was small and pale, with delicate features and dark hair that she wore pulled back from her face. She slipped into the water and stayed there. She had just gotten out of the bath, her skin flushed, when somebody knocked on the front door. It was about 7:00. The children assumed it must be Helen with their dinner.

But when they opened the door, a gang of people burst inside. It happened so abruptly that none of the McConville children could say precisely how many there were—it was roughly eight people, but it could have been ten or twelve. There were men and women. Some had balaclavas pulled across their faces; others wore nylon stockings over their heads, which twisted their features into ghoulish masks. At least one of them was carrying a gun.

As Jean emerged, pulling on her clothes, surrounded by her frightened children, one of the men said, gruffly, "Put your coat on." She trembled violently as the intruders tried to pull her out of the apartment. "What's happening?" she asked, her panic rising. That was when the children went berserk. Michael, who was eleven, tried to grab his mother. Billy and Jim threw their arms around her and wailed. The gang tried to calm the children, saying that they would bring Jean back—they just needed to talk to her; she would be gone for only a few hours.

Archie, who, at sixteen, was the oldest child at home, asked if he could accompany his mother wherever she was going, and the members of the gang agreed. Jean McConville put on a tweed overcoat and a head scarf as the younger children were herded into one of the bedrooms. While they were ushering the children away, the intruders spoke to them, offering blunt assurances—and addressing them by name. A couple of the men were not wearing masks, and Michael McConville realized, to his horror, that the people taking his mother away were not strangers. They were his neighbors.

Divis Flats was a nightmare from an Escher drawing, a concrete warren of stairways, passages, and overcrowded apartments. The elevators were perpetually out of order, and Jean McConville was borne by the rough little scrum out of her flat, through a corridor, and down a set of stairs. Normally there were people about at night, even in the wintertime—kids kicking a ball through the hallway or laborers coming home from work. But Archie noticed that the complex seemed eerily vacant, almost as if the area had been cleared. There was nobody to flag down, no neighbor who could sound the alarm.

He kept close to his mother, shuffling along, and she clung to him, not wanting to let go. But at the bottom of the stairs, a larger group was waiting, as many as twenty people, casually dressed and masked with balaclavas. Several of them had guns. A blue Volkswagen van sat idling at the curb, and now suddenly one of the men wheeled on Archie, the dull glint of a pistol arcing through the darkness, and pressed the tip of the barrel into his cheek, hissing, "Fuck off." Archie froze. He could feel the cold metal pressing into his skin. He was desperate to protect his mother, but what could he do? He was a boy, outnumbered and unarmed. Reluctantly, he turned and ascended the stairs.

On the second level, one of the walls was perforated by a series of vertical slats, which the McConville children called "pigeon holes." Peering through these openings, Archie watched as his mother was bundled into the van and the van drove out of Divis and disappeared. It would later strike him that the gang never had any intention of allowing him to chaperone his mother—they were simply using him to get Jean out of the flat. He stood there in the awful, wintry silence, trying to comprehend what had just happened and what he should do now. Then he started back toward the flat. The last words that his mother had said to him were "Watch the children until I come back."

ALBERT'S DAUGHTERS

WHEN DOLOURS PRICE WAS a little girl, her favored saints were martyrs. Dolours had one very Catholic aunt on her father's side who would say, "For God and Ireland." For the rest of the family, Ireland came first. Growing up in West Belfast in the 1950s, she dutifully went to church every day. But she noticed that her parents didn't. One day, when she was about fourteen, she announced, "I'm not going back to Mass."

"You have to go," her mother, Chrissie, said.

"I don't, and I'm not going," Dolours said.

"You have to go," Chrissie repeated.

"Look," Dolours said. "I'll go out the door, I'll stand at the corner for half an hour and say to you, 'I've been to Mass.' But I *won't* have been to Mass."

She was headstrong, even as a child, so that was the end of that. The Prices lived in a small, semidetached council house on a tidy, sloping street in Andersonstown called Slievegallion Drive. Her father, Albert, was an upholsterer; he made the chairs that occupied the cramped front room. But where another clan might adorn the mantelpiece with happy photos from family holidays, the Prices displayed, with great pride, snapshots taken in prisons. Albert and Chrissie Price shared a fierce commitment to the cause of Irish republicanism: the belief that for hundreds of years the British had been an occupying force on the island of Ireland—and that the Irish had a duty to expel them by any means necessary.

When Dolours was little, she would sit on Albert's lap and he would tell her stories about joining the Irish Republican Army when he was still a boy, in the 1930s, and about how he had gone off to England as a teenager to carry out a bombing raid. With cardboard in his shoes because he couldn't afford to patch the soles, he had dared to challenge the mighty British Empire.

A small man with wire-framed glasses and fingertips stained yellow by tobacco, Albert told violent tales about the fabled valor of long-dead patriots. Dolours had two other siblings, Damian and Clare, but she was closest with her younger sister, Marian. Before bedtime, their father liked to regale them with the story of the time he escaped from a jail in the city of Derry, along with twenty other prisoners, after digging a tunnel that led right out of the facility. One inmate played the bagpipes to cover the sound of the escape.

In confiding tones, Albert would lecture Dolours and her siblings about the safest method for mixing improvised explosives, with a wooden bowl and wooden utensils—never metal!—because "a single spark and you were gone." He liked to reminisce about beloved comrades whom the British had hanged, and Dolours grew up thinking that this was the most natural thing in the world: that every child had parents who had friends who'd been hanged. Her father's stories were so rousing that she shivered sometimes when she listened to them, her whole body tingling with goose bumps.

Everyone in the family, more or less, had been to prison. Chrissie's mother, Granny Dolan, had been a member of the IRA Women's Council, the Cumann na mBan, and had once served three months in Armagh jail for attempting to relieve a police officer from the Royal Ulster Constabulary of his service weapon. Chrissie had also served in the Cumann and done a stretch in Armagh, along with three of her sisters, after they were arrested for wearing a "banned emblem": little paper flowers of orange, white, and green, known as Easter lilies.

In the Price family—as in Northern Ireland in general—people had a tendency to talk about calamities from the bygone past as though they had happened just last week. As a consequence, it could be difficult to pinpoint where the story of the ancient quarrel between Britain and Ireland first began. Really, it was hard to imagine Ireland *before* what the Prices referred to simply as "the cause." It almost didn't matter where you started the story: it was always there. It predated the distinction between Protestant and Catholic; it was older than the Protestant church. You could go back nearly a thousand years, in fact, to the Norman raiders of the twelfth century, who crossed the Irish Sea on ships in search of new lands to conquer. Or to Henry VIII and the Tudor rulers of the sixteenth century, who asserted England's total subjugation of Ireland. Or to the Protestant emigrants from Scotland and the North of England who filtered into Ireland over the course of the seventeenth century and established a plantation system in which the Gaelic-speaking natives became tenants and vassals on land that had previously been their own.

But the chapter in this saga that loomed largest in the house on Slievegallion Drive was the Easter Rising of 1916, in which a clutch of Irish revolutionaries seized the post office in Dublin and declared the establishment of a free and independent Irish Republic. Dolours grew up hearing legends about the dashing heroes of the rising, and about the sensitive poet who was one of the leaders of the rebellion, Patrick Pearse. "In every generation, the Irish people have asserted their right to national freedom," Pearse declared on the post office steps.

Pearse was an inveterate romantic who was deeply attracted to the ideal of blood sacrifice. Even as a child, he had fantasies of pledging his life for something, and he came to believe that bloodshed was a "cleansing" thing. Pearse praised the Christlike deaths of previous Irish martyrs and wrote, a few years before the rising, that "the old heart of the earth needed to be warmed with the red wine of the battlefield."

He got his wish. After a brief moment of glory, the rebellion was mercilessly quashed by British authorities in Dublin, and Pearse was court-martialed and executed by a firing squad, along with fourteen of his comrades. After the Irish War of Independence led to the partition of Ireland, in 1921, the island was split in two: in the South, twenty-six counties achieved a measure of independence as the Irish Free State, while in the North, a remaining six counties continued to be ruled by Great Britain. Like other staunch republicans, the Price family did not refer to the place where they happened to reside as "Northern Ireland." Instead it was "the North of Ireland." In the fraught local vernacular, even proper nouns could be political.

A cult of martyrdom can be a dangerous thing, and in Northern Ireland, rituals of commemoration were strictly regulated under the Flags and Emblems Act. The fear of Irish nationalism was so pronounced that you could go to jail in the North just for displaying the tricolor flag of the Republic. As a girl, Dolours donned her best white frock for Easter Sunday, a basket full of eggs under her arm and, pinned to her chest, an Easter lily, to commemorate the botched rebellion. It was an intoxicating ritual for a child, like joining a league of secret outlaws. She learned to cover the lily with her hand when she saw a policeman coming.

She was under no illusions, however, about the personal toll that devotion to the cause could extract. Albert Price never met his first child, an older daughter who died in infancy while he was behind bars. Dolours had an aunt, Bridie, one of Chrissie's sisters, who had taken part in the struggle in her youth. On one occasion in 1938, Bridie had been helping to move a cache of explosives when it suddenly detonated. The blast shredded both of Bridie's hands to the wrist, while disfiguring her face and blinding her permanently. She was twenty-seven when it happened.

Against the projections of her doctors, Aunt Bridie survived. But because she was so incapacitated, she would require care for the rest of her life. With no hands or eyes, she couldn't change her clothes or blow her nose or do much else for herself without assistance. Bridie often stayed for stretches in the house on Slievegallion Drive. If the Price family felt pity for her, it was secondary to a sense of admiration for her willingness to offer up everything for an ideal. Bridie came home from the hospital to a tiny house with an outside toilet, no social worker, no pension—just a life of blindness. Yet she never expressed any regret for having made such a sacrifice in the name of a united Ireland.

When Dolours and Marian were little, Chrissie would send them upstairs with instructions to "talk to your aunt Bridie." The woman would be stationed in a bedroom, alone in the gloom. Dolours liked to tiptoe as she ascended the stairs, but Bridie's hearing was extra sharp, so she always heard you coming. She was a chain-smoker, and from the age of eight or nine, Dolours was given the job of lighting Bridie's cigarettes, gently inserting them between her lips. Dolours hated this responsibility. She found it revolting. She would stare at her aunt, scrutinizing her face more closely than you might with someone who could see you doing it, taking in the full horror of what had happened to her. Dolours was a loquacious kid, with a child's manner of blurting whatever came into her head. Sometimes she would ask Bridie, "Do you not wish you'd just died?"

Taking her aunt's stumpy wrists into her own small hands, Dolours stroked the waxen skin. They reminded her, she liked to say, of "a pussycat's paws." Bridie wore dark glasses, and Dolours once watched a tear descend from behind the glass and creep down her withered cheek. And Dolours wondered: How can you cry if you have no eyes?

. . .

On the cold, clear morning of January 1, 1969, a band of student protesters assembled outside City Hall in Donegall Square, in the center of Belfast. Their plan was to walk from Belfast to the walled city of Derry, some seventy miles away, a march that would take them several days. They were protesting systemic discrimination against Catholics in Northern Ireland. Partition had created a perverse situation in which two religious communities, which for centuries had felt a degree of tension, each came to feel like an embattled minority: Protestants, who formed a majority of the population in Northern Ireland but a minority on the island as a whole, feared being subsumed by Catholic Ireland; Catholics, who represented a majority on the island but a minority in Northern Ireland, felt that they were discriminated against in the six counties.

Northern Ireland was home to a million Protestants and half a million Catholics, and it was true that the Catholics faced extraordinary discrimination: often excluded from good jobs and housing, they were also denied the kind of political power that might enable them to better their conditions. Northern Ireland had its own devolved political system, based at Stormont, on the outskirts of Belfast. For half a century, no Catholic had ever held executive office.

Excluded from the shipbuilding industry and other attractive professions, Catholics often simply left, emigrating to England or America or Australia, in search of work they couldn't find at home. The Catholic birth rate in Northern Ireland was approximately double the Protestant birth rate—yet during the three decades prior to the march on Derry, the Catholic population had remained virtually static, because so many people had no choice but to leave.

Perceiving, in Northern Ireland, a caste system akin to the racial discrimination in the United States, the young marchers had chosen to model themselves explicitly on the American civil rights movement. They had studied the 1965 march by Dr. Martin Luther King and other civil rights leaders from Selma to Montgomery, Alabama. As they trudged out of Belfast, bundled in duffel coats, daisy-chained arm in arm, they held placards that read CIVIL RIGHTS MARCH, and sang "We Shall Overcome."

One of the marchers was Dolours Price, who had joined the protest along with her sister, Marian. At eighteen, Dolours was younger than most of the other marchers, many of whom were at university. She had grown up to be an arrestingly beautiful young woman, with dark-red hair, flashing blue-green eyes, and pale lashes. Marian was a few years younger, but the sisters were inseparable. Around Andersonstown, everyone knew them as "Albert's daughters." They were so close, and so often together, that they could seem like twins. They called each other "Dotes" and "Mar," and had grown up sharing not just a bedroom but a bed. Dolours had a big, assertive personality and a sly irreverence, and the sisters plodded through the march absorbed in a stream of lively chatter, their angular Belfast accents beveled, slightly, by their education at St. Dominic's, a rigorous Catholic high school for girls in West Belfast, their repartee punctuated by peals of laughter.

Dolours would later describe her own childhood as an "indoctrination." But she was always fiercely independent-minded, and she was never much good at keeping her convictions to herself. As a teenager, she had started to question some of the dogma upon which she had been raised. It was the 1960s, and the nuns at St. Dominic's could do only so much to keep the cultural tides that were roiling the world at bay. Dolours liked rock 'n' roll. Like a lot of young people in Belfast, she was also inspired by Che Guevara, the photogenic Argentine revolutionary who fought alongside Fidel Castro. That Che was shot to death by the Bolivian military (his hands severed, like Aunt Bri-

Dolours and Marian Price.

die's, as proof of death) could only help to situate him in her menagerie of revolutionary heroes.

But even as tensions sharpened between Catholics and Protestants in Northern Ireland, Dolours had come to believe that the armed struggle her parents championed might be an outdated solution, a relic of the past. Albert Price was an emphatic conversationalist, a lively talker who would wrap his arm around your shoulders, tending his everpresent cigarette with the other hand, and regale you with history, anecdote, and charm until he had brought you around to his way of seeing things. But Dolours was an unabashed debater. "Hey, look at the IRA," she would say to her father. "You tried that and you lost!"

It was true that the history of the IRA was in some ways a history of failure: just as Patrick Pearse had said, every generation staged a revolt of one sort or another, but by the late 1960s, the IRA was largely dormant. Old men would still get together for weekend training camps south of the border in the Republic, doing target practice with antique guns left over from earlier campaigns. But nobody took them very seriously as a fighting force. The island was still divided. Conditions had not improved for Catholics. "You failed," Dolours told her father, adding, "There *is* another way."

Dolours had started attending meetings of a new political group, People's Democracy, in a hall on the campus of Queen's

University. Like Che Guevara, and many of her fellow march-ers, Dolours subscribed to some version of socialism. The whole sectarian schism between Protestants and Catholics was a poi-sonous distraction, she had come to believe: working-class Prot-estants may have enjoyed some advantages, but they, too, often struggled with unemployment. The Protestants who lived in grotty houses along Belfast's Shankill Road didn't have indoor toilets either. If only they could be made to see that life would be better in a united—and socialist—Ireland, the discord that had dogged the two communities for centuries might finally dissipate.

One of the leaders of the march was a raffish, articulate young socialist from Derry named Eamonn McCann, whom Dolours met and became fast friends with on the walk. McCann urged his fellow protesters not to demonize the Protestant work-ing people. "They are not our enemies in any sense," McCann insisted. "They are not exploiters dressed in thirty-guinea suits. They are the dupes of the system, the victims of the landed and industrialist unionists. They are the men in overalls." These people are actually on our side, McCann was saying. They just don't know it yet.

.   .   .

Ireland is a small island, less than two hundred miles across at its widest point. You can drive from one coast to the other in an afternoon. But from the moment the marchers departed Done-gall Square, they had been harried by counterprotesters: Protes-tant "unionists," who were ardent in their loyalty to the British crown. Their leader was a stout, jug-eared forty-four-year-old man named Ronald Bunting, a former high school math teacher who had been an officer in the British Army and was known, by his followers, as the Major. Though he had once held more progressive views, Bunting fell under the sway of the ardently anti-Catholic minister Ian Paisley after Paisley tended to Bunting's dying mother. Bunting was an Orangeman, a member of the Protestant fraternal organization that had long defined itself in opposition to the Catholic population. He and his supporters jostled and jeered the marchers, attempting to snatch their protest banners, while raising a flag of their own—the Union Jack. At one point, a journalist asked Bunting whether it might not have been better just to leave the marchers be and ignore them.

"You can't ignore the devil, brother," Bunting said.

Bunting may have been a bigot, but some of his anxieties were widely shared. "The basic fear of Protestants in Northern Ireland is that they will be outbred by Roman Catholics," Terence O'Neill, the prime minister of Britain's devolved government in Northern Ireland, said that year. Nor did it seem entirely clear, in the event that Protestants *were* eventually outnumbered in such a fashion, that London would come to their rescue. Many people on the English "mainland" seemed only faintly aware of this restive province off the coast of Scotland; others would be happy to let Northern Ireland go. After all, Britain had been shedding colonies for decades. In the words of one English journalist writing at the time, the unionists in Northern Ireland were "a society more British than the British about whom the British care not at all." To "loyalists"—as especially zealous unionists were known—this created a tendency to see oneself as the ultimate defender of a national identity that was in danger of extinction. In the words of Rudyard Kipling, in his 1912 poem "Ulster," "We know, when all is said, / We perish if we yield."

But Major Bunting may have had a more personal reason to feel threatened by this march. Among the scruffy demonstrators with their hippie songs and righteous banners was his own son. A student at Queen's with heavy sideburns, Ronnie Bunting had drifted into radical politics during the summer of 1968. He was hardly the only Protestant among the marchers. Indeed, there had been a long tradition of Protestants who believed in Irish independence; one of the heroes of Irish republicanism, Wolfe Tone, who led a violent rebellion against British rule in 1798, was a Protestant. But Ronnie was surely the only member of the march whose father was the architect of a nettlesome counter-protest, leading his own band of loyalist marchers in a campaign of harassment and bellowing anti-Catholic invective through a bullhorn. "My father's down there making a fool of himself," Ronnie grumbled, shamefaced, to his friends. But this oedipal dynamic seemed only to sharpen the resolve of both father and son.

Like the Price sisters, Ronnie Bunting had joined People's Democracy. At one meeting, he suggested that it might be better if they did not proceed with the march to Derry, because he thought that "something bad" was likely to happen. The police had cracked down violently on several earlier protests. Northern Ireland was not exactly a bastion of free expression. Due to fears of a Catholic uprising, a draconian law, the Special Powers Act, which dated to the era of partition, had created what amounted to a permanent state of emergency: the government could ban meetings and certain types of speech, and could search and arrest people without warrants and imprison them indefinitely without trial. The Royal Ulster Constabulary was overwhelmingly Protestant, and it had a part-time auxiliary, known as the B-Specials, composed of armed, often vehemently anti-Catholic, unionist men. One early member, summarizing how the B-Specials were recruited, said, "I need men, and the younger and wilder they are, the better."

As the march progressed through the countryside, it kept running into Protestant villages that were unionist strongholds. Each time this occurred, a mob of local men would emerge, armed with sticks, to block the students' access, and a cordon of police officers accompanying the march would force them to detour around that particular village. Some of Major Bunting's men walked alongside the marchers, taunting them. One carried a Lambeg drum—the so-called big slapper—and its ominous thump echoed through the green hills and little villages, summoning other able-bodied counterprotesters from their homes.

If there *was* a violent clash, the students felt prepared for it. Indeed, some of them welcomed the idea. The Selma march had provoked a ferocious crackdown from the police, and it may have been the televised spectacle of that violent overreaction, as much as anything else, that sparked real change. There was a sense among the students that the most intractable injustice could be undone through peaceful protest: this was 1969, and it seemed that young people around the world were at the vanguard. Perhaps in Northern Ireland the battle lines could be redrawn so that it was no longer a conflict of Catholics against Protestants, or republicans against loyalists, but rather the young against the old—the forces of the future against the forces of the past.

On the fourth and final day of the march, at a crossroads ten miles outside of Derry, one of the protesters shouted through a bullhorn, "There's a good possibility that some stones may be thrown." It appeared there might be trouble ahead. More young people had joined the procession over the days since it departed Belfast, and hundreds of marchers now filled the road. The man with the bullhorn shouted, "Are you prepared to accept the possibility of being hurt?"

The marchers chorused back, "Yes!"

·   ·   ·

The night before, as the marchers slept on the floor of a hall in the village of Claudy, Major Bunting had assembled his followers in Derry, or Londonderry, as Bunting called it. Inside the Guildhall, a grand edifice of stone and stained glass on the banks of the River Foyle, hundreds of hopped-up loyalists gathered for what had been billed as a "prayer meeting." And there, ready to greet his flock, was Ian Paisley.

A radical figure with a rabid following, Paisley was the son of a Baptist preacher. After training at a fringe evangelical college in Wales, he had established his own hard-line church. At six foot four, Paisley was a towering figure with squinty eyes and a jumble of teeth, and he would lean over the pulpit, his hair slicked back, his jowls aquiver, and declaim against the "monster of Romanism." The Vatican and the Republic of Ireland were secretly in league, engineering a sinister plot to overthrow the Northern Irish state, he argued. As Catholics steadily accrued power and numbers, they would grow into "a tiger ready to tear her prey to pieces."

Paisley was a Pied Piper agitator who liked to lead his followers through Catholic neighborhoods, sparking riots wherever he went. In his basso profundo, he would expound about how Catholics were scum, how they "breed like rabbits and multiply like vermin." He was a flamboyantly divisive figure, a maestro of incitement. In fact, he was so unsympathetic, so naked in his bigotry, that some republicans came to feel that on balance, he might be *good* for their movement. "Why would we kill Paisley?" Dolours Price's mother, Chrissie, had been known to say. "He's our greatest asset."

Though the population of Derry was predominantly Catholic, in the symbolic imagination of loyalists, the city remained a living monument to Protestant resistance. In 1689, Protestant forces loyal to William of Orange, the new king, had managed to hold the city against a siege by a Catholic army loyal to James II. In some other part of the world, an event of such faded significance might merit an informative plaque. But in Derry, the clash was commemorated every year, with marches by local Protestant organizations. Now, Paisley and Bunting suggested, the student protesters who were planning to march into Derry the following morning might as well be reenacting the siege.

These civil rights advocates might pretend they were peaceful protesters, Paisley told his followers, but they were nothing but "IRA men" in disguise. He reminded them of Londonderry's role as a bulwark against papist encroachment. Did they stand ready to rise once again in defense of the city? There were cheers of "Hallelujah!" It was Paisley's habit to whip a crowd into a violent lather and then recede from the scene before any actual stones were thrown. But as his designated adjutant, Major Bunting instructed the mob that anyone who wished to play a "manly role" should arm themselves with "whatever protective measures they feel to be suitable."

In the darkness that night, in fields above the road to Derry, local men began to assemble an arsenal of stones. A local farmer, sympathetic to the cause, provided a tractor to help gather projectiles. These were not pebbles, but sizable hunks of freshly quarried rock, which were deposited in piles at strategic intervals, in preparation for an ambush.

.   .   .

"We said at the outset that we would march non-violently," Eamonn McCann reminded Dolours and the other protesters on the final morning. "Today, we will see the test of that pious declaration." The marchers started moving again, proceeding slowly, with a growing sense of trepidation. They were massed on a narrow country lane, which was bordered by tall hedges. Up ahead was a bottleneck, where Burntollet Bridge, an old stone structure, crossed the River Faughan. Dolours and Marian and the other young protesters continued trudging toward the bridge. Then, beyond the hedge, in the fields above, where the ground rose sharply, a lone man appeared. He was wearing a white armband and swinging his arms around theatrically in an elaborate series of hand signals, like a matador summoning some unseen bull. Soon other figures emerged, sturdy young men

The ambush at Burntollet Bridge.

popping up along the ridgeline, standing there in little knots, looking down at the marchers. There were hundreds of people on the road now, hemmed in by the hedges, with nowhere to run. More and more men appeared in the fields above, those white bands tied around their arms. Then the first rocks sailed into view.

To Bernadette Devlin, a friend of Dolours who was one of the organizers of the march, it looked like a "curtain" of projectiles. From the lanes on each side of the road, men and boys materialized, scores of them, hurling stones, bricks, milk bottles. Some of the attackers were on the high ground above the road, others behind the hedges alongside it, others still swarming around to head the marchers off at the bridge. The people at the front of the group sprinted for the bridge, while those in the rear fell back to avoid the barrage. But Dolours and Marian were stuck in the middle of the pack.

They clambered over the hedge, but the stones kept coming.

And now the men started running down and physically attacking the marchers. It looked to Dolours like a scene from some Hollywood western, when the Indians charge into the prairie. A few of the attackers wore motorcycle helmets. They descended, swinging cudgels, crowbars, lead pipes, and laths. Some men had wooden planks studded with nails, and they attacked the protesters, lacerating their skin. People pulled coats over their heads for cover, stumbling, blind and confused, and grabbed one another for protection.

As marchers fled into the fields, they were hurled to the ground and kicked until they lost consciousness. Someone took a spade and smacked a young girl in the head. Two newspaper photographers were beaten up and stoned. The mob seized their film and told them that if they came back, they would be killed. And there in the midst of it all was Major Bunting, the grand marshal, swinging his arms like a conductor, his coat sleeves blotted with blood. He snatched one of the banners from the protesters, and somebody set it on fire.

The marchers did not resist. They had agreed in advance to honor their pledge of nonviolence. Dolours Price found herself surrounded by young people with gashes in their faces and blood running into their eyes. She splashed into the river, the icy water sloshing around her. In the distance, marchers were being pushed off the bridge and into the river. As Dolours struggled in the water, she locked eyes with one attacker, a man with a club, and for the rest of her life she would return to that moment, the way his eyes were glazed with hate. She looked into those eyes and saw nothing.

Finally, an officer from the Royal Ulster Constabulary waded into the river to break up the fracas. Dolours grabbed his coat and wouldn't let go. But even as this sturdy cop helped usher her to safety, a terrifying realization was taking hold. There were dozens of RUC officers there that day, but most of them had done little to intervene. It would later be alleged that the reason the attackers wore white armbands was so that their friends in the police could distinguish them from the protesters. In fact, many of Major Bunting's men, the very men doing the beating, were members of the police auxiliary, the B-Specials.

Later, on the way to Altnagelvin Hospital, in Derry, Dolours cried, seized by a strange mixture of relief, frustration, and disappointment. When she and Marian finally got back to Belfast and appeared, bruised and battered, at the doorstep of the little house on Slievegallion Drive, Chrissie Price listened to the story of her daughters' ordeal. When they had finished telling it, she had one question. "Why did you not fight back?"

EVACUATION

JEAN McCONVILLE LEFT FEW traces. She disappeared at a chaotic time, and the children she left behind were so young that many of them had yet to form a rich catalog of memories. But one photograph of Jean survives, a snapshot taken in front of the family's home in East Belfast in the mid-1960s. Jean stands alongside three of her children, while her husband, Arthur, squats in the foreground. She stares at the camera, arms folded across her chest, lips pursed into a smile, eyes squinting against the sun. One detail that several of her children would recall about Jean McConville is a nappy pin—a blue safety pin, which she wore fastened to her clothes, because one child or another

Jean McConville, with Robert, Helen, Archie, and her husband, Arthur.

was always missing a button or needing some other repair. It was her defining accessory.

She was born Jean Murray, in 1934, to Thomas and May Murray, a Protestant couple in East Belfast. Belfast was a sooty, gray city of chimneys and steeples, flanked by a flat green mountain on one side and the Belfast Lough, an inlet of the North Channel, on the other. It had linen mills and tobacco factories, a deepwater harbor where ships were built, and row upon row of identical brick workers' houses. The Murrays lived on Avoniel Road, not far from the Harland & Wolff shipworks, where the *Titanic* had been built. Jean's father worked at Harland & Wolff. Every morning when she was a child, he would join the thousands of men plodding past her house on their way to the shipworks, and every evening he would return as the procession of men plodded home in the opposite direction. When the Second World War broke out, Belfast's linen factories produced millions of uniforms and the shipyards churned out navy vessels. Then, one night in 1941, not long before Jean's seventh birthday, air raid sirens wailed as a formation of Luftwaffe bombers streaked across the waterfront, scattering parachute mines and incendiary bombs, and Harland & Wolff erupted into flame.

Educating girls was not much of a priority in working-class Belfast in those days, so when Jean was fourteen, she left school and went in search of work. She ended up finding a job as a servant for a Catholic widow who lived on nearby Holywood Road. The widow's name was Mary McConville, and she had a grown son—an only child named Arthur, who served in the British Army. Arthur was twelve years older than Jean and very tall. He towered over Jean, who stood barely five feet in her shoes. He came from a long line of soldiers, and he told her stories about how he had gone off to fight the Japanese in Burma during the war.

When Jean and Arthur fell in love, the fact that they came from different sides of the religious divide did not go unnoticed by their families. Sectarian tensions were less pronounced during the 1950s than they had been in the past or would become again, but even so, "mixed" relationships were rare. This was true not just for reasons of tribal solidarity but because Protestants and Catholics tended to live in circumscribed worlds: they resided in different neighborhoods, attended different schools, worked different jobs, frequented different pubs. By entering Arthur's mother's house as a domestic employee, Jean had crossed these lines. When she took up with Arthur, his mother resented it. (Jean's mother may not have been delighted, either, but she accepted the marriage, though one of Jean's uncles, a member of the Orange Order, gave her a beating for the transgression.)

The young couple eloped to England in 1952 and lived in an army barracks where Arthur was posted, but eventually they returned to Belfast and moved in with Jean's mother, in 1957. Jean's first child, Anne, suffered from a rare genetic condition that would leave her hospitalized for much of her life. Anne was soon followed by Robert, Arthur (who was known as Archie), Helen, Agnes, Michael (whom everyone called Mickey), Thomas (whom everyone called Tucker), Susan, and, finally, the twins, Billy and Jim. Between Jean, her mother, her husband, and her children, there were a dozen or so people crammed into the tiny house on Avoniel Road. Downstairs was a small front parlor and a kitchen in the back, with an outdoor bathroom, an open fire for cooking, and a cold-water sink.

In 1964, Arthur retired from the army with a pension and set up a small building-repair business. But he struggled to stay employed. He found a new job in the Sirocco engineering works but eventually lost it when his employers discovered that he was Catholic. He held a job in a ropeworks for a time. Later, the children would recall this period—when the photo was taken—as a happy interlude. There were privations, to be sure, but nothing out of the ordinary for a working-class childhood in postwar

Belfast. Their parents were alive. Their existence seemed stable. Their life was intact.

But during the 1960s, the mutual suspicion between Catholics and Protestants gradually intensified. When members of the local Orange Order conducted their triumphal summertime marches, they would make a point of starting right outside the McConvilles' door. For years, Ian Paisley had been exhorting his Protestant brethren to seek out and expel Catholics who lived among them. "You people of the Shankill Road, what's wrong with you?" he would bellow. "Number 425 Shankill Road—do you know who lives there? Pope's men, that's who!" This was retail ethnic cleansing: Paisley would reel off addresses—56 Aden Street, 38 Crimea Street, the proprietors of the local ice cream shop. They were "Papishers," agents of Rome, and they must be driven out. There was no television in the house on Avoniel Road, but as the civil rights movement got under way and Northern Ireland became embroiled in riots, Jean and Arthur would visit a neighbor's house and watch the evening news with a growing sense of trepidation.

·   ·   ·

Michael McConville was eight when hell broke loose in 1969. Every summer in Derry, a loyalist order known as the Apprentice Boys held a march to commemorate the young Protestants who shut the city gates to bar the Catholic forces of King James in 1688. Traditionally, the marchers concluded their festivities by standing on the city's walls and hurling pennies onto the sidewalks and houses of the Bogside, a Catholic ghetto, below. But this year the provocation did not go unchallenged, and violent riots broke out, engulfing Derry in what would become known as the Battle of the Bogside.

As word of the clash in Derry reached Belfast, the riot spread like an airborne virus. Gangs of Protestant youths tore through

Catholic neighborhoods, breaking windows and torching homes. Catholics fought back, throwing stones and bottles and Molotov cocktails. The RUC and the B-Specials responded to this unrest, but the brunt of their authority was felt by Catholics, who complained that the cops would simply stand by while the loyalists committed crimes. Barricades sprang up around Catholic neighborhoods as people hijacked school buses and bread vans and turned them on their sides to block off streets and create defensive fortifications. Young Catholics pried up paving stones to pile onto the barricades or to throw at police. Alarmed by this onslaught, the RUC deployed squat armored vehicles, known as Pigs, which lumbered through the narrow streets, their gun turrets swiveling in all directions. Stones rained down on them as they passed. Petrol bombs broke open on their steel bonnets, blue flame spilling out like the contents of a cracked egg.

There were moments of anarchic poetry: a bulldozer that someone had left on a building site was liberated by a couple of kids, who sat atop the huge machine and drove it jauntily down a West Belfast street, to great whoops and cheers from their compatriots. At a certain point the boys lost control of their hulking steed and crashed into a telegraph pole—where somebody immediately lobbed a petrol bomb at the bulldozer and it burst into flames.

Loyalist gangs started moving systematically through Bombay Street, Waterville Street, Kashmir Road, and other Catholic enclaves, breaking windows and tossing petrol bombs inside. Hundreds of homes were gutted and destroyed, their occupants put out onto the street. As the rioting spread, ordinary families all across Belfast boarded up their doors and windows, as if for an approaching hurricane. They would move their old furniture away from the front room so there was less to burn, in the event that any incendiary material came crashing through the window. Then they would huddle in the back kitchen, grandparents clasping their rosaries, and wait for the chaos to pass.

Nearly two thousand families fled their homes in Belfast that summer, the overwhelming majority of them Catholic. Some 350,000 people lived in Belfast. Over the ensuing years, as much as 10 percent of the population would relocate. Sometimes a mob of a hundred people would converge on a house, forcing the inhabitants to leave. On other occasions, a note would come through the letter box, instructing the owners that they had a single hour to vacate. People crammed into cars that would shuttle them across the city to safety: it was not unusual to see a family of eight squeezed into a single sedan. Eventually, thousands of Catholics would queue at the railway station—refugees, waiting for passage on a southbound train to the Republic.

It was not long before the mob came for the McConvilles. A gang of local men visited Arthur and told him he had to leave. He slipped out under cover of darkness and sought refuge at his mother's house. At first, Jean and the children stayed behind, thinking the tensions might subside. But eventually they, too, were forced to flee, packing all the belongings they could into a taxi.

The city that they traversed was transformed. Trucks whizzed to and fro with whatever furniture people could gather before moving. Men staggered through the streets under the weight of aging sofas and armoires. Cars burned at intersections. Firebombed schoolhouses smoldered. Great plumes of smoke blotted out the sky. All the traffic lights had been shattered, so, at some intersections, young civilians stood on the street, directing traffic. Sixty buses had been commandeered by Catholics and placed along streets to form barricades, a new set of physical battle lines delineating ethnic strongholds. Everywhere there was rubble and broken glass, what one poet would memorably describe as "Belfast confetti."

Yet, in the midst of this carnage, the hardheaded citizens of Belfast simply adapted and got on with their lives. In a momentary lull in the shooting, a front door would tentatively crack open and a Belfast housewife in horn-rimmed glasses would stick her head out to make sure the coast was clear. Then she would emerge, erect in her raincoat, a kerchief over her curlers, and walk primly through the war zone to the shops.

The taxi driver was so fearful of the chaos that he refused to take Jean McConville and her children any farther than the Falls Road, so they were forced to lug their belongings the rest of the way on foot. They rejoined Arthur at his mother's house, but Mary McConville had only one bedroom. She was half-blind, and because she had always disapproved of the former domestic employee who married her son, she and Jean did not get along. Besides, there were frequent gun battles in the area, and Jean and Arthur were concerned that a timber yard behind the house might be torched and the fire could spread. So the family moved again, to a Catholic school that had been converted into a temporary shelter. They slept in a classroom on the floor.

The housing authority in Belfast was building temporary accommodation for thousands of people who had suddenly become refugees in their own city, and eventually the McConvilles were offered a newly constructed chalet. But when they arrived to move in, they discovered that a family of squatters had beaten them there. Many displaced families were squatting wherever they could. Catholics moved into homes that had been abandoned by Protestants, and Protestants moved into homes vacated by Catholics. At a second chalet, the McConvilles encountered the same problem: another family was already living there and refused to leave. There were new chalets being built on Divis Street, and this time Arthur McConville insisted on staying with the workmen until the moment they finished construction, so that nobody else could get in first.

It was a simple structure, four rooms with an outside toilet. But it was the first time that they had a place they could legitimately call their own, and Jean, delighted, went straight out and bought material to make curtains. The family stayed in the chalet until February 1970, when they were offered permanent accommodation in a new housing complex known as Divis Flats, which had been under construction for several years and now loomed into view, throwing the surrounding neighborhood into shadow.

.   .   .

Divis Flats was meant to be a vision of the future. Built between 1966 and 1972 as part of a "slum clearance" program, in which an ancient neighborhood of overcrowded nineteenth-century dwellings, known as the Pound Loney, was razed, the flats consisted of a series of twelve interconnected housing blocks, containing 850 units. Inspired by Le Corbusier, the flats were conceived as a "city in the sky" that would alleviate housing shortages while also providing a level of amenities that would seem downright luxurious to ordinary Belfast families like the McConvilles. Residents of Divis Flats would have a shower and an indoor toilet, along with a hot-water sink. Each level of the housing block had a wide concrete terrace running from one end to the other, onto which the apartments opened. This was meant to evoke the little streets outside the row houses of the Pound Loney—a recreational area where children could play. Each door was painted a candy hue, and the reds and blues and yellows offered a vibrant pop of optimistic color against Belfast's many shades of gray.

The McConvilles moved into a four-bedroom maisonette in a section of the flats called Farset Walk. But any excitement they may have felt about their new accommodation soon dissipated, because the complex had been constructed with little consideration for how people actually live. There were no social amenities in Divis Flats, no green spaces, no landscaping. Apart from two bleak football pitches and an asphalt enclosure with a couple of swing sets, there were no playgrounds—in a complex with more than a thousand children.

When Michael McConville moved in, Divis seemed to him like a maze for rats, all corridors, stairwells, and ramps. The interior walls were cheap plasterboard, so you could hear every word of the dinnertime conversation of your neighbors. And because the exterior walls were built with nonporous concrete, condensation developed, and a malignant black mold began to creep up the walls and across the ceilings of the apartments. For a utopian architectural project, Divis had yielded dystopian results, becoming what one writer would later describe as a "slum in the sky."

The same summer that the McConvilles were ousted from their home in East Belfast, the British Army had been sent to Northern Ireland in response to the Battle of the Bogside and the riots. Young, green-jacketed soldiers arrived on ships, thousands of them pouring into Belfast and Derry. Initially they were greeted warmly by Catholics, who welcomed the soldiers as if they were the Allied troops who'd liberated Paris. The Catholic population had been so furious at the RUC and the B-Specials, whom they regarded as sectarian authorities, that when the army (which appeared neutral by comparison) showed up, it seemed to hold the promise of greater security. In West Belfast, Catholic mothers ventured up to the army's sandbagged posts and offered the soldiers cups of tea.

Michael's father was more circumspect. As a retired army man himself, Arthur McConville did not like it when the soldiers came around on patrol, speaking informally to him, as if he no longer held a place in the chain of command. On one end of the Divis complex, a twenty-story tower had been constructed, becoming the tallest building in Belfast that wasn't a church. The first eighteen floors consisted of flats, but the British Army took over the top two for use as an observation post. As tensions mounted below, army lookouts could monitor the whole city with binoculars.

The troops had scarcely arrived before they began to lose the goodwill of the community. The young soldiers did not understand the complicated ethnic geography of Belfast. They soon came to be seen not as a neutral referee in the conflict, but rather as an occupying force—a heavily armed ally of the B-Specials and the RUC.

Catholics had started to arm themselves and to shoot at loyalist adversaries, at the police, and eventually at the army. Gun battles broke out, and a few Catholic snipers took to the rooftops by night, lying flat among the chimneys and picking off targets below. Incensed by such aggression, the army and the police would shoot back, with heavier weaponry, and the neighborhoods echoed with the crack of M1 carbines and the harsh clatter of Sterling submachine guns. Thinking that it would make them harder for the snipers to spot, the B-Specials used revolvers to shoot out the streetlights, which plunged the city into darkness. British troops patrolled the empty streets in their half-ton Land Rovers with their headlights off, so as not to present a target. For all the chaos, the number of people actually killed in the Troubles was initially quite low: in 1969, only nineteen people were killed, and in 1970, only twenty-nine. But in 1971, the violence accelerated, with nearly two hundred people killed. By 1972, the figure was nearly five hundred.

With a population that was almost entirely Catholic, Divis Flats became a stronghold for armed resistance. Once the McConvilles moved into the complex, they were introduced to something that local residents called "the chain." When police or the army came to the front door of a particular flat in search of a weapon, someone would lean out the back window of the flat and pass the gun to a neighbor who was leaning out her back window in the next apartment. She would pass it to a neighbor on the other side, who would pass it to someone farther along, until the weapon had made its way to the far end of the building.

It was at Divis Flats that the first child to die in the Troubles lost his life. It happened before the McConvilles moved in. One August night in 1969, two policemen were wounded by sniper fire near the complex. Prone to panic and untrained in the use of firearms in such situations, the police hosed bullets from an armored car indiscriminately into Divis. Then, during a pause in the shooting, they heard a voice ring out from inside the building. "A child's been hit!"

A nine-year-old boy, Patrick Rooney, had been sheltering with his family in a back room of their apartment when a round fired by the police pierced the plasterboard walls and struck him in the head. Because intermittent volleys of gunfire continued, the police refused to allow an ambulance to cross the Falls Road. So eventually a man emerged from the flats, frantically waving a white shirt. Beside him, two other men appeared, carrying the boy, with his shattered head. They managed to get Patrick Rooney to an ambulance, but he died a short time later.

Michael McConville knew that Divis was a dangerous place. Patrick Rooney had been close to his age. At night, when gun battles broke out, Arthur bellowed, "Down on the floor!" and the children would drag their mattresses to the center of the apartment and sleep there, huddled in the middle of the room. Sometimes it felt as if they spent more nights on the floor than in their beds. Lying awake, staring at the ceiling, Michael would listen to the sound of bullets ricocheting off the concrete outside. It was a mad life. But as the anarchy persisted from one month to the next, it became the only life he knew.

.   .   .

One July afternoon in 1970, a company of British soldiers descended into the warren of alleys around Balkan Street, off the Falls Road, looking for a hidden stash of weapons. Searching one house, they retrieved fifteen pistols and one rifle, along with a Schmeisser submachine gun. But as they climbed back onto their armored vehicles and prepared to pull out of the neighborhood, a crowd of locals confronted them and started throwing stones. In a panic, the driver of one of the Pigs reversed into the crowd, crushing a man, which further enraged the locals. As the conflict escalated, a second company of troops was sent in to relieve the first, and soldiers fired canisters of tear gas into the crowd.

Before long, three thousand soldiers had converged on the Lower Falls. They axed down doors, bursting into the narrow houses. They were officially searching for weapons, but they did so with the kind of disproportionately destructive force that would suggest an act of revenge. They disemboweled sofas and overturned beds. They peeled the linoleum off the floors, prying up floorboards and yanking out gas and water pipes. As darkness fell, a military helicopter hovered above the Falls Road and a voice announced over a loudspeaker, in a plummy Eton accent, that a curfew was being imposed: everyone must remain in their houses or face arrest. Using the tips of their rifles, soldiers unspooled great bales of concertina wire and dragged it across the streets, sealing off the Lower Falls. Soldiers patrolled the streets, wearing body armor and carrying riot shields, their faces blackened with charcoal. From the windows of the little homes, residents stared out at them with undisguised contempt.

It may have been the gas, as much as anything, that brought West Belfast together in virulent opposition. A cartridge would skitter across the pavement, trailing a billowing cloud, and send the adolescent rock throwers scattering. Over the course of that weekend, the army fired sixteen hundred canisters of gas into the neighborhood, and it gusted through the narrow laneways and seeped into the cracks in drafty old homes. It crept into people's eyes and throats, inducing panic. Young men bathed their faces with rags soaked in vinegar and went back out to throw more stones. One correspondent who reported on the siege described the gas as a kind of binding agent, a substance that could "weld a crowd together in common sympathy and common hatred for the men who gassed them."

. . .

Michael McConville made the most of this turbulent boyhood. He grew up with a healthy skepticism of authority. The British Army was no different from the police, in his view. He watched them throwing men against the wall, kicking their legs spread-eagle. He saw soldiers pull fathers and brothers out of their homes and haul them away, to be detained without trial. Arthur McConville was unemployed. But this was hardly unusual for Divis Flats, where half of the residents relied entirely on welfare assistance to support their families.

When the children left the flat in Divis, Jean would tell them not to stray too far. "Don't wander away," she would say. "Stay close to home." Technically, there was not a war going on—the authorities insisted that this was simply a civil disturbance—but it certainly felt like a war. Michael would venture out with his friends and his siblings into an alien, unpredictable landscape. Even in the worst years of the Troubles, some children seemed to have no fear. After the shooting stopped and the fires died down, kids would scuttle outside and crawl through the skeletons of burned-out lorries, trampoline on rusted box-spring mattresses, or hide in a stray bathtub that lay abandoned amid the rubble.

Michael spent most of his time thinking about pigeons. Dating back to the nineteenth century, the pigeon had been known in Ireland as "the poor man's racehorse." Michael's father and his older brothers introduced him to pigeons; for as long as he could remember, the family had kept birds. Michael would set out into the combat zone, searching for roosting pigeons. When he discovered them, he would take off his jacket and cast it over them like a net, then smuggle the warm, nervous creatures back to his bedroom.

On his adventures, Michael sometimes picked his way through derelict houses. He had no idea what dangers might lurk inside—squatters, paramilitaries, or bombs, for all he knew—but he had no fear. Once, he came upon an old mill, the whole façade of which had been blown out. With a friend, Michael scaled the front, to see if any pigeons might be roosting inside. When they reached an upper floor, they suddenly found themselves staring at a team of British soldiers who had set up camp there. "Halt or we'll fire!" the soldiers shouted, training their rifles on Michael and his friend until they clambered back down to safety.

About a year after the Falls Curfew, Michael's father began to lose a great deal of weight. Eventually, Arthur grew so weak and shaky that he could no longer hold a cup of tea. When he finally went to see a doctor for tests, it emerged that he had lung cancer. The living room became his bedroom, and Michael would hear him at night, moaning in pain. He died on January 3, 1972. As Michael watched his father's casket being lowered into the frigid ground, he thought to himself that things could not possibly get any worse.

AN UNDERGROUND ARMY

DOLOURS PRICE WAS WALKING through Belfast with her mother, Chrissie, one day in 1971 when they rounded a corner and saw a British Army checkpoint. Pedestrians were being questioned and searched. Chrissie slowed her pace and murmured, "Are you carrying anything?"

"No," Dolours said.

"Are you carrying anything?" Chrissie asked again, more forcefully. In the distance, Dolours could see young men being thrown up against armored vehicles and ordered by the soldiers to take off their jackets.

"Give it to me," Chrissie said.

Dolours produced the pistol she had been carrying and discreetly handed it to her mother, who concealed it under her own coat. When they reached the checkpoint, Dolours was forced to take off her jacket, while Chrissie, being older, was waved through. Back at the house on Slievegallion Drive, Chrissie meticulously cleaned the gun, oiling each metal component. Then she wrapped it in some socks and buried it in the garden. Later, a quartermaster from the IRA stopped by to exhume the weapon.

"Would your ma join?" he asked Dolours, only half in jest. "She's terrific at storing weapons."

· · ·

The Falls Road and the Shankill Road run roughly parallel as they move into the center of Belfast, drawing closer together but never touching. The Falls Road was a stronghold for Catholics, and the Shankill for Protestants, and these two arteries were connected by a series of narrow cross streets that ran between them at right angles, and featured rows of identical terraced houses. At some point along each of these connecting streets, Catholic territory ended and Protestant territory began.

During the riots of 1969, barricades went up around the neighborhoods, formalizing the sectarian geography. These would eventually be replaced by so-called peace walls, towering barriers that separated one community from another. Paramilitaries took to policing their respective enclaves, and teenage sentries manned the border lines. When the Troubles ignited, the IRA was practically defunct. The group had engaged in a failed campaign along the border during the 1950s and early '60s, but the effort drew little support from the community. By the late sixties, some members of the IRA's leadership in Dublin had begun to question the utility of the gun in Irish politics, and to adopt a more avowedly Marxist philosophy, which advocated peaceful resistance through politics. The organization dwindled to such a degree that when the riots broke out in the summer of 1969, there were only about a hundred IRA members in Belfast. Many of them, like Dolours's father, Albert Price, were seasoned veterans of earlier campaigns but were getting on in years.

For an army, they were also conspicuously unarmed. In a surpassingly ill-timed decision, the IRA had actually sold off some of its remaining weapons in 1968, to the Free Wales Army. There was still some residual expertise in how to manufacture crude explosives, but the IRA had developed a reputation as an outfit whose bombers had a tendency to blow themselves up more often than their targets.

Traditionally, the Catholic minority in Northern Ireland

had turned to the IRA for protection during periods of sectarian strife. But when the clashes started in 1969, the organization could do little to stop jeering loyalists from burning Catholic families out of their homes. In the aftermath of these purges, some people began to suggest that what IRA really stood for was "I Ran Away."

There was a faction in Belfast that wanted to take a more aggressive stand—to rekindle the IRA's identity as an agent of violent change. In September 1969, an IRA commander named Liam McMillen held a meeting of the leadership in a room on Cyprus Street. McMillen was widely blamed for the organization's failure to protect the community during the riots. Twenty-one armed men burst into the meeting, led by Billy McKee, a legendary IRA street fighter. Born in 1921, months after the partition of Ireland, McKee had joined the youth wing of the IRA when he was only fifteen. He had spent time behind bars in every decade since. A devout Catholic who attended Mass every day and carried a gun with him at all times, he had pale blue eyes and the conviction of a zealot. "You are a Dublin communist and we are voting you out," he growled at McMillen. "You are no longer our leader."

One of Albert Price's old friends, the writer Brendan Behan, famously remarked that in any meeting of Irish republicans, the first item on the agenda is the split. To Dolours, a split in the IRA came to seem inevitable. By early 1970, a breakaway organization had formed. Known as the Provisional IRA, they were explicitly geared to armed resistance. The old IRA became known as the Official IRA. On the streets of Belfast, they were often distinguished as the "Provos" and the "Stickies," because Officials would supposedly wear commemorative Easter lilies that stuck on their shirtfronts with adhesive, whereas the more dyed-in-the-wool Provos wore paper lilies affixed with a pin. In 1971, forty-four British soldiers were murdered by paramilitaries. But even as the two wings of the IRA intensified their battle with loyalist mobs, the RUC, and the British Army, they now began to wage bloody war against each other.

. . .

Andersonstown, where Dolours Price grew up, sits above the Falls Road, at the foot of the flat-topped Black Mountain, which looms over the city in the distance. As the situation grew dire in 1969, normal life had been suspended. Children could no longer safely walk to school, so many stopped going. Two of Dolours's aunts moved to the neighborhood after getting burned out of their homes in other areas. The army frequently raided Andersonstown, in search of IRA suspects or their weapons. One local house doubled as a bomb school: a clandestine explosives factory where Provisional IRA recruits could learn how to rig devices and handle incendiary material. Local residents resented incursions by the authorities, and the presence of armed and uniformed representatives of the British crown only reinforced the impression that Belfast had become an occupied city.

This dynamic of wartime siege led whole neighborhoods to pull together and collaborate in opposition. "The local people had suddenly changed," Dolours Price later recalled. "They'd become republicans." When the authorities were coming, housewives and little children would dash out of their homes, tear the metal lids from their rubbish bins, kneel down on the sidewalk, and crash the lids, like cymbals, against the paving stones, sending up a great gnashing din that reverberated through the back alleys, alerting the rebels that a raid was under way. Scrappy school-age kids would lounge on rubble-strewn street corners and unleash a piercing finger whistle at the first sign of trouble.

It was an invigorating solidarity. As the violence intensified, grandiose funerals became routine, with rousing graveside orations and caskets draped in tricolor flags. People took to joking that there was no social life in Belfast anymore, apart from wakes.

These ceremonies, with their pageantry of death and nationalism, held a certain allure for Dolours Price. She had returned
to high school after the march at Burntollet Bridge. For years,
she had aspired to go to art school, but after applying, she was
bitterly disappointed to learn that she had not been accepted.
Instead she secured a place at St. Mary's Teacher Training College, at the foot of the Falls Road, to earn a bachelor's degree in
education.

Albert Price was an intermittent presence in these years,
because he was involved in the new struggle. When the IRA
needed guns, Albert went out looking for them. In the evening,
Dolours would find groups of men huddled in her front room,
scheming in low tones with her father. At a certain point, Albert
went on the run, hiding out across the border in the Republic.
Dolours started at St. Mary's in 1970. She was naturally smart
and inquisitive, and applied herself to her degree. But something
had changed in her after the ambush at Burntollet Bridge. Both
Dolours and Marian had been altered by that experience, their
father would later say. After they got back to Belfast, "they were
never the same."

One day in 1971, Dolours approached a local IRA commander and said, "I want to join." The formal induction took
place in the front room of the Price home on Slievegallion
Drive. Someone said, casually, "Hey, come in here a minute,"
and Dolours went in and raised her right hand and recited a declaration of allegiance: "I, Dolours Price, promise that I will promote the objectives of the IRA to the best of my knowledge and
ability." She vowed to obey any and all orders issued to her by
a "superior officer." Even as Dolours partook in this momentous
rite, her mother sat in the next room, nursing a cup of tea and
behaving as though she had no inkling of what was going on.

Since the moment she locked eyes with the loyalist who beat
her at Burntollet Bridge, Dolours had concluded that her fantasy
of peaceful resistance had been naïve. *I'm never going to convert*

these people, she thought. No amount of marching up and down the road would bring the change that Ireland needed. Having strayed, in her youth, from the bedrock convictions upon which her family had built its legacy, she would come to regard the moment when she joined the IRA as a "return"—a sort of homecoming.

Marian joined the Provos, too. During the day, the sisters continued to attend school. But at night they would disappear, not returning to the house until late. In such situations, parents in West Belfast tended not to ask questions. Young people could vanish for a week at a time, and when they got home, nobody would inquire about where they had been. There was a reason for this. Because the IRA was a banned organization, and even admitting to being a member was grounds for arrest, the group was fanatical about secrecy. Youths who joined the IRA tended not to tell their parents about it. In some cases, parents might disapprove: Belfast was dangerous enough already; to sign on as a paramilitary was simply tempting fate. Occasionally a young IRA gunman would go out on a sniper mission, only to round a corner and bump smack into his own mother. Unfazed by the assault rifle in his hands, she would drag him home by the ear.

But even if your parents were ardent supporters of the IRA, there were reasons not to tell them that you had joined. If the police or the army broke down the door to interrogate them, the less they knew, the better. One of Dolours's friends was a big, square-jawed boy named Francie McGuigan. Like the Prices, the McGuigans were a staunch republican family, and because their parents were friends, Dolours and Francie had known each other all their lives. When Francie joined the IRA, he knew that his father was a member as well—yet they never discussed it. This could be comical at times, with the two of them living under the same roof. Francie's father was a quartermaster, in charge of weapons and ammunition. But when Francie needed bullets, he wouldn't ask his father; he would ask his friend Kevin instead: "Kevin, does my father have any rounds?" Kevin would ask Francie's father, who would give the rounds to Kevin, who would give them to Francie. It may not have been the most efficient way of doing business, but it meant that certain things could be left unsaid.

.   .   .

The chief of staff of the Provos was a man named Seán Mac Stíofáin. A moonfaced teetotaler in his early forties, with a cockney accent and a dimple in his chin, he'd been born John Stephenson in East London, and was raised by a mother who told him stories about her Irish upbringing in Belfast. After serving in the Royal Air Force, he had learned the Irish language, married an Irish girl, adopted an Irish name, and joined the IRA. It would later emerge that Mac Stíofáin was not Irish at all: his mother, who was given to storytelling, had been born not in Belfast but in Bethnal Green, in London. But sometimes it's the myths that we believe most fervently of all. (Some of Mac Stíofáin's IRA colleagues, when they wanted to get a rise out of him, would "forget" to use his Irish name and call him John Stephenson.)

Mac Stíofáin, though born a Protestant, was a devout Catholic who had done prison time in England for taking part in an IRA raid on an armory in 1953. He was a "physical force" republican, an unwavering advocate of armed struggle as the only means of ousting the British; he once summarized his personal military strategy with three words: "escalate, escalate, escalate." Mac Stíofáin's embrace of violence was such that he became known, to some of his contemporaries, as Mac the Knife.

In a passage in his 1975 memoir, Mac Stíofáin recalled how Dolours Price approached him. "She was planning a teaching career," he wrote, "and though she came from a Republican family, she had been convinced until then that non-violent protest would succeed in overcoming the injustice in the North." He pinpointed the ambush at Burntollet Bridge as the moment that changed her mind. Initially, Mac Stíofáin proposed that Dolours join the Cumann na mBan, the female auxiliary wing of the IRA. This was the same unit in which Chrissie Price and Aunt Bridie and Granny Dolan had all served. The women of the Cumann did serious jobs: they would care for injured men or take a gun, still piping hot from use, and spirit it away after a shooting.

But Price was offended by Mac Stíofáin's offer. Her feminism—in combination, perhaps, with a certain air of entitlement, as the scion of a notable republican family—meant that she had no intention of being relegated to a supporting role. "I wanted to fight, not make tea or roll bandages," she later recalled. "Army or nothing." Price insisted that she was equal to any man, and she wanted to do exactly the same work that a man would do. What she wanted, she told Mac Stíofáin, was to be a "fighting soldier."

A special meeting of the Provisionals' Army Council was convened, and it was determined that for the first time in history, women could join the organization as full members. This was likely driven in large measure by the ambition (and unimpeachable republican lineage) of Dolours Price. But Price herself would speculate that another factor may have played a role: because men were being locked up en masse by the authorities, the Provos may have felt that they had little choice but to start admitting women.

If Price thought that being female—or coming from republican royalty, or having an education that was fancy by the standards of the IRA—might win her any breaks, she was quickly disabused of such notions. After her swearing-in, she was summoned by her commanding officer to a house in West Belfast where several IRA men had gathered. There, Price was presented with a heap of filthy, mismatched, rusty bullets that had been dug up from some arms dump God knows where. Then somebody handed her a clump of steel wool and said, *Clean the bullets.*

This, Price decided with a sniff, was the most menial job imaginable. Any adolescent lad could do it. Was this really necessary? Come to think of it, were these bullets even functional? Was anybody ever actually going to *shoot* them? She pictured the IRA men sitting in the kitchen, chortling over the spectacle of her debasement. She was tempted to march in and say, "You know what you can do with these bullets?" But she stopped herself. She had vowed to obey orders. All orders. This might be a hazing ritual, but it was also a test. So Price took the steel wool and started scrubbing.

.   .   .

"You'd spent your life being taught that this was a *glorious* way of life," Price recalled. But if she was well acquainted with the romance of her new vocation, she was also aware of the risks. The IRA had just embarked on a shooting war with the British, and whatever her fellow recruits might say about their chances, the odds of success looked slim. In the likely event that you were outwitted or outgunned in any given operation—or in the whole campaign—you could expect the same fate as Patrick Pearse and the heroes of the Easter Rising: the British would end your life, then the Irish would tell stories about you forevermore. New recruits to the Provos were told to anticipate one of two certain outcomes: "Either you're going to jail or you're going to die."

Chrissie Price knew these risks, too, and for all of her devotion to the cause, she worried about her daughter. "Would you not finish your education?" she implored.

"Like the revolution's going to wait until I finish my education," Dolours replied.

Most nights, when Dolours came home from operations, Chrissie would silently take her clothes and put them in the washer without asking any questions. But on one occasion, Dolours returned late at night to find her mother crying, because news had reached Chrissie of a bomb going off somewhere and she had been seized by a fear that it might have killed her daughter.

Not long after the Price sisters joined the Provos, they were sent across the border to attend an IRA training camp in the Republic. These camps were a ritualized affair. Recruits would be driven in a car or minibus along winding country roads to a remote location, usually a farm, where a local guide might appear—a housewife in her apron, or a sympathetic parish priest—and escort them to a farmhouse. The camps could last from a few days to more than a week, and they involved intensive training in revolvers, rifles, and explosives. The Provos were still working with a limited arsenal of antiquated weapons, many of them dating back to the Second World War, but recruits learned to oil and disassemble a rifle and how to set a charge and prime explosives. They marched in formation, just as they might have done in basic training if they were serving in a conventional army. There was even a uniform, of a sort. Day to day, the young rebels wore standard civilian garb of jeans and woolly sweaters. But during funerals, they dressed in dark suits, sunglasses, and black berets, and stood in cordons along the sidewalks, like a resolute, disciplined street army. The authorities could take photographs at such events, and frequently did. But their intelligence on this new crop of paramilitaries was still rudimentary, and they often could not match the faces of these young recruits to names or any other identifying information.

If the image of an "IRA man" in Belfast during the 1960s entailed a gin-blossomed barstool radical, a shambling has-been, full of tales about the old days, the Provisionals set out to upend this caricature. They aimed to be clean, disciplined, organized, ideological—and ruthless. They called themselves "volunteers," a name that harked back to the doomed heroes of the Easter Rising and captured the sense that patriotism is a transaction in which the patriot must be prepared to pay dearly. As a volunteer, you stood ready to sacrifice everything—even your own life—in service to the cause. This pact tended to inculcate, among the revolutionaries, an intoxicating sense of camaraderie and mission, a bond that could seem indestructible.

. . .

The Price sisters may have wanted to serve as frontline soldiers, but initially they worked as couriers. This was an important job, because there was always money or munitions or volunteers to ferry from one place to another, and moving from place to place could be risky. Dolours had a friend, Hugh Feeney, who owned a car, which she would sometimes use to make runs. The bespectacled son of a pub owner, Feeney was a middle-class boy who, like Dolours, had been a member of People's Democracy and was training to be a teacher when he fell in with the IRA.

Even after becoming active volunteers, Dolours and Marian remained in college. This served as an excellent cover. They would come home after their classes, put away their books, and head out on operations. As women, the Price sisters were less likely than their male counterparts to attract attention from the authorities. Dolours would often cross the border several times a day, flashing a fake license that said her name was Rosie. She crossed so frequently that the soldiers manning the border checkpoints came to recognize her. They never grew suspicious, instead assuming that she must hold some dull job near the border that required her to cross back and forth. Dolours had a chatty, ingratiating, slightly flirtatious manner. People liked her. "Rosie!" the soldiers would say when they saw her coming. "How are you today?"

Often, the Price sisters transported incendiary material.

They came to know the scent of nitrobenzene, an ingredient of improvised explosives: it smelled like marzipan. Bomb-making materials were prepared in the Republic and then smuggled north across the border. On one occasion, Marian was driving a car packed with explosives when she spotted an army checkpoint. She was still a teenager and was driving without a license. The explosives were concealed behind a panel in the driver's-side door. As a soldier approached to inspect the car, he reached for the door handle, and Marian realized that if he opened it, he would instantly register the weight of the hidden payload.

"I can manage!" she said, hastily opening the door herself. She stepped out and stretched her legs. Miniskirts were all the rage in Belfast, and Marian happened to be wearing one. The soldier noticed. "I think he was more interested in looking at my legs than he was with the car," Marian said later. The soldier waved her through.

There were some in the more starchy and traditional Cumann na mBan to whom the presence of women in such operational roles—women who might deploy their own sexuality as a weapon—was threatening, even mildly scandalous. Some Cumann veterans referred to these frontline IRA women as "Army girls," and insinuated that they were promiscuous. As tactics evolved in the conflict, IRA women occasionally set so-called honey traps, trolling bars in the city for unsuspecting British soldiers, then luring them into an ambush. A story circulated about three off-duty Scottish soldiers who were out drinking in central Belfast one afternoon in 1971 and were allegedly approached by a couple of girls who invited them to a party. The bodies of the soldiers were discovered by a lonely road outside of town. They had stopped to urinate and somebody had shot all three of them in the head. The Price sisters disdained such operations. Dolours made a point of asking that she never be assigned to a honey trap. There were laws of war, she maintained: "Soldiers should be shot in their uniforms."

The spectacle of women as avatars of radical violence may have felt bracingly novel, but in other parts of the world, such figures were finding a place in the iconography of revolution. While Belfast was burning in the summer of 1969, a twenty-five-year-old Palestinian terrorist named Leila Khaled hijacked a TWA flight from Rome to Tel Aviv and, with it, the attention of the world. Khaled diverted the flight to Damascus, becoming the first woman to hijack an airplane. She emerged as a kind of pinup for the new militancy. Her photo was splashed across glossy magazines, her dark eyes and cut-glass cheekbones framed by a keffiyeh, an assault rifle clutched in her hands. A few years later, a famous photo captured the American heiress Patty Hearst brandishing a sawed-off carbine and wearing a beret. One close friend of Dolours Price's suggested that at least part of the allure for her, in those years, was "rebel chic."

Stories about the Price sisters began to circulate among British troops stationed in Belfast and to find their way into the accounts of visiting war correspondents. They developed an outsize reputation as deadly femmes fatales who would venture into the mean streets of Belfast with an assault rifle hidden "down a bell-bottomed trouser leg." Marian was said to be an expert sniper and was referred to, among British squaddies, as "the Widowmaker." Dolours would become known in the press as "one of the most dangerous young women in Ulster."

It is hard to judge how seriously to take such folklore. Some of it was the kind of frisky sexualized rumor that occasionally circulates in times of violent upheaval. A society that had always been a bit fusty and repressed was suddenly splitting apart in the most cataclysmic fashion. The perceived threats of sexual liberation and paramilitary chaos converged in the mythical specter of a pair of leggy, rifle-toting libertines.

But if this image was to some degree a battlefield fantasy, one of the key people projecting it was Dolours Price herself. "Would you like to be shown round our bomb factory?" she asked a visiting reporter in 1972, adding, "We had *Paris Match* magazine taking pictures of the place last week." Eamonn McCann, the activist from Derry who befriended Price on the Burntollet march, would still see her from time to time. She never told him explicitly that she had joined the Provos, but McCann knew. He was dismayed. He desperately wanted revolutionary change in Ireland, but he was certain that violence was not the way to achieve it. He told his friends who joined the armed struggle, "Nothing is going to come out of this that is commensurate with the pain that you will put into it."

When he saw Price, McCann was always struck by her sheer glamour. Most of the republican women he had known growing up were stern and pious—if not the Virgin Mary, exactly, then the Virgin Mary with a gun. The Price sisters were something else altogether. Dolours always dressed elegantly, her hair and makeup impeccable. "They were sassy girls," McCann recalled. "They weren't cold-eyed dialecticians or fanatics on the surface. There was a smile about them." In those days, there was a discount store in Belfast called Crazy Prices, and, inevitably, Dolours and Marian became known among their friends as the Crazy Prices.

Once, officers from the Royal Ulster Constabulary barged into the house on Slievegallion Drive at six in the morning and announced that they were arresting Dolours as a suspected member of an illegal organization. "She's not going out of here until she's had her breakfast," Chrissie said. The police, cowed by this small but formidable woman, agreed to wait, and Chrissie instructed her daughter to go and put on makeup. She was buying time so that Dolours could collect her wits. When Dolours was ready to go, Chrissie put on a fur coat, which she normally reserved for special occasions. "I'm going with her," she announced.

For a moment, Dolours was embarrassed, thinking, I'm in the IRA and my *mother* is coming with me to get arrested. But

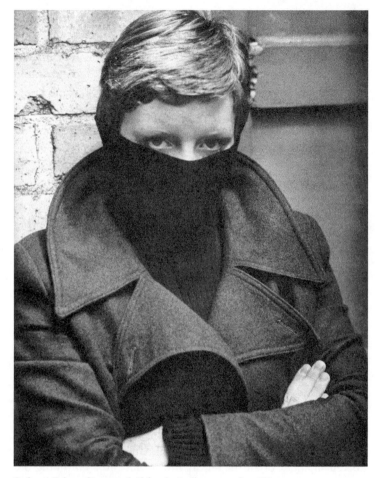

Dolours Price, photographed for the Italian magazine *L'Europeo*.

off they went. At Castlereagh police station, she was interrogated. She knew the rules, however, and she gave the police no information, repeating only "I have nothing to say." Eventually, she was released without charges. It would be difficult to make a case against Dolours: after all, she was still a student, with good marks and an attendance record to show for it. Before they left the station, Chrissie paused to admire the mug shot that the police had taken of her daughter.

"Can I keep that?" she deadpanned. "That's a nice one."

.　　.　　.

As a fund-raising initiative, the Provos took to robbing banks. *Lots* of banks. One day in the summer of 1972, three fresh-faced nuns walked into the Allied Irish Bank in Belfast. Just as the branch was about to close, the nuns reached under their habits and came out with guns—then proceeded to stick up the place. It was the Price sisters, along with another female volunteer. A month after the original robbery, three women walked into the very same bank and robbed it again. (The identity of the thieves was never ascertained, but it was tempting to wonder whether the sisters had not returned for seconds.) On another occasion, Dolours hijacked a post office lorry, because the IRA had received intelligence that it was transporting sacks of money.

For all the horror unfolding around them, there was a sense of adventure for Dolours and her comrades, a fantasy that they were dashing outlaws in a society in which all order had broken down. When one of Dolours's close colleagues in the IRA, a man named James Brown, was taken from prison to a hospital in Antrim with a burst appendix, the Price sisters carried out an audacious rescue mission, raiding the hospital, disarming the policemen there, and springing Brown free. It was a small miracle that the sisters managed to evade apprehension by the army or the police. Perhaps their ability to play the part of demure Catholic schoolgirls anytime they were confronted was enough to divert suspicion. But the authorities were also simply overwhelmed by the level of violence during this period.

The ranks of the Provos were filled with interesting characters. Dolours became friendly with an older man named Joe

Gerry Adams.

Lynskey, who had grown up on Cavendish Street, off the Falls Road, and still lived with his parents and his sister as he neared his fortieth birthday. Lynskey had trained as a monk during the 1950s, at an abbey in Portglenone, taking a vow of silence and rising before dawn each morning to pray. But he ended up leaving the order and joining the IRA. Lynskey was a bit of an overgrown child, having sat out his adolescence at the monastery. He was regarded as something of an oddball by the younger volunteers. They called him the "Mad Monk." But he had kind eyes and a gentle manner, and Dolours grew very fond of him.

Another person Price became associated with was a tall, angular young man named Gerry Adams. He was an ex-bartender from Ballymurphy who had worked at the Duke of York, a low-ceilinged pub in the city center that was popular with labor leaders and journalists. Like Price, Adams came from a distinguished republican family: one of his uncles had broken out of Derry jail with her father. Adams had gotten his start as an activist with a local committee that protested the construction of Divis Flats. He never attended college, but he was a fearsome debater, smart and analytical, like Dolours. He had joined the IRA a few years before she did, and he was already rising quickly through the Belfast leadership.

Price had been loosely acquainted with Adams since childhood. When they were both kids, she used to see him riding with his family on the same buses she did, to republican commemorations at Edentubber or Bodenstown. But now he had reappeared as a firebrand. The first time she recognized him on the back of a lorry, addressing a crowd, she exclaimed, "Who does Gerry think he is, standing up there?" Price found Adams intriguing, and faintly ridiculous. He was a "gawky fella with big black-rimmed glasses," she would recall, and he had a quiet, watchful charisma. Price was irrepressibly outgoing, but she found it difficult to get a conversation started with Adams. He carried himself with an aloof air of authority and referred to her, affectionately, as "child," though he was only a couple of years older than she was. The day after Price sprang James Brown from the hospital, Adams expressed concern about her operational security. "It said in the paper that the women were not wearing disguises," he murmured, adding reproachfully, "I hope that isn't true."

Price assured him that the press account was inaccurate, because the sisters had been decked out in blond wigs, bright lipstick, and garish head scarves, "like two whores at a hockey match." Adams took himself pretty seriously, Price thought. But she could laugh at anyone. For security, Adams did not sleep in his own home, and would bed down instead in various billets, some of which were not homes at all, but local businesses. He had taken to sleeping, lately, at a West Belfast mortician. Price found that hilarious. She joked that he slept in a coffin.

"It was an exciting time," she said later. "I should be ashamed to admit there was fun in it." But there was. She had only just turned twenty-one. Another family might disapprove of what Dolours and Marian were doing, but to Albert and Chrissie Price, there was a sense in which the girls were simply taking up a household tradition, and while you could blame a man for hitting someone, you could not blame him for hitting back. "The Provo army was started by the people to set up barricades against the loyalist hordes," Albert explained at the time. "We beat them with stones at first, and they had guns. Our people had to go and get guns. Wouldn't they have been right stupid people to stand there? Our people got shotguns at first and then got better weapons. And then the British, who were supposed to protect us, came in and raided our homes. What way could you fight? So you went down and you blew them up. That was the only thing left. If they hadn't interfered with us, there probably would be no Provo army today."

When British troops were killed, Albert would freely acknowledge the humanity of each individual soldier. "But he is in uniform," he would point out. "He is the enemy. And the Irish people believe that this is war." He was against death, he insisted, but ultimately this was a question of means and ends. "If we get a united socialist Ireland," Albert Price concluded, "then maybe it will all have been worth it."

As if to underline the futility of nonviolent resistance, when Eamonn McCann and a huge mass of peaceful protesters assembled in Derry one chilly Sunday afternoon in January 1972, British paratroopers opened fire on the crowd, killing thirteen men and wounding fifteen others. The soldiers subsequently claimed that they had come under fire and that they only shot protesters who were carrying weapons. Neither of these assertions turned out to be true. Bloody Sunday, as it would forever be known, was a galvanizing event for Irish republicanism. Dolours and Marian were in Dundalk when they heard reports of the massacre. The news filled them with an overpowering anger. In February, protesters set fire to the British embassy in Dublin. In March, London suspended the hated Unionist parliament in Northern Ireland and imposed direct rule from Westminster.

That same month, Dolours Price traveled to Italy to speak in Milan and help to spread the word about oppression of Catholics in Northern Ireland. She lectured about "the ghetto system" and the lack of civil rights. "If my political convictions had led me to take part in murder, I would confess without hesitation," she told an interviewer, employing the sort of deliberately evasive syntactical construction that would become typical when people described their actions in the Troubles. "If I had been commanded to go to kill an enemy of my people I would have obeyed without the slightest fear." In a photograph from her appearance there, Price posed like an outlaw, with a scarf pulled across her face.

ST. JUDE'S WALK

THE McCONVILLE FAMILY HAD two dogs, named Provo and Sticky. After Arthur passed away, his oldest son, Robert, might have stepped in to assume responsibility for the family, but in March 1972, when he was seventeen, Robert was interned on suspicion of being a member of the Official IRA—the Stickies. Jean McConville, who had been delicate by temperament to begin with, fell into a heavy depression after her husband's death. "She had sort of given up," her daughter Helen later recalled. Jean did not want to get out of bed and seemed to subsist on cigarettes and pills. Doctors in Belfast had taken to prescribing "nerve tablets"—sedatives and tranquilizers—to their patients, many of whom found that they were either catatonically numb or crying uncontrollably, unable to get a handle on their emotions. Tranquilizer use was higher in Northern Ireland than anywhere else in the United Kingdom. In some later era, the condition would likely be described as post-traumatic stress, but one contemporary book called it "the Belfast syndrome," a malady that was said to result from "living with constant terror, where the enemy is not easily identifiable and the violence is indiscriminate and arbitrary." Doctors found, paradoxically, that the people most prone to this type of anxiety were not the active combatants, who were out on the street and had a sense of agency, but the women and children stuck sheltering behind closed doors. At night, through the thin walls of their apartment in Divis Flats, the McConville children would hear their mother crying.

Increasingly, Jean became a recluse. Some weeks, she would leave the house only to buy groceries or to visit Robert in prison. It might have simply felt unsafe to venture out. There was a discomfiting sense in Belfast that there was no place where you were truly secure: you would run inside to get away from a gun battle, only to run outside again for fear of a bomb. The army was patrolling Divis, and paramilitaries were dug in throughout the complex. The year 1972 marked the high point for violence during the entirety of the Troubles—the so-called bloodiest year, when nearly five hundred people lost their lives. Jean made several attempts at suicide, according to her children, overdosing on pills on a number of occasions. Eventually, she checked into Purdysburn, the local psychiatric hospital.

Nights were especially eerie in Divis. People would turn out all of their lights, so the whole vast edifice was swathed in darkness. To the McConville children, one night in particular would forever stand out. Jean had recently returned from the hospital, and there was a protracted gun battle outside the door. Then the shooting stopped and they heard a voice. "Help me!" It was a man's voice. Not local.

"Please, God, I don't want to die." It was a soldier. A British soldier. "Help me!" he cried.

As her children watched, Jean McConville rose from the floor, where they had been cowering, and moved to the door. Peeking outside, she saw the soldier. He was wounded, lying in the gallery out front. The children remember her reentering the apartment and retrieving a pillow, which she brought to the soldier. Then she comforted him, murmuring a prayer and cradling his head, before eventually creeping back into the flat. Archie—who, with Robert in prison, was the oldest child there—admonished his mother for intervening. "You're only asking for trouble," he said.

"That was somebody's son," she replied.

The McConvilles never saw the soldier again, and to this

day the children cannot say what became of him. But when they left the apartment the next morning, they found fresh graffiti daubed across their door: BRIT LOVER.

.   .   .

This was a poisonous allegation. In the febrile atmosphere of wartime Belfast, for a local woman to be seen consorting with a British soldier could be a dangerous thing. Some women who were suspected of such transgressions were subjected to an antique mode of ritual humiliation: tarring and feathering. A mob would accost such women, forcibly shave their heads, anoint them with warm and sticky black tar, then shower a pillowcaseful of dirty feathers over their heads and chain them by the neck to a lamppost, like a dog, so that the whole community could observe the spectacle of their indignity. "Soldier lover!" the mob would bray. "Soldier's doll!"

In an environment where many married men were being locked up for long stretches, leaving their wives alone, and where cocky young British soldiers were patrolling the neighborhoods, deep-seated fears of infidelity, both marital and ideological, took hold. Tarring and feathering became an official policy of the Provisional IRA, which the leadership publicly defended as a necessary protocol of social control. When the first few cases showed up at local hospitals, the befuddled medical personnel had to consult with the maintenance crews who took care of their buildings about the best method for removing black tar.

It felt to Michael McConville as if he and his family were strangers in a strange land. Expelled from East Belfast for being too Catholic, they were outsiders in West Belfast for being too Protestant. After their home was marked with the graffiti, what few local friends they had no longer wanted anything to do with them. Everywhere they turned, they found themselves in an adversarial situation. Archie was badly beaten by the youth wing of the Provos and had his arm broken for refusing to join the organization. Helen and a friend were harassed by a regiment of soldiers. Helen would later suggest that her mother may have further alienated the family from their neighbors by declining to take part in "the chain," the hand-to-hand system for hiding weapons during police searches of the complex; Jean feared that if she was caught with a gun in the house, she might lose another child to prison. At a certain point, the family dogs, Provo and Sticky, vanished. Someone had shoved the animals down a rubbish chute, where they died.

Michael had asthma, and Jean worried that the gas heating in the flat was aggravating it. She requested a transfer, and the family was granted a new apartment, in another section of Divis Flats called St. Jude's Walk. They packed their belongings and made the short move into the new space. It was slightly larger than the previous one, but otherwise not much different.

Christmas was coming, but the city was hardly festive. Many shops were boarded up and closed, because they had been bombed. Jean McConville's only indulgence in those days was a regular excursion to play bingo at a local social club. Whenever she won anything, she would give the children twenty pence each. Occasionally, she would bring home enough to buy one of them a new pair of shoes. One night after the family had moved into the new apartment, Jean went with a friend to play bingo. But on that particular evening, she did not come home.

Shortly after 2 a.m., there was a knock at the door. It was a British soldier, who informed the McConville kids that their mother was at a barracks nearby. Helen raced to the barracks and found Jean, bedraggled and shoeless, her hair all over the place. Jean said that she had been at the bingo hall when someone came in and told her that one of the children had been hit by a car, and that someone was waiting outside to take her to the hospital. Alarmed, she left the bingo hall and got into the car. But it was a trap: when the door opened, Jean was pushed onto the floor and a hood was placed over her head. She was taken to a derelict building, she said, where she was tied to a chair, beaten, and interrogated. After she was released, some army officers found her wandering the streets, distressed, and brought her to the barracks.

Jean couldn't—or wouldn't—say who it was that had abducted her. When Helen wondered what kinds of questions they had been asking, Jean was dismissive. "A load of nonsense," she said. "Stuff I knew nothing about." Jean could not sleep that night. Instead she sat up, her face bruised, her eyes black and blue, and lit one cigarette after another. She told Helen that she missed Arthur.

The children would later recall that it was the following evening that Jean sent Helen out to fetch fish and chips for dinner. She drew a bath, to try to soothe the pain of the beating she had taken the night before. As Helen was leaving, she said, "Don't be stopping for a sneaky smoke."

. . .

Helen made her way through the labyrinthine passages of Divis to a local shop where she ordered dinner and waited for it. When the food was ready, she paid, took the greasy bag, and started to walk back. As she entered the complex, Helen noticed something strange. People were loitering on the balconies outside their apartments. This was the sort of thing that local residents did in the summertime. There were so few places for recreation in Divis that kids would play ball on the balconies and parents would hang about on temperate evenings, leaning in the doorways, gossiping over cigarettes. But not in December. As Helen got closer to the new apartment and saw the people gathered outside, she broke into a run.

THE DIRTY DOZEN

A VACANT HOUSE STOOD on Leeson Street, opposite the short block known as Varna Gap. Such derelict properties pockmarked Belfast's landscape—burned out, gutted, or abandoned, their windows and doors covered in plywood. The people who lived there had simply fled and never come back. Across the street from the vacant house, Brendan Hughes stood with a few of his associates from D Company. It was a Saturday, September 2, 1972.

Looking up, Hughes noticed a green van appear some distance away and begin to approach, along Leeson. He watched the van closely, something about it making him uneasy. He usually carried a handgun, but that morning an associate had borrowed it so that he could use it to steal a car. So Hughes found himself unarmed. The van drove right past him, close enough for Hughes to briefly glimpse the driver. It was a man. Not one he recognized. He looked nervous. But the van kept moving, right on down through McDonnell Street and onto the Grosvenor Road. Hughes watched it disappear. Just to be on the safe side, he sent one of his runners to fetch a weapon.

At twenty-four, Hughes was small but strong and nimble, with thick black eyebrows and a mop of unruly black hair. He was the officer commanding—"the OC"—for D Company of the Provisional IRA, in charge of this part of West Belfast, which made him a target not just for loyalist paramilitaries, the police, and the British Army but for the Stickies (the Official IRA) as well. Eighteen months earlier, Hughes's cousin Charlie, his pre-decessor as OC of D Company, had been shot and killed by the Officials. So Hughes was "on the run," in the parlance of the IRA: he was living underground, a man targeted by multiple armed organizations. In rural areas, you could stay on the run for years at a time, but in Belfast, where everybody knew everybody, you would be lucky to stick it out for six months. Someone would get you eventually.

Hughes had joined the Provos in early 1970. It was through his cousin Charlie that he initially got involved, but he soon established himself in his own right as a shrewd and tenacious soldier. Hughes moved from house to house, seldom sleeping in the same bed on consecutive nights. D Company's territory embraced the Grosvenor Road, the old Pound Loney area, the Falls Road—the hottest territory in the conflict. Initially, the company had only twelve members, and they became known as the Dogs, or the Dirty Dozen. Hughes adhered to a philosophy, instilled in him at a young age by his father, that if you want to get people to do something for you, you do it with them. So he wasn't just sending men on operations—he went along on the missions himself. Dolours Price first met Hughes when she joined the IRA, and she was dazzled by him. "He seemed to be a hundred places at the one time," she recalled, adding, "I don't think he slept." Despite his small stature, Hughes struck Price as a "giant of a man." It meant something to her, and to others, that he asked no volunteer to do anything he would not do himself.

D Company was carrying out a dizzying number of opera-tions, often as many as four or five each day. You would rob a bank in the morning, do a "float" in the afternoon—prowling the streets in a car, casting around, like urban hunters, for a British soldier to shoot—stick a bomb in a booby trap before supper, then take part in a gun battle or two that night. They were heady, breakneck days, and Hughes lived from operation to operation—robbing banks, robbing post offices, sticking up trains, planting bombs, shooting at soldiers. To Hughes, it seemed like a grand adventure. He thought of going out and getting into gunfights the way other people thought about getting up and going to the office. He liked the fact that there was a momentum to the operations, a relentless tempo, which fueled and perpetuated the armed struggle, because each successful operation drew new followers to the cause. In the words of one of Hughes's contemporaries in the IRA, "Good operations are the best recruiting sergeant."

As the legend of Brendan Hughes, the young guerrilla commander, took hold around Belfast, the British became determined to capture him. But there was a problem: they did not know what he looked like. Hughes's father had destroyed every family photograph in which he appeared, knowing that they could be used to identify him. The soldiers referred to him as "Darkie," or "The Dark," on account of his complexion, and the name stuck, a battlefield sobriquet. But the British did not know what his face looked like, and on many an occasion, Hughes had walked right by the soldiers' sandbagged posts, just another shaggy-haired Belfast lad. They didn't give him a second look.

The soldiers would go to his father's house and roust the man from bed, looking for Hughes. Once, when they hauled his father in for questioning, Hughes was incensed to learn that after two days of interrogation, the old man had been forced to walk home barefoot. The soldiers told his father that they weren't looking for Brendan in order to arrest him; their intention was to kill him.

This was not an idle threat. The previous April, an Official IRA leader named "Big Joe" McCann had been walking, unarmed, one day when he was stopped by British troops. He tried to flee but was shot. McCann had dyed his hair as a disguise, but they recognized him. He was only wounded by the initial shots, and he staggered away. But rather than call an ambulance, the soldiers fired another volley to finish the job. When they searched his pockets, they found nothing that could plausibly be described as a weapon, just a few stray coins and a comb for his hair.

The runner had not yet returned with a gun for Hughes when the van reappeared. Five minutes had passed, yet here it was once more. Same van. Same driver. Hughes tensed, but again the van drove right past him. It continued on for twenty yards or so. Then the brake lights flared. As Hughes watched, the rear doors swung open, and several men burst out. They looked like civilians—tracksuits, sneakers. But one had a .45 in each hand, and two others had rifles; as Hughes turned to run, all three of them opened fire. Bullets swished past him, slamming into the façades of the forlorn houses as Hughes tore off and the men gave chase. He sprinted onto Cyprus Street, the men pounding the pavement behind him, still firing. But now Hughes began to zigzag, like a gecko, into the warren of tiny streets.

He knew these streets, the hidden alleys, the fences he could scale. He knew each vacant house and laundry line. There was a quote attributed to Mao that Hughes was partial to, about how the guerrilla warrior must swim among the people as a fish swims through the sea. West Belfast was his sea: there was an informal system in place whereby local civilians would assist young paramilitaries like Hughes, allowing their homes to be used as shortcuts or hiding places. As Hughes was scrambling over a back fence, a rear door would suddenly pop open long enough for him to dart inside, then just as quickly close again behind him. Some of the residents were intimidated by the Provos and felt they had little choice but to cooperate, while others assisted out of an unforced sense of solidarity. When property was damaged in one of his operations, he would pay compensation to the family. He cultivated the community, knowing that without the sea, the fish cannot survive. There was a local invalid who lived on Cyprus Street, "Squire" Maguire, and at the height of the madness, with fires and police raids and riots in the street, residents in the area would occasionally see Brendan Hughes carrying Maguire on his back a few doors down to the pub so that Maguire could have a pint, then dutifully returning to bring him home a short while later. Once, a British soldier in the Lower Falls area caught Hughes in the sights of his rifle. Finger on the trigger, he was ready to open fire when an elderly lady stepped out of some unseen doorway and planted herself in the path of his weapon, then informed him that he would not be shooting anybody on her street on that particular evening. When the soldier looked up, Hughes was gone.

With his pursuers still clomping after him, firing wildly, Hughes veered onto Sultan Street. He had a specific destination in mind: a call house on Sultan. Call houses were usually regular homes, occupied by ordinary families, that happened to double as clandestine Provo facilities. Behind one particular door, on a street of identical brick houses with identical wooden doors, would be a secret refuge that could function as a safe house, a waiting room, or a dead drop. The families that lived in these homes deflected any suspicion from authorities. You might show up after midnight, haggard from a grueling day on the run, and they would lift slumbering children out of their beds, affording you a precious night of rest.

At the corner of Sultan, a baker's van was delivering bread, and as Hughes ran by it, the men behind him let off a volley of bullets, which punctured the van and shattered its windows. He kept pushing, sprinting the length of Sultan, desperate to reach the house before one of those bullets caught him. In addition to its other uses, a call house sometimes functioned as an arms depot. Hughes had become known to the British Army for his willingness to flit around the streets of the Falls area and engage their high-caliber weapons with his little World War II–era .45. The troops had developed what one later described as a "grudging admiration for this little bugger who had taken on an elite military unit with a handgun." But Hughes recognized at a certain point that he needed heavier weapons if he was going to compete. One day, a sailor of his acquaintance came back from a voyage to America with a catalog for the Armalite rifle—a lightweight, accurate, powerful semi-automatic that was easy to clean, easy to use, and easy to conceal. Hughes fell in love with the weapon. He convinced the Provos to import the Armalite, employing an audacious scheme. Cunard Lines had recently launched the *Queen Elizabeth II*, a luxury cruise liner that would crisscross the Atlantic, transporting well-heeled passengers between Southampton and New York. A thousand crew members worked on the ship, many of them Irish. Some of them also happened to work for Brendan Hughes. In this manner, Hughes used a ship named after a British queen to smuggle weapons to the IRA. When the guns arrived, fresh graffiti on the walls of West Belfast heralded a game change: GOD MADE THE CATHOLICS, BUT THE ARMALITE MADE THEM EQUAL.

Hughes was tearing along so fast that he almost passed the call house, and when he staggered to a sudden stop and swung open the door, he had acquired so much momentum that he went crashing, instead, right through the front window. He tumbled into the front room, got his bearings—and retrieved an Armalite. Then he stepped outside, saw his pursuers barreling toward the house, trained the Armalite on them, and started shooting. The men scrambled for cover and fired back. Then, out of nowhere, two Saracen armored vehicles materialized, racing down the road. They stopped abruptly, and suddenly the men were gone. Hughes stood there, panting, processing what he had just witnessed. The gunmen had been dressed like civilians. But they had escaped in a British Army vehicle. They weren't civilians—they were British Army. That was when Hughes looked down and realized he was bleeding.

. . .

Hughes had grown up surrounded by Protestants, in a predominantly Protestant enclave of West Belfast. When he was a child, during the 1950s, many of his friends were Protestant kids. There was an old lady who lived on the street who would spit every time he passed her house and ask if he had blessed himself with the pope's piss that morning. But for the most part he coexisted peacefully with the Protestants around him. Hughes was not yet ten years old when his mother died of cancer, leaving his father, Kevin, a bricklayer, to care for six children alone. Kevin never remarried. Two of Brendan's brothers emigrated to Australia, in search of work, and he stepped up, helping his father raise his younger siblings. Kevin would go out to work, and Brendan would be in charge of the kids at home. His father described him, in a modest expression that still counted as the highest praise, as a "lad you could depend upon."

In 1967, Hughes joined the British Merchant Navy and went to sea. He voyaged to the Middle East and to South Africa, where he witnessed up close the horrors of apartheid. By the time he returned two years later, Belfast had erupted into violence. Though he never spoke of it, Brendan's father had been a member of the IRA in his youth. One of Kevin's friends from that era was Billy McKee, the famous hard-line paramilitary who had helped to establish the Provos, and Brendan was raised to revere McKee as a legendary patriot and gunman. When the family walked to Mass on Sunday mornings, they would pass McKee's house on McDonnell Street, and Brendan felt as though he should genuflect out of respect for the man. Once, in some scullery where tea was being made after a funeral, he spotted McKee in conversation with some other adults. Brendan deliberately brushed against him and felt the bracing hardness of the .45 under his belt. Unable to control his own curiosity,

Brendan asked McKee if he could see the weapon, and McKee showed it to him.

When Brendan Hughes left to join the merchant navy, his father made a peculiar request: "Never get a tattoo." It was common for sailors to tattoo their bodies, and Hughes would have found himself in various tattoo parlors across Europe and the Far East, waiting while his mates submitted to the needle. But he honored his father's request. Kevin never gave any specific rationale for the admonition, apart from suggesting, vaguely, that a tattoo was an "identifiable mark." But years later, Brendan would reflect on that moment, wondering whether his father might have had some premonition about the road that he would end up taking.

At the call house on Sultan Street, he was losing blood quickly. But not from a gunshot. When he crashed through the front window, the broken glass had severed an artery in his wrist. The call house was blown now; it would not be safe to remain there. So several colleagues hustled Hughes along the sidewalk to another house a short distance away. He badly needed medical attention, but getting him to a hospital was out of the question: the army had sent men to execute him, and there was no policy of sanctuary that might protect him in a medical facility. The alternative was getting a doctor to come to Hughes, but that would pose a different sort of challenge. The men who tried to kill him had disappeared, but Saracens were still patrolling the neighborhood, no doubt searching for him. Hughes was trapped inside the house, like some wounded animal, the blood pumping out of his arm with each beat of his heart.

Half an hour went by. Things were looking grim. Then Gerry Adams arrived, with a doctor. Adams might have been the best friend that Brendan Hughes had. They had met two summers earlier, during the riots of 1970, when Adams was directing rioters. Hughes couldn't remember Adams himself actually throwing stones or petrol bombs, but he was very effective at orchestrating others. That was Adams's role, in Hughes's view—he was "the key strategist" for the Provos, whereas Hughes was more of a tactician. Fearless and cunning, Hughes could mastermind any operation, but Adams had the sort of mind that could perceive the broader political context and the shifting tectonics of the conflict. Like a general who stays behind the battle lines, Adams was known for avoiding direct violence himself. If a convoy of cars loaded with Armalites arrived in the neighborhood, Adams would ride in the "scout" car—the one without any weapons—whereas Hughes tended to be wherever the guns were. Dolours Price liked to joke that she never saw Hughes without a gun and she never saw Adams with one. To Adams, it seemed that Hughes was always very much in the thick of things. He had a "tremendous following" among the lads on the street, Adams later observed, adding that Hughes "compensated for any inability to articulate politically at great length by doing the right things instinctively."

If there was something faintly patronizing about this observation, it fit, more or less, with the role Hughes saw for himself in the conflict. He regarded himself as a soldier, not a politician.

A later photo of Gerry Adams and Brendan Hughes.

He considered himself a socialist, but he wasn't consumed by ideology. He considered himself a Catholic, too, but Adams said the rosary and read his Bible every night, whereas it was an effort for Hughes to get to Mass. Hughes sometimes remarked that his reverence for Adams was such that if Adams told him that tomorrow was Sunday when he knew that it was Monday, it would be enough to make him stop and think twice. Brendan's own little brother, Terry, remarked that Brendan's real family was the IRA—and his brother was Gerry Adams.

The doctor whom Adams had summoned was a local heart surgeon. But because he had come in such a hurry, he had no equipment. So someone fetched a needle and thread and a pair of tweezers, and the surgeon plunged the tweezers into the wound in Hughes's arm, grasping blindly for the recessed end of the severed vessel. Securing it, finally, between the tweezers' prongs, he pulled the vein down so that he could carefully sew it up. This rough procedure was conducted in close quarters, without anesthetic, but Hughes could not scream, because the army was still looking for him, patrolling the street outside. At one point while the doctor was working, a Saracen pulled up right in front of the house and lingered there, its powerful engine rumbling, while they all waited, frozen, wondering if men with rifles were about to break through the door.

. . .

That Adams would come personally meant a great deal to Hughes, because it was risky for him to do so. According to the Special Branch of the RUC, Adams had been commander of the Ballymurphy unit of the Provisionals, and later became the officer commanding of the Belfast Brigade—the top IRA man in the city. He was a marked man, more wanted by the authorities than even Hughes.

But Adams felt a deep bond of loyalty to Hughes. In addition to the genuine affection they shared, it mattered to Adams that when Hughes went "on the run," he remained on the streets of Belfast, rather than flee the city and retreat to the countryside or across the border to the Republic. He could have fled to Dundalk, just over the border, which had become a sort of Dodge City for republicans who were hiding out; they would sit in the pubs, getting drunk and playing cards. Instead, Hughes stayed in the city, close to his loyal soldiers in D Company, and he never let up the frantic pace of operations. "Local people knew he was there," Adams remarked. "And that was the kind of incentive they wanted."

Adams saved Hughes's life that day, and Hughes wouldn't forget it. He could have sent someone else, but he came himself. When Hughes was stitched up and the doctor had left, Adams ordered his friend to get out of Belfast and lie low for a while. He had clearly been targeted for assassination—it was a sure bet that they would try to kill him again. Hughes didn't want to leave, but Adams insisted. So Hughes traveled to Dundalk and booked a room in a bed-and-breakfast. But he was not one for R&R: he was itchy, impatient to get back to Belfast. In the end, he lasted only a week—which, given the pace of events in those days, felt to Hughes like an eternity.

·　·　·

In the vacant building across from where Hughes stood when the green van first discharged the shooters, something stirred. Behind the partially bricked-up façade, a team of British soldiers had spent the night. The paramilitaries were not the only ones to repurpose local real estate in service of their tactical objectives. The abandoned house, in the heart of D Company's territory, was being used as a clandestine observation post.

In the secret internal records of the British Army, a brief account of this botched mission survives. A write-up by the army, which has since been declassified and released, acknowledged that soldiers in civilian dress had engaged in what was described, for the purposes of the official record, not as an effort at targeted assassination, but as a "snatch attempt." From their hidden observation post, the soldiers had been conducting surveillance on Brendan Hughes and his associates from right inside their own territory. They had failed to kill or capture him this time. But now they knew what he looked like.

THE LITTLE BRIGADIER

FRANK KITSON, LIKE DOLOURS PRICE and Gerry Adams, was born into a family tradition. His father was an admiral in the Royal Navy. His brother was in the navy as well. His grandfather had served in the Indian Army. Kitson joined the British Army's Rifle Brigade and ended up marrying a colonel's daughter. But by the time he became a soldier, at eighteen, it felt as though he might have gotten started too late: it was 1945, and Kitson was sent to Germany, where the fighting had ended and the only thing left to do was watch the postscript to the war. There didn't seem to be much prospect of another world war, so Kitson spent his time living the life of a gentleman officer—going to the opera, racing horses, fishing—and trying to suppress the nagging suspicion that he might have missed his moment.

In 1953, he was assigned to Kenya, which was then still a British colony, to help put down an uprising by an elusive rebel group known as the Mau Mau. As he packed his bags for this assignment, Kitson's greatest fear was that by the time he actually arrived in Kenya, the "colonial emergency," as it was called, might have ended, and he would be forced to come home again without ever having seen any action.

He needn't have worried. When Kitson arrived in Kenya, he took immediately to what he called "the game." He was a methodical type, so he wrote down his ambition on a little piece of paper: "To provide the Security Forces with the information they [need] to destroy the Mau Mau." He tucked the paper into the Bible that he kept by his bed.

Kitson was short and stocky, with piercing eyes and a jutting chin. He carried himself ramrod straight, as if on a parade ground, and swung his shoulders as he walked, which gave the impression that he was a larger man than he was. Beneath his peaked and tasseled army cap, he was gradually losing his hair, and as the years went on he was seldom photographed without the cap. He had a slightly nasal voice and was prone to a sportsman's vernacular, describing people as "off net" and seasoning his conversation with other clubby expressions. He was known to dislike small talk. One story about Kitson that circulated in the army (and was almost certainly apocryphal, but revealing nonetheless) involved a dinner party at which the wife of one of Kitson's colleagues found herself seated next to him and announced that she had made a bet with a friend that she could get "at least half a dozen words" out of him.

"You've just lost," Kitson said, and did not speak another word to her all evening.

In Kenya, he found himself in a completely new environment: the forest. Before leaving on a night mission, he would apply black camouflage to his hands and face and, to complete the disguise, pull an old African bush hat over his head. By "blacking up" in this manner, he supposed he might be mistaken, at a distance and in poor light, for a native. Like a character out of Kipling, Kitson would plunge into the bramble, in search of the mysterious Mau Mau. As he navigated the dense bush, he was struck by how quickly you could adapt to the most alien milieu. In a memoir of his time in Kenya, he wrote, "Everything is strange for the first few moments, then after a time normal existence seems strange."

One day, Kitson came across a group of Kenyans draped from head to toe in white robes. Their faces were completely obscured, with thin slits cut in the fabric for their eyes, noses, and mouths. When Kitson inquired about who these strange men were, he learned that they were Mau Mau who had been induced to betray their fellow rebels and work with the British Army. With their identities shielded by the robes, they could observe a group of prisoners, then tell their British handlers who was who.

This was an epiphany for Kitson, a defining episode, as it introduced him to the "counter-gang," a concept that he immediately perceived could be fashioned into a highly effective weapon. In fighting an insurgency, Kitson realized, quality intelligence is essential, and one way to obtain that intelligence is to inveigle some members of the insurgency to switch sides. He began to devote a great deal of thought to how one could best go about persuading a rebel to betray his compatriots. Clearly, trust was a key ingredient, because any potential source, by agreeing to assist his enemy, would effectively be placing his life in the enemy's hands. But trust is a bond that can be cultivated. When Kitson was courting a new recruit to work as his agent, he would take the man on patrol with him. When they were deep in the bush, Kitson would hand his own pistol to the man, keeping only a machete for himself. This was a risky gesture, but Kitson believed that entrusting his secret agent with a weapon was a way of conveying "that he was absolutely one of the team."

The British eventually suppressed the rebellion, but at a staggering human cost. Nobody knows precisely how many Kenyans were slaughtered, but the number may reach the hundreds of thousands. Some 1.5 million people were detained, many in internment camps. Mau Mau suspects were subjected, during interrogations, to electric shocks, cigarette burns, and appalling forms of sexual torture. This brutal campaign did not forestall the British withdrawal from Kenya, in 1963. Yet, back in London, the operation against the Mau Mau was celebrated as a great success. Kitson had been awarded the Military Cross, for valor, in 1955, for his "gallant and distinguished services in

Kenya." "I wondered if perhaps some of my good fortune might have been due to the fact that I did think just a little bit more like a terrorist than some of our commanders," he mused afterward. "I wondered how much of the African mentality I had absorbed. Was I becoming callous and ruthless and treacherous—to mention some of their less attractive characteristics?"

Kitson had found his calling. There might be no more world wars to fight, but there were plenty of colonial insurgencies. In 1957, he ventured to Malaya, where he battled communist guerrillas in the jungles of Johore and was awarded a second Military Cross. From there he was dispatched to the Sultanate of Muscat and Oman, to contend with a rebellion in the desert. Next he did two stints in Cyprus, where Greek and Turkish Cypriots had gone to war, and was given command of his own battalion.

In 1969, Kitson spent a quiet year away from the battlefield, on a fellowship at Oxford University. Amid the Gothic architecture and manicured quads, he embarked on a new project: an effort to systematize his thinking about counterinsurgency. He studied Mao and Che Guevara and drew on his own combat experience, to produce a manuscript with the anodyne title *Low Intensity Operations*. In this book, Kitson advanced an argument that would become a cornerstone of later counterinsurgency

Frank Kitson in Kenya.

thinking: it is important not merely to put down an uprising but to win the hearts and minds of the local population. The book also focused heavily on the gathering of intelligence. It made a point so obvious that it almost went without saying: if you want to defeat an insurgency, it helps to know who the insurgents are. By the time Kitson finished the book, in 1970, he had emerged as perhaps the preeminent warrior-intellectual of the British Army. When he finished up at Oxford, he was promoted to brigadier and sent to the site of Britain's latest small war: Northern Ireland.

.   .   .

Army headquarters at Lisburn lay eight miles outside of Belfast, behind fortified blast walls lined with sandbags and barbed wire. The number of British troops in Northern Ireland had escalated dramatically in a short period of time: during the summer of 1969, there were 2,700; by the summer of 1972, there were more than 30,000. The soldiers were often just as young and inexperienced as the paramilitaries they were fighting: gangly, pimply, frightened young men who were scarcely out of their teens. They were spread across the country, at bases and barracks and makeshift billets. Two companies of Black Watch soldiers were billeted in a vast aircraft hangar. Another company resided in a bus depot, where soldiers bunked down in empty buses. The soldiers were being deployed to Northern Ireland for four-month tours, before rotating home again.

But it could be a hugely dangerous assignment, with a multitude of armed factions blending into close-knit communities. In light of the constant risk of getting picked off by a sniper or torn apart by a homemade bomb, some of the more introspective soldiers were forced to wonder: What would success look like? How would you define victory? They had been sent to Northern Ireland to quell the unrest during the summer of 1969, but since their arrival, the bloodshed had only intensified. What would they have to achieve before they could all go home? The army that deployed in the Troubles was not the army that had fought the Nazis. It was an organization that had come of age fighting small wars of colonial disentanglement. But what was Northern Ireland? Was it part of the United Kingdom? Or was it one of those restive colonies?

When Frank Kitson arrived, in 1970, he was not the overall commander of British forces. But he was in charge of the army's 39 Airportable Brigade, which had responsibility for Belfast, and his influence far exceeded his station. As one of Kitson's subordinates later put it, "Within his area of responsibility he was the sun around which the planets revolved, and he very much set the tone."

The biggest challenge facing the army when Kitson arrived was a shortage of solid intelligence. The men and women who became paramilitaries, whether republican or loyalist, looked like everyone else in the civilian population. So how to identify them? In previous decades, membership in the IRA had been relatively static—the same names came up year after year. But the old police files were in desperate need of an update, now that there were new recruits flocking to the cause every week. This difficulty was only exacerbated by the blunderbuss approach favored by the army. "When I was first there, the tactics were rather to stand in a line, pump the place full of gas, and let people chuck bricks at you until they got tired of it," Kitson later recalled. "Not a very good idea because the gas did so much damage to the local people. It made them hostile."

In *Low Intensity Operations,* Kitson had observed that the aim in counterinsurgency situations should be to "destroy the subversive movement utterly." But it's difficult to destroy a target that you cannot see. Kitson became obsessed with intelligence. The first challenge is always "getting the right information," he liked to say.

In particular, Kitson was interested in D Company of the Belfast Brigade, the IRA unit operated by Brendan Hughes and the one that was doing the most damage. British soldiers referred to Hughes's operational area in West Belfast as "the reservation"—Indian country, where soldiers should tread carefully, if at all. Among themselves (and occasionally in the press) the soldiers would decry their adversary's lack of humanity, saying, "These people are savages." Hughes and his men were out there, invisible and silent, embedded in the community. At Palace Barracks, outside the city, where many of the soldiers were stationed, you could hear the bombs going off in Belfast at night. The windowpanes would shudder.

With blasts in central shopping areas, you might suppose that the army would have no trouble finding frightened or disaffected civilians who were willing to help them by furnishing information. But soldiers complained that in West Belfast, a "wall of silence" protected the IRA. Informers were known as "touts," and for centuries they had been reviled in Irish culture as the basest species of traitor. So there was a profound social stigma against cooperating with the British.

Brendan Hughes was not the only one with a habit of quoting that Mao line about the fish and the sea. Kitson liked it, too. But he put his own spin on the sentiment. A fish can be "attacked directly by rod or net," he advised. "But if rod and net cannot succeed by themselves it may be necessary to do something to the water."

.   .   .

Just before dawn one morning in August 1971, three thousand British troops descended on nationalist areas across Northern Ireland. Soldiers broke down doors and dragged men from their beds, hauling them off to internment. Under the Special Powers Act, it was legal to hold someone indefinitely without trial, and internment had been used periodically in Northern Ireland. But not on this scale. Of the nearly 350 suspects arrested that day, not a single one was a loyalist, though there were plenty of loyalist paramilitaries engaged in terrorism at the time. This disparity in treatment only compounded the impression, in the minds of many Catholics, that the army was simply another instrument of sectarian oppression. In planning the sweep, the army had relied on intelligence from the RUC, and, as one British commander later acknowledged, the largely Protestant police force consisted of people who were "partial to one extent or another, in many cases, to a considerable extent."

But the lists of suspects that the RUC produced were not merely skewed to target Catholics—they were also out of date, and included many people who had no involvement whatsoever in the armed struggle. Because of the Irish tradition of naming sons after their fathers, elderly men were dragged off under the mistaken assumption that they were their sons, and sons were arrested because the authorities thought they were their fathers. (Sometimes, finding both father and son at home and uncertain about which one they were after, the army simply took both.) Nearly a third of the suspects seized that morning were released after two days. The army had arrested a bunch of people it wasn't looking for while failing to arrest most of the people it *was* looking for, all while further embittering a Catholic population that was highly embittered to begin with. An official study by the British Ministry of Defence later conceded that internment had been "a major mistake." In the words of one British officer who took part in the sweep, "It was lunacy."

As the presiding counterinsurgency intellectual in Northern Ireland, Frank Kitson would forever be associated with internment. But he would later insist that he had not approved of the decision—that, on the contrary, he had warned his superiors that such a measure would prove counterproductive. His quarrel was not so much with the use of the practice in general as with the specifics of its application in this instance. Kitson had endorsed the use of internment in Kenya and elsewhere. While allowing that it was "not an attractive measure to people brought up in a free country," he argued that internment could nevertheless shorten a conflict "by removing from the scene people who would otherwise have become involved in the fighting." He reportedly quipped, of locking people up without trial, "It's better than killing them." This view may seem callous in retrospect, but the sentiment was echoed at the time in the British press. The *Telegraph* suggested that some of the Catholics who were locked up without charge "admit to preferring internment to the chances of being shot outside."

Kitson's chief critique of internment in Northern Ireland was that it did not come as a surprise. Brendan Hughes, who knew a thing or two about intelligence himself, was never picked up in the raid—because he knew in advance that it was coming. In late July, the army did a kind of dry run, conducting searches and arrests, and the operation looked to Hughes like an effort to gather information. He was right. The army had devised this preparatory phase in order to make sure the addresses on their list were up to date. Another hint about the army's intentions was rising from the ground twelve miles outside of Belfast: on the premises of a former air force base, a capacious new prison camp was being constructed, a facility capable of housing large numbers of detainees. If you were paying attention, it was not a question of *whether* mass internment would be introduced, but when. Brendan Hughes, having realized this well in advance of the raid, simply went underground, along with his men. After the sweep, the IRA held a press conference to announce, with smug satisfaction, that the massive operation had succeeded in netting hardly any Provos at all.

.   .   .

Dolours Price was not one of those picked up. When the raids happened, she was out of town, on a visit to London. The army had come for her father, but he wasn't there, either. He knew they were coming and was already on the run. But Dolours's childhood friend Francie McGuigan was arrested. It was not just Francie and his father, John, who were involved in the armed struggle; his entire family was. Francie was the oldest of seven children, all of whom would end up doing time. When the raid happened that summer, his mother, a sturdy woman named Mary McGuigan, was already locked up, serving a sentence of almost a year in Armagh jail for taking part in a peaceful protest. It was around four in the morning and Francie was asleep in bed when the door burst open and soldiers flooded the room. They dragged him out of the house in his underpants while another soldier pulled his father onto the street. John McGuigan collapsed on the pavement, but Francie could not come to his aid. He was thrown into the back of a lorry. As the lorry drove off, Francie looked out the back window and caught a glimpse of his father, still on the ground.

John McGuigan ended up being held by the police for several days. When he got out, he could not find his son. Francie had not come home, so John assumed that he must still be in custody. But when he telephoned Crumlin Road jail, where many of the internees had been taken, they said there was no Francis McGuigan there. Next John telephoned the army, but they told him that everybody arrested in the raid had subsequently been turned over to the police. People were getting killed in the streets, and John began to fear that Francie might be dead. He saw a local man he knew, who confirmed his worst suspicions. "There's a boy down in the morgue," the man said. "I think it's your Francie." Distraught, John made his way to the morgue and asked to see the body.

It was another boy. It wasn't Francie. John was overcome with relief. But if Francie wasn't dead, and he wasn't being held by the army or the police—then where was he?

What John McGuigan did not know was that his son had

been selected, along with eleven others, for a special fate. A thick hood was placed over his head, muffling his senses. It had the stale smell of dirty laundry. Francie was loaded, along with several other prisoners, onto a Wessex helicopter. They flew for a period of time; it was hard to say how long. Nobody would tell Francie where they were going. Then, under the roar of the helicopter's rotor, he heard a sucking sound and a louder roar and realized that, though they were still flying, someone had just slid open the helicopter's door. Now Francie felt hands on him, jostling him, moving him. His handcuffs were removed and he managed to wrap his arms around his knees and draw them tight to his body, folding himself into a compact ball. He still couldn't see anything because of the hood, and he was panicking, and now he felt the hands pushing him out the open door of the helicopter and he was falling.

But another set of hands was on him now, and he felt the ground beneath him. What had seemed, in his blindness, to be a free fall to certain death ended up being just a few feet: the helicopter had been hovering close to the ground. Now the people who had caught him were hustling him into a mysterious facility. It was a remote barracks on an old Second World War airfield in County Derry. But Francie McGuigan did not know that at the time, since he was still hooded, and, technically, it was an undisclosed location, selected by the army because it was remote, anonymous, and far from any mechanism of accountability. McGuigan and his fellow detainees were stripped naked and examined by a doctor, then subjected to a series of procedures that were classified, in the army's euphemistic bureaucratese, as "interrogation in depth."

For days, the prisoners were deprived of food, water, and sleep and made to stand for long periods in stress positions, their vision negated by the hoods over their heads. They were also subjected to piercing, high-pitched noises. The British had learned these techniques by studying the experiences of soldiers who were held as prisoners of war by the Nazis or by the North Koreans and the Chinese during the Korean War. As it happened, Anthony Farrar-Hockley, who until the month before had served as commander of land forces in Northern Ireland, had himself once been tortured as a prisoner of war in North Korea. "The IRA call themselves soldiers and say they're carrying out warfare, so they must be prepared to be frightened if they're captured and interrogated," he remarked.

Initially, the techniques had been taught to British soldiers as a way to resist harsh interrogation and torture. But eventually these methods migrated from the portion of the curriculum that was concerned with defense into the portion that dealt with offense. They had been employed for nearly two decades against insurgents in British-controlled territories—in Palestine, Malaya, Kenya, Cyprus. But they had never been memorialized in any written manual and instead were passed down from one generation of interrogators to the next, an oral tradition of human cruelty.

"What's your position?" the interrogators asked McGuigan. "Who is on the Belfast Brigade staff?" They wanted names—names like Gerry Adams and Brendan Hughes, the names of McGuigan's commanding officers and his fellow volunteers. As one day bled into the next, with no sense of time, McGuigan's psyche became warped by sleep deprivation and hunger and the relentless noise. He felt as if he was starting to lose his mind. When the interrogators asked him to spell his own name, he would garble the answer. When they instructed him to count to ten, he found that he couldn't. For a long time, they had him chained to a cast-iron radiator, and the cuffs chafed his wrists until the skin was raw and tender. Many of the men began to suffer from hallucinations. At one point, convinced that he would never make it out alive, McGuigan bashed his own head against the radiator until blood seeped down his face.

When the torture ended, after a week, some of the men were

so broken that they could not remember their own names. Their eyes had a haunted, hollow look to them, which one of the men likened to "two pissholes in the snow." Another detainee, who had gone into the interrogation with jet-black hair, came out of the experience with hair that was completely white. (He died not long after being released, of a heart attack, at forty-five.) When Francie McGuigan was finally returned to Crumlin Road jail, he saw his father, and the older man broke down and cried.

There is no record, at least in the public domain, of Frank Kitson's views on "interrogation in depth." But it seems unlikely that he was troubled by it. Rough tactics were a signature of the colonial campaigns in which he specialized. When his treatise on counterinsurgency was released, one review noted that "the four Geneva conventions of 1949, many parts of which are explicitly relevant, and which Britain has signed, are not mentioned." A subsequent investigation by the British government found that some of the interrogation techniques used against the so-called Hooded Men constituted criminal assault. But in a controversial 1978 decision, the European Court of Human Rights held that the techniques, while "inhuman and degrading," did not amount to torture. (In the aftermath of the terrorist attacks of September 11, 2001, when the American administration of George W. Bush was fashioning its own "enhanced interrogation" techniques, officials relied explicitly on this decision to justify the use of torture.)

. . .

But perhaps the most concrete application of Frank Kitson's colonial philosophies in the context of the Troubles was the MRF. This was an elite unit so murky and clandestine that nobody seemed to agree even on the baseline matter of what precisely the acronym MRF stood for. It might have been Mobile Reconnaissance Force. Or *Military* Reconnaissance Force. Or

Military *Reaction* Force. The MRF consisted of thirty or so special operators, both men and women, who were handpicked from all across the British Army. They dressed in plain clothes, wearing bell-bottoms and jean jackets, and grew their hair long. Within the army, they were known as the Bomb Squad, because one of their responsibilities was reconnaissance, and they would stake out locations where they expected paramilitaries to plant a bomb. Soldiers of Irish origin were deliberately recruited, in order to blend in with the locals.

Members of the MRF drove around republican enclaves, conducting covert surveillance. But they also got out of their vehicles, in the heart of Indian country. They posed as road sweepers and dustmen. They huddled with the vagrants drinking methylated spirits by the side of the road. They also began to set up secret observation posts, creeping into shops and homes that had been damaged by rioting or fire. A single brick would be extracted from a walled-up façade, allowing an MRF member hiding inside to look out upon the neighborhood. One woman who worked for the MRF went door-to-door, selling cosmetics and gathering intelligence as she went. In December 1971, Kitson wrote a memo entitled "Future Developments in Belfast," in which he explained that one critical means of bringing the fight to the IRA was "building up and developing the MRF."

But the unit was doing more than gathering intelligence. It was assassinating people, too. Men in plain clothes would drive around in an unmarked Ford Cortina, with a Sterling submachine gun hidden under the seat. They had to keep the weapon out of sight, one MRF member would later explain, because they were camouflaged so effectively that if they passed an army outpost and were spotted with a gun, their own British colleagues "would open fire and we would be shot." It was an MRF team that had burst out of the green van in West Belfast and attempted to murder Brendan Hughes. These hit squads deliberately carried particular makes of weapons that were used by the paramilitaries, so that when someone was murdered, the ballistics would suggest that it was the IRA or loyalist killers who were responsible, rather than the army.

"We wanted to cause confusion," one MRF member recalled. If people believed the paramilitaries were responsible, it would erode their standing in the community and preserve the image of the army as a law-abiding neutral referee. This was particularly true in those instances where the MRF, seeking to assassinate a target, ended up inadvertently killing an unaffiliated civilian instead. One summer night in 1972, a twenty-four-year-old woman named Jean Smyth-Campbell was sitting in the passenger seat of a car at a bus terminal on the Glen Road when a bullet pierced the window and then her head. At the time, the police announced that "no security forces were involved" in her death and implied that there might be some connection to "political bodies" (a shorthand for paramilitary groups) in the area. Smyth-Campbell's family came to believe that she had been shot by the IRA. In fact, it would be four decades before they learned that she was actually killed by the MRF.

Frank Kitson was a maestro of press manipulation. In the aftermath of a spasm of violence, he would summon the local *Guardian* correspondent, a young writer named Simon Winchester, to visit him at army headquarters for a briefing. Kitson would proceed to spell out, with great certainty, the circumstances of the relevant incident, citing the army's classified intelligence files on the victims. Winchester, feeling lucky to have the scoop, would then dutifully report that the dead man in question had been a quartermaster or an ordnance expert or a senior marksman for the Provos. Winchester liked Kitson, whom he thought of as "the little Brigadier," and they became friends; the young correspondent would make social visits to Kitson's family at their home on the army base and play cards with Kitson's daughter. It was only later that Winchester came to realize how shoddy British intelligence on the Provos was at that stage, and to suspect that much of the information he had parroted was simply wrong. He eventually concluded, and acknowledged publicly, that he had been used by Kitson as a "mouthpiece" for the army.

Kitson's Strangelovean attributes made him an object of obsession for the IRA. The Provos studied *Low Intensity Operations* and featured Kitson in their propaganda. In the fevered imaginations of the paramilitaries, he became an outsize antagonist, talked about but rarely seen, "Kits the Butcher of Belfast." Already prone to wartime superstition, the Provos began to attribute any freak occurrence that they could not otherwise explain to the mind games of the shifty British strategist, as if he were some sort of poltergeist. There were plans to kidnap Kitson, though none of them ever came to fruition. The Provos were said to have a "death list," with the names of priority targets for assassination; Frank Kitson was right at the top.

But the Provos were not the only ones to keep a death list. As the MRF conducted its surveillance and developed intelligence, the unit had its own catalog of targets whom the operatives were authorized to shoot on sight. In the MRF's secret briefing room in the heart of Palace Barracks, the walls were plastered with surveillance shots of the biggest "players" among the Provos— their targets. According to an account by one former member of the MRF, the key figures on the wall included Brendan Hughes, Gerry Adams, and Dolours and Marian Price.

THE CRACKED CUP

A PRISON FLOATED IN Belfast Lough. The HMS *Maidstone* was a five-hundred-foot ship that had been used during the Second World War to service submarines for the Royal Navy. When the Troubles broke out, the vessel was hastily recommissioned as an emergency accommodation for two thousand British troops arriving in Belfast, then recommissioned again, as HMP *Maidstone*—Her Majesty's Prison. The ship slouched in the harbor, at a jetty, twenty feet from land. The prison quarters consisted of two bunkhouses beneath the deck: stuffy, overcrowded spaces in which prisoners were confined in three-tiered bunks. The light was dim, filtering through a few small portholes. The space was "not fit for pigs," as one prisoner put it.

One day in March 1972, armed guards escorted a high-profile prisoner onto the *Maidstone*. It was Gerry Adams. After being on the run for months, Adams had been snatched by troops in a dawn raid on a West Belfast home, and now he was ushered roughly into the hold of the ship. He was greeted warmly by friends and relatives who were being held there, but he soon came to hate the place, which he thought of as a "brutal and oppressive sardine tin." He may have been a hardened revolutionary, but Adams was not a man who was indifferent to nourishment. He liked a good meal, and the food on the ship was foul.

Adams was also in pain. When he was arrested, he had refused to acknowledge that he was in fact Gerry Adams. Instead he made up a pseudonym—Joe McGuigan—and insisted that was his name. He was taken to a police barracks and interrogated, and eventually one of the few RUC officers who actually knew Adams by face came in, took one look at him, and said, "That's Gerry Adams." Adams didn't care. He continued to insist, stubbornly, that his captors had the wrong guy. Adams had been ruminating, lately, about counter-interrogation techniques. "I had seized upon the device of refusing to admit I was Gerry Adams as a means of combating my interrogation," he later recalled. "By continuing to assert that I was Joe McGuigan, I reasoned that I would thwart the interrogation by bogging it down on this issue."

The interrogators beat Adams, but he wouldn't say a word. They tried good cop, bad cop—one guy going completely berserk, pulling out his gun and threatening to shoot Adams, only to be restrained by the other—but Adams didn't break. It was only when he sensed that the interrogation was finally coming to an end that Adams acknowledged what everybody already knew: that he was Gerry Adams. By that time, his interrogators had been arguing with him for so long over the simple question of what his name was that Adams had managed to tell them nothing of any substance. "Of course, my strategy had been reduced to a charade by this time, but it had given me, I felt, a crutch to withstand their inquisition," he later observed. "To remain silent was the best policy. So even though they knew who I was, it was irrelevant. I couldn't answer their questions, on the basis that I wasn't who they said I was."

When he was hauled onto the *Maidstone,* Adams had a visit with the prison doctor and explained that, after all the beating, his ribs felt tender.

"Is it sore?" the doctor asked.

"It's sore when I breathe," Adams replied.

"Stop breathing," the doctor said, without a flicker of a smile.

If the staff on board the *Maidstone* seemed bitter, and security was particularly tight, there was a reason. One frigid January evening a couple of months earlier, seven republican prisoners had stripped to their underwear, slathered their bodies in butter and black boot polish to insulate against the cold, sawed through an iron bar, squeezed through a porthole, dropped one by one into the icy water of the Musgrave Channel, and swum several hundred yards to the opposite shore. The prisoners had come upon the idea for the escape after watching a seal navigate the barbed-wire netting that had been placed in the water around the ship.

All seven men made it to the far shore and scrambled out of the water. They were soaking wet, dressed in their under-wear, and smeared with shoe polish. Looking as if they had just crawled out of the Black Lagoon, they proceeded to hijack a bus. Fortuitously, one of the escapees had been a bus driver before joining the IRA, and he piloted this unlikely getaway vehicle into central Belfast. When they stopped in a neighborhood that was home to many republican sympathizers, local kids immediately set upon the bus, like a swarm of locusts, and started stripping it for parts. The prisoners hastened into the nearest pub, still mostly naked, and the patrons who stood around the bar looked up abruptly, shocked by this sudden, surreal intrusion. Then, without hesitation or, really, much need for explanation, the barflies started stripping off their own clothes and offering them to the fugitives. One of the patrons produced his car keys and tossed them to the men, saying, "Away youse go." By the time the army mobilized six hundred troops for a manhunt, the men had vanished. After slipping across the border, they held a triumphant press conference in Dublin, where the newspapers anointed them "the Magnificent Seven."

.   .   .

Not long after Adams arrived on the *Maidstone,* British authorities elected to close the ship. The new prison that had been under construction for some time at the airfield outside Belfast was now complete. It was known as Long Kesh. One day, Adams was handcuffed to another prisoner, loaded into an army helicopter, and flown to the new facility. Long Kesh was an eerie place. The paramilitaries who were confined there, adamant that they were not criminals but political prisoners, called it a concentration camp. And it *looked* like a concentration camp: on a windswept, desolate plain, a series of corrugated steel huts housed the prisoners, amid barbed-wire fences, floodlights, and sentry towers.

Long Kesh came to occupy a vivid place in the Irish republican imagination. But Adams would not be staying long. One day in June 1972, a couple of months after his arrival, someone shouted, "Adams—release!" At first he thought this must be some practical joke. Or, worse, a trap. But when Adams had gathered his belongings and stepped out of the prison, he saw Dolours and Marian Price waiting there for him, with a car to take him home. They drove him into Andersonstown, for a meeting with other members of the republican leadership on a matter of utmost delicacy.

While Adams was locked up, a secret back channel had been developing between the Provos and the British government. After some preliminary contacts, it seemed that an opportunity might exist to negotiate a possible cease-fire. One of Adams's confederates in the IRA, a hard man named Ivor Bell, had insisted that a necessary precondition for any discussions with the British was the release from internment of Gerry Adams. He was still only twenty-three years old, but Adams had become such an instrumental figure in the IRA that there could be no peace talks without him. "No fucking cease-fire unless Gerry is released," Bell said.

On June 26, the IRA initiated a cease-fire, and the British Army agreed to reciprocate. There had been a crescendo of bombings and shootings just prior to the cease-fire; some suggested that this may have been a deliberate IRA strategy, in order to underline the contrast when the shooting stopped. But once the truce was called, IRA leaders committed to honoring it, vowing, in an unintentionally comical flourish, that anyone who violated the cease-fire would be shot. The Provos announced that they had formulated a "peace plan," which they would reveal "at the appropriate time."

Many people in Northern Ireland objected on principle to any such dialogue, insisting that there should be no negotiation whatsoever with IRA terrorists. But that July, Adams and a small contingent of fellow IRA members boarded a British military plane, under conditions of great secrecy. Along with Adams, the group included Seán Mac Stíofáin; Ivor Bell; a gregarious, curly-haired young man named Martin McGuinness, who was the OC in Derry; and two other IRA leaders, Dáithí Ó Conaill and Seamus Twomey. They landed at an air force base in Oxfordshire, where two immense limousines stood waiting.

If this mode of conveyance seemed ostentatiously swanky, it was also grounds for suspicion. Adams was a former bartender. Ivor Bell had worked as a mechanic. McGuinness had trained as a butcher's assistant. Hyper-attuned to any hint of British pomposity, the rebels would not allow themselves to be patronized or cowed. In advance of the trip, Bell had announced that, while they might be an official delegation to a peace summit, he, for one, would not be putting on a suit and tie. If history had taught him anything, Bell said, it was that the British liked nothing more than to make the Irish feel ill at ease. If their hosts were conspicuously formal, he would answer with extravagant informality. Let *them* feel uncomfortable for a change. Gerry Adams took a similar view on the wardrobe issue: he selected a pullover with a hole in it for the occasion.

The limousines ferried the group into London and deposited them at a grand old house in Chelsea, facing the Thames. As they walked inside, a little awed despite themselves, Adams

noticed a plaque out front that said the painter James McNeill
Whistler had once lived there.

The Irishmen were escorted up a staircase and into a book-
lined drawing room. Then William Whitelaw, Her Majesty's
secretary of state for Northern Ireland, walked in and offered
the men a genial greeting. Whitelaw was smooth and polished.
He made a show of pronouncing Seán Mac Stíofáin's adopted
name correctly—a touch that Mac Stíofáin could not help but
appreciate. But as they went round and shook hands, Adams
noticed that Whitelaw's palms were sweating.

Whitelaw began by saying that, in light of the long history
between England and Ireland, he could understand why his
guests might regard the British with suspicion, but that he hoped
that "in me, you will see a British minister you can trust." That
was the high point of the meeting. Mac Stíofáin had prepared
a statement, which he proceeded to read out loud. It consisted
of a list of demands: the Provos wanted a public declaration
from the British government acknowledging the right of *all* Irish
people—in the North and the South—to self-determination.
They also wanted the British to declare their intent to withdraw
all forces from Irish soil by January 1, 1975.

One of the British participants, an intelligence officer named
Frank Steele, watched this presentation with quiet dismay. Mac
Stíofáin was laying down his demands as if the IRA had already
fought the British to a standstill. When Steele was initially sent
to Northern Ireland, the view of the British government had
been that they didn't want to talk to the IRA—they wanted to
defeat it. After the massacre on Bloody Sunday, many British
officials were forced to realize that they were unlikely to win
the war through military might alone. Steele had been working, in great secrecy, with the IRA representatives in advance
of the meeting. He regarded these men with a certain disdain-
ful amusement, particularly for their insistence on adopting the

lingo and trappings of a conventional military organization. "It was all rather sweet, really," Steele later observed. "They wanted to depict themselves as representing an army and not a bunch of terrorists."

When the men strode into the meeting with Whitelaw and laid down their hard line, Steele found their posture to be hopelessly naïve. In demanding that the British withdraw from Northern Ireland, they were asking that the government give up the guarantee that it would not abandon the Protestant population in the North, a concession that it simply could not make. As the meeting progressed, Whitelaw grew frustrated. In his memoirs, he described the encounter as "a non-event," sabotaged by the "absurd ultimatums" of the IRA.

Gerry Adams said little during the meeting, but Steele watched the rangy, thoughtful young rebel and was impressed. He had been told that Adams represented the IRA in the North and that he was a senior officer in the Belfast Brigade. Steele had expected some arrogant, streetwise ruffian. But when he initially encountered Adams, at a preliminary meeting before the trip, he found him to be personable, articulate, and self-disciplined. These were appealing qualities in an interlocutor, Steele thought, but they also made Adams a dangerously effective adversary. As Adams was leaving one of the preliminary meetings, Steele took him aside. "You don't want to spend the rest of your life on the run from us British," he said. "What do you want to do?"

"I want to go to university and get a degree," Adams replied.

"We're not stopping you," Steele pointed out. "Renounce violence and you can go to university."

Adams grinned and said, "I've got to help to get rid of you British first."

.   .   .

When the cease-fire was first declared that June, it had seemed to Brendan Hughes as though the war might soon be over. For people who had been on the run, the abrupt cessation of hostilities meant that they could venture out of hiding, go home, and reconnect with family. Ordinary civilians emerged, tentatively, from behind the barricades. It would be the first peaceful summer since the outbreak of violence three years earlier. Shops reopened. There was a sense of tentative optimism in the air.

For Hughes, the cease-fire meant that he could spend time with his new wife. In early 1972, just before his twenty-fourth birthday, he had married a local girl named Lily, who was nineteen. By the time the truce began, Lily was pregnant. Brendan's father had disapproved of the union, on the grounds that Brendan could never be a husband to Lily in any conventional way. Having a family could be dangerous for a man on the run. Adams had also recently married, and it was because he was married that the authorities had been able to capture him and lock him up on the *Maidstone*: they had targeted the house where his bride, Colette, was living, and raided the place on a night when Adams had snuck in for a visit. Brendan's wife, Lily, grew accustomed to raids by British troops who were looking for her fugitive husband. It made her too anxious to sleep at night, fearful that the door might be kicked in at any moment.

The truce meant that Brendan could slow down and see Lily. They could pretend for a while that they had a normal relationship. But the peace lasted scarcely two weeks. After the inconclusive talks in London, the parties had agreed to meet a second time, but the meeting never happened. On the ninth of July, fighting broke out once more, on Lenadoon Avenue, after the army refused to allow Catholic refugees to take up residence in homes that had been abandoned by Protestants. Announcing an end to the truce, Seán Mac Stíofáin said that he had instructed his men to resume their campaign of violence with the "utmost ferocity." An order was passed down the chain of command until it reached Brendan Hughes: *Get back to work.*

Hughes set about planning one of the Provos' most ambitious operations. A key element of the IRA's strategy had been to detonate bombs in commercial districts in Northern Ireland. Because most businesses were owned by unionist or British companies, and because the government controlled the infrastructure, an attack on commercial property was regarded as a direct hit at the enemy. These operations may have been staged in civilian areas, but Hughes and his fellow rebels insisted that they were not *directed* at civilians. The point was to destroy property, not to murder people. Warnings were called in to the police and the media in advance of the blasts so that civilians could (in theory) vacate the area. Of course, these warnings had an added propaganda value: a panicked news bulletin alerting shoppers that the city was about to blow up only magnified the spectacle of each bomb.

.   .   .

One Friday that July, an IRA team planted nearly two dozen bombs—an unprecedented number—in bus stations, railway depots, and shopping areas all across Belfast. Shortly after 2 p.m., when the city was thronged with shoppers enjoying the midsummer afternoon, the devices began to detonate, and for the next hour, a new bomb would go off every few minutes. People screamed and scrambled, but in many cases they would flee a blast in one area only to run into an adjacent area just as a new bomb was about to explode. Several buses were ripped apart. Nine people were killed, including a fourteen-year-old boy; 130 were wounded. The city was totally unprepared for the carnage. As a pall of smoke hung over central Belfast, one woman staggered through the rubble and spotted a strange shape on the ground. She thought it looked like something that had fallen off a meat lorry. Then she realized it was a human torso. Police officers picked through the rubble, retrieving stray body parts and placing them gingerly in plastic bags.

"This city has not experienced such a day of death and destruction since the German blitz of 1941," the *Belfast Telegraph* declared, citing the "callous lack of remorse now so typical of the Provos." *The Irish Times* pointed out, in an editorial, that the main victims of the attack were not the British Army or even big business, but "the plain people of Belfast and Ireland." The article went on to wonder, "Can anyone now believe that anything worthwhile can be established by these methods? That the country of anyone's vision can live with more memories of this kind?"

As one of the key architects of the operation, Brendan Hughes had hoped it would be a "spectacular" event. But when the bombs started going off, he was stationed on Leeson Street, holding an Armalite, and he could hear the pace of the explosions—*boom, boom, boom.* "There's too much here," he thought to himself. Some of the volunteers in the Lower Falls area were cheering as they heard the blasts, but Hughes shouted at them to get off the streets. They had planted too many bombs. They had overestimated the ability of the authorities to deal, in real time, with a calamity on this scale. Hughes would insist for years that his aim had not been to kill people, just to destroy property. Whatever the truth of his intentions, the episode filled him with guilt. At the time, however, he did not have much opportunity to dwell on it, because he was embroiled in a very different sort of crisis.

·   ·   ·

Hughes was in Belfast one night, just before the cease-fire, when one of his men told him that a Provo named Joe Russell had been shot. Hughes immediately went to see Russell and found him clutching a wound. He hadn't gone to the hospital—too risky—so there was still a bullet lodged in his gut. Hughes made arrangements to have Russell taken over the border, to a hospital in Dundalk that was known for offering treatment to wounded republicans, with "no questions asked."

But a mystery remained: Who was the shooter? Russell had been home at the time. A man came to his front door and, when Russell opened it, the man shot him and then ran off. Russell told Hughes that he thought his assailant was a member of the Stickies—the Official IRA. This theory was endorsed by Joe Lynskey, the soft-featured Provo intelligence officer whom people called the Mad Monk.

During the Troubles, unlicensed drinking clubs opened up in neighborhoods all over Belfast. These establishments were known as "shebeens." Many of the traditional pubs had been burned out or bombed, and in this notoriously thirsty city, such informal watering holes sprang up to meet a need. It had become so risky to venture outside of one's own safe ethnic enclave that when shebeens were established in residential neighborhoods—often in former homes that had been abandoned—they provided a safe and convenient alternative. By the end of 1972, some two hundred shebeens were operating throughout Belfast. They were open seven days a week, with no fixed hours. The booze was often stolen from hijacked trucks, and the proceeds frequently went to whatever paramilitary group controlled the neighborhood in question.

A number of these shebeens were operated by the Official IRA, and members of the Officials liked to congregate in them. One was called the Burning Embers. (Brendan Hughes set fire to it once, and he liked to joke that he had burned the Burning Embers.) Another Official shebeen was the Cracked Cup, an outfit on Leeson Street so named because it occupied a former shop that had sold secondhand crockery. The place was not much to look at. The floorboards were rotting, the lighting was dim, and patrons sat on rickety chairs, huddled around their pints. There were pictures of the Virgin Mary and Patrick Pearse on the wall.

Looking for the man who had shot Joe Russell, Hughes dispatched a posse of gunmen to the Cracked Cup. They strode in, weapons drawn, and barred the entrance. One of the patrons that night was a man named Desmond Mackin. He had come out to celebrate Father's Day with his wife, Margaret, and his seventy-year-old mother. Mackin was not a member of the Official IRA; as it happened, he had a son who had recently joined the Provos. But as Hughes's gunmen ordered the men to kneel on the floor and jostled Mackin's wife and mother, Mackin made the mistake of resisting. A spurt of gunfire lit the gloom, and a bullet pierced Mackin's thigh.

The shooter was a young Provo, barely out of his teens. It would later emerge that by the time the gunmen crashed into the Cracked Cup that night, they may have all been quite drunk. Mackin's wife collapsed over his body, screaming. But the Provos would not let anyone summon an ambulance, for fear of attracting the authorities. For fifteen long minutes, they all stayed inside the Cracked Cup while Desmond Mackin bled to death on the floor.

The press would characterize the shooting that night as a "power struggle" between the Officials and the Provos, and, at a glance, that certainly appeared to be the case. One newspaper suggested that the incident might spark an "all out war." But, really, Desmond Mackin was just an innocent bystander, collateral damage in a badly botched operation. And when Hughes continued his inquiries into who it was that shot Joe Russell, he made an alarming discovery. It hadn't been the Officials at all. On the contrary, it was one of his own men.

.   .   .

Of all the social conventions the Troubles upended, one that was seldom discussed was romantic relationships. With its combination of Catholic and Scots Presbyterian cultures, Belfast could be an oppressively prudish society. But as the violence warped everyday life, long-established social mores began to loosen. The omnipresence of mortal danger drove some people to live their lives with a newfound, and sometimes reckless, intensity.

The Mad Monk, Joe Lynskey, had entered the monastery when he was only sixteen years old. When he left the priesthood, in his twenties, and returned to Belfast, he found a job at a silk-and-rayon factory in the Clonard area and began to reclaim the youth he had lost to his years of prayer and pious contemplation. He was, in the words of one relative, "very much into running after women and doing the normal things that young people would have done." In the monastery, Lynskey had received a solid education. He studied history and, in particular, the matter of the injustices suffered by working-class Catholics in Ireland. He did not come from a republican family; his father was a timid man who would not have wanted his children to become involved in that sort of activity; his older brother was in the Royal Navy. But Lynskey eventually decided to join the IRA. He grew close with Dolours Price, who was fond of his awkward but gentle manner. "He was a mature man but he was in many ways immature in the ways of the world," she observed. Brendan Hughes had always seen Lynskey as "a strange fella," an odd artifact of the older generation. He was smart and erudite, a chain-smoker, and he carried in his pocket a book about his hero, the Irish revolutionary Michael Collins. But he could be a bit aloof. What Hughes did not know about Joe Lynskey was that he was having an affair with Joe Russell's wife.

After the shooting at the Cracked Cup, the Provos conducted an internal inquiry and discovered that Lynskey had ordered a younger IRA gunman to murder his fellow volunteer—his lover's husband—Joe Russell. The gunman undertook this mission assuming, because Lynskey told him so, that Russell had become an informant to the authorities. But when Russell came to the door, the gunman, losing his nerve, shot him in the stomach, then ran off. In the initial hunt for the shooter, when Hughes and his men started asking around, they consulted the brigade intelligence officer, Joe Lynskey. Rather than confess that he had tried to murder his love rival, Lynskey placed the blame on the Stickies.

For a group with an alarming tendency to kill people by accident, the IRA had an elaborate internal mechanism for determining whether to kill people on purpose. Lynskey would have to face a court-martial for having endeavored to murder one of his fellow volunteers, and for having sought to cover up his crime in such a manner that another innocent man lost his life. This was a choreographed process designed to provide a form of internal accountability that was putatively less arbitrary than a quick bullet in the back of the head. But IRA court-martials were not exactly known for acquitting people. And given the gravity of Lynskey's crimes, his fate looked dire.

.   .   .

Inside the Provisionals, a new squad had recently been established. Like some black-ops government program, it was a unit that ostensibly did not exist—a tiny, elite cell called the "Unknowns." The commander of the Unknowns was a diminutive, serious-minded operator named Pat McClure, a man Brendan Hughes called "Wee Pat." McClure was in his thirties, which made him fairly old by the standards of the Provos at the time. He had actual military experience (and an unusually intimate familiarity with the enemy), having served in the British Army prior to the outbreak of the Troubles. McClure kept a scrupulously low profile. But he was regarded by those who knew him as an exceedingly capable and dedicated soldier.

The Unknowns did not fit neatly into the regimented org chart of the Provos. Instead, they answered directly to Gerry Adams. Brendan Hughes came to think of them as "head hunters," a handpicked team that did dangerous, secretive, sometimes unsavory work. McClure was soft-spoken and enigmatic. He didn't socialize with his soldiers; he had a family, and an air of responsibility about him, but he looked out for the people on his team. One winter night, a major gun battle broke out in Ballymurphy, and some of his young volunteers grabbed their weapons and announced that they were going to join the fight. "No, you're not," McClure told them. The British soldiers had been trained to shoot at night, but the volunteers hadn't, he pointed out. "You'll be shooting at newspapers blowing in the street," he said. "If they take the gloves off, you have no idea. They'll wipe you out." The members of the Unknowns were taken to the country for special training. They stayed in a remote farmhouse and did drills in which they clambered through a river while an instructor fired live rounds into the water around them.

The responsibility for transporting Joe Lynskey across the border to his court-martial and likely execution fell to the Unknowns, and to one member of the unit in particular: Dolours Price. She had joined the Unknowns with her friend Hugh Feeney, the bespectacled pub owner's son. Marian Price joined, too. Though the cease-fire that summer had lasted only a couple of weeks, Dolours had enjoyed the respite from violence. There was a festive, giddy quality to those days: soldiers walked around without flak jackets; local children took rides in their Jeeps. Dolours derived a certain mischievous satisfaction from flirting with the troops. Once, the soldiers, with their berets, asked her to pose for a photo with them, and she obliged. There was one British officer, Ian Corden-Lloyd, who would come to the house in Andersonstown and chat with her. He must have known, or at least suspected, that she was herself a member of the IRA, but they would argue, amiably, about politics as if they were a couple of graduate students, rather than adversaries in a bloody guerrilla war. At one point, Corden-Lloyd told her that he would love to come back and see her in ten years' time, "and we could all tell each other the whole truth."

Traditionally, the IRA killed as an example: murdering a traitor in a public fashion was a means of reinforcing social norms. But in the case of Joe Lynskey, the Provos would break that tradition. At a certain point, Lynskey simply disappeared. No announcement was made about the verdict of his court-martial. No body was dumped on the street. Nor, indeed, was any explanation ever offered to the Provo rank and file about the true shooter of Joe Russell, or the sordid backstory of the shooting at the Cracked Cup. Nobody said a word.

Because Lynskey's work often took him away for long stretches, when he initially vanished, in August 1972, his family did not realize that anything was amiss. A rumor took hold that Joe was in America—that he had gone to start a new life, as many people during those days did. This was a deliberate campaign of misinformation. At one point, a nephew of Lynskey's was in New York City and met a local Irish republican who told him, "You just missed Joe. He was here the other week." When Lynskey's mother died, three years later, she believed that her son must be alive and well and living in the United States.

By that time, he was already long dead. In a twist that represented either a small kindness or a terrible cruelty, when death came for Joe Lynskey, it was in the person of a friend. Dolours Price arrived at Lynskey's sister's house to take him across the border. She did not tell Lynskey that he was being summoned to his execution. She said there was a meeting in the Republic that he needed to attend.

Lynskey descended the stairs, freshly bathed and shaven and clutching an overnight bag, as if he were leaving for a weekend in the country. They got into the car and drove south toward the Republic. Lynskey did not say anything much, but Price realized that he knew exactly where they were going. It was just the two of them in the car. He was stronger than she was; he could have overpowered her. But instead he sat there meekly, holding his little bag in his lap. At one point, he tried to explain to her what had happened, and she said, "I don't want to know, Joe. I don't want to know. I just have this very difficult thing to do."

He was sitting in the back seat, and she looked at him in the rearview mirror. *I'll take him to the ferry,* she thought. *I'll take him to the ferry and say he ran off.* He could escape to England and never come back. But instead she kept driving. *Why doesn't he jump out of the car?* she wondered. *Why doesn't he smack me on the head and run away? Why doesn't he do something to save himself?* But as she drove on, she realized that he could not act to save himself for the same reason that she could not act to save him. Their dedication to the movement would not allow it. She had vowed to obey all orders, and Lynskey, it seemed, had chosen to accept his fate.

When they arrived in County Monaghan, just across the border, a group of men were waiting for them under a lamppost. Lynskey thanked her for driving him and told her not to worry. He reached out and shook her hand.

"I'll be seeing you, Joe," Price said. But she knew that she wouldn't be, and she cried the whole way home.

ORPHANS

ONE DAY IN JANUARY 1973, a television crew from the BBC arrived at St. Jude's Walk. They were looking for the McConville children. Jean had been gone for more than a month. The local press had become aware of the story after an initial article was published in the newsletter of the Northern Ireland Civil Rights Association. Under the headline WHERE IS JEAN MCCONVILLE, the article described how the widowed mother of ten had been missing since December 7, "when she was unceremoniously removed from her home." Picking up on that original item, the *Belfast Telegraph* ran a short article on January 16, SNATCHED MOTHER MISSING A MONTH, which noted that none of the children had reported the abduction of their mother to the police. The next day, the paper appealed for help in solving the "mystery disappearance."

The BBC crew discovered Helen and the younger children living alone in the flat. After the cameras had been set up, the children sat huddled on the couch, framed by a backdrop of striped yellow wallpaper, and described their ordeal. "Four young girls come into the kitchen. They ordered all the kids up the stairs and they just walked in and took my mummy," Agnes said quietly. "Mummy walked out in the hall, she put on her coat and left."

"What did your mummy say when she left?" the interviewer asked.

"She had a big squeal," Agnes said.

"Do you know why your mummy was taken away?"

They didn't. Helen was a lovely-looking teenager, with the same pale and narrow face as her mother, her dark hair swept to either side. She sat with Billy on her lap and nervously averted her eyes from the camera. The boys were fair and ginger. Tucker was sitting on Agnes's lap, wearing a blue turtleneck and shorts, though it was the dead of winter, revealing his knobby knees. The kids were twitchy, their eyes roving all over the place. Michael sat to Helen's side, nearly cut out of the shot. He stared at the camera, blinking.

"Helen, I believe you're looking after the family," the reporter said. "How are you managing to cope?"

"Okay."

"When do you think you'll see your mummy again?"

"Don't know."

"Nobody's been in touch with you at all?"

Agnes mentioned that they had seen Granny McConville.

"She must be a fairly old lady by now," the reporter said.

"She's blind," Agnes said. Agnes was thirteen. She noted, hopefully, that her mother had been wearing red slippers when she was taken away. It was like an image from a fairy tale. A clue. Agnes said that the siblings would "keep our fingers crossed and pray hard for her to come back."

Granny McConville may have been part of the reason that the children had not reported Jean's disappearance to the police. She told people that she was afraid to, though she did not spell out precisely why. The children believed, fervently, that their mother would soon come home. But things began to look bleak. They were able to draw on Jean's pension. But where one might expect the close-knit community in Belfast to rally around and care for such a family, dropping by with a hot meal or assisting Helen with the children, nobody did. Instead, it was as if the whole community in Divis simply chose to ignore the flat-ful of abandoned children on St. Jude's Walk. It might simply

Michael, Helen, Billy, Jim, Agnes, and Tucker McConville.

have been that this was a time of crisis in Belfast and people had worries of their own, or there could have been some darker reason. But in any case, nearly everyone in the community simply looked the other way.

A social worker did visit the children not long after Jean was taken. The authorities had received a call about a pack of siblings who had been looking after themselves. A bureaucrat created a new file and indicated that the children's mother appeared to have been abducted by "an organisation"—shorthand for a paramilitary group. The social worker spoke with Granny McConville, who did not seem overly perturbed. According to notes from the meeting, Jean's mother-in-law asserted, primly, that Helen was "a very capable girl" and seemed to be managing with the children. Helen did not get along with Granny McConville any more than Jean had. "No fondness there," the social worker wrote.

This was not exactly a healthy environment for young children, and the social worker recommended putting the kids "into care"—turning them over to the state, to be raised at a group home. But the McConville children flatly refused. Their mother would be returning any day now, they explained. They needed to be home when she got back.

They held on to one another, marooned inside the flat. Bedtime was suspended and dishes piled up in the sink. The neighbors, rather than help, started to complain to the authorities that they couldn't sleep at night because the children were making so much noise, with nobody to supervise them, and you could hear the racket through the walls. Even the Catholic Church declined to intervene. One report from the social worker, just a week before Christmas, noted that a local parish priest was aware of the children's predicament but was "unsympathetic." As other local kids were composing Christmas lists, the McConvilles were running out of food. They didn't have much money coming in. Only Archie, who worked as an apprentice roof tiler, had a job. The children started getting into trouble. Michael would stay out late and shoplift food. Eventually he was caught, along with one of his brothers, stealing chocolate biscuits from a shop in town. Asked by the police why he had done it, Michael said that he and his siblings had not eaten in several days. They were starving. Michael was eleven years old. When the authorities questioned the McConville kids about their parents, Jim told them, "My daddy is dead and the IRA took my mummy away."

. . .

There is no record in the files of the Royal Ulster Constabulary of any investigation into the disappearance of Jean McConville. She was abducted at the end of the most violent year of the conflict, and this sort of incident, horrible though it was, may not have risen to such a level that the police felt the need to concern themselves. A detective from Springfield Road police station did stop by the flat on January 17, but the police were not able to offer any substantive clues and do not appear to have pursued

the matter. Two local members of Parliament, when they discovered what had happened, decried the kidnapping as "a callous act" and appealed for help in finding Jean. But nobody came
forward with information.

Belfast could sometimes feel more like a small town than
a city. Even before the Troubles, the civic culture of the place
was clotted with unsubstantiated gossip. Almost as soon as Jean
McConville had disappeared, rumors began to circulate that
she had not been kidnapped at all—that, on the contrary, she
had absconded of her own free will, abandoning her children to
shack up with a British soldier. The children, who were already
seized with worry, became aware of these stories. They would
hear people whispering, feel the hot glare of judgment when
they saw their neighbors in the shop or on the street. Back at the
flat, some of them would wonder aloud if it could be true. Could
she really have left them? It didn't seem possible. But how else to
explain the fact that she had not returned? Archie McConville
would later conclude that all that whispering amounted to more
than just salt in the wound. It was a kind of poison, he decided:
"an attempt to wreck our minds."

One by-product of the Troubles was a culture of silence.
With armed factions at war in the streets, an act as innocent
as making inquiries about a vanished loved one could be dangerous. One day that February, a posse of boys from the youth
wing of the IRA seized Michael McConville. They took him to
a room where they tied him up and stabbed him in the leg with
a penknife. They let him go with a warning: *Don't talk to anyone
about what happened to your mother.*

. . .

The interlude of freedom did not last. By February, social
services had initiated the process of relocating the children to
orphanages. One day, three women showed up at the flat and

declared that they had been granted tenancy and were ready to move in. This was happening all the time in Belfast, a cruel expediency of wartime. It was like an awful game of musical chairs: no sooner was one family uprooted than another uprooted family would take their home. The children refused to leave. But the state had decided, and ultimately the kids were made "wards of the court."

The act of disappearing someone, which the International Criminal Court would eventually classify as a crime against humanity, is so pernicious, in part, because it can leave the loved ones of the victim in a purgatory of uncertainty. The children held out hope that they had not been orphaned, and that their mother might suddenly reappear. Perhaps she had developed amnesia and was living in another country, unaware that she had left a whole life behind in Belfast.

But, even then, there was reason to believe that something terrible had happened to Jean McConville. About a week after she was kidnapped, a young man whom the children did not know had come to the door of the flat and handed them their mother's purse and three rings she had been wearing when she left: her engagement ring, her wedding ring, and an eternity ring that Arthur had given her. Desperate for information, the children asked where Jean was. "I don't know anything about your mother," the man said. "I was just told to give you these."

Years later, Michael McConville would look back and isolate that encounter as the moment he realized that his mother must be dead.

THE FREDS

ONE AUTUMN DAY IN 1972, a laundry van pulled into the Twinbrook estate, on the outskirts of Belfast, and Sarah Jane Warke got out and walked up to one of the houses. The van was a regular presence in the neighborhood. There were not a lot of shops in the area, so it was common to see traders going door-to-door, offering their wares. The company was called Four Square Laundry, and once a week Sarah would come to the door, pick up a pile of dirty laundry, and then return it, clean and neatly folded, several days later. People liked the service; the prices were cut-rate. And people liked Sarah, a pretty, ingratiating young woman. The driver, Ted Stuart, was a young man from County Tyrone, who mainly stayed behind the wheel. But he was an easygoing fellow, and the local customers liked him, too. The kids on the estate called him Teddy. Twinbrook was home to both Catholics and Protestants, but it was relatively calm by the standards of Belfast at the time.

Sarah walked up to one of the residences. A housewife came to the door, and she and Sarah were exchanging a few words when suddenly they were interrupted by a loud cracking noise. Sarah spun to see that two men had appeared. One of them held a machine gun; the other had a rifle. They were standing in a nimbus of smoke, crouched, with their backs to Sarah, spraying bullets from close range into the driver's side of the laundry van, where Ted was sitting. Sarah stood frozen in the doorway, watching helplessly as Ted was killed. Then one of the gunmen turned in her direction.

.   .   .

After the debacle of the internment raids, the British Army and the Special Branch of the Royal Ulster Constabulary had continued to focus, with ever greater intensity, on cultivating sources within both loyalist and republican paramilitary groups. Brendan Hughes started to develop a suspicion, in 1972, that he might have an informant in D Company. His intelligence officer told him that a young volunteer, a former asphalt layer named Seamus Wright, had been arrested earlier in the year—and that ever since his arrest, he would go missing from time to time.

Wright, who was twenty-five, had recently gotten married, and Hughes paid a visit to his wife, Kathleen. She said that Seamus had been arrested in February and held by the British, but then he had telephoned a shop near her home and left a message for her, saying that he had "scarpered"—run away. Seamus was in England now, Kathleen continued. He was in Birmingham; she had an address. Hughes suggested that perhaps Kathleen should go there and see Seamus. He was enlisting the young bride of a suspected spy to serve as a spy herself: she would pay Seamus a visit and try to get him to return with her. Then she would report back to Brendan Hughes.

Kathleen flew to England. But when she got there, Seamus refused to come home. So she returned alone and met Hughes at a house on Leeson Street. During this debriefing, Kathleen confirmed his worst fears. Seamus had been turned by the British, she said. When she saw her husband, he had been accompanied by an Englishman—some sort of handler. But there was a catch, she continued: Seamus wanted out. He planned to flee, to escape his handlers. But he wanted a guarantee that if he came back to

Belfast, he wouldn't be shot by the IRA. This was a bold proposal from someone who had violated the trust of the Provos and gone into business with the enemy, a transgression that was generally punishable by death. But sensing an opportunity to learn how the British were going about their recruitment of double agents, Hughes consented, and gave the guarantee.

Not long afterward, Seamus Wright returned to West Belfast, where he was interrogated in a house for two days. He explained that during his initial arrest by the British, they had told him that they could link him to an explosion that had killed a member of the security forces. They were so adamant that they had the goods on him that Seamus began to suspect he had been grassed—given up to the authorities by a "supergrass," a paid informer. Once his handlers had secured his cooperation, they asked him about guns and explosives. But what they really wanted to know about was the Dirty Dozen. They told Seamus that if he would just give them the names of everyone in D Company, he would not be charged with any crime.

Hughes was dismayed to discover that he had a traitor in his company—a traitor who had revealed the identities of the Dirty Dozen. One irony of the Provos' pretense to being a legitimate army was that in those early days, they were structured much like the British Army, with battalions and companies and a clear, legible chain of command. What this meant, in practice, was that if the enemy succeeded in turning someone—even a relatively junior player like Seamus Wright—they could discern the org chart of a large swath of the organization.

.   .   .

After agreeing to be an informant, Wright said, he was flown to England, for training as a double agent. Then he was flown back to Northern Ireland, with the understanding that he would now begin to gather intelligence on the Provos. As Hughes listened intently, Wright described a secret compound at Palace Barracks, where the army housed its prized informants. There was a clandestine unit inside the army, Wright said—they called it the MRF, and it managed both republican and loyalist informants. Wright explained that the army controlled a stable of individuals who had been induced to switch sides and were now working undercover for the British. Members of the MRF would show them newsreel footage of funerals and surveillance pictures of suspects, then ask them to pick out the people they knew. Sometimes Wright's handlers would load him into an armored personnel carrier and drive into the Falls. As they prowled through the narrow streets, Wright would peek through the vehicle's gun slits and identify the pedestrians they passed.

The MRF had a name for this secret coterie of traitors. They called them the "Freds." Nobody in the Provos ever learned the source of the nickname, but there was no way to read the work of Brigadier Frank Kitson and not recognize that the Freds were a counter-gang. Now the eye slits in those white hoods that Kitson's Mau Mau informants wore back in Kenya had been replaced by the gun slits in a Saracen armored vehicle. Wright said that the compound where the Freds were kept was segregated, so he could not identify most of the other informants. But there was one he could name. "There is a guy I have seen in there," Wright said. "He is one of us."

The man Wright named was a young Provo, a boy, really, a member of Ballymurphy company named Kevin McKee. He was still a teenager, a handsome adolescent with big blue eyes, shaggy dark hair, and a slight overbite. People called him "Beaky." He had grown up in West Belfast and liked to sit in the front room of the family home, listening to records on the old-fashioned radiogram. He joined the youth wing of the IRA, throwing stones at the British Army and the RUC. When loyalists would string a Union Jack up on a telephone pole, Kevin would shimmy up the pole and pull the flag down, to cheers from the people below. He was a charismatic kid, caught up in the romance and intrigue of the Troubles. There was an innocence to him. But he also went on "snipes" (as sniping operations were known) and planted bombs. As one of his IRA contemporaries in Ballymurphy put it, "He didn't lack balls."

One night, Kevin McKee was arrested and hauled into Springfield Road army barracks. Two of his aunts ventured to the barracks to see what had happened to him, but when they arrived, they were told that he had escaped. Eventually the family received letters from Kevin in England, and assumed that he must have moved there to hide from the army and the police.

But the truth was, he had become an informant. A British Army log from the night when Kevin was arrested noted that after being taken into custody, he "gave information" about a particular property. The log then listed a series of weapons that were recovered from an IRA arms dump at that address. According to the log, McKee was arrested just before 11 p.m. that night, and the house was searched just after midnight. So he must have flipped almost immediately. Seamus Wright told Hughes that McKee "loved" his involvement in the Freds. And the members of the military units in the MRF took a shine to the cocksure teenager. They liked his bravado.

When Frank Kitson was recruiting captured Mau Mau in Kenya to work in counter-gangs, he found that they needed to be "tamed," in a process he described as if it were the breaking of a horse. He avoided fanatical believers, who were too difficult to bring across to the other side, and focused instead on recruiting people who had joined the movement for a reason that was essentially social: because their friends were joining. In one of his books, Kitson noted that the very best recruits were the ones with "a spirit of adventure," people who "thought that it would be fun to be a gangster and carry a pistol." They were "the easiest to handle because they were the easiest to satisfy." In Kenya, these were the types of recruits to whom Kitson would give his own gun, letting them carry it on patrol to indulge their sense of adventure and make them feel like a trusted part of the team. In Belfast, the MRF gave Kevin McKee a pistol and a shoulder holster, which he wore around, flaunting the costume as if he were a Chicago gangster. As a Fred, he was entitled to carry the weapon and make use of the firing ranges on the army base.

McKee was wearing the shoulder holster when the Provos tracked him down. Under interrogation, he confessed to his betrayal, just as Seamus Wright had. But now the Provos found themselves in an interesting position. On the one hand, they had identified two defectors, who had betrayed the organization by agreeing to work with the British. Normally, they would have been court-martialed, found guilty, shot in the back of the head, then dumped by the side of the road. But the British did not appear to *know* that Hughes had discovered this breach in the IRA's security—and Wright and McKee would do anything, now, to save their own lives. If their confessions were to be believed, the British Army had orchestrated an elaborate spy operation targeting the Provos, yet the precise dimensions and operational details of that effort remained unclear. So Hughes was presented with an opportunity: rather than execute Wright and McKee, he could use them to gather intelligence on the British, as triple agents.

For Wright and McKee, such a move might be risky, but it was preferable to the alternative of a speedy execution. Wright actually went back to work for the Freds, with instructions, this time, to provide his British handlers with only low-level information or, better still, misinformation. Asked to identify a Provo on a street corner, Wright could tell the British he was a Sticky instead. This was a dangerous game. If the army discovered the deception, Wright could be sent to jail. He could also be shot by the MRF, which had shown little compunction about the occasional extrajudicial killing. But by demanding that Wright and McKee supply him with intelligence, Hughes was offering each man an opportunity to earn his life back: if they could deliver for the IRA, Hughes promised them, they would be granted "immunity" for their initial crime.

The men delivered. What they described to Hughes was an extensive intelligence-gathering network that the British had developed around Belfast. The centerpiece of the operation was a laundry service, with an office in the city center. Four Square Laundry operated an actual door-to-door laundry service, picking up clothing and linens and then subcontracting to an industrial laundry in Belfast to wash the clothes. But before they got there, the clothes were analyzed by British authorities. Traces of explosives could be detected on garments in order to determine whether bombs were being made or stored at a property. Analysts could also compare the clothing being picked up at a given residence with the number, age, and gender of the people ostensibly living there; a mismatch might indicate that it was an arms drop or a call house. The laundry van had been specially configured with a hollow roof, in which a sapper could conceal himself, snapping photos of people and houses outside through a hidden opening.

As soon as Hughes learned about the laundry operation, he wanted to sweep in and upend it. But Gerry Adams cautioned him to hold off. "Sit back," Adams said. "Do more intelligence." Hughes and his men learned that, in addition to the laundry service and the office in the city center, the MRF was operating a massage parlor above a house on the Antrim Road, where customers would sometimes find themselves so blissfully relaxed that they casually disclosed things to the chatty masseuse. By early October, Hughes and his team decided that they had gathered enough intelligence. It was time to move. They couldn't hit these locations one by one: as soon as they attacked the first one, the MRF would know that the whole operation was blown. So the Provos would launch three near-simultaneous strikes—on the van, the office, and the massage parlor. The objective was to wipe out the whole intelligence-gathering apparatus in the space of a single hour.

.   .   .

The man behind the wheel of the Four Square Laundry van, Ted Stuart, was an undercover British sapper with the Royal Engineers. Ever since childhood, he had wanted to be a soldier. He was twenty and had been serving in Northern Ireland only since June. As the Provo hit team fired on the van, he died almost instantly.

When the gunmen turned on Stuart's partner, Sarah Jane Warke, she plunged into the house of the local woman she had been talking to. Warke was also an undercover soldier, a member of the Women's Royal Army Corps. She pulled the woman and her children in with her and—thinking quickly—told them that this must be a loyalist ambush. The woman helped Warke scuttle out the back door and escape.

The gunmen had orders not just to kill the young pair who operated the laundry service, but to strafe the ceiling of the van with bullets, in order to kill the sapper inside. In their haste, or panic, however, they did not do so, and if there was a third soldier concealed in the van, he escaped alive. Elsewhere in Belfast, another team of gunmen shot up the massage parlor, and a third shot up the office, though neither managed to hit any other members of the MRF.

The Four Square Laundry operation marked a major victory for the Provos. Hughes was proud of how it had played out, and in a memoir, decades later, Gerry Adams would call it "a devastating blow" to the British. The question now was, what to do with Wright and McKee?

On the day of the Four Square operation, Wright came

home and told his wife, Kathleen, that he would have to be careful, because before his release by the British, he had signed some papers relating to the Official Secrets Act. Then, that night, he disappeared. A car drove up to his family's door on Bombay Street. Wright exchanged a few words with the driver, got into the passenger seat, and drove off. When he did not return, Kathleen went to Leeson Street to ask the Provos what had become of him. They told her that Seamus had not been taken by the IRA. After hearing that, Kathleen became convinced that her husband might have been snatched by the army. But the army, too, denied any involvement in his abduction. Military sources suggested to the press that Wright could have run off on his own and might be hiding out in Scotland.

At around the same time, McKee vanished as well. One of his aunts had told him, "The IRA's been looking for you."

"I've done nothing wrong," McKee replied, confident as ever.

When he disappeared, the family chose not to contact the police. The authorities would likely be more harm than help. But there were rumors: that McKee had gone off to art school; that someone had spotted him in England.

The truth was that both men had been taken by the IRA. They had played their final card by giving the information on the MRF and the Four Square Laundry. The moment the simultaneous raids were complete, Wright and McKee no longer possessed any leverage. Brendan Hughes may have assured them that they had immunity, but this was not really an assurance he was authorized to give. By initially betraying the Provos, they had committed an unforgivable sin—one that was not diminished by their subsequent work as triple agents. The Unknowns were summoned, and Dolours Price drove both men across the border to the Republic.

It was just Price driving the two of them. She had a particular loathing for informers. She had been brought up to revile them. But if she felt contempt for Wright and McKee, she kept it hidden, and on the drive south, they were relaxed. After the success of the Four Square Laundry operation, they believed that they had earned their lives back. Someone had told Wright and McKee that they were going for a week of R&R across the border. "You're just going to get a rest and get your strength back," Price assured them. As far as she knew, it was true, though she had her suspicions to the contrary. In any case, she had her orders. In Monaghan, she dropped them off with the local unit.

McKee ended up in a house in County Monaghan, which belonged to the family of a dead IRA man, Fergal O'Hanlon, who had been killed in the 1950s and had become the subject of a famous ballad, "The Patriot Game." He was obliged to wait for a period of time so that some senior leaders could come across the border for his court-martial. The people who were minding him grew fond of him; he was a good cook, a fun guy, a personality. At one point, McKee telephoned his mother, from the home of a nearby priest, and asked her to bring him a change of clothes. She and his aunts drove down, but when they arrived at the house, Kevin was gone. A man was there. "Take the clothes with you," he said. "He'll not be back."

When it came time to execute Kevin McKee, the local volunteers who had been holding him hostage found themselves unable to shoot him. They had grown too fond of him. When Hughes heard about this, it seemed like a sort of Stockholm syndrome in reverse—the hostage taker gradually falling for the hostage. In their stead, a pair of dispassionate gunmen were sent from Belfast. Before the killing, they summoned a priest. This was not unusual: there were certain priests in that era who grew accustomed to the late-night phone call. They would be summoned outside by gruff men who were about to perform an execution and asked to deliver the last rites. The act of killing itself had a ritual character, a practiced choreography that would have been familiar to McKee. A bag is placed over your head. Your hands are bound behind your back. You kneel in the soft grass. Then you flop forward when the bullet hits your brain.

Brendan Hughes felt betrayed by the decision to disappear Wright and McKee. He had given them his word that they would not be killed. It would trouble him for the rest of his life.

.   .   .

The Four Square operation might have been a success, but Hughes and Gerry Adams could hold off the army for only so long. One afternoon the following summer, in July 1973, Adams was heading to a meeting at a call house on the Falls Road. As officer commanding for Belfast, he met daily with Hughes, his operations officer, and a man named Tom Cahill, who handled the finances. July was a tricky time to be on the run in Belfast: because it was the peak season for loyalist marches, most Catholics who could afford to get out of town for a week or two chose this time of year to do it. With fewer people on the streets in Catholic neighborhoods, it was harder to move around unnoticed. When he was about fifty yards from the call house, Adams hesitated, eyeing the building, observing the area for any signs of suspicious activity. He loitered there a minute, leaning on the hood of a parked car. Then he noticed that there was someone in the car, a businessman, consulting some papers in the front seat. Adams gave a little wave. The man waved back.

When he was convinced that the location had not been compromised, Adams crossed the street and entered the call house. Inside, he met up with Hughes and Cahill. But the men had not been talking long when there was a knock at the door. This was not, in itself, grounds for alarm; the British patrolled republican neighborhoods, and it was standard to knock on the door and ask for a look around or a chat. They might not realize the significance of the house they had happened to stumble upon. A hasty decision was made: Cahill would answer the door while Hughes and Adams escaped out the back. But when they got into the yard, Hughes peered over the back wall and was startled to behold a sea of British troops. As soldiers flooded into the house, Adams casually pulled out some matches and lit his pipe.

The businessman in the car that Adams had leaned on was not a businessman. While Adams did surveillance on the house, the man behind the wheel was doing surveillance on him. An ambitious operation had been planned, with soldiers secretly massing on the perimeter, but they had orders not to start the raid until both Adams and Hughes were inside the house. When Adams opened the front door, he triggered the operation.

The Provos were taken to a police station on Springfield Road, where they were beaten and tortured for hours. Adams was beaten so badly that he passed out. His captors doused him with a bucketful of water to revive him, then started beating him again. One of the interrogators, a tall man in a pin-striped suit, pulled out a pistol and put it to Hughes's head, then cocked it. He said that he was going to kill Hughes, then dump his body on the Black Mountain and say that the loyalists had done it.

The British forces were hugely pleased: in one swoop, they had caught several of their most high-profile targets—including Hughes, who had never been captured before. William Whitelaw, who had met with Adams in London the summer before, came personally to congratulate the men involved, and he brought with him a load of champagne. The soldiers took turns posing for "trophy" photographs with the two captives, who had been so severely beaten that they could hardly walk. Even so, Hughes was defiant. "I'm going to escape," he told them.

He and Adams were loaded into a Saracen and taken to a helicopter, which transported them on the short ride to Long Kesh. When the helicopter touched down, they were marched, handcuffed, into the prison. As they were walking in, the whole place erupted in a massive cheer. To the republican prisoners in Long Kesh, Adams and Hughes were iconic figures, celebrities. When they entered the heavily fortified installation, they were hailed as conquering heroes. Hughes would later count that moment—black and blue, manacled, borne into prison on that great wave of enthusiasm—as one of the greatest in his life.

book two

HUMAN SACRIFICE

CLOSE ENGLAND!

THE CROCUSES WERE ALREADY in bloom around London's parks and monuments on March 8, 1973. It was a Thursday, a crisp, crystalline early-spring morning. After a wet English winter, people were venturing outdoors, beckoned by the sun. The Queen left Buckingham Palace to inspect the first blooms in her garden. There was a transit strike that day, and with train service suspended, commuters were forced to drive into the city. As a result, central London was overrun with automobiles. In order to accommodate the surge of vehicles, the city had suspended parking restrictions for the day. Cars were everywhere—in loading zones and other areas that were usually off-limits, or at meters that had long since expired.

Just after lunchtime, at around 2 p.m., a phone rang at the headquarters of *The Times* of London. A young woman named Elizabeth Curtis, who had just started working on the news desk at the paper, picked up the call. She heard a man's voice, speaking very quickly, with a thick Irish accent. At first she couldn't make out what he was saying, then she realized that he was reeling off the descriptions and locations of a series of cars. He spoke for just over a minute, and, though she was still confused, she transcribed as much as she could. Before hanging up, the man said, "The bombs will go off in one hour."

A journalist named Martin Huckerby was on duty that day in the newsroom. He overheard Curtis dictating details about the bombs to one of her colleagues. The nearest of the locations she mentioned was the Old Bailey, the central criminal court in London, just a short walk from *The Times*. Huckerby bolted out of the office. He was looking for a green Ford Cortina Estate with a license plate that, assuming Curtis had transcribed it correctly, read YNS 649K. Huckerby left the office at 2 p.m. and arrived at the monumental stone courthouse a few minutes later. Built at the turn of the century, the Old Bailey had been the site of many celebrated trials. A great dome sat atop the heavy masonry, with a bronze figure of Justice, her arms outstretched, holding a sword and a set of scales.

Dozens of cars were parked around the building, and Huckerby began checking them to see if he could find the Cortina. Before long, he spotted it, parked right in front of the courthouse: a green Cortina Estate with the license plate YFN 469K, close enough to what he was looking for that he was sure this was it. Peering through the glass at the car's interior, he saw a pair of black gloves on the floor and an aerosol can. Huckerby waited for the police to come, and eventually, after what seemed like an eternity, two uniformed officers arrived at 2:33 and inspected the Cortina. They started evacuating people in the area, cordoning off the road. Huckerby took cover in a doorway, about twenty-five yards from the Cortina, and waited.

. . .

The plan to bring the bombing campaign to England had been, at least in part, Dolours Price's idea. The IRA had detonated hundreds of bombs in commercial centers throughout Northern Ireland. If the goal was to cripple the economy, this effort had been a success. But the collateral damage was considerable. For civilians in Northern Ireland, whether Catholic or Protestant, the routine bombings could make life impossible: suddenly you were taking your life into your hands when you went to the shop for a dozen eggs. It might not have been the intention of the IRA to create civilian casualties, but there *were* civilian casualties, lots of them, and they were borne by Catholics and Protestants alike. Bloody Friday was an especially grave debacle, but it was hardly unique—countless smaller bombing operations had claimed limbs and lives, steadily eroding support for a violent campaign among moderate Irish nationalists. Worst of all, because the toll of all this bombing was largely confined to Northern Ireland, it did not appear to be registering all that strongly with the intended target—the British. The English public, removed on the other side of the Irish Sea, seemed only dimly aware of the catastrophe engulfing Northern Ireland. It was a case study in strategic insanity: the Irish were blowing up their own people in a misguided attempt to hurt the English, and the English hardly even noticed. It bothered Price. "This is half their war," she would say to Wee Pat McClure, the head of the Unknowns, as they sat around call houses between operations. "Only half of it is our war. The other half is *their* war, and some of it should be fought on their territory." She became convinced that "a short, sharp shock—an incursion into the heart of the Empire—would be more effective than twenty car bombs in any part of the North of Ireland."

After making the case to Seán Mac Stíofáin, who approved of the idea, Price worked with McClure and Gerry Adams on an initial plan, to firebomb London. The firebombs were made and smuggled into London, and the idea was that a team of girls would fly over and deposit them in department stores on Oxford Street. But before they could put the bombs in place, they discovered that the acid in the devices had leaked, ruining them. So Price, who was already in London, abandoned the mission and walked down to the banks of the Thames, where she gently slid each faulty bomb into the river.

When firebombs didn't work, they resolved to plant car bombs instead. The idea took shape within the Belfast Brigade. When it came time to recruit a team for the mission, volunteers from different units assembled at a call house in the Lower Falls. Gerry Adams explained that they were planning a very dangerous job. Any volunteers who signed up for it would have to be away from home for a while. As Adams spoke, Price sat perched on the arm of his chair. In the interests of operational security, Adams was vague about the mission when he spoke to this larger group, offering few details, but he stressed that anyone who participated must be prepared to face the full wrath of the state. "This could be a hanging job," he said. "If anyone doesn't want to go, they should up and leave now." He instructed them to exit through the back door, at ten-minute intervals, so as not to attract attention.

Price thought Adams was being melodramatic. She suspected he might have picked up that flourish about ten-minute intervals from a book about Michael Collins. But, sure enough, people started to get up and walk out. "Don't knock me down in the rush, lads," Price said drily.

When this small exodus had concluded, about ten people remained: there was Price's friend and fellow Unknown Hugh Feeney. He was erudite, bespectacled, in his early twenties. Feeney would be the quartermaster, in charge of all the money for the operation; he was armed with a thick roll of five-pound notes. There was Gerry Kelly, a handsome young man from the Lower Falls, whom Price was meeting for the first time. Kelly had been on the run, after escaping from prison, where he had been serving a sentence for bank robbery. Price thought he was a grand lad. And there was Marian, of course. There was always Marian.

They were all very young. Kids, really. The oldest member of the crew, William Armstrong, a window cleaner with slicked-back hair, was twenty-nine. The youngest member was Roisin McNearney, a wide-eyed eighteen-year-old. She had been working as a typist before she joined the Provos six months earlier. She still lived with her parents.

As head of the Unknowns, Wee Pat wanted smart people

running the operation. So he selected Dolours to take the lead. She was appointed, in her own words, "the OC of the whole shebang." Reporting to her would be two lieutenants—Hugh Feeney and Marian Price. None of the recruits had any experience serving behind enemy lines, so Wee Pat arranged for them to go across the border for intensive training with explosives and timers.

As Aunt Bridie could testify, bomb making in the IRA was a hazardously inexact science. Brendan Hughes would tell stories about his great-grandfather, who, during the War of Independence, was trying to throw a grenade at an armored car when it detonated and blew his arm off. Bomb making had improved dramatically in recent years, because the Provos had taken every opportunity to practice. It was not that IRA volunteers no longer blew themselves up with their own bombs, which they continued to do. Rather, as one writer observed, these mishaps came to function as "a gruesome form of 'natural selection,' " weeding out the incompetent bombsmiths. Those who survived took greater care, and eventually the Provos produced some legendary bomb makers. They developed a fifty-page illustrated manual, which apprentice explosives specialists could study. It provided instructions on how to make booby traps using a remarkable variety of household implements—candle grease, clothes-pegs, a nail bomb made from a beer can, a soda straw used as a fuse.

The car bomb, which was first introduced to the conflict in early 1972, represented a terrifying departure, because up to that point the size of most bombs had been limited by the sheer weight of explosives that a few paramilitaries could carry. Hiding the bomb inside an automobile meant that you could prepare a massive payload, then simply drive the device to the target and walk away. Whereas a suitcase or a plastic bag left in a busy shop might attract attention, cars were the perfect camouflage, because they were everywhere. "The car bomb provided an efficient container and an efficient delivery system,"

Seán Mac Stíofáin wrote in 1975. "It yielded far greater administrative, industrial and economic damage for a given operation. And it required fewer volunteers to place it on the target." In the streets of Belfast, an empty, unattended car became, all by itself, a source of terror that could prompt people to flee the area and authorities to descend, whether the car actually contained a bomb or not.

In February, six cars were hijacked at gunpoint in Belfast and driven to the Republic. By the time the cars reemerged on the streets of Dublin in early March, they had been repainted and equipped with phony license plates. Ultimately, only four of the cars would make the journey to England: a Ford Corsair, a Hillman Hunter, a Vauxhall Viva—and the green Ford Cortina. Each was carefully fitted with a mammoth incendiary device, more than a hundred pounds of powder explosives hidden in plastic bags, along with a sausage of gelignite. Each payload was concealed beneath the rear seat and was connected by a length of detonating cord to a box under the front passenger seat that contained a timer fashioned from a household alarm clock.

About a month before the operation, Dolours Price had traveled to London on a scouting mission, along with Martin Brady, a muscular member of her team with bushy eyebrows, who had worked previously at a restaurant in the West End and knew his way around the city. The Unknowns had selected the targets themselves, before presenting them to the leadership in Belfast for approval. The targets were carefully chosen to "evoke particular political questions," Gerry Kelly later explained. The British public may have become inured to catastrophic headlines from Northern Ireland, but a series of bombs in central London would change all that. Nor was the timing of the operation an accident. They selected the day of a referendum in Northern Ireland on whether the territory should remain part of the United Kingdom. The mission, Kelly felt, was to bring "the reality of colonialism" home to England.

.   .   .

On March 5, the group split into two teams. Hugh Feeney led the first team across the Irish Sea, driving the Cortina and the Viva onto the Dublin–Liverpool ferry. The next day, a second team, led by Marian Price, drove the Corsair and the Hillman Hunter. But when the ferry reached Liverpool and their cars were passing through customs, the Hunter was held up. There seemed to be a problem with the license plate. Martin Brady was behind the wheel, while the young Roisin McNearney sat in the back. The inspectors appeared suspicious that they might be trying to bring a foreign car, from the Republic of Ireland, into the United Kingdom without paying any import tax. As they spoke, McNearney was fidgeting in the back seat, increasingly nervous. She announced that she needed to use the toilet and got out of the car.

When she returned a few minutes later, the inspector who had been questioning Brady was called away to deal with a lorry that was impeding the flow of traffic. The young IRA members stayed where they were, unsure what the inspector might do when he came back. But now they were holding up traffic themselves, and another customs official impatiently waved them through. According to the original plan, the two remaining stolen cars were supposed to follow on another ferry, bringing the total number of bombs to six, but after the scare at customs, the team sent a message back to Ireland instructing their colleagues not to send the last two cars, in case the authorities had been tipped off.

As the leader of the group, Dolours Price did not take the ferry. She flew from Dublin, under an assumed name, Una Devlin. By Wednesday, March 7, the whole crew had filtered into London, left the cars, with their hazardous cargoes, in public garages, and checked into different hotels.

The plan was simple. Early the following morning, the team

would drive the cars into position at four locations in the city: a British Army recruiting center in Whitehall; the British Forces Broadcasting Service, on Dean Stanley Street; New Scotland Yard; and the Old Bailey. A telephone warning would be issued in advance. Mindful of the disastrous civilian toll on Bloody Friday, the team had been given orders to avoid casualties. The warnings would be initiated just before 2 p.m. local time, and precisely one hour later, the alarm clock timers would trigger the detonations. By that time, Price and the others would already be back in Ireland—having returned to Dublin on a late-morning flight from Heathrow.

On Wednesday, after they had all checked into their hotels, members of the team did reconnaissance of the locations. "You don't know each other," Price told them. "You've never seen each other before when you meet each other on the street." She added, emphatically, that there should be "no drink involved." Before sundown, Price assembled everyone in the portico of the National Gallery, in Trafalgar Square, to finalize arrangements and to hand out plane tickets for the following day.

Then they had the night off. You might suppose that on the eve of a coordinated terrorist strike on a major city, the participants would devote the final hours to anxious preparation. But on account of their youth, perhaps, or the almost hallucinatory fever of their own righteousness, Price and her compatriots seemed eerily detached from the gravity and potential consequences of the mission they were about to undertake. Besides, they were in London, a city more vast and freewheeling than their own. The heart of empire it may have been, but London was also, indisputably, a fun place to visit. So the young terrorists went sightseeing. Roisin McNearney paid a visit to Buckingham Palace. Some of the men defied Price's admonition and went out and got drunk, so drunk that one of them would later have to be carried out of the pub.

Price, who was more high-minded, went to the theater,

along with Marian. Hugh Feeney ended up joining them but arrived late, because he had wanted to perform one final check on the car bombs. It did not strike any of them as the least bit incongruous that they might go to see a play on the night before a bombing. On the contrary, Feeney figured that, should something go awry the next morning, it might be a while before they had a chance to see any good theater. As it happened, their visit to London coincided with a production at the Royal Court of *The Freedom of the City*, a new show by the Irish playwright Brian Friel. The play, which was directed by Albert Finney, told a story that was fictional but highly topical, a story that could only have resonated with Dolours Price: three civil rights protesters seek refuge from gas and rubber bullets in the Guildhall, in Derry—the same hall where Ian Paisley and Major Bunting whipped up their followers the night before the ambush on the march at Burntollet Bridge. The play turns on a misunderstanding. While the peaceful protesters hole up inside the Guildhall, on the outside, the press and the British Army come to assume that they are actually terrorists, engaged in an armed occupation. The play was inspired, in part, by Bloody Sunday, which Brian Friel had witnessed personally. It was about the hysteria, the mythmaking, and the misunderstanding that had twisted the peaceful civil rights movement in Northern Ireland into a violent conflagration. The three marchers ultimately die in the play—shot by the British troops. In an echo of the cover-up following Bloody Sunday, a tribunal is assembled to investigate, and concludes that the shooting was justified.

This was delicate material for a London audience, and crowds for the show had been sparse, and notably uneasy. One of the three leads in the production, a young actor named Stephen Rea, later remarked that it had been received by London audiences "in a frost of ignorance." Though he was an emerging star at the Royal Court, Rea was a Belfast native himself, a beguiling-looking young man with soft features, quizzical eyes, and a shock of black hair that always looked recently slept on. As it happened, he and Dolours Price knew each other: Rea had studied at Queen's, and they had met during the civil rights movement in the late 1960s. They ended up falling out of touch as she joined the Provos and he became a prominent actor, doing parts in Dublin and Edinburgh before joining the company at the Royal Court. But here Dolours Price was, about to bomb London, watching this dashing, intelligent, intriguing young man play the part of a civil rights marcher who gets mistaken for a member of the IRA.

·   ·   ·

The bombers had arranged for wake-up calls before dawn. They rose, dressed, checked out of their hotels, then went to retrieve the cars and drive them into position while good parking spots were still available. The transit strike had created ideal circumstances for a car bombing: because parking rules were suspended, vehicles that might normally be towed were being left alone by the police. All four cars were driven to their destinations: the Hillman to the army recruiting office; the Corsair to New Scotland Yard; the Vauxhall to the British Forces Broadcasting Service; and the Cortina to the Old Bailey. By 7:30, the bombs were in place, with their timers set to detonate at 2:50 that afternoon. Just after 10 a.m., most of the crew caught a bus from Cromwell Road to Heathrow, where they were set to catch an 11:20 plane to Dublin. (The Price sisters and Hugh Feeney were scheduled to take a slightly later flight.)

·   ·   ·

The officers of London's Metropolitan Police rose early that day as well. At 7 a.m., just as the bombers were navigating their cars into position, the Special Patrol Group received a briefing at

Cannon Row Police Station, in Westminster, about an impending IRA attack. The officers were instructed to go out and look for suspicious vehicles. In particular, they were ordered to check in the vicinity of likely targets such as government buildings. The transit strike compounded the challenge: at the very moment when they needed as few vehicles as possible in central London, there was instead a tremendous influx. Later that morning, a couple of constables were patrolling the area around Scotland Yard when they noticed a green Corsair with no tax disc. As they examined the vehicle, they discovered that it was a 1968 model but had 1971 plates. They noticed another anomaly: whereas a number plate normally had two drill holes in it, this one had four. Peering in the windows, the officers spotted a thin white cord snaking from the front seat to the back, partially hidden under the carpet on the floor.

A team of bomb disposal experts was summoned. They discovered nearly two hundred pounds of explosives packed beneath the rear seats. It was, in the assessment of one of the investigators, "a monstrous, tremendously powerful bomb." The interior of the Corsair reeked of explosives, and the timer, in its box, was audibly ticking. One of the bomb experts looked up and saw that the windows of the surrounding buildings were filled with the faces of people looking down, watching them work. "Get those stupid bastards away from the windows!" he shouted. One member of the bomb squad held the cord to the timing device while his partner gingerly severed it.

It didn't blow. They had defused the bomb. Examining the position of the hour hand on the timer, the investigators deduced that it would have detonated at around 3 p.m., though it was hard to say for certain, because the minute hand on the clock had been removed. They realized two things immediately. One was that if there were other bombs hidden in the city, they had to find them before 3 p.m. The other was that the long fuse on the timer indicated that the bombers might be trying to flee the country before the blast. A bulletin was sent to Special Branch officers at every port and airport: CLOSE ENGLAND. Lock down all the exit points. Question any Irish people looking to leave.

In trying to explain how the police had managed to be so far ahead of the bombers, British authorities would later make it sound as though they had simply been brilliantly lucky. But it was also suggested in the press that the police in London may have had prior notice that an attack was coming, and that it would involve more than one bomb. The Price sisters, for their part, would always believe that the operation had been betrayed by an informant. Hugh Feeney shared their suspicion, declaring later, "We were set up."

They were right: decades after the bombing mission, a retired Special Branch officer would reveal that he had been tipped off fourteen hours before the bombs were set to blow, and that his source had been a senior member of the Provisionals. The officer knew in advance that there would be four bombs rather than six. He also knew that the bombing team would include a young Provo named Gerry Kelly and "two sisters named Price."

Even so, as police fanned across central London in search of the other three bombs, the city looked like one big parking lot, completely clogged with stationary automobiles. They searched frantically for suspicious vehicles but, having no clue as to the rough locations, they were unable to locate any of the other cars. The bombs could literally be anywhere. Just before 2 p.m., the warning call was received at *The Times,* spelling out the locations and descriptions of the cars. But even then, there was a miscommunication within the police department, which caused a delay in getting officers to the scenes of the three remaining bombs. Martin Huckerby, the *Times* reporter, beat the police to the Cortina outside the Old Bailey by more than twenty minutes, and additional precious minutes ticked by before the bomb squad arrived and the officers began running into surrounding buildings to evacuate people.

Inside the Old Bailey itself, several criminal trials were under way: a drug conspiracy case was wrapping up in one courtroom, a judge was addressing the jury for a murder trial in another. Someone burst into the courtrooms and told everyone to get out—a bomb was about to go off right outside the building. A pub called the George, which stood opposite the courthouse, was full of patrons nursing afternoon pints when somebody ran in and shouted that there was a bomb in the street. Some of the customers simply moved deeper into the pub, crowding the back parlor. But others looked out at the serene, sunny afternoon and, figuring this could only be a hoax, decided to stay put. London had not experienced any serious bombings since the Blitz, three decades earlier. It was as if people could not imagine the idea. Some gawkers pressed their faces against the glass to watch the bomb squad work. The technicians were trying to defuse the bomb, but without success, and the timer in the front seat kept ticking. As three o'clock approached, the police were still struggling to clear the area when a school bus rolled up, not fifty yards from the Cortina. Inside the bus were forty-nine schoolchildren, on a field trip to visit St. Paul's Cathedral. As the hand on the timer ticked toward three, the children began to disembark.

.   .   .

Most of the bombing team were on a bus to Heathrow airport when the BBC put out a report about the first bomb being discovered and defused. The bombers did not hear the bulletin, so they arrived at the airport unaware that they were now the subject of a manhunt. As far as they knew, the mission was proceeding as planned and they were about to return unnoticed to Ireland. They arrived at Terminal 1, headed to Gate 4, and presented their tickets for the British European Airways flight to Dublin, which was scheduled to depart at 11:20. Several of the bombers had actually filed onto the airplane and taken their seats when officials entered the plane and instructed everyone to get off.

Dolours, Marian, and Hugh Feeney were scheduled to take an Aer Lingus flight at 12:30. By the time they arrived at Heathrow, the rest of the team was supposed to be in the air. But when they entered the terminal, Special Branch officers were waiting. "Are you flying to Dublin?" one of the officers asked. "Would you mind coming with me?"

They were taken into custody and ushered into a holding area for questioning. But because the plan had been predicated on the idea that the team would be out of the country before any of the bombs were discovered, none of the volunteers had concocted any sort of cover story that was remotely convincing. Some claimed they had come to London in search of work. Others said they had been staying on the Belgrave Road and had gotten drunk at a local pub (which, at any rate, had elements of the truth). They all offered fake names—Dolours stuck with her pseudonym, Una Devlin—and denied that they knew one another. Asked about the bombs, they responded with sullen silence. (What authorities did not know then but would learn later was that one member of the group—an eleventh bomber—was missing. He had slipped away before the others were arrested at the airport, and gone to ground in London. He has never been identified or captured.)

"I don't intend to tell you anything," Marian Price said when she was questioned by a senior police officer. "You've no right to keep me here." She continued to stonewall, refusing to say a thing. It was already after 2 p.m., and the detectives knew they were running out of time. They pressed Marian about where the other bombs were, but she would not say. She wore a locket around her neck, and she kept putting it in her mouth and chewing on it anxiously. It suddenly occurred to the chief inspector who was interviewing her that the locket might contain some kind of poison, like a cyanide pill. He snatched it from her, only to see that it was a crucifix. His frustration growing, the inspector called her "an evil little maniac" and said she would not be seeing the sunshine again for some time.

But Marian Price said nothing. There was something robotic, almost trancelike, about her demeanor, and that of her fellow bombers. The detectives began to wonder if they had undergone some instruction in how to resist interrogation. They would fix their eyes on an object and just stare at it, as if hypnotized, refusing to say a thing. Then, just before 3 p.m., Marian raised her wrist and looked pointedly at her watch.

In a quiet fury, the chief inspector said, "Am I intended to gather that the timing on the other bombs has just expired?"

Marian Price just smiled.

.   .   .

In Whitehall, people were ambling back from lunchtime in the pleasant weather when the police finally discovered the Hillman Hunter parked in front of the army recruiting center. The officers stormed into the surrounding buildings, clearing everybody out. With five minutes to go before detonation, an explosives expert from the Royal Army Ordnance Corps broke a window and climbed into the car, then attempted to disarm the device. But there wasn't time now, and he scrambled out. Using a hook attached to a long line, he snagged the detonating cord connecting the timer to the explosives, then took cover around the corner of a building and started to pull. The resistance was significant, so he asked a sergeant who was with him for help. The two of them had just started pulling on the cord again when the timer's hand reached its terminus.

The Hillman split apart, ripped open by a sheet of flame that rose forty feet in the air. There was a dull thud, and a reverberation so strong that it lifted people in the surrounding area clean off the pavement. Windows shattered in the offices and shops for a quarter mile around. The blast blew the helmets off the policemen's heads and sent tiny missiles of glass and metal whizzing in every direction.

A sooty mushroom cloud rose above the street, and acrid smoke billowed among the buildings. A gas main ruptured, spewing more smoke and starting a blaze as firemen arrived and began dragging hoses through the carnage. People staggered about, dazed, their skin lacerated by glass. Dozens of cars were hollowed out and twisted up like crumpled paper.

The clap of the blast echoed throughout central London. On Dean Stanley Street, authorities had just managed to find and dismantle the third bomb, in the Vauxhall Viva, in front of the British Forces Broadcasting Service building. But by the time police had identified the car at the Old Bailey, it was too late. An officer ran toward the school bus and shouted at the children who had just gotten off, telling them to run for their lives. They did, screaming and shouting, hurrying around a corner for cover.

A police photographer was taking pictures of the car when suddenly he was hurled across the street. The blast was enormous. The façade of the George pub was torn away, exposing the lounge as if it were a room in a dollhouse. A police officer was evacuating jurors from the Old Bailey when the blast threw him twenty feet. Another policeman was riding by on his bicycle when he was hurled against a wall, the force of the blast ripping away his uniform. Martin Huckerby, the *Times* journalist, was cut on his face and hands and taken to St. Bartholomew's Hospital. People with blood running down their faces staggered through the smoke, trying to escape or to help others. But the whole vicinity of the explosion was consumed in a dense cloud of hot dust, making it difficult to see. The schoolchildren had managed to make it to safety, but injured victims lay sprawled out on the sidewalk. Everywhere there was a thick carpet of broken glass, swishing around people's feet, like sand at the beach.

This sort of scene might have become commonplace in

One of the London bombs explodes.

Northern Ireland, but it felt deeply jarring in London. To those witnesses who were old enough to remember, it was reminiscent of the Blitz. Between the two bombs that detonated, nearly 250 people were injured, and ambulances rushed in to deal with casualties. As luck would have it, there was not only a transit strike that week but also a strike of nonmedical workers at area hospitals. Even so, when they saw the bloodied patients being carried into emergency wards, the striking workers abandoned their picket lines and ran inside to help. Frederick Milton, a fifty-eight-year-old caretaker who worked at Hillgate House, right next to the Old Bailey, was covered in blood by the blast, but he resisted the call from medics to go to the hospital, insisting on helping other injured survivors. Milton collapsed a few hours later from a heart attack and died in the hospital.

An autopsy subsequently revealed that his heart attack had actually started prior to the explosion, so the medical evidence did not support a charge of murder. Dolours Price would blame the casualties from the blast on British authorities, for moving too slowly after the telephone warnings to locate and defuse the bombs and to alert civilians. Other members of the bombing team took the same view. This was clearly a convenient excuse, and as a moral matter it was conspicuously disingenuous. But as a factual matter, Price was not altogether wrong. The police themselves admitted, in the aftermath of the attack, that "human error" in their control room had garbled the message about the Old Bailey bomb, significantly delaying their response.

A British prosecutor would later speculate that the intention of the IRA mission was to kill people, and that it was no coincidence that the warning call had been made only after the gang had been arrested at the airport. He suggested that the warning was nothing but a selfish, last-minute bid to mitigate the severity of the punishment, once the IRA knew that their comrades had been captured. But however callous and incompetent the bombers were, it seems unlikely that their objective, when they journeyed to London, was mass slaughter. "If the intention was to kill people in London, it was quite easy to kill people in London, to kill civilians," Brendan Hughes said later. As with Bloody Friday, the London mission was envisaged as a symbolic, and ideally bloodless, attack. But powerful explosives leave no margin for serendipity, and the plan unraveled, with devastating results. Hughes was not particularly focused on the human toll of the bombs. What he regretted more acutely was not "burying" the bombers in England—letting them hide out in place, in or around London, to filter back home in ones and twos once the hysteria subsided. Instead, the IRA had tried to get them out as quickly as possible, a mistake that would have momentous consequences.

From Heathrow, the members of the bombing team were transported to a nearby police station. Their clothing was stripped from their bodies so that it could be forensically tested for residue of explosives. Dolours Price was photographed naked. When they were offered prison uniforms, some of the team accepted them. But the Price sisters and several others refused. This was a republican principle: they thought of themselves not as criminals but as captured soldiers from a legitimate army—as political prisoners. Given this distinction, they would not accept the prison scrubs of the ordinary criminal. Dolours and Marian draped rough prison blankets over their bodies. Hugh Feeney refused even a blanket and stood in his cell, brazenly naked. The prisoners were all separated, but at one point Dolours and Marian crossed paths briefly in an interview room, and Dolours hissed at her sister, "Don't say a word."

THE BELFAST TEN

THOMAS VALLIDAY WAS A prisoner at Long Kesh, where he held a job as an orderly. This required him to ride around in the rubbish lorry, picking up refuse from different corners of the prison camp and loading them into the truck. Life inside any prison tends to boil down to the deadening repetition of a daily routine, and Valliday's job was no exception: you made your rounds, you picked up the trash, you threw it in the lorry. Sometimes, in addition to the standard garbage, Valliday would find an old mattress that had been discarded because it was soiled or damaged. The prisoners would leave them, alongside the trash, outside the barbed-wire "cages" surrounding the half-cylinder Nissen huts where they lived. One Saturday morning in December 1973, the truck stopped outside a cage where a rolled-up mattress had been left. When Valliday went to pick up the mattress, it was considerably heavier than usual. But he got his arms around it and heaved it up onto the bed of the truck. If Valliday evinced no sign of suspicion that what appeared to be just a mattress might weigh as much as a small man, it was because he knew that nestled inside, wrapped up like a sausage in a bun, was Brendan Hughes.

Hughes had informed the police, upon his capture, that he intended to escape from prison, and he wasn't kidding. Within thirty-six hours of arriving at Long Kesh the previous summer, he had begun to scheme with comrades about how best to get out. Gerry Adams felt that, given the importance of operations to the current phase of the struggle, and the instrumental role that Hughes played in spearheading such operations, it should be Hughes who escaped first, before even Adams. But only two people had ever managed to break out of Long Kesh, which was ringed with barbed wire and surrounded by troops, and neither of them had "broken out," per se. The first was Dolours Price's childhood friend Francie McGuigan, the former "Hooded Man" who had been tortured at the secret army facility. One day in February 1972, McGuigan donned a set of borrowed black robes and, mingling with a visiting delegation of priests, walked right out the front door. Eighteen months later, another man, John Francis Green, managed to escape using the exact same ruse. (Green's brother, who actually was a priest, came for a visit, and the two of them switched clothes.)

It seemed prudent to assume that any further holy men seeking to depart Long Kesh might be subjected to a heightened degree of scrutiny, so if Hughes was going to escape, he would have to find another method. Somebody came up with the idea of leaving the camp by hitching a ride on the underside of one of the rubbish lorries. As a stratagem, this was reminiscent of Homer's *Odyssey*, in which Odysseus and his men escape the cave of the Cyclops by clinging to the bellies of his sheep. The prisoners constructed a special harness for Hughes to wear so that he could attach himself to the undercarriage of the truck. He rehearsed on one of the bunk beds in the cages, gripping the underside of the top bunk. But Hughes was still weak from the beating he had taken during his interrogation, and it was not certain that he would have the strength to cling to the lorry until it had cleared the outer fence. So eventually they abandoned that plan. This may have been disappointing for Hughes at the time, but it would turn out to be a stroke of exceptionally good luck: when another prisoner, Mark Graham, tried to escape using a similar method some months later, the truck went over a ramp and snapped his spine, leaving him paralyzed for life.

In late October, the Provos had engineered perhaps their most audacious escape to date. The IRA leader Seamus Twomey was being held at Mountjoy Prison, in Dublin, when a hijacked helicopter suddenly appeared in the sky and touched down in the prison yard just long enough for Twomey and a couple of his associates to hop aboard. This sort of precedent emboldened Hughes and his fellow prisoners, but it also meant that security was tight. The Provos knew that the trash lorry made its rounds twice a day before leaving the facility to go to the dump. They had heard that, before the truck was permitted to leave the grounds, guards would stab each trash bag with a spear, to make sure nobody was hidden inside. But the IRA had cultivated its own intelligence network inside the prison, and these informants suggested that lately the guards had not been bothering with the spears.

On the day in question, Hughes climbed into the center of an old mattress while others helped to roll it around him. With the assistance of Thomas Valliday, he ended up on the back of the truck, which proceeded to drive around the camp, stopping periodically so that garbage could be dumped on top of Hughes. All he had to do was wait. But the cheap prison mattress was filled with sawdust, and it was everywhere: fibrous, itchy, smothering. Hughes had brought an orange that he could suck for fluid and blood sugar, and he kept it jammed in his mouth, but the sawdust was getting in his nose, making it hard to breathe. The truck trundled around the camp, in no particular hurry. Then it stopped, and Hughes heard Valliday whispering to him. They could not leave the prison yet, Valliday said. The truck was going to stay to collect more trash. He advised Hughes to get out and sneak back to his cage. There would be a head count at 4 p.m. If Hughes was missing, the guards would lock down the facility and raise the alarm.

He stayed put. Valliday had disappeared, but Hughes was well hidden, and the truck had to leave at some point. Inside the mattress, he couldn't see what was going on around him, but now he heard the unmistakable accents of British soldiers. The lorry had ended up in the British Army compound, where the soldiers lived. Rather than take him through the gates to freedom, it had conveyed him directly into the most dangerous part of the camp. The sawdust had crept into his eyes, irritating them so much that he couldn't open one of them. Hughes lay quietly, hoping nobody would discover him.

After a small eternity, the truck began to move again and made its way toward the exit. Hughes knew exactly what to expect at this point: there would be two ramps, and then the truck would make a right turn and leave Long Kesh. But just before they reached the ramps, the truck stopped again. Hughes lay very still. Then, suddenly, a giant spear plunged down through the refuse, just to the left of his body.

Apparently his intelligence had been off. Hughes lay there, frozen. Then a spike impaled the bags on the other side of him. Now he decided he would just stand up and shout, just surrender, because to lie still would be suicide. If the spike came down again, it would surely kill him. He pictured it: the spear running straight through him. What a ridiculous way to die, harpooned in the back of a garbage truck, covered in sawdust, with an orange in your mouth. Hughes had two young children back in Belfast. This was madness. He was just about to identify himself to the men above when, with a rumble, the truck began to move again. It passed over one security ramp. Then it passed over the next. Finally, Hughes felt the truck make a right turn, and that was when he knew they had left the camp.

As the lorry moved along the open road, Hughes pulled out a small penknife he had brought with him and endeavored to cut himself out of the mattress. But the knife was not up to the task, and the blade simply bent back. He clawed and kicked his way out of the mattress, knocking some trash onto the roadway in the process. He feared that the driver might notice the refuse in the rearview mirror, but the truck kept moving.

At the top of the Hillsborough Road, Hughes knew there was an area where they would make a sharp right turn, followed by a sharp left. This seemed like the optimal moment to jump out the back undetected. So as the lorry made the turns, Hughes hopped down to the street. He watched the truck as it drove off, nervous that the driver might have spotted him. But it continued on in the direction of the dump.

Hughes stood there, caked in filth, one eye swollen shut. Gerry Adams had arranged for a car to meet him outside, but because the lorry had taken so much longer than expected on its rounds, Hughes had apparently missed the rendezvous, and the car wasn't there. Nor was this the kind of town where Hughes might just pop into the local pub, like the Magnificent Seven after they escaped from the *Maidstone,* and expect the patrons to donate a change of clothes and a getaway car. On the contrary, Hughes now found himself in the middle of a loyalist area. Not only was this hostile territory, but he had not put enough distance between himself and Long Kesh. As soon as they realized he was missing at the head count, the whole surrounding area would be flooded with troops. He had to get to the Republic. He was now the most wanted man in Northern Ireland, and he didn't have much time.

.   .   .

Michael Mansfield was sitting in the library on the top floor of the Old Bailey when the bomb detonated outside. A huge boom echoed below, and Mansfield was showered with broken glass. At thirty-two, Mansfield was an ambitious, slightly flamboyant English lawyer, with floppy hair and a sonorous voice. He had recently scored his first major legal triumph, in a months-long trial, at the Old Bailey, of the so-called Angry Brigade, a group of homegrown British anarchists who had tried to spark worldwide revolution by planting bombs in the homes of conservative ministers. Mansfield's client in that case, a young woman named Angela Weir, was acquitted. The case against her turned on handwriting evidence, and Mansfield was able, through his examination, to thoroughly discredit the government's experts. He had become politically radical as a student, and found that he was drawn to cases in which difficult questions were raised, questions about the nature of authoritarian power and resistance. With the money he made from the Angry Brigade case, Mansfield bought a car—a little secondhand Triumph 2000.

Because of the transit strike, Mansfield drove to work on the day of the bombing. He was running late and was worried about finding a parking space, but he discovered that parking restrictions had been waived, so he thought he might be able to find a spot right by the main entrance of the Old Bailey. He lucked out: there was one empty space, not far from a green Ford Cortina.

Mansfield was not seriously injured when the bomb exploded, but the Triumph was ripped apart. Not long afterward, Mansfield was asked if he would like to take on the case of the very people who had blown it up, the young Irish bombers Dolours and Marian Price. A long tradition existed in the legal profession of enterprising litigators taking on notorious clients, not least because the exposure often raised the profile of their practice. But the IRA bombing was considered such a deep affront to London that many established lawyers would not take the case, on principle.

Mansfield would. He was very curious to meet the sisters. When he did, he was struck immediately by their beauty and by the intensity of their commitment. They sat balled up on plastic chairs, hugging their knees, and told him about the abuses of Catholics in the North, about internment, about Bloody Sunday. They recalled being pummeled by the loyalist mob at Burntollet Bridge. Mansfield wasn't that much older than they were. He prided himself on his radical politics, but he had chosen to pursue those politics through the less-than-revolutionary vocation of the law. It struck him that the Price sisters had chosen a different sort of life, a life that was truly "on the edge."

. . .

Dolours and Marian were charged, along with the eight others who had been captured, with conspiring to cause "an explosion of a nature likely to endanger life." Normally, there would be an obvious venue for such a trial: the Old Bailey. But the building was still being repaired from the bombing and the government wanted to fast-track the proceedings. Besides, it might have been construed as prejudicial to try a group of defendants in a courthouse on charges of endeavoring to destroy that very courthouse. So the trial, which commenced in the fall of 1973, was relocated to the Great Hall of Winchester Castle, an imposing thirteenth-century chamber of medieval stone, marble col-

Mug shots of Dolours and Marian Price.

umns, and stained glass. It was in this same room that Sir Walter Raleigh was found guilty of treason in 1603, for plotting to overthrow King James I. An enormous oak replica of the surface of King Arthur's round table hung on one wall, with bands of green paint radiating from a Tudor Rose.

The Price sisters and their codefendants sang rebel songs on the prison bus to Winchester. Each morning throughout the trial, the defendants would be escorted in and out by a convoy of motorcycles and police cars. The bombings had occasioned such hysteria that the proceedings were marked by an extreme, almost theatrical devotion to security. A complete daytime parking ban was imposed on the whole surrounding area, to prevent car bombs. Police marksmen patrolled surrounding rooftops. (This may not have been entirely unreasonable: it would later emerge that republicans had tried to purchase a house directly across the street from the prison where the defendants were being held, with an eye to digging a tunnel under the street and directly into the cellblock, to spring them out. The plan was abandoned after the local woman who owned the home developed second thoughts about selling, for sentimental reasons.) As the bus drove into the complex under heavy armed guard, Dolours and Marian flashed V signs to the spectators outside.

The trial was a huge event, attracting widespread fascination. The actress Vanessa Redgrave, who was famous for her role in *Blow-Up,* volunteered to post bond for the defendants and offered up her own house in West Hampstead, should any of them need a place to stay. (None of the bombers were released from custody to take her up on this magnanimous proposal.) The English public and press became particularly fixated on Dolours and Marian. They were dubbed the "Sisters of Terror" and depicted as hugely dangerous. To *The Times,* Dolours became a paradigm of political radicalism and countercultural instability, with her "enthusiasm for the wider concept of violent world revolution and support for the diverse aims of Che

Guevara, the Black Panthers and the Palestinian guerrillas." She might have been the more dominant sister, the paper continued, but "Marian's soft speaking voice and apparent innocence disguise a 19-year-old well-versed in the arts of guerrilla warfare," whose ease with a rifle had earned her the nickname "the Armalite widow." Detecting, in the sisters, evidence of a disturbing trend, the *Daily Mirror* noted that "the legend that women are passive, peace-loving creatures who want only to stay at home and look after children has been finally exploded in a thunder of bombs and bullets." The tabloid drew a direct line from the Price sisters to Leila Khaled, the Palestinian hijacker, and diagnosed the violence of these women as a dangerous by-product of feminism—"a lethal liberation."

At the opening of the trial, in September, the attorney general, Sir Peter Rawlinson, a debonair barrister with a mellifluous voice, whom the newspapers described as the "Laurence Olivier of the bar," pointed out that the car bomb, while a novelty in London, was part of everyday life in Northern Ireland. "Those who place car bombs can walk away to safety," Rawlinson said. "When the bomb explodes, they are safe and sound many miles away. It is a very cowardly practice." As he laid out the details of that awful day, Rawlinson singled out Dolours Price as the leader of the group, "the girl who plays a major part in this operation."

The sisters were resolutely defiant. Apart from one member of the team, nineteen-year-old William McLarnon, who pleaded guilty on the first day of the trial, all of the defendants maintained their innocence. Dolours said that she had flown to London on the day before the bombing for a short holiday with her sister and their friend Hugh Feeney. She used the pseudonym Una Devlin because, as the daughter of a well-known republican, she was always getting hassled by the authorities, and offering a false name had become practically second nature. The girls were sassy and carefree in the courtroom, even upbeat.

They chuckled when the prosecution showed a photo of Michael Mansfield's wrecked Triumph. (Mansfield, less amused, pointed out to them that he could have been in it.)

For much of the ten-week trial, the defendants simply stonewalled. But there was a mountain of circumstantial evidence connecting them with the crime. Rawlinson spelled out the sequence of events leading up to the bombings and the particular charges against each individual, in a statement that took twelve hours, over several days. When Dolours was stopped by the officers at Heathrow, she had been carrying a black canvas shopping bag. Inside, along with a program for the Brian Friel play and what was described as a "large quantity of makeup," the police discovered two screwdrivers and a spiral-bound notebook. Some pages in the notebook were filled with idle jottings: theological musings about the Virgin Mary on one page, a list of foods with their corresponding calorie counts on the other. But investigators also noticed that some pages had been torn out. An expert forensic witness examined the remaining blank pages in the notebook and revealed for the jury the ghostly indentation of what had been written. It was a diagram of the timing device for a bomb.

This was a difficult turn for Mansfield's defense. Despite his past success in discrediting evidence from handwriting experts, he was unable to blunt the force of the notebook. But even as he was contending with that incriminating exhibit, Mansfield was faced with a more daunting challenge: one of the defendants had decided to cooperate.

. . .

When Roisin McNearney, the typist from Belfast who was the youngest member of the team, was initially questioned by police in the hours after the bombings, she stuck to the same story as the other bombers, insisting that she was not a member of the IRA. "I don't know what you are talking about," she said. "I am only over here for a holiday."

But as the interrogation continued, small fractures began to show in her façade. "I believe in the united Ireland," she told the investigators. "But I don't believe in violence." They continued to work on her, and finally she blurted, "I can't tell you everything, or I will get a bullet in my head."

She had joined the IRA only six months earlier, she said. Out at a pub one night, she was singing along to patriotic songs when someone approached her and asked if she was ready to do something for Ireland. She told the police about her role in the bombing operation but insisted that she was a minor, ineffectual figure, very much on the periphery of the gang. Notwithstanding her confession and cooperation with the authorities, McNearney pleaded not guilty. Though she had given a detailed confession after the bombing, the others did not realize until the trial began that she had betrayed them.

If the likelihood of an acquittal looked vanishingly small for the Price sisters and their fellow defendants, this did little to dampen their spirits. During the trial, Dolours and Marian sat at the end of the dock, and they would smile and wave to supporters in the gallery. When their old friend Eamonn McCann, the activist from Derry who had first encountered them on the Burntollet march, came to sit with their family in the spectators' gallery, they winked and waved. Albert and Chrissie Price had flown to London to attend the trial, and McCann marveled at the posture of the older Prices, ramrod straight and proud. It struck him that, behind their ferocious composure, they must have been suffering greatly to watch their daughters face a life sentence.

The defendants wore their own clothes for the trial, and Dolours selected eye-catching ensembles—smocks, pinafores, sweaters. She had always been attuned to performance, and there was an unmistakable sense that the trial had become a stage. As the proceedings dragged on, her red hair, which had been pixie short at the time of the bombings, gradually began to grow out.

But if there were moments when Dolours seemed to take the process lightly, she could also show flashes of fiery resolve. When Peter Rawlinson asked her if she supported the "aims and principles" of the IRA, Dolours replied that she might, "provided Sir Peter's interpretation of 'aims and principles' are the same as mine." When he asked her to elaborate on what she thought those aims were, Dolours said that, in her view, the IRA regarded "the long-term aim to be the reunification of Ireland with full civil religious liberties for all."

The judge, Sebag Shaw, interjected to ask whether she believed that violence should be employed in furtherance of these aims. "I did not say that," Price said—she had been speaking of objectives, not of the means that might justifiably be employed to achieve them. She jousted in this manner with both the prosecutor and the judge, unflustered by their bewigged solemnity, unintimidated by the grandeur of the surroundings or the phalanx of security personnel or the gravity of the charges against her. As the trial wore on, Price and her fellow defendants began to openly heckle Judge Shaw, refuting the moral authority of the court, mocking the witnesses, and reveling in their shared contempt for the whole proceeding.

·   ·   ·

On the November day that the verdict was delivered, Dolours Price dressed in a green sweater and tied a pink ribbon in her hair. Security was tight at the courthouse, with everyone who entered frisked at the door. As they were escorted up to the dock, the defendants were accompanied by fifteen prison officers, who crowded into seats behind them. To Michael Mansfield, it seemed that all the security had been designed to establish "an atmosphere of guilt." Throughout the trial, a bodyguard had sat, unseen, just behind Judge Shaw's seat, but today he sat out in the open, right next to the judge on the bench. There had been a series of bomb scares at nearby department stores, and the public gallery in the makeshift courtroom was crowded with rowdy Irish people who had come over to support the defendants. When the all-male jury filed in to deliver the verdict, four rows of plainclothes detectives came in and sat behind them. As the proceedings were about to get under way, guards took one final security precaution, bolting the doors to the courthouse.

Before sentencing Price and the other defendants, Judge Shaw announced that the jury was acquitting Roisin McNearney. Addressing McNearney—a small girl with penciled eyebrows, in a white shawl and a pink blouse—Shaw said that he hoped she had learned "not to dabble in murderous enterprises." Referring to her decision to betray her comrades, he said, "I do not know when you leave this court what other dangers may confront you." As McNearney was ushered out of the hall, the remaining defendants began to hum a tune, in ominous unison. It was "The Dead March" from Handel's *Saul,* a standard feature of the musical repertoire at funerals. Hugh Feeney reached into his pocket and came out with a coin. He hurled it at McNearney, shouting, "Here's your blood money!" She rushed out of the courtroom, sobbing.

The remaining defendants were convicted. When it came time to sentence them, Shaw delivered the maximum penalty— a so-called life sentence, which for five of the bombers would mean twenty years, in practice. For Dolours and Marian Price and for Hugh Feeney, Shaw handed down a more severe punishment, on account of their leadership role: thirty years. Dolours said, audibly, "That's a *death* sentence."

Seeming to shy away, himself, from the harshness of this penalty, Shaw announced that he would reduce the sentence for the Price sisters and Feeney to twenty years. But the defendants were making their displeasure known. A flustered Shaw ordered them to keep quiet in his courtroom. "No!" both Price sisters replied.

Having refused to say a word throughout the proceedings about their membership in the IRA, the defendants now all began to talk at once, making shrill political speeches as their relatives and friends applauded from the public gallery. "I stand before you as a volunteer of the IRA!" Marian Price announced. "I consider myself a prisoner of war!"

"Up the Provisionals!" the spectators shouted. "No surrender!"

"You must not regard the dock as a political arena," Judge Shaw cried. "It's a court of law!" But now that the sentence had been delivered, nobody was listening.

"Victory is within the grasp of the Irish Nation!" exclaimed Hugh Feeney. "She will not bend the knee!"

.   .   .

Roisin McNearney was hustled away, surrounded by a retinue of armed guards. Arrangements were made to create a new identity for her. She was given a new name and new documents and told that she could never return to Northern Ireland. Her belongings were taken from her family home in Andersonstown and put into storage, to be shipped to her once she had started her new life. "Make no mistake about it," one Provisional leader in Belfast told the press. "There is no hiding place for her." But the Provos never caught McNearney. She vanished from the courtroom, became another person, and disappeared.

Before they were removed from Winchester Castle, Dolours and Marian Price made an announcement: they were going on a hunger strike. They would refuse food until they were granted status as political prisoners and returned to Northern Ireland to serve their sentences. The sisters were taken to Brixton Prison. It was an all-male facility, but they were perceived as so dangerous that housing them there would represent a justifiable exception. From prison, Dolours wrote a letter to her mother, Chrissie, in which she suggested that either the British government would accede to their demands and send them back home to serve their sentences there or they would die of starvation and their bodies would be shipped to Belfast for burial: "We will be back in Northern Ireland one way or the other by the New Year."

THE TOY SALESMAN

ARTHUR McALLISTER WAS A toy salesman. He rented an apartment on the ground floor of an elegant brick home on Myrtlefield Park, in a middle-class neighborhood on the outskirts of Belfast. Even at the height of the Troubles, it could occasionally seem, in the leafier suburbs, that sectarian strife and paramilitary gun battles were chiefly a working-class phenomenon, one that seldom touched the area's more stable, well-heeled precincts. McAllister's flat was fronted by a lattice of ivy and surrounded by old trees and a gracious lawn. Each morning, he would leave the house carrying a case full of toy samples and catalogs. He would climb into his car and crisscross the greater Belfast area, popping into shops to see if he might interest the proprietors in his wares. He was a small, punctilious man, always clean-shaven, his hair carefully trimmed. He dressed in a manner that might have seemed unnecessarily formal for his chosen line of work: McAllister was ultimately just a door-to-door salesman, but when he made his rounds, he looked like a banker, attired in a three-piece suit.

One morning in the spring of 1974, the quiet of the suburban neighborhood was ruptured when a convoy of police cars and armored vehicles coursed through the streets and came to an abrupt halt right outside the house on Myrtlefield Park. The British Army had been staking out the property. In fact, a soldier dressed in camouflage had spent the previous night hiding in a rhododendron bush in the front garden. The lookout was in position so long that his fellow soldiers worried he might not have enough to eat. An effort to subtly resupply him had gone awry when someone walked by with an order of fish and chips but accidentally threw the food into the wrong bush.

The target of this surveillance, and of the morning raid, was the toy salesman himself. As the vehicles screeched into place, soldiers and police stormed the house, where they found McAllister and shoved him against a wall. With great indignation, he protested his innocence and expressed his effrontery that the authorities might barge into the home of a blameless civilian. But the officials did not appear to believe that he was actually a toy salesman, or even that his name was McAllister.

"Come on, Darkie," one of the officers said. "You've had a long enough run."

.   .   .

After he escaped from Long Kesh in the rubbish lorry, Brendan Hughes had eventually managed to hitch a ride from a vanful of gypsies, and then another ride from a driver who turned out to be English. Sitting in the passenger seat, it occurred to Hughes that the Englishman might be an off-duty guard from the very prison from which he happened to have just escaped. But if the man was a Long Kesh employee, he never figured out the identity of his hitchhiker. Hughes got as far as Newry, where he was able to access some money that he had stashed away for this type of eventuality. From there, he took a taxi across the border to Dundalk.

As soon as he was safe in the Republic, Hughes started to feel the tug of Belfast. Having lost months behind the wire at Long Kesh, he was eager to get back to running operations, but he knew that he could not return to his old patch of West Belfast. It was too hot, and he was too known. If his arrest with Adams the previous summer had marked a colossal success for the authorities, his escape was an even more colossal embarrassment. The only way for Hughes to safely return to Belfast would be to go incognito. So he decided to forge a new identity. He rented the property on Myrtlefield Park and began to construct an alter ego, adopting the name Arthur McAllister, shaving his trademark mustache, cutting and dyeing his hair, and endeavoring to appear the very opposite of the scruffy lout the police had photographed after his arrest with Adams in the Falls. Arthur McAllister was a real person, or had been—he had died as an infant but would have been about Brendan's age. By using this name and constructing a personality around it, Hughes had created what spies call a "legend"—a coherent double identity. (He would later suggest that this cloak-and-dagger tradecraft had been inspired by the thriller *The Day of the Jackal,* which was released in 1973.)

Becoming Arthur McAllister, middle-class toy salesman from Myrtlefield Park, meant that he could return to Belfast. What's more, it opened the city up to him: suddenly he could traverse the sectarian lines, toting his briefcase full of toys, conducting clandestine meetings wherever he wanted. Sometimes he would be stopped by British troops on his travels, but they always bought his story—after all, he had his case of toys and a driver's license that said "Arthur McAllister." The Provos knew that it would madden the British to think of Hughes out on the streets, at large, and they occasionally tempted fate by boasting publicly after he made appearances in disguise. At one point, following an Easter commemoration at Milltown Cemetery, which the authorities would have been monitoring closely, the IRA announced that Hughes had been in attendance, "under the noses of the British Army."

"My job at that time was to bring the war to the Brits," Hughes said later. "I was good at what I done and I done it." In the guise of Arthur McAllister, he was planning a number of ambitious operations. But his most audacious scheme during that period was a successful effort to wiretap army headquarters. The British were not the only ones with a taste for espionage. Hughes had appealed to republican technical experts to see if there was some way to penetrate the army's communications. A local telephone engineer visited army headquarters at Thiepval Barracks, in Lisburn, to install a new backup exchange. The engineer was not an IRA member, but a supporter, and he secretly installed a tap on the telephone of the army's intelligence cell, attaching a voice-activated recorder to the line. Because army intelligence liaised regularly with Special Branch, this would, at least in theory, provide Hughes with precious insight into the internal operations of both organizations.

The same technician who put the bug in place began to visit the house in Myrtlefield Park every few days, dropping off a fresh batch of tapes. But there was a problem: the tapes were garbled, unintelligible. They sounded, to Hughes, like Mickey Mouse. It appeared that, as an added precaution, the army had scrambled its calls. There was a device that could be used to unscramble such calls, but it was not the sort of thing you could walk into a consumer electronics shop and purchase. In fact, the only place where such a piece of equipment could be found was back at army headquarters. So Hughes ordered the technician to return to Lisburn, with instructions to steal an unscrambling device from the army. And he did.

· · ·

Hughes may have been spying on the authorities, but he failed to realize that, at a certain point, the authorities were also spying on him. They had somehow gotten wind of his hideout and established that the dapper toy merchant, in his ivy-covered home, was in fact the escaped IRA commander Brendan Hughes. It was not at all clear how the police and the army might have come by such a compromising piece of information, but for observers at the time, it raised an obvious possibility. As one report noted after Hughes was taken into custody, "The Provisionals are certain to launch an intensive inquiry into whether they have a big-time informer in their midst."

When the police raided the house where Hughes was staying, they discovered four rifles, a submachine gun, and more than three thousand rounds of ammunition, as well as half a dozen tapes of tapped phone calls from army headquarters. They also found a cache of materials that outlined a contingency scenario that would become known as the IRA's "doomsday plan." The situation envisaged by the documents was one of all-out sectarian war, in which Hughes and his colleagues would be forced to defend Catholic areas. There were maps showing evacuation routes, and a prepared statement that read, "An Emergency has been forced upon us and the IRA has no alternative to defend its people. It may be necessary to impose harsh measures to ensure that this succeeds militarily." The documents predicted a kind of apocalypse. They indicated that an IRA radio station would broadcast information about food supplies.

The first time Hughes was arrested, his captors had beaten him and taken trophy photographs while they posed alongside him. This time was different. What they wanted to do now was recruit him, just as they had recruited Seamus Wright and Kevin McKee. When they had him in custody, Special Branch officers told Hughes that, in his role as the nerve center for operations in Belfast, he was ideally situated to help them. They were just trying to stop the conflict—he could play a vital role in putting an end to all this bloodshed. Hughes told them that he was not interested. Perhaps he might be induced in some other fashion? The men offered him a suitcase full of money. But he declined. "I was offered fifty thousand pounds to become an informer," Hughes later recalled. "I told them fifty million wouldn't sway me."

THE ULTIMATE WEAPON

BRIXTON PRISON WAS A grim colossus surrounded by a high brick wall. For a period in the nineteenth century, it had housed female convicts, but by the time Dolours and Marian Price became residents there, shortly after their conviction at Winchester Castle, they were the only women held in the whole facility, and the atmosphere was overwhelmingly and oppressively male: the prison was overcrowded, and there were men everywhere, pacing their cells, loitering in the recreation areas in undershirts and brown prison scrubs, walking to the showers with towels slung over their shoulders. Dolours and Marian were segregated in their own individual cells, but as they took exercise in the yard for half an hour each day or were escorted through Brixton's endless corridors, they attracted a stream of verbal commentary from their fellow inmates. A rumor went around that men in the prison were selling seats at their windows overlooking the exercise yard during the time when the sisters were let out. It seemed to Dolours that Brixton even *smelled* like men. Every inch of the place was redolent of cooped-up males. The cells were adorned with collages of pornography.

"You didn't go anywhere without a screw beside you every step of the way," Dolours later recalled. A screw was a guard, in the prison vernacular. The sisters were given numbers—Dolours was Prisoner No. 286185—a new institutional identity that they would wear, in theory, for the next twenty years.

Except that neither sister had any intention of remaining behind bars for anywhere near that long. They had already stopped eating by the time they entered Brixton, refusing to take anything but water. Some of the other convicted members of their bombing crew dabbled with short-term hunger strikes, but Dolours and Marian intended to strike until death if necessary. Hugh Feeney and Gerry Kelly, who were being held at different prisons, both joined them.

Marian and Dolours in prison.

Their demand was simple: that they be repatriated to serve out their sentences as political prisoners in jails in Northern Ireland.

By electing this particular mode of protest, the Price sisters were invoking a long-standing tradition of Irish resistance. Dating back to the Middle Ages, fasting had been used by the Irish to express dissent or rebuke. It was a quintessential weapon of passive aggression. In a 1903 play about a poet in seventh-century Ireland who launched a hunger strike at the gates of the royal palace, W. B. Yeats described

> *An old and foolish custom, that if a man*
> *Be wronged, or think that he is wronged, and starve*
> *Upon another's threshold till he die,*
> *The common people, for all time to come,*
> *Will raise a heavy cry against that threshold.*

In 1920, an Irish republican poet and politician named Terence MacSwiney, who had been imprisoned in Brixton on charges of sedition, refused food for seventy-four days, demanding that he be released. The British would not let him go, and he perished. MacSwiney's death sparked an international furor, and before he was buried, in the uniform of the IRA, tens of thousands of people filed past his coffin to pay their respects, and thousands more rallied in protest in cities around the world. He had eloquently articulated a philosophy of self-sacrifice that would help define the emerging traditions of Irish republican martyrdom. "It is not those who inflict the most but those who suffer the most who will conquer," MacSwiney declared. When somebody dies on a hunger strike, the moral calculus of causation can be tricky. It may have been MacSwiney who, in the strictest sense, chose to take his own life, but by announcing that he would eat again only if the British acceded to his demands, he seemed to transfer the responsibility for whether he lived or died into the hands of his captors. His coffin bore an inscription in Gaelic: MURDERED BY THE FOREIGNER IN BRIXTON PRISON.

When the Price sisters stopped eating, prison officers would leave a tray of food in their cells, to tempt them. The sisters would not touch it. Eventually the officers stopped leaving the food. A kindly Polish nurse still brought a jug of orange juice every morning.

"Water only, sister," Dolours would say.

"I leave, anyway," the nurse would reply.

The sisters had been strapping and healthy when they went into prison. As they started shedding weight, Dolours made light of it. "My chubby cheeks have gone," she wrote in a letter to her family that January. "I must be growing up, losing my 'puppy fat'!!" She joked that Marian's big brown eyes now took up half her face. But Dolours had always enjoyed a little gallows humor, and she recognized from the outset that a hunger strike is ultimately a contest of wills—the will of the striker to carry on starving, and the will of her opponent to continue refusing her demands. Terence MacSwiney may have lost his life, but he won his standoff with the British: his death generated unprecedented publicity and international support for the cause of Irish independence. "He who blinks first is lost," Dolours later observed. "I knew that at a very early age."

.   .   .

The notion that two young Irishwomen might die on hunger strike in the very prison where MacSwiney met his fate had the ingredients of priceless propaganda. The sisters, who had already been the subject of widespread press coverage during the trial, now became the stars of a different sort of serialized tabloid drama, with breathless daily updates in newspapers and on the radio about their steadily deteriorating condition. They were the "bomb girls," and the coverage tended to play not on the fortitude with which they continued to swear off nourishment, but on their youth and gender, their frail femininity. (Hugh Feeney and Gerry Kelly, who also continued their strike, received much less attention and were never referred to as "boys.")

"Soup, turkey, ham, potatoes, Christmas pudding and brandy sauce," a newspaper ad from the Provisional Republican Movement read over the holidays. "Merry Christmas everyone. Dolours Price is dying." The brinksmanship between the Price sisters and the British was described in language that recalled not just MacSwiney, but the Great Famine of the nineteenth century, in which a million people in Ireland were allowed to die of disease and starvation, and another million or more were forced to migrate. Even as the Irish starved during the famine, ships laden with food were leaving Irish harbors—for export to the English. Many in Ireland and elsewhere had taken the view that the British bore a responsibility for the famine, one that exceeded callous neglect and began to look more like deliberate murder. One of the first widely circulated tracts about the famine described it as "The Last Conquest of Ireland."

If the British had employed hunger as a weapon during the famine, it would now be turned around and used against them. Dolours Price had always felt that prison was where an IRA volunteer's allegiance to the cause was truly tested. Now, she told anyone who would listen, she stood more than ready to die. "Volunteers died on the streets of Belfast for our cause and our deaths will be no different from theirs," she pointed out in a letter. "We'll be the first women, I think, and are very proud to be so. If we are left to die in Brixton, we'll feel honored to die in the same prison as Terence MacSwiney, over 50 years later." Such an outcome, she felt, would be proof that the empire never learned from its mistakes. The British had always outmanned and outspent and outgunned the Irish, but the "ultimate weapon," Dolours believed, was "one's own body."

Confronted with this peculiar form of defiance, the leaders of the British government were under no illusions: if any of the hunger strikers died, it would be a disaster. If such a thing should happen, officials feared "massive retaliatory violence." But rather than bend to the sisters' demands, the government imposed a blunt alternative solution. On December 3, when the strike had been going on for two and a half weeks, a group of doctors and nurses marched into Dolours's cell. They took her to a room where they forced her into a chair that was bolted to the floor and began tying her up with bedsheets, to secure her. She tried to struggle, but she was weak; she hadn't eaten in more than two weeks. Once they had restrained her, she watched in terror as a pair of hands prized open her jaws. An object was shoved roughly into her open mouth. It was a wooden bit with a hole in the center of it. Another pair of hands produced a thin length of rubber hose, then inserted the tip through the hole in the bit and began to slide this tube down her throat. She could not catch her breath as the tube snaked past her tonsils, and she gagged, nearly suffocating. She tried to bite the tube, but the wooden contraption prevented it. Several officials held her body back, and then she felt liquid coursing down the rubber coil and into her belly.

It took only a few minutes for the substance to slosh down into her, but to Dolours it felt like an eternity. Before they had even removed the tube, she vomited the food up. "The feed," as she came to think of this forcibly administered diet, consisted of a combination of foods that had been whipped together in a blender—raw eggs, orange juice, and liquid Complan, a concentrated blend of milk, minerals, and vitamins. After the force-feeding, Dolours was released to the exercise yard, where she saw Marian, who had not yet been subjected to it. Dolours told her sister about the ordeal and said that she did not think she could go through with it again. You don't need to, Marian said. You can come off the strike.

No, Dolours replied. We'll come off together or not at all.

Two days later, the prison doctors started force-feeding Marian as well. It became a gruesome ritual. Each morning at 10 a.m., the crew of doctors and nurses would arrive in their cells, tie them down, and pour the food down their throats. "We are learning to breathe a bit more easily when the tube is down," Dolours wrote in a letter.

Force-feeding was a controversial practice that had been used on another group of unruly women, the British suffragettes. After being force-fed in Holloway Prison in 1913, one of the suffragettes, Sylvia Pankhurst, called it torture, noting that "infinitely worse than any pain was the sense of degradation."

"I don't want the stuff forced down me," Dolours wrote in a letter. "And while I am not in a position to offer physical resistance, that's not to say that I can't mentally resist and reject the whole horrible happening." Sometimes one of the sisters would vomit while the tube was still down her throat and nearly choke to death. Some of their letters were published in the press, and there was a great outcry about the force-feeding. The Home

Office responded, at least initially, with a claim that these measures were being taken simply in the interests of helping the strikers, and that British prison officials were not in the habit of allowing their inmates to kill themselves.

In January, Bernadette Devlin, the student leader from the People's Democracy march at Burntollet Bridge, who had gone on to win a seat at Parliament in Westminster, paid a visit to the Price sisters. Devlin was shocked by the sight of Dolours. Her hair, which had been a rich dark red, "has lost color to the extent that it is fair, and actually white at the roots," Devlin said. Because she had begun to struggle with her captors during the feed, biting down on the wooden bit, Dolours's teeth had started to loosen and decay. Both sisters' complexions had grown waxy. They shuffled when they walked.

Some of the personnel who administered the force-feeding were cruel. One doctor mocked the sisters' conviction, joking during feeding sessions that it was "all for the cause." A female attendant made a comment about the Ulster Irish breeding "like rabbits" and living off the English.

"We built your roads!" Dolours snapped back, not so enfeebled that she would shrink from an argument. "We were happy in our own country 'til you English took it away from us... The Irish are here because of yous!"

Other officials were more kind. The sisters had a good rapport with the prison doctor, a man named Ian Blyth. He called them "my girls," and as the hunger strike progressed, he would challenge them to arm-wrestling contests. They gamely played along, knowing full well that the purpose of this pantomime was to register how rapidly their strength was dissipating. A psychiatrist was sent by the Home Office to examine them. He certified that the Price sisters knew exactly what they were doing. In summarizing his diagnosis, Marian said, "The problem was we were too sane." The psychiatrist knew Roy Jenkins, the British home secretary, and Marian asked him if Jenkins might come himself to see them. Jenkins would never meet them face-to-face, the psychiatrist told her, because he knew that if he did, he would send them right home.

. . .

For the government, this was an impossible crisis. Even as their bodies continued to shrink and wither, the Price sisters took on an iconic dimension. "They were the stuff of which Irish martyrs could be made: two young, slim, dark girls, devout yet dedicated to terrorism," Jenkins later recalled. He feared that the ramifications of "the death of these charismatic colleens" would be incalculable. Privately, Jenkins regarded their demand for repatriation to be "not totally unreasonable." But he felt that the government could not appear to be making any concessions under such duress. Terrorism was a "contagion," Jenkins believed. Bending to the demands of the hunger strikers would only validate their methods and encourage others to adopt them.

But if the alternative was force-feeding, it was turning out to be a public relations fiasco. Many members of the British public regarded the practice as a form of torture. According to their medical records, the Price sisters sometimes fainted during the procedure. On one occasion, when the sisters resisted the feeding, they were forcibly gagged, and a radio was turned up to cover their screams. Speaking at a protest outside the home of the British ambassador in Dublin, a psychiatrist decried the practice, likening it to rape. "The doctor here told us that he thought the first couple of times they force-fed Dotes they'd break her," Marian wrote in a letter to her family. "But it takes more than that to break our kid, some pup she is."

Some parents, seeing their daughters, who were barely out of high school, proposing to starve themselves to death, might prevail upon them to give up the fight. Not the Prices. "An awful lot of people come onto earth, eat, work and die and never contribute anything to the world," Albert Price told a reporter. "If they die, at least they will have done something."

Their mother, Chrissie, sounded a similar note. "I raised them to do their duty to their country," she said. "I am heartbroken looking at them suffering, yet I am proud of them. I will not ask them to give up. I know they will win in the end."

When Chrissie saw her daughters in prison, she kept a brave face, chatting animatedly about everything but the hunger strike until the end of the visit. Then, just as she was about to leave, she said, "What are you taking now?"

"We're taking water, Mum. We're just drinking water," Dolours said.

"Well," Chrissie said, with gruff composure, "drink plenty of water."

There is a morbid but undeniable entertainment in watching a hunger strike unfold. As a test of the limits of human endurance, it can become a spectacle for rubberneckers, a bit like the Tour de France, except that the stakes are life and death. It is also a game of chicken between the strikers and the authorities. The case became hugely notorious. Bands like the Dubliners played benefit concerts in support of the Price sisters, Hugh Feeney, and Gerry Kelly. There were regular protests outside the walls of Brixton Prison. Sixty women showed up at Roy Jenkins's London home, chanting in support of the strikers. The father of a young girl who had been badly injured in the London bombing called for the sisters to be returned to Ireland. Even one of the loyalist paramilitary groups, the Ulster Defence Association, asked the British government to either return the girls to Northern Ireland or simply let them die. (Dolours was "amazed" by that endorsement, she wrote to her family, adding, "It just goes to show that when it comes to the crunch, we're all Irish together.")

The sisters closely monitored their own coverage, listening to daily broadcasts about their condition. This was a strange experience for Dolours. She processed the stories of these two

Irish girls on hunger strike as if they were about somebody else. She could never quite believe that they were talking about her. Nevertheless, she was well attuned to the propaganda value of such coverage, and she knew that the letters she wrote home about her condition would be circulated to the press. After a lifetime of being introduced as one of "Albert's daughters," Dolours was tickled to have achieved a notoriety of her own. She tweaked Albert about it, telling Chrissie, in one letter, to ask him "how does he like being called 'Dolours and Marian's father'?"

.   .   .

Nearly a year had passed since the bombings, and the sisters were still being force-fed, when the case took a bizarre turn. In February 1974, a seventeenth-century painting by Vermeer, of a young girl plucking a narrow guitar, was stolen from a museum in Hampstead. A pair of anonymous typewritten letters arrived at *The Times* of London, demanding that Dolours and Marian Price be returned to Northern Ireland and threatening that if they weren't, the painting would "be burnt on St. Patrick's night with much cavorting about in the true lunatic fashion." As proof that this threat was sincere, one of the letters contained a sliver of canvas from the Vermeer. In a strange coincidence, on a trip to London two years earlier, Dolours had visited Kenwood House, where the Vermeer hung—and had stopped to look at that very painting. In a statement, Chrissie Price appealed to whoever it was that took the artwork to return it unharmed. She noted that Dolours—"who is an art student"—had made a special plea on behalf of the painting.

One evening in May, a suspicious package appeared in a churchyard near Smithfield Market, in London. It was wrapped in newspaper and tied with string. A squad of officers arrived at the Church of St. Bartholomew the Great. In this atmosphere of heightened tension, the package could be a bomb. But it wasn't: it was the painting, which had been returned, just as Dolours had requested.

During this same period, a second art heist was perpetrated in the name of the Price sisters. A collection of old masters worth millions of pounds was stolen from a house in County Wicklow, in Ireland. Among the paintings that went missing were a Velázquez, a Vermeer, a Rubens, a Goya, and a Metsu. Once again, a ransom letter appeared, demanding that the hunger strikers be returned "at once to serve their sentences in Ireland." These paintings, too, were later recovered.

In June, an elderly Irish earl and his wife returned to their home in Tipperary after a formal dinner one night to discover several strange men lurking in their driveway. One of the men pistol-whipped the earl. Then they dragged his wife across the gravel, shoved them into a vehicle, blindfolded them both, and drove away. The kidnappers informed the couple that they were being held as "hostages for the Price sisters." They were confined for several days in a dark room at gunpoint, but the prisoners ended up taking a liking to their captors and came to regard the whole experience as something of an adventure. The kidnappers "could not have been kinder," the earl said afterward, adding that he had been well fed with a full Irish breakfast each morning and steaks and chops for lunch. The hostage takers had even supplied him with the racing pages. The earl and his wife were eventually released, because of a dramatic turn in the case.

·   ·   ·

In May, the British government had decided to stop force-feeding the Prices. Up to that point, the sisters had suffered through the procedure with as much dignity as they could muster. They did not want to show any fear. But at a certain point, it seemed that they had reached a stalemate: the force-feeding might be inflicting mental and physical trauma on them, but it was also keeping them alive. So, rather than endure the feeding in hostile submission, the sisters opted to change their strategy. One day, they offered "maximum resistance," as Dolours recounted in a letter, "which involved the expected, undignified scenes of struggling, holding down, steel clamps, and—in my case—screaming, because believe me, that steel clamp hurts the old gums." It was a battle. The sisters struggled so hard that it became difficult for the doctors to insert the tubes safely into their stomachs. The Prices informed the doctors that they were giving them "the privilege of killing us" if something went wrong. After a few of these fraught encounters, the doctors simply stopped, refusing to continue with the procedure, because it was just too dangerous. It was a clinical judgment, not a political one, that ended the force-feeding.

Just the same, it would fall to Roy Jenkins to explain the change in policy, and he announced that after carrying out the "distasteful task" of artificial feeding for 167 days, the doctors at Brixton had stopped because "the minimal cooperation necessary for this process was withdrawn by the sisters." Jenkins laid some blame on Albert and Chrissie Price, who, rather than discourage their daughters from a "slow suicide," had instead "urged them on."

Dolours and Marian were thrilled that the force-feeding had stopped. Almost immediately, they began to lose one pound a day. Dolours counted each pound as she shed it, weighing herself at intervals, marveling at her control over her own body. "We are now reinforced by the fact that we no longer desire or crave food," she wrote to a friend. She began to see her own organism in the most clinical, mechanical terms. "I am now my own tool," she mused. "I am also the craftsman wielding the tool. I am carving away at myself."

There was talk, in Brixton, of a place called the terminal ward. It had always sounded ominous to Dolours, but when she and Marian were finally moved there, it seemed positively luxurious. Now, rather than live in separate cells, the sisters could be in the same room. There was even a private toilet next to the room, so when they needed to urinate (because all they produced at this point was urine), they no longer had to rely on a chamber pot. "Getting nearer to Paradise by the minute!" Dolours joked. There was a mirror in the cell, and she would stare at herself, her long nightdress hanging from her skeletal frame, and imagine that she looked like the ghost of some former inmate, haunting the wing.

By this point, in the assessment of one of the doctors treating them, the Price sisters were "living entirely off their own bodies." They had become so weak that even walking across the room could leave Dolours fatigued, her heart thumping in her rib cage like a drum. They could not sit or lie in any one position for long or they would get bedsores from their bones pressing against their skin; to alleviate this, their beds were fitted with "ripple mattresses" that had a thin cushion of circulating air.

"Each day passes and we fade a little more," Dolours wrote to her mother. The sisters lay side by side in their beds, with three prison officers on constant guard. Dolours worried about Marian—worried that she was more anxious to die, more ready to accept it. Sometimes Dolours would be talking to her, reminiscing or gossiping, a valiant facsimile of their old animated chatter, and she would look across and see Marian, dreadfully pale and thin, her eyes closed, her lips ajar, her fingers long and spindly from starvation. The sight of her sister frightened Dolours, and she would say, "Marian, wake up." *Don't go first,* she would think. *Don't go first.*

"The likelihood that the sisters may end their lives must now clearly be envisaged," Jenkins warned in early June. He had considered going to see the Prices, hoping, perhaps, that he might be able to dissuade them from dying. But he decided against it, on the grounds that, as the person charged with deciding their fate, he had a duty to "stand back a little" and be dispassionate.

Albert Price, after a visit with his daughters in the terminal ward, emerged and told the press that they were ready to meet their fate. "They are happy," he said. "Happy about dying." The Provisionals braced for violence, warning that if the sisters died, "the consequences for the British Government will be devastating."

Reports in the press claimed that a priest had visited the sisters and administered last rites. In a letter to a friend, Dolours wrote, "Well, please give our love to our family and all our friends." She concluded, "We're ready for what is ahead."

·   ·   ·

Then Britain blinked. On June 3, another Irish hunger striker, Michael Gaughan, died in Parkhurst Prison, on the Isle of Wight. Gaughan was also an IRA volunteer, though he had played no role in the bombing mission. He was imprisoned for robbing a bank in London, and when he went on hunger strike, Dolours Price had been annoyed. She'd been striking since November when he started in April, and she felt that Gaughan was a Johnny-come-lately, "getting in at the heels of my hunt." She was watching TV when the news was announced, and when she heard the words "One of the IRA prisoners on hunger strike has died," her stomach seized and she wondered if it was Hugh Feeney or Gerry Kelly. The authorities would claim that Gaughan had died of pneumonia, but his family suspected that his death had been precipitated by complications associated with force-feeding, a scenario that was hardly difficult to imagine.

Roy Jenkins was starting to have what he later described as "forebodings of menace." He had been thinking, lately, of Terence MacSwiney and the huge wave of recrimination to which his death had given rise. What kind of reaction might ensue if the Price sisters died? Jenkins was loath to give the impression that he would make any decision under duress, but privately he began to fear that if Dolours and Marian succeeded, he himself could be a target for the rest of his life. This wouldn't just mean that he would have to forgo holidays in South Armagh. The Irish were *everywhere*. No place would be safe: if those damned girls delivered on their intention, he worried, "I might never again be able to walk in freedom and security down a street in Boston or New York or Chicago." Reluctantly, Jenkins decided that he had no choice but to capitulate.

On June 8, Dolours, Marian, Gerry Kelly, and Hugh Feeney released a statement. "We went on hunger strike 206 days ago in support of our demand for Political Prisoner status and transfer to prison in Northern Ireland," they wrote. Roy Jenkins had assured them that they would be returned to Northern Ireland, they continued. So they had decided to terminate the strike. "Ours was never a suicide mission," they maintained, "since we did not set out to kill ourselves but only to secure just and indeed minimal demands."

The transfer was not immediate. Instead of being shipped back to Ireland, Dolours and Marian were relocated to the women's wing at Durham Prison. But one day in March 1975, at lunchtime, all the prisoners at Durham were ordered into their cells. Something in Dolours's heart told her that this might be the day. She went to her cell and started packing. She put on her coat, gathering her few belongings. Then the prison governor walked in and announced that they were going home. "Or—not home. You're going to Armagh."

"That's near enough for me," she said.

Marian ran into her cell and they hugged each other so tightly they could hardly breathe. They shoveled the last of their belongings into bags, and the screws rushed them out into the hall. Dolours was so drunk with excitement that she hugged the prison governor.

The sisters were taken to an air force base. The flight took off, and England receded in the distance. On board the plane, a man in uniform made coffee. They had been flying over water for some time when Dolours looked out the window and suddenly glimpsed green land below. She burst into tears.

"That's not Ireland yet," Marian said. "That's the Isle of Man."

They flew some more. Then Dolours looked out and saw green in the distance again. "Is that it, Marian?" she asked.

"I think that's it," Marian said.

As the Price sisters disembarked, British Army photographers took their picture, the flashbulbs lighting up the early evening sky. The two women were overjoyed to be home, but distressed about the timing of their arrival. In February, Bridie Dolan, their aunt, had died. As a minor republican icon, she was treated to a big funeral; the authorities sent photographers to snap surveillance shots of the mourners. Four days after the funeral, Chrissie Price died of pancreatic cancer. Until very recently, it had looked as though the mother would outlive her daughters, not the other way round, and Dolours and Marian were distraught. They petitioned for compassionate leave to attend Chrissie's funeral, but the request was denied. Instead they sent a wreath of Easter lilies. Four hundred people joined the slow-moving cortege from Slievegallion Drive to Milltown Cemetery. Albert walked alongside the coffin, his head bowed. The whole solemn procession was led by a young girl playing bagpipes. She wore the black beret and dark glasses of the IRA.

CAPTIVES

FOR WEEKS AFTER THEIR mother disappeared, the McConville children clung together, trying to hold on to the family home. They had to be there, in the event that Jean returned. But eventually the social welfare authorities intervened, and two cars arrived at Divis Flats to take the children into care. Helen McConville loaded her younger siblings into the vehicles, promising that they were going away only "'til Mummy comes back." As the children piled into the seats, Helen looked up and saw their neighbors from Divis gathered on the concrete balconies, watching silently. "Fuck yous all," she muttered. Then they drove away.

The oldest child, Anne, was still in the hospital. Robert was still interned, Archie was old enough to work and take care of himself, and Agnes remained with Granny McConville. But Helen, Michael, Tucker, Susan, Billy, and Jim were brought to South Belfast and up a long, curving drive to an imposing four-story redbrick orphanage called Nazareth Lodge. It proved to be a wretched environment. Many of the children living there had been wards of the state since infancy and seemed numbly accustomed to institutional living. But the McConville kids had grown up in a home. They were haunted by their mother's disappearance, and by their father's death before that, and they had now been living wild for several months. The orphanage was run by an order of stern nuns who were legendary for their sadism. One former resident described the facility as "something out of Dickens," a bleak, pinched place where beatings and harsh punishment were routine.

It was around this time that Michael McConville became a master of escape. From the moment he was removed from the flat at Divis, he would contrive ways to sneak out and run back to West Belfast. He was a restive, streetwise child—a child of the Troubles—and he was angry. At one point when he was dealing with the welfare authority, an official suggested that his mother had "abandoned" the children. "That's lies!" Michael shouted.

In March 1973, the same month that Dolours Price was bombing London, Michael and Tucker were summoned to court in Belfast on a shoplifting charge, and a decision was made to move them out of Nazareth Lodge—out of Belfast altogether, in fact, to the De La Salle Boys' Home, twenty-two miles away in County Down, near the village of Kircubbin. The drive to their new home did not take long, but as far as Michael was concerned, it could have been a hundred miles. The institution occupied a converted Victorian mansion nestled in the deep-green countryside, as well as a series of newer cottages where the children were housed. The property was vast—250 acres—and it felt wide and wild and open after a lifetime spent in the brick-and-concrete confines of Belfast. The grounds included a school, a swimming pool, tennis courts, and a football pitch. They even had a billiard table.

Kircubbin was, in the words of one person who resided there in those years, "a pure nightmare." A subsequent government investigation revealed that a "culture of physical force" had pervaded the establishment, and both monks and lay employees would resort to violence on the merest of pretexts. Children were pummeled with fists, strapped with belts, and lashed across the knuckles with a thin wooden cane that snapped down with such ferocity it felt like it might sever their fingertips.

For all his grit and savvy, Michael was still just eleven years old. Tucker was nine. There were older children there, in whom this culture of abuse had already been well ingrained. They bullied the McConville boys without mercy. The Christian brothers who ran the orphanage purchased clothing for their charges in bulk, so the kids walked around in garments that did not fit—shirtsleeves that rode up past the elbow, capacious adult trousers that needed to be cinched with a belt, urchin ensembles that compounded the sense that this was a storybook purgatory for Belfast's misbegotten. The adults at Kircubbin put the children to work. Sometimes the staff would hire them out to neighboring farms, as rental labor, to pick potatoes.

In the evenings, as everyone watched a program in the darkened TV room, monks in their long robes would instruct certain children to come and sit on their laps. Sexual abuse was rampant at the home. Michael was never molested himself, but at night he would watch from under the covers as shadowy adults entered the dormitory with a flashlight and plucked sleeping boys from their beds.

Michael and Tucker ran away. They felt a duty to be back in Belfast in the event that their mother reappeared. But each time the boys ran off, they were returned, and each time they came back, they were beaten. The McConville boys ran away so frequently that eventually the staff at Kircubbin took their shoes away, on the theory that even if they managed to get off the grounds and as far as the country road where they might thumb a ride back to Belfast, it would slow them down if they were barefoot.

The authorities may simply not have realized at the time the kind of predatory behavior that was happening inside the walls of Kircubbin, but if they did get any inkling of the environment at the home, it did not stop them from sending other children there. Eventually the twins, Billy and Jim, were reassigned from Nazareth Lodge to Kircubbin. As the car made its way from Belfast down the coast of the Strangford Lough in the direction of the orphanage, the boys sat in the back seat, consumed by apprehension. They were seven years old. They became the youngest children at Kircubbin, and it was as if they had been fed to the wolves. They were physically assaulted by the older kids and Billy was sexually abused by the grown-ups. The boys could not turn to any of the adults for help, because so many of the staff were molesting children that the behavior was silently tolerated. All of the Christian brothers, one former resident explained, "were in it together." Some of the McConville children were so scarred by their encounters in the Catholic institutions of Northern Ireland that they developed a fear of priests in general. Even as adults, the mere sight of a man of the cloth could fill them with anxiety. (The De La Salle Brothers later admitted that widespread sexual abuse took place at Kircubbin during this period. The Sisters of Nazareth, who administered Nazareth Lodge, have also acknowledged a pattern of physical abuse at the home.)

Helen McConville was too old to be kept in care against her will but still too young to be legal guardian to her siblings, so she struck out on her own, staying with Archie or with friends. She found work at a company that made funeral shrouds, and as a waitress. During her stay at Nazareth, she had briefly met a boy her age named Seamus McKendry, who was working as an apprentice carpenter at the orphanage. After that initial encounter, they fell out of touch, but two years later, when Helen was waitressing, they crossed paths again—and fell in love. They married when she was eighteen.

There were times when it seemed that there was no home that could hold Michael McConville. Eventually, after escaping on one too many occasions, he was moved once again, sent this time to a "training" school not far from the town of New-townards. Known as Lisnevin, this school had recently been established, over protest from the surrounding community, as a "secure" residential facility for boys. Even calling the place a school was a bit of a euphemism: Lisnevin was a juvenile detention facility for kids who were too rough or too willful for places like Kircubbin. Michael's new housemates included serial escapees like him, along with a rogues' gallery of misfit adolescents who had been arrested for burglary, assault, and paramilitary activity. The main building was a converted mansion, the centerpiece of some once grand country seat. It now featured "isolation rooms"—cells stripped of furniture, with bars on the windows, in which errant children could be locked in solitary confinement. The property was surrounded by a tall perimeter fence, which was electrified and equipped with an alarm that would sound if anyone should try to escape.

Lisnevin might have seemed like a gulag, but Michael loved it. He would later joke, wryly, that Lisnevin was the best home he ever had. The staff liked to say that the fences were for keeping people out, not keeping people in, and it may be that by sealing out some of the tragedy and mania of the Troubles, Lisnevin created a space in which a victim like Michael McConville could finally settle down and begin to heal. The facility was nondenominational, and there were regular sectarian skirmishes between Catholic and Protestant residents. But Michael steered clear of trouble. He got to know a kindly nun, Sister Frances, who looked out for him. She befriended his siblings as well, and for years afterward, even after she moved away to America, she would send them cards every Christmas, with a dollar folded inside. It was a minor gesture, but to the motherless McConvilles, it meant the world.

Michael was eligible for weekend leave, like a furlough from prison, so he would go back to visit Belfast, staying with Archie or Helen. When they were together, the children never spoke about what had happened to their mother. It was too painful. But their sense of the family as a unit had begun to erode. Increasingly, they were each alone, fending for themselves in unforgiving territory. As soon as Michael turned sixteen, he left Lisnevin and set out in search of a job and a place to live—in search of a life. He had been living in institutions for nearly a third of his years. But this was how it worked: when you reached sixteen, they opened the door. They did very little to prepare you for this abrupt emancipation. Nobody taught you how to rent a flat or find a job or boil an egg. They simply let you go.

.   .   .

When Brendan Hughes returned to Long Kesh after being apprehended in his guise as a toy salesman, Gerry Adams was still there, doing time. Adams had tried, twice, to escape. But he was not the tactician that Hughes was, and he had been caught and given a sentence for his efforts. Adams had settled into life in Long Kesh. Compared with life on the outside—on the run, sleeping in a different bed every night, fearing the knock on the door, never knowing if you might be recognized on the street and shot on sight—he found the predictable routine of prison life relaxing. The wire enclosures surrounding the Nissen huts where the prisoners lived were known as "cages," and each had a number. Hughes and Adams shared Cage 11. The two revolutionaries had been close before this stint in confinement, but now their bond grew tighter as they cohabited in the intimate confines of a cell. The hut was drafty and Spartan, and chill winds whipped through the camp. In the winter, they wore socks over their hands, like gloves, to keep warm.

They nurtured themselves on endless conversation. Adams, who had always had a scholarly bent, encouraged the men around him to harden their minds. The prisoners organized lectures and discussion sessions. They would meet at "the wire"—the fences separating the different enclosures—and discuss politics, history, and the latest news from the war outside. A fresh-faced, headstrong young IRA prisoner organized cultural classes. He wrote poetry and would become the official press officer for the republican prisoners. His name was Bobby Sands. The place came to feel, Adams later remarked, like "our barbed wire ivory tower." Adams was a witty, engaging interlocutor with a piercing mind. But for all his gregariousness, there were aspects of his personality that he kept to himself. Whereas Hughes had come to regard himself not just as unreligious but anti-religious, Adams was quietly immersed in Catholicism. At night, Hughes read speeches by Fidel Castro; Adams recited the rosary.

By the mid-1970s, Adams was confronting a dilemma. From the moment the Provisionals emerged in 1969 and began to bring the fight directly to the unionist establishment, there had been a sense that it might take just one final, furious push to drive the British into the sea. It was this strategic thesis that accounted both for the frantic pace of operations during the early years of the Troubles and for the high morale that drove recruitment and galvanized the lads. As the conflict entered its sixth year, however, it appeared that matters might not be so simple. After years of violence, the brunt of which was often felt by the very citizenry the IRA claimed to represent, public support for the Provos had tapered. The British, meanwhile, seemed to be settling in for a conflict of indefinite duration. When Adams and Hughes met their subordinates for conversations at the wire, they could see a new set of installations being built at the prison—the so-called H Blocks, which, once they were completed, would have the capacity to house many more paramilitary detainees.

Adams's father, Gerry Sr., had been an IRA man as well, and had taken part in a campaign during the 1940s that fit squarely into the long republican history of noble failure. When Adams was growing up, he would see veterans of earlier conflicts hanging out at the Felons Club, a social club that his father had helped to found, where men like Albert Price would drink and tell war stories and ruminate about what could have been. It was almost as if "defeat suited them better than victory," in the words of one historian, "for there was a sense in which Irish republicanism thrived on oppression and the isolated exclusivity that came with it." During the early 1970s, it had become commonplace for the Provos to declare, every January, that *this* was the year they would eject the British once and for all. For people of Adams's generation, who had beheld the fall of Saigon, the sudden toppling of regimes seemed like something that was readily achievable. But after a few years and a great abundance of spilled blood, those January resolutions were beginning to seem delusional. To be sure, there was a doomed romance in the notion of republican failure, a poetry in those archetypes of futility. But Gerry Adams was not a romantic.

This time, he told his men, the struggle must come to something. This generation of Irish republicans would not simply pass the baton to the next one; they must force change within their own lifetimes. Even as he made this case, however, Adams began to argue that it would be naïve to expect immediate results. What the republican movement should do, instead, was hunker down for what would come to be known as the "long war." Stop telling people victory is just a year away. Better to marshal your resources and plan for a fight that could take much longer.

This was not an easy argument to make. The foot soldiers of the Provos had been beaten by loyalists, shot at by the army, and tortured by the police. They had abandoned their families to go on the run, and now they found themselves locked up alongside Adams and Hughes at Long Kesh. They could readily embrace a message that said, "If you just fight a little harder right now, this will all be over soon." But it was quite another thing to tell them, "Get used to this, because the fight won't end after our next big offensive. It could take years. Even decades."

Adams also began to subtly modulate the language in which he talked about what victory itself might mean. It was important to fight the long war, but also to recognize that the end of the conflict would likely result not merely from a military triumph, but from some variety of political settlement. The armed struggle is simply a means to an end, Adams would tell the young IRA men at the wire. It is not the end itself.

"Youse are politicians," he told them.

"We're not, really. We're army," they replied.

"No, you have to develop your consciousness in here," Adams insisted. "Politics is important."

Adams commanded respect and loyalty inside the walls of Long Kesh, but he wanted to get his message to the volunteers fighting the war in Belfast and Derry. So in 1975, he began writing a series of articles for *Republican News,* the movement's propaganda newspaper. Because it was illegal to be a member of the IRA, writing such articles under his own name might be risky, so Adams adopted a pseudonym, "Brownie." After composing each fresh column, he would smuggle it out of the camp. Secret documents—or "comms," as they were known—regularly made their way in and out of Long Kesh. These memos and letters would be etched in tiny handwriting on cigarette paper, then palmed to a visiting friend or spouse. In this manner, the IRA's command structure inside the prison remained in near constant contact with their counterparts on the outside.

Republican News was edited by a baby-faced propagandist named Danny Morrison. Sometimes the Brownie columns were lighthearted, showcasing Adams's dry humor. Sometimes they were treacly, though his sentimentality tended to feel more calculated than sincere. Often, the articles served the purpose of educating people on the outside about the conditions in which the prisoners lived. But Adams also used the columns to wrestle with his own emerging philosophy of the conflict. He frequently handed drafts to Brendan Hughes for feedback before he sent them out to be published. But Hughes had never been quite so analytically inclined. Sometimes he had to read a column three times just to get the thrust of Adams's argument.

In 1977, Adams was released. On his final day, he paced around the yard with Hughes, talking strategy. He had come to believe that Sinn Féin, the political entity associated with the IRA, needed to operate more "in tandem" with the armed organization. He also believed that the Provos had to be restructured. Traditionally, the IRA had imitated the hierarchical configuration of the British military. But Adams believed that the Provos should reinvent themselves, adopting the type of cellular structure more typical of paramilitary organizations in Latin America. They would be more secure this way: if the authorities managed to interrogate and flip one gunman, he would know only the contacts in his particular cell, rather than the whole command. What Adams was proposing was an ambitious reorganization. It was also the blueprint for an IRA that could fight the long war. On that final day at Long Kesh, with his belongings in a brown paper bag, Adams gave Hughes a hug before he walked to the gate. He joked that of the two of them, Hughes had the more enviable job, staying behind to keep things under control in Long Kesh. Adams may have been a free man, now, but he would have the more daunting task of reinventing the IRA.

.   .   .

The truth was that the job Hughes had would be anything but easy. Toward the end of 1975, internment had officially ended. From now on, rather than being detained indefinitely as political prisoners, paramilitary suspects would be charged like ordinary criminals. This might have seemed like mere semantics, a simple matter of classification, but the distinction cut to the core of the republican identity. To call IRA volunteers criminals was to delegitimize the very basis upon which they had taken up arms. Even in the face of bombs and bloodshed, the government in London might stubbornly refuse to call the Troubles a war, but as far as the IRA was concerned, Hughes and his comrades were soldiers, and, if captured, they should be held as prisoners of war. Internment had its own problems—you could be arrested without charge and confined without a trial for years. But people who were interned were generally permitted to wear their own clothes behind bars, and they could freely associate with their paramilitary colleagues. Now, with internment ending, anyone convicted of paramilitary activity was confined to an individual cell in the new facility at Long Kesh, the H Blocks. The prison issued uniforms, and it didn't matter if you were an IRA volunteer or a common thief—you got the same uniform.

In the fall of 1976, the republican prisoners rebelled, refusing to wear the clothes issued by the prison and initiating a so-called blanket protest, in which prisoners wrapped themselves, naked, in blankets, just as the Price sisters had done following their arrest in London. One ditty that the protesters sang captured the stakes:

> I'll wear no convict's uniform
> Nor meekly serve my time
> That Britain might
> Brand Ireland's fight
> Eight hundred years of crime.

What the protesters wanted was "special category" status, which would effectively classify them as prisoners of war. But the authorities refused to grant it. Inside Long Kesh, relations between the inmates and the screws deteriorated, and a grinding game of mutual escalation took hold. The protesters refused to wear clothes, but, initially, they would leave their cells to shower and use the toilet. The guards, frustrated by their defiance, would sometimes subject them to beatings on these trips, and restricted their use of towels to cover and dry themselves. So the protesters started refusing to leave their cells at all. The guards were obliged to go from cell to cell, gathering chamber pots to be emptied. But the prisoners started tipping the pots so that piss sluiced under the cell door and out into the corridor. And so the blanket protest, which had become a "no-wash protest," now blossomed into the "dirty protest." A great tide of urine coursed through the prison, which the guards now had to clean. This left the issue of what the protesters should do with their shit, and when they raised this dilemma with Hughes, who was the commanding officer inside the prison, he made a suggestion: *Daub it on the walls.*

Hughes and his men were naked and filthy, with wild beards and long, matted, unwashed hair, and now they began to paint the walls of the prison with their own solid waste, swirling it into van Gogh moons and lunatic patterns. The place took on the aspect of a madhouse. As maggot infestations set in and the threat of disease began to assert itself, a team of screws would barge into the squalor-encrusted cells and haul the scrawny prisoners out, then hose the men down while another team attacked the filthy space with water and disinfectant. But even placing a protesting inmate in a fresh cell made little difference. A single metabolic cycle would furnish him with the tools to despoil it. A visiting priest, surveying the prison, compared the men to "people living in sewer-pipes in the slums of Calcutta."

If, on the face of it, there was something comically grotesque about this whole ordeal—an avant-garde experiment in the theater of the absurd—underlying it was something more familiar: yet another game of brinksmanship. The demands of the prisoners were relatively simple. They wanted the right not to wear the prison uniform, to be able to associate freely with other prisoners, and to receive mail. But with each escalating gesture, they seemed only to harden the resolve of their adversaries. Who would yield first?

. . .

Though Adams was no longer in prison, he remained in close contact with Hughes, via smuggled comms. He succeeded in reorganizing the Provos, shifting the center of gravity away from Dublin by creating a Northern Command. Adams was becoming increasingly vocal about his view that the long war could not be won unless the struggle had a political dimension. "We cannot build a republic on the IRA's military victories," he declared at one event in 1980. "We must realize, as have the imperialists, that victory through military means alone is impossible."

Adams might be advocating for a political movement to run in parallel with the armed struggle, but he was not counseling any abandonment of violent means. In August 1979, Lord Louis Mountbatten, a cousin of Queen Elizabeth II who had served as the last viceroy of India, was on his fishing boat in Donegal Bay, off the coast of County Sligo, when a radio-controlled bomb detonated, splintering the vessel to matchsticks and killing him, along with two family members and a local boy from Enniskillen.

That year, a new prime minister took residence at 10 Downing Street in London. Margaret Thatcher was the leader of the Conservative Party, and she was already known for her fierce resolve. When she was a girl in the East Midlands of England during the Second World War, her hometown, Grantham, had been bombed by the Nazis. Her closest adviser on Northern Ireland was Airey Neave, a hawkish aide who had served as her campaign manager; Neave had been a prisoner of war himself and had escaped from the infamous Nazi prison camp at Colditz Castle. Influenced, in part, by her conversations with Neave, Thatcher came into office regarding Northern Ireland as somewhat akin to the Sudetenland, those parts of Czechoslovakia that were predominantly ethnic German and had been annexed by Hitler on the eve of the war. Like the Sudetenland Germans, the Catholics in Northern Ireland might have been the victims of an accident of geography, but in Thatcher's view, that did not give them the right to simply break off and join a neighboring country. When she was briefed on the subtle demographic factors that fueled and perpetuated the Troubles, Thatcher would murmur, "So, it's like the Sudetenland."

If Thatcher seemed poised to be a hard-liner on the Irish question, her position was only reaffirmed by something that happened shortly before she took office. On March 30, 1979, Airey Neave was driving his car out of a parking garage at the House of Commons when a bomb under the driver's seat exploded, killing him. The bomb was set not by the Provos but by a different republican group, the Irish National Liberation Army, which took credit for the attack. Shortly after learning the news, a stricken Thatcher, laboring to preserve her trademark calm, said that Neave had been "one of freedom's warriors: courageous, staunch, and true." The murder, less than two months before she became prime minister, would set the stage for her uncompromising posture toward any form of Irish republicanism.

By the time Thatcher began her new job, several hundred men were participating in the dirty protest at Long Kesh. The willpower of the demonstrators was extraordinary. "You were going against your whole socialization of how you were brought up," one of them later recalled. "Everything you ever learned about basic hygiene and manners." As if tensions with the screws were not high enough, the Provos had started targeting and killing off-duty prison officers. But still, the British would not relent. After the government ended internment and special category status in 1976, the new secretary of state for Northern Ireland, Roy Mason, described the IRA prisoners as "thugs and gangsters." Thatcher would sound the same note. "There is no such thing as political murder, political bombing, or political violence," she maintained. "We will not compromise on this. There will be no political status." In a crisp formulation that would soon become famous, she asserted, "Crime is crime is crime."

In the fall of 1980, Brendan Hughes answered with a further escalation. He announced plans for a hunger strike and asked for volunteers. Morale among the prisoners was such that a hundred or more people came forward. A team of seven was selected.

Brendan Hughes on hunger strike.

They would be led by Hughes, who had decided to participate in the strike: he had always taken pride in not asking a subordinate to do anything he was not prepared to do himself. In the last week of October, the men began refusing food. For weeks, Hughes sat in his cell, growing weaker and more frail, his cheeks sunken, his ragged black beard and long hair giving him the look of an ancient soothsayer. The prison doctor was a man named David Ross. He was kind to Hughes. Each morning, Ross would come in and bring a flask of fresh spring water, explaining that it was better than the tap water in the prison. He would sit on the edge of the bed and talk to Hughes about fishing and about the mountains and the rivers and the streams.

Brendan Hughes had made his reputation as a peerless tactician, but at the very outset of the strike, he had made one significant tactical mistake. Because all seven men had embarked on the strike at the same time, eventually one of them would be the first to reach the brink of death, and the other six would be forced to choose between calling off the strike and saving him or pushing forward and letting him die. One of the younger strikers was a twenty-six-year-old from Newry named Sean McKenna.

Hughes had not wanted McKenna to take part in the strike, but McKenna had insisted. Once the fast began, he quickly grew ill, and was eventually confined to a wheelchair in the hospital wing. As the strike progressed, McKenna grew more fearful, and at one point he said to Hughes, "Dark, don't let me die." Hughes promised McKenna that he wouldn't.

Just before Christmas, McKenna started lapsing in and out of a coma. Hughes saw orderlies rushing him on a stretcher through the hospital wing. He saw two priests standing with Dr. Ross. If Hughes did not intervene, the boy would die, and he would have violated his promise, just as he had violated his promise of clemency to Seamus Wright and Kevin McKee. If Hughes did intervene, however, the strike would be over; the strikers would have blinked, squandering their leverage. Hughes could smell the festering bodies in the hospital ward. He was conscious of the smell of his own body eating itself. Finally, he shouted, "Feed him!" And like that, the strike was over.

A doctor instructed the orderlies to prepare some scrambled eggs. As he started to eat again after his fifty-three-day fast, Hughes slowly recovered and regained weight. But he felt deeply ashamed about botching the strike. The prisoners decided, almost immediately, to mount a second strike. This time they would stagger the strikers, so that one would begin, followed by another a week or so later, and then a third a week or so after that. This way, the decision of whether to continue would not be a collective one. It would be entirely up to each striker to decide whether or not to die. Because Hughes was still recovering, the prisoners selected a new leader for this second strike. He would be the first to start refusing food and, presumably, the first to die. They chose the young volunteer who had coordinated the arts program, Bobby Sands.

A CLOCKWORK DOLL

THE PRETTY CATHEDRAL TOWN of Armagh, about an hour's drive from Belfast, was built on seven hills, like Rome. The skyline was dominated by the towers of two cathedrals, and near them stood a Victorian stone prison for women. Prior to the Troubles, Armagh jail had rarely housed more than a dozen or so women at any time. Most of the inmates were locked up for charges of drunkenness, prostitution, or fraud. But during the 1970s, when Dolours and Marian Price arrived, the jail housed more than a hundred women, many of whom had been involved in republican activity. The decision to move the sisters to the women's prison had sparked some controversy, because of the formidable danger that they were said to pose. One unionist politician likened this custody arrangement to keeping "a python in a paper bag."

When the Price sisters stepped into the walled facility, a group of IRA women had assembled, holding a homemade banner that read, WELCOME HOME DOLOURS AND MARIAN. As they walked deeper into the prison, they saw other women staring at them and darting, nervously, in and out of cells. "Is it them?" someone whispered. They were celebrities. "We had heard so much about these girls and I expected to see two skeletons," one of their fellow prisoners later recalled. Instead, she thought, "they were like two film stars." The other women had made a point, prior to their arrival, of neatening up the place.

The sisters were introduced to Eileen Hickey, the no-

nonsense officer commanding of the IRA inside the prison. She was reputed to be so formidable that even the screws listened to her. But the guards at Armagh were more relaxed than any that Dolours Price had previously encountered. They would hang back, lounging on a windowsill, giving the prisoners plenty of space. One of the women fried up some potatoes. Dolours ate them with gusto. She hadn't tasted anything so good in years.

This ready-built community proved decidedly more hospitable than Brixton. But it was also the case that, after two years in confinement and the exertions and publicity of their hunger strike, the Price sisters were ready to retreat, somewhat, from their posture of political activism. Age has a way of curbing one's appetite for frontline revolution, and they were growing older. There may also have been a sense in which, having fought for a transfer back to Armagh, and having said from the start that they made no apologies for the bombing mission and would happily serve their time, the sisters had won. In March 1975, they were granted special category status, which meant that they did not have to work in the prison's laundry and sewing rooms, as other inmates were required to do. They were allowed to wear their own clothes and to stay in a newly constructed area that

Marian and Dolours Price, at left, in Armagh jail.

housed the special category prisoners. C Wing, as it was called, was relatively commodious. The space was set up like a suite in a hotel, with a TV room and an eat-in kitchen.

The head screw, a woman with protruding teeth whom the prisoners called Big Suzie, was not as unsympathetic as the guards in England. Security was much less tight, and the women were not forced to stay in their cells for long stretches. During the days, Dolours would paint and write letters. She and Marian were also able to take correspondence courses. They made handicrafts, which could be sold on the outside to raise money for the cause. Dolours did leatherwork, though she didn't enjoy it. In a letter to Fenner Brockway, a British member of the House of Lords who had been supportive of the sisters during their time in Brixton, she described a wallet she was making him for his ninety-second birthday, and joked that when she put it in the mail, he should not be alarmed at the sight of a "small parcel from N. Ireland"—it was not a bomb. At night, after lockup, the women talked to one another from their separate cells. Someone would lead them in the rosary, in Irish. Sometimes people told ghost stories. To Dolours, Armagh jail felt like boarding school without the teachers. In one snapshot from this period, the sisters struck poses alongside a smiling cohort of fellow prisoners and managed, somehow, to look glamorous despite their surroundings.

But if this new life was better than the old one, it was still life in prison, and it soon grew dull. One week stretched into the next, and Dolours began to fixate on the sky that she could see through the prison window, that little square of blue. Some of the women in Armagh had initiated their own dirty protest. But the Price sisters did not take part. They were beginning, in subtle ways, to draw back from the movement. "Things started going a bit askew and you started questioning things," Dolours said later. In February 1978, the IRA attacked the La Mon House hotel, outside Belfast, while it was crowded with civilians. The bomb killed twelve people and severely burned dozens more. "Things like that happened and you have to say, What is going on?" Dolours recalled. "Am I here because I want to burn people to death? Am I here because I want to incinerate people?" When the IRA ordered Dolours not to associate with other republican women who had chosen to abstain from the dirty protest, she resigned from the organization, because she could not obey the order. Both she and Marian had achieved legendary status in the IRA for the sacrifices they had made, but from then on Dolours would become, in her words, "a freelance republican."

In letters to Fenner Brockway, Dolours indicated that she had also begun to reconsider the efficacy of violence. "Dolours, like her sister Marian, [has] become convinced that the violence of the IRA is all wrong," Brockway wrote to Humphrey Atkins, the latest secretary of state for Northern Ireland. "I have told Dolours, as I did Marian, that if they were released from prison on the grounds that they had repudiated their previous action they would probably be shot by the IRA, and are therefore safer in prison." But by that time, the Price sisters were grappling with an affliction that was more pressing and immediate than politics.

. . .

"We didn't ever have a normal relationship with food or eating," Dolours said later. The months of starvation and force-feeding in England had irrevocably complicated their relationship with nourishment. During a hunger strike, Dolours pointed out, "your body is telling you it wants food, and you're telling your body, 'No, you can't have food... We will not win this struggle if I give you food.' So there you're setting up a very difficult mindset, which has to be rock solid, or you will eat food. Because, you know, that's what the body does. That's what we do. We eat food and then we live." After that experience of self-abnegation, Dolours continued, the force-feeding only compounded the trauma, because "it further alienated us from the process of sustenance, the whole process of putting food into your body." As a result, she concluded, "we both ended up with very, very, very distorted notions of the function of food and we both found it very difficult to reestablish a proper relationship with the process of eating."

There may have been some element of social contagion at play within the intimate confines of Armagh jail. Several other women in the facility had recently succumbed to anorexia. The sisters were no longer on hunger strike, but now they, too, stopped eating. Marian's weight began to drop precipitously. A confidential government assessment eventually concluded that "to leave her in prison would be to leave her to die (for crimes through which no one was killed)."

On April 30, 1980, Marian was released from jail and went voluntarily, under an assumed name, to the Royal Victoria Hospital, in Belfast. A government spokesman said that she had been receiving "intensive medical treatment for the past three years" but that she could no longer be treated in Armagh. On May 1, she checked out of the hospital. This news sparked an outcry. English tabloids implied that she had engineered a velvet prison break—that anorexia was simply the latest clever ruse by the IRA.

Dolours was elated to see her sister walk free. Marian had been close to death, and now she would live. But deep down, she felt conflicted. "All along, a little part of me had always hoped and thought that because we'd been through everything together, that again this would be a together thing," she reflected later. The sisters had always been lumped together—as Albert's daughters, as student protesters, as members of the Unknowns, and as prisoners and hunger strikers. Now, for the first time, they were uncoupled. To Dolours it felt "like I'd been separated from my Siamese twin."

·   ·   ·

Like Brendan Hughes, Bobby Sands had grown up Catholic in a Protestant neighborhood. But when Sands was seven years old, his neighbor discovered that he and his family were Catholics, and they were ejected from their home. Eventually, Sands had joined the IRA. On March 1, 1981, he stopped eating. His last morsel was a prison ration orange. It tasted bitter. "I am standing on the threshold of another trembling world," Sands wrote on a scrap of toilet paper as he commenced his strike. "May God have mercy on my soul." Two weeks later, a second protester initiated a strike, and one week after that, a third, until eventually there were ten men on hunger strike at Long Kesh. There was no reason to think that Margaret Thatcher would be any more sympathetic this time around than she was during the previous strike. "Faced with the failure of their discredited cause, the men of violence have chosen in recent months to play what might be their last card," Thatcher said.

But four days after Sands commenced his strike, a politician named Frank Maguire died, triggering a dramatic chain of events. Maguire was a nationalist who held a seat in the British House of Commons, representing Fermanagh and South Tyrone. His sudden death would necessitate a by-election. Initially, Maguire's brother considered running to take over his seat, but he was approached by some republicans who urged him to reconsider. An improbable but possibly ingenious plan was being hatched: Bobby Sands would run for the seat, from behind bars. This would be a publicity stunt, to be sure—but a resonant one. What better way to garner attention and support for a hunger strike than have one of the strikers run for office? If Sands were to win, it would upend the power dynamics of the strike: the British government might allow some unkempt blanketman to die in prison, but what about a member of Parliament?

This gambit marked a radical departure for the Provos. There had been moments in history when republicans ran candidates for elective office, but the movement had long been suspicious of the parliamentary process. For generations, many republicans had adhered to a tradition of "abstentionism"—staying out of politics altogether. There was a sense that one's revolutionary fervor could be diluted all too easily by the system. This had been part of the basis for the split in 1969 between the Official IRA and the Provisionals—a sense that the Officials had become too political and that politics would inevitably lead to accommodation.

"It has been a tradition down the decades, at least in the North, for republicans not to vote," Gerry Adams would say. But as he began to argue for greater political organization by the IRA and Sinn Féin, he saw, for the first time, the potential for a new mode of republican politics. "There will be a time," he vowed, "when Sinn Féin will be a power in the land."

To Adams, who had been thinking through ways in which the struggle could become more political, the Sands election represented an extraordinary opportunity. There were many people in Northern Ireland who might not support the violence of the IRA but would happily vote a republican hunger striker into elected office. Working with Danny Morrison, the editor of *Republican News,* Adams began to mold a new philosophy that, on the surface, seemed to embody a contradiction: Sinn Féin would run candidates for office while the IRA continued to bring a bloody war to the British. Morrison would eventually capture the strategy in a famous aphorism, asking, at a Sinn Féin gathering, "Will anyone here object if, with a ballot paper in one hand and an Armalite in the other, we take power in Ireland?"

On April 10, 1981, Bobby Sands was elected to Parliament. He had not eaten for forty-one days. But even then, his demands were not met. Sands's condition continued to deteriorate, and now Margaret Thatcher faced a crisis. On April 25, she spoke with Humphrey Atkins, her Northern Ireland secretary. "Sands is clearly determined," Atkins told her.

"He's only got a few days," Thatcher said.

"They are talking of two or three," he said. "But to be honest with you, Margaret, they really don't know."

"No," Thatcher said, with tart annoyance. "Because it's not a position with which anyone has very much experience."

Atkins noted that, because the strikers were staggered, even if Sands died and they could weather the backlash and bad publicity, the next striker would likely die a few weeks later. "One hopes very much that we can prevent the thing going on week after week," he said. "I think there is bound to be a weak link."

Thatcher speculated that the IRA leadership might not allow the strike to continue "if one died and then a second one died and then a third one died and nothing happened."

"It doesn't look very attractive," Atkins said.

"No," Thatcher agreed. "It doesn't."

. . .

Dolours Price followed the news of the hunger strike closely. But since Marian had left Armagh, she had started, gradually, to unravel. "I was lost without Marian," she recalled. Her weight was dropping rapidly, and she seemed increasingly isolated and unstable. At one point in May 1980, she swallowed a dozen sleeping pills. Whether this was a bona fide effort at suicide or a cry for help was not clear, but her stomach was pumped in the prison hospital.

"I move as a clockwork doll," she wrote to Fenner Brockway, describing numb, empty days in which her only refuge was sleep. As her thirtieth birthday approached, she reflected that nearly all of her twenties had been "wasted" in prison. She thought about having a child and noted that this "natural instinct" might never be fulfilled. "It does hurt me deeply," she wrote, "and will scar the rest of my life."

Marian Price had visited Dolours only a handful of times since her release. When she prepared to leave at the end of these visits, Dolours would cling to her, unable to let go. Having pledged, years earlier, to serve her time without complaint, provided she could do so in Northern Ireland, she was now feeling more indignant. "It is not fair," she wrote to Brockway. "I will have served eight years in March, even murderers don't serve that, I am doing life for causing an explosion." As a member of the Unknowns, Price had been involved in other operations that *were* genuinely deadly. But she hadn't been charged with those actions, and she did not mention them now. Instead she pointed out that she no longer even paid "lip service" to the IRA, and that she had been made "to feel an outcast, a traitor to their cause because I have declared it to be no longer mine." Even so, she pledged her allegiance to the hunger strikers in Long Kesh. "I will be eating (as well as any anorexic can!) but mentally I will live and starve each day with them," she wrote.

Brockway was so moved by these letters that he made a direct appeal to Margaret Thatcher, arguing that the sisters had been "caught up in adolescent emotion" when they perpetrated the bombing in London, and that they had assured him they took part in the operation only on the condition that "no human being would suffer." Brockway described himself as "almost their spiritual adviser" and said that both sisters had "become convinced that violence is wrong." He assured Thatcher that if Dolours were released, she would dedicate herself, "despite the dangers," to "urging her fellow Catholics to refrain from violence."

Thatcher was not so easily persuaded. "I recognize that you are convinced that Dolours has renounced violence," she wrote, delicately suggesting that Brockway may have been a bit too ready to take the wily Price sisters at their word. Thatcher wrote that she had made inquiries about Dolours's current health and that "the doctors consider that she is a much tougher personality than her sister." One thing puzzled Thatcher. In the margin of one of Brockway's letters, she jotted, "I am amazed that Marian goes to see her so rarely. That itself must be disturbing for a twin." It was indicative of the closeness of the Price sisters that Thatcher erroneously concluded that they were twins. But even so, Thatcher pointed out that Dolours seemed to harbor republican "sympathies," and, should she be released, "I doubt whether her old friends will let her alone."

As Bobby Sands stood for election, Dolours Price was declining rapidly. The writer Tim Pat Coogan, who visited her in C Wing at Armagh, was struck by her intelligence but thought she had a "lemur-like air." She "counteracted the effects of the disease by dressing tastefully and attending carefully to her hair and manicure," Coogan noted, but she had grown too exhausted for most activity.

On April 3, 1981, an Irish cardinal, Tomás Ó Fiaich, wrote to Thatcher that he had visited Price and that she had been confined for the past month to the infirmary, "listless and companionless, scarcely able to walk and requiring help on the stairs." The cardinal had visited with Dolours before, prior to her deterioration, and he remembered her as a vivacious character. What she had become, he noted, was "a gaunt spectre, prematurely aged and deprived of any further desire to live." He asked Thatcher to recognize "the stark fact that this girl is dying" and pointed out that, were she to die, it could precipitate an explosion of recriminatory violence. The cardinal begged Thatcher to release Price, saying that "even next week may be too late."

Still, Thatcher would not relent. She wrote back to Ó Fiaich saying that she understood the "anxiety" of the Price family but that she had no intention of releasing Dolours. "Miss Price's condition will continue to be very closely watched," she said. In mid-April, Price was rushed from Armagh to the secure ward in

Musgrave Park Hospital, in Belfast. By the time she was admitted, she weighed seventy-six pounds.

Outside the hospital, Northern Ireland was once again engulfed in rioting. Street fights were raging in Belfast and Derry. Every day, people in the hospital would say that Bobby Sands would be there soon, and it seemed, for a time, as though Price would be joined in the secure wing by the young hunger striker with whom she felt such an affinity. Even in her wan state, this was something to look forward to. She hoped that she would be able to offer Sands one final salute.

.   .   .

He never came. On May 5, 1981, Bobby Sands died. It was the sixty-sixth day of his strike, and just as Terence MacSwiney's death had six decades earlier, the story made headlines around the world. Gerry Adams later recalled Sands's death as having "a greater international impact than any other event in Ireland in my lifetime." One hundred thousand people poured onto the streets of Belfast to watch his coffin being carried to the cemetery. There was an overwhelming upsurge of support for the republican cause on both sides of the border in Ireland. Thatcher showed no remorse over taking a firm line. "Mr. Sands was a convicted criminal," she declared after his death. "He chose to take his own life. It was a choice his organization did not allow to many of its victims."

But while the world focused on her fatal contest of wills with Bobby Sands, Thatcher had quietly shown that she was capable of mercy when it came to Dolours Price. Two weeks before Sands died, Price had been released "on medical grounds," and the balance of her twenty-year sentence had been remitted. The official explanation for this decision was that she was "in imminent danger of sudden collapse and death."

For years afterward, Price would weep when she thought

of that moment, in which Bobby Sands perished and she was set free. The Price sisters had stared down the British crown on two occasions, and in both instances, the damage they inflicted upon their own bodies was enough to make them prevail. Sands may have been less fortunate, in that he perished, but he was more fortunate in the sense that he achieved more in martyrdom than he ever might have had he lived. And Humphrey Atkins and Thatcher had been wrong when they speculated that among the ten strikers there must be at least one weak link. After Sands died, another nine followed, starving to death one by one throughout that summer.

But the link that Dolours Price felt to Bobby Sands ran deeper still. "We were 'force-fed' for a long time, it meant we did not die," she wrote years later. "Once the British Medical Council refused to 'force-feed' prisoners, then the British Parliament rushed a bill through ... making it an impossibility to keep prisoners by shoving a tube down their throats!" Not long after the Price sisters concluded their strike, the World Medical Association had issued a landmark declaration finding that force-feeding was unethical. Once the determination was made to stop force-feeding Dolours and Marian, the policy had indeed changed in the United Kingdom, when Roy Jenkins announced that hunger strikers would no longer be subjected to force-feeding in British prisons. By triumphing in the particular manner that she had back in 1974, Dolours Price had unwittingly given rise to the circumstances that would allow ten hunger strikers to starve to death seven years later. In subsequent years, she would wonder if this did not make her, in some way, responsible.

FIELD DAY

WHEN THE NEWS THAT Dolours Price had been released became public, it prompted an angry outcry. Ian Paisley, the fanatical loyalist reverend and politician, described the suspension of her sentence as an "outrageous scandal," arguing that Price continued to pose a very real threat to society, because she had "murder in her heart." Some observers suggested that Humphrey Atkins had been "taken for a sucker" by the Price sisters—that Dolours and Marian were unrepentant terrorists who had deliberately cultivated eating disorders in order to secure their own release. Anorexia, which at that time was not widely understood, was described as "the slimmers' disease," as if what had instigated the affliction was not a hunger strike or force-feeding, but vanity. Paisley and others speculated darkly that Dolours might have been released as part of a secret deal associated with Bobby Sands and the other hunger strikers at Long Kesh.

Years later, Dolours would describe what it was like for a person "who spent many years in prison and came out to a new world, a different world, a world they had to learn to live in all over again." After more than eight years behind bars, she rejoined her family and began to recover. Slowly, she started to put on weight. Technically, she was released "on license," meaning that there were conditions attached to her freedom, and if she violated those conditions, she could be returned to prison at any time. One of those terms was that she was not to leave Northern Ireland. But several months after her release, she petitioned for permission to take a monthlong summer holiday in the Republic. Margaret Thatcher personally reviewed the request, and ultimately the permission was granted.

Price wanted more than a holiday in the South, however. She wanted to relocate altogether, to Dublin. The atmosphere in Dublin had always been looser, less pinched, and more culturally vibrant than in Belfast. With its cafés and canals, it could feel a world away from the conflict in the North, and it seemed like an ideal place for Price to pursue her new ambition: to become a writer. She found work almost immediately, writing freelance articles for newspapers. It was, in some ways, a natural vocation for her; she had always possessed a gadfly personality, and this would allow her to remain tangentially involved with political issues while keeping well away from the paramilitary front lines. In December 1982, a year and a half after her release, she published a story in *The Irish Press* about anorexia, in which she noted that as an illness it was really all about control, and that well-known women such as Princess Diana and Jane Fonda had suffered from it. She suggested, erroneously, that anorexia was correlated with a "higher than average IQ."

Both before and after she made the move to the Republic, Price was being monitored by British intelligence. Reports from this surveillance indicated that there was no evidence to suggest that she had ongoing involvement "with any illegal organization or with any kind of terrorist activity." In fact, one intelligence report noted that, not long after her release, she had been approached by her old IRA comrades and asked to take part in a mission, but she rebuffed them.

Price had always been interested in the arts, and now she spent her days working on a book about her experience in Brixton. She talked about getting it published. According to a small item in *The Irish Times* in 1982, the book would explain "the development of Dolours's thinking from her time as a member of the IRA to the point where she came to favor pacifism (and

eventually resign from the movement while at Armagh prison)."
It may be true that Price had come to embrace nonviolence as
a personal philosophy. But there is reason to be skeptical of any
suggestion that she had renounced altogether the republican tradition of armed resistance. Such an item, discreetly placed in
the press, was likely intended for the benefit of the British officials who were deciding how severely they should circumscribe
Price's post-prison life. Dolours gave her Brixton manuscript to
Eamonn McCann, who found it dull—just a day-by-day account
of her time there. But she managed to publish an excerpt in a
Galway literary magazine, and it showed flashes of lyricism,
recounting how the summer sun would warm the floor of the
terminal ward, and how she could feel "the warmth of its memory on my bare feet."

It was after her release from prison that Price reconnected
with Stephen Rea, the actor from Belfast whom she had initially
met during her student days and had seen onstage in London
on the night before the bombing. Rea, who was five years older
than Price, had a scrawny, crumpled beauty and a gentle manner. He had a laconic air about him, but he shared with Price

a mordant, rapscallion wit.
He would avert his eyes as
he was casually setting up a
joke, then suddenly look right
at you when he delivered the
punch line.

Rea had grown up in a
house full of women, with his
mother and father, his grandmother, and three sisters.
But whereas Price had been
reared in a republican family
in Andersonstown, Rea was a

Dolours Price and Stephen Rea.

Protestant who came of age at

a slightly earlier time, during the 1950s, and in a corner of Belfast where his cultural influences were more eclectic. "I grew up in a mixed area, with mixed neighbors and mixed friends and my father drank—rather a lot—with both sides because it was that kind of place," he once explained. In a children's production of "Little Red Riding Hood," Rea played the Wolf, and he decided, then and there, that he wanted to be an actor.

First he would have to flee Belfast. He loved the city but felt that there was no space to operate there, no room to become anything different. He may have been Protestant, but he was sympathetic to the nationalist cause. After half a century of repression, he felt, it was inevitable that the Catholic community would produce some form of resistance. Rea ended up living in West Belfast for a time, and when he took the stage in the local community festival, his fellow Protestants saw it as a betrayal.

He attended Queen's during the 1960s and first met Price during the student protests. But as the Troubles took hold and Dolours was pulled into revolutionary activity, Rea was in Dublin, working as an actor at the famous Abbey Theatre. He felt dissatisfied there, too, concluding that "Ireland squanders talent," and he moved again, this time to London. While Price was hunger-striking in Brixton and staring down Margaret Thatcher in Armagh, Rea was becoming a well-known actor in London, with a series of high-profile roles at the Royal Court, the Old Vic, and the National Theatre, as well as the odd part on British television.

During those years, Rea faced a common dilemma for Irish actors on the English stage: To what degree should he soften the edges of his spiky Ulster accent and reinvent himself as an Englishman? As a gifted mimic, he could certainly "play" English, and people advised him to do precisely that, in order to advance on the stage. But, like Price, Rea was headstrong, and he decided that he would rather be an unemployed Irishman than find work by sounding like he had grown up in Surrey. After all, it was one of the great achievements of Irish civilization to take the English language and adapt it, creating a different music. The Irish might have tended to lose in their political conflict with the British, Rea remarked, but "they have been triumphant in terms of the language."

On a Saturday in the fall of 1983, Price and Rea were married. For the ceremony, they chose St. Patrick's Cathedral in Armagh, a short walk up the hill from Dolours's former home in C Wing. The officiant was Father Raymond Murray, the chaplain at the jail, who had been active in lobbying for Dolours's release. Mindful, perhaps, of the spectacle that might attend the union of the Old Bailey bomber and a well-known London actor, they opted to marry in secret, with only two witnesses in attendance. When an English tabloid reached Father Murray afterward, he would furnish no details. "The couple have asked me not to discuss the wedding," he said. "I am sworn to secrecy."

.   .   .

Rea had also reconnected, during this period, with the playwright Brian Friel, whose play Rea had performed in on the night before the London bombing. In 1980, the two of them cofounded a new theater company, Field Day. The troupe was inaugurated with the world premiere of a play that would come to be regarded as Friel's masterpiece, *Translations*. Set in a school in Donegal in 1833, the play concerned a survey by the British Army that would identify local Irish place names and replace them with English translations or phonetic equivalents. The play opened at the Guildhall, in Derry. The building was a symbol of unionism, so much so that it had become a frequent target for the IRA. On opening night, scaffolding still clung to some parts of the building as workmen repaired damage from prior attacks. So there was something slightly arch about this choice of venue—but something hopeful about it, too.

Friel and Rea decided that their new theater group would produce one play each year and tour it around Ireland. The company came to include an illustrious assemblage of participants and boosters, among them the poets Seamus Deane and Seamus Heaney. The politics of Field Day were a sensitive matter. Friel had been raised Catholic, and some observers regarded the company as a nationalist outfit; one critic described Field Day as the "cultural wing of the Provos." But while there was often something obviously political about the plays that they performed, the politics tended to be oblique, and Rea stubbornly refused to be painted into any ideological corner. The work of Field Day was "political action in the widest sense," he said. Part of the idea for the company, according to Rea, was that if everyone all over Ireland was hearing the same story, on both sides of the border in a divided country, it might have some cohesive effect. The board consisted of three Catholics and three Protestants. ("All lapsed," one of them noted.) But there was not a unionist among them.

What this meant in practice was that Rea spent some five months a year on the road, touring. And, having joined the circus, in effect, by marriage, Dolours Price often went with him. Price helped manage the books and the correspondence for the company, keeping track of miles traveled and money spent on gas and taking the car in to the garage ("the car hospital," as she called it). They crisscrossed the island, north and south, touring parts of Ireland that had not seen a professional theater company in thirty years. In some rural areas, tractors would pull up and farmers would dismount and amble over to a makeshift stage to see the play.

Even so, a major career was beckoning Rea in London, and this posed an obvious problem for the relationship: technically, Price was defying the terms of her release by even living in Dublin and traveling with Field Day around the Republic. In England, a rumor circulated not long after Price and Rea were married that she was going to accompany him to London for the premiere of a new film. The British tabloids sounded the alarm: would the notorious "bomb girl" have the temerity to revisit the very city she had bombed? Price did not make the trip, in the end, but privately she did plead repeatedly with the British government to cancel the residency requirement, or at least grant her permission to visit her husband in England.

She was careful to mail these written appeals from the Price family home in Belfast. But as it happened, the authorities knew that she was already violating the terms of her release, by living most of the time in Dublin. When the requests made their way to Thatcher, who had always perceived Price to be a manipulator, she wrote to her subordinates, "I think we are just being played along here. Should resist firmly."

Having defied Thatcher and prevailed in the past, Price now proceeded to defy her once again. In May 1985, a police officer in Folkestone, a town in southeast England, across the Channel from France, pulled a car over. Inside were Stephen Rea and Dolours Price. Asked where they resided, they offered an address in London. The couple had taken up residence in a flat in Maida Vale, around the corner from the BBC studios and just a few miles from the Old Bailey.

To Thatcher, Price's return to London, in direct contravention of the terms of her release, was a thumb in the eye. After the incident in Folkestone, the secretary of state for Northern Ireland recommended that the government change the terms of Price's release in order to accommodate the fact that she was already in England, and simply allow her to stay. But Thatcher would have none of it. In November, an aide wrote that Price was "still living in Maida Vale with her husband." He pointed out that if she were to be locked up again, it would provoke an "immediate and adverse reaction" among Catholics in Northern Ireland. Besides, he ventured, if they *did* throw her into prison again, Price would probably just stop eating, and then they would be right back where they had started. The aide acknowledged that, while it was possible in theory for the couple to live in Northern Ireland, "it would be difficult for an established actor to continue his profession there." The only alternative, it seemed, was to change the terms of Price's release. A report by Special Branch indicated that "on present evidence there is no real basis for regarding her as a threat to Great Britain." But Thatcher would not change the terms. In fact, she would rather allow Price to flout the provision and simply pretend not to notice than acknowledge that she had been arm-twisted into altering her stance.

Some civil servants worried that the "anomalous position" of the couple "could well come to public notice and attract criticism." But Thatcher would not waver. "I do not think Mrs. Rea should be allowed to live here," she wrote. "She was transferred to Northern Ireland on conditions and if she and her husband wish to be together they can live in Northern Ireland." In a prim flourish of willful disassociation, she added, "If she were still in England she would be in prison."

The British newspapers, which had always taken such an interest in Price, soon figured out that she was in London and living the fashionable life of the bride of a well-regarded actor. Gleeful write-ups described the Old Bailey bomber "sipping champagne with the stars at the National Theatre." There was a brief scandal when Stephen Rea was slated to perform in the musical *High Society* at the Victoria Palace Theatre, and the Queen Mother was scheduled to attend the show. Would the convicted IRA terrorist be there? Would she shake the Queen Mum's hand? "Dolours has indicated that she will not be attending either of the Royal Gala performances," Rea's agent told the press. "It is a sensitive matter and entirely her decision but she has said she will be at home." For the purposes of propriety, the agent added that "home" meant Belfast.

Rea would later remark that his decision to marry a notorious ex-militant from the IRA had done nothing to hurt his career. "The people in my profession were enormously generous about it," he said. But inevitably, he was often questioned about his wife's past, and when this happened, he tended to bristle. Rea wanted the press to focus exclusively on his work and not get caught up in his biography, much less the history or politics of his spouse.

Nevertheless, he was obliged to give interviews to promote each new production, and he developed a reputation for abruptly terminating any interview that turned to the subject of the woman he had married. It became a joke among journalists covering Rea: *Never, ever mention the missus.*

But Rea did himself no favors with his choice of roles. He often seemed to end up playing the part of a soulful gunman—frequently, a gunman from the IRA. "What I bring is an understanding of how decent, ordinary people got involved," he said, "and how that spiraled into something out of control." On the rare occasion when he did speak of his wife's bombing raid on London, he emphasized that the one man who had perished that day did so from a heart attack.

Once, in an interview for a documentary in 1988, Rea was asked how far he himself would be prepared to go in service of a political cause. "I could never be a soldier," Rea said. "I couldn't do that. I mean I think what you're asking me is would I be prepared to be violent and all that." He paused. "I couldn't be, personally," he continued. "But I think the violence isn't just a moral thing. It's not just a moral choice at this stage. It's a kind of reflex, and there's a great deal of establishment violence, as well."

The interviewer asked him if political change could happen *without* violence.

"I don't know," Rea said. "Does it ever?"

·   ·   ·

The authorities were correct to judge that Dolours Price no longer posed a threat. She had abandoned violence as a means of fighting for a united Ireland, at least for her own part. But this was not to say that she abandoned republicanism. She canvassed for a Sinn Féin candidate for Belfast City Council. Though she came from a hard-line republican background, she adapted to the shift to electoral politics, and the strategy of the Armalite and the ballot box. In 1983, her old officer commanding, Gerry Adams, entered politics himself. A decade had passed since Adams sent Price to bomb London, and now he was seeking a parliamentary seat at Westminster, representing West Belfast. Adams trimmed his hair and gradually replaced the casual jumpers of his guerrilla days with a wardrobe of corduroy and tweed. With his silver tongue and his analytical mind, he had always had a touch of the professor about him, and now he *looked* professorial. He even smoked a pipe. Adams's decision to embrace an electoral strategy had grown, in part, from the success of Bobby Sands in standing for election, even if Sands had died before he could ever assume the position. In a nod to the traditional abstentionism of the IRA, Adams announced that, if elected, he would boycott Westminster and would not actually attend Parliament. Price supported him and took to the campaign trail. "Vote Sinn Féin!" she cried. "Vote Gerry Adams!" On Election Day, she ferried voters to the polling stations. And Adams won.

THE BLOODY ENVELOPE

THE SPRING OF 1988 was a season of funerals in Belfast. On March 6, Mairéad Farrell was shot to death, along with two associates, on the streets of Gibraltar. A slim, dark-haired thirty-one-year-old woman, Farrell had been a prisoner alongside Dolours and Marian Price in Armagh jail. But unlike the Price sisters, when she left prison, she returned to active service. Farrell journeyed to Gibraltar as part of an IRA team. They had traveled to the British territory on the southern tip of Spain with the intention of launching a bombing mission. But before they had a chance to carry out the attack, they were walking along, unarmed, one day when they were approached by plainclothes British commandos and executed, in what some would claim was an expression of a secret "shoot-to-kill" policy by the army. The bodies of the three volunteers were transported back to Northern Ireland with great fanfare, and a massive funeral procession bore their coffins through Belfast, trailing thousands of mourners.

Father Alec Reid would help officiate at the graveside. Reid was fifty-six, with a long, lined face and small hooded eyes. He had grown up in Tipperary, and, while still in his teens, he had joined the Redemptorists, an order of Catholic priests who dedicated themselves to the salvation of the poor and abandoned. Reid moved to Belfast before the outbreak of the Troubles, in the early 1960s, and joined Clonard Monastery, a great old Gothic structure, erected at the end of the nineteenth century, that straddled a line between the republican Falls Road and the loyalist Shankill. The founder of the monastery had come to regret this location, reportedly remarking, "I doubt if ever a more troublesome piece of property was acquired." But it gave Father Reid a vantage point from which to witness the Troubles up close.

He did more than pay witness. Some clergymen, Reid noticed, had a tendency to hide behind the scripture. But he was a priest "on the streets," he liked to say, always in the thick of things, a ghetto diplomat, quietly negotiating disputes. Occasionally he would find himself in the middle of a paramilitary feud. This could be dangerous, but, as Reid said to one fellow priest who questioned the wisdom of inserting himself into such dicey situations, "In for a penny, in for a pound." Reid possessed an unerring faith in the power of dialogue: if you could just get people to talk, he believed, the most bitter antagonists could discover common ground.

On regular visits to Long Kesh during the 1970s, Father Reid had grown close to Brendan Hughes and Gerry Adams. Adams, who lived near Clonard, had grown up going to the monastery once a week for religious instruction. After Adams was released from prison, Reid would shuttle messages between the young leader and his comrades, like Hughes, who were still locked up. Reid seemed so often to be engaged in one intrigue or another that Hughes gave him a nickname: "Behind the Scenes."

Reid may have assisted the Provos by playing messenger, but that did not mean he condoned their activities. On the contrary, he was deeply unsettled by the violence that had torn his community apart. Reid was a quiet man, and his fellow priests would often see him pacing the monastery garden, clutching a cigarette, deep in thought. His job, he felt, was to speak for the victims—to represent the next person who might be killed in the conflict. He had no particular party; his only allegiance was to those who had been (and would be) cut down. Reid believed that there were opportunities, even in the darkest times, for grace; that in the direst scenarios, one could still follow the example of Jesus; that war could call forth the very worst qualities of humankind, but also the best. "You meet God in the midst of the Troubles," he would say.

At IRA funerals, one perpetual source of tension was the presence of British security forces. With so many known IRA members out on the street, the RUC and the army rarely missed an opportunity to monitor these occasions, taking pictures and gathering intelligence. But to the mourners, this intrusion could feel disrespectful and intimidating, even smug—particularly when the people being buried had been felled by a British bullet. As the coffins of Mairéad Farrell and her two accomplices were carried through the streets of West Belfast, however, there was not a policeman or soldier in sight. Evidently, the authorities had been instructed to stay away. Amid a forest of Celtic crosses at Milltown Cemetery, in West Belfast, Gerry Adams and other notable republicans gathered around a freshly dug grave, surrounded by thousands of mourners, as the first coffin was lowered into the ground. Having been elected to Westminster five years earlier, Adams was now a member of Parliament. He often presided at republican funerals.

Father Reid began to intone a prayer. But as he spoke, he looked up and saw movement on the edge of the stationary crowd. A man, in the distance. A burly man dressed in a dark anorak. He was walking toward the mourners with unsettling purpose. Reaching into his jacket, he pulled out an object that looked like a smooth black egg. Reid thought immediately that it must be a stone—people were forever throwing stones in Belfast. Now, it seemed, this man had the nerve to transgress the sacred ritual of a funeral and throw one here. Sure enough, the man wound up and hurled the object. Then Reid heard the sharp crack of an explosion. It wasn't a rock; it was a hand grenade.

People flew into a panic, scrambling in every direction, diving behind the headstones, sliding in the mud of the freshly dug grave. Sensing the possibility of a stampede, Adams seized a megaphone and bellowed, "Will people please stay calm!" *Boom!* A second grenade exploded. Several mourners started to sprint toward the man, to take him down. But before they could reach him, he pulled out a pistol and began shooting.

A slow-motion chase ensued as the shooter backed out of the cemetery, firing shots and chucking grenades, down a sloping hill toward the M1 motorway, and dozens of mourners pursued him, weaving among the tombstones for cover, advancing cautiously. By the time he reached the M1, where cars whizzed by, the gunman had run out of ammunition. His pursuers converged on him and beat him unconscious. He was arrested, and identified as Michael Stone, an East Belfast loyalist who was a member of the Ulster Defence Association. He had gone to the funeral that day hoping to kill Gerry Adams and other top republicans. Stone did not succeed in hitting Adams, but he did kill three other mourners and wound more than sixty.

And so a second giant funeral was arranged, in order to bury the three victims of this attack. Tensions could scarcely run higher. Adams had darkly suggested, following the cemetery murders, that it was no accident that the authorities had chosen to steer clear of the funeral—that they may have done so in collusion with the loyalist gunman, quite aware of his designs.

The following Saturday, Father Reid attended the funeral Mass of Kevin Brady, one of the dead mourners, at St. Agnes's Church. When he walked out of the church, a huge funeral cortege was making its way along Andersonstown Road to the cemetery. Brady had been a cabdriver, so, in addition to the usual mourners, there was a small fleet of black taxis inching along, as a guard of honor. The victims would be buried in the same ground upon which they had been killed just days earlier. People were massed in the streets, angry and embittered. Gerry Adams was among the mourners. Father Reid walked out of the church and joined the procession, seeking out Brady's family, who were walking behind his coffin.

But just as Reid was reaching the family, there was a commotion. A car appeared, a squat silver Volkswagen, on the road at the edge of the crowd. The vehicle accelerated out of nowhere, then came to an abrupt stop, halted by the phalanx of black taxis that were leading the procession. A surge of anxiety radiated through the crowd. Was this another attack? The Volkswagen abruptly reversed, scooting backward at a dangerous clip, then it stopped and was immediately engulfed by people. There were two men inside the vehicle. As hundreds of mourners swarmed the little car, one of the men flashed something. "He's got a gun!" somebody cried. "It's the peelers!"—the cops—someone else shouted. One of the men had indeed waved a pistol and, in a panic, fired a shot in the air. But even as the mob immobilized the car and several men climbed on top of it and someone else kicked in the window and the mourners began to drag the men out of the car and pummel them and tear at their clothes, they never fired on the crowd.

They weren't police officers. They were soldiers: two British corporals, Derek Wood and David Howes, who had been driving in the area when they took what would prove to be a lethally misguided wrong turn. Upon realizing that they had driven into the path of the funeral, Howes and Wood had panicked and tried to escape. But by that time, they were hemmed in by black taxis and consumed by the crowd.

Somebody arrived with a lug wrench to smash the windscreen. Father Reid saw the men getting pulled out of the car, then dragged and shoved into a nearby park. There, the mob stripped their clothes off, so that the corporals were dressed only in their underwear and socks, then forced them onto the ground and beat them. There was a madness in the air—you could taste it—and Reid knew as he approached the scene that these men were about to get shot. Scrambling down onto the ground between the two soldiers, he wrapped one arm around each of them and lay there, hoping that this would prevent the attackers from pulling the trigger. "Would somebody get an ambulance!" he cried.

But a voice above him growled, "Get up or I'll fucking well shoot *you*," and a pair of rough hands heaved Reid off the ground.

The soldiers were thrown into a black taxi and driven to a vacant lot near Penny Lane, about two hundred yards away. Reid was running toward the area when he heard the crack of gunshots. David Howes was twenty-three; he had just arrived in Northern Ireland to begin his tour. Derek Wood, who was twenty-four, was scheduled to go home soon. The two men were left there, sprawled in the rubble, their limbs akimbo, pale and stranded like beached whales. In the sky above, a helicopter slowly circled. But nobody intervened.

Father Reid ran to the men. One of them was clearly dead, but the other stirred; when Reid leaned close, he could hear the sound of breathing. Reid looked up frantically at the people standing around and asked if anybody knew how to resuscitate someone. Nobody responded. They just stood there, watching. Reid crouched over the body and placed his mouth on the soldier's mouth, trying to breathe the life back into him. But eventually the breathing stopped, and someone said, "Father, that man is dead."

Reid looked up, and as he did, a photographer standing some distance away took a picture that would become perhaps the most indelible image of the Troubles: a priest, clad in black, on his knees, ministering to a man who has just died, lying with his arms splayed, like Christ, on the ground before him. Reid looks directly at the camera, a witness to the horror, his own thin lips smeared dark with the dead man's blood. Reid did not

Father Alec Reid, administering the last rites to Corporal David Howes.

know if either of the soldiers was Catholic, but he anointed them both, as he had anointed the bodies of the slain mourners at Milltown Cemetery several days earlier, and delivered the last rites.

It had been two decades since the violence began in the late 1960s, and Reid wore the weight of all that bloodshed heavily. "People have had enough," he said in an interview hours after the shooting. "What people have to do is listen to each other. People haven't been doing that." He added, "Physical force is a sign of the desperation of the poor." But as it happened, even while Reid defied the mob and ministered to the murdered soldiers that day, he was up to something behind the scenes. He was nurturing a plan: a clandestine, audacious plan to end the conflict.

·   ·   ·

Before he left the requiem Mass at St. Agnes's Church that morning, Father Reid had taken possession of a secret document. For years, he had tried to discourage paramilitaries and ordinary citizens on both sides of the sectarian divide from resorting to violence. But he had come to believe that the surest way to end the conflict would be to persuade the IRA to stop fighting. Reid broached the issue with Gerry Adams and discovered that he was prepared to entertain the idea. Perhaps Adams had a different vision for the future; perhaps he had found that the ballot and the bullet were not mutually reinforcing but were actually at cross-purposes; perhaps he was simply exhausted. Whatever the case, Reid found that when he made his initial appeal to Adams, he was "pushing an open door." Later, Reid would receive credit for having coaxed Adams onto the path of peace. But to Brendan Hughes, who knew both men intimately, it never seemed that Adams was being handled by the priest. Rather, Hughes recalled, "I believe it was, right from the start, Gerry handling him."

Adams saw in the priest an unimpeachable convener. "The only organization that can do anything is the Church," he told Reid. Only the Church had the status, the credibility, and the lines of communication with the relevant parties to achieve peace. The one conceivable scenario in which the IRA might willingly lay down its arms would be if there were a joint peace strategy that brought together the republicans, the nonviolent nationalists of the Social Democratic and Labour Party (SDLP), and the government of the Republic of Ireland.

This might sound appealing in theory, but it would pose major challenges in practice. The leader of the SDLP was John Hume, a rumpled but shrewd Derry politician who was eleven years older than Adams. Hume was a hero to moderate Catholics and had repeatedly condemned the violence of the IRA. "They bomb factories and shout about unemployment," he said in 1985.

"They shoot a teacher in a classroom, kill school bus drivers, kill people on campuses and then lecture us about education. They kill, maim and injure and they carry out attacks in hospitals, and then they tell us about protecting the National Health Service. They rob post offices, leaving people without benefit payments and then they preach to us about defending the poor." To Hume, the hypocrisy of the republican movement—the cynical shell game of the ballot and the bullet—seemed all too calculated. "The real strategy and objectives are clear," he said. "Have the military wing create as much discontent and deprivation as possible, the more unemployment the better. Then have your political wing feed off the people's discontent. One of these days, Sinn Féin will disappear up their own contradiction."

Six months after Hume made these remarks, Father Reid sat down and wrote Hume a long letter. "My only aim is to help those who, if the present situation continues, will be killed," the priest suggested. Because of his years of quiet work in the republican community, Reid noted, he enjoyed the trust of the IRA. "I am certain that if the situation is handled properly, the IRA can be persuaded to end their campaign," he wrote.

At the time Reid sent his letter, Hume was publicly committed to the idea that no dialogue with Sinn Féin would be acceptable as long as the IRA's campaign of violence continued. Hume had always said that he was prepared to talk with anyone, so long as the objective was peace. But the IRA did little to encourage such magnanimity. In the fall of 1987, the IRA detonated a powerful bomb at a Remembrance Day commemoration in the town of Enniskillen, killing ten civilians and one British soldier and wounding more than sixty others. The IRA announced afterward that the bombing had been a mistake: the intended target was actually a ceremony involving British soldiers nearby. Adams apologized for the attack, disassociating himself from it. But the bombing was roundly condemned, and it underlined the pariah status of the Provos. Hume criticized the attack as "an act of sheer savagery." It could be hazardous to antagonize the Provos in such a manner: several months earlier, the IRA had firebombed Hume's home. He was not in the house at the time, but his wife and youngest daughter were, and they only narrowly escaped.

Nevertheless, on January 11, 1988, Hume met with Gerry Adams at Clonard Monastery. They had spoken on several prior occasions—but in secret. It would be politically dangerous for Hume to be seen engaging with Adams. But it was just as dangerous—possibly more so—for Adams to be seen talking with a moderate like Hume. Adams had always walked a fine line within the ranks of the Provos, as a strategist rather than an operational man. If people suspected that he was initiating any sort of cease-fire negotiations, it might give rise to a perception that he had sold out the armed struggle. In 1988, that was the sort of perception that could get a person killed.

But Father Reid's faith in dialogue was not misplaced. The two adversaries got along. Hume experienced the same dissonance that the British negotiators had back in 1972: after all the frightening tales they had heard about Gerry Adams, when he actually walked into the room, he seemed nothing like the hot-blooded hobgoblin of lore. He was personable, tweedy, and straightforward, a man one could find a way to work with. A politician. Initially, Adams and Hume agreed to an exchange of documents, in which they would lay out the positions of their respective organizations in order to establish the parameters for a possible peace deal. In claustrophobic Belfast, the secrecy of this exchange necessitated a degree of spycraft. On the day the British corporals were killed, Father Reid had been instructed to attend the funeral Mass for Kevin Brady—where someone would slip him a document. At the requiem Mass, he took possession of a brown envelope containing a position paper from Sinn Féin. Reid was carrying the paper when he left the church, and it was in his pocket when he tended to the two murdered soldiers. As Reid ministered to the men and delivered mouth-to-mouth, he got fresh blood on his hands, and the blood smudged the envelope. After leaving the bodies, Reid returned to Clonard Monastery, where he transferred the documents into a clean envelope. Then he made his way to Derry with this fragile, precious seed of peace and delivered it personally to John Hume.

.   .   .

When Adams was first elected to Parliament, in 1983, the British government lifted a ban that had prevented him from traveling to the mainland, so that he would be able to take his seat at Westminster. But Adams had no intention of actually participating in Parliament, in any case. Throughout the 1980s, Adams played a delicate game. He was elected president of Sinn Féin in 1983. Yet he had become convinced that there would eventually have to be peace: a united Ireland could not be won through armed force alone.

He could not simply spring this new thesis on the rank and file of the IRA, because if the volunteers knew his intentions, they might oust him from the party, or just kill him. At the same time, as Adams grew more invested in the political side of the struggle, he faced a separate challenge: the IRA remained an illegal organization. Traditionally, when volunteers were asked if they were in the IRA, they would refuse to answer, because to acknowledge membership would be enough to put them in prison. But as Adams refashioned his persona from guerrilla leader to statesman, he took this gambit one step further: he began to tell people that he had always been a purely political figure, an ardent republican and a Sinn Féin leader—but not a volunteer, not someone who was in any way directly involved or implicated in the armed struggle. "I am not a member of the IRA, and have never been in the IRA," he would say.

Of course, to anyone who had been paying attention, this

was a laughable assertion. Adams had long been known to be not just a member, but one of the foremost *leaders,* of the IRA. As a young man, he had been photographed at funerals, standing at attention and wearing the black beret of the IRA. He was released from Long Kesh in 1972 and traveled to London to negotiate with the British government as part of an IRA delegation. (When Seán Mac Stíofáin was asked, years later, whether the delegation represented Sinn Féin or the IRA, he replied that they were IRA. Pressed on whether this included Adams, Mac Stíofáin growled, "*All* of them.") The media, dating back to the early 1970s, had characterized Adams as an IRA member. British security and intelligence forces had also long considered him to be a major figure in the IRA.

On the sixtieth anniversary of the Easter Uprising, in 1976, Adams had published an article in *Republican News.* Writing under his pseudonym, Brownie, he described an encounter with a priest who had come to see him in prison. Adams defended the morality of violence to the priest, arguing that paramilitarism was not a role IRA members had sought out but, rather, one that had been thrust upon them. "Rightly or wrongly, I am an IRA Volunteer," Adams wrote. "The course I take involves the use of physical force, but only if I achieve the situation where my people can genuinely prosper can my course of action be seen, by me, to have been justified."

A few years after writing those lines, Adams would start asserting that he had never been a member of the IRA. Thus, even as he emerged as an ever more prominent face of the armed struggle in Northern Ireland, he denied having been a part of that struggle himself. Sinn Féin's headquarters occupied a ramshackle building on the Falls Road. The space operated as a political office, a location where Adams could grant interviews to the press and meet with constituents. Opponents joked that the upstart political party had accounts at every bank in the country, which they regularly drew upon, at gunpoint. Asked about such allegations, Adams protested that Sinn Féin's community activities and electoral campaigns were funded not by paramilitary action but by raffles, donations, and "cake fairs." Yet the walls outside the headquarters featured colorful murals of masked IRA gunmen hoisting assault rifles. This paradox would become a signature of Adams's emerging persona: homespun whimsy mingled with armed insurrection, cake fairs with a dash of bloodshed.

Such contradictions may simply have been a matter of expediency. The Royal Ulster Constabulary, which had long nurtured a grudge against the man they perceived to be an architect of IRA violence, would not hesitate to arrest Adams if he admitted to his membership in the group. In fact, the British government had endeavored to prosecute Adams on a so-called membership charge in 1978, based on language he had used that seemed to acknowledge his role in the IRA. But he fought the charges, and the case was dismissed. "In a society where an organization like the Provisional IRA is illegal and its political wing legal, activists like Gerry Adams have an enigmatic role to play," observed a 1982 feature on Adams in *The Irish People*, a newspaper published by republican sympathizers in New York, adding that Adams "plays his part very adroitly." Adams appeared in a photograph wearing a turtleneck sweater and expressed great indignation, in an interview, about his treatment by the press. He was often asked "loaded questions" about whether he "continued" to condone violence, he said, adding, "I'm getting a bit fed up with it." Queried by *The Irish People* about whether he would justify Bloody Friday, the operation that Brendan Hughes oversaw in which bombs exploded all over civilian areas in Belfast, Adams responded, "I would certainly not attempt to justify any action in which civilians are killed. I naturally regret very much all such deaths." But, he continued, "since it is not the policy of the IRA to kill civilians, I could not, by the same token, condemn them for accidental killings."

Such calibrated sophistry became another Adams signature, always delivered with unwavering certainty, in his unflustered brogue, and many Adams critics came to loathe his caveated expressions of "regret." But Adams insisted that when it came to a moral accounting of violence, the IRA should be held to the same standard as the British state. "In any war situation, civilians unfortunately suffer and die," he pointed out. "The presence of the gun in Irish politics is not the sole responsibility of the Irish. The British were responsible for putting it there in the first place and they continue to use it to stay in Ireland." He added, "No amount of voting papers alone will get them out."

Adams had always been deeply enmeshed in his community, and, as MP for West Belfast, he demonstrated a surprising avidity for the quotidian busywork of local politics. Loping down the little streets, trailed by curious schoolchildren and loyal aides, he would go door-to-door, murmuring empathetically at his constituents' complaints about litter or their quarrels with the Housing Executive. "Brian'll phone them in the morning and then he'll nip round here to see what's happened, won't you, Brian?" he would assure them as Brian or some other aide dutifully scribbled details in a notebook.

With his smart blazers, carefully trimmed beard, and ever-present pipe, Adams had acquired the air of a hip, if slightly pompous, public intellectual. He published a book of gauzy remembrances about his childhood in the Falls. He stroked his beard. He appointed a press aide.

Sinn Féin began to open "advice centers," which could counsel constituents on prosaic matters like welfare claims. There was something slightly comical about this self-conscious metamorphosis from revolutionary cadre to retail political outfit: at one point, Sinn Féin determined, with great fanfare, that it no longer condoned "kneecapping" as a means of disciplining young people for antisocial behavior. The former Derry gunman Martin McGuinness, who had won a seat in the Northern

Gerry Adams, politician.

Ireland Assembly elections in 1982, solemnly announced that, "after some discussion, the IRA decided that shooting a young lad in the leg, leaving him crippled for life, is not a just and fair punishment." Instead, McGuinness continued, "we want to take a more socially involved, preventative approach." Some nationalists from the SDLP likened Sinn Féin's abrupt rebranding as a well-meaning troupe of community activists to the Virgin Birth.

Adams now maintained that he had never personally ordered or participated in any violence, but he would not renounce violent techniques. In his first address after getting elected president of Sinn Féin, he made it clear that violence should continue—in tandem with political activity. Indeed, even as Adams began to contemplate, and then act upon, a scheme to bring an end to the conflict, the IRA carried out more deadly operations. Just before Christmas in 1983, the Provos detonated a bomb at Harrods department store, in London, killing five people and injuring ninety. (Adams said that the bomb "had not gone right.") The following October, a volunteer placed a time bomb in a room at the Grand Brighton Hotel, where Margaret Thatcher and her cabinet would be staying during a conference. The bomb exploded, killing five people, but not Thatcher. The IRA issued a statement, eloquently capturing the strategic advantage of terrorism: "Today we were unlucky, but remember, we only have to be lucky once. You will have to be lucky always."

Adams defended the Brighton bombing as not merely justifiable but necessary. The fatalities, he said, "are sad symptoms of the British presence in this country." The bombing was not a blow against democracy, as some had charged. It was actually "a blow *for* democracy." Thatcher may have survived the attack, but she was shaken. Privately, she became convinced that the Provos would eventually succeed. "They'll probably get me in the end," she would say. "But I don't like to hand myself to them on a plate."

Adams shared with his nemesis a conviction that the conflict might kill him. After an arrest in 1983, when the RUC tried to stop a Sinn Féin motorcade from displaying tricolor flags, Adams was put on trial in Belfast in the spring of 1984. The MP for West Belfast faced charges of disorderly behavior and obstruction of the police. One day, during a lunch break from the proceedings, he left the Magistrates Court and climbed into a car with some associates for the short ride back to West Belfast. After years on the run, Adams tended to deliberately make his movements difficult to predict. But his trial was a major news story, and it was widely known that he would be at court in the center of Belfast that day. He had grown so fearful about his own safety that he had applied for a license to carry a firearm for self-defense. But the request had been rejected, to nobody's surprise, by the RUC. Adams had taken to predicting his own death, saying, "I think there is a ninety percent chance I may be assassinated."

Not long after the car left the court, it slowed in traffic on Howard Street, and a brown vehicle appeared, pulling alongside it. Two gunmen fired a dozen shots at Adams and his associates. Adams was hit three times, in the neck, shoulder, and arm, but not killed. (Three others in the car were also wounded, but none of them died.) "Christ said that those that take the sword shall perish by the sword," the Reverend Ian Paisley declared upon hearing of the shooting. "I have followed too many coffins over which Gerry Adams has rejoiced to feel any pain and sorrow over what has taken place today."

The shooters were quickly apprehended, and identified as members of the Ulster Freedom Fighters. But from his bed at Royal Victoria Hospital, Adams claimed that the authorities had known about the attack in advance and had hoped it would succeed. It was indicative of Adams's continued status as a political outcast that none of his fellow members of the British Parliament issued any expressions of sympathy or condemnation following this assassination attempt. They greeted the news of the shooting with glacial silence.

BLUE RIBBONS

WHEN BRENDAN HUGHES WAS finally released from Long Kesh in 1986, after nearly thirteen years, he went to live, initially, with Gerry Adams and his family in West Belfast. Hughes's marriage had foundered while he was inside. He learned from a fellow prisoner that Lily had become involved with another man. "I called her to the jail and told her there was no problem," he later recalled. "She was young and deserved a bit of happiness. She always said the war was my number one priority and she was right. I was selfish. I neglected my family." When he got out of prison, Hughes went to Lily's house and shook her new partner's hand.

After so many years behind bars, he was puzzled by the city he had returned to. Everything seemed different. Sometimes Hughes would go for a walk only to discover, as if in a dream, that the old streets he remembered were gone, and new, different streets had taken their place. Once, he got lost in his own neighborhood and a stranger had to guide him home. Prison life had a comforting, if monotonous, predictability. By contrast, Belfast seemed noisy, jarring, unsafe. Hughes found that he was uncomfortable in large crowds. He would venture out to the pub only in the afternoon, when it was quiet.

Hughes could sense that Adams was maneuvering politically, though he had no inkling of the nascent peace process. He still thought of himself as a soldier, and Adams, who had always been political, was now an actual politician. There were places in Belfast where hard men congregated, and Hughes could go and sit and be accepted among such men, but Adams could not, because even before his rote denials of IRA membership, he had never been perceived as much of a soldier. Even so, Hughes and Adams had always been a team, and Hughes maintained a deep sense of loyalty to his comrade. If Adams's lack of combat bona fides amounted to a liability, then Hughes hoped that his own reputation would buttress his friend's, and he could serve Adams as "his physical force arm within the movement." If Adams was the draftsman, then Hughes would be his instrument. He may not have fully appreciated just how useful it was to Adams for the two of them to be seen together as he accompanied Adams around the country, helping to secure the electoral base for Sinn Féin. This way, Adams could keep repeating that he was not a member of the IRA, but to anyone with eyes in their head, the value of such a bromide would be subtly counteracted by the presence, at his elbow, of the ferocious, mustachioed Brendan Hughes.

Hughes was keenly aware of the ways in which his role as a republican icon—Darkie Hughes, Hunger Striker—might be put to use as a political commodity. After his release, he agreed to make a trip to America, in an effort to raise morale and financial support for the armed campaign. There were vastly more Irish Americans than there were people in Ireland itself. This demographic anomaly was a testament to centuries of migration caused by poverty, famine, and discrimination, and there was strong support for the cause of Irish independence among the Irish in America. Indeed, it could occasionally seem that support for the armed struggle was more fervent in Boston or Chicago than it was in Belfast or Derry. The romantic idyll of a revolutionary movement is easier to sustain when there is no danger that one's own family members might get blown to pieces on a trip to the grocery store. Some people in Ireland looked askance at the "plastic Paddies" who urged bloody war in Ulster from the safe distance of America. But the IRA had long counted on the United States as a source of support. Indeed, it was from America that Brendan Hughes had first procured the Armalite rifle years earlier.

Hughes traveled to New York City and met with representatives from the Irish Northern Aid Committee, or "Noraid," a fund-raising group. At one meeting, an opinionated Irish American benefactor informed Hughes that the Provos were going about the war all wrong. What you should really be doing, the man told him, is widening your range of targets. Start shooting anyone who is in any way associated with the British regime— anyone who wears the crown on his uniform.

"Postmen?" Hughes interjected. "Shoot postmen?"

Of course you should be shooting postmen, the man replied.

"Right," Hughes said. "I'm going back to Belfast in a couple of weeks ... We'll get another ticket and you come back with me and *you* shoot the fucking postmen."

The man presented Hughes with a suitcase full of money for the cause. But the more they conversed, the more objectionable Hughes found his politics. Hughes still regarded himself as a revolutionary socialist, but he was discovering that among the conservative Irish Americans who supported the IRA during the 1980s, socialism was not exactly in vogue. Finally, in a fit of pique, Hughes blurted, "I don't want your fucking money!" So the man left and took his suitcase with him.

After his release from prison, Hughes had returned directly to active service with the IRA. He traveled around on both sides of the border, planning operations. But as he interacted on these missions with frontline volunteers, he was struck by a feeling of unease in some quarters, a lurking sense that the IRA might have become too political. At times, Hughes wondered whether, as a pure soldier, he had been overtaken by history and grown outmoded. On a visit to Dublin, he went to Sinn Féin headquarters, on Parnell Square. The place was abuzz with aboveboard political activity. But as Hughes glanced around, he could not escape the sensation that he had no role to play in this new tableau—that he was not really a part of it. He paid a visit to Seamus Twomey, the former chief of staff of the IRA, who had been sprung from Mountjoy Prison in a helicopter back in 1973. Twomey was three decades older than Hughes. He had been sidelined, squeezed out of the IRA's Army Council by Gerry Adams and the people around him, and Hughes found him living alone in a small Dublin flat. The place, Hughes noted, was quite run-down. This was a man who had spent his whole adult life in the IRA. It occurred to Hughes, when he beheld the meager circumstances in which Twomey would spend his final years, that there wasn't much of a pension plan for the movement. When Twomey died, a few years later, Hughes drove his coffin from Dublin back to Belfast. Apart from Twomey's wife, there was nobody to greet the coffin when it got there.

.   .   .

A few days after New Year's in 1989, Dolours Price and Stephen Rea had a baby, a little boy named Fintan Daniel Sugar ("to be known as 'Danny,'" the birth announcement said). Just over a year later, they had a second son, Oscar, who was named after Oscar Wilde. "The poor fella looks like me (I think) but he may grow out of that," Price noted in a letter to a friend, adding, "Know any babysitters?" She was besotted with her children, "cracked about them," Rea said. Seamus Heaney composed an original poem for the boys. He wrote it on a Japanese fan, which the couple hung on the wall in their home. (It has never been published.) In prison, Price had feared that she might never have a child, but now here she was, getting a chance at something like a normal life. The family lived in London but continued to keep a home in Belfast. "I want them to have an Irish childhood, to grow up with Irish accents," Stephen Rea said of his sons. "I'd find it kind of phony to bring up two English kids."

Price was still working on her autobiography and talking, periodically, with various publishers. But, as Rea explained in one interview, "It's never the right time to publish." Price had retreated from politics. Yet her husband maintained an unusual connection to her old commanding officer, Gerry Adams. When he emerged as a presence on the international scene, Adams had become a hate figure in England. With his unnerving calm and his baritone erudition, he was a deeply polarizing and palpably dangerous figure: a righteous, charismatic, eloquent apologist for terrorism. Fearful, perhaps, of his powers of ideological seduction, the Thatcher government imposed a peculiar restriction, "banning" the IRA and Sinn Féin from the airwaves. What this meant in practice was that when Adams appeared on television, British broadcasters were prevented, by law, from transmitting the sound of his voice. His image could be shown, and the content of his speech could be conveyed, but his *voice* could not be heard. So broadcasters devised a work-around that was practical, if also slightly ridiculous: when Adams appeared on television, an actor would dub his voice. The face was recognizably Adams, and the words were his words, but the voice saying them would belong to somebody else.

A handful of Irish actors provided voice-overs for the Sinn Féin president; Adams was in the press with sufficient frequency that there was plenty of work to go round. One of the actors was Stephen Rea. "There was nothing to stop us employing the best actor we could find," one news producer said in 1990 when asked about Rea, adding, "We're not interested in who he's married to. Anyway, I think he's Protestant." For his part, Rea explained the decision to serve as a surrogate for Adams not as an expression of any particular ideological affinity, but as a reaction against censorship. Whatever people thought of Adams, they should at least hear what the man had to say, Rea argued: "The problems will never be solved unless we are allowed to know what all the elements are."

As Rea's acting career continued to flourish, he still balked at questions about Price or her past. But he did not shy away, in his work, from the subject of the Troubles. In 1992, Rea achieved a new level of international renown when he starred in the film *The Crying Game,* directed by a close collaborator of his, Neil Jordan. Rea's character in the film is an IRA gunman, Fergus, who is given the task of guarding a doomed prisoner—a British soldier, played by Forest Whitaker. Over several days, the guard and his captive develop a relationship, to the point that, when the time comes for Fergus to pull the trigger, he finds himself unable to do so. The scenario eerily evoked the dirty work that Dolours Price had done for the Unknowns two decades earlier: crying behind the wheel as she chaperoned her friend Joe Lynskey to his death; taking Kevin McKee to County Monaghan, where his captors grew so fond of him that they refused to shoot him and another team of gunmen had to be summoned from Belfast to do it.

One of the characters in the film, played by Miranda Richardson, is a redheaded IRA woman. "I spent a few days in Belfast soaking up the atmosphere," Richardson said, years later, when she was asked about the part. "Stephen introduced me to his wife, Dolours Price, who had been a member of the Provisional IRA and a hunger striker, and who was a real heroine there. We went out to a pub, which was an extraordinary experience. She was treated like a film star."

Rea insisted that the part of Fergus was not in any way based on his spouse. But he did allow that Price might have influenced his interpretation. "The only thing I can say is that I wouldn't regard anyone involved in that conflict as essentially evil, which is what we're told to believe," he said. "There may have been some empathy with Dolours's situation, but...it never consciously crossed my mind." Discussing the themes of the film, Rea added, in a line that could be the Price family credo, "Redemption through suffering. That's my fave."

On the subject of his own ideology, Rea was elusive. "You mustn't assume that my politics are the same as my wife's, and you mustn't assume that her politics are the same as they were twenty years ago," he told *The Times* of London in 1993. This was a canned answer, rehearsed for the publicity tour, and for the most part Rea stuck to it. But occasionally he would slip. After repeating the same evasive sentiment in an interview with *Entertainment Weekly,* he added, "I don't feel ashamed of my wife's political background, and I don't think she should either. I feel that the people who administered the North of Ireland for the last twenty years should be ashamed." Realizing that he had strayed off script, he added, tartly, "There you are. That's a political statement."

In December 1992, Rea and Price traveled with the children to New York, to stay for a couple of months while Rea performed in a play on Broadway. The city agreed with Price. In another life, she might have just been a theater person. With her quick tongue, flaming red hair, and peacock personality, she might have fit in as another eccentric bohemian. "She would have been ideally suited to be someone's crazy aunt who moved to New York and was in the theater and flounced around with scarves," one of her friends remarked. "That's who she would've been had it not been for the Troubles."

In *The Crying Game,* Fergus ends up walking away from the armed struggle. To Rea, it was a story about someone "remaking" himself, "going through some appalling experience yet coming out better, enriched." There were ordinary, decent people who became involved in the republican movement only to see the conflict spiral into something that they could no longer control. For some of these people, Rea pointed out, a moment arrived when they found themselves saying, "I've had enough."

.   .   .

In August 1994, the IRA declared a cease-fire. It appeared that the secret negotiations brokered by Father Alec Reid had borne fruit. Dolours Price and other republicans were summoned to a social club in West Belfast to be told about the decision. Three representatives sat behind a table and summarized the plan. The cease-fire was presented as a positive move—not a victory, certainly, but not a defeat, either. Some people struggled to understand why the IRA would lay down its weapons without any sort of promise from the British that they would withdraw from Ireland in exchange. There was talk about the enormous number of people who had died. Price raised her hand and asked, "Are we being told that with hindsight we should never have undertaken an armed struggle?"

There had always been a certain absolutism about the hard edge of Irish republicanism. "Whatever soul searchings there may be among Irish political parties now or hereafter, we go in the calm certitude of having done the clear, clean, sheer thing," Patrick Pearse, the doomed hero of the Easter Rising, once declared. "We have the strength and the peace of mind of those who never compromise." But the nature of a cease-fire and a peace process is precisely negotiation, soul searching, and compromise. Much blood had been spilled over a quarter of a century in the name of a stark and absolute ambition: *Brits out.* Yet that ambition had not been realized. This left some members of the movement feeling confused. The leadership assured past and current foot soldiers that they had not *given up* their weapons, that the cease-fire was a tactical move, that it could be undone at any time. But this felt like a sop, a line concocted to placate the troops, in order to avoid another split in the ranks like the one that had divided the Provisionals from the Officials back in 1969. The one major concession that the IRA received in the cease-fire negotiations was a greater acceptance, by the

British, of Sinn Féin. As one former IRA volunteer remarked, "In return for ending the armed insurrection, Sinn Féin was given an opportunity to present itself as a conventional political party and, perhaps more important, as a party that could help deliver an end to the long years of conflict in Northern Ireland."

One day the following summer, a press conference was held in central Belfast at the Linen Hall Library, which occupies a handsome old building on Donegall Square. A new organization had been formed to address the fate of the "disappeared"—people who had been abducted and murdered during the Troubles and whose bodies had never been found. Participants mingled, wearing sky-blue ribbons on their lapels. Jean McConville's daughter Helen was one of the speakers. "Four women and eight men came into our home in 1972 and took my mother away," she said. "We never saw her again, and I now say, to those women in particular, how can they look at their own children and not feel guilt about what they did to my mother?"

Helen was thirty-seven—nearly the same age Jean had been when she disappeared. She had a stable marriage to Seamus McKendry, and children of her own. But the McConvilles had never managed to function as a normal family after their mother's abduction. At one point, an opportunity had emerged for Helen to relocate with Seamus and the children to Australia. But she felt that she could not go, because, as Seamus explained, "she always had this wee thing that her mother might come back."

If childhood had been difficult for the McConville children, adulthood had not been much easier. Some had struggled to find work. Several grappled with drug and alcohol addiction. Jim McConville, who, along with his twin brother, Billy, was the youngest of the siblings, had been detained in a young offenders' center in the 1980s and had served a prison sentence in England for armed robbery. Michael was, in many respects, one of the most stable of the children. After leaving Lisnevin, the high-security group home, at sixteen, he had lived with Archie for a while, and then with Helen. But Michael and Helen had clashed, and for a time Michael ended up living on the street. He would stay with friends—a night here, a night there. But eventually he found work. At a dance one evening when he was seventeen, he met a girl named Angela. They became a couple and eventually got married. Michael held various jobs. For a time, he worked at the DeLorean plant in Belfast, where an assembly line produced futuristic cars with gull-wing doors.

In 1992, Jean McConville's oldest child, Anne, who had been ill all her life, died at the age of thirty-nine. Helen peered into the coffin at her older sister and was struck by how much she resembled Jean. She pledged to do what she could to find out what had happened to her mother. Seamus started to ask around Belfast. Once, he ventured into a bar on the Falls Road that was known as an IRA hangout. But when he mentioned the name of his mother-in-law, the place went quiet. An old fellow slipped McKendry a bookie's docket and asked him to go next door to make a bet. On the docket, the man had written: *Get away.*

There were other families in the area with loved ones who had disappeared. One was a formidable woman named Margaret McKinney, whose son Brian had been abducted in 1978. "I'm away Mammy," he had told her, before climbing into his sister's car and driving off. He was twenty-two. She never saw him again. Over the years, there were rumors that Brian had emigrated to England or to Mexico. McKinney was left with a nagging uncertainty, a dull, ever-present pain that she likened to a toothache. Eventually she rallied a group of families who were haunted by their own disappearances. After years of frightened silence, there was relief, if not catharsis, in being able to speak openly with others about the enduring trauma of this kind of loss. The families had mostly given up any hope of their relatives returning alive, but they still wanted to recover their bodies. "I could accept now that Brian was dead," McKinney said. "I could not accept not having a grave to go to." For years, she had refused to change the linens on her son's childhood bed. "I used to just get into his bed and wrap his clothes around me to see if I could just dream. Sleep and dream that I could see him," she recalled. But she would wake each time to find that he was still gone.

When the families of the disappeared found one another, they discovered that they had been plagued by the same set of persistent, chilling questions: When had their loved one been killed? Had he suffered before he died? Was she tortured? Was he dead before they put him in the hole? Occasionally, people came forward with information. Father Alec Reid would hear things sometimes and pass along the odd tip. At one point, a rumor went around that some of the bodies had been buried on the Black Mountain, overlooking the city. But a search turned up nothing. After the cease-fire, the families felt secure enough, finally, to go public. In hopes of raising awareness, they wore the blue ribbons, as a symbol of remembrance for the disappeared, and sent ribbons to prominent figures like Bill Clinton and Nelson Mandela.

When the McConvilles and other families finally aired these revelations, the press responded with shock that a tactic more familiar from grisly civil conflicts in places like Chile or Argentina might have been employed against British citizens. This was a parallel that the families were only too happy to highlight: the group that they established was inspired by the mothers of the disappeared who gathered at the Plaza de Mayo, in Buenos Aires. Fewer than twenty people disappeared during the Troubles. Because the country is so small, however, the impact of each disappearance reverberated throughout the society. There was Columba McVeigh, a teenager who was abducted by the IRA in 1975 and never seen again. There was Robert Nairac, a dashing British Army officer who was working undercover when he disappeared in south Armagh in 1977. There was Seamus Ruddy, a thirty-two-year-old Newry man who was working as a teacher in Paris when he vanished in 1985.

That this push by the families for answers would coincide with the peace process and the IRA cease-fire could only have been embarrassing for Gerry Adams. Just as he was positioning himself as a visionary who could see beyond the horizon of the conflict, the families of the disappeared were directing a series of loud and increasingly indignant queries at him by name. "We have a simple message for Gerry Adams and the IRA: our families have suffered far too much. Please bring this nightmare to an end," Seamus McKendry said in 1995. He continued, pointedly, "We feel it is hypocritical for Sinn Féin to expect the status of a full democratic party while this issue remains unresolved."

McKendry had visited the Sinn Féin leadership and asked them to conduct some kind of internal investigation to determine what had happened to Jean. One day, he bumped into Adams at the supermarket and confronted him, blurting, "Gerry, are you trying to make an idiot of my wife?" At the end of the summer in 1995, Adams issued a carefully worded statement, pledging to help locate the bodies. "I call upon anyone who has any information about the whereabouts of these missing people to contact the families," he said.

· · ·

book three

A RECKONING

A SECRET ARCHIVE

ONE COLD NOVEMBER DAY in 1995, Bill Clinton went to Derry to deliver a speech. Since assuming office three years earlier, he had taken an interest in the peace process in Northern Ireland. He had granted a visa to Gerry Adams to visit the United States, a crucial step in ending the isolation of Sinn Féin and legitimating Adams as an acceptable interlocutor. He had also met with John Hume in Washington on several occasions. In Derry, it was Hume who introduced Clinton, describing how the American president had a dream, "that we will have a land in the next century where for the first time in our history there will be no killing in our streets, and no emigration of our young people to other lands."

Clinton took to the podium outside the Guildhall, beneath a display of winking Christmas lights. Bundled in a dark overcoat, he looked young, robust, and optimistic. People were everywhere, clotting the narrow streets of Derry, teeming beneath the arches of the ancient city walls. "This city is a very different place from what a visitor like me would have seen just a year and a half ago, before the cease-fire," Clinton said. "The soldiers are off the streets. The city walls are open to civilians." He spoke of "the handshake of reconciliation" and quoted a passage from a poem by Heaney:

History says, Don't hope
On this side of the grave

But then, once in a lifetime
The longed-for tidal wave
Of justice can rise up
And hope and history rhyme.

The chilly air was charged with a buoyant sense of possibility. The cease-fire would eventually end, in 1996, when the IRA detonated a bomb in London's Docklands, injuring more than one hundred people. The group issued a statement blaming the British government's refusal to negotiate with Sinn Féin until the IRA had decommissioned its weapons. There was some speculation in the press that Adams might not have known about the bombing in advance—that in his dedication to the peace process, he may have grown alienated from the IRA's armed wing. But a second cease-fire was initiated in 1997, and this one held. For a week in April 1998, negotiators holed up in a drab office complex on the grounds of Stormont Castle, outside Belfast, and hashed out the details of a peace agreement. The new British prime minister, Tony Blair, personally attended the negotiations, subsisting on sandwiches and Mars bars and leaving the building only once in three days. The chief negotiator was an American, former Maine senator George Mitchell. He was a quiet man, with great patience. But he likened his own commitment to forging a peace agreement to the uncompromising orthodoxy of a terrorist; he had what one observer described as "the tenacity of a fanatic."

The various representatives bluffed and quarreled over dry bureaucratic questions regarding the structure of a new national assembly in Northern Ireland, the decommissioning of paramilitary weapons, the status of prisoners, and future relations between the six counties in the North and the governments of Ireland and Britain. Outside, as flurries of sleet battered the building, Protestant and Catholic schoolchildren gathered at the gates, singing songs and asking for peace. Gerry Adams came out and brought them a tray of drinks.

Eventually, on Good Friday, the parties emerged and announced that they had arrived at a pact to which all sides could agree—a mechanism to end the three-decade conflict. Northern Ireland would remain part of the United Kingdom, but with its own devolved assembly and close links to the Republic of Ireland. The agreement acknowledged that the majority of people on the island wanted a united Ireland—but also that a majority of people in the six counties favored remaining part of the United Kingdom. The key principle was "consent": if, at some juncture, a majority of people in the North wanted to unite with Ireland, then the governments of the U.K. and Ireland would have a "binding obligation" to honor that choice. But until that time, Northern Ireland would remain part of the U.K., and Sinn Féin agreed to set aside its principle of abstention and allow its representatives to serve in the newly created assembly.

"We'll deliver the end of British rule in our country, and until we do, the struggle will continue," Adams said in a speech at the grave of Wolfe Tone, a few months after the agreement. Adams had played an instrumental role in securing the deal, and the very ambiguity that he had cultivated around his own persona may have been what made it possible for the various negotiators to deal with him. Even after the agreement, Bill Clinton would wonder about Adams. "I don't know what the real deal is between him and the IRA," Clinton mused to Tony Blair on a telephone call in 1999. But the fiction that Adams had never been a paramilitary created a political space in which interlocutors who might not want to be seen negotiating with terrorists could bring themselves to negotiate with him.

In his speech, Adams couldn't exactly declare victory. But he was upbeat, saying, "The Good Friday Agreement marks the conclusion of one phase and the beginning of a new phase of struggle." He wanted to see "a new Ireland," he said. "An Ireland in which the guns are silent. Permanently. An Ireland in which all of the people of this island are at peace with each other and with our neighbors in Britain. An Ireland united by a process of healing and national reconciliation."

.   .   .

Two years later, across an ocean, Paul Bew was enjoying a stint as a visiting scholar at Boston College. Bew, who was normally based at Queen's University, was a professor of Irish history. He had also served as an adviser to David Trimble, the leader of the Ulster Unionist Party, who had played a major role in the Good Friday negotiations and was now serving as first minister for Northern Ireland. Boston College had a dignified legacy as a bastion of scholarship on Irish history and literature. In the spring of 2000, the college administration was looking for a way to mark the end of the three-decade conflict in Northern Ireland, and Bew mentioned to Bob O'Neill, the head of the John J. Burns Library, that the college might consider some way of documenting the Troubles. Perhaps, Bew suggested, the college could gather some sort of testimony from people who had participated in the Troubles, in order to create a historical record of the conflict. "This will be for graduate students a generation from now," Bew said. O'Neill liked the idea. But the new project would need a director. Bew proposed a longtime Belfast journalist named Ed Moloney, who had been a respected reporter and editor at *The Irish Times* and the *Sunday Tribune*.

Moloney was a bold choice, a sharp-minded, sharp-elbowed chronicler of the Troubles. He had been a student at Queen's during the 1960s and had witnessed, firsthand, the emergence of the civil rights movement and the dawn of the Troubles. He took part in demonstrations himself and got to know Dolours Price, Eamonn McCann, Bernadette Devlin, and other radicals of the day. As a newspaperman, Moloney covered the conflict with painstaking attention, breaking important stories at a frantic clip. Physically, he was unprepossessing: as an infant, he had contracted polio, so all his life he had walked stiffly, with metal braces on his legs. But he was known for his fearlessness and his unwillingness to back down from a fight. His disability had endowed him with a lifelong sympathy for the underdog. When the hair on his head went gray, his eyebrows remained thick and black, which gave him the appearance of a tenacious badger. Once, in 1999, the government used a court order to try to force Moloney to turn over his interview notes from a meeting with a loyalist paramilitary. He refused, risking prison. Then he took the government to court, and won.

Moloney had written a critical biography of Ian Paisley and developed extensive sources in both the republican and loyalist communities. There had been a time when he was quite friendly with Gerry Adams. Once, when Adams was on the run, the two men sat up chatting in a hotel room, and, because it was unsafe for anybody to leave, Moloney spent the night sleeping on the floor. As Adams grew more political in the 1980s, Moloney would go and see him every few months at the Sinn Féin offices on the Falls Road. Adams would make a pot of tea and the two of them would sit in a back room and talk. But eventually the relationship soured. Moloney had grown convinced that Adams was deliberately misleading the rank and file of the IRA. He suspected that Adams had privately resolved early on to give up the army's weapons in the interests of the peace process but that he and the people around him had kept this closely guarded secret from the rest of the organization. Moloney had begun work on a new book, *A Secret History of the IRA,* which would draw on his decades of reporting to tell the story of this process. But as he broke stories that conflicted with the Sinn Féin party line, he encountered hostility. Martin McGuinness nicknamed him "Ed Baloney." One night, someone slashed his tires. In 2001, Moloney left Belfast and moved to the Bronx, to be closer to his wife's family but also because he was beginning to feel some discomfort in Northern Ireland. Besides, he figured, he had spent his career covering the Troubles, the biggest story in Europe at the time. And now the story was over.

Moloney took Bew's general notion of documenting the Troubles and proposed something more specific: Boston College should conduct an oral history, in which combatants from the front lines could speak candidly about their experiences. There was a challenge, however. Because of the traditional prohibition on talking about paramilitary activity, the details of many of the key events of the Troubles were shrouded in a fog of reticence. The peace process might have normalized Sinn Féin as a political party, but the IRA remained an illegal organization. Just admitting to having been a member could result in criminal prosecution. And if the paramilitaries feared the authorities, they were even more afraid of one another. Anyone who violated the credo of silence could be branded a "tout," as informers were known. And touts got killed. Militants tend to be clannish, and deeply suspicious of outsiders. But perhaps, Moloney thought, you could figure out a way to interview people now, with a promise that their testimony would not be released until after they were dead. That way, you could reach the players who were at the cutting edge of the conflict while they were still alive and their memories were fresh, but then assure them that their confidentiality would be protected, because the archive would be sealed up, like a time capsule, until they were no longer around to be prosecuted by the government or chastised by their peers. Paul Bew was enthusiastic about this idea. He talked about "laying down the tapes" as if they were bottles of old claret.

The academics at Boston College may have been prepared to make assurances that such interviews would be used only for posterity, but why would anyone believe them? In fact, it seemed unlikely that any team of notebook-toting PhD students would get very far at all in persuading hardened gunmen to open up. So Moloney proposed a decidedly unorthodox, but possibly ingenious, solution: if ex-paramilitaries wouldn't spill their secrets to a grad student, perhaps they would talk to another former paramilitary.

.   .   .

One evening in the summer of 2000, Moloney and the librarian from Boston College, Bob O'Neill, went to dinner at Deanes, a sleek, upscale seafood restaurant in central Belfast. Founded by a local chef who had cooked at Claridge's, in London, before returning home in the 1990s, Deanes was a very New Belfast establishment, a snapshot of the kind of cosmopolitan future that peace might bring. The men were there to meet Anthony McIntyre. A hulking man with an unkempt goatee and forearms that were thickly tattooed, McIntyre was known, to everyone, by his nickname, Mackers. He had grown up in South Belfast. At sixteen, he lied about his age and joined the Provos, then served seventeen years in prison for the murder of a loyalist paramilitary. Mackers had never finished high school before he was locked up, but in prison he got sick of reading the Bible and developed an interest in education. He did this in part to appease his mother, who had always been disappointed that he'd abandoned his studies. But it was also a good way to spend the evenings. Mackers grew to cherish those quiet hours late at night when other prisoners went to sleep and he was left to read in solitude.

By the time he was released from prison in 1992, Mackers had obtained an honors undergraduate degree. When he got out, he enrolled in a PhD program at Queen's, where his adviser was Paul Bew. After writing a dissertation about the republican movement, he received his doctorate. But the degree did not provide him with any steady work. When he initially got out of prison, he had been reduced, for a time, to shoplifting. In

2000, he met a young American woman named Carrie Twomey, a freckled brunette with big blue eyes who had recently moved to Belfast. They fell in love, married, and had two children.

Ed Moloney had first met Mackers at a republican funeral in 1993, and the ex-IRA man had subsequently become one of his sources. Mackers spoke the language of both the academy and the street, and Moloney felt that he would be an ideal interviewer for the Boston College project. Bew endorsed the idea of enlisting his former advisee, and was comforted to think that the university might put some money in Mackers's pocket. In 2001, Boston College received a grant of $200,000 from a wealthy Irish American businessman who was willing to support the initiative. The plan was to interview former paramilitaries from both the republican and loyalist sides. (Originally, Moloney had wanted to include testimony from members of the police force as well, but that idea was eventually abandoned.) For the loyalist interviews, Moloney recruited an East Belfast man named Wilson McArthur, who had strong connections in loyalist circles and had also obtained a degree from Queen's. Before they finished dinner at Deanes, Moloney, O'Neill, and Mackers agreed that, because of the great sensitivity of the subject matter, it was of paramount importance that this whole undertaking remain secret.

.   .   .

The Belfast Project, as it became known, seemed to address an obvious shortcoming in the Good Friday Agreement. In their effort to bring about peace, the negotiators had focused on the future rather than the past. The accord provided for the release of paramilitary prisoners, many of whom had committed atrocious acts of violence. But there was no provision for the creation of any sort of truth-and-reconciliation mechanism that might allow the people of Northern Ireland to address the sometimes murky and often painful history of what had befallen their country over the previous three decades. After apartheid ended in South Africa, there had been such a process, in which people came forward and told their stories. The explicit understanding in that case was that there was an exchange: if you told the truth, then you could receive legal immunity. The South African model had flaws: critics claimed that the accounting was incomplete, and often political. But at least there was some effort at an accounting.

Part of the reason that such a process may have been feasible in South Africa was that in the aftermath of apartheid, there was an obvious winner. The Troubles, by contrast, concluded in a stalemate. The Good Friday Agreement envisioned a "power sharing" arrangement. But there was a sense in which neither side had really emerged triumphant. There were some cosmetic changes: the RUC was rebranded the Police Service of Northern Ireland; the structural discrimination that the civil rights protests sought to challenge had mostly gone away. Northern Ireland had always been devoted to the theater of historical commemoration. But there was no formal process for attempting to figure out how to commemorate, or even to understand, the Troubles.

This queasy sense of irresolution was only complicated by Gerry Adams's refusal to acknowledge that he was ever in the IRA. If people in Northern Ireland were wondering whether it was safe, yet, to come clean about their own roles in the conflict, the continued denials by Adams would suggest that it most definitely wasn't. "O land of password, handgrip, wink and nod," Seamus Heaney wrote in a poem about the Troubles called "Whatever You Say, Say Nothing." There was a sense that, even as people greeted the new day with great enthusiasm, the sulfurous intrigue of the past would continue to linger.

In 2001, Martin McGuinness broke the IRA's code of silence when he acknowledged that he had been a member of the Provos, serving as the second-in-command in Derry during the early 1970s. But McGuinness did so in the context of an inquiry into the events of Bloody Sunday—a circumstance in which he would receive immunity from prosecution. As a political party, Sinn Féin was now on the ascendant, more powerful than ever. The IRA had ostensibly been sidelined by the peace process, going so far as to agree to decommission its weapons. But it could seem, even so, that, having cast so profound a shadow over Irish life for such a long time, the paramilitary army was unlikely to simply fade away. Once, in the summer of 1995, Adams gave a speech at a rally in Belfast. He looked like a politician, in a crisp summer suit, consulting his cue cards. But during a pause in his prepared remarks, someone in the crowd shouted, "Bring back the IRA!"

As the audience cheered, Adams chuckled and smiled. Then he leaned into the microphone and said, "They haven't gone away, you know."

.   .   .

To the small cohort who knew about the Belfast Project, the penumbra of silence and innuendo that still hung over Northern Ireland only added urgency to the need to establish a space in which people could talk candidly about their experiences. Tom Hachey, a professor of Irish studies at Boston College who became involved in the project, said that the ambition of the archive was not traditional scholarship, but an effort to create a corpus of material that future generations could ponder; a study, as he rather grandly put it, of "the phenomenology of sectarian violence."

But in order for such an endeavor to be carried out, conditions of absolute secrecy would have to prevail. People who agreed to tell their own stories would be provided with a contract stipulating that their testimony would not be publicly released without their consent until after they died. It wasn't just the interviews themselves that would remain under wraps: the very *existence* of the project was sub-rosa. The participants would be describing crimes in which they had participated. If the authorities knew that such confessions existed, they might make an effort to seize them. This was part of what made Boston College so attractive as a repository for the oral history, Ed Moloney believed: on the other side of the Atlantic Ocean, it stood at a great remove, both physically and legally, from the police in Britain and Ireland. The United States was neutral ground. Even if the authorities did somehow learn about the existence of the project, the protections of the First Amendment—and the institutional clout of Boston College—would render any effort to obtain the interviews a nonstarter.

In the spring of 2001, Mackers started conducting interviews. He had many friends in republican circles. But even so, he needed to be careful. For a clandestine outfit, the IRA was notoriously prone to gossip. In truth, it wasn't that nobody talked. *Everybody* talked. They just tended to do so only among themselves. The author of some notorious crime might be widely known in West Belfast, but breathe a word to an outsider about it—to a journalist, or to the Brits—and you were a tout. Interviewers from Boston College were outsiders, whatever their previous bona fides. If word got out that ex-gunmen were unburdening themselves to anyone in possession of a tape recorder, people were liable to get killed.

Mackers was also an outsider in another critical respect. Like many Provo foot soldiers, he was disillusioned by the Good Friday Agreement. Patrick Pearse once wrote that "the man who in the name of Ireland accepts as a 'final settlement' anything less by one iota than separation from England is guilty of so immense an infidelity, so immense a crime against the Irish nation...that it were better that he had not been born." This kind of absolutism formed the marrow of republican mythology:

the notion that any acceptance of incremental change was tantamount to betrayal. In Mackers's view, Sinn Féin had settled for too little when it acceded to a scenario in which British dominion over Ireland would continue. Adams, Mackers believed, had sold out the armed struggle.

The Sinn Féin leadership was well aware of this strain of opinion and had taken to discrediting critics like Mackers as "dissident" republicans or "opponents of the peace process." The IRA had always excelled at internal discipline and, as an emerging political party, Sinn Féin was heavily invested in preserving a particular narrative about the Troubles and the peace process. No Sinn Féin official ever seemed to be off message. In this manner, the party maintained what one scholar described as a "monopoly over the memory of republican armed struggle."

Given Mackers's position as a Sinn Féin critic, what this meant in practice was that neither Gerry Adams nor anyone aligned with him was likely to agree to sit down and record an oral history. In fact, Mackers was reluctant even to *ask* them, because if the leadership had any inkling of the project's existence, they would almost certainly shut it down, putting the word out that anyone who participated would be punished.

So for the next several years, Mackers sought out republicans who, for one reason or another, were no longer close to Adams. As he did so, he was at pains to avoid detection. He used encrypted email to communicate with Moloney and tried to minimize any paper trail associated with the project. He would tuck a digital MiniDisc recorder into his backpack and venture out into Belfast and beyond, conducting interviews. He met with his subjects multiple times, spending ten hours or more with each person, spread out over several sittings. When his interviews with a particular individual were complete, Mackers would have them transcribed by a trusted typist. Then he would mail both the recordings and the transcripts to Boston College, where Bob O'Neill would store them in the most secure part of the Burns Library, the Treasure Room. O'Neill was an expert on "archival security." He had published a book on the subject. "To be responsible custodians of the treasures that have been entrusted to their care, all librarians and archivists must look hard and carefully at security," he maintained.

As an added precaution, when Mackers mailed the interview materials to Boston College, he would withhold the name of the individual who was supplying the oral history and substitute a letter of the alphabet. It was only in a separate set of documents—the contracts that each individual signed, in which they were assured that their testimony would be kept confidential—that the alphabetical code name for each participant was linked to an actual name.

One day, Mackers went out to see a former IRA man he had known for years, having first met him in prison in 1974. The two of them were close, so these interviews would have an easygoing, intimate quality. Like Mackers, the man had found himself deeply disillusioned with the peace process, and had cut ties with Gerry Adams and Sinn Féin. Now he had a story to tell. In the materials that Mackers would eventually mail to Boston College, the man was identified only by his code name, "C." His real name was Brendan Hughes.

ON THE LEDGE

BY THE TIME ANTHONY McINTYRE started interviewing him in 2001, Brendan Hughes was living in what was left of Divis Flats. In 1993, the apartment block from which Jean McConville had once been abducted was demolished, along with all the other low-rise blocks, after an outcry from activists about the appalling conditions in the complex. During the 1980s, a so-called demolition committee had formed—a group of agitators whose mission was to make the place uninhabitable. Each time an apartment was vacated, these self-appointed wrecking crews would swoop in with sledgehammers, before another family could move in, and tear out baths, sinks, toilets, and electrical fittings, shattering windows and ripping good doors off their hinges. Eventually the government bulldozed the whole place, making way for a new development full of tidy redbrick houses fronted by tiny cement gardens. All that remained of Divis Flats was the twenty-story tower. The British Army continued to occupy the roof and the top two floors. Below them, on the tenth floor, lived Brendan Hughes.

It was a fitting residence for Hughes, high above the streets of West Belfast, where he was considered a war hero. Even after the bombings had stopped and the Good Friday Agreement brought peace to Northern Ireland, the walls of Belfast still jostled with colorful murals depicting heroes of the armed struggle, and among them was the grinning, dark-eyed visage of a young Brendan Hughes. But in recent years, Hughes's mood had turned increasingly bleak. "Welcome to my cell," he would tell visitors when they came to see him. There were times when he wouldn't leave the flat for days, preferring to stay inside, drinking and smoking in solitude. He was in his fifties now, the famous dark hair gone gray and thinning. He was living on a disability benefit. He had worked various menial jobs on building sites, but, apart from his youthful stint in the merchant marine, he had never held a real civilian job, and he struggled to find steady employment. "You never really leave prison," he would say.

The apartment was decorated with multiple photographs of Hughes's hero, Che Guevara: pictures of Che laughing, smoking, drinking coffee. Hughes felt warmly toward these iconic images, yet they also functioned as a taunt. Che had what you might argue was the good fortune of being martyred when he was still young. He was not yet forty when he was executed by the Bolivian army, in 1967, his skin still smooth, his beard untinged by gray. But Hughes was also stuck with the feeling that, whereas Che's revolution in Cuba had succeeded, the revolution that Hughes and Gerry Adams had undertaken in Northern Ireland had failed.

To Hughes, Good Friday had symbolized the ultimate concession: formal acceptance by the republican movement that the British would remain in Ireland. Hughes had killed people. He had done so with the conviction that he was fighting for a united Ireland. But it now became clear to him that the leadership of the movement may have been prepared to settle for less than absolute victory and had elected—deliberately, in his view—not to inform soldiers like him. For Hughes, this strategic sleight of hand was deeply personal: he placed the blame directly on his dearest comrade, Gerry Adams. A framed photograph hung on one wall in his flat, alongside the tributes to Che. It was an old snapshot, taken at Long Kesh during the 1970s, of Hughes and Adams with their arms around each other. Adams wore a big splayed collar and shaggy locks that hung around his shoulders;

Hughes in his flat in Divis Tower.

Hughes wore a tight white T-shirt that said MELBOURNE IRISH CLUB. Both of them were grinning, against a backdrop of barbed wire. Hughes no longer had any love for Adams, but he kept the picture on the wall, to remind him of the way things had once been. For decades he had shared an intimate bond with Adams, but it was never a relationship of equals. Lately he had taken to joking, darkly, that, like the weapons of the IRA, he had been used and then discarded—"decommissioned."

Hughes was increasingly anxious. The man who had engineered Bloody Friday now avoided crowded areas of central Belfast. He liked Divis Tower because he found comfort in its architecture of parameters: like a prison cell, it was an insular space that he could control. He found a measure of temporary relief in alcohol. His doctor told him to stop drinking, but he couldn't.

Mackers still remembered when he first got to know Hughes. At the time, Mackers was only sixteen. Hughes came into Long Kesh as a famous figure. He was a decade older than Mackers, but he took a liking to the younger man, and the two became close friends. In conducting his interviews, Mackers had found that, for former paramilitaries, the experience of speaking after decades of silence could often be profoundly cathartic. It was sometimes hard to get his subjects to start talking. But once they started, it was often difficult to get them to stop. Years of war stories and terrifying experiences and hysterical jokes and private grievances came tumbling out. Mackers was a sympathetic listener, murmuring encouragement, rewarding humor with sincere and raucous laughter, and volunteering the occasional personal anecdote of his own. He would punctuate his questions by saying, "Could you fill out for the future students of Boston some detail on that for me?"

Just as Ed Moloney had predicted, the fact that Mackers knew so many of the players—had lived alongside them, carried out operations with them, gone to prison with them—endowed him with a particular credibility. Over a series of interviews, Hughes and Mackers would sit in the flat, smoking and talking. At one point Hughes joked that he wanted Boston College to pay for his cigarettes for the rest of his life. Then, when he got cancer, he would turn around and sue the university. They spoke about Hughes's childhood, about how his father coped after his mother died, about his travels with the merchant marine, his awakening as a socialist, the hundreds of operations he had masterminded, and the long years in prison. They spoke about Bloody Friday. "There was no intention to kill people that day," Hughes insisted, adding, "I have a great deal of regret about that."

But above all, Hughes talked about Gerry Adams. Mackers had overlapped with Adams at Long Kesh, and he understood the close bond that Adams and Hughes had enjoyed. But now Hughes was filled with anger toward his erstwhile compatriot. Hughes hated the Good Friday Agreement. He joked that GFA, the acronym by which the accord had become known, actually stood for Got Fuck All. "What the fuck was it for?" he would ask. The lives he had taken, the young volunteers he had sent to die: his understanding of those sacrifices had always been that they would ultimately be justified by the emergence of a united Ireland. Instead, Adams had become a well-heeled statesman, a peacemaker; he had positioned himself for a prominent role in a post-conflict Northern Ireland. To his supporters, Adams was a historic figure, a visionary, a plausible candidate for the Nobel Prize. But it seemed to Hughes that Gerry Adams might have been duped by his own ambition—or, worse, manipulated by the British. In prison, when the Provos conducted educational workshops on strategy, one fundamental lesson was that a central pillar of Britain's approach to counterinsurgency was "to mould leaderships whom they could deal with." Hughes believed that in the aftermath of the peace agreement, Adams might have unwittingly allowed himself to be molded in just this manner.

One burden of command, in any armed conflict, is that the senior officer is obliged to make choices that may get subordinates killed. Hughes was traumatized by the orders he had given to send young volunteers—and innocent civilians—to their deaths. He replayed these events on a loop in his head. On Bloody Friday, he told Mackers, he had been the man on the ground. But it was Adams who was calling the shots. "Gerry was the man who made the decisions," he said.

By denying that he had ever played a role in the conflict, Adams was, in effect, absolving himself of any moral responsibility for catastrophes like Bloody Friday—and, in the process, disowning his onetime subordinates, like Brendan Hughes. "I'm disgusted with the whole thing," Hughes said. "It means that people like myself... have to carry the responsibility of all those deaths." If all of that carnage had at least succeeded in forcing the British out of Ireland, then Hughes might be able to justify, to himself, the actions he had taken. But he felt robbed of any such rationale for absolution. "As everything has turned out," he said, "not one death was worth it."

Even as Hughes contended with these demons, he was struck by the fact that Adams appeared to be completely free of any such painful introspection. He seemed, instead, to glide along from one photo opportunity to the next, like a man who was not in any way shackled by his own past. It maddened Hughes. Of course he was in the IRA! "Everybody knows it," he told Mackers. "The British know it. The people on the street know it. The *dogs* know it on the street. And he's standing there denying it."

. . .

Hughes may have seemed to possess credentials, as a veteran of the armed struggle, that would render him unimpeachable in republican circles. But when he refused to endorse the peace process and drifted apart from Adams, Sinn Féin, with its fetish for conformity, proceeded to shun him. It humiliated Hughes to be living on public benefits and to see others—people "who never fired a shot," people who were "never actually involved in the revolution but hung on to the aprons of dead volunteers"—establishing themselves as power brokers in postwar Belfast. He grumbled that Adams and his cohort seemed to be enjoying a lavish lifestyle that was at odds with their ostensible politics as revolutionary socialists. He called them "the Armani suit brigade."

Hughes worried, also, that the armed struggle was now being sanitized and reified, turned into a bumper sticker. The republican movement had always venerated its martyrs, but it seemed to Hughes as though some of those martyrs, who were still alive and struggling from the aftereffects of their contributions, were now being cast aside, upstaged by their own portraits in graffiti. "Painting murals on walls to commemorate blanket men after they have died a slow and lonely death from alcohol abuse is no use to anyone," he would say. "I would hate for young people now to have this romanticized version of the events of that time." He added, "The truth is so very far removed from that and I suppose I'm living proof."

It had not taken long for word to reach Adams of his old comrade's disloyalty. In 2000, the two men met, and Adams challenged Hughes about why he had chosen to go public with his critique, questioning him about some of the people he had been associating with and saying, as Hughes remembered it, "that I had got myself into bad company and I should get myself out of it." Hughes felt that this overture was an effort to censor him. It only intensified his resentment. At one point, Hughes discovered a listening device in his flat: a small black microphone. There was a time when such a device would almost certainly have been planted by the British military. But now he was convinced that it had been installed there by the IRA.

.   .   .

This sense of disillusionment was a theme in other interviews that Mackers conducted. One of his subjects was Ricky O'Rawe, a compact man in his late forties who had shared a prison cell with Hughes and been a close friend of Bobby Sands's. During the 1981 hunger strike, O'Rawe had served as the lead spokesman for the strikers. When Mackers first approached O'Rawe and told him about the Belfast Project, O'Rawe was reluctant to participate. As it happened, he had been nursing a dark secret for two decades, and he worried that if he spoke about his experiences in the IRA, the secret might slip out. But eventually Mackers persuaded O'Rawe to talk and started coming over to his house in the evenings with his recorder. The initial interviews were anodyne. O'Rawe spoke about his family history, how his father had been an IRA man in the 1940s, how he had grown up singing rebel songs and joined the Provos himself when he was still a teenager. O'Rawe talked about how he was interned on the *Maidstone,* alongside Gerry Adams, and about how he once conducted a "freelance" robbery to score some money for booze. His IRA masters punished him by shooting him in the legs—a penalty that he felt, on balance, was entirely justified. Mackers and O'Rawe were doing an interview when the news broke that two planes had crashed into the World Trade Center, in New York. Both men were horrified. If either of them saw any affinity between the Irish tradition of political violence and the mass murder of Al Qaeda, they did not dwell on it.

"I'm not going to talk about the hunger strike," O'Rawe told Mackers on a number of occasions. And for the first eight interviews, he didn't. But on the night of their final interview, the subject came up and O'Rawe found himself sharing the one story he had promised himself he would hold back.

In the summer of 1981, after Bobby Sands and three other hunger strikers had died, O'Rawe was helping to lead the negotiations from inside the prison. According to O'Rawe, the prisoners received a secret offer from Margaret Thatcher that would have granted almost all of their demands. It wasn't a complete capitulation, but it guaranteed that they would be able to wear their own clothes—one of their chief requirements—as well as other key concessions. O'Rawe and another negotiator smuggled a message to the Provo leadership outside the prison, indicating that they were inclined to accept the British offer and call an end to the strike. But word came back from the outside—specifically, from Gerry Adams—that what Thatcher was proposing was not enough, so the strikers should hold out.

Six more men died before the strike concluded. The public narrative had always maintained that it was the prisoners themselves who insisted on persevering with the strike, and O'Rawe had never spoken out to question this version of history, deferring to what he came to think of as the "carefully scripted myths" that had solidified around these dramatic events. But privately, he felt enormous guilt for not standing up at the time and being more forceful. He wondered why Adams and those around him would have sustained the strike rather than take an offer that the men on the inside had been prepared to accept.

Over years of private rumination, O'Rawe began to develop an awful theory. When Bobby Sands ran for his parliamentary seat, the spectacle of a peaceful protester seeking public office engendered popular support for republicanism on a scale that the IRA had never achieved through violence. After Sands died, on May 5, 1981, as many as a hundred thousand people took to the streets. O'Rawe wasn't privy to the discussions of the Army Council, which made the decision; but he came to believe that Adams had deliberately perpetuated the hunger strike in order to capitalize on the broad-based sympathy and support that it produced. In terms of republican policy, the hunger strike was the moment that "split the atom," O'Rawe concluded. For the first time, Adams saw the potential for change through electoral politics. In prolonging the strike, he recognized an unprecedented opportunity to dramatically expand the support base for the republican movement. It only cost six lives.

Once O'Rawe started telling Mackers the story, he found that he could not stop. He began to cry, choking up at first, then bawling uncontrollably like a child. For twenty years, he had been walking around with the weight of those six dead strikers on his conscience, and after two decades of silence he felt purged, emotionally, to be talking about it. "I don't give a fuck anymore, this is coming out," he told Mackers. "Guys died here for fucking nothing!"

But when he reflected on the notion that Adams might have cynically determined that a steady supply of martyrs was indispensable in launching Sinn Féin as a viable political party, O'Rawe was forced to concede a jarring possibility: were it not for that decision, the war might never have ended. As Ed Moloney subsequently wrote, "The hunger strike made Sinn Féin's successful excursion into electoral politics possible: the subsequent tension between the IRA's armed struggle and Sinn Féin's politics produced the peace process and ultimately the end of the conflict. Had the offer of July 1981 not been undermined, it is possible, even probable, that none of this would have happened. There will be those who will say that the end justified the means, that the achievement of peace was a pearl whose price was worth paying." To O'Rawe it seemed that anyone capable of playing such a long and calculating game and dispatching six men to an unnecessary death must be a genius of political strategy—but also a sociopath.

.   .   .

Brendan Hughes nurtured his own survivor's guilt when it came to the hunger strikes, and he dwelled on it in his interviews with Mackers. Hughes often thought about the initial, abortive strike, which he had called off after the young striker Sean McKenna slipped into a coma. Playing a similar game of if/then counterfactuals, Hughes would consider what might have happened had he just allowed McKenna to die. Could the second strike have been prevented altogether? Could that have saved the lives of ten men? He ran the arithmetic in his head. It could be overwhelming. At one point, long after the strike, Hughes bumped into McKenna in Dundalk. McKenna had brain damage, and his eyesight had been permanently affected by the strike. "Fuck you, Dark," McKenna said to Hughes. "You should have let me die."

There were times when Hughes thought about killing himself. Like McKenna, he bore physical scars from the strike. Eventually, his eyesight would start to go. He took to wearing an eye patch, which gave him the piratical appearance of an outlaw in winter. He would sit in his flat and stare for hours out the window, chain-smoking, gazing at the jagged lines of the city, the schoolyards and church steeples, and, in the distance, the shipworks, where a century earlier the *Titanic* had been built. It seemed to Carrie Twomey, Mackers's wife, that Hughes was stuck there. "I always got the sense that he lived a large part of his life in that windowsill," she recalled. "He couldn't commit to either jump out and end it all or jump back in and start really living."

"I have a clear image now of the prison hospital," Hughes told Mackers at one point. "I can still smell the—there is a smell when you die, there's a *death* smell—and it hung over the hospital the whole period during the hunger strike. And I still have recurring thoughts of that. I can even smell it sometimes, that stale death smell. And for years, I mean, I couldn't have spoke like this a few years ago. I couldn't. I wasn't able to do it. I put it out of my head."

Hughes recalled Dr. Ross, the kind physician who had tended to him during his hunger strike and brought him fresh water gathered from a mountain spring. Bobby Sands had never trusted Ross. He called him a "mind manipulator." But the doctor's kindness had meant a lot to Hughes. Later, he learned that after watching all ten men die in the hunger strike, Dr. Ross had taken his own life, with a shotgun, in 1986.

Hughes acknowledged to Mackers that there was a level of candor he could adopt in these conversations because he knew that the interviews would be sealed until his death. He told Mackers that Gerry Adams had authorized the bombing mission to London in 1973, the mission that ended up putting Dolours Price and her fellow bombers behind bars. "I mean, there's things that you can say and things you can't say," he reflected. "I'm not going to stand up on a platform and say I was involved in the shooting of a soldier or involved in the planning of operations in England. But I'm certainly not going to stand up and *deny* it. And to hear people who I would have died for, and almost did on a few occasions, stand up and deny the part in history that he has played—the part in the war that he has played, the part in the war that he *directed*—and deny it is totally disgusting and a disgrace to all the people who have died."

Hughes remembered Pat McClure, "Wee Pat," and his clandestine squad, the Unknowns, in which Dolours Price had served. McClure ended up disappearing during the 1980s. He had dropped out of active service at some point and gone to work driving a black taxi. Someone asked him if he would go back, to fight the long war. But McClure said no. He was done. Hughes heard that he emigrated to Canada and died there. If it was McClure who had day-to-day command of the Unknowns, Mackers asked, who had ultimate authority for the unit? Who was giving the orders?

"They were always Gerry's squad," Hughes said.

When Mackers asked about the disappearance of Jean McConville, Hughes told him that Gerry Adams had known about and approved the operation. In Hughes's view, the murder had been justified.

"She was an informer," he said.

TOUTS

EVERYONE IS RECRUITABLE. IN *The Informer,* an Irish novel published in 1925, the author Liam O'Flaherty tells the story of Gypo Nolan, a police informer. Gypo identifies a Dublin republican who is wanted for murder. The man is subsequently killed by the police. From the moment Gypo delivers the information to authorities, he is acutely aware that he has become an "outcast" in his close-knit city. He feels paranoid and doomed, terrified of exposure: "the customary sound of a human footstep had, by some evil miracle, become menacing." The tout occupies an outsize place in the Irish imagination, as a folk devil—a paragon of treachery. Gerry Adams once remarked that informants are "reviled in all aspects of society in this island." But the truth is that the English have employed spies and cultivated double agents in Ireland for hundreds of years. Frank Kitson's insights, back at the onset of the Troubles, eventually blossomed from the rudimentary "counter-gangs" of the MRF into an extraordinarily broad and sophisticated effort, by British military and intelligence and by the Royal Ulster Constabulary, to penetrate paramilitary circles.

Trevor Campbell was a burly and imposing Belfast cop who worked for the Special Branch of the RUC. After two years in Derry (which was always and only "Londonderry" to Campbell), he was transferred to Belfast in 1975 and spent the next twenty-seven years embroiled in the conflict. Campbell's specialty was the handling of informants.

"In the beginning, there were no real rules. No law. It was catch as catch can," he recalled. The authorities were not systematic about who they targeted or how they managed their informants. But, gradually, the science on the ground improved. The biggest challenge of running touts in Northern Ireland was the petri-dish dimensions of the place. You couldn't meet a Belfast source in Belfast; the city was just too small. So you would have him travel to the suburbs or to the country. But these were often quite parochial individuals, who had grown up in one pocket of the city and never ventured beyond it. Too many buses and trains and they were liable to get lost. Campbell would take informants out of town for a meeting in a beachside village and they would stand there in awe, as if a single bus transfer had deposited them at the end of the earth. Campbell liked to meet his contacts in the countryside, but not too far into the countryside. In some rural areas, like South Armagh, the locals knew every car. The presence of a single unfamiliar automobile was enough to put the neighbors on alert.

The challenge of finding a safe location in which to meet was often secondary to the challenge of communicating the need for a meeting in the first place. During the early years of the Troubles, many homes in Northern Ireland did not have their own telephones. If they did have a phone, it was generally a shared line, upon which prying neighbors could eavesdrop—not a great solution for communicating with a clandestine informant. In theory, the tout could use a pay phone. But virtually all of the pay phones in wartime Belfast had been destroyed by vandals, and in the event that the tout was lucky enough to find one that functioned, some nosy acquaintance was liable to happen by, spot him in the phone booth, and demand to know who he'd been talking to.

So Campbell devised creative ways to notify his informants when he needed to meet. Initially, he employed crude tricks from the playbook of Cold War espionage, like a chalk mark on a brick wall. But he soon developed other, more innovative techniques. Sometimes Campbell would launch a sudden, clamorous raid on a Belfast house—not the house of his source, but the residence of some unsuspecting civilian who had the misfortune of living across the street. This could be tough for the innocent family whose home was raided, Campbell allowed. But it was an unmistakable way to deliver a message: *We need to meet.*

Belfast is not Berlin—it's not even East Berlin—and playing these types of spy games in such a small, provincial city could give rise to surreal situations. Once, Campbell was interviewing a hardened IRA man at Castlereagh, the fortresslike East Belfast interrogation center, which was notorious as a site of rough questioning and torture. The man had been arrested on other occasions, and Campbell had endeavored, without success, to recruit him. Now, the police could legally hold him for three days before they had to either charge him or let him go, and for three days Campbell sat face-to-face with him in a stale, windowless interrogation room and talked. In such encounters, some IRA prisoners would maintain a stony silence, staring daggers at Campbell and never uttering a word. Others would talk and talk, working *him,* trying to elicit information: Where did he grow up? What rugby club did he support? Did he have a family? Where did they live? Campbell wanted to build rapport with his interrogation subjects, but he knew that any stray detail he let slip might amount to a death sentence. So he endeavored to keep the banter flowing without offering up any hard details about himself. On this occasion, the IRA man was a talker. But he was just as disciplined as Campbell was: he wouldn't reveal anything that Campbell could work with, and he certainly wasn't going to allow himself to be recruited. He was just shooting the shit, with a casual, jocular menace that Campbell could not help but respect. Waiting out the clock. After three days, time was up, and Campbell had no choice but to let him go.

Campbell had not spent any time with his wife in seventy-two hours, and she was grumbling that he never took a night off. So, when the man was released, Campbell went home to clean up and take his wife on a date. They drove to a nice fish restaurant down the coast. It was a bustling spot, popular with tourists, and Campbell and his wife sat at a table with a view of the water and ordered their meals. They had just finished their first course when Campbell glanced up and saw someone standing at the bar. He had his back to Campbell, but there was a large mirror behind the bar, and now, in the reflection above the liquor bottles, the two of them locked eyes. It was the man Campbell had been questioning for the past three days.

"We may not be staying for the main course," Campbell announced to his wife, without taking his eyes off the man. He was generally careful about watching the road when he was driving, and he did not think that they had been followed to the restaurant. Instead, this appeared to be a wild coincidence. But it felt like a dangerous one. Without elaborating to his wife about the delicacy of this predicament, Campbell excused himself, walked over to the bar, and greeted the IRA man with the kind of gruff nonchalance he would normally reserve for someone whom he saw every day.

The man returned the greeting. Then he said, casually, "Is that your wife?"

"It's somebody's wife," Campbell replied.

"Knowing you, it's probably somebody else's wife," the man said with a smirk.

Campbell acknowledged the joke with a thin smile. Then, selecting his words with care, he said, "Are you going to sit at this bar all night? Or are you going to go to the phone and call someone?"

After a carefully attenuated pause, the man murmured, "Go back to the good woman. Enjoy your meal. Then fuck off out of here."

"Who was that?" Campbell's wife asked when he rejoined her.

"Guy I know, workwise," Campbell replied, and left it at that.

.   .   .

Campbell lived by a principle: Everyone is recruitable. Sometimes you just need to find the right button. You could haul the same person in fifteen times and he would not break; then, the sixteenth time, something would happen. Circumstances change. The man suddenly found himself on the outs with his crew. Or he was in a spot and needed money. Informants from the ethnic ghettos that breed Belfast paramilitaries were often unemployed, scraping by on public benefits. If you timed your overture right, you could offer a bailout at the moment when they most desperately needed it.

If there was someone you really wanted to target and his circumstances *didn't* change, you might just change those circumstances for him. "You'd arrange for him to lose his job," Campbell recalled. "Or lose his house." For a man or woman with a family to feed, nothing sharpens the mind like the prospect of homelessness. If the potential recruit relied on a car to get to work, Campbell could arrange for the car to have a problem that would necessitate expensive repairs. "When you know he's down-and-out, that's when you bring him in," Campbell would say.

Money might have been an effective hook with which to ensnare an informant, but it could be dangerous as well. Some informants were what are known as "five-pound touts": little fish, local people who could furnish occasional low-level tips for a minimal gratuity. But when you had someone who was more fully compromised—someone who was delivering valuable intelligence and acting as an agent of the British state—it could be difficult to pay such a person in a manner that would not blow his cover. Most of these people lived in run-down enclaves where nobody had ever had much money. How do you pay someone in that environment hundreds or even thousands of pounds and expect it to go unnoticed? You might concoct a story about a windfall. A banner day at the races. But that works exactly once. What do you say about the next payment?

The best informants worked for the authorities for years, often decades. It was hazardous to pursue such a double existence, in a land where the punishment for touting was a bullet in the head and a lifetime of shame for one's family. It was also lonely. Campbell's informants often came to rely on him emotionally. He may have been exploiting their preparedness to risk death. He may have blackmailed them into cooperating with him in the first place, or blackmailed them into staying an informant when they wanted to quit. But he was also, quite often, the only person who knew their secret. As such, he became doctor, social worker, and priest. The tout's problems became his problems: repairs to the house, Christmas presents for the kids.

Conventional wisdom had it that every handler wants a highly placed source. But Campbell found that the best informants often were "access agents"—not the intelligence target himself, but the man standing right beside him. Recruit the guy who drives Gerry Adams's car and you may get more valuable intelligence than you would if you recruited Adams himself. (Roy McShane, who served as Adams's personal chauffeur during the 1990s, was outed as a British informant in 2008.)

The IRA was hardly oblivious to the dangers of British penetration. When Brendan Hughes and his men first interrogated Seamus Wright and Kevin McKee back in the 1970s, they learned about the "Freds" and the Kitsonian scheme to subvert the republican movement from within. Later that decade, the Provos established a dedicated internal security unit, which could vet new recruits and interrogate suspected touts.

This cadre of inquisitors would become known as the Nutting Squad—because when a traitor confessed, they would "nut" him, or put a bullet in his head.

For decades, the most fearsome spy hunter on the Nutting Squad was Alfredo "Freddie" Scappaticci. A barrel-chested bricklayer with a handlebar mustache, Scappaticci had grown up in South Belfast, in a family of Italian immigrants. His father owned a popular ice cream truck, which bore the family name, and people called Freddie "the Wop" or, more often, simply "Scap." He joined the republican movement at the beginning of the Troubles and was interned at Long Kesh.

Along with a man named John Joe Magee, Scap would interrogate any IRA member who was suspected of possible cooperation with the British. His method seldom varied: he would bring the suspect to a safe house, blindfold him, and sit him in a chair facing the wall. Then Scap would question him for hours, and often days, threatening him, belittling him, and eventually beating and torturing him until he agreed to confess. "Every army attracts psychopaths," Brendan Hughes liked to say. But Scap was a special case. Often, he would promise a suspect that if he only confessed, Scap would spare his life. When the man blubbered out the truth of his transgressions—or lied just to make the torture stop—Scap would record the confession. But whatever he told his hapless victims while he was torturing them, the penalty for betraying the IRA was always death. The signs of Scap's handiwork would suddenly materialize in stretches of wasteland at the edge of town or alongside rutted lanes in the country: corpses, their limbs bound, their flesh singed and battered from torture, their eyes ghoulishly blotted out with scraps of masking tape.

After the bodies surfaced, Scap liked to visit the families of the dead, to play the recorded confession aloud and explain precisely why their loved one had been executed. Occasionally he would tell them, in detail, about the killing. Trevor Campbell knew about Scappaticci. He was all too aware of the fate that awaited those who were summoned by the Nutting Squad. Once, a Provo quartermaster named Frank Hegarty supplied his handlers in British intelligence with the location of a cache of weapons that the IRA had obtained from Libya. Hegarty fled to England, where he went into hiding at an MI5 safe house. He might have survived, had he stayed away for good. But he got homesick and telephoned his mother back in Derry. She told him that Martin McGuinness had been coming round to see her and that he had offered his personal assurance that if Hegarty came back to Derry and explained everything to the IRA, his life would be spared. When Hegarty returned, he was questioned by the Nutting Squad, and his body turned up by the side of a road along the border. (In 2011, McGuinness insisted that he had played "no role whatsoever" in the execution. But in 1988, two years after Hegarty was killed, McGuinness had pointed out in an interview that republican activists knew the repercussions for "going over to the other side." Asked to clarify what those repercussions might be, McGuinness said, "Death, certainly.") When Trevor Campbell was working with his own informants, he would tell them: "Whatever happens, never confess. If you confess, you're dead."

. . .

During his Boston College oral history with Anthony McIntyre, Brendan Hughes declared with conviction that Jean McConville had been executed because she was a tout. According to Hughes, McConville had been discovered to have a "transmitter" in her house—a radio, presumably supplied by the British. McConville, Hughes said, "had her own kids gathering information for her, watching the movements of IRA volunteers around Divis Flats."

Hughes told Mackers that McConville first came to the

attention of the Provos when a local foot soldier encountered one of her children and the boy mentioned that his "mammy" had something in the house. "I sent a unit, a squad, over to the house to check it out," Hughes recalled. There, Hughes said, they discovered the radio. The IRA arrested McConville, Hughes continued, taking her away for interrogation. According to Hughes, she confessed that she had been passing information to the British Army using the radio to communicate. Hughes cautioned Mackers that he himself had not been "on the scene at the time," so his recollections were based on secondhand information from his subordinates. But he said that after the confession, his men confiscated the transmitter and let Jean McConville return to her children, with a warning.

Several weeks later, Hughes said, a second transmitter was discovered in the McConville flat. "I warned her the first time," he recalled, but now, "I knew she was being executed." Even if one were to accept Hughes's account that McConville was an informer, it is difficult to conceive of a scenario in which she could have furnished anything but low-level tidbits. That didn't matter to Hughes and his comrades. However minor the practical impact of the alleged betrayal might have been, to the IRA, a tout was a tout, and the penalty was death.

Hughes insisted that he personally did not know that McConville was going to be secretly buried, "or 'disappeared,' as they call them now." He had always identified as a left-wing freedom fighter, yet here was a tactic that seemed synonymous with tyranny. In Mackers's view, "the disappearance of people is a calling card of the war criminal, whether it's in Chile or Kampuchea." Even in the chaos of 1972, the Provos did not kill and disappear someone lightly, Hughes insisted. As barbaric as it might seem in retrospect to bury a mother of ten in an unmarked grave, the decision to do so was the product of an earnest debate.

As Hughes related the story, one local IRA leader in particular, Ivor Bell, had argued that McConville should not be buried. Bell was a hard-liner, a veteran of the 1950s campaign who had accompanied Gerry Adams to the unsuccessful peace talks in London in the summer of 1972. Less than six months after the London summit, Hughes said, Bell and the Provisional leadership in Belfast argued about what to do with Jean McConville. "If you are going to kill her, put her on the fucking street," Hughes recalled Bell saying. "What's the sense of killing her and burying her if no one knows what she was killed for?" Better to send a lesson to other locals who might consider becoming touts in the future. If you didn't leave the body out, Bell suggested, then the murder would be "pure revenge."

But Bell was overruled, Hughes said—by Gerry Adams.

"Adams rejected this logic?" Mackers asked.

"He rejected it," Hughes said.

"And ordered her to be disappeared?"

"To be buried," Hughes said. There may have been concern, Hughes hypothesized, that because McConville was a woman, and a widowed mother, her murder could damage the reputation of the IRA. Yet the Provos had identified her as an informer, and that necessitated the ultimate sanction. So a decision was made to kill McConville in secret and have her simply disappear. In the hierarchical IRA, Hughes suggested, there was no ambiguity about who it was that ultimately authorized this decision. "There was only one man who gave the order for that woman to be executed," Hughes told Mackers. "That fucking man is now the head of Sinn Féin."

The Nutting Squad did not yet exist in 1972. So, Hughes said, for the sensitive job of transporting Jean McConville across the border, Adams had turned to the secret squad run by Wee Pat McClure. It was the Unknowns who were responsible for escorting McConville to her execution, and one member of the group in particular: Dolours Price.

. . .

As it happened, Price was one of Mackers's closest friends. They had found each other in the aftermath of the Good Friday Agreement and discovered that they both nurtured a deep sense of disaffection. She was living in Dublin, where the family had moved in the mid-1990s. She liked the city, though she hoped that her sons would not lose their Belfast accents. Her marriage to Stephen Rea, which had grown strained in recent years, eventually ended in 2003. Price continued to live in the large family home in Malahide, a prosperous suburb on the coast north of Dublin. There, she surrounded herself with memorabilia from her days of notoriety: framed press clippings, faded photos, and patriotic banners lined the walls. Her relationship with food had never returned to normal. She would invite a guest for tea and lay out a fresh coffee cake, then watch the guest eat but decline to have a slice herself. "I don't particularly enjoy food," she would say.

Price's aspirations for a writing career had not amounted to much. She never did publish her memoir. But for a time, she went back to school, enrolling in a law course at Trinity College, in Dublin. To the young students in the program, Price cut an unusual figure, an older eccentric who wore brightly colored hats and would sit in lectures with her head cocked quizzically to one side. She didn't raise her hand before offering her own interjections, and she took pleasure in amiably heckling the lecturers.

One day, Price entered the women's lavatories to discover a long line of students waiting to use the facilities. The bathroom was undergoing repairs, and several of the stalls lacked doors. "What are ye all waiting for?" Price asked.

"There's no doors on those toilets," one of the women in line explained.

"You'd know you had never been to prison!" Price exclaimed, striding over to one of the doorless cubicles and attending to her business.

Price clung to her acid wit. She could seem, at times, to marinate in it. But there were signs, also, that she was haunted. She felt as though she spent a great deal of time rummaging around her own head, coming up with bits and pieces of her past. She was troubled by her experiences as a young woman—by things she had done to others, and to herself. Many of her old comrades were suffering from PTSD, flashing back to nightmarish encounters from decades earlier, waking with a start in a cold sweat. From time to time, when Price was driving her car with her sons in the back seat, she would glance up at the rearview mirror and, instead of Danny or Oscar, see her dead comrade Joe Lynskey staring back at her. One day, during a lecture at Trinity on political prisoners, Price stood up in a fury and began to rattle off the names of republican hunger strikers, before storming out of the classroom. She never came back.

To Price, the Good Friday Agreement felt like an especially personal double cross. "The settlement betrayed what she had been born into," her friend Eamonn McCann recalled. "It had a more intense and deep-seated effect on Dolours than it did on many other people." She had set bombs and robbed banks and seen friends die and nearly died herself, in the expectation that these violent exertions would finally achieve the national liberation for which generations of her family had fought. "For what Sinn Féin has achieved today, I would not have missed a good breakfast," she said in an interview on Irish radio. "Volunteers didn't only die," she pointed out. "Volunteers had to kill, as well, you know?"

There is a concept in psychology called "moral injury," a notion, distinct from the idea of trauma, that relates to the ways in which ex-soldiers make sense of the socially transgressive things they have done during wartime. Price felt a sharp sense of moral injury: she believed that she had been robbed of any ethical justification for her own conduct. This sense of grievance was exacerbated by the fact that the man who steered republicanism

on a path to peace was her own erstwhile friend and commanding officer, Gerry Adams. Adams had given her orders, orders
that she faithfully obeyed, but now he appeared to be disowning
the armed struggle in general, and Dolours in particular. It filled
her with a terrible fury.

At a republican commemoration in County Mayo in 2001,
she stood up and announced that it was "too much" for her to
listen to people say that they had never been in the IRA. "Gerry
was my commanding officer," she exclaimed. This sort of outspokenness was not welcomed by Sinn Féin, and on more than
one occasion, stern men came to tell Price to quiet down. But if
Sinn Féin had a conspicuous devotion to message control, this
only intensified Price's anger. As the IRA moved toward a peaceful strategy during the 1990s, various armed splinter groups had
formed, some of which were committed to further violence.
Price occasionally attended meetings of these groups, but she
was not a joiner. "What are you going to get out of going back to
war?" she would ask them.

Even so, she could not let go of the past. Her boys, Danny
and Oscar, were not political. Price joked that when she spoke
about the tumultuous events of her youth, it seemed as distant
to them as "the stone age." After a series of sectarian murders
in 1998, Stephen Rea had remarked, "Everyone has become so
used to the state of war that it becomes impossible for them to
imagine anything else." Now Price was having trouble reconcil-
ing herself to peace. Mackers had started a magazine called *The
Blanket,* which featured writing by disaffected republicans, and
Price became a regular contributor. Her columns often took the
form of poison pen letters addressed directly to Adams. "What
Gerry Adams is saying, and saying gently so as not to panic the
grass-roots, is, 'They will go away, you know,'" she wrote in
2004. "The IRA will disband ... the guns will be sealed in concrete ... A few will get the political jobs, others will get satisfac-

tory jobs (community work and the like), some will get shops to run, taxis to drive, a racket here, a scam there. It is the way of the world."

Like Brendan Hughes, Price was keenly attuned to the commodification of republican martyrs. She pounced on a suggestion, by Adams, that, had Bobby Sands only lived, he would have embraced the shift to politics. "Bobby, he told us, would be fully behind the Peace Process," Price wrote. "I often wonder who would speak for me had my circumstances in Brixton Prison reached their expected conclusion? What praises would I be singing of the Good Friday Agreement?" (As it happened, Sands's own family would come to resent Sinn Féin's use of Bobby's name and image for fund-raising, and ask the party to stop.) Price noted, bitterly, that when Adams was speaking before certain republican audiences, he would invoke the name of her sainted aunt Bridie. She often found herself reflecting on the Troubles in their entirety. *Is this what we killed for?* she would ask herself. *Is this what we died for? What was it really all about?* Occasionally, she saw Adams in her dreams.

Even so, she retained a ferocious pride in her own headlong personal history. When an American graduate student named Tara Keenan visited her in 2003, Price said, "I would like to think that what I did was to illustrate to the world the ability of any regular human being to push themselves to the limits and beyond, physically and mentally, because of some deeply felt belief." She spoke as if she had been some kind of endurance athlete rather than a paramilitary. "An ordinary person was able to react in a kind of extraordinary way," she continued. "It's like a woman who can lift cars off her children. None of us know the limits of our ability."

When Mackers told Price about the Belfast Project, she agreed to participate. They would meet at her house and talk for hours. With Mackers's recorder rolling, she spoke about her proud republican lineage, about her radicalization as a teenager during the civil rights movement, about the bombing mission to London and the years in prison and on hunger strike.

Before one of their interviews, Price said that she wanted to talk about the role she had played in the disappearance of Jean McConville. The whole reason that Mackers had been selected to conduct the Boston College interviews was that he was anything but objective. He came from the same community as the people he was interviewing. Price had become his dear friend. She attended his wedding to Carrie, dressed in a gown of shimmering gold, and posed for a photograph with her arms around Brendan Hughes. When Mackers's son was born, Price agreed to be his godmother. Now, as Price announced that she was prepared to unlock one of the most awful secrets of the Troubles, Mackers found himself hesitating before turning on his recorder. "As an historian, I would love to get this," he told Price. "But as a friend, Dolours, I have to warn you. You have children. If you commit to being involved in the McConville disappearance, your children will bear the mark of Cain."

When Mackers hit RECORD, Price chose not to tell the story. When he sent the recordings and transcripts of the Dolours Price interviews off to Boston College, marked with her alphabetical cryptonym—"H"—they did not contain a single reference to Jean McConville.

"I was disappointed," Mackers reflected later. "She took my advice."

BOG QUEEN

GEOFF KNUPFER STALKED THE moors. Knupfer was a retired English detective. He had penetrating blue eyes and a clipped mustache, and when he came to Ireland in search of bodies, he wore a high-visibility coat of vivid orange. It made him pop out in the landscape of heather and mossy green, like a beacon. For three decades, Knupfer had served as a detective in Manchester. He had worked robberies and homicides and eventually retired as detective chief superintendent. But along the way he developed a morbid talent for the recovery of human remains.

One of the most notorious cases in the history of Manchester was the so-called Moors Murders, in which a couple of deranged lovers, Myra Hindley and Ian Brady, killed five local children over a two-year period, starting in 1963, and buried them in the countryside outside of town. Initially, only two of the bodies were discovered. But in 1986, more than two decades after the murders, Geoff Knupfer was introduced to Myra Hindley. She was serving a life sentence in prison, but she agreed to help him search for the body of another victim, and she was flown in a police helicopter to the moors. Overweight and in poor health, Hindley was unsteady on the rough terrain. But Knupfer took her hand, guiding her across the windswept mire, and his team eventually discovered the unmarked grave of Pauline Reade, who had been sixteen years old and on her way to a dance when Hindley and Brady murdered her. Trapped for decades in dense peat, her body had remained eerily preserved. But the moment it was exposed to the atmosphere, Knupfer recalled, "she began to deteriorate before our eyes."

With this grim qualification, Knupfer would eventually become involved in the search for the disappeared in Ireland. In April 1999, as part of the peace process, the governments of the United Kingdom and Ireland created a new binational entity, the Independent Commission for the Location of Victims' Remains. Dating back to the *Iliad,* ancient Egypt, and beyond, burial rites have formed a critical function in most human societies. Whether we cremate a loved one or inter her bones, humans possess a deep-set instinct to mark death in some deliberate, ceremonial fashion. Perhaps the cruelest feature of forced disappearances as an instrument of war is that it denies the bereaved any such closure, relegating them to a permanent limbo of uncertainty.

"You cannot mourn someone who has not died," the Argentine-Chilean writer Ariel Dorfman once observed. In Chile, more than three thousand people were disappeared during the military dictatorship of Augusto Pinochet. In Argentina, the number may have been as high as thirty thousand. In tiny Northern Ireland, the figure was much smaller. The commission ultimately identified sixteen individuals who had been disappeared through the whole course of the Troubles. Even that was a reflection of the extraordinary smallness of the province: in some other countries, there were debates about the aggregate numbers of people who were buried in unmarked graves. In Northern Ireland, you could list the victims on the back of an envelope: Joe Lynskey, Seamus Wright, Kevin McKee, Jean McConville, Peter Wilson, Eamon Molloy, Columba McVeigh, Robert Nairac, Brendan Megraw, John McClory, Brian McKinney, Eugene Simons, Gerard Evans, Danny McIlhone, Charlie Armstrong, Seamus Ruddy. But to name the dead was one thing. To find them was another.

Investigators drove small country lanes and met with local

people. Ex-gunmen. Barmen. Farmers. Priests. Their plea was simple: *Tell us what you've heard, tell us what you remember, help us find the bodies.* The legislation that established the commission speci-fied that anyone coming forward with information would receive a limited grant of immunity from prosecution. One morning in the spring of 1999, scarcely a month after the legislation to form the commission was passed, a pair of Catholic priests escorted police officers to a medieval graveyard outside Dundalk. Under a rhododendron bush in a quiet corner of the cemetery, the offi-cers discovered a new coffin, which had been hastily deposited aboveground. It held the remains of Eamon Molloy, who was twenty-one when he was killed by the IRA in 1975, for being an informant. It appeared that Molloy's remains had been dug up and placed in the coffin, then left in the graveyard overnight.

When Molloy's family recovered his body, they held a funeral and reburied him. Not long afterward, they were approached by a priest who had heard about the discovery on the news and said that he had a story to tell. His name was Eugene McCoy, and he recalled one night, a quarter century earlier, when he was startled by a knock at the door and summoned by a group of men to a mobile home in a remote area of County Louth. There, he found a young man, tied up on a bed. It was Eamon Molloy. The men were going to execute him that night, but Molloy had asked to confess to a priest before they did. Father McCoy had left in such haste that he forgot to bring his rosary beads. The man whom he took to be the head of the execution squad drew out a set of his own and, handing them to the priest, said, "Use mine."

The boy was frightened. He knew that he was about to die. He asked Father McCoy to deliver one last message to his fam-ily: *Tell them I'm not an informer.* This wasn't true. It would sub-sequently be well established that Molloy had indeed been an informer. But his dying wish was that his family be told oth-erwise. Members of the clergy were often thrust into morally fraught situations during the Troubles, and they didn't always do the right thing. After Father McCoy left that night, he did not track down the boy's family to deliver the message. Nor did he ever report the incident to the police.

.   .   .

A month after Molloy's body was discovered, the commission exhumed two more corpses from a bog in County Monaghan: Brian McKinney, son of Margaret McKinney, who had advocated for the families of the disappeared, along with his friend John McClory. They had been killed for stealing a gun from a Provo arms dump and using it to rob a bar. The search for bodies seemed to be gathering momentum, and one day that summer the children of Jean McConville had assembled on a beach at the tip of the Cooley Peninsula, in County Louth. It was a bleak and lonely spot, rocky and raked by the breeze, fifty miles or so from Belfast. Information had surfaced, passed along by the IRA, that their mother had been buried at a spot along this stretch of the coast. Massive backhoes lumbered around the site like prehistoric beasts, their craned arms churning up the soil and sand. Police officers in fluorescent jackets worked pneumatic drills, pickaxes, shovels, and rakes while the McConville children watched and waited.

This vigil was a reunion for the siblings, but a dissonant one. As children, they had fiercely resisted any effort by the state to split the family up, as though they knew in advance that once they were pried apart, they might never come back together. They had gone their separate ways, staying in touch only sporadically. As they gathered now, in the hopes of finally recovering their mother, some of them worried that they would no longer know how to relate to one another as siblings. The physical resemblance among them remained striking. Most of Jean's children shared her narrow face, sharp cheekbones, and small, pursed mouth. But the siblings, who were in their thirties and

forties now, looked older than their years; their faces were haggard, and the hands and forearms of the men were etched with
inky, blue-black tattoos. They were fractious and edgy around
each other. When they spoke of Jean, each tended to use the
singular possessive rather than the plural—"*my* mother"—as if
they were all only children.

Jim McConville, who was six when his mother was abducted,
had been in and out of prison. Archie, like several of the siblings,
had struggled with alcohol, and with his temper. "If someone
says the wrong thing, you would explode," he said. "If something is said that hits the right spot, you can't hold back." The
children hadn't had any counseling to speak of, so their grief
and anger were still raw and unprocessed. They were particularly incensed at the IRA—over the decision to disappear their
mother but also, perhaps even more so, over the suggestion that
Jean McConville might have been an informant. The whispers
about Jean had started not long after her death, the notion that
she might have been executed for being a tout. As if it were not
misfortune enough to be orphaned at a young age and cast into
austere and predatory Irish orphanages, the children had come
of age bearing that incendiary stigma.

The previous year, IRA representatives had acknowledged
to Helen that the Provos were responsible for disappearing Jean.
But in a statement in the spring of 1999, the organization said that
McConville had "admitted being a British army informer." The
children were gratified that the IRA was finally at least acknowledging their mother's murder and might now cooperate in the
effort to track down her remains, but they fiercely disputed any
intimation that she had been a tout. Jean was a victim of bigoted
animus, they argued, a Protestant widow in a nationalist Catholic neighborhood at the apex of sectarian tension. They told and
retold the story about how Jean had tended to the wounded British soldier in Divis Flats shortly before her death, and how those
words—BRIT LOVER—were scrawled in paint, like a scarlet let-

The McConvilles stand vigil at the beach: Archie, Michael, Jim, Susan, Helen, Robert, Agnes, and Billy.

ter, across their door. "I fought a lot of times with people who called my mother a tout," Jim said, recalling a life of merciless ostracism. "People wouldn't look at us. When we walked into the pubs, they would make a space for us. We sat there by ourselves."

What the children wanted now was to clear Jean's name. Archie wondered whether her murder had been a case of mistaken identity: the IRA had been searching for a woman who was a suspected double agent at Divis and might simply have taken the wrong person. Michael scoffed at any notion that his mother could have been some sort of spy. She was an overworked, depressed, psychologically fragile mother of ten who had just lost her husband to cancer. She spent her days cocooned in her flat, smoking cigarettes and juggling children and doing laundry by hand. What information could she possibly provide? As to the claim that Jean might have confessed, Helen said, "While they were torturing her, she would have admitted anything."

Each day, the backhoes turned more soil, but there was no sign of Jean McConville. At one point, there was a momentary flurry of excitement when the investigators unearthed a set of bones. But it turned out to be the skeleton of a dog. Nerves frayed. Sympathetic locals turned up at the dig site with warm meals for the family. Someone donated a mammoth carton of cigarettes.

"Where are we going to bury her?" Michael asked his siblings one day.

"West Belfast," Helen responded. "They were the ones that killed her. They were the ones that robbed us of a mother." Helen wanted to bury Jean at Milltown Cemetery, among the republican tombs, with a headstone that read JEAN MCCONVILLE. KIDNAPPED AND MURDERED BY THE IRA.

Her siblings might have shared her anger, but they were wary of antagonizing the Provos. "We're not discussing the IRA and what they done. Everybody knows it," Jim said. "We all live in republican areas and we don't want no hassle from them." He continued, "Them boys who done it, they'll suffer for the rest of their lives. It is time to say forgive."

"I don't know about youse, but I'll never forgive," Billy snapped. "I don't forgive them bastards for what they done."

It was painful for Michael McConville to see his siblings quarrel, and to join the quarrels himself. "I'd hoped we'd come together a bit over this," he said. "But it's tearing us even further apart."

.   .   .

Inside the IRA, the disappeared, as they came to be known, were regarded as a political liability—and as a source of shame. In 1995, Bill Clinton had made a point of pressuring Gerry Adams and Sinn Féin on the issue. "There are families that have still not had the chance to grieve in peace, to visit the graves of their loved ones, to reunite after years of separation," Clinton said. "It is time to allow families to be whole again." In 1998, a longtime IRA man named Bobby Storey, who was a close confidant of Gerry Adams's, began knocking on the doors of former

Provos, inquiring about their memories of what had happened to Jean McConville. He sought out Ivor Bell, who had argued that McConville should be murdered and left out in the street. He also approached Dolours Price, who was startled to think that Adams might send anybody to ask *her* what had become of Jean McConville. She advised Storey that if he wanted to find out the truth, perhaps he should "go and see Gerry."

As it happened, Adams was meeting during this period with the McConville children. He had initially visited Helen and her husband, Seamus, in 1995, arriving at their house accompanied by bodyguards, "like he was a celebrity," Helen thought. Like the McConvilles, Adams had grown up in a family of ten children, and he expressed his condolences. But Helen noticed that he would not meet her eye. During a meeting with Michael McConville, Adams said, "For what it's worth, I apologize for what the republican movement did to your mother." Adams excelled at this type of dissimulation. He would assume no personal responsibility himself. After all, he had never been in the IRA. "These killings happened twenty-five years ago, when the war here was at its height," Adams told one newspaper. "During war, horrible things are done."

At one of his initial meetings with the McConvilles, Adams made it clear that he had what was, in effect, an alibi. "Thank God I was in prison when she disappeared," he said. This was not true. He had been released from Long Kesh in June 1972, in order to fly to London for the peace talks. Jean was abducted in December, and Adams was not locked up again until the following July. ("That shouldn't be taken out of context," Adams said later. "I got confused about the dates.")

To Brendan Hughes, it was appalling that Adams would go to Jean McConville's children and pledge to get to the bottom of what had happened to their mother, as though it were some great mystery to him. "He went to this family's house and promised an investigation into the woman's disappearance," Hughes told

Mackers in one of his Boston College sessions. "The man that gave the fucking order for that woman to be executed! Now tell me the morality in that." Only a "Machiavellian monster" could do such a thing, Hughes concluded.

It was beginning to appear that the search for the bodies would take longer than expected. "The IRA were able to deliver a body on Friday in a coffin," Helen's husband, Seamus, said after the discovery of Eamon Molloy. "They should get down here and do the same for us." But while a few of the graves had been easy to locate, others were proving more elusive. The graves were unmarked precisely so that they would blend in with the surroundings. People had grown old, memories had faded. Also, the topography had changed. Someone might recall a particular location with reference to a barn, but the barn had been torn down decades earlier. What had been a row of delicate saplings in the 1970s might be a grove of sturdy trees today. "The IRA leadership approached this issue in good faith," the Provos declared in a statement, sounding a bit defensive. Their efforts had been hampered, they said, by the passage of time.

The McConvilles found some solace in other families whose loved ones had disappeared. Several of the families would convene at a "cross-community" trauma center called Wave, which became a source of support for the relatives of the disappeared. Some had been through indescribable anguish. After Kevin McKee disappeared, his mother, Maria, went slightly mad. Some nights, she would roust her other children from bed and bundle them into their coats, insisting that they head out into the city on fruitless searches. She would accost neighbors, pounding on their front doors, shouting, "Where's my son? What have you done with Kevin?" Other nights, she would prepare a plate of food and tell her children, "Put that in the hot press to keep it warm for Kevin," as if he had just stepped out to run an errand.

After a gun was discovered on a police raid of the McKee house, Maria ended up getting arrested and spending several months at Armagh jail, where she happened to overlap with the Price sisters. She allowed Dolours Price to do her hair, unaware that this was the woman who had driven her son across the border to be shot. When Eamon Molloy's body was recovered, Maria McKee attended the funeral and experienced the blissful delusion that she was burying her own son. But they still had not found Kevin when she died. Maria's extended family kept the memory of him alive by naming children Kevin. Sons. Cousins. Nephews. Whenever a baby boy was born, it seemed, they'd call him Kevin.

.   .   .

The Irish landscape is dominated by peat bogs, and the anaerobic and acidic conditions in the densely packed earth mean that the past in Ireland is occasionally subject to macabre resurrection. Peat cutters sometimes churn up ancient mandibles, clavicles, or entire cadavers that have been preserved for millennia. The bodies, which in some cases date back to before the Bronze Age, often show signs of ritual sacrifice and violent death. These victims, cast out of their communities and buried, have surfaced vividly intact, from their hair to their leathery skin. At the height of the Troubles, during the 1970s, Seamus Heaney became fixated on "bog people" after encountering a book, published in 1969, about the preserved bodies of men and women found in bogs in Jutland, who appeared to be the victims of ritual sacrifice. The photographs of these gnarled bodies, naked, some with their throats cut, reminded Heaney of certain "barbarous rites," past and present, in Ireland. Heaney wrote a series of poems about such figures, including "Bog Queen," in which he assumes the voice of a woman, long buried, who is disinterred, "barbered / and stripped / by a turfcutter's spade."

Heaney grew up harvesting peat as a boy on his family's farm. He once described the bogs of Ireland as "a landscape that remembered everything that had happened in and to it." Reviled though the practice of disappearing people might be, it was not new in Ireland. In fact, the old IRA disappeared people during the War of Independence, back in the 1920s. Nobody knows precisely how many people were secretly buried, but the bodies still crop up occasionally, bones dyed such a deep brown by peat that they look like tree roots rather than anything human.

At the beach on the Cooley Peninsula, the backhoes excavated for fifty days, digging a crater that grew to the size of an Olympic swimming pool. The McConvilles kept assembling by the shore each day, holding out hope that the earth might yield up some clue: a button, a bone, a slipper, the nappy pin their mother always wore. Some nights, the children would sit in the warmth of a car, staring out over the darkening Irish Sea, as the waves beat against the shore. But eventually the search was called off. It appeared that, in supplying the coordinates of the grave, the IRA had been mistaken. "They made a laughingstock of us" when Jean was kidnapped, Agnes said, her mascara dissolving in tears. "They're making another laughingstock of us now."

The siblings parted ways, left the beach, and returned to their respective homes. But everywhere there were reminders of their mother. They may not have known who ordered Jean's murder or who carried it out, but they still remembered the young neighbors who had barged into their flat that December night and ushered her out the door. The members of the abduction team had grown up, married, had families of their own. This was a cruel twist: some of the children could no longer remember what their mother had looked like, apart from the one surviving photo of her, but they still recognized the faces of the people who took her away. Once, Helen took her children to McDonald's and found herself staring at one of the women who she knew had taken her mother. The woman was there with her own family. She shouted at Helen to leave her alone.

On another occasion, Michael climbed into the back of a black taxi on the Falls Road, only to look up and see that the driver was one of Jean's abductors. The car pulled away from the curb and the two men rode in silence. Michael didn't say a word. What could he say? Instead he sat, unspeaking, until they reached his destination, then he handed the man the money for his fare.

AN ENTANGLEMENT OF LIES

THE THIEVES WERE DRESSED in suits, as if they had come on official business. There were three of them, in a car, purring up to the gates of the Castlereagh complex just after ten o'clock on a Sunday night. It was St. Patrick's Day 2002, and East Belfast was quiet. Only twenty or so people were on duty throughout the entire heavily fortified police compound. Trevor Campbell wasn't there that night. After decades of interrogating and flipping paramilitaries, he was preparing to retire. In fact, four months earlier, in accordance with the Good Friday Agreement, the Royal Ulster Constabulary itself had ceased to exist; rechristened as the more neutral-sounding Police Service of Northern Ireland, it had a new mission to be more inclusive in its hiring and less closely associated with the Protestant community.

Even so, Castlereagh still had the look of a forward operating base in a war zone, encircled by high walls garnished with barbed wire. It was said to be one of the most secure buildings in all of Europe. At the gate, the thieves casually flashed their credentials—what appeared to be army identification badges—and a guard waved them into the complex. In addition to the police, Castlereagh housed members of the British Army, along with certain faceless, nameless individuals who worked for the intelligence community. It was a busy facility, not some local precinct house where a guard might be expected to know every face, and besides, even the boldest criminal would not be so foolish as to break into a heavily guarded installation that was crawling with armed soldiers and cops. Bad things happened to people who got locked up at Castlereagh. It was a place paramilitaries fantasized about breaking *out* of—not into. At the front desk, the men produced their identification a second time, and an inattentive night-duty guard waved them into the building.

The thieves moved through a series of corridors with a purpose that suggested this expedition had been carefully planned. They were headed to one room in particular, an office. As it happened, the room that the office normally occupied was being renovated, so the whole operation had been temporarily relocated to a different space elsewhere in the facility. But the men knew this in advance. They proceeded deep inside the building to the temporary location of what was known as 220—the secret, round-the-clock nerve center of the security forces' spy network in Belfast, where hundreds of informants all across the city could call into a special hotline and make contact with their handlers in the police force, the army, and MI5.

A solitary Special Branch constable was in the room that night, manning the phones. He had no reason to suspect that anyone would knock on the door with bad intentions, so he opened it, and a fist connected, powerfully, with his jaw. The constable went down. Moving quickly and saying little, the men taped his mouth shut, tugged a hood over his head, and trussed him to an office chair. Then they placed a pair of headphones blaring music from a Walkman over his ears. With a set of keys that was lying, unhidden, on the desk, the men began to unlock drawers and file cabinets, pulling out documents. Periodically, one of them would return to the bound police constable, check his pulse, and make sure he was breathing properly. But eventually, they stopped checking. With the blindfold and headphones, the constable had no way of knowing whether they were still in the room. Eventually, he started trying to wriggle out of his binding, and nobody intervened to stop him. By the time he got the blindfold off, the thieves were long gone and the shelves were empty. The men had made off with a precious trove of highly classified information—notebooks and files containing details and code names of informants working inside the IRA and other paramilitary groups. Nobody noticed them leaving the building. They left behind only one clue—a lapel pin that one of the men had been wearing. In what was either one stray element of a convincing disguise or a smug joke on the part of the thieves, the pin said: SAVE THE RUC.

This was a brazen heist: three men had walked, unmasked and unarmed, into the inner sanctum of anti-terrorist operations in Belfast and escaped with a bonanza of sensitive intelligence. The police immediately flew into a panic, contacting informants to let them know they could be compromised and ultimately relocating more than three hundred people. Suspicion turned to the IRA. One security source told the BBC that the break-in was a willful violation of the peace process—indeed, that it constituted "an act of war." The IRA responded that, on the contrary, this was an inside job by the authorities. Most observers ultimately concluded that the break-in had indeed been carried out by the Provos. But the thieves appeared to have had help from within the building. A man who worked as a cook at Castlereagh was sought for questioning; it turned out he was an associate of Denis Donaldson, an ex-IRA leader who now worked at Stormont as a Sinn Féin official. One press report speculated that the break-in may have been carried out with the aim of uncovering "the identity of one informer in particular," an individual who had achieved "mythological status as one of the highest-ranking informers working for the police within the Provisionals." According to the article, the code name of this supposed spy was "Steak Knife."

There had been rumors for years about an informant operating at the very highest echelons of the republican movement. At some point, a code name had leaked out: sometimes it was written "Stakeknife," other times "Steak Knife" or "Stake Knife."

But the visual implication was always the same: a lethal stiletto, a dagger in the heart of the IRA. In one 1999 account, Stakeknife was described as "the crown jewel" of British intelligence in Ulster.

Dolours Price had heard the rumors. "You know this Stakeknife character they talk about? The informer of all informers," she said to a visitor at her Dublin home in March 2003. "He's meant to be high, high up in the republican hierarchy. I certainly have not figured out who it is." In her moments of anger, Price admitted, she sometimes joked that it could be Gerry Adams himself. "But I don't think he's Stakeknife," she said.

The very idea of Stakeknife was so unnerving to republicans that it was tempting to wonder whether the British had not simply concocted the rumor with the explicit aim of demoralizing them. During the Cold War, the CIA official James Jesus Angleton became convinced that his agency was being undermined by a Russian mole. He paralyzed the agency for years, trying to find this double agent, but it is generally accepted now that he was chasing shadows. Mole hunting can become a self-destructive madness, a paranoid condition elegantly captured by Angleton himself, who described the counterintelligence business as a "wilderness of mirrors." For years, Freddie Scappaticci and his associates on the Nutting Squad had been interrogating and killing suspected informants. Between 1980 and 1994, no fewer than forty people were executed by the IRA on suspicion of being touts, their bodies dumped unceremoniously. Of the people who were murdered, many had indeed been cooperating in some fashion with the authorities. But not all of them. As the IRA would subsequently acknowledge, some of the Nutting Squad's victims had never been informers at all. And for all the corpses deposited in country lanes along the border, the IRA never could seem to eliminate the problem. Arms dumps kept getting discovered. Missions kept getting foiled. No matter how many people Scappaticci and his colleagues killed, there always seemed to be at least one more traitor lurking in the ranks.

When Brendan Hughes got out of prison, an IRA associate named Joe Fenton offered him an apartment. Fenton worked as a real estate agent on the Falls Road. He also secretly worked for the British, providing "safe houses" to the IRA that had in fact been wired for sound. Fenton used to tell his IRA friends that he had connections who could procure brand-new, presumably stolen color televisions. The TVs were bugged as well. Eventually Fenton's betrayal was discovered. He was questioned by Scappaticci and confessed. Before he could be executed, he broke away and made a run for it, but the Nutting Squad shot him in the back, then in the face, and left him in an alley on the outskirts of Belfast.

Hughes found that he was increasingly uneasy. "I discovered something here that was murky, was high-level," he told Mackers. "I didn't trust Belfast." There seemed to be spies everywhere. He spoke to Gerry Adams about it, but Adams told him not to worry, that he was being paranoid. Hughes was right to worry. James Jesus Angleton may have conjured infiltrators where there weren't any, but the IRA was, in actual fact, hopelessly penetrated by double agents. In a subsequent submission to a tribunal in Dublin, one handler who worked in British military intelligence estimated that by the end of the Troubles, as many as one in four IRA members worked, in some capacity, for the authorities. At the most senior levels of the IRA, he suggested, that figure might be closer to one in two. Of course, that also is the kind of story that could be fabricated, as a psy-op to undermine republican leadership, and Adams and other Sinn Féin officials would discount any such statistics that emanated from the British as inherently unreliable.

But just over a year after the Castlereagh break-in, several newspapers in England and Ireland published a bombshell story. Stakeknife was no figment of anyone's fevered imagination. He was a real spy, who for decades had been a paid informant of British Army intelligence. His information was so prized that British ministers were regularly briefed on it, and he made the careers of a generation of spymasters. Stakeknife was "our most important secret," in the words of one British Army commander in Northern Ireland. He was "a golden egg." Stakeknife wasn't Gerry Adams. He was Freddie Scappaticci.

.   .   .

"I am not guilty of these allegations," Scappaticci said. After being exposed in the press, he appeared at the Belfast office of his solicitor. Short, jowly, and puffy around the eyes, he seemed remarkably composed for a man who would now have a hefty price on his head. But then, Scappaticci knew a thing or two about how to comport yourself when someone is accusing you of being a spy. *Never confess,* Trevor Campbell used to tell his informants. *Confess and you're dead.* Before anyone managed to nut Scappaticci, he vanished from Belfast and went into hiding, with the assistance, presumably, of his handlers. He had been a double agent for a quarter of a century, since initially offering his services to the authorities in 1978. In fact, Scappaticci was reportedly a walk-in. It has been suggested that he was motivated, in the moment, by revenge, having recently received a beating at the hands of other members of the IRA. But it may never be known what precisely impelled him to become the most important double agent of the Troubles.

For the IRA, this was a devastating paradox: the man the organization had entrusted to root out moles was a mole himself. For the British, having an informant at the heart of the IRA's own internal security unit had been a singular coup. In order to thwart penetration by spies, the Provos had reorganized, in the late 1970s, into a cellular configuration, in which each operational node would have limited insight into the activities (or

even the existence) of the others. But as an army-wide internal affairs unit with a mandate that always seemed urgent, the
Nutting Squad had access to everything: personnel, weapons
supplies, attack plans. As one former Provo put it, the security
unit was like a junction box for the whole organization, and for
most of the Troubles, the British had a man placed right inside
it. If the IRA burgled Castlereagh in the hopes of uncovering
Stakeknife's identity, they failed; Scappaticci's name was presumably so sensitive that it was not kept in the files there. In fact,
when Scappaticci was outed by the press, the shock in republican
circles was so intense that a number of Sinn Féin leaders cast
doubt on the idea that Scap really was Stakeknife at all, caution-
ing people to be skeptical of the "unsubstantiated allegations"
against him.

"I still can't believe it," the Sinn Féin official Dennis Donaldson, who was one of Gerry Adams's most trusted apparat-
chiks, told a visiting American journalist after Scap was exposed.
"My God," he said, shaking his head.

But then, Donaldson was a spy himself. In December 2005,
at a hastily assembled press conference, Adams announced that
Donaldson had confessed to being a paid informer for British
intelligence over the previous twenty years. Nearly eight years
after the Good Friday Agreement, Adams said, some segments
of the military and intelligence establishment refused to accept
that "the British war in Ireland is over." As if in warning to others who might consider betraying the movement in the future,
Adams noted that those who become British agents are "blackmailed, bullied, coerced, bought, broken, used, abused, and then
thrown to one side."

Donaldson went into hiding, in an isolated Donegal cottage
that predated the nineteenth-century famine. Like a portal into
Ireland's miserable agrarian past, the place had no running water
or electricity. But a lucky horseshoe hung above the door. Donaldson grew a penitential beard and chopped wood in order to

heat the place. Then, one day, someone arrived at the cottage and killed him. (It has never been ascertained who precisely shot Donaldson, or who ordered the shooting. But both Gerry Adams and the Provisional IRA have denied that they played any role.)

.   .   .

How could such informants, at such high levels, remain hidden for so long? In the case of Scappaticci, there was one obvious explanation: he was a killer. Nobody in the IRA was under any illusions about the willingness of the state to embrace unsavory tactics in this dirty, undeclared war. But even so, the conspicuous savagery of a man like Scap might seem, at least in theory, to be grounds for disqualification as an agent of the crown. "The one preconception the IRA had is that if you are dirty—that is, if you have killed—then you cannot be an agent," the British military intelligence handler Ian Hurst once remarked. For Scappaticci, he continued, the best protection may simply have been "to keep killing."

If an agent is a murderer, and his handlers know that he is murdering people, does that not make the handlers—and, as such, the state itself—complicit? British Army sources would subsequently claim that Scappaticci's efforts saved 180 lives. But they allowed that this number was a "guesstimate," and this sort of thinking can degenerate pretty quickly into a conjectural mathematics of means and ends. Scappaticci would ultimately be linked to as many as fifty murders. If a spy takes fifty lives but saves some larger number, can that countenance his actions? This kind of logic is seductive, but perilous. You start out running numbers in your head, and pretty soon you are sanctioning mass murder.

For years, when the Provos made claims about collusion between the RUC or the army and loyalist paramilitaries, it was dismissed as propaganda. After all, the image that the British state had scrupulously cultivated for decades was that of the reluctant, impartial referee, stepping into the fray when nobody else would, to sort out two warring tribes. But the truth was that, from the beginning, the authorities perceived the Provos as the main enemy, where their energies should be focused, and regarded loyalist terror gangs as a sideshow—if not an unofficial state auxiliary.

As early as 1975, an army officer in Belfast wrote a letter to his boss warning about connections between loyalist paramilitaries and members of British intelligence and Special Branch, who appeared to have formed "some sort of pseudo gangs in an attempt to fight a war of attrition by getting paramilitaries on both sides to kill each other." In another letter, the following month, the officer expressed the view that the exploding violence of the Troubles could be attributed largely to British intelligence agents' "deliberately stirring up conflict."

Loyalist gangs, often operating with the tacit approval or outright logistical assistance of the British state, killed hundreds of civilians in an endless string of terror attacks. These victims were British subjects. Yet they had been dehumanized by the conflict to the point that organs of the British state often ended up complicit in such murders, without any sort of public inquiry or internal revolt in the security services. All those bright lines that bureaucrats and legal scholars draw to delimit the government's monopoly on the legitimate use of force, those boundaries that are meant to separate order from barbarism, had been transgressed. "We were not there to act like an army unit," one former British officer who served in the MRF later acknowledged. "We were there to act like a terror group."

One day in the late 1980s, Raymond White, a senior Special Branch officer who oversaw the handling of informants, met with Margaret Thatcher and explicitly raised the danger of paramilitary collusion. "I'm sitting here, with the agents and handlers out there, and I feel somewhat uncomfortable," White told the prime minister. "Because I'm asking them to do things that technically could be construed as criminal acts." White's remit was to recruit sources inside the paramilitaries. But paramilitaries steal vehicles. They build bombs. They kill people. "To be a paramilitary is *itself* a criminal act," White said. He wanted a set of clear legal guidelines, he told Thatcher, that would spell out just what the state could authorize its informants to do—and what it couldn't. To continue functioning in a gray area could be dangerous, he felt. Thatcher considered the request. But in the end, she would offer him no such boundaries. To White, the message was clear: "Carry on doing what you're doing. But don't tell us the details."

Stakeknife was hardly the only paid double agent who also happened to be a murderer. One of the top British informants on the loyalist side was Brian Nelson, a former army officer who became a paramilitary with the Ulster Defence Association. After a stint in prison during the 1970s for kidnapping a disabled Catholic civilian and torturing him with a cattle prod, Nelson became an informant for the Force Research Unit (FRU), a shadowy army intelligence outfit that was a successor to the MRF. (It was the FRU that employed Scappaticci.)

In his day job as a loyalist paramilitary, Nelson's responsibility was to gather intelligence, and, particularly, to assemble dossiers on republicans who might make worthy targets for assassination. Nelson was every bit as prolific as Scappaticci when it came to killing. He, too, would end up linked to some fifty murder plots. When Gerry Adams was wounded in the shooting by loyalist paramilitaries in 1984, he had suggested that the authorities must have known about the attack in advance. At the time, this charge may have seemed ludicrous—if the government had known beforehand of a plot to assassinate a member of Parliament in a drive-by shooting during the lunch hour in busy central Belfast, surely it would have prevented the attack—but in fact the government *did* know about the plot, because Nelson had tipped off his handlers. The government allowed it to proceed.

One night in February 1989, a thirty-nine-year-old solicitor, Pat Finucane, was at home eating Sunday dinner with his wife, Geraldine, and their three children in a prosperous neighborhood in North Belfast when gunmen crashed through the front door with a sledgehammer and murdered Finucane, shooting him a dozen times. His wife was hit by a ricocheting bullet. His young children witnessed the whole thing. As an attorney, Finucane had advised many republicans. But he was not a member of the IRA himself. Nevertheless, the authorities felt that he had become too close to the organization. Members of the RUC had complained about lawyers who were "effectively in the pockets of terrorists." It was Nelson who gathered information about Finucane in advance of the shooting and supplied it to the execution team. The weapons used in the attack were supplied by a different man, who had also been a police informant. A subsequent inquiry stopped short of concluding that there had been "an over-arching State conspiracy to murder Patrick Finucane," but it did say that he would not have been murdered without "involvement by elements of the state." (Finucane's family, convinced that there had indeed been an overarching conspiracy, rejected the findings of the inquiry as a cover-up and a "sham.")

On one occasion in 1987, Brian Nelson saved Freddie Scappaticci's life. A loyalist boss had given Nelson a list of Provisional IRA members who were being targeted for possible assassination. Nelson dutifully passed the list along to his handlers in the FRU. One of the names on the list was Freddie Scappaticci. At that point, Stakeknife had already been a valuable informant for a decade, and he stood poised to deliver an untold bounty of intelligence in the future. As an investment, he was still maturing nicely, so the presence of his name on a loyalist kill list prompted panic among his British handlers. Nelson himself did not know that Scappaticci was also an informant. Any given mole rarely knew about the others. So the FRU devised a scheme to try and divert the murderous intentions of Nelson's loyalist associates. In the words of one member of the unit at the time, "The aim was to switch attention to another individual."

The British Army handlers fed Brian Nelson the name of a different potential target: Francisco Notarantonio. A Belfast Italian, like Scappaticci, Notarantonio was a former taxi driver. At sixty-six, he was a pensioner, a father of eleven, and a grandfather. What he wasn't was a member of the IRA. But Nelson's handlers made him out to be a major figure, a Provo godfather, someone easily on par with Scappaticci. One morning, Notarantonio was at home in his bedroom with his wife of thirty-nine years when gunmen climbed the stairs and shot him to death in his bed. When he was buried, a few days later, hordes of mourners came out to the funeral procession. One of them was Freddie Scappaticci, who had no inkling that the innocent man in the coffin had just been sacrificed so that he might live.

"In almost thirty years as a policeman I had never found myself caught up in such an entanglement of lies and treachery," said Lord John Stevens, a top English police official. Stevens had been selected to conduct an investigation into the FRU and collusion between loyalist paramilitaries and the state, but his efforts were obstructed along the way. In 1990, a fire broke out in the office where Stevens and his team had been working. A subsequent police investigation concluded that the fire was an accident. But Stevens remained convinced that it was sabotage—an act of deliberate arson designed to destroy evidence of state collusion.

In 2012, the British prime minister, David Cameron, acknowledged the existence of "frankly shocking levels of state collusion." The Good Friday Agreement had contained a few specific clauses on criminal justice. There was a provision to free paramilitary prisoners who were being held at the time of the agreement, and under this framework, any sentence delivered in the future for Troubles-related crimes would be capped at two years. Beyond that, however, there were no suggestions in the peace agreement for how to address the crimes of the past. There was no mechanism through which amnesty might be granted in exchange for testimony. Nor would the kinds of murders that Scappaticci and Nelson engaged in—and the state facilitated and condoned—be prosecuted as war crimes, because, whatever the reality on the ground might have been, the Troubles was never declared a war. What this meant was that the many unsolved murders of the Troubles would remain open criminal cases, in which ex-paramilitaries and ex-soldiers might yet be prosecuted. There was one notable exception: under the 1999 legislation designed to help recover the bodies of the disappeared, a limited amnesty would be provided if people with knowledge of the particulars of these cases came forward to share it voluntarily with the authorities.

.   .   .

One late-summer evening in 2003, eighteen months after the Castlereagh heist, a man named John Garland was walking along Shelling Hill Beach, near Carlingford, in the Republic. Garland had just taken his son and daughter for a visit to his mother's grave in a nearby cemetery, and now they were strolling back along the beach. The tide was going out, and the children wanted to catch crabs. As they capered on the damp shore, Garland's eye fell on something, a snatch of fabric sticking out of the sand. Approaching it, he picked up a piece of driftwood and used it to try to drag the material out of the sand. But it wouldn't budge. Curious, Garland pulled harder. Then he stopped, suddenly, as the material came loose and he caught sight of human bones.

"These were the disarticulated remains of an adult," a subsequent pathologist's report concluded. "There were no soft tis-

The coffin of Jean McConville passes Divis Tower.

sues adherent to the bones and the bones were crumbling. There was some evidence of plant growth on the bones." It was the skeleton of a woman. After counting the ribs and enumerating the other intact bones, the report noted, "There was a single gunshot wound to the back of the head which would have been sufficient to cause her death." A flattened lead bullet was recovered not far from the skull.

Four years after their long vigil in the summer of 1999, the McConville children reassembled on this stretch of beach, several hundred yards from the area that had been so comprehensively excavated in the earlier search. A series of recent storms had caused heavy erosion in the area, so, after remaining hidden for decades, the grave had gradually been uncovered by the elements. The skeleton's left femur was sent away for genetic profiling, along with DNA samples from Archie and Agnes McConville. But in the meantime, there was that fabric, a few tangled garments that had swaddled the bones over the decades in their unmarked grave. At a nearby morgue, the children of Jean McConville were ushered into a room, one by one, so that they could examine the clothing, which was laid out on a table. Tights, underwear, the remains of a skirt, a pink woollen top, the sole of a single shoe. Archie went in first, but he couldn't bring himself to look.

Instead he asked a question: "Is there a nappy pin?"

A police officer surveyed the garments and said no, there wasn't. Then he folded over a corner of fabric, and there it was. Thirty-one years after Jean McConville vanished, her body had been found. "My mother was a very good mother to all of us," Archie declared at a subsequent inquest. "All of our lives has been hell without her."

Jean was reburied that November. The coffin was decorated with a spray of flowers, and the children accompanied it through the streets of West Belfast, pausing for a moment of silence when they passed Divis Tower, where Brendan Hughes still lived. Father Alec Reid, who had been so instrumental in the peace process, attended the funeral. But some others who accompanied the coffin felt that West Belfast was oddly quiet, as if the locals had been told to stay away, as if they were shunning the McConville family once again.

When the remains of other individuals who had been disappeared were discovered, the chief focus was on recovering the bodies and burying them in consecrated ground. But the coroner in the McConville case ruled that Jean's body did not fall under the limited amnesty agreement governing the disappeared, because she was found not through the assistance of the IRA but by a random member of the public who happened to walk the beach. This had one very serious implication, the coroner declared: "The criminal case remains open."

THE LAST GUN

FATHER REID KEPT AN eye on the gunman. He had agreed to serve as a witness to the decommissioning of the IRA's weapons, along with a Methodist minister, Harold Good. The process had unfolded in phases, and the precise technique that the IRA used to render its weaponry "beyond use" was a closely held secret, but it was said to involve sealing the weapons in concrete. Now, in 2005, the two clergymen had been summoned to oversee the destruction of the final batch. As they watched the process, Reid was distracted by the presence of one Provo official who stood nearby, holding an AK-47. "Everywhere we went, this Kalashnikov was there, and I could see it was loaded," Reid said later. The gun was on display, he concluded, not because of any fear about what the clergymen might do, but because the Provos needed to guard against an ambush by dissident paramilitaries who were not quite ready to give up fighting and might endeavor to repossess the arsenal.

The destruction proceeded without incident, however, and once the clattering assortment of assault rifles, flamethrowers, mortars, and shoulder-fired missiles had been disposed of, the only weapon that remained was the Kalashnikov in the gunman's hand. Father Reid watched the man as he solemnly handed it over, and noticed that he had become emotional. The man seemed very aware, Reid thought, that this was "the last gun."

While the IRA was decommissioning, Brendan Hughes was fulfilling a lifelong dream. With his brother Terry, he flew to Cuba. The two graying Irishmen visited the Che Guevara memorial in Santa Clara and paid their respects at the mausoleum. They met some aging veterans of Cuba's revolution and bonded with the men. They posed for photos where Che fought. Brendan was delighted.

When he got back to Belfast, Hughes grew increasingly ill, struggling with a range of infirmities that dated back to his hunger strike twenty-five years earlier. One day in 2008, he fell into a coma. His family surrounded him at the hospital, and veterans of D Company began to appear, knowing that their former commander was close to death, to pay their respects. One night, Gerry Adams slipped into the hospital. This caused some discomfort among Brendan's siblings, who knew that if he were awake, he might not welcome Adams. Hughes had taken to telling people, "There was a time in my life when I would have taken a bullet for Gerry Adams. Now, I'd put one in him." But the family chose not to intervene, and Adams went into the hospital room alone and sat in silence by Brendan's bed. Hughes died the next day. He was fifty-nine.

The funeral, on a frigid day in February, was a massive affair. Dolours Price attended, as did Mackers, along with his wife, Carrie. At one point, Price looked over and saw a familiar figure cutting through the crowd. It was Adams. For the Sinn Féin leader to show up at all was awkward. When Adams traveled the world now, he was embraced. He was a government minister, a peacemaker. People would queue just to shake his hand. They would reach out to touch his sleeve. But not here. Surrounded by men and women who had once taken his orders, at the funeral of a man who had been one of his closest friends, Adams was an outsider. In the judgment of Terry Hughes, Brendan's brother, Adams had little choice but to make an appearance. Brendan was a republican icon. In the symbolic calculus of IRA politics, in which every funeral is a stage, Adams could afford to disassociate himself from Hughes in life, but not in death.

Watching Adams, Price felt something unexpected: a pang of sympathy. He looked so uneasy in this crowd, she thought. He looked lonely. Still, he was nothing if not determined. Adams plunged into the cortege, maneuvering across the throng. Then he shouldered his way into the clutch of men carrying the coffin. "We were there in grief, not for photo opportunities," Price complained afterward. But it was a bit late to be accusing Adams of a single-minded fixation on politics. After the burial, Adams told the Sinn Féin newspaper *An Phoblacht* that although Hughes had "disagreed with the direction taken in recent years," he was still held "in high esteem" by all who knew him. "He was my friend," Adams remarked, before concluding with a Gaelic aphorism that translates roughly as "He is on the way of truth." It was a sentiment that would soon prove to be more apt than Adams could possibly imagine.

.   .   .

At the time Hughes died, the existence of the Belfast Project was still a closely guarded secret. But there were already indications that Sinn Féin's complete control of the narrative of IRA history during the Troubles was beginning to fray. When Ricky O'Rawe did his oral history with Mackers, he waited until the final session to reveal his long-held secret about how the Adams leadership had spurned an offer by the British government that might have ended the 1981 hunger strike before the last six strikers died. But O'Rawe found the experience of unburdening himself so invigorating that as soon as he finished the interview, he resolved not to wait until his own death in order to release the story to the world. O'Rawe had a big, round face, close-cropped gray hair, and a jovial sensibility. He was still relatively young and in good health. It could be decades before he died. Besides, he didn't want to restrict his story to the future students of Boston College. He wanted to tell it to the world.

What O'Rawe really wanted to do was write a book. The idea sounded slightly outlandish, and potentially dangerous. When Ed Moloney, the director of the Belfast Project, learned of O'Rawe's plan, he tried to warn him. The allegation that O'Rawe aimed to make public—that Gerry Adams had knowingly sacrificed the lives of six hunger strikers in order to advance the electoral prospects of Sinn Féin—was simply too explosive. "If you publish this, you'll be nailed to the cross," Moloney said.

But O'Rawe was undeterred. "If I die before this comes out, all these geezers will be off the hook," he said. In 2005, he published the book. It was called *Blanketmen,* and it portrayed Adams as a coolheaded visionary, but also a slippery operator. "No matter how history chooses to judge Adams" in relation to the strike itself, O'Rawe wrote, "without him and the hunger strikers, there would be no semblance of peace in Ireland today."

This sort of nuance did nothing to placate those who perceived the publication of *Blanketmen* as a weaponized personal history aimed squarely at Gerry Adams. The Sinn Féin president did not respond to O'Rawe directly, preferring to remain aloof. Instead, as O'Rawe put it, he "unleashed his Dobermans": an assortment of proxies and allies took to the press to hammer the book. Bik McFarlane, who had worked closely with O'Rawe during the hunger strikes, derided the book as "totally fictitious," claiming that no deal had ever been offered by the British, so Adams couldn't have sent a message directing the prisoners not to accept it. (Several years later, McFarlane changed his story and acknowledged that a secret offer *had* been made, but he insisted that it was the hunger strikers themselves, rather than the leadership, who deemed the offer unworthy and opted to continue the strike.)

If the attacks on *Blanketmen* were intended to silence O'Rawe, they had the opposite effect. He never missed an opportunity to publicly debate anyone who might question the particulars of his story, and he decided that he would now write a *second* book about the strike and its aftermath. He also found that his willingness to tell a story that was at odds with republican orthodoxy won him supporters. In a review in *The Blanket,* Dolours Price praised O'Rawe, thanking him for providing "access to this vital piece in the jigsaw."

Brendan Hughes had admired *Blanketmen* as well, and he came to its defense before he died. "I am a former prisoner whom O'Rawe talked to on a number of occasions about the things that concerned him and which eventually appeared in his book," Hughes wrote, in a letter to *The Irish News.* In his final years, Hughes had gotten together with O'Rawe from time to time, to share memories of their years in prison. "Dark, you should write all this down," O'Rawe would tell him.

"Don't worry," Hughes said. "I've made tapes."

.   .   .

One day in 2009, Dolours Price was arrested and charged with trying to steal a bottle of vodka from a Sainsbury's supermarket. Price maintained that she had not *intended* to steal the bottle. The store had automated checkout counters, with electronic scanners, and she simply got confused about the mechanism. Price elaborated that it was not in her "temperament or breeding to take things from shops without paying for them." She was subsequently acquitted of shoplifting, but the truth was that Price had been struggling for some time with alcohol and drug addiction, and with PTSD. In 2001, she was caught with stolen pharmaceutical prescriptions and was found guilty of theft. A few years later, she was thrown out of Maghaberry Prison, where she had gone to visit a dissident republican prisoner. Officials at the prison said that she was drunk, though she denied it. Friends were concerned. Price still spoke once a week to Eamonn McCann, her old friend from Derry. She often wanted to talk about the past, but McCann would endeavor to steer her to other subjects. "Don't," he would say. "I don't want to know." Like Ricky O'Rawe, Price wanted to write about her days in the IRA. But McCann cautioned her against it. "Write about your childhood," he said. "Don't write about the IRA."

Speaking out still invited fierce censure. In 2009, another IRA veteran, Gerry Bradley, wrote a memoir. Like Price, Bradley had contempt for "the Shinners," as people often called members of Sinn Féin. Many of them, he felt, were "free-loading on the IRA's achievements." Bradley told his co-author, a respected scholar of the Troubles named Brian Feeney, "The only thing I know is that I'm not an informer." Yet as soon as the book was published, Bradley's North Belfast neighborhood was tagged with graffiti identifying him as a tout. "I'm just telling my story," he protested, insisting that he only wanted to "put on record the truth of life in the IRA." Eventually Bradley was forced to flee Belfast, seeking exile in Dublin. Ostracized and in poor health, he drove one day to a parking lot beside a Norman castle on Belfast Lough and took his own life.

"Are *they* the only ones allowed to write books?" Ricky O'Rawe asked indignantly after Bradley's death. "Is history never to be recorded properly?"

As it happened, Brendan Hughes had made arrangements before he died. He asked Mackers and Ed Moloney to promise him that his own recollections would be published in book form. When the time came, Moloney volunteered to write the book. Using the Boston College transcript of Hughes, and that of another participant in the project, a loyalist paramilitary with the Ulster Volunteer Force named David Ervine, who had also recently died, Moloney wrote a book called *Voices from the Grave.* It was published in 2010. In a preface, Bob O'Neill and Tom Hachey, from Boston College, described it as "the inaugural volume of a planned series of publications drawn from the Boston College Oral History Archive on the Troubles."

The secret of the archive was officially out. The book would quote Hughes by name not just asserting that Gerry Adams had been an IRA commander, but describing how Adams had personally ordered murders. Here was Hughes, saying in his own words that it was Adams who sent him to America to procure Armalites. It was Adams who sent Dolours Price to bomb London. It was Adams who ordered the killing of Jean McConville. The publisher, Faber & Faber, promised that *Voices from the Grave* would "make it impossible for certain forms of historical denial to continue in public life."

The publication generated enormous attention—and a swift and lacerating backlash. "I knew Brendan Hughes well," Adams said when he was asked about the book. "He wasn't well and hadn't been for a very long time, including during the time he did these interviews. Brendan also opposed the IRA cessations and the peace process." Adams, who would soon be elected to a seat in the Dáil Éireann, the legislature of the Republic of Ireland, rejected "absolutely" any suggestion that he had played a part in the Jean McConville case, "or in any of the other allegations that are being promoted by Ed Moloney." Sinn Féin issued a blanket pronouncement that anyone who participated in the Belfast Project had "a malign agenda."

Attention soon turned to Anthony McIntyre, who was identified in the book as the person who had interviewed Hughes. Mackers had long since fallen out with people in the circle around Adams, but now he began receiving threats. One night, someone smeared the house of one of his neighbors with excrement—wrong address, apparently—a gesture whose combination of vindictiveness and clumsiness had all the hallmarks of the IRA. In one press report, an unnamed republican said that Mackers would "go the same way as Eamon Collins," a Newry man who was stabbed to death in 1999, not long after publishing his own memoir about life in the IRA.

But *Voices from the Grave* received strong reviews, and Ed Moloney went on a book tour. He had plans to launch a documentary on Irish television that would include audio from Hughes's oral history. Then, one day in the summer of 2010, Danny Morrison, the longtime friend and ally of Gerry Adams, contacted Boston College and requested access to the Hughes tapes.

During the Troubles, Morrison had been the chief propagandist for the IRA, the man who is credited with coining the phrase "the Armalite and the ballot box." If Hughes delivered the oral history to Boston College with the understanding that it would not be made public until his death, and if Hughes was now dead, then surely Morrison could access not just Ed Moloney's book but the original tapes themselves? When the college forwarded this request to Moloney and Mackers, they panicked. Under no circumstances should Morrison be granted access, Moloney said. "Morrison played a key role in the IRA's spycatchers unit," Mackers wrote in an email to Tom Hachey at Boston College. "Danny Morrison has no intellectual interest in the tapes. He is not an academic or investigative writer but a propagandist."

It may simply have been the flush of euphoria when the Belfast Project was originally conceived, in the aftermath of the Good Friday Agreement, but at no point had any of the project's architects contemplated a scenario like this. In fact, there were quite a few fairly important points upon which their original conception of the project had been ambiguous. For instance, Wilson McArthur, Anthony McIntyre's counterpart, who conducted all of the interviews in the loyalist community, had been under the impression, as he was gathering the oral histories, that *none* of the interviews would be made public until *all* of the participants had died. He was caught off guard by the news that Moloney intended to publish *Voices from the Grave* just a few years after the last of the interviews had concluded, thereby revealing the existence of the archive when the first participants had died, rather than waiting decades until the last ones had.

The men had also never decided just who would be allowed to access the interviews. The conversations had always been about "the future students of Boston College." But the history department at the college had not known, until the publication of Moloney's book, that the project was happening at all. In fact, the archive had been so secret that almost nobody at Boston College, apart from Hachey and O'Neill, knew that it existed. One history professor, when he learned about the project, sent a PhD student he was supervising to the Burns Library to consult the Hughes and Ervine interviews for her thesis. But when he found out about this arrangement, Ed Moloney objected. "I would strongly urge you now to close the archives to any and all further access," Moloney wrote to Hachey. There should be a strict protocol, he proposed. Anyone could apply to access the interviews, but the list of applicants should be sent to Moloney for "vetting."

In an email to Mackers, Hachey expressed his indignation. If the perception had been from the outset that the project would be "mothballed for a lengthy time," Boston College might not have been so supportive, he pointed out. "We never got as much as a hint that there was any expected fallout," he complained. The university could not be expected to close the archive "to the entire scholarly and/or journalistic world—other than to Ed Moloney."

From the beginning, the two Irishmen and the two Americans—Moloney, McIntyre, Hachey, and O'Neill—had enshrouded the Belfast Project in secrecy, because they recognized just how sensitive and potentially dangerous an undertaking it was. Out of this concern for operational security, they kept the circle of people who knew anything about the project extremely small, and, for the better part of a decade, until the publication of Moloney's book, they scrupulously preserved this need-to-know ethos. But the very smallness of the circle may have led them to take certain things for granted and prevented them from asking important questions about how to manage the process if the whole thing unraveled and their most paranoid, worst-case-scenario fears came true.

·   ·   ·

Just prior to the publication of *Voices from the Grave*, in February 2010, Gerry Adams gave a long interview to *The Irish News*, in which he was asked about Joe Lynskey, the "Mad Monk" of the IRA, who was the first person to be disappeared in the Troubles after he was court-martialed for ordering a hit on his love rival, which led to the shooting at the Cracked Cup. When the IRA acknowledged, in 1999, that it had disappeared people, and released a list of names, including the informants Seamus Wright and Kevin McKee, as well as Jean McConville, Lynskey was not on the list. In fact, it had been Ed Moloney who first informed the Lynskey family, before publishing the story in *Voices from the Grave*, that Joe had been disappeared by the IRA. When the *Irish News* interviewer questioned Adams about Lynskey, he said, casually, "He was a neighbor of mine." Asked if he had been friends with Lynskey, Adams said, "Oh, yeah. I knew him and he disappeared." He added that he would encourage anyone who might have information about Lynskey's disappearance to come forward now.

At her home outside Dublin, Dolours Price read the interview, and it made her furious. She might not have spoken to Adams for years, but she maintained a conversation, of sorts, with him through her articles in *The Blanket*. "I knew you way back when," she reminded Adams in one column. Was it the "interfering cleric" who had diverted Adams from the cause, she wondered, in a possible reference to Father Alec Reid? Or was it "the flattery of the Americans"? Did it "go to your head," she asked him, "did the ego soar and at last did you see the possibility that you might be somebody?" Again and again, she came back to her feeling of personal and political betrayal. "You didn't do it for a couple of houses and a good suit on your back, surely?" she asked. "I'm all curiosity."

Adams never responded to these provocations, and Price, spurned anew, could occasionally turn menacing. "I look forward to the freedom to lay bare my experiences," she wrote in 2005, adding, "This is the only freedom left to me."

Price had taken lately to telephoning journalists when she felt like talking. She would be sitting at home, sometimes with a glass of something in her hand, and slide into a doleful reverie about the past. It wasn't just that she was lonely. It was that she was seized, in these moments, by a defiant impulse to set matters straight. To testify. "Dolours, what the fuck are you doing?" Eamonn McCann would protest, pointing out just how hazardous it could be for her to ring up a journalist for a chat about her history. But to McCann, it seemed that Price was filled with "a great rage" she could scarcely control. When she read the Adams interview about Lynskey in February 2010, she reached for the telephone.

The next morning, a Belfast journalist named Allison Morris got to work at *The Irish News* and discovered a stack of messages waiting for her. Price, it seemed, had been ringing the night desk at the newspaper all night. As it happened, Morris had grown up in Andersonstown, where Price did. She was an aggressive reporter, blond and slightly brassy, with impeccable republican sources. She made the trip to Dublin, where Price was waiting to meet her. Morris had interviewed her fair share of ex-paramilitaries, and she was acquainted with the relevant hazards: warped by trauma, such men and women often navigated their days in a fog of liquor and prescription drugs. She had interviewed Brendan Hughes on a number of occasions before he died, and she sometimes had to stop the interviews because he was drunk. But when Price came to the door and greeted Morris and her photographer, she seemed sober and coherent.

Her hair was short and dyed a platinum blond, and she wore a cardigan and a red scarf looped around her neck. Morris was struck by her poise and beauty. Price seemed to her, as she did to so many, like a theater person, a bohemian.

Price wanted to talk about the disappeared. What had set her off was the blitheness with which Adams discussed the disappearance of her old friend Joe Lynskey, as though it were some act of God rather than an atrocity that Adams himself had ordered. Lynskey was "a gentleman," Price told Morris. She should not have allowed him to go to his death. She should have helped him flee the country. "It devastated me, it still does," she said. "I should have done more."

"You do realize you're implicating yourself?" Morris said.

"I don't care anymore," Price said. "The man's a liar."

The two women had been talking for some time when Morris looked up and was startled to see a boy hovering uncertainly in the doorway. He had pale skin and dark, shaggy hair. He was the spitting image, Morris thought, of Stephen Rea. It was Danny, Dolours's son. He was holding a telephone. "My aunt Marian wants to speak with you," he said to Morris.

When Morris got on the phone, Marian Price was furious that she might be conducting an interview. She explained that Dolours had been receiving treatment at St. Patrick's, a mental health facility in Dublin. "She is not well," Marian said. "She should not be talking to people."

"Your sister's a grown woman," Morris protested. But Marian was insistent.

After leaving the house, Morris consulted with her boss and tried to think of a way to salvage the interview. The solution she ended up devising was to write a slightly anodyne version of the story and say that Dolours Price intended to confess to the Independent Commission for the Location of Victims' Remains—because anyone who approached the commission with information would, in theory, receive immunity from prosecution. The article was published a few days later, under the headline DOLOURS PRICE'S TRAUMA OVER IRA DISAPPEARED. It said that Price had "vital information" to share about the disappearances of Joe Lynskey, Seamus Wright, and Kevin McKee. But it did not spell out any of the details. Morris also noted that Price had information about "the final days of mother-of-10 Jean McConville." Before the article ran, Morris telephoned Price and asked if she had contacted the commission. Price lied and said that she had.

.   .   .

Three days after Morris's article was published, a Belfast tabloid called *Sunday Life* put out an article of its own. Under the headline "Gerry Adams and the Disappeared," this article featured precisely the types of details that Morris had omitted from hers, and it attributed these details to the "Terrorist in a Mini-Skirt Who Married a Movie Star," Dolours Price. According to *Sunday Life,* Price fingered Adams directly, saying he had "played a key role in disappearing victims." When Price picked up Joe Lynskey before he was killed, she did so "on the orders of Gerry Adams." Price said that she had also driven Jean McConville across the border to her death. Some members of the IRA had "wanted Jean's body dumped in the middle of Albert Street." But, Price maintained, Gerry Adams "argued against that," saying that doing so would be bad for the image of the Provos.

These charges were devastating in their specificity, and dovetailed quite precisely with the account by Brendan Hughes. But there was something peculiar about the article in *Sunday Life.* To begin with, the author, Ciarán Barnes, did not appear to have spoken to Dolours Price himself. Instead he cited a "tape recorded confession" by Price, "which *Sunday Life* has heard." But what was this confession? Elsewhere in the article, Barnes wrote that Price "has made taped confessions of her role in the abduc-

tions to academics at Boston University." Apart from the erroneous name—Boston University and Boston College are separate
institutions—the implication was unmistakable: it appeared that
Ciarán Barnes, a Belfast tabloid journalist, had somehow listened
to the Boston College tapes of Dolours Price, and had done so
before her death.

When Ed Moloney learned about the *Sunday Life* story, he
reacted with alarm. The article clearly intimated that Barnes
had accessed the archive at Boston College. But Moloney knew
that this could not be true. The recordings had been held under
lock and key, in the Treasure Room at the Burns Library. What's
more, Moloney could point to another reason why Barnes
could not have had access to the tapes: in her recorded interviews with Mackers, Dolours Price had never mentioned Jean
McConville—because Mackers had warned her against doing
so. "Dolours Price did not once mention the name 'Jean McConville,'" Moloney wrote in a subsequent affidavit.

If Barnes hadn't heard the Boston tapes, then which confession was he referring to? As they tried to fathom what had happened, Moloney and Mackers arrived at a theory. Allison Morris
and Ciarán Barnes were friends and former colleagues who had
worked together in the past, at the *Andersonstown News*. Moloney
and Mackers knew about the abortive *Irish News* interview that
had been halted by Marian Price. They concluded that, after
publishing her own defanged version of the Price story, Morris must have shared the tape of her interview with her friend
Barnes. In the article, Barnes wrote about hearing a "taped confession" and also said that Dolours Price had made a "taped confession" for the Belfast Project. The article implied that there
was only one taped confession. But in fact there were two.

Allison Morris denied sharing her interview with Barnes;
Barnes would say only that he "would be remiss" to talk about
his sources. Gerry Adams, meanwhile, angrily contested Price's
claims, noting that she was "a long-standing opponent of Sinn

Féin and the peace process." Price was suffering from "trauma," Adams pointed out, adding, "There obviously are issues she has to find closure on for herself." It was the same criticism Adams had leveled at Hughes, whom he characterized as having "his issues and his difficulties."

If Adams had indeed been the commanding officer of both Price and Hughes, this talking point could be interpreted as surpassingly callous: both were indignant because Adams had ordered them to take brutal actions, then disowned them, claiming that they alone bore moral responsibility, because he was never in the IRA. When each finally spoke up, Adams maintained that they were lying—and, in order to discredit them, pointed to the genuine trauma they were experiencing. Adams himself seemed conspicuously undaunted by the past. So many others were tortured by what they had experienced in the Troubles. But he never looked as though he had lost a night's sleep. "Brendan said what Brendan said," he told one interviewer. "And Brendan's dead. So let it go."

THE MYSTERY RADIO

FOR THE McCONVILLE FAMILY, the nearly simultaneous revelations of Ed Moloney's book about Brendan Hughes and the newspaper stories about Dolours Price were painful. Both Hughes and Price had insisted that Jean was an informant, and Hughes had described in detail how she was discovered in possession of a radio. This new information appeared to reopen a matter that the McConvilles had felt was conclusively settled. In 2006, the police ombudsman for Northern Ireland, Nuala O'Loan, released a report on the death of Jean McConville. O'Loan found that the authorities had never conducted any sort of proper investigation into the abduction. But she located intelligence files from the time that recorded rumors suggesting that "McConville had been abducted by the Provos because she is an informer." When she searched old military and police files, however, O'Loan was unable to locate any records that mentioned McConville prior to her disappearance—or any suggestion that she might have been working as an agent in Divis Flats. In her report, O'Loan pointed out that the United Kingdom has a policy to neither confirm nor deny whether any particular individual has served as a clandestine agent of the state. Nevertheless, she wrote, this situation was unique. "That family has suffered extensively because of the allegation that their mother was an informant," she noted, and because Jean was long since dead, no harm could come to her now. "She is not recorded as having been an agent at any time," O'Loan wrote, before concluding, more forcefully, "She was an innocent woman who was abducted and murdered."

This emphatic declaration felt like a vindication to Jean's children, who for decades had asserted that their mother was unfairly maligned because she came to the assistance of a wounded British soldier. "I am glad my mother's name was cleared," Michael McConville said after the report was released. "We knew throughout all the years, it was lies."

Not everyone was ready to accept O'Loan's report as the final word, however. Even after her findings were announced, the Provos stuck to their original position, saying, in a new statement, that the IRA had conducted a "thorough investigation" of its own into the circumstances surrounding McConville's murder and had confirmed that she was "working as an informer for the British army." The statement singled out Michael McConville by name and acknowledged that he might dispute the Provos' account, before adding, acerbically, "The IRA accepts he rejects this conclusion."

Ed Moloney and Anthony McIntyre also continued to believe that McConville had been an informant. Their confidence in the oral history of Brendan Hughes was unshakable. To Moloney, it seemed that Nuala O'Loan, influenced by her obvious sympathy for the McConville children, simply chose to arrive at the categorical conclusion that would be most comforting for them. As a hard-nosed reporter, Moloney had an outlook that was more clinical and unsparing. In his view, the fact that O'Loan could not retrieve any records indicating that McConville was a spy hardly settled the matter. Which of the many secret archives of British military records had O'Loan consulted? She refused to specify. Perhaps there were records that she had not discovered. Had she really left no stone unturned? Mackers believed that the army or the police might have deliberately covered up Jean's involvement. If she had been a tout, and she was warned by the IRA to stop, it would look pretty terrible for the authorities to

Soldier with a handheld radio in Divis Flats.

give her another radio and send her back to work, when such a move was so likely to get her killed.

There was also a mystery relating to the detail of the radio itself. Some former police officers, like Trevor Campbell, maintained that neither the army nor the police were using handheld radios to communicate in those days, much less to communicate with informants. But Ed Moloney, working with a researcher who had served in the British Army, dug through old British files and found evidence of a small radio that *was* used by the army in Belfast in 1972. They even managed to track down a photograph of a British soldier, squatting against a wall in full battle flak, holding this type of radio—in Divis Flats.

Even if such a radio did exist, however, it would be folly to give the device to a low-level informant who lived with a bunch of children in an intensely republican area. And what about those thin walls in Divis Flats? You couldn't have a casual conversation over a cup of tea without the neighbors in the next flat overhearing. So making covert transmissions on a clandestine radio would pose serious risks. When Michael McConville studied the recollections of Brendan Hughes, he was struck by the fact that Hughes never said that he had *personally* seen the radio in question. Perhaps this was just a rumor that got passed around Belfast for long enough that over the years it became accepted as fact. Perhaps it was a story that the people who murdered Jean McConville told one another (or told themselves) in order to feel less awful about what they'd done. Michael also wrote off as ludicrous and insulting the suggestion, by Hughes, that the McConville siblings might somehow have assisted their mother in any conspiracy to spy on their neighbors.

But there was another mystery that was compounded by the publication of the Brendan Hughes account. It involved the timeline of Jean McConville's disappearance. In her investigation, Nuala O'Loan was not able to recover any official documents giving a precise date for the night Jean McConville disappeared. The children had always maintained that one evening in early December, Jean had gone to play bingo and then been seized, questioned, and beaten before she was discovered wandering in a daze by the army and brought home to Divis Flats. It was the following evening that she was taken away, according to the children's memory: she was still nursing the bruises from her beating. While the children could not be absolutely certain about the date, they believed that Jean was abducted on December 7, 1972.

This timeline would seem to contradict the story told by Brendan Hughes, who recalled McConville being questioned and having the radio seized, then returning to work as an informant and, some time later, being caught with a second radio. The story that Hughes told, which Dolours Price endorsed and the IRA officially maintained in its statements, was that Jean McConville was not just an informant but a recidivist: that she was warned to stop helping the British, and then murdered only after she defied the warning. But if McConville was questioned and warned on the night of December 6 and then abducted from her flat the following night, the timeline Hughes asserted would make no sense. Even in a scenario in which McConville's ostensible British handlers were callous enough to put her back to work after the warning, it seems unlikely that they would do so—and even supply her with a new radio—within twenty-four hours.

The McConville children embraced O'Loan's report as a complete exoneration of their mother, a decades-overdue affirmation of everything they had been saying for years. But in a few significant particulars, the report was actually at odds with the family's version of events. In her review of historical documentation, Nuala O'Loan discovered an official record that seemed to describe the night Jean was taken from the bingo hall by the IRA for questioning. According to an old police log, a woman was found wandering the streets in West Belfast one night at 11 p.m. She had been beaten. The log noted that her name was Mary McConville, but clearly this was Jean—her address was listed as St. Jude's Walk, in Divis Flats. The log stated that the woman had been "accosted by a number of men and warned to stop giving information to the military."

Setting aside the question of whether the IRA was correct or mistaken in believing Jean to be a tout, this document appeared to corroborate the claim that a warning had been issued to McConville. But the police log was a significant clue for another reason as well: according to the log, McConville was found wandering the streets after the beating and the warning not on the night of December 6, as the children's account suggested, but seven nights earlier, on November 29.

Michael McConville and his siblings were just kids in 1972. They lived in a war zone, their mother had been taken, and they were forced to steal and scavenge for food. In the midst of tumult and tragedy, nobody is consulting the calendar. And memory is a strange thing. Helen remembers that on the day after Jean was taken from the bingo hall, the younger children went to school; Michael remembers that they stayed home. It could be that the McConville siblings simply got the dates mixed up in retrospect and that Jean was actually questioned on November 29 and taken away on November 30. But from the very first press interviews and accounts to social services that they gave beginning in January 1973, the children were emphatic that their mother was taken in early December, not late November. If the date of the abduction is accurate, and the police log that O'Loan discovered is reliable, then it would seem that more than a single night may have elapsed between the initial interrogation and warning and the moment Jean McConville was taken away. If *that* were the true chronology, then it would look a lot more like the timeline proposed by Brendan Hughes.

.   .   .

There was one final confounding detail in O'Loan's report. For decades, the McConville kids had talked about the night their mother came to the aid of the wounded British soldier in Divis Flats. More than one of the children could recall vivid details from that evening: the family huddled in the darkness of the flat; the staccato pop of gunfire in the concrete corridors; the soldier's anguished moan outside the door. But when O'Loan consulted army records from the period, she could find no evidence of a British soldier being wounded in the vicinity of Divis Flats. Perhaps the records were incomplete? Or perhaps there was some mistake regarding the nature of the soldier's injuries, or the period in the lives of the McConvilles when the episode took place. But it was tempting to wonder whether the children of Jean McConville, like the people who abducted her, had not constructed a legend around the vanished woman that they could live with.

Brendan Hughes may have been dead by the time it was revealed that he had direct knowledge of the McConville disappearance. But Dolours Price was still alive. When the *Sunday Life* article was published, in 2010, the McConvilles were shocked that Price would speak so freely about her involvement in an operation that had been a closely guarded secret for so many years. Ravenous for more information, Michael sent a message, through intermediaries, that he would like a meeting with Price. But he never heard back from her. Helen greeted the story with an angry challenge to the authorities. "Arrest the pair of them, Adams and Price," she said. "It's disgusting that the people involved in my mother's murder are still walking the streets." The Sinn Féin president and his outspoken antagonist might not have "pulled the trigger," Helen allowed. But they were "as guilty as the people who did."

One bright, chilly morning the following spring, Ed Moloney was at home in the Riverdale section of the Bronx when he received a phone call that filled him with alarm. Boston College had just received a subpoena. The U.S. Department of Justice, acting under a mutual legal assistance treaty with the United Kingdom, was passing on an official request from the Police Service of Northern Ireland. The request was made, the subpoena stated, in order to assist the authorities "regarding an alleged violation of the laws of the United Kingdom, namely, murder." Specifically, the subpoena demanded "the original tape recordings of any and all interviews of Brendan Hughes and Dolours Price."

THE BOSTON TAPES

"I ALWAYS, PROBABLY TO the point of being boring, asked about the legal status and confidentiality," Mackers fumed. "Total confidentiality and total protection. This was the whole reason for putting them in a U.S. university!" An emergency conference call had been convened among the chief architects of the Belfast Project to discuss what to do about the subpoena. Along with Mackers and his wife, Carrie, outside Dublin, the call was joined by Ed Moloney (in New York), Wilson McArthur, who had conducted the loyalist interviews (in Belfast), and Tom Hachey and Bob O'Neill, at Boston College. Hachey announced that he had spoken with the president of the college, William Leahy, and that Leahy had assured him, "We are not going to allow our interviewers or interviews to be compromised."

Mackers and Moloney were in a state of panic. During the years when they were compiling the oral history archive, they had never believed that British authorities might seriously endeavor to access the recordings. The very idea seemed ludicrous: just a few months earlier, the British government, along with the government of Ireland, had entrusted a raft of sensitive documentation associated with the post-Troubles disarmament process to Boston College, on the understanding that the records would be sealed for up to thirty years. Could officials from the same government really be seeking, now, to violate a similar embargo at the very same university?

Administrators at Boston College had been consulting with lawyers, and it was not yet clear how the university would respond. On the call, Hachey and O'Neill were unflustered, and reassuring. But Mackers expressed a fear that BC might ultimately comply with the request and turn over the tapes—that the interviewers and the ex-paramilitaries who shared their secret histories might simply be "hung out to dry."

Moloney shared this fear, and, as a form of insurance against any quiet, dead-of-night handover, he had already gone public. He contacted *The New York Times,* which ran a front-page story, "Secret Archive of Ulster Troubles Faces Subpoena." He also spoke to *The Boston Globe,* suggesting in an interview that Boston College might be left with no choice but to "destroy" the tapes rather than turn them over to the authorities. To Moloney and Mackers, it seemed that nothing less than the principles of free speech and academic freedom hung in the balance, and the more publicity the case received, the more likely Boston College would be to do the right thing. But Hachey scolded Moloney for going straight to the press without consulting university administrators first, and he complained that the threat about destroying the archive had been "over the top."

Nobody in the group knew what was driving this sudden request for the interviews, but Moloney had a suspicion. The Police Service of Northern Ireland might be striving, on paper, to become a new kind of department, but while the cops had changed the name of the constabulary, they were still, in many instances, the same cops. For decades, the men of the RUC had perceived Gerry Adams to be their chief antagonist, the figurehead of a paramilitary outfit that murdered nearly three hundred police officers over the course of the Troubles. Many old hands in the PSNI had lost loved ones—fellow cops, childhood friends, fathers—at the hands of the IRA. Now they had become aware that, across an ocean at Boston College, there existed an archive featuring testimony by former subordinates of Gerry Adams, and that these secret interviews might furnish the kind of proof that had eluded British authorities for decades: evidence that could put Adams away not just for IRA membership, but for murder.

"This is a vendetta that is being waged," Tom Hachey said on the conference call, agreeing with Moloney. "They're out to try to find something that they can nail a person like Gerry on." He added, "I'll be goddamned if they're going to use our archives to indict him, because that's not what we undertook this enterprise for." Hachey certainly sounded adamant. But as he and Bob O'Neill questioned the others about the particulars of the project, Moloney thought that he detected, in the line of questioning, a hint that Boston College might not be feeling quite so resolute as Hachey was making it sound. They were very curious about the precise guarantees that McIntyre and Wilson McArthur had made at the time they conducted the interviews. What exactly had the interview subjects been promised in the way of confidentiality? Before he interviewed his loyalist subjects, McArthur said, he had assured them that there was an "ironclad" guarantee of confidentiality. Their testimony would be released to no one, nor would it even be acknowledged that they had participated in the project at all, until their death. McArthur reminded Hachey and O'Neill that they themselves had used that word—*ironclad*—when they first discussed the archive, a decade earlier. When he encountered skittish participants, McArthur would tell them that "Boston College's legal counsel" had vetted the whole arrangement.

As it turned out, this was not actually true. When Ed Moloney was preparing the contracts that the participants would sign, in early 2001, he emailed some proposed language to Bob O'Neill, writing, "You may want to refer this to your legal people before we use it." The following day, O'Neill wrote back to say that he was working on the wording of the contract and would run it by the university's lawyers. But in the end, it appears, he never did. A lawyer would likely have advised him that the contracts should specify that any guarantee of confidentiality they might contain would not necessarily be able to protect the archive from a court order. The contract that each participant signed did not contain any such qualification, and no lawyer at Boston College ever reviewed those agreements.

Hachey ended the conference call on an upbeat note, like a quarterback breaking up a huddle, as though the men would brace themselves and march into this battle as a team. But while they would exchange a few further emails, that was the last time that Hachey or O'Neill would speak with any of their partners in the Belfast Project. Before the end of May, Boston College turned over the Brendan Hughes interviews, on the grounds that Hughes was now dead and much of the content of his oral history had already been published in Moloney's book. But whereas *Voices from the Grave* had been carefully edited to shield certain identities for legal and security reasons, the Hughes transcripts and recordings were unredacted. Moloney was irate to learn that the PSNI had come into possession of this material. "The authorities now have information upon which to act," he emailed Hachey. "I would bet the mortgage that at this moment there are teams of lawyers working in the bowels of the British government trying to discover ways to force BC to surrender the names of other possible interviewees."

Moloney proposed that, in order to avert a "huge disaster," Hachey and O'Neill should immediately pack the entire archive into FedEx envelopes and overnight it to Mackers in Ireland. Boston College might not have the stomach for a protracted legal fight, but Mackers did. Before he would ever turn the tapes and transcripts over, Moloney said, Mackers would "happily go to jail." For the academics to mail the material out of the country at that point might have constituted obstruction of justice. But Mackers agreed with Moloney that Boston College had a moral obligation to honor its commitment to confidentiality, and this preempted any niceties of law. People had risked their lives to entrust their stories to the Belfast Project; the least Boston College could do was engage in a little civil disobedience to protect them. Now that the authorities had the Brendan Hughes material, Moloney predicted, there was a "strong possibility" that they would return with a second subpoena, seeking other interviews, based on what they had gathered from Hughes.

In a terse email, Hachey said that under "no circumstances" would the university transfer the documents out of the country. In a line that would come to seem ironic in retrospect, he pointed out that promises had been made to the participants and argued that the *safest* place for their recollections was Boston College. The university agreed to fight the Price subpoena, arguing, in a motion to federal court, that releasing the material would violate the agreements made with the participants, undermine academic freedom, jeopardize the peace process in Northern Ireland, and throw into danger the lives of people associated with the project. "The IRA imposes a code of silence akin to the concept of 'omerta' in the Mafia," the brief noted. As such, people like Dolours Price were willing to participate in the oral history only with the assurance "that the interviews would be kept locked away." In an affidavit, Moloney noted that "it is an offense punishable by death" for IRA members to reveal details of their paramilitary careers to outsiders.

But the U.S. government hit back aggressively with its own arguments for why the Price interview should be turned over, suggesting that Moloney, McIntyre, and Boston College had "made promises they could not keep—that they would conceal evidence of murder and other crimes until the perpetrators were in their graves." The Belfast Project was not a work of journalism, and, as a legal matter, there was no "academic privilege" that would shield the interviews from a court order. As for

Moloney's arguments about the dangers of revealing the archive, the government argued, Moloney *himself* had widely publicized the project. He published a book about it! Nobody had assassinated Mackers when it was revealed that he had interviewed Brendan Hughes and others for the project. So how dangerous could it really be?

The government also suggested, erroneously, that the Price interview had already been unsealed and shared with the reporter Ciarán Barnes for his article in *Sunday Life*. Lawyers for Boston College pointed out, in a filing to the court, that this was false—that U.S. officials had clearly been duped by the ruse with which Barnes implied that he had heard the Boston tapes, without ever saying explicitly that he had. But by August, Moloney's dire prediction had come true, and a second subpoena arrived at BC, demanding any and all tapes related to "the abduction and death of Mrs. Jean McConville." In December, a federal judge ruled against the university and ordered BC to turn over the tapes and transcripts to the court for review. The university chose not to appeal this ruling—a capitulation that Moloney and Mackers greeted with ire, if not surprise. So the two Irishmen hired their own lawyers and appealed the decision.

.   .   .

Unfortunately for the Irishmen, the legal case was cut-and-dried: there were few legal or constitutional protections that the men could invoke. But in parallel with their efforts in the courts, Moloney and Mackers, along with Carrie Twomey, pursued a political strategy, appealing to anyone they could for support. John Kerry, then a senator from Massachusetts, had close ties to Boston College (where he'd received his law degree) as well as to Ireland. Kerry wrote to the secretary of state, Hillary Clinton, urging her to work with British authorities on the issue, because the subpoenas might jeopardize the peace process. The Massachusetts branch of the American Civil Liberties Union filed a friend-of-the-court brief opposing the subpoenas.

In making their case that this controversy represented a crisis for academic freedom, Moloney and Mackers, and the university itself, might have turned to BC's faculty for support. But by the time the subpoenas arrived, most faculty members had soured on the Belfast Project. Because of the secrecy surrounding the archive, almost nobody on campus had known about it before the publication of Moloney's book. When it was originally conceived, the project was supposed to have a board of overseers from the university who could monitor its academic rigor, but, like the close reading of the contracts by lawyers, that idea never came to fruition. When the details of the project did come to light, some members of the faculty took issue with what they learned: Anthony McIntyre might have had a PhD, but he was hardly a seasoned practitioner of oral history. Nor was Wilson McArthur. Both men appeared to be ideological fellow travelers—and, in some cases, close friends—with their interview subjects. Hardly a model of academic objectivity. Then there was the fact that Mackers had served nearly two decades in prison for murder.

Tom Hachey was regarded with suspicion by the faculty. He was an old friend of President Leahy's, and he seemed to enjoy a sinecure with few actual departmental responsibilities. The same might be said of Bob O'Neill, who presided over the Burns Library. Neither man had a strong scholarly constituency on campus to which he could turn for backup. In an email to Moloney, Hachey remarked that there was "no visible support emerging from outraged academics." Moloney may not have done the project any favors in this regard by endeavoring to bar access by graduate students to the archive. When the Boston College history department finally released a statement about the Belfast Project, in 2014, it did so not to come to the defense of academic freedom, but to make clear that the undertaking "is not and never was" in any way associated with the department. "Nobody trusted the integrity of the project," one faculty member explained. Professors in the department believed in academic freedom. "But this was such a bad case to hang that principle on."

Moloney and Mackers brought their case to the First Circuit Court of Appeals and lost. They obtained a stay, which barred the university from turning over the interviews pending an appeal to the Supreme Court. But in the spring of 2013, the Supreme Court refused to hear the case. In determining which of the interviews would be responsive to the second subpoena, which requested any material relating to the abduction and murder of Jean McConville, the judge, William Young, had asked Mackers for help. For security, each interview had been logged at Boston College without the name of the interview subject, and with the alphabet code name instead. But Mackers knew the identities of all of the people he had interviewed, and he might recall which of them had discussed Jean McConville. He declined to help, however, saying that assisting the court would "lead me across the boundary that firewalls academic research from police investigation." Judge Young asked Bob O'Neill for assistance, but he, too, demurred, claiming that he had not read the interviews. So over several days one Christmas, the judge read through the transcripts of all of the republican interviews himself. He found that six of the participants mentioned Jean McConville, though one had done so only glancingly. As a result, Young authorized the release of all the recordings associated with five of the participants.

One of those participants was Dolours Price. Mackers and Moloney had both been adamant that Price never spoke about McConville in her oral history. "Dolours Price did not mention Jean McConville nor talk about what had happened to her in her interviews for the Belfast Project," Moloney said in a press release in September 2012. "The subject of that unfortunate woman's disappearance was never mentioned, not even once," he wrote in an affidavit that same month. This assertion had significant legal implications, as Moloney explained. "The truth is that the interviews that Anthony McIntyre conducted with Dolours Price are notable for the absence of any material that could ever have justified the subpoenas."

Technically, this was true. Dolours Price spent some fifteen hours in recorded conversations with Mackers, and on those recordings she never once mentioned McConville. But there was another set of recordings in the archive in which Price *did* discuss the disappearance of Jean McConville, in great detail. The interviewer wasn't Anthony McIntyre, however. It was Ed Moloney.

.   .   .

When the *Irish News* reporter Allison Morris went to interview Dolours Price at her home in Malahide in February 2010, the Belfast Project had long since concluded. Mackers and Wilson McArthur had finished the last of their interviews by 2006, and the archive lay in the Treasure Room at the Burns Library, apparently complete. But not long after Price spoke with Morris, Moloney visited her in Dublin, to conduct an interview of his own. What he proposed was not to publish his own version of her story, but to ask her about her past, in a level of detail that would go beyond her conversations with Mackers, and then safeguard the interview on the same terms that had applied to the Belfast Project: he would not release her account until after her death.

Price agreed. At the time, she was staying at St. Patrick's Hospital, where she was being treated for depression and PTSD. One morning, Moloney visited her there and the two of them spoke for several hours in her room. Moloney recorded the conversation on a digital recorder. A few days later they met again, outside the hospital, in a rented apartment. This time, Moloney had assembled a small camera crew to film the interview. In both conversations, Price was sober and coherent, her hair tousled and platinum blond, her eyes lined with mascara. She told Moloney about her aunt Bridie, about how, when Bridie came home, blinded and maimed after the accident in the IRA arms dump, Granny Dolan had put the house into mourning. Bridie's sisters were not allowed to go out dancing, Price said. "It was like having a wake with a living body." It was Bridie's suffering, in part, that had obliged her to join the struggle, she said, because it "vindicated her sacrifice." She talked about getting beaten at Burntollet Bridge and joining the IRA, and then the Unknowns.

When Moloney asked about the practice of disappearing people, Price said that she never believed in it. "Pat McClure and myself and other volunteers would have discussed it among ourselves, that we didn't know that it was such a smart idea to be doing it this way," she said. "But we were told, 'This is the way it's being done.'"

"Do you think it's a war crime?" Moloney asked her.

"I think it's a war crime, yes. I think it's a war crime," she said. "I certainly advocated and said that...their bodies should be thrown out in the street. To put the fear of God and the republican movement into anybody who would choose that form of life."

Price had already been helping to disappear people for some time when she was ordered to take McConville across the border, she said. Up to that point, she had not known the woman, or known of her. But McConville had confessed to being an informer, Price insisted. A transmitter had been discovered at her flat. There was also another detail: Price said that Jean McConville had been spotted by some IRA volunteers at a barracks on Hastings Street. "She was concealed behind a blanket with a slit in it that she could see through," Price said.

Like the Mau Mau cloaked in sheets with slits in them so

that they could identify their countrymen for Frank Kitson, Jean McConville was, in Price's telling, hiding behind a blanket and picking out IRA men from a lineup. Except that the blanket did not reach all the way to the floor, Price continued, and one of the men "recognized the slippers."

When McConville was taken for questioning, Price continued, she "made an admission." She said that she had been an informer. "For money."

With a level gaze, Price told Moloney, "We believed that informers were the lowest form of human life. They were less than human. Death was too good for them."

Along with Wee Pat McClure and one other volunteer, Price picked Jean McConville up at a house in West Belfast where she was being held, and they drove toward the border. Price's friend Joe Lynskey might have known from the moment he got in the car with her that he was being ferried to his death, but Jean McConville had no such premonition. Price told her that she was going to be turned over to the Legion of Mary, a Catholic charity, who would take her away to a place of safety.

"Will my children be brought to me?" McConville asked.

Price had not realized until that moment that she had children.

"Yes, I'm sure they will," she lied.

"Will they give me money?" McConville asked. "Will they get me a house?"

According to Price, McConville felt no fear, having already confessed everything to the IRA. Along the way they stopped, and Price bought McConville fish and chips and cigarettes. Price told Moloney that she did not like McConville. "She said at one point, 'I knew those Provo bastards wouldn't have the balls to shoot me.' And the 'Provo bastards' who were driving her thought, *Oh, wouldn't they?*" Price said coldly, adding, "She talked too much. And condemned herself out of her own mouth."

Was this true? It was such a specific recollection, and so

starkly at odds with the memories that the McConville children had of their mother. The woman they recalled was not some coarse-tongued instigator, but a cowed and tentative recluse. Could McConville really have lashed out in such a suicidally impetuous manner, when her encounter with Price was so obviously fraught with danger? Was Price consciously lying about the woman? Or had she coped with her own sense of culpability by remembering Jean McConville as something less than human? For most of her conversation with Moloney, she maintained her steely resolve. But it could sometimes feel like a pose, a form of armor. And occasionally her tone would falter.

"I don't know the specifics of what she did and what she didn't do," Price said immediately after her condemnation of McConville. She had no firsthand knowledge of McConville's alleged crimes; what she knew was that the organization had come to the improbable conclusion that the mother of ten was an informer. Even if the charge was true—and Price believed that it was—she doubted, deep down, that the penalty was appropriate. "What warrants death?" she said to Moloney. "I have to ask myself. What warrants death?" She continued, "I certainly knew nothing of the nature of the children or the number. I knew none of that. And had it been a situation where I was brought into the discussion of what happened, I might have advocated a lesser punishment." Perhaps McConville could have been expelled from the country rather than killed, she suggested.

Instead, Price said, they crossed the border and she left Jean in Dundalk, with the local unit of the IRA.

. . .

Then what happened? Moloney asked.

"She stayed there for a while," Price said. She hesitated. Then she said, "This is where it gets dangerous for me."

If Price continued to malign McConville's character at least in part to assuage her own nagging conscience, it may have been because she had done more than simply drive the widow to the border.

"I need to know the facts," said Moloney.

"Okay, well, we were called back," Price said. "She'd been there for about four to five days. And we were called back to Dundalk." The local unit had dug a hole in the ground. All they had to do was take McConville across a field to the freshly dug grave and shoot her. But they hadn't. "They didn't want to do it," Price said. It was because McConville was a woman, she thought.

"So you guys had to do it," Moloney said.

Price said nothing, just made a small murmur.

"Is that right?" he pressed.

She murmured again. Then she uttered, "Yeah."

"Do you want to talk about that, or not?" Moloney asked.

There were three members of the Unknowns with McConville when she died, Price said: Wee Pat McClure, another volunteer, and Price herself. They had only one gun, and they worried about their consciences and decided that they would each take a shot, so that they could never say for certain who it was that dealt the killing blow. This is an old trick used by firing squads—one of the gunmen's rifles will be loaded with a blank so that afterward, each of the shooters can tell himself that he *might* not have been the one to take a life. It can serve as a comforting fiction, though in this case, because they had only one gun, there would not be much ambiguity about which of them did the killing. "We each in turn fired a shot," Price said. When Price fired hers, she deliberately missed. Then one of the others pulled the trigger, and McConville collapsed.

"We left her in the hole," Price said. Then the local Dundalk unit sealed the grave.

.   .   .

"Then you went back to Belfast?" Moloney asked.

"Then we went back to Belfast."

"And what happened then?"

"Well," Price said, "we were pretty distraught. And Pat went and reported it."

"To Gerry?" Moloney asked.

"Yeah," Price said.

Suddenly shifting his tone from patient confessor to stern cross-examiner, Moloney said, "There's no doubt in your mind, being part of all that operation, that the chain of command was such that the order which had originated with Gerry Adams—"

"Yes," Price said.

"And reporting went back to Gerry Adams. You're sure of that?"

"I'm sure," she said. Then, her pace quickening, she said, "And he tried to pretend he was in Long Kesh when that happened. He *wasn't* in Long Kesh when that happened. He wasn't. And, um, that's very hard, a very hard thing." She was upset. "Those experiences, I mean..." She trailed off. "These people do come into my mind, come into my head," she said. Lynskey, Wright, McKee, McConville. "I think about them and," she continued, "I won't tell a lie: I'm not a great one for prayer. But I do occasionally say the odd one in the middle of the night. I do occasionally say, 'Well, God bless them. I hope they are in a better place.'"

As an IRA volunteer, Price said, "I was often required to act contrary to my nature." Sometimes she had to obey orders that were not easy to obey. At the time, she always did as she was instructed. But later, she had the opportunity to ask herself "all the complex questions that you don't ask in the heat of the moment." She added, "I've spent a lot of time talking to a lot of doctors about all of this."

After several hours, Moloney and Price stopped talking.

They parted ways, and he assured her that he would protect the things she had said. He would bring the tapes back to America and deposit them in the safest place he knew—the Belfast Project archives, in the Treasure Room at Boston College.

They were still there three years later when two detectives from the Police Service of Northern Ireland flew to Logan Airport, in July 2013, and made their way to Chestnut Hill to retrieve the material they had been authorized by Judge Young to collect. The interviews that Moloney conducted with Price were not technically part of the Belfast Project at all. But in trying to keep them safe, he had actually been placing them in jeopardy. Moloney pleaded with Bob O'Neill not to include this material in the collection that the university turned over. The subpoenas were written broadly enough, however, that the university, which had never had much of a fight in it to begin with, chose to give up Moloney's interviews along with everything else. One day the following spring, Gerry Adams was arrested by the PSNI, in relation to the abduction and murder, forty-one years earlier, of Jean McConville.

DEATH BY MISADVENTURE

AT MASSEREENE BARRACKS ON Saturday nights, the young British soldiers liked to order pizza. Stuck on the army base, they would telephone a nearby Domino's. Over the course of a given Saturday evening, the Domino's might dispatch twenty different orders to the barracks. The soldiers were good customers. A few minutes before ten o'clock on the night of March 7, 2009, a couple of young soldiers ventured out to the brick gatehouse at the entrance of the base. Dressed in desert camouflage, they were scheduled to fly a few hours later, in the dead of night, on a transport plane to Afghanistan for a six-month tour of duty. But first they would fill up on pizza. One delivery car pulled up, and then a second—overlapping orders both from the same Domino's, two different delivery guys withdrawing hot square boxes from insulated bags. Then a third car pulled up, a green sedan, and there was a sudden hail of automatic gunfire. There were two gunmen, dressed in dark clothing, their faces sheathed by balaclavas. After a sustained initial volley, they approached the two soldiers, who were lying on the ground, and stood above them, firing repeatedly from close range. Having discharged more than sixty rounds in half a minute, the gunmen scrambled back into the green sedan and disappeared. The two soldiers were killed. Patrick Azimkar was twenty-one, from North London. Mark Quinsey was twenty-three, and from Birmingham. Two other soldiers were wounded in the attack, along with both

Domino's deliverymen. One of them was a local kid, the other an immigrant from Poland.

Twelve years had passed since the last British soldier was killed in Northern Ireland. In a phone call to a Dublin newspaper, an armed dissident group, the Real IRA, claimed responsibility. Even the deliverymen were legitimate targets, a spokesman for the group asserted, because they were "collaborating with the British by servicing them." In a statement, the chief constable of the PSNI, Hugh Orde, said, "This was an act by a small group of increasingly desperate people who are determined to drag ninety-nine percent of this community back to where they don't want to go."

A huge investigation was launched, and several arrests were made. Then, eight months after the shooting, a team of heavily armed police officers burst into a house in Andersonstown. Authorities had traced the telephone used by the Real IRA to claim responsibility for the attack. It was a pay-as-you-go phone that had been purchased at a Tesco supermarket in Newtownabbey the day after the shooting. Consulting CCTV footage from the store, police spotted a pale woman in late middle age who was bundled in a heavy, dark coat. As she stood at the checkout counter and reached into her wallet to purchase the phone, the woman's gaze wandered upward until, suddenly, she was looking directly into the surveillance camera. It was Marian Price.

Dolours might have loathed the Good Friday Agreement, but she could not commit herself to any of the republican splinter groups that were devoted to continuing the violence. Her sister had no such compunction. "Armed struggle *does* have a place in the present and in the future," Marian would say. She was in her late fifties, with grown daughters and arthritis, but she was not yet ready to put down the gun. After two days of interrogation about the barracks shooting, she was released without charges. But eighteen months later, she was detained by the authorities again, and this time they did not let her go. Marian was ultimately charged with "providing property for the purposes of terrorism." There was another charge as well, relating to a dissident rally in Derry, at which a masked Real IRA man read a statement threatening police officers, saying that, as an occupying force, they were "liable for execution." While he recited the statement, Marian Price stood beside him, holding his script, unmasked.

For the next two years, Marian was held in prison, including long stretches in solitary confinement. Her psoriasis was acting up, and she started losing weight. In her head, it could seem at times as if she was back in jail in England, institutionalized again, as if the past thirty years had not actually happened, as if she had never gotten married or had children or enjoyed a life outside prison walls. Dolours was distraught with worry for her sister. She took part in a "Free Marian Price!" campaign, outside the prison. Earnest letters were written and little rallies were held. Supporters described Marian as a "victim of psychological torture and internment without trial." It was all conspicuously reminiscent of the movement to free the Price sisters back in the early 1970s.

But this campaign did not garner the kind of popular support among Irish republicans that the Price sisters had enjoyed decades earlier. Marian might not have moved on, but the world had; it had changed in profound and irrevocable ways. The war had taken its toll, and there was a new spirit of compromise and reconciliation in the air. The very month that Marian was taken into custody, Queen Elizabeth II made a state visit to Ireland—the first by a British monarch since 1911, a century earlier, when the whole island was still part of the United Kingdom. A former schoolmate of Dolours's, Mary McAleese, had grown up to become president of Ireland. She welcomed the historic occasion of the royal visit, saying it was "absolutely the right moment for us to welcome on to Irish soil Her Majesty the Queen." Marian was still in prison the following year when Martin McGuinness, the former Derry gunman turned deputy first minister of Northern Ireland, met with the Queen and shook the woman's hand. McGuinness and Gerry Adams seemed capable of finding common ground with anyone. They even reconciled with the vitriolic Ian Paisley, with whom McGuinness came to work closely in government. "In politics, as in life, it is a truism that no one can ever have one hundred percent of what they desire," Paisley said, appearing alongside McGuinness at Stormont. "They must make a verdict when they believe they have achieved enough."

But just because everybody else was now ready to give up fighting didn't mean that Marian was. She readily acknowledged that her recalcitrance on this matter was fundamentally antidemocratic—that only a tiny minority of people in Northern Ireland were supportive of further bloodshed in the name of expelling the British. "But being a republican isn't about entering a popularity contest," she observed. "It never has been." She had announced, back in 2001, that "another generation is going to have to take up the torch of republicanism and fight on." But whereas she took the torch from her parents, just as they had taken it from theirs, Marian's own daughters, like her sister's sons, showed little inclination to devote themselves to armed struggle. Marian had raised two civilians, young women who were creatures not of the troubled twentieth century but of the globalized twenty-first. One of her daughters was a journalist; she worked for the BBC.

Some of Marian's friends worried that she was being used by her young dissident associates, that these wannabe revolutionaries humored her because she was a Price sister—because she conferred, as a poster girl of the truly dire years of the struggle, some vicarious, if slightly retro, credibility. In 2013, after two years in custody, Marian pleaded guilty to both charges against her and was sentenced to twelve months in prison, though, due to her declining health and the time she had already served, the judge suspended the sentence. At the hearing, she was frail, and approached the dock with the aid of a walking stick.

In prison, Marian had sustained herself with a cultural diet that seemed less characteristic of a radical agitator than of a middlebrow, apolitical pensioner. She did the word puzzles in the *Daily Mail*. She read Stieg Larsson novels. And she spent hours watching her favorite TV show, the lush English confection of manor house nostalgia, *Downton Abbey*.

. . .

It was about a year after Marian Price was released from custody that her old comrade Gerry Adams found himself under arrest. Armed with the Boston College interviews, the PSNI had already arrested a number of people by that point and questioned them about the abduction and murder of Jean McConville. Some of these individuals had lived in the Divis area at the time McConville was taken. But in 1972, many of them had been teenagers, so if they played any role in the affair it was likely a minor one—they may have assisted the scrum of locals who removed McConville from her flat that night—and after their interviews with the police, they were all released. Only one person had actually been charged: Ivor Bell, the veteran republican who, according to Brendan Hughes, had argued that Jean McConville should not be disappeared but should be killed and left in the street, and who was overruled, in Hughes's telling, by Gerry Adams. Bell faced charges of aiding and abetting the murder, and of IRA membership—because even after the Troubles, you could still be prosecuted for having been a member of a paramilitary organization in the past.

Adams had plenty of notice that the authorities wanted to take him into custody. Since 2011, he had been a legislator in the Republic of Ireland, so he enjoyed certain courtesies. The police had contacted him in advance, through his lawyers, and asked him to come to a PSNI station in Antrim. Adams insisted that he would come of his own accord and that they could arrest him *inside* the barracks: he was, by this stage, an emeritus professor of political optics, and he wanted to deny the police the opportunity to arrest him outside the station, in the parking lot, where a gaggle of press photographers, tipped off in advance, could snap a photograph of him in cuffs. Just after eight o'clock on a Wednesday evening, April 30, Adams glided into the station. His belt, watch, and tie were removed, and he was escorted into a room where two officers, a man and a woman, proceeded to inundate him with questions.

Given how frequently Adams had been questioned about the fate of the disappeared, you might suppose that he would have a selection of burnished defenses at the ready. But the answers that he tended to put forth in these situations were never particularly compelling. Questioned about the oral histories of Brendan Hughes and Dolours Price, Adams tended to repeat his assertion that, because they were aggrieved opponents of the peace process, their accounts must be dismissed in their entirety. He wasn't wrong in suggesting that Hughes and Price nursed grudges. Price herself had once acknowledged that she had given the interviews to Boston College "for a kind of score settling reason." But Adams never seemed to be able to account for how it was that Hughes and Price had independently come up with stories about him that were so identical in their particulars.

Yes, they resented Adams, and *yes,* they had demons, and *yes,* they were bitter, and *yes,* that was probably why they put their accusations on the record, Eamonn McCann wrote in *The Irish Times.* "But he isn't obviously right in suggesting that these feelings caused them to concoct wicked lies to discredit him. It is at least as likely that they broke the IRA's code of secrecy because they believed it had been rendered meaningless by the strategy adopted by Adams and his close associates." McCann concluded that "what they'd been driven to do was not to tell lies but to tell the truth." As Price herself said, "I wanted very much to put Gerry Adams where he belonged—and where he had been."

On the particular question of the disappeared, Adams tended to feign a level of ignorance that was difficult to reconcile with the role he had played in Belfast at the dawn of the Troubles. Joe Lynskey was "a neighbor of mine. He lived across the street," Adams had acknowledged. Yet he had no memory of asking any questions when Lynskey abruptly disappeared. There were "numerous rumors over the last forty years," Adams told *The Irish News,* noting that there had supposedly been sightings of Lynskey in Birmingham, Manchester, and Australia. How was Adams to know that the IRA had murdered him and buried him in an unmarked grave?

When a Belfast investigative journalist named Darragh MacIntyre questioned him about Seamus Wright and Kevin McKee, the informants who were disappeared after the Four Square Laundry operation, Adams claimed to have known nothing about the IRA's decision to kill them, either. But in his own memoir, Adams had written glowingly about the IRA's discovery of the Four Square Laundry, MacIntyre pointed out. How could he have known about that yet not known that the Provos discovered the operation only after Wright and McKee confessed to being double agents? Adams could offer no coherent answer. MacIntyre pressed: *You weren't at all curious about the fate of these two young men?*

"I learned a long time ago," Adams replied, "if you don't ask, you can't tell."

Dating as far back, perhaps, as his own childhood, Adams had excelled at the fraught art of willful denial. In 2009, a woman named Áine Tyrrell, who was Adams's niece, the daughter of his brother Liam, revealed on a news program that her father had raped her during her childhood and molested her for almost a decade, beginning when she was four years old. In an interview on the program, Gerry Adams admitted that he had known about Áine's allegations—and believed them—for twenty-two years. Yet he had never approached the police. In fact, Liam Adams became an active member of Sinn Féin, one who specialized in working with young people. He ended up getting a job counseling local children at a youth center in Gerry's own Belfast constituency. Gerry would subsequently claim that he had intervened to persuade Liam that this might not be the best environment for him. But by the time he did so, Liam had been on the job for more than a year.

Reeling from the exposure that he had long known his brother was a monster, Adams offered a revelation of his own: their father, Gerry Sr., had been a predator as well, who "emotionally, physically, and sexually" abused members of the family. Adams said that he had not been abused himself, and he would not specify which of his nine siblings had been victimized in this way. He maintained, moreover, that he had not known about the abuse until he was an adult. Adams acknowledged that there was a "culture of concealment" in Irish life regarding the issue of sexual predation. But he was going public now, he said, to help "other families who are in the same predicament."

On the one hand, this was an astounding turn, and a window into how Adams became the cipher that he was: here was a man who had grown up in a penumbral world of secrets and who had cultivated the quick and unsentimental reflexes of a survivalist. At the same time, some observers detected in this jarring announcement the deft hand of public relations. Áine Tyrrell would later allege that her uncle, whom she called "the Beard," had urged her not to go public and had done everything in his power to prevent the revelations about Liam from coming out. When he came forward with his own story of growing up in an abusive household, Adams was breaking, belatedly, a code of silence that had allowed abuse to flourish. But why come forward with the story of his father now, days after the exposure of his brother? As one political journalist in Belfast noted, "He must have known, and been advised by his media handlers, that it could move the story on from Liam." Adams possessed an uncanny grasp of the metabolism of the news media. The new story "would provide a follow-up, give things a new twist," perhaps even "attract sympathy for Adams."

When he was asked about the disappeared, Adams always flatly denied knowing anything about the decision-making behind this controversial tactic. But it *would* have been a decision: even in the antic, bloody days of late 1972, the Provos were an assiduously hierarchical organization in which one didn't go about executing people, much less disappearing them, without authorization from the brass. Dumping bodies in unmarked graves was not an accident. It was a policy. Dolours Price told Ed Moloney that the decision to disappear someone was made by the Belfast Brigade. The brigade staff "would have had to sit and thrash it out," she said. And Gerry Adams was the brigade commander.

In the police station at Antrim, the cops asked Adams about the Boston College interviews. Presumably, they walked through the statements by Price and Hughes and others and spelled out what they knew about the structure of the Belfast Brigade. But Adams had a simple, implacable answer to all of that. There was just one problem with their theory: he could not have been the commanding officer of the Belfast Brigade in 1972, because he never joined the IRA in the first place. Describing his own theory of how best to survive under interrogation, Adams had once recalled the time he was arrested as a young man and questioned before being locked up on the *Maidstone*. That was the interview in which he stubbornly insisted that his name was not Gerry Adams. The whole pretense had been an obvious charade, he conceded later, but it was also "a crutch to withstand their inquisition." To remain silent was the best policy, he had decided as a young man. "So even though they knew who I was, it was irrelevant. I couldn't answer their questions, on the basis that I wasn't who they said I was."

.   .   .

In some other political party, in some other place, the arrest of a politician in a cold-case investigation involving the notorious murder and secret burial of a widowed mother of ten would more than likely mean the swift end of a political career. But Gerry Adams was a special case. Even as Sinn Féin had thrived as a political party, not just in Northern Ireland but in the Republic, and achieved stature and influence beyond the most ambitious imaginings of its leaders, the party's fortunes still seemed tied, inextricably, to those of its charismatic president. Sinn Féin had plenty of young, polished representatives who, having grown up after the worst of the Troubles were over, bore no compromising taint of paramilitary violence. This new cohort did not lack for ambition. But they were unwilling, or unable, to shuffle the old men of the IRA off the stage. When it emerged that Adams had effectively covered for his pedophile brother, nobody in his party breathed a word, in public, that was less than supportive. Sinn Féin still retained an unmatched capacity to project the appearance of a unified front, and the leadership now argued that the arrest of Gerry Adams was nothing short of an attack on the party itself.

Overnight, a team of artists painted a new mural on the Falls Road, depicting a smiling Adams alongside the words PEACEMAKER, LEADER, VISIONARY. At a rally to unveil the mural, Martin McGuinness announced that the arrest was "politically biased." He cited upcoming local government and EU elections in the coming weeks and suggested that the timing of Adams's humiliation was designed to hurt Sinn Féin's electoral prospects. McGuinness blamed "an embittered rump of the old RUC" that still persisted within the police department and now was out to "settle old scores whatever the political cost." With Divis Tower visible in the distance, hundreds of supporters milled around, holding placards that read DEFEND THE PEACE PROCESS, RELEASE GERRY ADAMS, above a photo of Adams alongside Nelson Mandela.

While McGuinness delivered his remarks, a great bear of a man stood at his elbow. The man had close-cropped gray hair, a high forehead, and a knit brow, and he stood chewing gum, holding the script from which McGuinness was reading. It was Bobby Storey, a longtime IRA enforcer who was known affectionately, in republican circles, as Big Bobby. Given all the rhetoric about how Gerry Adams was getting antagonized for being such a peacemaker, Big Bobby was a discordant presence at the occasion. He had joined the IRA as a teenager, in the early 1970s, and ultimately served twenty years in prison. After the peace process, he had become the chair of Sinn Féin in Belfast, but he was often described as the IRA's top spymaster. In fact, he was reputed to have been the architect of the break-in at the Castlereagh barracks, in 2002. Storey was also widely believed to have been involved in another heist, the Northern Bank robbery, in which thieves made off with twenty-six million pounds. It was the largest bank robbery in the history of the United Kingdom at the time. And it was the timing of the heist that proved most significant: the bank was robbed in December 2004, years after the Good Friday Agreement. The IRA no longer needed money to buy weapons. In fact, at the time the robbery happened, the group was *giving up* its weapons; the decommissioning process overseen by Father Reid was at that point almost complete. For critics of Sinn Féin, the robbery solidified the impression that the IRA had morphed into a mafia organization. "Call me old fashioned if you like, but there used to be standards," Dolours Price wrote in the aftermath of the robbery. "The War is over, we are told ... so what is all this money needed for?"

Big Bobby was a close confidant of Adams's. But he had the

Belfast graffiti.

mien of a thug. Standing in front of the mural, he took the micro-phone and bellowed about the arrogance that might prompt authorities to "dare touch our party leader." His indignation ris-ing, Storey shouted, "We have a message for the British govern-ment, the Irish government, for the cabal that's out there." Then he said, "We ain't gone away, you know."

To anyone in Belfast who heard those words, the echo was unmistakable. Storey was quoting, quite intentionally, one of the most famous sound bites of the Troubles: the moment, nineteen years earlier, when Adams was interrupted during a speech by a heckler who shouted, "Bring back the IRA!" and Adams responded, "They haven't gone away, you know." Hear-ing those words from Big Bobby, Michael McConville felt a chill. The McConville children had been pushing to get access to the Boston College tapes, and had felt gratified by the arrest of Gerry Adams. Yet here was what seemed like an unambigu-ous threat.

Mackers, too, saw pure menace in the remark. "He didn't mean *Sinn Féin* hadn't gone away," he said. "He meant the IRA." To the people who had participated in the Belfast Project, the message was clear. "I don't even care about Sinn Féin and the political process. I don't give a fiddler's fuck," Ricky O'Rawe said. "All I care about is the truth." Yet Storey was informing those who might dare to tell their tales that they had crossed not only Gerry Adams, but the IRA. To O'Rawe, the city suddenly felt unsafe. The IRA itself wouldn't necessarily need to sanction some action against him. With rhetoric like Storey's, it could be some kid, heeding the call to arms, looking to please the leadership, itching to earn his spurs.

A new epithet, BOSTON COLLEGE TOUTS, began to appear in graffiti on buildings around Belfast. In an article titled "The Boston Time Bomb," *Sunday World* described the "state of panic" in republican circles about the Belfast Project, and outed a number of additional individuals who had purportedly given interviews to Anthony McIntyre. "Mackers has managed to do what countless RUC men failed to do, he has turned good people into touts," one former IRA figure told the paper. Mackers had instructed his children that they should no longer answer any knock at the door, and had taken to checking the area around the house for signs of an explosive device.

"There was a sustained, malicious, untruthful and sinister campaign alleging involvement by me in the killing of Jean McConville," Adams declared when he was released after four days of questioning. "I am innocent of any involvement in the abduction, killing, or burial of Mrs. McConville." At a press conference, he denounced the allegations against him as a "sham" and challenged Ed Moloney to explain why he had done the follow-up interview with Dolours Price in 2010. "It is *that* interview," along with the Brendan Hughes and Ivor Bell interviews, "which formed the mainstay for my arrest," Adams said. It was important to focus on the future now and not the past, he stressed. "The IRA is gone," Adams insisted, somewhat less than convincingly, in light of Storey's comments. "It's finished."

· · ·

After releasing Adams, the PSNI forwarded a file on him to the Public Prosecution Service, which would now determine whether enough evidence existed to bring murder charges against him. It looked as though Adams might be in very real jeopardy—a development that, it seems fair to say, Dolours Price would surely have appreciated.

But by that time, Price was already dead. She had been well aware of the court battle in the United States over her Boston College interview, though she claimed to be indifferent to it. "I have put that away to the back of my head," she said in the summer of 2012. "I will not lose a night's sleep over it." Her drinking intensified, however, as did her depression. The following January, she was briefly hospitalized after falling, drunk, down a flight of stairs. She discharged herself, went back to her house in Malahide, and continued to drink and to take Valium. On the day she died, her son Danny checked in on her before he left the house in the morning and found her in bed, asleep. When he came back that evening, she had not moved. "She wasn't breathing," he said later. "I knew straight away that she was dead." A postmortem discovered a toxic combination of antidepressants, sedatives, and antipsychotics in her bloodstream. (There was no alcohol in her system at the time she died.) She was sixty-two.

In 1975, when the Price sisters petitioned for compassionate leave from prison to bury their mother, permission was denied. But in 2013, the authorities allowed Marian to leave prison for a few hours so that she could attend the wake of her sister in the family home on Slievegallion Drive. The following day, black flags hung from the lampposts lining Andersonstown Road as Stephen Rea and his sons carried the coffin through a cold rain and into St. Agnes's Church, trailed by a long cortege.

A bespectacled priest with a wreath of white hair said the requiem Mass. He was Monsignor Raymond Murray, who had been the chaplain at Armagh jail when Dolours and Marian were prisoners there and had married Dolours and Stephen, in the secret ceremony at the Armagh cathedral, in 1983. "In a strange way, she lived up to her name, Dolours," Murray said. "A baptismal name given to her no doubt in devotional memory of Our Lady of Sorrows." He recalled her early years as a student protester and the lifelong toll of her hunger strike. Her old friend and codefendant Hugh Feeney was at the Mass. He pointed out that forty years earlier, he and Gerry Kelly had been on hunger strike along with Dolours and Marian. Now Dolours was getting buried, Feeney was at her funeral, Marian was back in prison, and Gerry Kelly was in politics. Kelly, who had become a Sinn Féin politician and had long since fallen out with Price, did not attend the funeral. Nor did Price's old commanding officer, Gerry Adams.

Outside, the rain came pouring down. It was a dismal, windswept Belfast winter day, and as the mourners left the church and began the trudge to Milltown Cemetery, hundreds of black umbrellas popped open. The coffin was wrapped in a bright tricolor flag, and for a moment it seemed to float, borne along on that dark tide, like a raft on an unquiet sea.

"We cannot keep pretending forty years of cruel war, of loss, of sacrifice, of prison, of inhumanity, has not affected each and every one of us in heart and soul and spirit," Price's old friend Bernadette Devlin, who had led the student protests in the 1960s, said when the mourners reached the grave. "It broke our hearts and it broke our bodies. It changed our perspectives, and it makes every day hard."

The other graveside oration was delivered by Eamonn McCann. He spoke of Price's contradictions and said that he had loved her for forty years. "If Dolours had a big fault, it was perhaps that she lived out too urgently the ideals to which so many others also purported to be dedicated," McCann said. "She was a liberator but never managed to liberate herself from those ideas." The mourners huddled under their umbrellas as the rain pounded the sodden ground. "Sometimes," McCann said, "we are imprisoned within ideals."

When the coroner asked Danny Rea if his mother had ever talked about killing herself, he replied that she had expressed no direct intention but had commented on "the self-destructive nature of her condition." The coroner ruled out suicide. There was no letter or note. But Carrie Twomey, who was close with Price in her final years, believed that she had effectively taken her own life. "Brendan, too," Twomey said, speaking of Hughes. "They committed suicide for years."

"The body is a fantastic machine," Hughes told Mackers in one of his Boston College interviews, recounting the grueling sequence of a hunger strike. "It'll eat off all the fat tissue first, then it starts eating away at the muscle, to keep your brain alive." Long after Hughes and Price called an end to their strikes and attempted to reintegrate into society, they nursed old grudges and endlessly replayed their worst wartime abominations. In a sense, they never stopped devouring themselves. The official pronouncement in the coroner's report for Dolours Price was "death by misadventure."

When the graveside orations were finished, the mourners fell silent and there was only the thrum of the driving rain and the distant buzz of a police helicopter hovering in the gray sky overhead. Before the coffin was lowered into the earth, someone retrieved the flag of Ireland, folded the bright rain-soaked fabric, and handed it to Price's sons.

THIS IS THE PAST

IN THE FALL OF 2015, Theresa Villiers, the secretary of state for Northern Ireland, released a report about paramilitary activity, which had been produced by the PSNI and British intelligence. "All the main paramilitary groups operating during the period of the Troubles remain in existence," the report announced, specifying that this included the Provisional IRA. The Provos continued to function, albeit in "much reduced form," and still had access to weapons. Big Bobby Storey was right: they hadn't gone away.

Gerry Adams dismissed the report as "nonsense." But it caused a firestorm. One claim Villiers made was that, in the view of rank-and-file Provos, the IRA's Army Council—the seven-member leadership body that for decades directed the armed struggle—continues to control not just the IRA, but also Sinn Féin, "with an overarching strategy." Secretly, behind the scenes, the army was still calling the shots. The report was careful to indicate that the organization was no longer engaged in violence, and now had a "wholly political focus." Even so, as one columnist in *The Irish Times* suggested, it seemed to reinforce "the notion of men and women in balaclavas running the political show."

Nearly two decades had passed since the Good Friday Agreement, and Northern Ireland was now peaceful, apart from the occasional dissident attack. Yet the society seemed as divided as ever. The borders between Catholic and Protestant neighborhoods were still inscribed in the concertina wire and steel of the so-called peace walls that vein the city, like fissures in a block of marble. In fact, there were *more* peace walls now than there had ever been at the height of the Troubles. These towering structures maintained some degree of calm by physically separating the city's populations, as if they were animals in a zoo. But the walls were still tagged with runelike slurs—K.A.T., for "Kill all Taigs," a derogatory term for Catholics, on one side; K.A.H., for "Kill all Huns," a reference to Protestants, on the other.

The center of Belfast seemed bustling, almost cosmopolitan. It was dominated by the same chain stores—Waterstones, Caffè Nero, Kiehl's—that you would find in any other small, prosperous European city. The local film production facility, Titanic Studios, had become famous as the place where the television show *Game of Thrones* was filmed. There was even a popular tourist attraction, the Troubles Tour, in which ex-combatant cabdrivers guided visitors to flashpoints from the bad years, decoding the ubiquitous murals that conjured famous battles, martyrs, and gunmen. The effect was to make the Troubles seem like distant history.

But the truth was that most residents still lived in neighborhoods circumscribed by religion, and more than 90 percent of children in Northern Ireland continued to attend segregated elementary schools. Bus stops in some parts of Belfast were informally designated Catholic or Protestant, and people would walk an extra block or two to wait at a stop where they wouldn't fear being hassled. Hundreds of Union Jacks still fluttered in Protestant neighborhoods, while Catholic areas were often decked out with the tricolor, or with Palestinian flags—a gesture of solidarity but also a signal that, even now, many republicans in the North regarded themselves as an occupied people. For a time, the American diplomat Richard Haass chaired a series of multiparty negotiations about unresolved issues in the peace process. But the talks foundered, in no small measure, over the issue of flags. Tribalism and its trappings remained so potent in Belfast that the various sides could not agree on how to govern the display of regalia. When the Belfast City Council voted, in 2012, to limit the number of days that the Union Jack could be raised above City Hall, protesters tried to storm the building, and riots erupted throughout the city, with unionist demonstrators throwing bricks and petrol bombs.

In light of this ongoing discord, the Villiers report made one fascinating observation. "The existence and cohesion of these paramilitary groups since their cease-fires has played an important role in enabling the transition from extreme violence to political progress," it asserted. This was a counterintuitive finding, and a subtle enough point that it was overlooked in the storm of press coverage that greeted the report. The continued existence of republican and loyalist outfits didn't hurt the peace process—but *helped* it. It was because of the "authority" conferred by these persisting hierarchies that such groups were able to "influence, restrain and manage" their members, the report maintained, noting that there have been only "limited indications of dissent to date," which were quickly dealt with "by the leadership."

To Brendan Hughes or Dolours Price or Marian Price or Anthony McIntyre, Sinn Féin's tendency to brook no opposition seemed self-interested, illiberal, and cruel. But perhaps, as the Villiers report appeared to suggest, it was only through such ruthless discipline—and the insistence that Irish republicanism must be a monolith, with zero tolerance for outliers—that Adams and the people around him had managed to keep the lid on a combustible situation, and prevent the war from reigniting.

.   .   .

At around the time the Villiers report was released, prosecutors in Belfast announced that they intended to try Ivor Bell

386 PATRICK RADDEN KEEFE

in connection with the murder of Jean McConville. "A decision has now been taken to prosecute this defendant," a government lawyer said. Bell was nearly eighty years old, a stooped figure, dressed in a cardigan, with a snow-white mustache and the wispy eyebrows of an aging wizard. He had trouble climbing the courthouse stairs. But this development looked as though it could signal a dangerous turn for Gerry Adams, who had been arrested and released but not yet charged. If Bell was tried for "aiding and abetting" the murder of Jean McConville, then presumably the testimony would touch on who it was that actually ordered the murder, and who carried it out. Some other loyal Sinn Féin functionary, like Bobby Storey, might be willing to go to jail to protect the boss, but Bell was anything but loyal to Adams.

In the early years of the Troubles, Bell and Adams were allies. They worked intimately together on the Belfast Brigade and did time together at Long Kesh. It was Bell who'd insisted that the 1972 peace talks could happen only if Adams was released from prison, and it was Bell who'd made the trip to London with him. Bell was a great proponent of physical force and had served as the IRA's "ambassador" to Muammar Qaddafi's Libya, procuring huge shipments of heavy weaponry from the pariah state. By the mid-1980s, he had risen to become chief of staff of the IRA. But after Sinn Féin embraced an electoral approach during the hunger strike of Bobby Sands and started running other candidates for office, Bell grew concerned that resources and attention were being diverted from the armed struggle in order to campaign for seats. Too much ballot box, not enough Armalite. Eventually, Bell and some allies grew so dubious of this strategy that they plotted to overthrow Gerry Adams. But word of this defection reached Adams, and he moved swiftly, court-martialing Bell for treachery—a charge that could lead to a death sentence. Bell was found guilty, but when it came to the penalty, Adams stepped in—out of loyalty to his old friend, perhaps, or out of consideration for the optics of such a move—and spared his life.

So Bell retreated from the movement, with a possible death sentence still hanging over his head, and lived a quiet life in West Belfast. He had refused, ever since, to speak to journalists about his experiences in the IRA. When Big Bobby Storey made the rounds during the 1990s, asking former Provos what they knew about the Jean McConville case, Bell was unhelpful. "Go and ask Gerry," he said, offering Storey the same line that Dolours Price had. "He's the man."

In fact, there was only one context in which Bell had been willing to go on the record and recount the story of his IRA career: an oral history for the Belfast Project, with Anthony McIntyre. In court, a prosecutor suggested that an individual who had participated in the project, who was referred to only as "Z," had acknowledged, in the Boston tapes, playing a role in the McConville murder. (The charges against Bell were eventually changed from "aiding and abetting" to "soliciting" the murder.)

But Bell's lawyer, a prominent Belfast attorney named Peter Corrigan, argued that the Boston tapes were "totally inadmissible." The oral history archive was "an intellectual, academic project, but was riddled with inaccuracies," Corrigan contended, and because it was so "unreliable and subjective," it did not match the rigorous standards required for evidence in a criminal case. In any event, Corrigan said, his client hadn't even been in Belfast during the period in 1972 when McConville was abducted, and he could present an alibi to prove it.

Such arguments were secondary, however, to the more audacious central thrust of Bell's defense: he wasn't Z. When Mackers was doing his interviews for the Belfast Project, he would never append the actual name of the interview subject to the recordings and transcripts, just the alphabet code name. The real identity of each individual was contained in a separate form. These forms were the only documents that translated the code names to real names. Because they were so sensitive, they had not been sent electronically, but rather were hand-delivered to

Bob O'Neill, the director of the Burns Library. It now emerged, however, that in the intervening years, Boston College had *lost* some of the forms—including the form for Z. The prosecutors could produce no piece of paper that proved that the interviewee named Z was really Ivor Bell. Of course, Ed Moloney and Anthony McIntyre knew exactly who Z was. But they let it be known that they had zero intention of cooperating with the court. This is "a one issue case," Peter Corrigan said. "Is the person on the tape Ivor Bell? And that cannot be proven."

Taken aback, perhaps, by this bold gambit, the prosecutors announced that they intended to summon a voice analyst. Experts in "forensic phonetics" occasionally testify in court, and they compare not just the tone and frequency of voices, but the lexicon, the syntax, and the use of characteristic filler words like "um" and "ah." There was a sense, though, in which Bell saying that he wasn't Z was a bit like Gerry Adams saying he wasn't in the IRA: it was a pretense that turned into a farce. Most of the Belfast Project participants spoke to Mackers for hours on end, and in his solicitous, collegial manner, Mackers often slipped, and addressed them by their first names. So the Z recording more than likely included instances in which Mackers referred to Z as Ivor. Besides, the context of the rest of Bell's interview would make it impossible to deny that he was Z: How many IRA men accompanied Adams to the peace talks in 1972, served as ambassador to Libya, then became chief of staff, before getting court-martialed for treachery?

The voice analyst ended up testifying that Z was "likely" Ivor Bell. But Corrigan said that, even if the government could prove that his client was Z, Bell was still innocent of the charges. If you listen to the recording itself, Corrigan suggested, "Z explicitly states that he was *not* involved with the murder of Jean McConville." A PSNI detective who had also heard the interview disagreed, saying that Z does acknowledge playing "a critical role in the aiding, abetting, counsel and procurement of the murder."

If the case was going to focus on the abetting, the question remained: abetting whom? Brendan Hughes and Dolours Price were both steadfast in their assertion that it was Adams who ordered the murder. But Adams, now, seemed safe from prosecution. After he was questioned by the PSNI in 2014, his file had been forwarded to the prosecution service. But the director of public prosecutions, a man named Barra McGrory, had to recuse himself from the case, because his father, who was also a lawyer, had previously represented Adams. This sort of potential conflict of interest was everywhere in Northern Ireland. The PSNI official who signed off on the decision to arrest Adams was a man named Drew Harris. His father had been murdered by the IRA. After prosecutors listened to the Boston tapes, however, they concluded that the evidence against Adams amounted to uncorroborated allegations, which would not be a successful basis for prosecution. If indeed Adams had ordered the execution of Jean McConville, then, with this ruling, he had officially gotten away with murder. It appeared that an oral history in which one implicated oneself could be used to prosecute, whereas an oral history in which one implicated others could not. Ivor Bell would have done better to heed the credo that Adams had so resolutely clung to since his youth: *Never say anything.* It might have saved him.

.   .   .

Who should be held accountable for a shared history of violence? It was a question that was dogging Northern Ireland as a whole. "My client is entitled to be treated equally before the law," Peter Corrigan said of Ivor Bell. Would the British soldiers who shot unarmed civilians on Bloody Sunday be subjected to the same justice? he asked. "Why is everybody not being treated equally for conflict-related offences?" Because there was never any mechanism established for dealing with the past, the official approach to decades-old atrocities was entirely ad hoc, which left everyone unhappy. There were inquests and investigations by the police ombudsman and special government inquiries. The past was big business for criminal justice. Every day, the Belfast papers carried reports of some new cold case that would now be reexamined. The PSNI had a "legacy" unit devoted exclusively to investigating Troubles-related crimes. It had a backlog of nearly a thousand cases.

Even if one took for granted the good faith and intentions of the police—which many didn't—there was no way to undertake such a project without being accused of bias. The authorities had limited resources. Budgets were getting slashed. And the police had to continue actually policing Northern Ireland in the present day. For the detectives in the legacy unit, it could seem, at times, as though they were living out a scenario from the *Twilight Zone:* in your life outside of work, the year is 2018, but on the job it is always 1973, or 1989, or some other bloody moment from the distant past. The head of the team was a Catholic cop named Mark Hamilton, the son of one of the few Catholic officers in the old RUC. By the time Hamilton joined the department in 1994, the peace process was already under way. He was a "cease-fire cop," he liked to say. He just wanted to be a regular police officer; he didn't want to spend his career relitigating the Troubles.

Sometimes Hamilton would go to public hearings about one long-ago bloodbath or another and, as the representative of the police, he would dutifully play the role of whipping boy. Grieving families would express their frustration, having suffered for decades without answers. They did not trust the authorities, and felt they had good reason not to. Sometimes they would shout abuse at him. Usually Hamilton just took it. This was part of the job, and he felt tremendous empathy for victims whose lives had been upended by violence. But occasionally, he would protest. "When this crime happened, I was a *baby*. I was in *nappies*," he would say. "I am not the enemy here."

Sometimes, historical investigations were so big or so sensitive that they were taken out of the department altogether. In 2016, a new investigation into Stakeknife was launched. Led by Jon Boutcher, the chief constable of Bedfordshire, in England, it would involve fifty detectives working for up to five years, with a budget that might exceed thirty million pounds. "With both the passage of time and the very nature of these crimes, the truth will be a difficult and elusive prey," Boutcher acknowledged.

There was reason to believe that neither Freddie Scappaticci nor his British handlers would ever be held accountable for the dozens of murders in which they appear to have colluded. Scappaticci was still in hiding, reportedly living under an assumed name, in a witness protection program administered by the very government that now claimed to be investigating him. But in January 2018, he was picked up by the British police. "A 72-year-old man has been arrested," Boutcher said in a carefully worded statement. "He is currently in custody at an undisclosed location." Scappaticci was released without charges after several days of questioning. It seemed unlikely that British authorities would ever really get to the bottom of the Stakeknife conspiracy, because to do so would thoroughly implicate the British state.

Scappaticci would also be a dangerous man to prosecute, knowing what he knew about the extent to which the butchery of the Nutting Squad had been countenanced, or facilitated, by Her Majesty's Government. It would be exceedingly risky for the state to put Stakeknife into any position where he might feel the need to start talking. When it came to his former comrades in the IRA, Scappaticci may have enjoyed a similar immunity. He knew too much about too many people. Perhaps he had a cache of secret evidence, a dossier locked in a safe somewhere, to be released in the event that anything should happen to him.

When his father died, in the spring of 2017, there were rumors in Belfast that Freddie had slipped back into town to attend the funeral. The procession was led by the family ice cream truck. It would have been a prime opportunity for anyone with a grudge against the ultimate IRA tout to confront him. But if he was there, nobody did.

If Scappaticci wasn't criminally prosecuted, perhaps he could be sued. In the vacuum of accountability left by the criminal justice system, private lawyers had taken to signing up clients and bringing civil suits. The families of numerous victims initiated lawsuits against Scappaticci. The Hooded Men, who were tortured during internment, were also pursuing legal action against their former captors. In 2015, the counterinsurgency guru Brigadier Frank Kitson was sued. He was an old man now, long since retired. He had briefly resurfaced in 2002, to testify before an inquiry into the events of Bloody Sunday, praising the paratroopers who shot thirteen unarmed civilians as a "jolly good" unit who were "ready to go at the drop of a hat." But otherwise, he lived a quiet life. Lately, he had been assisting his wife, Lady Elizabeth Kitson, with an inspirational book she was writing about a show pony she had owned in her youth.

A woman named Mary Heenan sued Kitson. Her husband had been murdered by loyalists in 1973. "Nobody cared," she said. "We were just left there. We knew nothing." In her suit, Heenan claimed that, as the architect of British counterinsurgency strategy in the early years of the Troubles, Kitson was "reckless as to whether state agents would be involved in murder." When she was challenged about the appropriateness of subjecting an old man to such a lawsuit, Heenan, who was eighty-eight, pointed out that Kitson was "a year younger than me."

The little Brigadier denied the charges, observing that he had already left Ireland by 1973. He had been a mere commander of troops, he argued, not someone who set official policy or could be blamed for the broader thrust of British strategy in the Troubles. He added, lamely, "We never instigated the use of paramilitary gangs."

.   .   .

When police and prosecutors pursued cases against former British soldiers, they were accused of a "witch hunt" against young men who were just trying to do their jobs in a difficult environment. To such charges of bias, the top prosecutor, Barra McGrory, responded that there had been no "imbalance of approach" and that investigations of terrorist atrocities far outnumbered cases against the state. But was that not itself a kind of bias? Was it possible to appropriately calibrate the number of investigations of republican murders with those of loyalist murders? Would anything but a perfect one-to-one ratio suffice? People in Northern Ireland talked about the danger of a "hierarchy of victims." Outrage is conditioned not by the nature of the atrocity but by the affiliation of the victim and the perpetrator. Should the state be accorded more leniency because, legally speaking, it has a monopoly on the legitimate use of force? Or, conversely, should we hold soldiers and cops to a higher standard than paramilitaries?

According to one scholar, the "ideal victim" in the Troubles was someone who was not a combatant, but a passive civilian. To many, Jean McConville was the perfect victim: a widow, a mother of ten. To others, she was not a victim at all, but a combatant by proxy, who courted her own fate. Of course, even if one were to concede, for the sake of argument, that McConville was an informer, there is no moral universe in which her murder and disappearance should be justified. Must it be the case that how one perceives a tragedy will forever depend on where one sits? The anthropologist Claude Lévi-Strauss once observed that, "for the majority of the human species, and for tens of thousands of years, the idea that humanity includes every human being on the face of the earth does not exist at all. The designation stops at the border of each tribe, or linguistic group, sometimes even at the edge of a village." When it came to the Troubles, a phenomenon known as "whataboutery" took hold. Utter the name Jean McConville and someone would say, *What about Bloody Sunday?* To which you could say, *What about Bloody Friday?* To which they could say, *What about Pat Finucane? What about the La Mon bombing? What about the Ballymurphy massacre? What about Enniskillen? What about McGurk's bar? What about. What about. What about.*

After it was revealed that the PSNI was seeking the Boston tapes related to the killing of Jean McConville, there were some who accused the service of bias. This was the embittered rump of the old RUC, perverting justice in a last bid to get their nemesis, Gerry Adams. If the police were interested in historical crimes, why not ask for the loyalist interviews? Loyalists did plenty of murdering during the Troubles, too. Boston College itself said in a statement that, by "ignoring the tapes of the UVF members," the police lent support to the charge that the subpoenas had been politically motivated. The British government's reaction to this critique was not to withdraw its request for the republican interviews, but to ask that a loyalist interview be turned over, as Boston College had practically invited it to do.

The police obtained a new subpoena, for the recordings of a former paramilitary, Winston Churchill Rea, a onetime member of a group called the Red Hand Commando. Rea, who went by the misleadingly innocuous nickname "Winkie" and was no relation to Stephen Rea (much less Winston Churchill), filed a legal challenge to prevent Boston College from turning over his tapes. But he fared no better than Moloney and Mackers had, and the tapes were handed to the police. Rea was eventually charged with offenses including conspiracy to murder two Catholic men in 1991. When he showed up in court to deny the charges, he was confined to a wheelchair, a slumped figure with white stubble and milky eyes. In a statement, Ed Moloney decried the "cynical attempt by the PSNI to show even-handedness in their pursuit of the Boston College tapes." Winkie Rea, Moloney said, was "the token Prod."

Anthony McIntyre was also harshly critical of the effort to prosecute Rea. How will the truth of what really happened during the Troubles ever come out, he asked, if the authorities file murder charges against anyone who has the nerve to talk about it? "I would describe the PSNI stance as one of *prosecuting* truth, rather than procuring truth," he said in an interview.

The PSNI was well aware of Mackers's criticism. People in the department had been following his public commentary closely. He was a garrulous type; he liked talking to journalists, and they liked talking to him. Given his attachment to the idea of speaking truth to power, he was not one to hold his tongue when it came to the perfidy of the authorities. But the PSNI took a particular interest in something that Mackers had let slip in a television interview in 2014. On the subject of the sensitivity and confidentiality of the Boston archive, he said, "I won't go into any detail, but I exposed myself to exactly the same risks as anybody else was exposed to."

Mackers didn't just gather republican oral histories as an interviewer. He recorded an oral history of his own. In a letter to the Public Prosecution Service, a PSNI detective cited the television interview, noting that "not only did he discuss his own terrorist activities … but also that he is opposed to PSNI obtaining the interview content. Implicit is the belief that he fears that prosecutions could be mounted as a result of the interviews being released to investigators."

One day in April 2016, Mackers was at home in Drogheda when he opened his email to find a message from a lawyer in Boston. "I am writing to inform you that Boston College has been served with the enclosed subpoena seeking your Belfast Project interview," it said. The authorities were alleging that Mackers had been implicated in an assortment of crimes, from membership in a paramilitary organization and being in possession of an imitation firearm while he was in prison, in 1978, to involvement in an operation in which a pipe bomb exploded in Belfast. Mackers was terrified: the whole oral history was a chronicle of his years in a banned organization. His account, like the accounts of other former paramilitaries, was *full* of stories about illegal things he'd done. If government officials were out to get him, as he believed they were, and if there was no statute of limitations on these crimes, then the state could fish happily from his oral history and bring trumped-up charges against him forever.

The best indication of the government's bad faith, in Mackers's view, was the shoddiness of the allegations against him. Had the police actually checked their own records, they would have discovered that Mackers couldn't have taken part in the pipe bombing—because he was *in police custody* when it happened. It seemed unlikely that the authorities would ultimately pursue any formal proceedings against him, but this brought him little comfort. Both Mackers and his wife, Carrie, had been unemployed for some time. They had kids to feed, and they had now spent the better part of a decade dealing virtually full-time with the aftermath of the Belfast Project. They continued to fear retaliation by the IRA, and now they had to contend with the government whose effort, Mackers was convinced, was motivated purely by revenge—revenge for his public criticism of the PSNI, but also revenge because he had refused to cooperate with the authorities in identifying Z. He found himself wishing, almost daily, that he had left history alone and never undertaken the Belfast Project in the first place.

.   .   .

In the countryside, the digging continued. In 2010, the body of Peter Wilson, a young man with learning disabilities who had been murdered by the IRA, was discovered. His remains were exhumed at a picturesque beach in County Antrim. Over the decades since he disappeared, Wilson's family had often visited that beach, little knowing.

The scandal of the Boston tapes had been frustrating for the Independent Commission for the Location of Victims' Remains. The commissioners felt obliged to assure the public that, notwithstanding the Boston College fiasco, anyone who might have information regarding the whereabouts of the disappeared could share it with the commission in "complete confidence." In the fall of 2014, they received a tip indicating that the remains of Joe Lynskey might be found in a particular area of County Meath. A team led by the retired Manchester detective Geoff Knupfer got to work. They brought in a cadaver dog and a forensic anthropologist and used ground-penetrating radar to find anomalies in the earth. In December, Lynskey's niece Maria was cautiously optimistic. "We hope and pray that Joe's remains are found and he can be given a proper burial," she said. But for months they continued to dig and did not find him.

Then, one day the following summer, at lunchtime, someone shouted, "Something's here!" Dispensing with the mechanical excavators, the investigators crouched in the dirt and started delicately clearing the earth away with trowels. Gradually, they uncovered a set of bones. In his quiet, methodical way, Knupfer was hugely excited, though there was, inevitably, a bittersweetness to these moments of discovery. Someone alerted Maria Lynskey, and she drove to the site.

The team was still working that evening when, at around 8:30, there was a sudden cry from the grave site. Investigators had discovered something in the grave, lying underneath the bones: a second set of human remains. In an instant, the searchers realized what had happened. There were two bodies buried together, lying one on top of the other. All this time, they had been looking for Joe Lynskey. But they had discovered the young triple agents whom Dolours Price had driven to their deaths, Seamus Wright and Kevin McKee. Maria Lynskey was devastated, but also happy for the families of Wright and McKee. At a requiem Mass for Seamus Wright, his sister, Breige, issued a special plea for any information relating to Lynskey and the other victims who had yet to be discovered.

.   .   .

In 2016, the Abbey Theatre, in Dublin, premiered a provocative new play by the East Belfast playwright David Ireland called *Cyprus Avenue*. It is a scabrous black comedy, the story of a Belfast loyalist named Eric Miller. His daughter has recently given birth to a baby girl, but Eric is seized by a mad delusion: he thinks that the baby looks like Gerry Adams. At first, this is played for a joke. Eric asks his daughter whether the Sinn Féin president is not in fact the father of her child. At one point, when he is alone with the baby, he takes a big magic marker and scribbles a black beard onto the child's cheeks. "The Gerry Adams beard is part and parcel of the Gerry Adams persona," Eric points out. "It symbolizes his revolutionary ardor, his passion for constitutional change. And now as it whitens it cements his status as *éminence grise*, aging philosopher king."

Eric was played by Stephen Rea. He had worked steadily since the death of his ex-wife, in film and in theater, and had still not spoken in any substantial way about the life or legacy of Dolours Price. But now he was playing a man who is undone by his own obsession with Gerry Adams. Eric's delusion intensifies, and Adams seems to represent, for him, all that threatens his identity as a Belfast Protestant and as a loyalist. He comes to believe that the baby actually *is* Gerry Adams. When he encounters a loyalist gunman named Slim in a local park, Eric confides, "I think that Gerry Adams has disguised himself as a new-born baby and successfully infiltrated my family home."

Slim, without skipping a beat, replies, "That's *exactly* the kind of thing he'd do!"

The play is hilarious and absurd, but it ends in horrific violence. It is a study in the derangement of bigotry, a portrait of Northern Ireland as a land consumed by feverish pathology, an inquiry into the inability to shake free of what has come before.

"This is the past," Eric tells Slim at one point.

"No, this is the *now*," Slim corrects him.

"No," Eric says. "It's the past."

.   .   .

In the summer of 2017, the McConville children came together once again when one of the two youngest brothers, Billy, died of cancer. Before his death, Billy had testified, along with several of his siblings, at an inquiry into child abuse at institutions in Northern Ireland. "After a while I was like—what do you call it?—like a robot; you know what I mean? Because I was so institutionalized," he said. As he was succumbing to cancer, Billy asked his family, as a dying wish, that he be carried into the church for his funeral feetfirst, in a final gesture of defiance.

"You were so strong and unbelievably brave, braver than anyone I knew," Billy's daughter said at the funeral. He had been only six years old when Jean was taken away. He died at fifty. "The whole world knows the name of a simple Belfast mother who loved her children and who was cruelly abducted, murdered, and secretly buried, in December 1972," a priest said. Her disappearance was an "act of inexcusable wickedness," which "plunged Billy and his brothers and sisters into a lifelong nightmare."

It remained unclear whether the children would ever get their wish of seeing someone held accountable. Michael and his siblings attended the hearings in the case of Ivor Bell, sitting silently in the public gallery, serving as a kind of moral witness.

But at a hearing in December 2016, a lawyer representing Bell announced that he could not fairly be tried in the case—because he was suffering from vascular dementia and wouldn't be able "to properly follow the course of proceedings." The government announced that it wanted to inspect Bell's medical record and have him seen by its own specialists. But it seemed increasingly unlikely that anyone would ever face trial for the murder.

After prosecutors said that they would not bring charges against Gerry Adams, Helen consulted with a London-based law firm that had won a landmark multi-million-dollar settlement in a case against four members of the Real IRA over a 1998 car bomb attack in Omagh. The firm announced that Helen had instructed them to explore the possibility of launching a civil suit against Adams. "The McConville family is going to stay to the bitter end," Michael said. "We have already been fighting for justice for 40-odd years and we are not going to stop now."

THE UNKNOWN

ACCORDING TO THE CENSUS, some thirty-three million Americans—roughly 10 percent of the total population—claim Irish heritage. I'm one of them. My forebears on my father's side emigrated from Cork and Donegal in the nineteenth century. I'm actually more Australian than Irish—my mother is from Melbourne—but I grew up in Boston, where Irish Americans who have never set foot in the old country can still feel an intense emotional connection to the place. With my conspicuously Irish name, you might think that I would, too.

But, at least when I was growing up, I didn't. If the unionists of Ulster were a people "more British than the British," the Irish Americans of Boston could sometimes seem more Irish than the Irish, and I found that I did not always relate to the clover-and-Guinness clichés and the sentimental attitudes of tribal solidarity. In the Boston I grew up in, during the 1980s, there was a fair degree of ambient support for the IRA, even as the group perpetrated some of its most devastating acts of terror. I can still remember my father telling me that inside the local Irish pub, down the street from my childhood home, a man would circulate among the patrons with a jar full of money, soliciting contributions "for the lads." A black wreath hung above the bar, in tribute to the IRA dead. But I never felt any particular interest in the conflict in Northern Ireland. My heritage notwithstanding, I read about it with the detached concern you might accord to any story about a war in a foreign country.

In my career as a journalist, I had never written about the Troubles, or felt any particular urge to do so, until January 2013, when Dolours Price died and I read her obituary in *The New York Times*. The article related the dramatic contours of her biography but also mentioned the battle, which was then still brewing, over the secret archive at Boston College. One theme that I had become fascinated with as a journalist was collective denial: the stories that communities tell themselves in order to cope with tragic or transgressive events. I became intrigued by the idea that an archive of the personal reminiscences of ex-combatants might be so explosive: what was it about these accounts that was so threatening in the present day? In the intertwining lives of Jean McConville, Dolours Price, Brendan Hughes, and Gerry Adams, I saw an opportunity to tell a story about how people become radicalized in their uncompromising devotion to a cause, and about how individuals—and a whole society—make sense of political violence once they have passed through the crucible and finally have time to reflect.

As I was finishing this book, after four years of research and writing, certain stubborn mysteries remained, and I had resigned myself to the conclusion that the whole truth of this dark saga might never be widely known, because the handful of individuals who still knew the truth would take it with them to their graves. Then, just as I was completing the manuscript, I made a startling discovery.

When Dolours Price unburdened herself to Ed Moloney about the final moments in Jean McConville's life, she spoke about how she and two other members of the Unknowns had accompanied McConville to the lip of a freshly dug grave. One of the two associates with her was Wee Pat McClure, the head of the Unknowns.

For a long time, I could not figure out what had happened to McClure. I knew that he had disappeared in the 1980s. I interviewed a man who had seen McClure just after the notorious bombing of the La Mon restaurant, the horrific incident in Belfast in 1978 in which a device containing a napalm-like substance killed a dozen people and horribly burned thirty others. McClure had been arrested after the blast and held by the police for a week. He was badly shaken by the experience, and he worried about the information that Special Branch appeared to have on the Provos. "I'm out," McClure told the man. People who had known McClure in Belfast told me that he left the country and relocated to Canada, where he died at some point in the 1980s.

There are a lot of McClures in Canada, and when I tried to track down the family of Pat McClure, I couldn't find them. Then, one day, I learned from a friend that the reason I couldn't locate Wee Pat's family in Canada was that they hadn't ended up there at all. Instead, when McClure escaped Belfast with his wife and children not long after the La Mon bombing, he moved to the United States. In fact, his family had been living all along in Connecticut, not far from where I live, in New York.

McClure died in 1986. For five years before his death, he had worked as a guard at the Cheshire Correctional Institution, a high-security prison. When I saw Hugh Feeney, the fellow Unknown who had bombed London with the Price sisters and gone on hunger strike, he was quietly appalled to learn that McClure, a man he had revered, might have ended up becoming "a screw." I approached McClure's widow, Bridie, and their children, to see if they might speak with me. After all, Dolours Price had put Pat at the graveside of Jean McConville and described his involvement in other notorious incidents during the Troubles. But the family had no interest in talking, and it struck me that they probably had not realized that the husband and father they knew and loved had also been a war criminal. An obituary for McClure noted that he was a parishioner at his local Catholic church. I wondered whether, before his death, he had confessed.

For several years, I made periodic trips to the Bronx, to meet with Ed Moloney. Eventually he shared with me an unpublished transcript of one of the two long interviews he conducted with Dolours Price. The document consisted of thirty dense, single-spaced pages. Before entrusting it to me, Moloney had made one key redaction—he removed certain identifying details about the third executioner who was at McConville's grave. His rationale was simple: Price and McClure were both dead, but this third person was still alive. Moloney's decades-long project of recording the facts of the Troubles had by this point created quite a bit of legal difficulty for any number of people, and he may have felt that he didn't want to create any more.

I had been able to gather a few details about this mystery individual, however. Some time earlier, over dinner one night in Drogheda, Anthony McIntyre had told me that Dolours Price never spoke about the fate of Jean McConville in her recorded interviews for Boston College, but "off tape," she had told him what happened. She related to Mackers the same story she did to Moloney, about the three-person death squad and the unmarked grave. Like Moloney, Mackers told me that Pat McClure had been there with Price. Also like Moloney, Mackers declined to tell me the identity of the third person. What he did say was that it was this third individual who fired the shot that killed Jean McConville. And he gave me one further clue: at some point, Mackers said, Gerry Adams had asked the shooter to become his personal driver.

This seemed like a promising revelation. It couldn't be too difficult, I figured, to track down all of the people who had been drivers for Adams over the years. But Mackers then told me that the killer had never actually *taken* the job, instead declining Adams's offer. So after dangling this tantalizing detail, he left me more or less where I had started. Eventually, I concluded that I would never learn the identity of the actual shooter. It would remain, quite literally, an Unknown.

When Moloney gave me the transcript of his interview with Price, I devoured the whole document quickly and then kept returning to it, poring over particular sections for days, extracting details that were relevant to the events I was covering in this book. Before finishing the manuscript, I decided to reread the whole interview from beginning to end, on the off chance that I had overlooked any important details. Twelve pages into the document, I encountered something that I had somehow missed before, and I sat bolt upright.

In the transcript, Moloney asks about the positions that Gerry Adams held in the various brigades and battalions of the IRA during the early 1970s. At a certain point, Price says, "Actually, he may have been moved to Brigade at that stage—because he wanted my sister to be his driver."

She says it casually, in passing, and Moloney does not press her on it or interject.

"You know, he always had to have a driver," Price goes on. "And she refused, because it was such a boring job."

.   .   .

Marian Price would not speak to me for this book. Her lawyer in Belfast stonewalled my various overtures. When I tracked down one of her daughters, she requested, politely, that I never contact her again. Dolours Price had become so associated with the disappearance of Jean McConville in the public imagination that it had never occurred to me that her sister might also have played a part in the killing.

Of course, there may have been some slim chance that this was all just an extraordinary coincidence, and that the mosaic of details I had assembled did not actually incriminate Marian Price. There must have been other people, over the years, who declined an offer to become Gerry Adams's chauffeur. A representative for Adams, for what it is worth, told me that any suggestion that Adams might have made such an offer to the killer of Jean McConville was, "like so many other claims made in relation to this case, entirely bogus."

It's also important to note that, while Moloney might have redacted clues about the identity of the shooter from the interview transcript he supplied to me, the Police Service of Northern Ireland are also in possession of the original transcript, which they obtained from Boston College—and that version is *not* redacted. If Dolours Price implicated her own sister in the murder of Jean McConville, and the police in Belfast knew about it, wouldn't they have charged Marian Price with the crime?

Not necessarily. Price also implicated Gerry Adams, and the Brendan Hughes oral history corroborated her account—yet Adams was never charged. The legal actions against Ivor Bell and Anthony McIntyre appear to suggest that if a person implicates himself in a Belfast Project oral history, those utterances can be used against him in court, but if he implicates somebody else, that is simply hearsay, rather than admissible evidence.

The more I mulled the suggestion that Marian Price was the third Unknown at the graveside and may have fired the shot that ended Jean McConville's life, the more it made sense. After all, the sisters were both members of the Unknowns. They both reported to Pat McClure. As Dolours liked to say, they did everything together. If Dolours had condemned Jean McConville in the fiercest terms to Ed Moloney and insisted, at times, that the killing was justified, it may have been an expression of the strain she felt in struggling to reconcile not just her own conduct with some plausible moral code, but the even graver conduct of her sister.

In the spring of 2018, I flew to Belfast one final time and took the train down to Drogheda. I had told Mackers and Carrie that I needed to speak with them about something important, and we met one evening at a restaurant on the banks of the River Boyne. As the sun set outside the window, I laid out for them the reasons that I believed it was Marian Price who had murdered Jean McConville. Mackers had ordered a whiskey, and he stared into it as I spoke. He acknowledged that he had told me the story about the offer from Gerry Adams, but he said that he would never confirm, one way or the other, whether Marian was the shooter. Carrie reminded me that when she and Mackers got married, Marian had been their maid of honor. Marian was in poor health, they pointed out, and the publication of such an allegation might have unfortunate repercussions for her adult children. But when we finished our meal and parted ways that night, neither of them had told me that I was wrong.

There was one more person I wanted to speak with, someone whom Dolours had known and confided in before she died. I explained what I had deduced and asked whether Dolours had ever mentioned Marian playing a role in the McConville killing. This person confirmed that she had—that Dolours had said the execution of Jean McConville was "something that the sisters had done together."

Finally, I wrote to Marian's lawyer in Belfast, spelling out what I had learned and intended to publish, and asking whether Marian would deny it. He never wrote back.

· · ·

At the end of 2017, Gerry Adams announced that he would retire from his position as president of Sinn Féin and hand over authority to the party's longtime deputy, Mary Lou McDonald. At forty-eight years old, McDonald had come of age, professionally, in the period after the Good Friday Agreement, so she was untinged by paramilitary history. Some observers wondered if Adams might continue to exercise power behind the scenes, but he promised that he had no interest in playing "puppet master," and that he intended, genuinely, to retire.

Adams would soon turn seventy. He was still vigorous, but

his movements had slowed ever so slightly, and his voice, which had always been one of his greatest assets, was no longer quite so formidable. The famous beard had gone a snowy white. The previous spring, Martin McGuinness, Adams's longtime comrade in both war and peace, had died of a rare genetic disease. "Martin McGuinness was not a terrorist," Adams intoned, to applause, in a speech at McGuinness's grave. "Martin McGuinness was a freedom fighter."

Of course, to his supporters and his detractors alike, Adams himself retained a hint of danger. According to polls, even Sinn Féin voters did not believe his claims about never being in the IRA, and it is often said in Northern Ireland that he still has "the whiff of cordite" about him. But Adams is nothing if not enigmatic, and, as he prepared to retire from politics, he had succeeded in modulating his public persona once again. He often played the role, now, of twinkle-eyed celebrity grandfather— an iconic but approachable grandee. This development found its surreal culmination on Twitter, where Adams tended his popular account, interspersing studiously boring tweets about small-bore political issues with a barrage of cat pictures and encomiums to sudsy baths, rubber duckies, and teddy bears. ("I do love teddy bears," he told the BBC. "I have a large collection of teddy bears.") One Irish writer likened such flourishes to "Charles Manson showing you his collection of tea cosies," and it could seem, at times, that this assertive expression of whimsy was a form of cynical calculation. The West Belfast journalist Malachi O'Doherty suggested, in a biography of Adams, that the Sinn Féin leader is prone to "propagandizing for his own humanity."

But, cumulatively, Adams's tweets suggest the giddiness of a man who has defied some very long odds. He was shot and nearly killed by loyalist gunmen and imprisoned and tortured by the British state. Improbably, he survived the conflict, helped bring the fighting to an end, and built a hugely successful political party that was a force not just in Northern Ireland but in the Republic as well. The historian Alvin Jackson has written that, for Adams, democratic action "was a way of liquidating the otherwise unrecoverable political capital amassed by the gunmen."

In one of his conversations with Anthony McIntyre, Brendan Hughes said something similar, in the form of a metaphor. Think of the armed struggle as the launch of a boat, Hughes said, "getting a hundred people to push this boat out. This boat is stuck in the sand, right, and get them to push the boat out and then the boat sailing off and leaving the hundred people behind, right. That's the way I feel. The boat is away, sailing on the high seas, with all the luxuries that it brings, and the poor people that launched the boat are left sitting in the muck and the dirt and the shit and the sand, behind."

It is hard not to sympathize with Hughes emotionally. But politically, it would be folly not to sympathize with Adams. He may have possessed a sociopathic instinct for self-preservation, and there is something chilling about how Adams, secure in his place on the boat, does not cast so much as a backward glance at those comrades, like Hughes, who are left behind. But, really, it was history that was leaving Hughes behind. Northern Ireland had suffered enough. Whatever callous motivations Adams might have possessed, and whatever deceptive machinations he might have employed, he steered the IRA out of a bloody and intractable conflict and into a brittle but enduring peace.

Even after the Good Friday Agreement, Adams always insisted that he had never given up the cornerstone republican aspiration for a united Ireland; it was just that the means for getting there had changed. In the long run, the war may be won by demography. By some estimates, Catholics may outnumber Protestants in Northern Ireland as soon as the year 2021. This doesn't necessarily mean that the British will soon be voted off the island. After the 2008 fiscal crisis and the subsequent recession in Dublin, some polls found that most Catholics in the

North preferred to remain part of the United Kingdom. "Out-breeding Unionists may be an enjoyable pastime for those who have the energy," Adams once remarked. "But it hardly amounts to a political strategy."

In the summer of 2016, the British people voted by a thin margin to exit the European Union. Only after the referendum passed did the public in Britain fully consider the implications of such a move. Since the Good Friday Agreement, the border between Northern Ireland and the Republic has seemed, at times, to have virtually disappeared. The soldiers and sand-bagged checkpoints are long gone, and every day, tens of thousands of people and countless trucks full of goods crisscross the national boundary in one direction or the other. Northern Ireland is able to enjoy the benefits of being part of the United Kingdom and part of Europe at the same time. But Brexit, inevitably, complicates that split identity, and, depending on how the measure is implemented, it might ultimately force Northern Ireland to make a choice.

Adams is attuned to such possibilities. "Those of us who want a United Ireland need to be very careful that we are not accused of trying to exploit Brexit," he said. "But I just think the notion of Irish unity, in terms of public debate, is now much more prevalent." He announced that within five years, he would like to see a new referendum on whether Northern Ireland should remain part of the United Kingdom.

It would be ironic, to say the least, if one inadvertent long-term consequence of the Brexit referendum was a united Ireland—an outcome that three decades of appalling bloodshed and some thirty-five hundred lost lives had failed to achieve. But this is, in a way, the defining question hanging over the legacy of Gerry Adams. As a young man, he justified the use of political violence with one important caveat, writing that "only if I achieve the situation where my people can genuinely prosper can my course of action be seen, by me, to have been justified."

Adams will probably not live to see a united Ireland, but it seems that such a day will inevitably come. The real question is whether it would have happened eventually anyway, without the violent interventions of the IRA. This is the sort of conundrum that bedeviled Dolours Price and Brendan Hughes, but in his final years, Adams seemed free of any such tortured introspection. When an interviewer asked him, in 2010, if he had blood on his hands, he responded, "I don't. I am perfectly at peace. Absolutely."

.　.　.

Behind the airy, modern house that Michael McConville built for his family in a rural area outside Belfast lies a bright-green expanse of lawn, lined by a series of wooden enclosures. These little houses hold hundreds of small cubbyholes, in which dozens of pigeons warble and bob and shift their feet. Having picked through the ruins of wartime Belfast as a child in search of pigeons in the wild, Michael grew up to keep hundreds of the birds, and to race them competitively. "Through the whole Troubles, there was never any hassle between Protestants and Catholics raising pigeons," he said, delicately cupping one of the creatures in his hand. It eyed him nervously, rolling its neck, so that its slate-gray feathers flashed magenta and teal, suddenly iridescent, like a peacock's.

Pigeons were one of the first animals to be domesticated by humans, more than five thousand years ago. They're monogamous and fiercely protective of their offspring. A pigeon builds endurance in the same way that a human athlete does, flying progressively longer distances. Irish pigeon racers can travel as far as England or France and release their birds and they will fly home across the water, through foul weather, covering hundreds of miles to return to their roost. Sometimes, when they get home after a long race, they will have burned off half their body weight from the exertion. But nurture and husband them with seeds and comfort and they will build up their strength to race again.

On race days, Michael released his birds, and they would disappear over the horizon. Then, eventually, they would come home. He always loved that about pigeons. They wander. But their natural instinct is to fly back to the place where they were born.

ACKNOWLEDGMENTS

My first thanks go to Jean McConville's children, several of whom spent time speaking with me. Those were difficult conversations. The McConvilles have experienced unimaginable suffering with great dignity. I hope that I have related the story of what happened to their family as truthfully and comprehensively as possible.

I owe thanks to the staffs of numerous libraries and archives, particularly the Linen Hall Library in Belfast, the National Library of Ireland in Dublin, the National Archives of the United Kingdom in Kew, the Churchill Archives Centre at the University of Cambridge, the New York Public Library, the Tamiment Library and Robert F. Wagner Archives at New York University, and the John J. Burns and Thomas P. O'Neill, Jr., Libraries at Boston College. The Conflict Archive on the Internet (CAIN) at Ulster University was also an invaluable resource.

Ed Moloney was extremely patient in relating his own story and his broader insights about the Troubles. He also shared crucial material that he has assembled over decades of research, and I deeply appreciate the collegial spirit in which he was willing to do so. Anthony McIntyre, Carrie Twomey, Ricky O'Rawe, and Hugh Feeney were particularly generous with their time and recollections. Sandra Peake of the Wave Trauma Centre, Dennis Godfrey of the Independent Commission for the Location of Victims' Remains, and Liz Young of the Police Service of Northern Ireland were all helpful. For hospitality, friendship, and guidance in Belfast, I'm indebted to Gerry and Shelagh Moriarty, Alison Millar, and Paul Howard (and their son Sam), Rachel Hooper, Darragh MacIntyre, and my old pal Steve Warby. Oorlagh George and I first met in Los Angeles, then reconnected in Belfast. Along the way, she shared a few observations about the Troubles that have been rattling around in my head ever since and have informed the book in subtle but important ways. In Dublin, dear friends John Lacy, Sean O'Neill, and Clodagh Dunne took care of me. A particular thanks to Adam Goldman of *The New York Times,* who found Pat McClure. Tara Keenan-Thomson graciously shared the transcript of her 2003 interview with Dolours Price. James Kinchin-White, a tenacious archival researcher with a particular interest in the Troubles, uncovered several of the government documents cited here.

Book writing can be a lonely enterprise, but I've been fortunate to work with a series of talented research assistants. Some helped track down one-off items, others did work that spanned years, and they all made the book feel more like a collaboration. Deep thanks to Ruby Mellen, Linda Kinstler, Giulia Ricco, Katy Wynbrandt, Colson Lin, Jake McAuley, Rachel Luban, and particularly Victoria Beale. Emily Gogolak and Ruth Margalit fact-checked the original article. The precise, indefatigable Fergus McIntosh fact-checked the book. Needless to say, any errors that remain are entirely my own.

During 2016–17, I spent a year as an Eric and Wendy Schmidt Fellow at the New America foundation. My thanks to the Schmidts for supporting this project, and to Anne-Marie Slaughter, Peter Bergen, Konstantin Kakaes, and Awista Ayub for that opportunity. The book first started to feel like a book in April 2016, when I spent several precious weeks at the Rockefeller Foundation's Bellagio Center, on Lake Como, where I had the time and space to start getting words on paper. Thanks to Claudia Juech, Elena Ongania, and Pilar Palaciá for that extraordinary experience. I workshopped sections of the book at New

America and Bellagio, and also at the New York Institute for the Humanities, and I remain deeply grateful to my fellow fellows at each of these institutions for their insightful critiques.

I've been reading *The New Yorker* since I was a kid, and I'm still a little gobsmacked that a publication I so cherish has become my professional home. Thanks to David Remnick, Pam McCarthy, Dorothy Wickenden, and Henry Finder for all they do for the magazine, and for enabling me to do this work. A particular, profound thanks to Daniel Zalewski, ingenious editor and steadfast friend, who makes everything he touches so much better. I'm grateful to all of my colleagues but particularly Fabio Bertoni, Andrew Marantz, Tyler Foggatt, Raffi Khatchadourian, Rachel Aviv, David Grann, Philip Gourevitch, George Packer, Sheelah Kolhatkar, Jonathan Blitzer, and Siobhan Bohnacker. Without Bruce Diones, I might still be locked out of the building.

Bill Thomas at Doubleday saw promise in this story from our initial conversation about it and edited the manuscript with his usual keen eye and steady hand. Enormous thanks to Bill and also to Margo Shickmanter, Michael Goldsmith, Todd Doughty, Daniel Novack, Leila Gordon, Will Palmer, Maria Massey, and everybody else at Doubleday. I'm also very grateful to Arabella Pike for her encouragement and guidance on the manuscript, and to all of her colleagues at William Collins in London. Thanks, as ever, to my agent, the wonderful Tina Bennett, and to Anna DeRoy, Tracy Fisher, and Svetlana Katz at WME. Thea Traff, with her impeccable eye, helped me track down the photos. I'm indebted to my friend and colleague, the supremely gifted Philip Montgomery, who took the author photo, and to Oliver Munday, who designed the beautiful cover.

Thanks, for various reasons, to Michael Shtender-Auerbach, Sai Sriskandarajah, Michael Wahid Hanna, Sarah Margon, Dan Kurtz-Phelan, Ed Caesar, Linc Caplan, William Chan, Alex Gibney, Jason Burns, David Park, Andy Galker, Nate Lavey, Jean Strouse, Melanie Rehak, Eric Banks, Maya Jasanoff, Simon Carswell, Trevor Birney, Nuala Cunningham, Gideon Lewis-Kraus, and Matthew Teague.

There is no summarizing my gratitude to my parents, Frank Keefe and Jennifer Radden. They still read every word I write before almost anyone else does, and when I think about the kind of person (and the kind of parent) I want to be, they still provide the model. Special thanks to Beatrice Radden Keefe and Greg de Souza, and to Tristram Radden Keefe and Carlota Melo. A big hug, also, to baby E.

I am so fortunate in my in-laws, Tadeusz and Ewa, without whose last-minute childcare interventions this book could never have been written.

But my biggest thanks go to their beautiful, sharp-minded daughter, Justyna. It's been twenty years since we first met, yet a day doesn't go by when I'm not reminded of how lucky I am to share my life with her. (Indeed, she is often the one who reminds me.) As for our sons, Lucian and Felix, Lucian said to me just now, "Write that we basically did all the work." I can't say that they accelerated the progress of this project, exactly, but they were a daily reminder of life's antic consolations, and the book is dedicated to them.

A NOTE ON SOURCES

Say Nothing is based on four years of research, seven trips to Northern Ireland, and interviews with more than one hundred people. But in the spirit of the book's title, there were many people who refused to speak with me, or who started to and then had a change of heart. It may seem strange that events from nearly half a century ago could still provoke such fear and anguish. But, as I hope this book makes clear, in Belfast, history is alive and dangerous.

Memory is a slippery thing, so I have sought wherever possible to establish corroboration for individual recollections. In instances where there are discrepancies among different accounts, I have used the most plausible version of events in the main text of the book and elaborated on alternative accounts, or other nuances, in the notes.

This is not a history book but a work of narrative nonfiction. No dialogue or details have been invented or imagined; in instances where I describe the inner thoughts of characters, it is because they have related those thoughts to me, or to others, as detailed in the notes. Because I have elected to tell this particular story, there are important aspects of the Troubles that are not addressed. The book hardly mentions loyalist terrorism, to take just one example. If you're feeling whataboutish, I would direct you to one of the many excellent books cited in the notes that address the Troubles more broadly or your favored subject in particular. Because the history of the Troubles is so vexed, and so often inflected by partisan predispositions, some of the episodes described in this book are the subject of controversy and divergent interpretation; rather than burden the central narrative with frequent digressions, I have tended to address such debates in the notes.

In addition to interviews, the book is based on extensive archival research, including many contemporary newspaper accounts, as well as unpublished letters and emails, recently declassified government papers, published and unpublished memoirs, contemporary propaganda, affidavits, depositions, inquest reports, coroners' reports, witness testimony, diaries, archival footage and photographs, and the recordings of phone conversations. In recounting the history of the Price family, I relied heavily on two extensive unpublished interviews with Dolours Price, one conducted by Tara Keenan-Thomson in 2003, the other by Ed Moloney in 2010.

Though the book is based chiefly on my own original reporting, it incorporates the groundbreaking work of a series of longtime chroniclers of the Troubles, chief among them Susan McKay, David McKittrick, Ed Moloney,

Peter Taylor, Mark Urban, Martin Dillon, Richard English, Tim Pat Coogan, Malachi O'Doherty, Suzanne Breen, Allison Morris, and Henry McDonald. In the early chapters, I also made use of the marvelous dispatches of Simon Winchester and Max Hastings. I have drawn heavily on many terrific documentaries, particularly *Disappeared* (1999), *The Disappeared* (2013), and Ed Moloney's film *I, Dolours* (2018).

Gerry Adams frequently gives interviews, but when he learned the subject of my inquiry, he declined to speak with me. Through a representative, he sent a statement that said, in part, that the Boston College oral history project "is a deeply flawed, shoddy and self-serving effort," and that Ed Moloney and Anthony McIntyre are "well known opponents of the Sinn Féin leadership and the party's peace strategy." Adams continues to deny that he ordered the murder of Jean McConville or that he was ever a member of the IRA. But the downside of denying something everyone knows to be true is that the value of anything you say inevitably starts to depreciate. In creating the portrait of Adams, I relied on the recollections of numerous people who served alongside him in the IRA, on scores of other interviews that Adams has given, and on his own autobiographical writings.

When I started this project in 2014, Ed Moloney gave me the complete, unredacted transcript of Brendan Hughes's Boston College interview, which became an indispensable source. But apart from that oral history, nobody involved in the Belfast Project would share any of the interviews with me. I never had access to the oral histories of Dolours Price, Ivor Bell, or any of the other participants referenced in the book, though I was able to reconstruct some of the conversations by interviewing Anthony McIntyre. The Boston tapes were supposed to lie untouched, like bottles in a wine cellar, until some future date when the participants were dead and scholars could study their testimony to make sense of the Troubles. Instead the tapes became criminal evidence—and a political weapon. They might be used to prosecute old crimes. But it seems likely, now, that they will never become available to researchers.

Several years ago, Boston College started informing people who had participated in the project that they could have their interviews back. The university, burned by its own carelessness in handling such incendiary material, wanted to jettison its responsibility as custodian of the tapes. Many of the participants took the university up on it. One of them was Ricky O'Rawe. One day, he received a box from Boston College containing the recordings and transcripts of his conversations with Mackers from more than a decade earlier. At first, O'Rawe could not decide what to do with them. Then he had an idea. He took the CDs and transcripts into the study in his house and lit a fire in the fireplace. Then he opened a nice bottle of Bordeaux and poured himself a glass. The firelight reflected in framed photographs that lined the walls, pictures of old friends and comrades from the Troubles, many of them now dead. There was a copy of the 1916 Proclamation, in which Patrick Pearse declared an independent Ireland, and a photograph of Brendan Hughes. O'Rawe tossed his testimony into the flames. Then he drank the Bordeaux and watched it burn.

NOTES

ABBREVIATED SOURCES

Interviews

H-BC   Brendan Hughes/Anthony McIntyre Boston College oral history transcript.

P-EM   Unpublished Dolours Price interview with Ed Moloney, 2010.

P-TKT   Unpublished Dolours Price interview with Tara Keenan-Thomson, 2003.

Legal Proceedings

Archie McConville deposition

Deposition of Arthur (Archie) McConville, Inquest on the Body of Jean McConville, Coroner's District of County Louth, April 5, 2004.

BC Motion to Quash

Motion of Trustees of Boston College to Quash Subpoenas, June 2, 2011 (U.S. District Court of Massachusetts, M.B.D. No. 11-MC-91078).

Government's Opposition to Motion to Quash

Government's Opposition to Motion to Quash and Motion for an Order to Compel, July 1, 2011 (U.S. District Court of Massachusetts, M.B.D. No. 11-MC-91078).

Moloney Belfast affidavit

First Affidavit of Ed Moloney in the Matter of an Application by Anthony McIntyre for Judicial Review (High Court of Justice in Northern Ireland, September 12, 2012).

Moloney Massachusetts affidavit

Affidavit of Ed Moloney, June 2, 2011 (U.S. District Court of Massachusetts, M.B.D. No. 11-MC-91078).

O'Neill affidavit

Affidavit of Robert K. O'Neill, "In Re: Request from the United Kingdom Pursuant to the Treaty Between the Government of the

United States of America and the Government of the United Kingdom on Mutual Assistance in Criminal Matters in the Matter of Dolours Price," June 2, 2011 (U.S. District Court of Massachusetts, M.B.D. No. 11-MC-91078).

Price affidavit
Affidavit of Dolours Price, *Price & Price v. Home Office* (High Court of Justice, Queen's Bench Division), April 23, 1974.

Other Reports and Transcripts

De Silva Report
The Report of the Patrick Finucane Review, December 12, 2012.

HIA transcript
Historical Institutional Abuse Inquiry, hearing transcript, 2014.

May 16, 2011, conference call
Recording of a conference call between Ed Moloney, Anthony McIntyre, Carrie Twomey, Wilson McArthur, Bob O'Neill, and Tom Hachey, May 16, 2011.

Police Ombudsman's Report
"Report into the Complaint by James and Michael McConville Regarding the Police Investigation into the Abduction and Murder of Their Mother Mrs. Jean McConville," Police Ombudsman for Northern Ireland, July 18, 2006.

PROLOGUE

3 The Jesuits who founded: Charles Donovan, Paul FitzGerald, and Paul Dunigan, *History of Boston College: From the Beginnings to 1990* (Chestnut Hill, Mass.: University Press of Boston College, 1990), pp. 2–3.

3 sell to Sotheby's: "FBI Busts Librarian Accused of Stealing Books," United Press International, October 8, 1986.

3 call the FBI himself: "Librarian Helps Foil the Theft of Irish Artifacts," *New York Times,* September 1, 1991.

3 It is a secure space: O'Neill affidavit.

4 One summer day in 2013: "U.S. Hands Over Bomber Dolours Price's Secret Interview Tapes to PSNI," *Belfast Telegraph,* July 8, 2013; interview with Ed Moloney.

4 There were MiniDiscs containing: Interviews with Ed Moloney and Anthony McIntyre.

CHAPTER I

9 Jean McConville was thirty-eight: "Snatched Mother Missing a Month," *Belfast Telegraph,* January 16, 1972. There have been conflicting accounts of Jean's date of birth. Her daughter Helen has said that she was born in 1935, and the age of death cited on Jean's headstone—thirty-seven—would also suggest that she was born in 1935. Most press accounts describe her as having been thirty-seven when she disappeared. But according to her birth certificate, which I obtained, her actual date of birth was May 7, 1934, which means that she was thirty-eight.

9 sweet-eyed twins: Unless otherwise noted, details in this section are drawn from several interviews with Michael McConville. Ann McConville was born November 28, 1952, and died September 29, 1992; she suffered from tuberous sclerosis. The detail about the fourteen children being carried to term is from Susan McKay, "Diary," *London Review of Books,* December 19, 2013.

10 The stove in the new apartment: Interview with Archie and Susie McConville.

10 when somebody knocked: Ibid.

10 must be Helen: "Snatched Mother Missing a Month," *Belfast Telegraph,* January 16, 1972; Archie McConville deposition.

10 precisely how many there were: In most of the McConville children's recollections, the number is eight. See, for example, Archie McConville deposition. But in some accounts, the children have suggested that there were more. In an interview with Susan McKay, Helen maintained that the gang consisted of "four women and eight men," though Helen was not in fact at home at the time of the abduction and returned only later. See Susan McKay, "Diary," *London Review of Books,* December 19, 2013. In an interview with me, Michael McConville put the number between ten and twelve.

10 carrying a gun: Interviews with Michael, Archie, and Susie McConville.

10 "What's happening?": "Sons Recall 30 Years of Painful Memories," *Irish News,* October 24, 2003; Agnes McConville interview, *Marian Finucane Show,* RTÉ Radio, November 23, 2013.

10 children went berserk: Interview with Michael McConville.

10 only a few hours: Archie McConville deposition.

11 not strangers: Interview with Michael McConville.

11 There was nobody: Interview with Archie McConville; "Sons Recall 30 Years of Painful Memories," *Irish News,* October 24, 2003.

11 He kept close: "Sons Recall 30 Years of Painful Memories," *Irish News,* October 24, 2003.

11 barrel into his cheek: Interview with Archie McConville; Archie McConville deposition.

11 Reluctantly, he turned: Interview with Archie McConville.

12 "Watch the children": "Sons Recall 30 Years of Painful Memories," *Irish News,* October 24, 2003.

CHAPTER 2

13 one very Catholic aunt: Dolours Price interview in the documentary *I, Dolours,* directed by Maurice Sweeney, produced by Ed Moloney and Nuala Cunningham (New Decade Films, 2018).

13 "I'm not going back to Mass": P-EM.

13 The Prices lived: P-TKT.

13 he made the chairs: "Lest We Forget," *Daily Express,* June 1, 1974.

13 snapshots taken in prisons: Interview with Eamonn McCann.

14 When Dolours was little: "Protest Now, Before It Is Too Late!" *Irish People,* January 12, 1974; " 'Republicanism Is Part of Our DNA,' Says IRA Bomber Dolours Price," *Telegraph,* September 23, 2012.

14 cardboard in his shoes: P-EM.

14 fingertips stained yellow: "Lest We Forget," *Daily Express,* June 1, 1974.

14 digging a tunnel: Ibid. Details about the escape can be found in Uinseann Ó Rathaille Mac Eoin, *The I.R.A. in the Twilight Years 1923–1948* (Dublin: Argenta, 1997), p. 452.

14 bagpipes to cover: Tim Pat Coogan, *The IRA* (New York: St. Martin's Press, 2002), p. 185.

14 "a single spark": P-EM.

14 friends who'd been hanged: Ibid.

14 tingling with goose bumps: Ibid. and P-TKT.

14 relieve a police officer: Dolours Price, "Gerry Kelly: He's Not the Boy I Loved," *Fortnight,* September 2004.

14 "banned emblem": P-EM.

15 raiders of the twelfth century: In an unintentionally comical flourish, the "Chronology of Events" at the beginning of one of Gerry Adams's memoirs commences in the year 1169. Gerry Adams, *A Farther Shore: Ireland's Long Road to Peace* (New York: Random House, 2005), p. xi.

15 "In every generation": Peter de Rosa, *Rebels: The Irish Rising of 1916* (New York: Random House, 1990), p. 268.

15 Even as a child: Ruth Dudley Edwards, *Patrick Pearse: The Triumph of Failure* (Dublin: Poolbeg Press, 1990), pp. 7–8.

15 a "cleansing" thing: Ruán O'Donnell, *16 Lives: Patrick Pearse* (Dublin: O'Brien Press, 2016), pp. 18, 63.

15 Christlike deaths: O'Donnell, *16 Lives,* pp. 140–41.

15 "the red wine of the battlefield": De Rosa, *Rebels,* p. 89.

16 a firing squad: O'Donnell, *16 Lives,* p. 273.

16 rituals of commemoration: Flags and Emblems (Display) Act (Northern Ireland), 1954. The law was repealed in 1987.

16 cover the lily: Price, "Gerry Kelly: He's Not the Boy I Loved."

16 never met his first child: Ibid.

16 suddenly detonated: "Big Arms Haul in Belfast," *Irish Times,* May 30, 1938; "The Belfast Explosion," *Irish Times,* May 31, 1938.

17 for the rest of her life: P-TKT.

17 everything for an ideal: "Old Bailey Bomber Ashamed of Sinn Féin," *Village Magazine,* December 7, 2004.

17 a life of blindness: Ibid.

17 never expressed any regret: Price, "Gerry Kelly: He's Not the Boy I Loved."

17 "talk to your aunt Bridie": P-TKT.

17 lighting Bridie's cigarettes: P-EM.

17 found it revolting: Ibid.

17 scrutinizing her face: P-TKT.

17 "Do you not wish you'd just died?": Ibid.

17 How can you cry: Ibid.; Dolours Price, "Gerry Kelly," *Fortnight,* September 2004.

18 walk from Belfast: Interview with Eamonn McCann.

18 extraordinary discrimination: See, generally, Michael Farrell, *Northern Ireland: The Orange State* (London: Pluto Press, 1987).

18 For half a century: Michael Farrell, Introduction, in *Twenty Years On,* ed. Michael Farrell (Dingle, Ireland: Brandon, 1988), p. 14.

18 the Catholic population: Marc Mulholland, *Northern Ireland: A Very Short Introduction* (Oxford: Oxford University Press, 2002), p. 24.

19 civil rights movement: Daniel Finn, "The Point of No Return? People's Democracy and the Burntollet March," *Field Day Review* no. 9 (2013), pp. 4–21.

19 As they trudged: Archival footage.

19 At eighteen: Dolours is often reported to have been born on June 21, 1951, which would have made her seventeen at this time. According to her birth certificate, which I obtained, her actual birthday was December 16, 1950, so she was eighteen on January 1, 1969.

19 "Albert's daughters": Dolours Price to her family, January 28, 1974, in *Irish Voices from English Jails: Writings of Irish Political Prisoners in English Prisons* (London: Prisoners Aid Committee, 1979), p. 54.

19 They called each other "Dotes": Letters from Dolours and Marian Price to their family, both dated January 7, 1974, reproduced in "The Price Sisters," *Spare Rib* no. 22 (April 1974).

19 grown up sharing not: Dolours Price, "Afraid of the Dark," *Krino* no. 3 (Spring 1987).

19 Belfast accents beveled: P-TKT.

19 peals of laughter: Interview with Eamonn McCann.

19 childhood as an "indoctrination": Dolours Price, "Gerry Kelly," *Fortnight,* September 2004.

19 Like a lot of young people: "Ulster's Price Sisters: Breaking the Long Fast," *Time,* June 17, 1974. The former student leader Michael Farrell would subsequently describe the effect that Che's death had on his generation in Ireland in the introduction to his edited collection *Twenty Years On,* p. 11.

20 Albert Price was an emphatic: This description is drawn from archival video of Price and conversations with people who knew him, among them Tommy Gorman.

20 "and you lost!": Tara Keenan-Thomson, *Irish Women and Street Politics, 1956– 1973* (Dublin: Irish Academic Press, 2010), p. 146.

20 "You failed": Ibid., p. 146.

20 started attending meetings: P-EM.

21 poisonous distraction: P-TKT.

21 became fast friends: Interview with Eamonn McCann.

21 "They are not our enemies": Bowes Egan and Vincent McCormack, *Burntollet* (London: LRS, 1969), p. 26.

21 Though he had once: Max Hastings, *Barricades in Belfast: The Fight for Civil Rights in Northern Ireland* (London: Taplinger, 1970), p. 71; Walter Ellis, *The Begin-*

ning of the End: The Crippling Disadvantage of a Happy Irish Childhood (Edinburgh: Mainstream, 2006), p. 137; Ed Moloney and Andy Pollak, *Paisley* (Dublin: Poolbeg Press, 1986), p. 161.

22 "You can't ignore the devil": Hastings, *Barricades in Belfast,* p. 84.

22 "outbred by Roman Catholics": Marc Mulholland, *Northern Ireland at the Cross-roads: Ulster Unionism in the O'Neill Years* (London: Palgrave, 2000), p. 1.

22 In the words of one English: The commentator was Max Hastings. "Why Britain Is Committed in Northern Ireland," *Irish Times,* January 27, 1972.

22 "We perish if we yield": Rudyard Kipling, "Ulster," in *The Collected Poems of Rudyard Kipling* (London: Wordsworth Editions, 1994), p. 243.

22 Among the scruffy: P-EM; "Documents Shed More Light on Burntollet Attack," *Irish News,* October 15, 2010.

22 A student at Queen's: Ellis, *Beginning of the End,* pp. 124, 157.

23 "My father's down there": Interview with Eamonn McCann.

23 But this oedipal dynamic: Ellis, *Beginning of the End,* p. 138.

23 "something bad": P-EM. Ronnie Bunting would end up becoming a leader of the Irish National Liberation Army (INLA). In 1980, he was murdered in his bed, at the age of 32. See Martin Dillon, *The Trigger Men* (Edinburgh: Mainstream, 2003), pp. 95–96.

23 a permanent state of emergency: Laura K. Donohue, "Regulating Northern Ireland: The Special Powers Acts, 1922–1972," *Historical Journal,* vol. 41, no. 4 (1998).

23 "wilder they are, the better": Wallace Clark, *Guns in Ulster* (Belfast: Constabulary Gazette, 1967), p. 9.

23 cordon of police officers: Bob Purdie, *Politics in the Streets: The Origins of the Civil Rights Movement in Northern Ireland* (Belfast: Blackstaff Press, 1990), pp. 213–14.

24 One carried a Lambeg drum: Farrell, *Northern Ireland,* p. 249; "End in Sight After Long March," *Guardian,* October 27, 2001.

24 welcomed the idea: Some observers have suggested that the civil rights protesters were not so distinct from the IRA as they might have liked to suggest. Richard English has written that the movement was "an initiative which originated from within the old IRA, and which—as far as those old-IRA republicans were concerned—did so with the explicit intention of bringing down the Northern Ireland state." Richard English, *Armed Struggle: The History of the IRA* (New York: Oxford University Press, 2003), p. 82. Eamonn McCann told me that during the March to Derry, IRA gunmen materialized at night to "protect" the marchers. McCann was not happy to discover them.

24 sparked real change: Daniel Finn, "The Point of No Return? People's Democracy and the Burntollet March," *Field Day Review* no. 9 (2013).

24 "possibility of being hurt?": "Battling Through to Derry," *Irish Times,* January 6, 1969; archival footage. The man with the bullhorn was Michael Farrell.

24 The night before: Purdie, *Politics in the Streets,* pp. 213–14; Egan and McCormack, *Burntollet,* p. 22.

25 "monster of Romanism": Moloney and Pollak, *Paisley,* p. 159.

25 "multiply like vermin": Ibid., p. 201.

25 "Why would we kill Paisley?": Dolours Price, "Ideals Live On," *The Blanket,* November 29, 2006.

25 reenacting the siege: Egan and McCormack, *Burntollet,* p. 22.

26 "IRA men" in disguise: Ellis, *Beginning of the End,* p. 137.

26 defense of the city?: Egan and McCormack, *Burntollet,* p. 22.

26 to play a "manly role": Moloney and Pollak, *Paisley,* p. 168.

26 arsenal of stones: Tommy McKearney, *The Provisional IRA: From Insurrection to Parliament* (London: Pluto Press, 2011), p. 42.

26 "that pious declaration": Egan and McCormack, *Burntollet,* p. 26.

26 some unseen bull: Ibid., pp. 29–30.

26 other figures emerged: "Battling Through to Derry," *Irish Times,* January 6, 1969; Purdie, *Politics in the Streets,* p. 214.

27 "curtain" of projectiles: Bernadette Devlin, *The Price of My Soul* (New York: Vintage, 1970), pp. 139–41; "Battling Through to Derry," *Irish Times,* January 6, 1969.

27 still swarming around: "Battling Through to Derry," *Irish Times,* January 6, 1969.

27 stuck in the middle: P-TKT.

27 clambered over the hedge: P-EM.

28 some Hollywood western: P-TKT.

28 wore motorcycle helmets: "Attack on March—Bunting Fined," *Irish Times,* March 11, 1969; "Battling Through to Derry," *Irish Times,* January 6, 1969.

28 They descended: Egan and McCormack, *Burntollet,* pp. 31–32.

28 grabbed one another: Ibid., p. 33.

28 As marchers fled: Hastings, *Barricades in Belfast,* p. 86.

28 smacked a young girl: "Battling Through to Derry," *Irish Times,* January 6, 1969.

28 Two newspaper photographers: Ibid.

28 the grand marshal: "Attack on March—Bunting Fined," *Irish Times,* March 11, 1969.

28 blotted with blood: Ibid.

28 pledge of nonviolence: "Battling Through to Derry," *Irish Times,* January 6, 1969; "Riots Injure 120 on Belfast March," Reuters, January 5, 1969.

28 blood running into their eyes: "Battling Through to Derry," *Irish Times,* January 6, 1969.

28 She splashed into: P-EM.

28 pushed off the bridge: Egan and McCormack, *Burntollet,* p. 37.

28 glazed with hate: Dolours Price, "Gerry Kelly," *Fortnight,* September 2004.

28 into those eyes: Keenan-Thomson, *Irish Women and Street Politics,* p. 41.

28 grabbed his coat: P-TKT.

29 police could distinguish them: Purdie, *Politics in the Streets,* p. 215; Michael Farrell, "Long March to Freedom," in *Twenty Years On,* p. 58.

29 the B-Specials: Bob Purdie writes: "Many assailants wore white armbands which readily distinguished them from marchers. Egan and McCormack were able to identify a number of the attackers from photographs ... Many were B Specials; this was a good propaganda point for the civil rights movement, but since membership of the B Specials in the area was roughly coterminous with the status of adult, able-bodied male Protestants, this underlies the point that it was an attack by local people." Purdie, *Politics in the Streets,* p. 215.

29 on the way to Altnagelvin Hospital: Dolours Price, "Gerry Kelly," *Fortnight,* September 2004.

29 "fight back": Ibid. The torn-clothes detail comes from "Lest We Forget," *Daily Express,* June 1, 1974.

CHAPTER 3

30 one photograph: In an excellent piece based on an interview with Helen, Susan McKay says that the photo was taken in 1965. McKay, "Diary," *London Review of Books,* December 19, 2013.

31 defining accessory: In interviews with me, Michael, Susan, and Archie McConville each recalled the nappy pin. Helen told Susan McKay that she has no memory of it. This is a typical pattern for the McConville children, who often have conflicting memories of their traumatic childhood.

31 *Titanic* had been built: Author visit to Avoniel Road.

31 Jean's father worked: McKay, "Diary," *London Review of Books,* December 19, 2013.

31 plodded home: Séamus McKendry, *Disappeared: The Search for Jean McConville* (Dublin: Blackwater Press, 2000), p. 9.

31 Luftwaffe bombers: "Many Killed in Mass Air Attack on Belfast," *Irish Independent,* April 17, 1941; Ian S. Wood, *Britain, Ireland and the Second World War* (Edinburgh: Edinburgh University Press, 2010), pp. 174–75.

31 job as a servant: McKay, "Diary," *London Review of Books,* December 19, 2013.

31 He towered over: McKendry, *Disappeared,* p. 9.

31 fight the Japanese: Ibid. and McKay, "Diary," *London Review of Books,* December 19, 2013.

32 "mixed" relationships were rare: See Edward Moxon-Browne, "National Identity in Northern Ireland," in *Social Attitudes in Northern Ireland: The First Report,* ed. Peter Stringer and Gillian Robinson (Belfast: Blackstaff Press, 1991).

32 circumscribed worlds: Cormac Ó Gráda and Brendan M. Walsh, "Intermarriage in a Divided Society: Ireland a Century Ago," *Explorations in Economic History,* vol. 56 (2015).

32 crossed these lines: McKay, "Diary," *London Review of Books,* December 19, 2013.

32 member of the Orange Order: This is an area where the McConville children have differing accounts. In his book, Helen's husband, Séamus McKendry, suggests that Granny Murray did not seem concerned about the marriage, and it is a fact that Albert and the children did end up moving in with Mrs. Murray in East Belfast. But after the disappearance of Jean McConville, several of her children would suggest that Mrs. Murray had effectively disowned her daughter (and, by extension, her grandchildren) because Jean had married a Catholic. It may be that such social transgressions were easier to overlook in the 1950s than in the 1960s.

On the notion that Mary McConville was not overly troubled, and on the beating by the uncle, see McKendry, *Disappeared,* p. 10. Michael McConville told me, "My mother's family wouldn't have anything to do with us, because she'd married a Catholic." The same assertion is made in legal papers filed on behalf of James McConville: "Their mother's family had disowned her." Application to the Attorney General in Relation to the Death of Jean McConville, filed by Joe Mulholland & Co., Solicitors, on behalf of James McConville, May 23, 2013.

32 eloped to England: McKay, "Diary," *London Review of Books,* December 19, 2013; McKendry, *Disappeared,* p. 9.

32 a dozen or so people crammed: McKay, "Diary," *London Review of Books,* December 19, 2013.

32 Arthur retired: McKendry, *Disappeared,* p. 10.

32 job in a ropeworks: McKay, "Diary," *London Review of Books,* December 19, 2013.

33 starting right outside: McKendry, *Disappeared,* p. 10.

33 "You people of the Shankill Road": Moloney and Pollak, *Paisley,* p. 89.

33 There was no television: McKendry, *Disappeared,* p. 10; McKay, "Diary," *London Review of Books,* December 19, 2013.

33 Battle of the Bogside: English, *Armed Struggle,* p. 102. See also Russell Stetler, *The Battle of Bogside: The Politics of Violence in Northern Ireland* (London: Sheed and Ward, 1970).

34 pried up paving stones: Hastings, *Barricades in Belfast,* pp. 142–43.

34 blue flame spilling: Archival footage.

34 a bulldozer: Hastings, *Barricades in Belfast,* p. 143.

34 Loyalist gangs started moving systematically: An eyewitness account from the documentary *The Burning of Bombay Street* (BBC One Northern Ireland, 2011).

34 As the rioting spread: Seamus Brady, "Eye-witness Account of Events in Belfast," August 22, 1969, National Archives of Ireland. See also *Burning of Bombay Street.*

34 clasping their rosaries: McKearney, *The Provisional IRA,* p. 47.

35 two thousand families: *The Irish Times, The Guardian,* and other media sources cite the same figures, which appear to have originated with Tim Pat Coogan: 1,820 families are believed to have fled their homes between July and September 1969—315 Protestant and 1,505 Catholic. See "Day the Troops Marched in to Nationalist Welcome," *Irish Times,* August 14, 1999; Tim Pat Coogan, *The Troubles* (New York: Palgrave, 2002), p. 91.

35 Some 350,000 people: Census of Population, Belfast County Borough, 1971.

35 10 percent: Paul Doherty and Michael A. Poole, "Ethnic Residential Segregation in Belfast, Northern Ireland, 1971–1991," *Geographical Review,* vol. 87, no. 4 (October 1997).

35 converge on a house: McKay, "Diary," *London Review of Books,* December 19, 2013.

35 hour to vacate: Seamus Brady, "Eye-witness Account of Events in Belfast," August 22, 1969, National Archives of Ireland.

35 family of eight: Ibid.

35 southbound train: "Army Under Crossfire," *Telegraph,* July 16, 1972. See also "Thousands of Northern Refugees Streamed over the Border in the 1970s—Some Were Called 'Ungrateful,'" *TheJournal.ie,* December 27, 2014.

35 his mother's house: Interview with Michael McConville.

35 forced to flee: McKay, "Diary," *London Review of Books,* December 19, 2013; McKendry, *Disappeared,* p. 10.

35 staggered through the streets: See *Burning of Bombay Street.*

35 All the traffic lights: Hastings, *Barricades in Belfast,* pp. 146–47.

35 "Belfast confetti": Ciarán Carson, *Belfast Confetti* (Winston-Salem, N.C.: Wake Forest University Press, 1989).

36 war zone to the shops: There is archival footage of women heading to a shop on Omar Street during a lull in the shooting during the Falls Curfew, on Saturday, July 4, 1970.

36 lug their belongings: McKay, "Diary," *London Review of Books,* December 19, 2013; McKendry, *Disappeared,* p. 10.

36 She was half-blind: Interview with Michael McConville; social worker's report regarding the McConville children, December 13, 1972.

36 the fire could spread: McKay, "Diary," *London Review of Books,* December 19, 2013; McKendry, *Disappeared,* p. 11.

36 Many displaced families: "Flight: A Report on Population Movement in Belfast During August, 1971," Northern Ireland Community Relations Commission Research Unit, Belfast, 1971.

36 nobody else could get in first: McKay, "Diary," *London Review of Books,* December 19, 2013; McKendry, *Disappeared,* p. 11.

37 material to make curtains: McKay, "Diary," *London Review of Books,* December 19, 2013.

37 The family stayed in the chalet: Interview with Michael McConville; McKendry, *Disappeared,* p. 12; McKay, "Diary," *London Review of Books,* December 19, 2013.

37 Divis Flats was meant: *High Life,* documentary (BBC, 2011); Megan Deirdre Roy, "Divis Flats: The Social and Political Implications of a Modern Housing Project in Belfast, Northern Ireland, 1968–1998," *Iowa Historical Review,* vol. 1, no. 1 (2007).

37 "city in the sky": *High Life.*

37 four-bedroom maisonette: Interview with Michael McConville.

38 no playgrounds: Roy, "Divis Flats," *Iowa Historical Review,* vol. 1, no. 1 (2007).

38 maze for rats: Interview with Michael McConville.

38 hear every word: McKay, "Diary," *London Review of Books,* December 19, 2013.

38 malignant black mold: Roy, "Divis Flats," *Iowa Historical Review,* vol. 1, no. 1 (2007); *High Life.*

38 "slum in the sky": Lynsey Hanley, *Estates: An Intimate History* (London: Granta, 2000), p. 97.

38 soldiers cups of tea: Hastings, *Barricades in Belfast,* p. 147.

38 more circumspect: McKay, "Diary," *London Review of Books,* December 19, 2013.

39 complicated ethnic geography: Hastings, *Barricades in Belfast,* p. 147.

39 Gun battles broke out: Ibid., p. 144.

39 Incensed by such aggression: Ibid., p. 144.

39 city into darkness: Ibid., p. 145.

39 Land Rovers with their headlights off: "Belfast's Night Patrol: An Uneasy Tour," *Newsday,* September 17, 1971.

39 For all the chaos: David McKittrick, Seamus Kelters, Brian Feeney, and Chris Thornton, *Lost Lives: The Stories of the Men, Women and Children Who Died As a Result of the Northern Ireland Troubles,* 2nd ed. (Edinburgh: Mainstream, 2004), table 1, p. 1494.

39 stronghold for armed resistance: Roy, "Divis Flats," *Iowa Historical Review,* vol. 1, no. 1 (2007). Also see Jeffrey Sluka, *Hearts and Minds, Water and Fish: Support for the IRA and INLA in a Northern Ireland Ghetto* (Greenwich, Conn.: JAI Press, 1989).

39 residents called "the chain": McKendry, *Disappeared,* p. 15.

40 "A child's been hit!": Hastings, *Barricades in Belfast,* p. 144.

40 A nine-year-old boy: McKittrick et al., *Lost Lives,* p. 34.

40 frantically waving a white shirt: Hastings, *Barricades in Belfast,* p. 144.

40 "Down on the floor!": McConville, "Disappearance of Jean McConville," in *The Disappeared of Northern Ireland's Troubles* (Belfast: Wave Trauma Centre, 2012), p. 16.

40 anarchy persisted: Interview with Michael McConville.

40 One July afternoon: Simon Winchester, *In Holy Terror* (London: Faber, 1975), pp. 68–69.

41 three thousand soldiers: Ibid., p. 70.

41 They axed down doors: Patrick Bishop and Eamonn Mallie, *The Provisional IRA* (London: Heinemann, 1987), p. 123.

41 an act of revenge: Winchester, *In Holy Terror,* p. 73.

41 a military helicopter hovered: Ibid., pp. 71–72.

41 Using the tips of their rifles: Archival footage.

41 From the windows: Winchester, *In Holy Terror,* p. 72; archival footage.

41 A cartridge would skitter: Archival footage.

41 seeped into the cracks: Interview with Richard O'Rawe.

41 inducing panic: Winchester, *In Holy Terror,* p. 71.

41 Young men bathed: Ibid., p. 70; "Falls Road Curfew, 40th Anniversary," *Irish News,* June 30, 2010.

42 "weld a crowd together": Winchester, *In Holy Terror,* p. 32.

42 He watched them: Interview with Michael McConville.

42 Arthur McConville was unemployed: McKendry, *Disappeared,* p. 12.

42 welfare assistance: Roy, "Divis Flats," *Iowa Historical Review,* vol. 1, no. 1 (2007).

42 When the children: "Sons Recall 30 Years of Painful Memories," *Irish News,* October 24, 2003.

42 kids would scuttle outside: "How Belfast Feels Behind the Barricades," *Christian Science Monitor,* September 10, 1969.

42 "the poor man's racehorse": Kevin C. Kearns, *Dublin Street Life and Lore: An Oral History* (Dublin: Glendale, 1991), p. 63.

43 warm, nervous creatures: Interview with Michael McConville.

43 Eventually, Arthur grew so weak: McKendry, *Disappeared,* p. 13.

43 he had lung cancer: McKay, "Diary," *London Review of Books,* December 19, 2013; McKendry, *Disappeared,* p. 13.

43 Michael would hear him: Interview with Michael McConville.

CHAPTER 4

44 "Are you carrying anything?": This account is based on Tara Keenan-Thomson's book *Irish Women and Street Politics,* pp. 213–14, and on P-TKT.

45 The Falls Road and the Shankill: This description owes a debt to Tommy McKearney, *The Provisional IRA,* p. 47, and Winchester, *In Holy Terror,* p. 164.

45 peace walls: H-BC; "IRA Provisionals Put Up Barriers in Belfast," *Telegraph,* June 30, 1972.

45 The organization dwindled: Liam McMillen put the number at 120 as of 1969. Liam McMillen, "The Role of the I.R.A. 1962–1967" (lecture, Dublin, June 1972), reproduced in "Liam McMillen: Separatist, Socialist, Republican," Repsol Pamphlet no. 21 (1975). For a revisionist account, which argues that the narrative of a diminished (and more peaceful) IRA has been greatly exaggerated, see Brian Hanley, "'I Ran Away'? The IRA and 1969: The Evolution of a Myth," *Irish Historical Studies,* vol. 38, no. 152 (November 2013). He notes that British intelligence estimated that the IRA had perhaps 500 people throughout Northern Ireland in the spring of 1969, and that the organization's numbers in the Republic were much higher.

45 conspicuously unarmed: English, *Armed Struggle,* p. 84; H-BC.

45 tendency to blow themselves up: "Why Britain Is Committed in Northern Ireland," *Irish Times,* January 27, 1972.

46 "I Ran Away": H-BC; "The I.R.A., New York Brigade," *New York,* March 13, 1972. Hanley points out that the story, which has circulated widely in the historical literature, of graffiti on walls in Belfast saying I RAN AWAY is probably apocryphal: there were hundreds of journalists in the city, yet no press photo of such a slogan exists. But Hanley acknowledges that the formulation was in use as of 1970, and Hughes, in his BC oral history, does recall the phrase appearing on city walls.

46 There was a faction in Belfast: Interview with Billy McKee; "IRA Founder, 89, Has 'No Regrets,'" *Belfast News Letter,* May 17, 2011.

46 He had spent time: "Political Process Will Not Deliver a United Ireland," *Irish News,* March 30, 2016.

46 A devout Catholic: H-BC.

46 "You are a Dublin communist": Martin Dillon, *The Dirty War: Covert Strategies and Tactics Used in Political Conflicts* (New York: Routledge, 1999), p. 11; also see English, *Armed Struggle,* p. 105.

46 first item on the agenda is the split: John F. Morrison, *The Origins and Rise of Dissident Irish Republicanism* (London: Bloomsbury, 2013), p. viii.

46 To Dolours: Ibid., p. 54.

46 forty-four British soldiers: McKittrick et al., *Lost Lives,* table 1, p. 1494.

47 Two of Dolours's aunts: Price interview in *I, Dolours;* P-EM.

47 The army frequently raided: "Intelligence War by Army Cracks IRA Ranks," *Telegraph,* November 5, 1971.

47 One local house doubled as: "IRA Bomb School Uncovered by Army Swoop," *Telegraph,* January 8, 1972; "One Escapes After Seven Are Arrested at Bomb Lecture," *Guardian,* January 8, 1972.

47 Local residents resented: "London Bomb Campaign Decision Taken by IRA in Dublin," *Irish Times,* November 16, 1973.

47 "The local people had suddenly changed": Price interview in *I, Dolours.*

47 When the authorities were coming: Winchester, *In Holy Terror,* p. 164.

47 Scrappy school-age kids: "Soldiers Scurry in Sniper Country," *Baltimore Sun,* November 26, 1971.

47 People took to joking: "Army Under Crossfire," *Telegraph,* July 16, 1972.

48 she was bitterly disappointed: Interview with Anne Devlin.

48 Instead she secured a place: "London Bomb Campaign Decision Taken by IRA in Dublin," *Irish Times,* November 16, 1973.

48 When the IRA needed guns: P-TKT.

48 Albert went on the run: "Home Often Raided, Says Accused Girl," *Irish Times,* October 24, 1973; "London Bomb Campaign Decision Taken by IRA in Dublin," *Irish Times,* November 16, 1973; "Dolours Price Won Rapid Promotion As Gunmen Died," *Telegraph,* November 15, 1973.

48 "never the same": "Lest We Forget," *Daily Express,* June 1, 1974.

48 "I want to join": P-EM.

48 declaration of allegiance: P-TKT.

48 She vowed to obey: Price interview in *I, Dolours.*

48 nursing a cup of tea: P-TKT.

48 fantasy of peaceful resistance: P-EM.

49 No amount of marching: Price interview in *I, Dolours.*

49 Having strayed, in her youth: Keenan-Thomson, *Irish Women and Street Politics,* p. 149.

49 But at night they would disappear: "Lest We Forget," *Daily Express,* June 1, 1974; P-TKT.

49 Young people could vanish: Interview with Francis McGuigan.

49 Unfazed by the assault rifle: Interview with Hugh Feeney.

49 This could be comical: Interview with Francis McGuigan and Kevin Hannaway.

50 A moonfaced teetotaler: "Seán Mac Stíofáin: Obituary," *Telegraph,* May 19, 2001. Mac Stíofáin once said, "When I was very young, not more than seven, my mother said to me, 'I'm Irish, therefore you're Irish. You're half Irish, anyway. Don't forget it.'" This myth was sufficiently entrenched by the time he died that several obituaries erroneously said that his mother was from Belfast. See "Adams Leads Tributes As Mac Stíofáin Dies," *Irish Independent,* May 19, 2011; "Former Chief-of-Staff of the IRA Sean Mac Stíofáin Dies Aged 73," *Irish Times,* May 19, 2001.

50 "forget" to use his Irish name: "IRA Threatens to Kill Ceasefire Breakers," *Guardian,* June 24, 1972.

50 "escalate, escalate, escalate": Brendan O'Brien, *The Long War: The IRA and Sinn Féin* (Syracuse, N.Y.: Syracuse University Press, 1999), p. 119.

50 Mac the Knife: "Death of the Englishman Who Led the Provisionals," *Observer,* May 19, 2001.

50 In a passage in his: Seán Mac Stíofáin, *Revolutionary in Ireland* (Edinburgh: R & R Clark, 1975), p. 117.

51 Initially, Mac Stíofáin proposed: P-EM; P-TKT; "IRA Bomber Says Adams Ordered Terror Attacks on London Targets," *Irish Independent,* September 23, 2012.

51 The women of the Cumann: P-EM; "Irish Women Play a Growing Role in IRA Struggle Against British," *Washington Post,* April 11, 1972.

51 "Army or nothing": "IRA Bomber Says Adams Ordered Terror Attacks on London Targets," *Irish Independent,* September 23, 2012.

51 Price insisted that she was equal: P-EM.

51 "fighting soldier": "IRA Bomber Says Adams Ordered Terror Attacks on London Targets," *Irish Independent,* September 23, 2012.

51 A special meeting: Ibid.

51 But Price herself would speculate: Keenan-Thomson, *Irish Women and Street Politics,* p. 232.

52 *Clean the bullets*: P-TKT.

52 *"glorious* way of life": Price interview in *I, Dolours.*

52 New recruits to the Provos: H-BC.

52 "Like the revolution's going": P-TKT.

52 Most nights: Ibid.

53 But on one occasion: Ibid.

53 Not long after: P-EM; P-TKT.

53 They marched in formation: These details are drawn from H-BC.

53 But during funerals: Archival images of IRA funerals.

53 organized, ideological—and ruthless: H-BC.

54 they worked as couriers: P-EM; P-TKT; "London Bomb Campaign Decision Taken by IRA in Dublin," *Irish Times,* November 16, 1973.

54 Dolours had a friend: "Two Sisters from Belfast Republican Family—and Their Allies in IRA Unit," *Guardian,* November 15, 1973; "Girl out of Her Depth," *Telegraph,* November 15, 1973.

54 The bespectacled son of a pub owner: Interview with Hugh Feeney.

54 come home after their classes: Marian Price interview in the documentary *Car Bomb,* directed by Kevin Toolis (Many Rivers Films, 2008).

54 Dolours would often cross the border: P-EM.

54 "Rosie!" the soldiers would say: P-TKT.

55 the scent of nitrobenzene: "What Ever Happened to the IRA?" *Time,* March 28, 2008.

55 On one occasion, Marian was driving: *Car Bomb.*

55 Some Cumann veterans referred to: See Dieter Reinisch, "Cumann na mBan and the Acceptance of Women in the Provisional IRA: An Oral History Study of Irish Republican Women in the Early 1970s," in *Socheolas: Limerick Student Journal of Sociology,* vol. 5, no. 1 (September 2013).

55 A story circulated: "Three British Soldiers Shot Dead in Ulster," *Guardian*, March 11, 1971; Dillon, *The Dirty War*, pp. 214–15. A subsequent investigation, in 2020, indicated that this may not have been a honey trap at all. See "The Killings of the Three Scottish Soldiers," BBC *Spotlight*, February 25, 2020.

55 The Price sisters disdained such operations: P-EM; P-TKT. Also see Andrew Sanders, "Dolours Price, Boston College, and the Myth of the 'Price Sisters,'" *The United States of America and Northern Ireland* blog, January 24, 2013.

56 The spectacle of women as avatars: "Woman Hijacker Feels 'Engaged to the Revolution,'" *New York Times*, September 9, 1970.

56 Her photo was splashed across: "I Made the Ring from a Bullet and the Pin of a Hand Grenade," *Guardian*, January 25, 2001.

56 Patty Hearst brandishing: Jeffrey Toobin, *American Heiress: The Wild Saga of the Kidnapping, Crimes, and Trial of Patty Hearst* (New York: Doubleday, 2016), p. 157.

56 "rebel chic": Interview with Carrie Twomey.

56 Stories about the Price sisters: "Dolours Price Won Rapid Promotion As Gunmen Died," *Telegraph*, November 15, 1973.

56 They developed an outsize reputation: "The Sisters of Terror," *Observer*, November 18, 1973.

56 "the Widowmaker": "IRA Female Terrorists Work Havoc in Ireland," Associated Press, September 21, 1976.

56 "most dangerous young women": "Dolours Price Won Rapid Promotion As Gunmen Died," *Telegraph*, November 15, 1973.

56 frisky sexualized rumor: Similar stories got passed around in Vietnam during the same era. See chapter 9, "Sweetheart of the Song Tra Bong," in Tim O'Brien, *The Things They Carried* (New York: Houghton Mifflin, 1990).

57 "We had *Paris Match* magazine": "Dolours Price Won Rapid Promotion As Gunmen Died," *Telegraph*, November 15, 1973.

57 Eamonn McCann, the activist: Interview with Eamonn McCann.

57 Crazy Prices: Interview with Anthony McIntyre.

57 Once, officers from the Royal Ulster Constabulary: P-TKT.

59 Just as the branch was about to close: The robbery was reported in the press at the time, though the identity of the robbers was not known. "Spate of Robberies Throughout North," *Irish Times*, June 27, 1972; "'Nuns' Hold Up Belfast Bank," United Press International, June 27, 1972; "IRA Ceasefire Preceded by More Killing," *Guardian*, June 27, 1972; "Cease-fire Off to Uneasy Start in Northern Ireland," Associated Press, June 27, 1972.

59 It was the Price sisters: Price interview in *I, Dolours*.

59 The identity of the thieves was never: "A.I.B. Branch Robbed Again by Women," *Irish Times*, July 18, 1972.

59 hijacked a post office lorry: P-EM.

59 springing Brown free: "Hospital Gang Grab IRA Chief," *Telegraph*, December 30, 1972; "Two Sisters from Belfast Republican Family—and Their Allies in IRA Unit," *Guardian*, November 15, 1973; "IRA Leader Is Caught Year After Escape," *Times* (London), February 2, 1974. That Dolours Price was directly involved in this operation is confirmed in P-EM.

59 The ranks of the Provos: P-EM; "Disappeared IRA Victim and Provo 'Love Triangle,'" *Irish Independent*, December 7, 2014.

60 Lynskey had trained as a monk: Interview with a relative of Joe Lynskey's (who did not want to be identified more specifically); "Behind the Story: Allison Morris on How She Broke the Story of Joe Lynskey's IRA Execution," *Irish News*, June 25, 2015.

60 ended up leaving the order: Interview with a relative of Joe Lynskey's.

60 something of an oddball: Interview with Joe Clarke.

60 "Mad Monk": "Searching for the Mysterious 'Mad Monk' Who Fought for—and Was Killed by—the IRA," *Washington Post*, June 30, 2015.

60 Dolours grew very fond: Price interview in *I, Dolours*.

60 an ex-bartender from Ballymurphy: Gerry Adams, *Before the Dawn: An Autobiography* (Dingle, Ireland: Brandon, 2001), pp. 62–64.

60 Adams came from a distinguished: The uncle was Paddie Adams. Uinseann Ó Rathaille Mac Eoin, *The I.R.A. in the Twilight Years 1923–1948* (Dublin: Argenta, 1997), p. 453.

60 Adams had gotten his start: Adams, *Before the Dawn*, pp. 88–89.

60 He had joined the IRA: Adams insists that he has never been a member of the IRA, but any consultation of the evidence makes it impossible to countenance such a claim. There is general agreement in the scholarly literature that Adams seems to have joined the IRA as a teenager. See English, *Armed Struggle*, p. 110; Ed Moloney, *A Secret History of the IRA* (New York: Norton, 2002), p. 46; David Beresford, *Ten Men Dead: The Story of the 1981 Irish Hunger Strike* (New York: Atlantic Monthly Press, 1987), p. 23; Malachi O'Doherty, *Gerry Adams: An Unauthorised Life* (London: Faber, 2017), p. 24. As early as 1972, Adams was identified in the press as a leader of the IRA in Belfast. In December that year, the month that Jean McConville was abducted, *The Times* of London reported, "Gerry Adams, the 25-year-old ex-barman who now commands the Provisionals in [Belfast], wants to play a more political role in the Sinn Féin movement in the North but he cannot do so because he knows he would be arrested immediately" ("The High Stakes on Mr. Whitelaw's Luck," *Times* [London], December 1, 1972). In 2010, WikiLeaks released a secret U.S. diplomatic cable, from 2005, in which the U.S. ambassador in Dublin at the time, James Kenny, stated that the Irish government possessed "'rock solid evidence' that Gerry Adams and Martin McGuinness are members of the IRA military command" ("Peace Process: GOI Shaken by Second IRA Statement," U.S. diplomatic cable, February 4, 2005).

61 "Who does Gerry think he is?": P-EM.

61 he had a quiet, watchful charisma: Ibid.

61 sleeping, lately, at a West Belfast mortician: Ibid.

61 "It was an exciting time": "'Republicanism Is Part of Our DNA,' Says IRA Bomber Dolours Price," *Telegraph*, September 23, 2012.

61 "The Provo army was started by": "Hunger Strikers Seek Only to Serve Sentences in North," *Irish Times*, January 21, 1974.

62 "But he is in uniform": "Lest We Forget," *Daily Express*, June 1, 1974.

62 "maybe it will all have been worth it": Ibid.

62 chilly Sunday afternoon in January 1972: "Bloody Sunday in Derry," *New York Times*, February 1, 1972; " 'Bloody Sunday,' Derry 30 January 1972—Names of the Dead and Injured," CAIN.

62 The soldiers subsequently claimed: An initial inquiry, led by John Widgery, issued its conclusions just eleven weeks after Bloody Sunday and largely exonerated the British soldiers, taking at face value their suggestion that "they themselves came under fire and their own shooting consisted of aimed shots at gunmen and bomb throwers who were attacking them." Lord Widgery, *Report of the Tribunal Appointed to Inquire into the Events on Sunday, 30 January 1972* (April 1972). This investigation was widely condemned as a whitewash. It was only in 1998 that a subsequent inquiry, this one led by Mark Saville, was convened. In its 2010 report, the Saville inquiry concluded that, "despite the contrary evidence given by soldiers...none of them fired in response to attacks." *Independent Report of the Bloody Sunday Inquiry* (June 15, 2010).

62 filled them with an overpowering anger: P-TKT.

62 In February, protesters set fire: "Nation Mourns Derry's Dead," *Irish Times*, February 1, 1972.

62 In March, London suspended: "British Take Direct Rule in N. Ireland: Heath Suspends Ulster Self-Rule, Names Aide to Run Province," *Washington Post*, March 25, 1972.

62 Dolours Price traveled to Italy: Interview with Fulvio Grimaldi; "Misteriosa 'pasionaria' irlandese illustra l'attività rivoluzionaria dell'IRA," *Corriere della Sera*, March 24, 1972.

62 "the ghetto system": "Evidence Given on Handwriting," *Irish Times*, October 26, 1973; "Violence 'Not Included in IRA Principles,' " *Guardian*, October 26, 1973.

62 "If my political convictions": "Condannata all'ergastolo," *L'Europeo*, November 29, 1973.

63 In a photograph: "Espulsi dall'Italia, i 2 irlandesi dell'IRA," *Corriere Milano*, March 24, 1972.

CHAPTER 5

64 The McConville family had two dogs: McKendry, *Disappeared*, p. 14.

64 in March 1972, when he was seventeen: Interview with Michael McConville; McKendry, *Disappeared*, p. 13; "Snatched Mother Missing a Month," *Belfast Telegraph*, January 16, 1973.

64 "She had sort of given up": McKay, "Diary," *London Review of Books*, December 19, 2013.

64 subsist on cigarettes and pills: Ibid.

64 Tranquilizer use was higher: Eileen Fairweather, Roisín McDonough, and Melanie McFadyean, *Only the Rivers Run Free: Northern Ireland; The Women's War* (London: Pluto Press, 1984), p. 35.

64 "the Belfast syndrome": Jeffrey Sluka, "Living on Their Nerves: Nervous Debility in Northern Ireland," *Healthcare for Women International*, vol. 10 (1989). See also R. M. Fraser, "The Cost of Commotion: An Analysis of the Psychiatric

Sequelae of the 1969 Belfast Riots," *British Journal of Psychiatry,* vol. 118 (1971); "Mental Illness in the Belfast Trouble Areas," *Irish Times,* September 3, 1971.

64 Doctors found, paradoxically: "Mental Illness in the Belfast Trouble Areas," *Irish Times,* September 3, 1971.

64 At night, through the thin walls: McKay, "Diary," *London Review of Books,* December 19, 2013.

65 Increasingly, Jean became a recluse: McKendry, *Disappeared,* p. 13.

65 There was a discomfiting sense: "Jean McConville's Daughter: 'If I Give Up Fighting, They've Won,'" *Observer,* July 6, 2014.

65 1972 marked the high point: McKittrick et al., *Lost Lives,* table 1, p. 1494; table NI-SEC04, "Deaths (Number) Due to the Security Situation in Northern Ireland (Only) 1969–2002," assembled by the Conflict Archive on the Internet (CAIN).

65 several attempts at suicide: McKendry, *Disappeared,* p. 13. Also see McConville, "Disappearance of Jean McConville," p. 16.

65 Purdysburn, the local psychiatric hospital: Interview with Michael McConville.

65 Nights were especially eerie: "Helen McKendry: Some People Ignored Us… Others Didn't Give a Damn," *Belfast Telegraph,* April 13, 2015.

65 "Please, God, I don't want to die": Interview with Michael McConville; McKendry, *Disappeared,* p. 14.

65 As her children watched: Interview with Michael McConville; McKendry, *Disappeared,* p. 14.

65 Then she comforted him: Interview with Michael McConville; McKendry, *Disappeared,* p. 14; "Helen McKendry: Some People Ignored Us… Others Didn't Give a Damn," *Belfast Telegraph,* April 13, 2015.

65 "That was somebody's son": "Helen McKendry: Some People Ignored Us… Others Didn't Give a Damn," *Belfast Telegraph,* April 13, 2015; McKendry, *Disappeared,* p. 14.

66 BRIT LOVER: McKendry, *Disappeared,* p. 14; "Sons Recall 30 Years of Painful Memories," *Irish News,* October 24, 2003.

66 an antique mode of ritual humiliation: For a general account of how tarring and feathering fit into the larger context of social control in Belfast, see Heather Hamill, *Hoods: Crime and Punishment in Belfast* (Princeton, N.J.: Princeton University Press, 2011), pp. 76–77.

66 A mob would accost: Winchester, *In Holy Terror,* p. 110; "3 IRA Men Jailed for Tarring Incident," *Hartford Courant,* May 13, 1972.

66 "Soldier lover!": "Ulster Women Tar 2 Girls for Dating British Soldiers," *New York Times,* November 11, 1971; "Ulster Girl Who Was Tarred Secretly Weds British Soldier," *Boston Globe,* November 16, 1971; "Irish Girl Who Was Tarred Weds Her British Soldier," *New York Times,* November 16, 1971.

66 Tarring and feathering became an official policy: "Officers of IRA Group Give Account of Fights," *Irish Times,* March 18, 1971.

66 When the first few cases showed up: "Belfast Confetti," *The New Yorker,* April 25, 1994.

66 strangers in a strange land: Interview with Michael McConville.

66 After their home was marked: "Sons Recall 30 Years of Painful Memories," *Irish News,* October 24, 2003.

66 Archie was badly beaten: Interviews with Archie McConville and Michael McConville.

67 Helen and a friend were harassed: McKendry, *Disappeared,* pp. 13–14.

67 declining to take part in "the chain": Ibid., p. 15.

67 shoved the animals down a rubbish chute: "Sons Recall 30 Years of Painful Memories," *Irish News,* October 24, 2003.

67 Michael had asthma: McKendry, *Disappeared,* p. 15.

67 She requested a transfer: Interview with Michael McConville; McKendry, *Disappeared,* p. 15.

67 Christmas was coming: "Shops Suffer in Bomb Attacks," *Belfast Telegraph,* December 20, 1972.

67 Whenever she won anything: "Sons Recall 30 Years of Painful Memories," *Irish News,* October 24, 2003.

67 One night after the family had moved: McKendry, *Disappeared,* p. 15. There is some disagreement about the timing of the bingo night, but the McConville children maintain today that the episode occurred the night before their mother's abduction. This was also what they said in the immediate aftermath of the incident. On January 16, 1973, the *Belfast Telegraph* published a front-page story that quotes Helen describing the bingo night abduction and saying, "The following night she was taken" ("Snatched Mother Missing a Month," *Belfast Telegraph,* January 16, 1973).

67 Shortly after 2 a.m.: McKay, "Diary," *London Review of Books,* December 19, 2013. In the 1973 *Belfast Telegraph* article, Helen recalls, "My mother was robbed of her purse, handbag, shoes and coat and was badly beaten. She was found wandering the streets by soldiers who were then stationed in Albert Street Mill" ("Snatched Mother Missing a Month," *Belfast Telegraph,* January 16, 1973).

67 Jean said that she had been: McKendry, *Disappeared,* p. 16. This much of the account appears to be corroborated by official records consulted later by the police ombudswoman, Nuala O'Loan: "Police records show that on 30 November 1972 a report was received at 02.00 hrs from an army unit stating that at 23.00 hrs on 29 November 1972 a woman had been found wandering in the street. The woman had told them that she had been beaten and told not give (*sic*) information to the army. She was very distressed and the army stated her name was Mary McConville of St Jude's Walk. Jean McConville's mother-in-law was called Mary McConville. It is thought by the family that the woman found by the army may have been Jean McConville, who was asking for her mother-in-law" (Police Ombudsman of Northern Ireland, "Report into the Complaint by James and Michael McConville Regarding the Police Investigation into the Abduction and Murder of Their Mother Mrs. Jean McConville," August 2006, p. 4). There is an obvious discrepancy in the time lines between the November 29 date in this report and the suggestion by the McConville children that Jean was not abducted until December 7. This anomaly is explored at length in a later chapter.

68 "A load of nonsense": McKendry, *Disappeared,* p. 17.

68 lit one cigarette after another: Interview with Agnes McConville in *The Disappeared*, directed by Alison Millar (BBC Northern Ireland, 2013).

68 She told Helen that: McKay, "Diary," *London Review of Books*, December 19, 2013.

68 The children would later recall: Interviews with Michael, Archie, and Susan McConville.

68 She drew a bath: Interview with Michael McConville; "Sons Recall 30 Years of Painful Memories," *Irish News*, October 24, 2003.

68 "Don't be stopping for a sneaky smoke": McKendry, *Disappeared*, p. 18.

68 Helen noticed something strange: Ibid., p. 18.

CHAPTER 6

69 A vacant house stood: H-BC.

69 It was a Saturday, September 2, 1972: "British Troops May Have Exchanged Fire," *Irish Times*, September 4, 1972.

69 Looking up, Hughes noticed: H-BC. The fact that the van was green comes from "British Troops May Have Exchanged Fire," *Irish Times*, September 4, 1972.

69 Just to be on the safe side: H-BC.

69 At twenty-four, Hughes: In his Boston College interview, Hughes said that he was born in June 1948. He did not recall the date of this incident, but contemporary reports and subsequent research indicate that it was September 2, 1972. See Ed Moloney and Bob Mitchell, "British 'War Diary' Suggests Possible MRF Role in Effort to Kill Brendan Hughes While London Buries Secret Military Files for 100 Years," *The Broken Elbow* blog, February 23, 2013. Also see Margaret Urwin, "Counter-Gangs: A History of Undercover Military Units in Northern Ireland, 1971–1976," Spinwatch report (Public Interest Investigations, November 2012), p. 15.

69 He was the officer commanding: H-BC; Brendan Hughes, "IRA Volunteer Charlie Hughes and the Courage of the Brave," *The Blanket*, September 10, 2002.

70 In rural areas: "Portrait of a Hunger Striker: Brendan Hughes," *Irish People*, December 6, 1980.

70 Hughes had joined: H-BC.

70 Hughes moved from house to house: Brendan Hughes interview, *Radio Free Éireann*, WBAI, March 17, 2000.

70 D Company's territory: H-BC.

70 the Dogs, or the Dirty Dozen: Ibid.; Dolours Price, "Gerry, Come Clean, You'll Feel Better," *The Blanket*, February 26, 2008.

70 Hughes adhered to a philosophy: H-BC.

70 "He seemed to be a hundred places": P-EM.

70 "giant of a man": Dolours Price, "Brendan Hughes: Comrade and Friend," *The Blanket*, February 17, 2008.

70 D Company was carrying out: "Brendan Hughes: Obituary," *Guardian*, February 18, 2008. (The obituary is citing a quote that Hughes gave to the journalist Peter Taylor, which I am paraphrasing nearly verbatim here.)

70 They were heady, breakneck days: H-BC.

71 He thought of going out: Ibid.

71 "Good operations are the best": Bishop and Mallie, *The Provisional IRA,* p. 218.

71 they did not know what he looked like: H-BC.

71 The soldiers would go to his father's house: "Portrait of a Hunger Striker: Brendan Hughes," *Irish People,* December 6, 1980.

71 their intention was to kill him: Ibid.

71 The previous April: "Coffee? No Thanks, Said the Major—I Want a Tranquilizer," *Observer,* April 23, 1972.

72 When they searched his pockets: Ibid.

72 The runner had not yet returned: H-BC.

72 There was a quote attributed to Mao: The original quote is from Mao Tsetung, *On Guerrilla Warfare* (Champaign: University of Illinois Press, 2000), p. 93.

72 local civilians would assist young paramilitaries: For the perspective of a West Belfast Catholic who resented the presence of the Provos and felt coerced into this type of allegiance, see Malachi O'Doherty, *The Telling Year: Belfast 1972* (Dublin: Gill & Macmillan, 2007).

72 When property was damaged: H-BC.

72 He cultivated the community: "Portrait of a Hunger Striker: Brendan Hughes," *Irish People,* December 6, 1980.

73 When the soldier looked up: *Voices from the Grave,* documentary, directed by Kate O'Callaghan (RTÉ, 2010).

73 Call houses were usually regular homes: H-BC.

73 The troops had developed: *Voices from the Grave.*

74 One day, a sailor: H-BC. For more detail on the mechanics of this operation, see Taylor, *Behind the Mask: The IRA and Sinn Fein* (New York: TV Books, 1999), p. 131.

74 BUT THE ARMALITE MADE THEM EQUAL: Adams, *Before the Dawn,* p. 186.

74 Hughes was tearing along so fast: This event has become something of a legend. In addition to Hughes's account in his BC oral history, this incident was recounted in *The Irish People,* which noted that "the window did not shatter, there was just left a hole—perfectly round and small—for Brendan is not a big man." See "Portrait of a Hunger Striker: Brendan Hughes," *Irish People,* December 6, 1980.

74 The gunmen had been dressed like civilians: H-BC.

75 Hughes had grown up surrounded: "Portrait of a Hunger Striker: Brendan Hughes," *Irish People,* December 6, 1980.

75 "lad you could depend upon": Ibid.

75 In 1967, Hughes joined: H-BC.

75 When the family walked to Mass: Ibid.

76 "Never get a tattoo": Ibid.

76 When he crashed through: Ibid.

76 He badly needed: Ibid.

76 Then Gerry Adams arrived: Ibid.

77 Adams would ride in the "scout" car: Dolours Price interview in *Voices from the Grave.*

77 Dolours Price liked to joke: P-EM.

77 "tremendous following": "Portrait of a Hunger Striker: Brendan Hughes," *Irish People*, December 6, 1980.

77 He regarded himself as a soldier: H-BC.

78 Brendan's own little brother: Terry Hughes, quoted in *Voices from the Grave;* interview with Terry Hughes.

78 The doctor whom Adams had: Former IRA volunteer Paddy Joe Rice confirms the story about Adams bringing a doctor in *Voices from the Grave.*

78 So someone fetched a needle: H-BC.

78 According to the Special Branch: Mark Urban, *Big Boys' Rules: The SAS and the Secret Struggle Against the IRA* (London: Faber, 1992), p. 26. As Fintan O'Toole has pointed out, in 1996 Adams gave an enthusiastic endorsement of David Beresford's book *Ten Men Dead,* which described him as the commander of the Belfast Brigade from July 1972 to July 1973 (Fintan O'Toole, "The End of the Troubles?" *New York Review of Books,* February 19, 1998).

78 He could have fled to Dundalk: "'Provos' Go into Hiding," *Observer,* June 4, 1972.

79 "Local people knew he was there": "Portrait of a Hunger Striker: Brendan Hughes," *Irish People,* December 6, 1980.

79 Adams saved Hughes's life: H-BC.

79 In the secret internal records: Ed Moloney and a researcher discovered the corroborating paper trail in British Army files. The operation to kill Hughes was known as TOM TIME. See Ed Moloney and Bob Mitchell, "British 'War Diary' Suggests Possible MRF Role in Effort to Kill Brendan Hughes While London Buries Secret Military Files for 100 Years," *The Broken Elbow* blog, February 23, 2013. For a contemporary account of the shootout, see "British Troops May Have Exchanged Fire," *Irish Times,* September 4, 1972.

CHAPTER 7

81 His father was an admiral: Frank Kitson, *Gangs and Counter-Gangs* (London: Barrie Books, 1960), p. 1.

81 His grandfather had served: "The Guru of the New Model Army," *Times* (London), May 14, 1972.

81 Kitson joined the British Army's Rifle Brigade: Ibid.

81 But by the time he became a soldier: Kitson, *Gangs and Counter-Gangs,* p. 1.

81 In 1953, he was assigned to Kenya: Ibid., p. 7.

81 He needn't have worried: "The Guru of the New Model Army," *Times* (London), May 14, 1972.

82 He tucked the paper: Kitson, *Gangs and Counter-Gangs,* pp. 28, 90.

82 Beneath his peaked and tasseled army cap: *War School,* part 1: "Kitson's Class" (BBC documentary, 1980).

82 He had a slightly nasal voice: Ibid.

82 He was known to dislike small talk: Mike Jackson, *Soldier: The Autobiography* (London: Bantam Press, 2007), p. 81.

82 Before leaving on a night mission: Kitson, *Gangs and Counter-Gangs,* p. 163.

82 By "blacking up" in this manner: Ibid., p. 163. "Blacking up" was standard, if unfortunate, vernacular. It is invoked specifically in relation to Kitson's time in Kenya in Peter Taylor, *Brits: The War Against the IRA* (London: Bloomsbury, 2001), p. 127.

82 "Everything is strange for the first few moments": Kitson, *Gangs and Counter-Gangs,* pp. 180–81.

83 With their identities shielded by the robes: Ibid., p. 79.

83 This was an epiphany for Kitson: Ibid., p. 79.

83 This was a risky gesture: Ibid., p. 127.

83 staggering human cost: Caroline Elkins, *Imperial Reckoning: The Untold Story of Britain's Gulag in Kenya* (New York: Henry Holt, 2005), p. xvi.

83 Some 1.5 million people were detained: Ibid., p. xiv.

83 Mau Mau suspects were subjected: Ibid., pp. 54, 66.

83 Kitson had been awarded the Military Cross: Seventh Supplement to *London Gazette,* December 31, 1954. (The award was actually conferred on January 1, 1955.)

84 "I wondered how much of the African mentality": Kitson, *Gangs and Counter-Gangs,* p. 184.

84 Kitson had found his calling: "The Guru of the New Model Army," *Times* (London), May 14, 1972.

84 dispatched to the Sultanate of Muscat: Frank Kitson, *Bunch of Five* (London: Faber, 2010), pp. 155–201.

84 given command of his own battalion: Ibid., pp. 205–77; Dillon, *The Dirty War,* pp. 25–26.

84 he embarked on a new project: Frank Kitson, *Low Intensity Operations: Subversion, Insurgency, Peace-Keeping* (London: Faber, 1991), bibliography.

84 a cornerstone of later counterinsurgency thinking: Ibid., pp. x–xi.

85 by the summer of 1972: Table NI-SEC03, "British Army Personnel (Number) in Northern Ireland, 1969 to 2005," CAIN.

85 They were spread across the country: "Soldiers Scurry in Sniper Country," *Baltimore Sun,* November 26, 1971.

85 What would they have to achieve: Ibid.

86 Or was it one of those restive colonies?: See Niall Ó Dochartaigh, *From Civil Rights to Armalites: Derry and the Birth of the Irish Troubles* (Cork: Cork University Press, 1997), chapter 4.

86 When Frank Kitson arrived: Taylor, *Brits,* p. 53.

86 As one of Kitson's subordinates: Jackson, *Soldier,* p. 82.

86 "It made them hostile": "Paras Were 'Jolly Good' Says Bloody Sunday Brigadier," *Daily Mail,* September 25, 2002.

86 "destroy the subversive movement utterly": Kitson, *Low Intensity Operations,* p. 50.

86 The first challenge: *War School:* "Kitson's Class."

86 In particular, Kitson was interested: Dillon, *The Dirty War,* p. 33.

87 British soldiers referred to Hughes's: Taylor, *Brits,* p. 138.

87 "These people are savages": "Soldiers Scurry in Sniper Country," *Baltimore Sun*, November 26, 1971.

87 The windowpanes would shudder: Jackson, *Soldier*, p. 82.

87 "wall of silence": "Brigadier Denies T.D.'s Claims," *Irish Times*, November 11, 1971.

87 "necessary to do something to the water": Kitson, *Low Intensity Operations*, p. 49.

87 Just before dawn one morning in August 1971: Coogan, *The Troubles*, p. 150.

88 "partial to one extent or another, in many cases": Taylor, *Brits*, p. 67.

88 elderly men were dragged off: Winchester, *In Holy Terror*, p. 163.

88 the army simply took both: This happened with one of the Hooded Men and his son, both named Seán McKenna.

88 Nearly a third of the suspects: Taylor, *Brits*, p. 67.

88 study by the British Ministry of Defence: Ministry of Defence, *Operation Banner: An Analysis of Military Operations in Northern Ireland*, 2006, pp. 2–7.

88 "It was lunacy": Taylor, *Brits*, p. 67.

88 Frank Kitson would forever be associated: Dillon, *The Dirty War*, p. 26.

88 His quarrel was not so much with the use: Kitson, *Bunch of Five*, pp. 58–59.

89 "not an attractive measure": Ibid., p. 58.

89 He reportedly quipped: "The Laws of Emotion," *Guardian*, October 18, 1973.

89 echoed at the time in the British press: "Intelligence War by Army Cracks IRA Ranks," *Telegraph*, November 5, 1971.

89 Kitson's chief critique of internment: Winchester, *In Holy Terror*, pp. 154–55.

89 In late July, the army: Taylor, *Brits*, p. 66.

89 The army had devised this preparatory phase: Winchester, *In Holy Terror*, p. 154.

89 Another hint about the army's intentions: Ian Cobain, *Cruel Britannia: A Secret History of Torture* (London: Portobello, 2013), p. 139.

89 After the sweep, the IRA: "Joe Cahill," *Telegraph*, July 26, 2004.

89 When the raids happened: P-EM.

90 a sturdy woman named Mary McGuigan: Interview with Francis McGuigan. Also see "The McGuigans: One Radical Irish Family," *New York Times*, June 11, 1972, and "The Fighting Women of Ireland," *New York*, March 13, 1972.

90 It was around four in the morning: This account is based on an interview with Francis McGuigan and on a firsthand account McGuigan gave in Dennis Faul and Raymond Murray, *The Hooded Men: British Torture in Ireland, August, October 1971* (Dublin: Wordwell Books, 2016).

90 John McGuigan collapsed: Interview with Francis McGuigan.

90 John McGuigan ended up: Ibid.

90 his son had been selected: The initial group was twelve; two other men were later subjected to the same techniques. John McGuffin, *The Guinea Pigs* (London: Penguin, 1974), p. 46.

91 A thick hood was placed over his head: Faul and Murray, *The Hooded Men*, p. 58.

91 His handcuffs were removed: Interview with Francie McGuigan; "Hooded Man: 'They Asked Me to Count to Ten; I Refused In Case I Couldn't Do It,'" *Journal.ie*, March 24, 2018.

91 out the open door of the helicopter: McGuigan's story has varied somewhat in different tellings over the years. In the *Times* piece in 1972, he says that he hit the ground. In his account for Faul and Murray, he says the helicopter landed and he was carried out. In his interview with me and in other interviews he has done, he described being thrown out and then caught.

91 hustling him into a mysterious facility: "The Torture Centre: Northern Ireland's 'Hooded Men,'" *Irish Times,* July 25, 2015.

91 far from any mechanism of accountability: This account is based on interviews with Francis McGuigan, Kevin Hannaway, and Joe Clarke; as well as on Winchester, *In Holy Terror,* pp. 170–72; "The Torture Centre: Northern Ireland's 'Hooded Men,'" *Irish Times,* July 25, 2015; and the firsthand accounts in McGuffin's *The Guinea Pigs* and Faul and Murray's *The Hooded Men.*

91 For days, the prisoners were deprived: Cobain, *Cruel Britannia,* pp. 128–34; Taylor, *Brits,* p. 65.

92 tortured as a prisoner of war in North Korea: "Gen Sir Anthony Farrar-Hockley," *Telegraph,* March 14, 2006.

92 "so they must be prepared to be frightened": Taylor, *Brits,* p. 69.

92 Initially, the techniques had been taught: Cobain, *Cruel Britannia,* p. 131.

92 an oral tradition of human cruelty: Ibid., p. 130. Ian Cobain notes that in November 1971, after internment, Brigadier Richard Mansfield Bremner, of the British Army's Intelligence Corps, did produce a written memo outlining the evolution of British interrogation techniques since the Second World War. It was deemed sufficiently sensitive that it was initially classified for "at least 100 years." (It ended up being declassified after thirty.)

92 "What's your position?": Interview with Francis McGuigan.

93 "two pissholes in the snow": "The Torture Centre: Northern Ireland's 'Hooded Men,'" *Irish Times,* July 25, 2015.

93 Another detainee, who had gone into the interrogation: The man was Seán McKenna. John Conroy, *Unspeakable Acts, Ordinary People: The Dynamics of Torture* (Berkeley: University of California Press, 2000), p. 123.

93 (He died not long after being released): Ibid., p. 188.

93 When Francie McGuigan was finally returned: Interview with Francis McGuigan.

93 But it seems unlikely that he was troubled: "The Book Answer to the Guerrillas," *Times Literary Supplement,* February 11, 1972.

93 A subsequent investigation by the British government: Report of the Committee of Privy Counsellors Appointed to Consider Authorised Procedures for the Interrogation of Persons Suspected of Terrorism (the "Parker Report"), March 1972.

93 But in a controversial 1978 decision: *Case of Ireland v. the United Kingdom* (Application no. 5310/71), European Court of Human Rights, judgment, January 18, 1978. The court upheld this decision, in the face of a new challenge, in 2018: *Case of Ireland v. the United Kingdom* (Application no. 5310/71), European Court of Human Rights, judgment, March 20, 2018. Also see "Hooded Men Torture Ruling Is 'Very Disappointing,'" Amnesty International, March 20, 2018.

93 (In the aftermath of the terrorist attacks): See memorandum from Jay Bybee, Office of Legal Counsel, U.S. Department of Justice, to Alberto Gonzales, Counsel to the President, "RE: Standards of Conduct for Interrogation under 18 U.S.C. §§ 2340–2340A," August 1, 2002, p. 28.

93 But perhaps the most concrete application: Within the army, it was referred to, at least some of the time, as the Mobile Reaction Force. Major General W. G. H. Beach to Brigadier M. E. Tickell, February 17, 1972 (National Archives, Kew).

93 This was an elite unit so murky: Taylor, *Brits,* pp. 128–30. Some classified British government documents refer to the group as the Mobile Reaction Force, e.g., "Northern Ireland Visit," Loose Minute prepared by Maj. P. H. Courtenay, February 10, 1972 (National Archives, Kew).

94 The MRF consisted of thirty or so special operators: "Undercover Soldiers 'Killed Unarmed Civilians in Belfast,'" BBC, November 21, 2013.

94 They dressed in plain clothes: Ibid.

94 known as the Bomb Squad: Urban, *Big Boys' Rules,* p. 36.

94 Soldiers of Irish origin: Ibid.

94 They posed as road sweepers: "Undercover Soldiers 'Killed Unarmed Civilians in Belfast,'" BBC, November 21, 2013.

94 They also began to set up secret: Dillon, *The Dirty War,* p. 30.

94 One woman who worked for the MRF: Urban, *Big Boys' Rules,* p 36.

94 In December 1971, Kitson wrote: Frank Kitson, "Future Developments in Belfast by Commander 39 Airportable Brigade," December 1971. (This formerly confidential document was discovered in the archives at Kew by the Irish writer and researcher Ciarán MacAirt.)

94 submachine gun hidden under the seat: Dillon, *The Dirty War,* p. 42.

94 They had to keep the weapon out of sight: Ibid.

94 These hit squads deliberately carried: One former MRF soldier elaborated in 1978: "We were instructed in the use of the Russian AK47 assault rifle, the Armalite and a Thompson machine gun. All these weapons are favored by the Provos. I will leave it to your imagination why Brigadier Kitson thought this was necessary, as these weapons are not standard issue for the British Army." See Margaret Urwin, "Counter-Gangs: A History of Undercover Military Units in Northern Ireland, 1971–1976," Spinwatch report (Public Interest Investigations, November 2012), p. 9.

95 "We wanted to cause confusion": "Britain's Secret Terror Force," *Panorama* (BBC, 2013).

95 One summer night in 1972: "Woman, 24, Shot Dead," *Guardian,* June 9, 1972.

95 In fact, it would be four decades: "Undercover Army Unit Linked to Killing Previously Blamed on IRA," *Irish News,* June 9, 2015.

95 In the aftermath of: Interview with Simon Winchester. See also "Journalist Believes Army Used Him to Feed Stories," *Irish Times,* May 22, 2001, and "My Tainted Days," *Guardian,* May 22, 2001.

96 Kitson's Strangelovean attributes: Dillon, *The Dirty War,* p. 26.

96 "Kits the Butcher of Belfast": *War School:* "Kitson's Class."

96 the mind games of the shifty British strategist: Dillon, *The Dirty War,* p. 26.

96 There were plans to kidnap: "The Kidnap Target," *Daily Mail,* August 11, 1973.

96 The Provos were said to have: *War School:* "Kitson's Class."

96 In the MRF's secret briefing room: "Exposed: The Army Black Ops Squad Ordered to Murder IRA's Top 'Players,'" *Daily Mail,* November 16, 2013.

CHAPTER 8

97 A prison floated in Belfast Lough: J. J. Colledge, *Ships of the Royal Navy* (Newbury, U.K.: Casemate, 2010), p. 244.

97 HMP *Maidstone*—Her Majesty's Prison: "Seven IRA Suspects Swim to Freedom," *Guardian,* January 18, 1972.

97 The prison quarters consisted: "Mac Stíofáin Tells Why Escapers Were Chosen," *Irish Times,* January 25, 1972.

97 "not fit for pigs": Ibid.

97 He was greeted warmly: Adams, *Before the Dawn,* p. 192.

97 "brutal and oppressive sardine tin": Gerry Adams, *Cage Eleven* (New York: Sheridan Square Press, 1993), p. 2.

97 He liked a good meal: Adams, *Before the Dawn,* p. 192.

98 "refusing to admit I was Gerry Adams": Ibid., p. 189.

98 It was only when he sensed that: Ibid., pp. 191–92.

98 Adams had managed to tell them nothing: Ibid.

98 "Stop breathing," the doctor said: Ibid., p. 192.

98 One frigid January evening: This account is drawn from an interview with Tommy Gorman and from "7 At Large after Maidstone Swim," *Irish Times,* January 18, 1972; "Seven IRA Suspects Swim to Freedom," *Guardian,* January 18, 1972; "7 Maidstone Escapers Cross Border to Freedom," *Irish Times,* January 24, 1972.

99 The prisoners had come upon the idea: Interview with Tommy Gorman; Coogan, *The IRA,* p. 403; "7 IRA Guerrillas Tell of Prison Escape," *Globe and Mail,* January 25, 1972.

99 just crawled out of the Black Lagoon: "Thirty Years On—the Maidstone," *Andersonstown News,* September 9, 2000.

99 When they stopped in a neighborhood: Interview with Tommy Gorman.

99 Then, without hesitation: "Thirty Years On—the Maidstone," *Andersonstown News,* September 9, 2000.

99 By the time the army mobilized: "7 At Large after Maidstone Swim," *Irish Times,* January 18, 1972.

99 After slipping across the border: "Mac Stíofáin Tells Why Escapers Were Chosen," *Irish Times,* January 25, 1972.

99 The new prison: Adams, *Before the Dawn,* p. 196.

100 It was known as Long Kesh: Long Kesh would subsequently be renamed as Maze Prison. But most of the republican prisoners in this story continued to refer to it as Long Kesh, so in order to avoid confusion, I have opted to use that name throughout.

100 But Adams would not be staying: Ibid., p. 197.

100 At first he thought this: Ibid., p. 198.

100 a secret back channel had been developing: H-BC.

100 "No fucking cease-fire unless Gerry is released": Ibid.

100 On June 26, the IRA initiated a cease-fire: "IRA Ceasefire Follows MP's Peace Moves," *Guardian,* June 23, 1972.

101 anyone who violated the cease-fire would be shot: "IRA Threatens to Kill Ceasefire Breakers," *Guardian,* June 24, 1972.

101 The Provos announced that: "IRA Provisionals, British Agree to Indefinite Truce," *Boston Globe,* June 23, 1972.

101 Many people in Northern Ireland: "Truce by Provisional IRA Opens Way to Peace," *Irish Times,* June 23, 1972.

101 IRA members boarded a British military plane: Mac Stíofáin, *Revolutionary in Ireland,* p. 281; David McKittrick and David McVea, *Making Sense of the Troubles: The Story of the Conflict in Northern Ireland* (Chicago: New Amsterdam Books, 2002), pp. 84–85.

101 Hyper-attuned to any hint: Taylor, *Behind the Mask,* p. 164.

101 Gerry Adams took a similar view: Adams, *Before the Dawn,* p. 202.

101 The limousines ferried the group into London: In a 1982 interview, Adams recalled the plaque saying that Whistler's mother lived there. In fact, Whistler lived there himself. "Sinn Féin Vice-President Gerry Adams," *Irish People,* November 27, 1982.

102 The Irishmen were escorted: Mac Stíofáin, *Revolutionary in Ireland,* p. 281.

102 Then William Whitelaw: Ibid.

102 But as they went round: Adams, *Before the Dawn,* p. 204.

102 "in me, you will see a British minister you can trust": Ibid.

102 It consisted of a list of demands: Ed Moloney and Bob Mitchell, "British Cabinet Account of 1972 IRA Ceasefire Talks," *The Broken Elbow* blog, January 21, 2014. This draws on a "Secret and Personal" account of the meeting given to then prime minister Ted Heath by Whitelaw and Northern Ireland Office official Philip Woodfield, written just after the meeting.

102 They also wanted the British: Mac Stíofáin, *Revolutionary in Ireland,* p. 281; Adams, *Before the Dawn,* p. 204.

102 One of the British participants: Taylor, *Behind the Mask,* p. 169.

102 When Steele was initially sent: Taylor, *Brits,* p. 80.

102 After the massacre on Bloody Sunday: Ibid., pp. 107–8, 116–17.

103 "It was all rather sweet, really": Taylor, *Behind the Mask,* p. 164.

103 When the men strode into the meeting: Ibid., pp. 169–70.

103 In demanding that the British: "Adams and IRA's Secret Whitehall Talks," BBC, January 1, 2003.

103 sabotaged by the "absurd ultimatums": William Whitelaw, *The Whitelaw Memoirs* (London: Headline Books, 1989), pp. 128–29.

103 These were appealing qualities: Taylor, *Behind the Mask,* p. 165.

103 Adams grinned: Ibid.

104 When the cease-fire was first: Ibid., p. 166.

104 Ordinary civilians emerged: "IRA Ceasefire Follows MP's Peace Moves," *Guardian,* June 23, 1972.

104 Having a family could be dangerous: Terry Hughes, quoted in *Voices from the Grave.*

104 where his bride, Colette: Adams, *Before the Dawn,* p. 189.

104 Brendan's wife, Lily: "Portrait of a Hunger Striker: Brendan Hughes," *Irish People,* December 6, 1980.

104 It made her too anxious: Ibid.

104 But the peace lasted scarcely: "Ulster Truce Ends in Street Battle," *Guardian,* July 10, 1972.

104 "utmost ferocity": "IRA Truce Falls Apart, 5 Die in Hour," *Boston Globe,* July 10, 1972. See also *Behind the Mask,* documentary, directed by Frank Martin (BBC, 1991).

105 An order was passed down: Brendan Hughes interview in *Voices from the Grave.*

105 Hughes set about planning: McKearney, *The Provisional IRA,* pp. 112–13; Mac Stíofáin, *Revolutionary in Ireland,* p. 243.

105 Of course, these warnings had an added: McKearney, *The Provisional IRA,* pp. 112–13.

105 One Friday that July, an IRA team: Nineteen bombs exploded that day, according to the Northern Ireland Office. Some press accounts put the number of bombs at closer to twenty-four, but it may be that the IRA planted more bombs and only nineteen successfully detonated. "Timetable of Terror," brochure published by the Northern Ireland Office, July 1972.

105 People screamed and scrambled: "11 Die in Belfast Hour of Terror," *Guardian,* July 22, 1972.

105 Several buses were ripped apart: "Timetable of Terror."

105 Nine people were killed: Some initial reporting put the death count higher, but the Northern Ireland Office recorded nine deaths (seven civilians and two soldiers). "Timetable of Terror."

106 she realized it was a human torso: *Car Bomb.*

106 Police officers picked through: "Bombing Wave Kills 13, Injures 130 in Belfast," *Boston Globe,* July 22, 1972.

106 "This city has not experienced": "Bomb-a-Minute Blitz in Belfast: Many Injured," *Belfast Telegraph,* July 22, 1972.

106 "Can anyone now believe": "The Only Message," *Irish Times,* July 22, 1972.

106 Some of the volunteers in the Lower Falls: H-BC.

106 Hughes would insist for years: Ibid.

106 Hughes immediately went to see Russell: Ibid.

107 But a mystery remained: According to Ed Moloney, Russell was holding a child when he came to the door, which may explain why the shooter did not finish the job. Ed Moloney, *Voices from the Grave: Two Men's War in Ireland* (New York: PublicAffairs, 2010), p. 114.

107 his assailant was a member of the Stickies: H-BC.

107 This theory was endorsed: Interview with Joe Clarke; "Trio Vanished Forever," *Sunday Life,* February 21, 2010.

107 shebeens were established: "Thriving Shebeens Where Law and Order Has Ceased," *Irish Times,* December 29, 1972.

107 One was called the Burning Embers: H-BC; "IRA Volunteer Charlie Hughes and the Courage of the Brave," *The Blanket,* September 10, 2002.

107 Another Official shebeen was the Cracked Cup: "Disappeared IRA Victim and Provo 'Love Triangle,'" *Irish Independent,* December 7, 2014; Gerry Adams, *Falls Memories: A Belfast Life* (Niwot, Colo.: Roberts Rinehart, 1994), pp. 124–25.

107 The floorboards were rotting: Kevin Myers, *Watching the Door: Drinking Up, Getting Down, and Cheating Death in 1970s Belfast* (Brooklyn, N.Y.: Soft Skull Press, 2009), p. 247.

108 Looking for the man who had shot: H-BC; "Man Gets Life for Murder at Club," *Irish Times,* January 24, 1973.

108 One of the patrons that night: McKittrick et al., *Lost Lives,* p. 203.

108 A spurt of gunfire lit the gloom: "Club Death in IRA Power Struggle," *Telegraph,* June 20, 1972; "Man Gets Life for Murder at Club," *Irish Times,* January 24, 1973.

108 The shooter was a young Provo: "Man Gets Life for Murder at Club," *Irish Times,* January 24, 1973.

108 It would later emerge that: "Rejection of Provisional IRA Policy Urged," *Irish Times,* July 1, 1972.

108 For fifteen long minutes: "Club Death in IRA Power Struggle," *Telegraph,* June 20, 1972; "Whitelaw Move Gives New Status to Belfast Prisoners," *Guardian,* June 20, 1972.

108 The press would characterize: "Club Death in IRA Power Struggle," *Telegraph,* June 20, 1972.

108 One newspaper suggested: "Whitelaw Move Gives New Status to Belfast Prisoners," *Guardian,* June 20, 1972.

108 he made an alarming discovery: H-BC.

109 When he left the priesthood: Interview with a member of the Lynskey family.

109 "very much into running after women": These details, and this quote, are from an oral history interview with Maria Lynskey, "The Disappearance of Joe Lynskey," in *The Disappeared of Northern Ireland's Troubles,* p. 6.

109 He did not come from: Interview with a relative of Joe Lynskey's.

109 "He was a mature man but": Price interview in *I, Dolours.*

109 Brendan Hughes had always: H-BC.

109 He was smart and erudite: Interview with a relative of Joe Lynskey's.

109 carried in his pocket a book about his hero: Interview with Joe Clarke.

109 But he could be a bit aloof: Ibid.

109 What Hughes did not know: H-BC; Price interview in *I, Dolours;* "Disappeared Victim Killed Over Affair with IRA Man's Wife," *Irish News,* February 8, 2010.

109 Lynskey had ordered: Interview with Joe Clarke; Price interview in *I, Dolours;* "Disappeared Victim Killed Over Affair with IRA Man's Wife," *Irish News,* February 8, 2010; "Disappeared IRA Victim and Provo 'Love Triangle,'" *Irish Independent,* December 7, 2014.

110 The gunman undertook this mission: Price interview in *I, Dolours.*

110 But when Russell came to the door: H-BC; Moloney, *Voices from the Grave*, p. 114.

110 Rather than confess: "Disappeared IRA Victim and Provo 'Love Triangle,' " *Irish Independent*, December 7, 2014; "I Didn't Order Jean's Killing," *Sunday Life*, February 21, 2010.

110 Lynskey would have to face a court-martial: Price interview in *I, Dolours;* "IRA Man: I Held Lynskey Captive Until His Murder," *Irish News*, December 15, 2009.

110 Like some black-ops government program: Interviews with Hugh Feeney and Richard O'Rawe; H-BC.

110 McClure was in his thirties: "Patrick F. McClure," obituary, *Record-Journal* (Meriden, Conn.), December 5, 1986.

110 He had actual military experience: Interview with Hugh Feeney; H-BC.

111 But he was regarded: Interviews with Hugh Feeney and Richard O'Rawe.

111 they answered directly to Gerry Adams: H-BC; P-EM.

111 Brendan Hughes came to think of them as "head hunters": H-BC.

111 McClure was soft-spoken and enigmatic: Interview with Richard O'Rawe.

111 "You'll be shooting at newspapers": Interview with Hugh Feeney.

111 members of the Unknowns were taken: P-EM.

111 responsibility for transporting: Interview with Hugh Feeney; H-BC.

111 There was a festive, giddy quality: Interview with Colin Smith; "The Night the Truce Ended," *Observer,* July 16, 1972.

111 Dolours derived a certain mischievous: P-TKT; "The Sisters of Terror," *Observer,* November 18, 1973.

111 Once, the soldiers, with their berets: "Violence 'Not Included in IRA Principles,' " *Guardian,* October 26, 1973. One such photo was presented in her subsequent trial in London and published in the press. See "IRA Planning to Kidnap 10 Hostages from an English Village in Reprisal for Sentences," *Times* (London), November 16, 1973.

111 There was one British officer: P-TKT. They would never have the opportunity: Corden-Lloyd was killed in action in 1978, when the helicopter he was riding in crashed while under fire by the IRA.

112 Because Lynskey's work often: Interview with a relative of Joe Lynskey's.

112 "You just missed Joe": Ibid.

112 When Lynskey's mother died: Maria Lynskey interview, *Marian Finucane Show*, RTÉ Radio, April 4, 2015; "Emigration Rumor Hid Lynskey Murder," *Irish News*, December 8, 2009.

112 In a twist that represented: P-EM.

113 Lynskey did not say anything much: P-EM.

113 "I don't want to know, Joe": Price interview in *I, Dolours*.

113 *I'll take him to the ferry,* she thought: P-EM.

113 *Why doesn't he do something to save himself?*: Price interview in *I, Dolours*.

113 Their dedication to the movement: P-EM; Price interview in *I, Dolours*.

113 under a lamppost: P-EM.

113 He reached out and shook her hand: P-EM; Price interview in *I, Dolours*.

113 "I'll be seeing you, Joe": P-EM.

CHAPTER 9

114 a television crew from the BBC: Interview with Graham Leach, the BBC reporter who made the visit.

114 The local press had become aware: "Where Is Jean McConville," *Civil Rights,* January 14, 1973.

114 noted that none of the children had reported: "Snatched Mother Missing a Month," *Belfast Telegraph,* January 16, 1973.

114 the paper appealed for help: "Help Trace Kidnapped Mother—MP's Appeal to Falls," *Belfast Telegraph,* January 17, 1973.

114 "Four young girls": Archival BBC footage from January 17, 1973.

115 Granny McConville may have been: "Snatched Mother Missing a Month," *Belfast Telegraph,* January 16, 1973.

116 A social worker did visit the children: Social worker's report from a visit to the McConville children, December 13, 1972.

116 Jean's mother-in-law asserted, primly: Social worker's report from a visit to St. Jude's Walk, December 13, 1972.

116 Helen did not get along: Social worker's report, December 14, 1972.

116 But the McConville children flatly refused: Social worker's report, December 18, 1972.

116 Their mother would be returning: Interview with Michael and Susan McConville.

117 Bedtime was suspended: Social worker's report, January 10, 1973.

117 The neighbors, rather than help: Social worker's report, January 15, 1973.

117 a local parish priest was aware: Social worker's report, December 18, 1972.

117 the McConvilles were running out of food: "Sons Recall 30 Years of Painful Memories," *Irish News,* October 24, 2003.

117 They didn't have much money: Interview with Michael McConville.

117 The children started getting into trouble: Interview with Michael McConville; social worker's report, February 15, 1973.

117 Eventually he was caught: Interview with Michael McConville; Michael McConville interview, *Marian Finucane Show,* RTÉ Radio, November 23, 2013; McConville, "Disappearance of Jean McConville," p. 19.

117 They were starving: Interview with Michael McConville; Michael McConville interview, *Marian Finucane Show,* RTÉ Radio, November 23, 2013.

117 Michael was eleven years old: Social worker's report, January 24, 1973.

117 "My daddy is dead and the IRA took my mummy away": This detail is taken from a letter dated November 23, 2012, containing James McConville's instructions to his solicitors, in which he spells out his own experience.

117 There is no record in the files: Police Ombudsman for Northern Ireland, "Report into the Complaint by James and Michael McConville Regarding the Police Investigation into the Abduction and Murder of Their Mother Mrs. Jean McConville," August 2006.

117 the police were not able to offer any substantive clues: Social worker's report, January 17, 1973.

118 decried the kidnapping as "a callous act": The MPs were Paddy Devlin and Gerry Fitt. "Help Trace Kidnapped Mother—MPs Appeal to Falls," *Belfast Telegraph,* January 17, 1973.

118 rumors began to circulate: Interviews with Arthur, Susan, and Michael McConville.

118 "an attempt to wreck our minds": "Sons Recall 30 Years of Painful Memories," *Irish News,* October 24, 2003.

118 a posse of boys from the youth wing of the IRA: Interview with Michael McConville. There is also an army record of this event, dated February 11: "2 Catholic children were taken into a car by 3 masked men in Combat kit. One of the children has since returned, but Michael McConville (10-RC) is still missing," British Army Situation Report, "0700 Hrs Sunday 11 February to 0700 Hrs Monday 12 February 1973," Annex C to A/BR/30/8/M04, February 12, 1973 (National Archives, Kew).

118 *Don't talk to anyone about what happened to your mother*: Interview with Michael McConville.

118 The interlude of freedom did not last: Social worker's report, February 15, 1973.

118 One day, three women showed up at the flat: Social worker's report, February 27, 1973.

119 the kids were made "wards of the court": McConville, "Disappearance of Jean McConville," p. 19.

119 The act of disappearing someone: Rome Statute of the International Criminal Court (1998), Article 7(1)(i).

119 About a week after she was kidnapped: McKendry, *Disappeared,* p. 20.

119 "I was just told to give you these": Interview with Michael McConville.

119 the moment he realized that his mother must be dead: Ibid.

CHAPTER 10

120 One autumn day in 1972: "Shot Laundry Man Was British Agent," *Irish Times,* October 3, 1972.

120 The van was a regular presence: Ibid.

120 There were not a lot of shops in the area: Ibid.

120 people liked Sarah: "Medal for Van WRAC," *Guardian,* September 19, 1973.

120 The driver, Ted Stuart: "Shot Laundry Man Was British Agent," *Irish Times,* October 3, 1972.

120 he was an easygoing fellow: Dillon, *The Dirty War,* pp. 26–27. This description is derived from an interview with Ted Stuart's mother after his killing. See "Provos Admit Killing Army Secret Agent," *Belfast Telegraph,* October 3, 1972.

120 The kids on the estate called him Teddy: "Shot Laundry Man Was British Agent," *Irish Times,* October 3, 1972.

120 Twinbrook was home to both Catholics and Protestants: Ibid.

120 A housewife came to the door: Ibid.

120 spraying bullets from close range: Dillon, *The Dirty War,* pp. 26–27.

121 one of the gunmen turned in her direction: Ibid., pp. 26–27.

121 he might have an informant in D Company: H-BC; Dillon, *The Dirty War*, pp. 30–31; "IRA Never Got Spy's Secrets," *Guardian*, May 14, 1973.

121 Hughes paid a visit: "More Double Agents at Work," *Irish Times*, May 14, 1973.

121 He was in Birmingham: Taylor, *Brits*, p. 134.

121 He planned to flee: H-BC.

122 Seamus Wright returned: Ibid.

122 They told Seamus that if he would: Dillon, *The Dirty War*, pp. 31–32.

122 Hughes was dismayed: Taylor, *Brits*, p. 135.

123 Wright described a secret compound: Dillon, *The Dirty War*, pp. 32–34.

123 individuals who had been induced to switch sides: Ibid., pp. 32–34.

123 "There is a guy I have seen in there": Ibid., p. 34.

123 The man Wright named was a young Provo: H-BC; Dillon, *The Dirty War*, pp. 32–34.

123 He was still a teenager: "Kevin and the Pain That Has Never Disappeared," *Belfast Telegraph*, August 30, 2013. Some sources maintain that McKee was seventeen, but in this article, Philomena McKee writes that the family never knew whether Kevin made it to his seventeenth birthday, suggesting that he would have been sixteen when he disappeared.

123 big blue eyes: "The IRA and the Disappeared: Tell Us Where Kevin Is Buried and I'll Shake Hands," *Irish Times*, October 5, 2013.

123 People called him "Beaky": H-BC.

123 He had grown up in West Belfast: "The IRA and the Disappeared: Tell Us Where Kevin Is Buried and I'll Shake Hands," *Irish Times*, October 5, 2013; Phil McKee, "The Disappearance of Kevin McKee," in *The Disappeared of Northern Ireland's Troubles*, p. 10.

123 He joined the youth wing of the IRA: Marie McKee interview in *The Disappeared*.

124 But he also went on "snipes": Interview with Richard O'Rawe.

124 One night, Kevin McKee was arrested: Interview with Richard O'Rawe; McKee, "The Disappearance of Kevin McKee," p. 11.

124 Two of his aunts ventured to the barracks: McKee, "The Disappearance of Kevin McKee," p. 11.

124 the family received letters from Kevin in England: Ibid., p. 11.

124 A British Army log: Watch Keeper's Diary, C Company, 1 Battalion, King's Own Scottish Borderers, December 28, 1971–April 24, 1972 (National Archives, Kew).

124 Wright told Hughes that McKee "loved" his involvement: H-BC.

124 the MRF took a shine to the cocksure teenager: Dillon, *The Dirty War*, pp. 34–35.

124 the very best recruits: Kitson, *Gangs and Counter-Gangs*, p. 126.

125 the MRF gave Kevin McKee a pistol: H-BC.

125 McKee was wearing the shoulder holster: Dillon, *The Dirty War*, p. 35.

125 he confessed to his betrayal: Ibid., p. 35.

125 gather intelligence on the British, as triple agents: H-BC.

125 low-level information or, better still, misinformation: Dillon, *The Dirty War*, pp. 33–34.

126 they would be granted "immunity": H-BC.

126 The centerpiece of the operation: Adams, *Before the Dawn*, pp. 212–13.

126 "Sit back," Adams said. "Do more intelligence": H-BC.

126 in addition to the laundry service and the office: Ibid.; Dillon, *The Dirty War*, pp. 39–40.

127 launch three near-simultaneous strikes: See Taylor, *Brits*, p. 135, in which, without naming Adams, Taylor characterizes his position.

127 Ted Stuart, was an undercover British sapper: "Provos Admit Killing Army Secret Agent," *Belfast Telegraph*, October 3, 1972.

127 told them that this must be a loyalist ambush: Dillon, *The Dirty War*, pp. 26–27.

127 The woman helped Warke: Brendan Hughes interview in *Brits*, part 1: "The Secret War," directed by Sam Collyns (BBC, 2000).

127 if there was a third soldier concealed in the van: Dillon, *The Dirty War*, p. 39.

127 Elsewhere in Belfast, another team: Ibid., pp. 28, 37–39.

127 major victory for the Provos: H-BC; Adams, *Before the Dawn*, p. 213.

127 Wright came home: "More Double Agents at Work," *Irish Times*, May 14, 1973.

128 Wright exchanged a few words: This detail is from an interview Wright's wife, Kathleen, gave to Rev. Brian Brady of Trench House, in Andersonstown, in 1973. See "More Double Agents at Work," *Irish Times*, May 14, 1973; "IRA Never Got Spy's Secrets," *Guardian*, May 14, 1973.

128 not been taken by the IRA: "More Double Agents at Work," *Irish Times*, May 14, 1973.

128 might have been snatched by the army: "More Double Agents at Work," *Irish Times*, May 14, 1973; "IRA Never Got Spy's Secrets," *Guardian*, May 14, 1973.

128 Military sources suggested: "IRA Never Got Spy's Secrets," *Guardian*, May 14, 1973.

128 McKee vanished as well: *The Disappeared*.

128 both men had been taken by the IRA: P-EM.

128 It was just Price driving: Ibid.

129 McKee ended up in a house in County Monaghan: "Every Time We Met a Family We Found New Material, New Facts," *Irish Independent*, November 10, 2013.

129 people who were minding him grew fond: H-BC.

129 telephoned his mother: McKee, "The Disappearance of Kevin McKee," p. 12.

129 "He'll not be back": "The IRA and the Disappeared: Tell Us Where Kevin Is Buried and I'll Shake Hands," *Irish Times*, October 5, 2013; "Every Time We Met a Family We Found New Material, New Facts," *Irish Independent*, November 10, 2013.

129 found themselves unable to shoot him: H-BC.

129 dispassionate gunmen were sent from Belfast: Ibid.

129 they summoned a priest: Dillon, *The Dirty War*, p. 44.

129 The act of killing itself had a ritual: Ibid., p. 44. The journalist Martin Dillon has identified the two shooters as Jim Bryson and Tommy "Todler" Tolan (both now dead). Dillon, *The Dirty War*, p. 44.

130 Hughes felt betrayed by the decision: H-BC.

130 in July 1973, Adams was heading: Adams, *Before the Dawn*, pp. 217–18; H-BC; "IRA Chiefs Among 17 Held in Army Raids," *Guardian*, July 20, 1973.

130 As officer commanding for Belfast: H-BC.

130 July was a tricky time to be on the run: Adams, *Before the Dawn*, p. 217.

130 he noticed that there was someone in the car: Taylor, *Brits*, pp. 154–55; British soldier interviewed in *Brits:* "The Secret War."

130 A hasty decision was made: Adams, *Before the Dawn*, pp. 217–18.

131 startled to behold a sea of British troops: Ibid., pp. 217–18.

131 Adams casually pulled out some matches and lit his pipe: Ibid., p. 218.

131 The businessman in the car: Taylor, *Brits*, pp. 154–55.

131 they were beaten and tortured: H-BC.

131 water to revive him, then started beating him again: H-BC. Adams and Hughes raised charges of brutal treatment at the time. See "Brutality Against Adams Alleged," *Irish Times*, July 23, 1973.

131 dump his body on the Black Mountain: H-BC.

131 The British forces were hugely pleased: Taylor, *Brits*, p. 156.

131 "trophy" photographs with the two captives: H-BC; "Portrait of a Hunger Striker: Brendan Hughes," *Irish People*, December 6, 1980. One of the intelligence officers involved later acknowledged to journalist Peter Taylor that there were trophy photographs taken, adding that Hughes and Adams were "in a pretty bad way." Peter Taylor, *Provos: The IRA and Sinn Fein* (London: Bloomsbury, 1998), p. 158.

131 Hughes was defiant: H-BC.

132 one of the greatest in his life: Ibid.

CHAPTER 11

137 The crocuses were already in bloom: "Bombs in Placid London," *Christian Science Monitor*, March 10, 1973.

137 There was a transit strike that day: Ibid.

137 Just after lunchtime: "Police Admit 'Human Error' Which Garbled Bomb Warning," *Irish Times*, March 10, 1973; "Warnings on Phone Sent Reporters Rushing to Find Named Cars," *Irish Times*, September 21, 1973.

137 Huckerby was on duty that day in the newsroom: Interview with Martin Huckerby.

138 He was looking for a green Ford Cortina Estate: "Warnings on Phone Sent Reporters Rushing to Find Named Cars," *Irish Times*, September 21, 1973.

138 Before long, he spotted it: Interview with Martin Huckerby; "A Taste of Ulster's Violence," *Guardian*, March 9, 1973.

138 They started evacuating people: "Warnings on Phone Sent Reporters Rushing to Find Named Cars," *Irish Times*, September 21, 1973; "Police Holding 10 in London Blasts," *New York Times*, March 10, 1973.

138 Huckerby took cover in a doorway: "Warnings on Phone Sent Reporters Rushing to Find Named Cars," *Irish Times*, September 21, 1973.

139 The English public: This sentiment is expressed by Billy McKee in Taylor, *Provos*, p. 152.

139 "Only half of it is our war": P-EM.

139 "an incursion into the heart of the Empire": "IRA Bomber Says Gerry Adams Sanctioned Mainland Bombing Campaign," *Telegraph*, September 23, 2012.

139 Price worked with McClure and Gerry Adams: "IRA Bomber Says Gerry Adams Sanctioned Mainland Bombing Campaign," *Telegraph*, September 23, 2012; P-EM. Adams has denied any involvement in the plan to attack London, but both Price and Brendan Hughes maintain that he was involved. Hugh Feeney, who was also a member of the Unknowns and took part in the mission, confirmed to me that Adams was intimately engaged with the unit's activities during this period.

139 the acid in the devices had leaked: P-EM.

139 they resolved to plant car bombs instead: H-BC. Hughes, in his interview: "The initial idea, right, was discussed at Belfast Brigade meetings, right, with myself, Gerry Adams, Ivor Bell, Pat McClure, basically that group of people. Tom Cahill. We were, we would have been the main people in the Belfast Brigade at the time. And the discussion and the idea and the whole concept of the London bombings came out of that particular group of people." Also see "IRA Bomber Says Gerry Adams Sanctioned Mainland Bombing Campaign," *Telegraph*, September 23, 2012.

139 When it came time to recruit a team: H-BC.

140 Gerry Adams explained: "IRA Bomber Says Gerry Adams Sanctioned Mainland Bombing Campaign," *Telegraph*, September 23, 2012.

140 prepared to face the full wrath of the state: H-BC.

140 "This could be a hanging job": Adams denies having said this; he denies having been in the IRA at all. But there is ample testimony to his presence and to his remarks. These direct quotes from Adams are drawn from Dolours Price's recollection. See "'Republicanism Is Part of Our DNA,' Says IRA Bomber Dolours Price," *Telegraph*, September 23, 2012. Brendan Hughes describes the meeting in similar terms in his Boston College oral history.

140 exit through the back door: P-EM.

140 flourish about ten-minute intervals from a book: Ibid.

140 "Don't knock me down in the rush, lads": Ibid.

140 about ten people remained: Interview with Hugh Feeney; "Central London Bombs Trial Opens," *Irish Times*, September 11, 1973.

140 Gerry Kelly, a handsome young man: P-EM.

140 Kelly had been on the run: "Protest Now Before It Is Too Late!" *Irish People*, January 12, 1974; "Biography of an IRA Bomb Squad," *Times* (London), November 15, 1973; Gerry Kelly, *Words from a Cell* (Dublin: Sinn Féin Publicity Department, 1989), p. 8.

140 Price thought he was a grand lad: Dolours Price, "I Once Knew a Boy," *The Blanket*, July 17, 2004.

140 They were all very young: "Biography of an IRA Bomb Squad," *Times* (London), November 15, 1973.

140 she joined the Provos six months earlier: Bob Huntley, *Bomb Squad: My War against the Terrorists* (London: W. H. Allen, 1977), pp. 1–2; "Police Kept Watch on Group at London Airport," *Irish Times,* September 18, 1973.

140 She still lived with her parents: "Police Kept Watch on Group at London Airport," *Irish Times,* September 18, 1973; "Bomb Trial Court Told of Threat," *Irish Times,* October 6, 1973.

140 As head of the Unknowns: Interview with Hugh Feeney.

141 he selected Dolours to take the lead: "'Republicanism Is Part of Our DNA,' Says IRA Bomber Dolours Price," *Telegraph,* September 23, 2012.

141 None of the recruits: Interview with Hugh Feeney; Taylor, *Provos,* p. 153.

141 intensive training with explosives and timers: P-EM; H-BC.

141 detonated and blew his arm off: H-BC.

141 "gruesome form of 'natural selection'": Urban, *Big Boys' Rules,* pp. 32–33.

141 soda straw used as a fuse: "IRA Bomb Making Manual and Rocket Seized by Troops," *Telegraph,* January 11, 1972.

141 cars were the perfect camouflage: Mac Stíofáin, *Revolutionary in Ireland,* p. 243.

142 unattended car became, all by itself, a source of terror: "Empty Car Causes Panic," *Belfast Telegraph,* January 3, 1973.

142 In February, six cars were hijacked: Interview with Hugh Feeney.

142 repainted and equipped with phony license plates: "Central London Bombs Trial Opens," *Irish Times,* September 11, 1973.

142 only four of the cars: Ibid.

142 more than a hundred pounds of powder explosives: Huntley, *Bomb Squad,* p. 4; "A Taste of Ulster's Violence," *Guardian,* March 9, 1973; "London Explosions Came from Bombs in Cars Hijacked at Gunpoint in Ulster, Crown Says," *Times* (London), September 11, 1973.

142 traveled to London on a scouting mission: Huntley, *Bomb Squad,* pp. 2, 7; Taylor, *Provos,* p. 153; P-EM.

142 The Unknowns had selected the targets: Marian Price interview in *Car Bomb.*

142 "evoke particular political questions": Kelly, *Words from a Cell,* p. 9.

142 bring "the reality of colonialism" home to England: Ibid., p. 9.

143 the Hunter was held up: "Bombs Trial Jury Told Girl May Have Had Timing Circuit Sketch," *Times* (London), September 12, 1973.

143 problem with the license plate: Ibid.

143 Martin Brady was behind the wheel: Huntley, *Bomb Squad,* p. 8.

143 The inspectors appeared suspicious: "Bombs Trial Jury Told Girl May Have Had Timing Circuit Sketch," *Times* (London), September 12, 1973.

143 McNearney was fidgeting in the back seat: Huntley, *Bomb Squad,* p. 8; "Bombs Trial Jury Told Girl May Have Had Timing Circuit Sketch," *Times* (London), September 12, 1973.

143 When she returned a few minutes later: Huntley, *Bomb Squad,* p. 8; "Central London Bombs Trial Opens," *Irish Times,* September 11, 1973.

143 after the scare at customs: Interview with Hugh Feeney; P-EM.

143 under an assumed name, Una Devlin: "Central London Bombs Trial Opens," *Irish Times,* September 11, 1973.

143 By Wednesday, March 7, the whole crew: Ibid.

144 A telephone warning would be issued in advance: Taylor, *Provos,* p. 153.

144 the team had been given orders: Interview with Hugh Feeney.

144 "You don't know each other,": Price told them: P-EM.

144 Before sundown, Price assembled everyone: "Puncture Gives Raid Disastrous Start," *Telegraph,* November 15, 1973; Huntley, *Bomb Squad,* p. 10.

144 So the young terrorists went sightseeing: Huntley, *Bomb Squad,* p. 11.

144 Some of the men defied Price's admonition: Price interview in *I, Dolours;* "The Day of the Terror," *Daily Mirror,* November 15, 1973.

145 before they had a chance to see any good theater: Interview with Hugh Feeney.

145 new show by the Irish playwright Brian Friel: "Central London Bombs Trial Opens," *Irish Times,* September 11, 1973.

145 about the hysteria, the mythmaking, and the misunderstanding: Brian Friel, *The Freedom of the City,* in *Brian Friel: Plays 1* (London: Faber, 1996).

145 crowds for the show had been sparse: "London Preview of Friel's New Play," *Irish Times,* February 23, 1973. The production had previously been staged in Dublin. "Shows Abroad," *Variety,* February 28, 1973.

145 received by London audiences "in a frost of ignorance": "Stephen Rea's Tribute to Brian Friel: A Shy Man and a Showman," *Irish Times,* October 2, 2015.

146 he and Dolours Price knew each other: "Patriot Games," *People,* February 8, 1993.

146 while good parking spots were still available: "Central London Bombs Trial Opens," *Irish Times,* September 11, 1973.

146 All four cars were driven to their destinations: "London Explosions Came from Bombs in Cars Hijacked at Gunpoint in Ulster, Crown Says," *Times* (London), September 11, 1973.

146 By 7:30, the bombs were in place: "Central London Bombs Trial Opens," *Irish Times,* September 11, 1973.

146 set to catch an 11:20 plane to Dublin: Ibid.; Huntley, *Bomb Squad,* p. 16.

146 The officers of London's Metropolitan Police: Peter Gurney, *Braver Men Walk Away* (London: HarperCollins, 1993), p. 140.

146 briefing…about an impending IRA attack: Taylor, *Provos,* p. 154.

147 targets such as government buildings: "A Taste of Ulster's Violence," *Guardian,* March 9, 1973.

147 they needed as few vehicles as possible: Gurney, *Braver Men Walk Away,* p. 140.

147 They noticed another anomaly: Taylor, *Provos,* p. 154.

147 the officers spotted a thin white cord snaking: "Central London Bombs Trial Opens," *Irish Times,* September 11, 1973.

147 nearly two hundred pounds of explosives: "A Taste of Ulster's Violence," *Guardian,* March 9, 1973.

147 "monstrous, tremendously powerful": Huntley, *Bomb Squad,* p. 16.

147 the timer, in its box, was audibly ticking: "Bombs Trial Jury Told Girl May Have Had Timing Circuit Sketch," *Times* (London), September 12, 1973.

147 "Get those stupid bastards away from the windows!": Gurney, *Braver Men Walk Away*, p. 143.

147 his partner gingerly severed it: "Suspect Car Exploded As Expert Pulled on Line to Disconnect Fuse," *Irish Times*, September 15, 1973; "Central London Bombs Trial Opens," *Irish Times*, September 11, 1973.

147 They had defused the bomb: "Central London Bombs Trial Opens," *Irish Times*, September 11, 1973.

147 would have detonated at around 3 p.m.: Huntley, *Bomb Squad*, p. 16.

147 the minute hand on the clock: Gurney, *Braver Men Walk Away*, p. 144.

148 CLOSE ENGLAND: Huntley, *Bomb Squad*, p. 16.

148 simply been brilliantly lucky: "Central London Bombs Trial Opens," *Irish Times*, September 11, 1973.

148 prior notice that an attack was coming: "Police Admit 'Human Error' Which Garbled Bomb Warning," *Irish Times*, March 10, 1973.

148 always believe that the operation had been betrayed: Marian Price said to Andrew Sanders, "We knew from day one that we had been informed on... They stopped us at the airport, but they were actually waiting on us coming." Andrew Sanders, "Dolours Price, Boston College, and the Myth of the 'Price Sisters,'" *The United States of America and Northern Ireland* blog, January 24, 2013. Also P-EM.

148 "We were set up": Interview with Hugh Feeney.

148 his source had been a senior member of the Provisionals: George Clarke, *Border Crossing: True Stories of the RUC Special Branch, the Garda Special Branch and the IRA Moles* (Dublin: Gill & Macmillan, 2009), p. 7.

148 having no clue as to the rough locations: "Police Admit 'Human Error' Which Garbled Bomb Warning," *Irish Times*, March 10, 1973.

148 beat the police to the Cortina: Interview with Martin Huckerby.

149 Inside the Old Bailey: "Bombings: 'A Sickening Bang, a Pea-Soup Cloud of Dust,'" *Washington Post*, March 9, 1973.

149 Someone burst into the courtrooms: Ibid.

149 customers simply moved deeper into the pub: "A Taste of Ulster's Violence," *Guardian*, March 9, 1973.

149 could only be a hoax: Huntley, *Bomb Squad*, p. 21.

149 watch the bomb squad: Peter Gurney interview in *Car Bomb*.

149 a school bus rolled up: "Victims Remember," *Daily Express*, June 1, 1974.

149 forty-nine schoolchildren: Ibid.; "Police Admit 'Human Error,'" *Irish Times*; Huntley, *Bomb Squad*, p. 21.

149 the children began to disembark: "Police Admit 'Human Error' Which Garbled Bomb Warning," *Irish Times*, March 10, 1973; Huntley, *Bomb Squad*, p. 21.

149 The bombers did not hear the bulletin: Huntley, *Bomb Squad*, p. 16.

149 presented their tickets: "Central London Bombs Trial Opens," *Irish Times*, September 11, 1973; Huntley, *Bomb Squad*, p. 17; "Suspect Car Exploded as Expert Pulled on Line to Disconnect Fuse," *Irish Times*, September 15, 1973.

150 officials entered the plane: Huntley, *Bomb Squad*, p. 17; "Thousands Checked in Heathrow Hunt," *Irish Times*, September 19, 1973.

150 Dolours, Marian, and Hugh Feeney were scheduled: Huntley, *Bomb Squad*, p. 17.

150 Special Branch officers were waiting: "Police Kept Watch on Group at London Airport," *Irish Times*, September 18, 1973.

150 "Would you mind coming with me?": Marian Price interview in *Car Bomb*.

150 any sort of cover story that was remotely convincing: Huntley, *Bomb Squad*, p. 17.

150 Some claimed they had come to London in search of work: Ibid., p. 17.

150 Others said they had been: "Central London Bombs Trial Opens," *Irish Times*, September 11, 1973.

150 They all offered fake names: Huntley, *Bomb Squad*, p. 18.

150 one member of the group—an eleventh bomber—was missing: "Central London Bombs Trial Opens," *Irish Times*, September 11, 1973.

150 "You've no right to keep me here": Huntley, *Bomb Squad*, p. 18.

150 locket might contain some kind of poison: "Jury Told Why Crucifix Was Taken Off Girl," *Times* (London), October 10, 1973.

151 would not be seeing the sunshine again: "Girl Branded 'Evil Maniac,' Court Told," *Irish Times*, October 10, 1973.

151 something robotic, almost trancelike, about her demeanor: Ibid.

151 They would fix their eyes on an object: "Car-bomb Defendant Smiled at Watch in Interview, Court Told," *Irish Times*, October 9, 1973.

151 looked pointedly at her watch: Ibid.

151 police finally discovered the Hillman Hunter: "A Taste of Ulster's Violence," *Guardian*, March 9, 1973.

151 With five minutes to go before detonation: "Whitehall Shaken by Blast," *Guardian*, March 9, 1973.

151 the timer's hand reached its terminus: "Suspect Car Exploded as Expert Pulled on Line to Disconnect Fuse," *Irish Times*, September 15, 1973.

151 The Hillman split apart, ripped open by a sheet of flame: Huntley, *Bomb Squad*, p. 20.

151 a dull thud, and a reverberation so strong: "A Taste of Ulster's Violence," *Guardian*, March 9, 1973.

151 Windows shattered in the offices and shops: Ibid.

152 tiny missiles of glass and metal whizzing: "Whitehall Shaken by Blast," *Guardian*, March 9, 1973.

152 A sooty mushroom cloud rose: "Bombs in Placid London," *Christian Science Monitor*, March 10, 1973.

152 A gas main ruptured: "Shattering Day That Brought the Ulster Troubles Home," *Guardian*, March 6, 1993.

152 People staggered about, dazed: "A Taste of Ulster's Violence," *Guardian*, March 9, 1973.

152 cars were hollowed out and twisted up: "Shattering Day That Brought the Ulster Troubles Home," *Guardian*, March 6, 1993.

152 dismantle the third bomb: "A Taste of Ulster's Violence," *Guardian*, March 9, 1973.

152 An officer ran toward the school bus: "Bombings: 'A Sickening Bang, a Pea-Soup Cloud of Dust,'" *Washington Post,* March 9, 1973.

152 They did, screaming: Huntley, *Bomb Squad,* p. 21.

152 A police photographer: Ibid., p. 21.

152 The façade of the George pub was torn away: "A Taste of Ulster's Violence," *Guardian,* March 9, 1973.

152 A police officer was evacuating jurors: Ibid.

152 Another policeman: "Bombings: 'A Sickening Bang, a Pea-Soup Cloud of Dust,'" *Washington Post,* March 9, 1973.

152 Huckerby, the *Times* journalist, was cut: Interview with Martin Huckerby; "Warnings on Phone Sent Reporters Rushing to Find Named Cars," *Irish Times,* September 21, 1973.

152 People with blood running down their faces: "Bombings: 'A Sickening Bang, a Pea-Soup Cloud of Dust,'" *Washington Post,* March 9, 1973.

152 But the whole vicinity: Ibid.

152 injured victims lay sprawled: "Bombs in Placid London," *Christian Science Monitor,* March 10, 1973.

152 Everywhere there was a thick carpet of broken glass: "A Taste of Ulster's Violence," *Guardian,* March 9, 1973.

152 This sort of scene might have: "Car Bombs Wreak Terror and Havoc in London," *Irish Times,* March 9, 1973.

154 Between the two bombs that detonated: "Bombings: 'A Sickening Bang, a Pea-Soup Cloud of Dust,'" *Washington Post,* March 9, 1973; "London Is Shaken by Two Bombings," *New York Times,* March 9, 1973.

154 Even so, when they saw the bloodied patients: "London Is Shaken by Two Bombings," *New York Times,* March 9, 1973.

154 Frederick Milton, a fifty-eight-year-old caretaker: McKittrick et al., *Lost Lives,* pp. 1515–16.

154 Milton collapsed a few hours later: Huntley, *Bomb Squad,* p. 22; McKittrick et al., pp. 1515–16.

154 An autopsy subsequently revealed: Huntley, *Bomb Squad,* p. 22; McKittrick et al., *Lost Lives,* pp. 1515–16.

154 Dolours Price would blame: "Old Bailey Bomber Dolours Price Accused Gerry Adams of Being Behind Abductions of 'The Disappeared,'" *Telegraph,* May 2, 2014.

154 Other members of the bombing team: Roy Walsh, one of the bombers, subsequently said, "We believed our warnings were adequate. We thought an hour was plenty of time. We gave the description of the cars, their registration numbers and where they were parked. I think it was the slowness of the police reaction that caused the injuries." Taylor, *Provos,* p. 155.

154 But as a factual matter, Price was not altogether wrong: "Police Admit 'Human Error' Which Garbled Bomb Warning," *Irish Times,* March 10, 1973; "Our Blunder Say Police," *Daily Express,* March 10, 1973.

154 nothing but a selfish, last-minute bid: "Central London Bombs Trial Opens," *Irish Times,* September 11, 1973.

155 What he regretted more acutely: H-BC.

155 Their clothing was stripped: Huntley, *Bomb Squad,* p. 24.

155 Dolours Price was photographed naked: "Girl Branded 'Evil Maniac' Court Told," *Irish Times,* October 10, 1973; "Jury Told Why Crucifix Was Taken Off Girl," *Times* (London), October 10, 1973; "Bomb Trial Court Told of Threat," *Irish Times,* October 6, 1973; "Photo with No Blanket Alleged," *Guardian,* October 6, 1973.

155 But the Price sisters and several others refused: Huntley, *Bomb Squad,* p. 24; "Girl Branded 'Evil Maniac' Court Told," *Irish Times,* October 10, 1973; "Car-bomb Defendant Smiles at Watch in Interview, Court Told," *Irish Times,* October 9, 1973.

155 Dolours hissed at her sister: Huntley, *Bomb Squad,* p. 24.

CHAPTER 12

156 Thomas Valliday was a prisoner: H-BC.

156 it was considerably heavier than usual: "IRA Leader Escapes from Maze Prison," *Irish Times,* December 10, 1973.

156 he knew that nestled inside: H-BC. Valliday died in 1987, apparently choking on his own vomit after taking an overdose of drugs. See "Hooded Men Stalk Feud Opponents in Belfast," *Irish Times,* February 20, 1987. The sausage roll analogy is not mine: see Taylor, *Provos,* p. 160.

156 Within thirty-six hours of arriving at Long Kesh: Adams, *Before the Dawn,* p. 225.

157 Gerry Adams felt that, given the importance: H-BC.

157 McGuigan donned a set of borrowed black robes: "IRA Man Escapes from Long Kesh," *Irish Times,* February 8, 1972; "McGuigan Keeps Secret of Escape from Long Kesh," *Irish Times,* February 14, 1972.

157 another man, John Francis Green, managed to escape: "More Violence As IRA Factions Agree," Reuters, September 11, 1973.

157 the underside of one of the rubbish lorries: Adams, *Before the Dawn,* p. 225.

157 this was reminiscent of Homer's *Odyssey*: Homer, *The Odyssey,* trans. Robert Fagles (New York: Penguin, 1997), Book 9, p. 225.

157 But Hughes was still weak: H-BC.

157 when another prisoner: Ibid.; Adams, *Before the Dawn,* p. 225; "Provos Claim Chief Evaded Security Net," *Guardian,* April 8, 1974.

158 a hijacked helicopter suddenly appeared in the sky: "Helicopter Snatch from Dublin Gaol a Boost to Provos," *Guardian,* November 1, 1973.

158 The Provos knew: H-BC.

158 But the IRA had cultivated: Ibid.

158 center of an old mattress while others helped to roll it around him: Ibid.

158 making it hard to breathe: Adams, *Before the Dawn,* p. 227; Brendan Hughes interview, *Radio Free Éireann,* WBAI, March 17, 2000.

158 The truck trundled around: In the March 17, 2000, *Radio Free Éireann* interview, he says it was four to five hours.

158 Hughes heard Valliday whispering: H-BC.

158 There would be a head count at 4 p.m.: Ibid. Gerry Adams, whose recollection of this episode tracks very closely with that of Hughes, remembers that there was a "decoy" at the head count, so the escape was not discovered that day. See Adams, *Before the Dawn*, pp. 227–28. But Hughes recalls that the decoy had allowed him to escape in the first place, but that this ruse would be discovered at the afternoon head count.

159 The lorry had ended up in the British Army compound: H-BC.

159 The sawdust had crept into his eyes: Ibid.

159 Hughes lay quietly: Ibid.

159 a giant spear plunged down: Ibid.; Brendan Hughes interview, *Radio Free Éireann*, WBAI, March 17, 2000.

159 He pictured it: the spear running straight through him: H-BC.

159 Hughes had two young children back in Belfast: "Hunt on for Long Kesh Escapee," *Irish People*, December 22, 1973.

159 He was just about to identify himself: This detail and the rest of the account of this episode is drawn from H-BC.

160 in the library on the top floor of the Old Bailey: Interview with Michael Mansfield.

160 Mansfield was showered with broken glass: Michael Mansfield, *Memoirs of a Radical Lawyer* (London: Bloomsbury, 2009), p. 146.

160 an ambitious, slightly flamboyant English lawyer: "The Best Form of Attack," *Guardian*, October 25, 1997.

160 recently scored his first major legal triumph: Interview with Michael Mansfield; Mansfield, *Memoirs*, pp. 33–34.

161 questions about the nature of authoritarian power and resistance: "Meet Britain's Boldest Barrister," *Independent*, May 7, 2008.

161 money he made from the Angry Brigade case: "The Best Form of Attack," *Guardian*, October 25, 1997.

161 one empty space, not far from a green Ford Cortina: Mansfield, *Memoirs*, p. 146.

161 Triumph was ripped apart: Ibid., p. 146.

161 established lawyers would not take the case: Interviews with Michael Mansfield and David Walsh.

161 their beauty and by the intensity of their commitment: Interview with Michael Mansfield; Mansfield, *Memoirs*, p. 147.

161 They recalled being pummeled by the loyalist mob at Burntollet: Interview with Michael Mansfield.

162 a life that was truly "on the edge": Mansfield, *Memoirs*, p. 147.

162 "an explosion of a nature likely to endanger life": "Britain Charges Ten in London Bombings," *New York Times*, March 13, 1973.

162 the building was still being repaired from the bombing: Interview with Michael Mansfield.

163 It was in this same room: Raleigh Trevelyan, *Sir Walter Raleigh* (New York: Henry Holt, 2002), pp. 376–77.

163 replica of the surface of King Arthur's round table hung on one wall: Ruán O'Donnell, *Special Category: The IRA in English Prisons*, vol. 1: *1968–1978* (Sallins, Ireland: Irish Academic Press, 2012), p. 115.

163 sang rebel songs on the prison bus to Winchester: Dolours Price, "The UnHung Hero," *The Blanket*, August 3, 2004.

163 defendants would be escorted in and out by a convoy: "Central London Bombs Trial Opens," *Irish Times*, September 11, 1973.

163 marked by an extreme, almost theatrical devotion to security: "Security Precautions at Winchester Courthouse," *Times* (London), November 15, 1973.

163 Police marksmen patrolled surrounding rooftops: "Marksmen on Watch at Conspiracy Trial," *Times* (London), September 10, 1973.

163 republicans had tried to purchase a house directly across the street: O'Donnell, *Special Category*, vol. 1, p. 117.

163 Dolours and Marian flashed V signs to the spectators: "Central London Bombs Trial Opens," *Irish Times*, September 11, 1973.

163 Vanessa Redgrave…volunteered to post bond for the defendants: "Actress, Novelist, and MP Offer Bail for 10 'Bomb Plot' Accused," *Guardian*, March 28, 1973.

163 The English public and press became particularly fixated: "The Sisters of Terror," *Observer*, November 18, 1973.

163 political radicalism and countercultural instability: "Biography of an IRA Bomb Squad," *Times* (London), November 15, 1973.

164 earned her the nickname "the Armalite widow": Ibid.

164 a dangerous by-product of feminism: "Deadlier Than the Male," *Daily Mirror*, September 25, 1975.

164 a debonair barrister: "Lord Rawlinson of Ewell," *Telegraph*, June 29, 2006; "Central London Bombs Trial Opens," *Irish Times*, September 11, 1973.

164 "safe and sound many miles away": Ibid.

164 Rawlinson singled out Dolours Price: Ibid.

164 the defendants maintained their innocence: "Bomb Trial Court Told of Threat," *Irish Times*, October 6, 1973.

164 offering a false name had become practically second nature: "Accused Girl Says She Would Back IRA Aims," *Times* (London), October 25, 1973.

165 a photo of Michael Mansfield's wrecked Triumph: Interview with Michael Mansfield; Mansfield, *Memoirs*, p. 148.

165 Rawlinson spelled out the sequence of events: Peter Rawlinson, *A Price Too High: An Autobiography* (London: Weidenfeld and Nicolson, 1989), p. 229.

165 carrying a black canvas shopping bag: "Bomb Trial Jury Told of Tools in Shopping Bag," *Times* (London), September 20, 1973.

165 police discovered two screwdrivers and a spiral-bound notebook: "Police Say What Handbags Held," *Irish Times*, September 20, 1973.

165 Some pages in the notebook were filled: "Yard Man Describes Indentations in Notebook," *Times* (London), September 27, 1973; "Ulster's Price Sisters: Breaking the Long Fast," *Time*, June 17, 1974.

165 diagram of the timing device for a bomb: "London Bombs Trial Told About Handbag Secrets," *Irish Times,* September 12, 1973; "Bombs Trial Jury Told Girl May Have Had Timing Circuit Sketch," *Times* (London), September 12, 1973; "Court Moves to Darkened Room for Notebooks Demonstration," *Irish Times,* October 3, 1973.

166 "I don't know what you are talking about": "Bomb Trial Court Told of Threat," *Irish Times,* October 6, 1973.

166 She had joined the IRA only six months earlier: Huntley, *Bomb Squad,* p. 2; "Bomb Trial Court Told of Threat," *Irish Times,* October 6, 1973.

166 insisted that she was a minor, ineffectual figure: Huntley, *Bomb Squad,* p. 24.

166 the others did not realize until the trial began: O'Donnell, *Special Category,* vol. 1, p. 116.

166 the older Prices, ramrod straight and proud: Interview with Eamonn McCann.

166 Dolours selected eye-catching ensembles: "The Sisters of Terror," *Observer,* November 18, 1973.

166 She had always been attuned to performance: Ibid.

167 "the long-term aim" ... "I did not say that": "Violence 'Not Included in IRA Principles,'" *Guardian,* October 26, 1973; "Evidence Given on Handwriting," *Irish Times,* October 26, 1973.

167 began to openly heckle Judge Shaw: "Defiance from IRA Group Who Pledge Jail Protest," *Irish Times,* November 16, 1973.

167 On the November day that the verdict was delivered: "Defiant Right to the End," *Daily Express,* November 16, 1973.

167 with everyone who entered frisked: "Snipers on Rooftops in Huge Security Check," *Daily Mirror,* September 11, 1973.

167 accompanied by fifteen prison officers: "Sentences Today As Eight Are Convicted on All Charges," *Irish Times,* November 15, 1973.

167 designed to establish "an atmosphere of guilt": Interview with Michael Mansfield.

168 just behind Judge Shaw's seat: "Sentences Today As Eight Are Convicted on All Charges," *Irish Times,* November 15, 1973.

168 rowdy Irish people who had come over: "Marks in Notebook 'Showed Time Bomb Circuits,'" *Guardian,* September 12, 1973.

168 When the all-male jury filed in: "Hostage Threat As IRA Eight Are Convicted in London Bombs Trial," *Times* (London), November 15, 1973.

168 jury was acquitting Roisin McNearney: "Sentences Today As Eight Are Convicted on All Charges," *Irish Times,* November 15, 1973.

168 "I do not know when you leave this court": Ibid.

168 the remaining defendants began to hum a tune: Interview with Hugh Feeney; "Sentences Today As Eight Are Convicted on All Charges," *Irish Times,* November 15, 1973; "Hostage Threat As IRA Eight Are Convicted in London Bombs Trial," *Times* (London), November 15, 1973.

168 "Here's your blood money!": "But for Roisin Freedom and a Secret Hide-Out," *Daily Express,* November 15, 1973.

168 She rushed out of the courtroom, sobbing: Ibid.

168 Dolours said, audibly, "That's a *death* sentence": "IRA Eight Start Hunger Strike after Being Jailed for Life," *Times* (London), November 16, 1973.

168 Shaw announced that he would reduce: "Life Sentences for Winchester Eight," *Irish Times,* November 16, 1973.

168 defendants were making their displeasure known: "IRA Eight Start Hunger Strike after Being Jailed for Life," *Times* (London), November 16, 1973.

169 "I stand before you as a volunteer of IRA!" Marian Price announced. "I consider myself a prisoner of war!": Ibid.

169 "Up the Provisionals!" the spectators shouted: "Defiance from IRA Group Who Pledge Jail Protest," *Irish Times,* November 16, 1973.

169 "You must not regard the dock as a political arena": "Defiant Right to the End," *Daily Express,* November 16, 1973.

169 "Victory is within the grasp of the Irish Nation!": "Defiance from IRA Group Who Pledge Jail Protest," *Irish Times,* November 16, 1973.

169 McNearney was hustled away: "Hostage Threat As IRA Eight Are Convicted in London Bombs Trial," *Times* (London), November 15, 1973.

169 She was given a name and new documents: "IRA Planning to Kidnap 10 Hostages from an English Village in Reprisal for Sentences," *Times* (London), November 16, 1973.

169 "Make no mistake about it": "Deadliest Sentence of Them All," *Daily Mirror,* November 17, 1973.

169 they were going on a hunger strike: "IRA Eight Start Hunger Strike after Being Jailed for Life," *Times* (London), November 16, 1973.

169 They would refuse food until they were granted: Ibid.

170 "We will be back in Northern Ireland": "Sinn Féin Start Campaign over London Bombers," *Times* (London), November 24, 1973.

CHAPTER 13

171 He rented an apartment: Dillon, *The Dirty War,* p. 64.

171 a small, punctilious man, always clean-shaven: Taylor, *Brits,* p. 157.

171 he looked like a banker, attired in a three-piece suit: "Two Top IRA Men Captured in Flat in Fashionable Belfast Suburb," *Times* (London), May 11, 1974; H-BC. Press reports from that period often described the suit as "pin-striped," but according to Hughes it was a gray check.

171 convoy of police cars and armored vehicles: "IRA Terror Den Smashed," *Daily Express,* May 11, 1974.

171 a soldier dressed in camouflage: *Brits:* "The Secret War."

172 "Come on, Darkie," one of the officers said: Ibid.

172 Hughes had eventually managed to hitch a ride: H-BC.

173 He rented the property on Myrtlefield Park: Ibid.

173 had died as an infant but would have been: Taylor, *Brits,* p. 157.

173 inspired by the thriller *The Day of the Jackal:* Jonathan Stevenson, *We Wrecked the Place: Contemplating an End to the Northern Irish Troubles* (New York: Free Press, 1996), p. 32.

173 he had his case of toys and a driver's license: Brendan Hughes interview, *Radio Free Éireann,* WBAI, March 17, 2000; Dillon, *The Dirty War,* p. 63.

173 "under the noses of the British Army": "Bridegroom Guise in Kesh Escape," *Irish People,* April 27, 1974.

173 "I was good at what I done and I done it": H-BC.

173 But his most audacious scheme: Taylor, *Brits,* p. 158; Dillon, *The Dirty War,* p. 65.

174 Because army intelligence: Taylor, *Brits,* p. 158; Dillon, *The Dirty War,* p. 65.

174 the tapes were garbled, unintelligible: Taylor, *Brits,* p. 158; Dillon, *The Dirty War,* p. 65.

174 steal an unscrambling device from the army: *Brits:* "The Secret War"; "Provisionals Breach British Security," *Irish Times,* July 22, 1974. After this operation was revealed, a British Army spokesman insisted that Hughes had not compromised any significant intelligence, claiming that officials were careful not to say anything sensitive even on ostensibly scrambled lines. See "Phone Tapping 'Unimportant,' " *Irish People,* August 3, 1974.

174 They had somehow gotten wind of his hideout: "Army Smashes the Provos' Life at the Top," *Guardian,* May 11, 1974.

175 They also found a cache of materials: "Two Men Get 15 Years for Having Rifles," *Irish Times,* February 4, 1975; "British Army Aims to Press Charges after Disclosure About Lisburn Phone Tapping," *Irish Times,* July 23, 1974; Taylor, *Brits,* p. 159.

175 The documents predicted a kind of apocalypse: Dillon, *The Dirty War,* pp. 65–66.

175 Perhaps he might be induced: *Brits:* "The Secret War."

175 "I told them fifty million wouldn't sway me": "Decommissioned Provos Thrown on Scrap Heap of History," *Sunday Tribune,* April 16, 2006.

CHAPTER 14

176 Brixton Prison was a grim colossus: Price, "Afraid of the Dark," *Krino* no. 3 (Spring 1987), p. 7. Other details are drawn from a recollection by the writer Ronan Bennett, who spent nineteen months in Brixton in the late 1970s: "Back to Brixton Prison," *Guardian,* January 31, 2001.

176 Dolours and Marian were segregated: Dolours Price to her family, January 8, 1974, in *Irish Voices,* p. 46.

176 a stream of verbal commentary: O'Donnell, *Special Category,* vol. 1, p. 96.

176 selling seats at their windows: "The Price Sisters," *Spare Rib* no. 22 (April 1974).

176 Brixton even *smelled* like men: Price, "Afraid of the Dark," *Krino* no. 3 (Spring 1987), p. 9.

176 adorned with collages of pornography: "Back to Brixton Prison," *Guardian,* January 31, 2001.

176 "a screw beside you every step of the way": Dolours Price interview in *The Chaplain's Diary,* radio documentary, produced by Lorelei Harris (RTÉ Radio, 2002).

176 The sisters were given numbers: This prisoner number appears on multiple files relating to Price during her time at Brixton that are now held in the National Archives, in Kew.

177 Dolours and Marian intended to strike until death: Chronology of Events in Connection with the London Bomb Explosions of 8 March 1973 and Subsequent Events, Department of Foreign Affairs of the Republic of Ireland (1973), National Archives of Ireland.

177 Hugh Feeney and Gerry Kelly: Interview with Hugh Feeney.

177 fasting had been used by the Irish: Beresford, *Ten Men Dead,* p. 7.

177 In a 1903 play about a poet: The play is *The King's Threshold.* William Butler Yeats, *The Collected Works of W. B. Yeats,* vol. II: *The Plays* (New York: Scribner, 2001), p. 122.

178 The British would not let him go: "Mayor McSwiney Dies," *The Independent* (U.S.), November 6, 1920.

178 MacSwiney's death sparked: "MacSwiney's Funeral," *The Independent* (U.S.), November 13, 1920; "Tribute Paid in Chicago by Great Throng," *Chicago Tribune,* November 1, 1920; "10,000 in 'Cortege,'" *Washington Post,* November 1, 1920; "Thousands March in MacSwiney's Funeral Cortege in London," Associated Press, October 28, 1920.

178 articulated a philosophy of self-sacrifice: Padraig O'Malley, *Biting at the Grave: The Irish Hunger Strikes and the Politics of Despair* (Boston: Beacon Press, 1990), pp. 26–27.

178 MURDERED BY THE FOREIGNER: "Thousands March in MacSwiney's Funeral Cortege in London," Associated Press, October 28, 1920.

178 Eventually the officers stopped leaving the food: Marian Price to her family, February 3, 1974, in *Irish Voices,* p. 57.

178 "Water only, sister": Price, "Afraid of the Dark," *Krino* no. 3 (Spring 1987), p. 9.

178 "I must be growing up, losing my 'puppy fat'!!": Dolours Price to her family, January 10, 1974, in *Irish Voices,* p. 48.

179 "He who blinks first is lost": Dolours Price, "Once Again, the Big Transition," *The Blanket,* January 28, 2007.

179 stars of a different sort of serialized tabloid drama: Price, "Afraid of the Dark," *Krino* no. 3 (Spring 1987), p. 10.

179 youth and gender, their frail femininity: Ian Miller, *A History of Force Feeding: Hunger Strikes, Prisons and Medical Ethics, 1909–1974* (Basingstoke, U.K.: Palgrave Macmillan, 2016), p. 197.

179 "Merry Christmas everyone. Dolours Price is dying": "Protest Now Before It Is Too Late!" *Irish People,* January 12, 1974.

179 the Great Famine of the nineteenth century: These statistics are endlessly argued over in the literature, but these are both consensus estimates. See R. F. Foster, *Modern Ireland, 1600–1972* (New York: Penguin, 1989), pp. 323–24.

179 ships laden with food were leaving Irish harbors: "In the long and troubled history of England and Ireland no issue has provoked so much anger or so embittered relations between the two countries as the indisputable fact that huge quantities of food were exported from Ireland to England throughout the period when the people of Ireland were dying of starvation." Cecil Woodham-Smith, *The Great Hunger: Ireland, 1845–1849* (New York: Penguin, 1991), p. 75. This matter is more complex in its particulars than in the broad strokes: During the years in question, Ireland was a net importer of food, even if it did continue to export throughout the famine. Nor was Ireland a monolith: different parts of the country grew and consumed different crops; it was not merely the British but the landlord class in Ireland who were complicit in this diversion of food that could have been consumed at home; Catholic traders and farmers may have speculated on food for personal profit. For a revisionist discussion, see Colm Tóibín and Diarmaid Ferriter, *The Irish Famine: A Documentary* (New York: St. Martin's Press, 2001), pp. 6–16. See also, more broadly, Foster, *Modern Ireland,* chap. 14. Debates about the actual degree of moral accountability that should properly be attributed to the English are beside the point in this context: in the universe of Dolours and Marian Price, British guilt was taken for granted.

180 One of the first widely circulated tracts: John Mitchel, *The Last Conquest of Ireland (Perhaps)* (Glasgow: R. & T. Washbourne, 1861).

180 If the British had employed: Dolours Price, "Post Traumatic Stress Syndrome," *The Blanket,* June 29, 2006.

180 "We'll be the first women": Dolours Price to a friend, May 23, 1974, in *The Irish People,* June 22, 1974.

180 British had always outmanned: Dolours Price, "A Salute to Comrades," *The Blanket,* May 18, 2005.

180 "massive retaliatory violence": Roy Jenkins, *A Life at the Centre* (London: Macmillan, 1991), p. 382.

180 blunt alternative solution: Price affidavit; treatment notes of Dr. R. I. K. Blyth (National Archives, Kew).

180 she gagged, nearly suffocating: This description is derived from an account provided by Dr. R. I. K. Blyth, the principal medical officer at Brixton, in a letter to D. A. Watson, treasury solicitor, May 13, 1974 (National Archives, Kew), as well as from the following: Price affidavit; a statement about the experience that Dolours provided afterward, excerpted in "English Government Tortures Irish Prisoners by Force Feeding," *Irish People,* December 15, 1973; and a 2004 interview that Marian Price gave to Suzanne Breen about the experience, in "Old Bailey Bomber Ashamed of Sinn Féin," *Village,* December 7, 2004.

181 substance to slosh down into her: Price affidavit.

181 raw eggs, orange juice, and liquid Complan: Details of the feed are from: Dolours Price to her family, January 23, 1974, in *Irish Voices,* p. 53; "Concern Grows among Relatives of Four Hunger Strikers," *Times* (London), January 16, 1974; and "Old Bailey Bomber Ashamed of Sinn Féin," *Village,* December 7, 2004. The ingredients come from Dolours Price Medical Treatment Notes (Kew).

181 We'll come off together or not at all: "Old Bailey Bomber Ashamed of Sinn Féin," *Village,* December 7, 2004.

181 Two days later: Treatment Notes for Marian Price.

181 gruesome ritual: Dolours Price to recipient unknown, December 10, 1973, quoted in *The Irish People,* December 22, 1973.

181 After being force-fed in Holloway Prison in 1913: "Forcibly Fed: The Story of My Four Weeks in Holloway Gaol," *McClure's*, August 1913.

181 "I don't want the stuff forced down me": Dolours Price to her family, excerpted in "Concern Grows among Relatives of Four Hunger Strikers," *Times* (London) January 16, 1974.

181 nearly choke to death: Ibid.

182 not in the habit of allowing their inmates to kill themselves: Ibid.

182 Devlin was shocked by the sight: "Mrs. McAliskey Visits Price Girls," *Irish Times*, January 11, 1974; "Frightening Appearance of Dolours Price Described," *Irish Times*, February 7, 1974.

182 Dolours's teeth had started to loosen: "Letters on Force Feeding Treatment Forbidden," *Irish People*, February 2, 1974. This was confirmed by the dentist at Brixton. See "Ulster's Price Sisters: Breaking the Long Fast," *Time*, June 17, 1974.

182 Both sisters' complexions had grown waxy: "Sister Tells of Visiting Price Girls," *Irish People*, February 2, 1974.

182 One doctor mocked the sisters' conviction: "Letters on Force Feeding Treatment Forbidden," *Irish People*, February 2, 1974.

182 Ulster Irish breeding "like rabbits": Price, "Afraid of the Dark," *Krino* no. 3 (Spring 1987), p. 10.

182 register how rapidly their strength was dissipating: "Old Bailey Bomber Ashamed of Sinn Féin," *Village*, December 7, 2004.

182 "The problem was we were too sane": Ibid.

182 The psychiatrist knew Roy Jenkins: Ibid.

183 "the death of these charismatic colleens": Jenkins, *A Life at the Centre*, p. 378.

183 concessions under such duress: Ibid., p. 377.

183 Terrorism was a "contagion": Ibid.

183 According to their medical records: Treatment Notes for Marian Price (National Archives, Kew).

183 a radio was turned up to cover their screams: Miller, *A History of Force Feeding*, p. 210.

183 psychiatrist decried the practice, likening it to rape: "Effect of Force Feeding Like Multiple Rape Says Psychiatrist," *Irish People*, March 23, 1974.

183 "more than that to break our kid, some pup she is": Letter from Marian Price to her family, January 7, 1974, in "The Price Sisters," *Spare Rib* no. 22 (April 1974).

183 "An awful lot of people come onto earth": "Lest We Forget," *Daily Express*, June 1, 1974.

184 Their mother, Chrissie, sounded a similar note: "England, You Shall Pay Dearly," *Irish People*, March 2, 1974.

184 with gruff composure, "drink plenty of water": P-TKT.

184 Bands like the Dubliners played: "'Let the Price Sisters Starve,' Send Them Back Says MP," *Irish People*, February 16, 1974.

184 protests outside the walls of Brixton Prison: Entries in the diary of B. D. Wigginton, governor of Brixton Prison, for April 14 and May 20, 1973. Available on London's Oldest Prison website, maintained by Christopher Impey.

184 Sixty women showed up at Roy Jenkins's London home: "Bomb Victim's Father Now Supports Prices," *Irish People,* June 8, 1974.

184 The father of a young girl: Ibid.

184 Even one of the loyalist paramilitary groups: "UDA Back Price Girls," *Irish People,* February 16, 1974.

184 "when it comes to the crunch, we're all Irish together": Dolours Price to her family, February 4, 1974, in *Irish Voices,* pp. 58–59.

184 closely monitored their own coverage: Price, "Afraid of the Dark," *Krino* no. 3 (Spring 1987), p. 10.

184 She processed the stories: Ibid., p. 7.

185 "being called 'Dolours and Marian's father'?": Dolours Price to her family, January 28, 1974, in *Irish Voices,* p. 54.

185 a seventeenth-century painting by Vermeer: "Letter to 'The Times' Says That Vermeer Will Be Burnt on Sunday," *Times* (London), March 13, 1974.

185 one of the letters contained a sliver of canvas: Ibid.

185 Dolours had visited Kenwood House: "Price Sisters Ask That Painting Be Returned," *Irish People,* March 23, 1974.

185 Dolours—"who is an art student": "Threat to Destroy Stolen Vermeer," *Irish Times,* March 13, 1974.

185 suspicious package appeared in a churchyard: "Stolen Vermeer Found in a Churchyard," *Belfast Telegraph,* May 7, 1974.

186 A collection of old masters worth millions: "Demand by Art Thieves," *Irish Times,* May 4, 1974; "Ransom Note Offers Five Paintings If Prisoners Are Moved to Ulster," *Times* (London), May 4, 1974.

186 were later recovered: "Dr. Rose Faces Court Today," *Daily Express,* May 6, 1974.

186 In June, an elderly Irish earl: "Hostages Teach IRA Kidnappers All About Racing," *Irish Times,* June 10, 1974. Another hostage was not so fortunate. Thomas Niedermayer was a forty-five-year-old German industrialist who managed a plant in Dunmurry. He was abducted from his home on December 27, 1973. According to two of the conspirators involved in taking him hostage, the intention was to trade Niedermayer in an "exchange" for the Price sisters. But within days of his abduction, he died in a struggle with his captors. Niedermayer was secretly buried in a shallow grave. His remains were not discovered until 1980. Had they not been found, his name would likely be better known today as another instance of forced disappearance during the Troubles. See McKittrick et al., *Lost Lives,* p. 410.

186 as much dignity as they could muster: Dolours Price to a friend, May 23, 1974, reproduced in *The Irish People,* June 22, 1974.

187 "that steel clamp hurts the old gums": Ibid.

187 "the privilege of killing us": Ibid.

187 It was a clinical judgment: Jenkins, *A Life at the Centre,* p. 377.

187 artificial feeding for 167 days: "Jenkins Demands Ultimate: Death for Price Sisters," *Irish People,* June 8, 1974.

187 Dolours and Marian were thrilled: "Price Sisters Losing 1lb Weight a Day," *Irish Times,* May 27, 1974.

187 "we no longer desire or crave food": Letter from Dolours Price to a friend, May 23, 1974, reproduced in *The Irish People,* June 22, 1974.

187 "I am carving away at myself": Price, "Afraid of the Dark," *Krino* no. 3 (Spring 1987), p. 10.

188 "Getting nearer to Paradise by the minute!": Ibid., p. 10.

188 "living entirely off their own bodies": "Price Sisters Losing 1lb Weight a Day," *Irish Times,* May 27, 1974.

188 even walking across the room: Letter from Dolours Price to Chrissie Price, excerpted in "Price Sisters Threat," *Daily Mirror,* May 31, 1974.

188 "ripple mattresses": Price, "Afraid of the Dark," *Krino* no. 3 (Spring 1987), p. 9.

188 "Each day passes and we fade a little more": Dolours Price to Chrissie Price, May 27, 1974, in *Irish Voices,* p. 61.

188 three prison officers on constant guard: "Price Sisters Threat," *Daily Mirror,* May 31, 1974.

188 fingers long and spindly from starvation: Price, "Afraid of the Dark," *Krino* no. 3 (Spring 1987), pp. 11–12.

188 "stand back a little" and be dispassionate: "Jenkins Demands Ultimate: Death for Price Sisters," *Irish People,* June 8, 1974.

189 "Happy about dying": "Fears Havoc in Ulster If Daughters Die in London," Associated Press, June 1, 1974.

189 braced for violence, warning that if: "An IRA Warning If Sisters Die," *Belfast Telegraph,* May 30, 1974.

189 administered last rites: "Price Sisters' 'Last Rites,'" *Daily Mirror,* May 28, 1974.

189 "We're ready for what is ahead": Letter from Dolours Price to a friend, May 23, 1974, reproduced in *The Irish People,* June 22, 1974.

189 Michael Gaughan, died in Parkhurst Prison: Coogan, *The IRA,* pp. 415–17.

189 "getting in at the heels of my hunt": Price, "Afraid of the Dark," *Krino* no. 3 (Spring 1987), p. 12.

189 She was watching TV: Ibid., p. 12.

189 complications associated with force-feeding: "The Gaughan Funeral," *Irish Press,* June 19, 1974.

189 later described as "forebodings of menace": Jenkins, *A Life at the Centre,* p. 378.

190 No place would be safe: Ibid., p. 380.

190 "We went on hunger strike 206 days ago": "Statement from Dolours and Marian, Gerry Kelly and Hugh Feeney," June 8, 1974.

190 The transfer was not immediate: "Price Girls in Durham," *Irish Independent,* December 16, 1974.

190 "That's near enough for me": Dolours Price interview in *The Chaplain's Diary,* RTÉ Radio.

190 Marian ran into her cell: Dolours Price, "Brixton, Durham and Armagh Gaol, 1973," in *In the Footsteps of Anne: Stories of Republican Women Ex-Prisoners,* ed. Evelyn Brady, Eva Patterson, Kate McKinney, Rosie Hamill, and Pauline Jackson (Belfast: Shanway Press, 2011), p. 134.

190 Dolours was so drunk with excitement: Ibid., p. 134.

190 The sisters were taken to an air force base: Ibid., p. 134.

191 glimpsed green land below: Dolours Price interview in *The Chaplain's Diary,* RTÉ Radio.

191 flashbulbs lighting up the early evening sky: Price, "Brixton, Durham and Armagh Gaol, 1973," in Brady et al., *Footsteps of Anne,* p. 134.

191 Bridie Dolan, their aunt, had died: "Provisional Sinn Féin to Establish Its Own 24-Hour Centres to Monitor Ceasefire," *Irish Times,* February 12, 1975.

191 Chrissie Price died of pancreatic cancer: "A Voice Uncompromised by Prison, Hunger Strike, Years," *Sunday Tribune,* March 9, 2003.

191 petitioned for compassionate leave: "IRA Leaders at Price Funeral," *Irish Press,* February 19, 1975; "Price Sisters Send Wreaths As Mother Is Buried in Belfast," *Irish Times,* February 19, 1975.

191 Four hundred people joined the slow-moving cortege: Ibid.

CHAPTER 15

192 take the children into care: McKendry, *Disappeared,* p. 23.

192 "'til Mummy comes back": Ibid., p. 24.

192 gathered on the concrete balconies, watching silently: Ibid., p. 24.

192 The oldest child, Anne: Interview with Michael McConville.

192 four-story redbrick orphanage: *Report of the Historical Institutional Abuse Inquiry,* vol. 3, chap. 9, module 4: "Sisters of Nazareth, Belfast—Nazareth Lodge" (2017). The McConville children were initially moved to another home before being placed at Nazareth Lodge; for reasons of narrative economy I have had to condense the sequence of housing arrangements during this period.

192 numbly accustomed to institutional living: Ibid.

192 nuns who were legendary for their sadism: "The Nuns Poured Boiling Water on Our Heads," *Belfast News Letter,* May 7, 2016.

193 contrive ways to sneak out and run back to West Belfast: Interview with Michael McConville.

193 "That's lies!": Ibid.

193 to the De La Salle Boys' Home: Ibid.

193 it could have been a hundred miles: Ibid.

193 a school, a swimming pool, tennis courts, and a football pitch: HIA transcript; HIA witness statement.

193 even had a billiard table: *Report of the Historical Institutional Abuse Inquiry,* vol. 4, chap. 11, module 3: "De La Salle Boys Home, Rubane House."

193 "a pure nightmare": HIA transcript.

193 pummeled with fists, strapped with belts: *Report of the Historical Institutional Abuse Inquiry*: Rubane; HIA transcript; HIA witness statement.

193 There were older children there: HIA witness statement.

194 the kids walked around in garments that did not fit: *Report of the Historical Institutional Abuse Inquiry*: Rubane.

194 the staff would hire them out to neighboring farms: HIA witness statement. Some former staff members from Rubane House have contested this claim.

194 in the darkened TV room: *Report of the Historical Institutional Abuse Inquiry*: Rubane.

194 Sexual abuse was rampant: Ibid.

194 plucked sleeping boys from their beds: Interview with Michael McConville.

194 Michael and Tucker ran away: Ibid.

194 took their shoes away: HIA witness statement; "Sons Recall 30 Years of Painful Memories," *Irish News*, October 24, 2003.

194 Billy and Jim, were reassigned: HIA transcript.

195 "were in it together": HIA witness statement. Several of the McConville children offered testimony to the HIA. The transcripts of this testimony have been publicly released, but the individual names have been redacted, in order to preserve their anonymity. While I have honored that convention here, the testimony itself was a valuable resource in understanding conditions at the home. Billy McConville is now dead, but when he offered his testimony, he chose to waive anonymity. See "Son of Jean McConville Reveals Hell of Being Abused by Notorious Paedophile Priest Brendan Smyth," *Irish Mirror*, November 6, 2014; "I Was Victim of Abuse in Boys' Home, Jean McConville's Son Tells Inquiry," *Belfast Telegraph*, November 7, 2014; "McConville Children Abused in Home Following Murder of Their Mother," *Irish News*, January 21, 2017.

195 (The De La Salle Brothers later admitted): "Sisters of Nazareth Become Second Catholic Order to Admit to Child Abuse," *Guardian*, January 14, 2014.

195 she struck out on her own: McKendry, *Disappeared*, p. 29.

195 She found work at: Ibid., p. 29.

195 They married when she was eighteen: "Jean McConville's Daughter: 'If I Give Up Fighting, They've Won,'" *Guardian*, July 5, 2014; McKendry, *Disappeared*, pp. 2–6.

195 sent this time to a "training" school: Interview with Michael McConville.

195 Known as Lisnevin: *Report of the Historical Institutional Abuse Inquiry*, vol. 5, chap. 15, module 7: "Lisnevin."

195 kids who were too rough or too willful: Ibid.

196 tall perimeter fence, which was electrified: Interview with Michael McConville; *Report of the Historical Institutional Abuse Inquiry*: Lisnevin.

196 He would later joke: Interview with Michael McConville.

196 regular sectarian skirmishes: "Inquiry Told of 'Sectarian Abuse' at Co Down Training School," *Belfast Telegraph*, September 2, 2015.

196 Sister Frances, who looked out for him: Interview with Michael McConville.

196 children never spoke about what had happened: Ibid.

197 Adams had tried, twice, to escape: "Release of Long Kesh Men Cancelled After Car Bombings," *Times* (London), July 27, 1974; Adams, *Before the Dawn*, pp. 230–32.

197 predictable routine of prison life relaxing: Adams, *Before the Dawn*, p. 222.

197 Hughes and Adams shared Cage 11: H-BC.

197 their bond grew tighter: Adams, *Before the Dawn*, p. 242.

197 socks over their hands, like gloves: Ibid., p. 223.

197 prisoners organized lectures and discussion sessions: H-BC.

197 "our barbed wire ivory tower": Adams, *Cage Eleven,* p. 3. Also see Lachlan Whalen, " 'Our Barbed Wire Ivory Tower': The Prison Writings of Gerry Adams," *New Hibernia Review,* vol. 10, no. 2 (Summer 2006), pp. 123–39.

198 Hughes read speeches by Fidel Castro; Adams recited the rosary: H-BC.

198 As the conflict entered its sixth year: "Portrait of a Hunger Striker: Brendan Hughes," *Irish People,* December 6, 1980.

198 "defeat suited them better than victory": Moloney, *Secret History of the IRA,* p. 197.

199 toppling of regimes seemed like something: Ibid., p. 150.

199 they must force change within their own lifetimes: Ibid., p. 197.

199 what would come to be known as the "long war": Ibid., pp. 149–51.

199 Adams also began to subtly modulate: This recollection from Joe Doherty is quoted in a PhD thesis by John F. Morrison, *"The Affirmation of Behan?" An Understanding of the Politicisation Process of the Provisional Irish Republican Movement Through an Organisational Analysis of Splits from 1969 to 1997* (University of St. Andrews, 2010), pp. 184–85.

200 in 1975, he began writing a series: Adams has acknowledged that "Brownie" was his pen name. See Adams, *Cage Eleven,* p. 3.

200 etched in tiny handwriting on cigarette paper: Beresford, *Ten Men Dead,* p. 19.

200 baby-faced propagandist named Danny Morrison: Adams, *Before the Dawn,* p. 247.

200 But Adams also used the columns: H-BC.

200 he paced around the yard: Ibid.

201 But Adams believed that the Provos: Urban, *Big Boys' Rules,* pp. 30–31.

201 Adams gave Hughes a hug before he walked to the gate: H-BC; Adams, *Before the Dawn,* p. 251.

201 that of the two of them, Hughes had the more: H-BC.

201 internment had officially ended: "Cautious Reactions As the Last N.I. Detainees Are Set Free," *Irish Times,* December 6, 1975.

201 paramilitary suspects would be charged: Moloney, *Secret History of the IRA,* p. 177.

202 you got the same uniform: "One Man, One Cell," *Irish Times,* February 26, 1976.

202 In the fall of 1976, the republican prisoners rebelled: Tim Pat Coogan, *On the Blanket: The Inside Story of the IRA Prisoners' "Dirty" Protest* (New York: Palgrave, 2002), pp. 93–94.

202 *"Brand Ireland's fight"*: Francie Brolly, "The H-Block Song."

202 "special category" status: Coogan, *On the Blanket,* p. 93.

202 grinding game of mutual escalation: Beresford, *Ten Men Dead,* p. 17.

202 refusing to leave their cells at all: This phase was known as the "no-wash" protest. English, *Armed Struggle,* p. 191; Beresford, *Ten Men Dead,* p. 27; O'Malley, *Biting at the Grave,* p. 21.

202 blossomed into the "dirty protest": Beresford, *Ten Men Dead,* p. 17; "Rebels Refuse to Use Toilets in Ulster Jail," Reuters, April 25, 1978.

203 *Daub it on the walls*: Taylor, *Behind the Mask*, p. 257.

203 Hughes and his men were naked and filthy: Ibid., p. 258.

203 But even placing a protesting inmate: McKittrick and McVea, *Making Sense of the Troubles*, p. 140.

203 Though Adams was no longer: H-BC.

203 He succeeded in reorganizing: Moloney, *Secret History of the IRA*, pp. 159–60.

204 "We cannot build a republic": "Ballybofey Republican Reunion," *Irish People*, May 10, 1980.

204 In August 1979, Lord Louis Mountbatten: "IRA Bombs Kill Mountbatten and 17 Soldiers," *Guardian*, August 28, 1979.

204 When she was a girl in the East Midlands: Margaret Thatcher, *The Path to Power* (New York: HarperCollins, 1995), pp. 31–32.

204 Her closest adviser on Northern Ireland was Airey Neave: "The Airey Neave File," *Independent*, February 22, 2002.

204 "So, it's like the Sudetenland": This is per the accounts of Sir David Goodall and Michael Lillis in *Thatcher and the IRA: Dealing with Terror*, documentary (BBC, 2014).

205 On March 30, 1979, Airey Neave was driving: "Neave's Assassins Linked with North Political Killings," *Irish Times*, April 2, 1979.

205 after learning the news, a stricken Thatcher: "Commons Car Bomber Assassinates Neave," *Guardian*, March 31, 1979.

205 several hundred men were participating in the dirty protest: "A Look at Ulster's Maze and the 'Men on the Blanket,'" Associated Press, March 16, 1979.

205 "going against your whole socialization": Taylor, *Behind the Mask*, p. 258.

205 As if tensions with the screws were not high enough: Ibid., p. 254.

205 the new secretary of state for Northern Ireland: Ibid., p. 253.

205 "There is no such thing as political murder": Margaret Thatcher speech in Belfast, March 5, 1981.

205 "Crime is crime is crime": Margaret Thatcher remarks at a press conference in Riyadh, April 21, 1981.

205 In the fall of 1980, Brendan Hughes answered: Peter Taylor, who interviewed Hughes extensively, put the number at 170 (Taylor, *Behind the Mask*, p. 270); in his Boston College oral history, Hughes says it was "over ninety."

206 They would be led by Hughes: "Hunger Strike Begins," *Irish People*, November 1, 1980.

206 The prison doctor: H-BC.

206 Because all seven men had embarked: Beresford, *Ten Men Dead*, p. 28.

206 One of the younger strikers: "Don't Let Them Die!" *Irish People*, November 8, 1980.

207 McKenna grew more fearful: "Hunger Striker Fights for Eyesight," *Irish Republican News*, October 20, 2006.

207 McKenna started lapsing: Moloney, *Secret History of the IRA*, p. 206.

207 He saw two priests standing with Dr. Ross: H-BC.

207 Hughes could smell: Ibid.

207 Finally, he shouted, "Feed him!": Ibid.

207 A doctor instructed the orderlies: "Hunger Striker Fights for Eyesight," *Irish Republican News,* October 20, 2006.

207 But he felt deeply ashamed: O'Malley, *Biting at the Grave,* p. 35.

207 This time they would stagger the strikers: H-BC.

CHAPTER 16

208 Prior to the Troubles: Raymond Murray, *Hard Time: Armagh Gaol 1971–1986* (Dublin: Mercier Press, 1998), p. 7.

208 But during the 1970s: Margaretta D'Arcy, *Tell Them Everything* (London: Pluto Press, 1981), p. 11.

208 "a python in a paper bag": "Terror Sisters Flown Out," *Daily Express,* March 19, 1975.

208 WELCOME HOME DOLOURS AND MARIAN: Price, "Brixton, Durham and Armagh Gaol, 1973," in Brady et al., *Footsteps of Anne,* p. 134.

208 "Is it them?": Ibid., p. 135.

208 "like two film stars": Recollection of Geraldine McCann, in Brady et al., *Footsteps of Anne,* p. 48.

209 She was reputed: Recollection of Kathleen McKinney, in Brady et al., *Footsteps of Anne,* p. 142.

209 They would hang back: Recollection of Dolours Price in Brady et al., *Footsteps of Anne,* p. 135.

209 She hadn't tasted: Ibid.

209 In March 1975, they were granted: "Special Status for Sisters Expected," *Irish Times,* March 20, 1975.

209 They were allowed to wear their own clothes: Ibid.

210 The space was set up like a suite: Coogan, *On the Blanket,* pp. 236–37.

210 The head screw: Brady et al., *Footsteps of Anne,* p. 135.

210 Security was much less tight: Ibid.

210 Dolours would paint and write letters: Coogan, *On the Blanket,* p. 236.

210 able to take correspondence courses: Dolours Price to Fenner Brockway, September 29, 1977 (Brockway Papers, Churchill Archives Centre, University of Cambridge).

210 They made handicrafts: Brady et al., *Footsteps of Anne,* p. 144. On such handicrafts, see Máirtín Ó Muilleoir, "The Art of War: A Troubles Archive Essay," Arts Council of Northern Ireland, 2009.

210 Dolours did leatherwork: Brady et al., *Footsteps of Anne,* p. 136.

210 the sight of a "small parcel from N. Ireland": Dolours Price to Fenner Brockway, October 29, 1977 (Brockway Papers).

210 Someone would lead them: Brady et al., *Footsteps of Anne,* p. 216.

210 To Dolours, Armagh jail felt like: Ibid., p. 136.

210 Dolours began to fixate: Ibid.

210 Some of the women: Murray, *Hard Time,* p. 11.

210 "Things started going a bit askew": P-TKT.

210 In February 1978, the IRA: "La Mon Bomb Produced Ball of Fire 60 Feet in Diameter," *Irish Times,* July 26, 1978.

211 "Am I here because I want to incinerate people?": P-TKT.

211 "a freelance republican": Dolours Price, "Bun Fights & Good Salaries," *The Blanket,* March 27, 2007.

211 "Dolours, like her sister Marian": Fenner Brockway to Humphrey Atkins, June 27, 1980 (Brockway Papers).

211 "We didn't ever have a normal relationship": Dolours Price interview in *The Chaplain's Diary,* RTÉ Radio.

212 Several other women in the facility: "Mystery of the Four Who Got Away," *Daily Express,* April 24, 1981.

212 A confidential government assessment: "The Release of Marian Price," memorandum enclosed in a letter from R. A. Harrington, of the Northern Ireland Office, to Michael Alexander, of Downing Street, May 1980 (no exact date specified) (National Archives, Kew).

212 On April 30, 1980, Marian was released from jail: Ibid.

212 A government spokesman said: "Marian Price Set Free," *The Irish Times,* May 1, 1980.

212 On May 1, she checked out of the hospital: "The Release of Marian Price."

212 engineered a velvet prison break: "Mystery of the Four Who Got Away," *Daily Express,* April 24, 1981.

212 "like I'd been separated from my Siamese twin": Dolours Price interview in *The Chaplain's Diary,* RTÉ Radio.

213 But when Sands was seven years old: O'Malley, *Biting at the Grave,* pp. 36–37, 44–45; Beresford, *Ten Men Dead,* pp. 41–42.

213 On March 1, 1981, he stopped eating: O'Malley, *Biting at the Grave,* p. 3.

213 His last morsel: Beresford, *Ten Men Dead,* p. 57.

213 "I am standing on the threshold": Ibid., pp. 62–63.

213 "Faced with the failure of their discredited cause": McKittrick and McVea, *Making Sense of the Troubles,* p. 146.

213 But four days after Sands commenced: Beresford, *Ten Men Dead,* pp. 69–72.

213 If Sands were to win: Ibid., pp. 72–73.

214 This gambit marked: McKearney, *The Provisional IRA,* pp. 149–50.

214 This had been part of the basis: Moloney, *Secret History of the IRA,* p. 198.

214 "when Sinn Féin will be a power": "Sinn Féin Vice-President Gerry Adams," *Irish People,* November 27, 1982.

214 "ballot paper in one hand and an Armalite in the other": Coogan, *The Troubles,* p. 282; Moloney, *Secret History of the IRA,* p. 202.

214 On April 10, 1981, Bobby Sands: "Sands Election a Propaganda Win for Hunger Strike," *Irish Times,* April 11, 1981.

215 On April 25, she spoke with Humphrey Atkins: "Prime Minister's Telephone Conversation with the Secretary of State for Northern Ireland on Saturday Evening, 25 April 1981," Prime Minister's Office Records, National Archives (Kew).

215 But since Marian had left: Dolours Price interview in *The Chaplain's Diary,* RTÉ Radio.

215 she swallowed a dozen sleeping pills: Unsigned letter from the Northern Ireland Office to Fenner Brockway, June 17, 1980 (Brockway Papers).

215 As her thirtieth birthday approached: Dolours Price to Fenner Brockway, dated "20 Somethingth October, 1980" (Brockway Papers).

216 Marian Price had visited Dolours: M. W. Hopkins (Northern Ireland Office) letter to Michael Alexander (10 Downing Street), November 2, 1980 (National Archives, Kew).

216 When she prepared to leave: Dolours Price to Fenner Brockway, dated "20 Somethingth October, 1980" (Brockway Papers).

216 "I will have served eight years in March": Ibid.

216 "become convinced that violence is wrong": Fenner Brockway to Margaret Thatcher, October 25, 1980 (Brockway Papers).

216 Brockway may have been a bit: Margaret Thatcher to Fenner Brockway, November 11, 1980 (Brockway Papers).

217 "That itself must be disturbing for a twin": Margaret Thatcher handwriting on Fenner Brockway letter to Margaret Thatcher, October 25, 1980 (Brockway Papers).

217 "counteracted the effects of the disease": Coogan, *On the Blanket,* pp. 236–37.

217 On April 3, 1981: Tomás Ó Fiaich to Margaret Thatcher, April 3, 1981 (National Archives, Kew).

217 "Miss Price's condition will continue to be very closely watched": Margaret Thatcher to Tomás Ó Fiaich, April 13, 1981 (National Archives, Kew).

217 In mid-April, Price was rushed: M. W. Hopkins to Michael Alexander, April 10, 1981 (National Archives, Kew).

218 Street fights were raging: "Worst Violence in Eight Nights Hits Northern Ireland," Associated Press, April 23, 1981.

218 Every day, people in the hospital: Dolours Price, "Post Traumatic Stress Syndrome," *The Blanket,* June 29, 2006.

218 On May 5, 1981, Bobby Sands died: O'Malley, *Biting at the Grave,* p. 3.

218 "a greater international impact than": Adams, *Before the Dawn,* p. 297.

218 One hundred thousand people: Beresford, *Ten Men Dead,* p. 103.

218 "It was a choice his organization": Taylor, *Behind the Mask,* p. 283; McKittrick and McVea, *Making Sense of the Troubles,* p. 144.

218 But while the world focused: "Price Release Sparks Protest," *Irish Times,* April 23, 1981.

218 For years afterward, Price: Dolours Price, "Post Traumatic Stress Syndrome," *The Blanket,* June 29, 2006.

219 After Sands died, another nine followed: O'Malley, *Biting at the Grave,* p. 64.

219 "Once the British Medical Council refused to 'force-feed'": Dolours Price, "Post-Traumatic Stress Syndrome," *The Blanket,* June 29, 2006.

219 World Medical Association had issued: Steven H. Miles and Alfred M. Freedman, "Medical Ethics and Torture: Revisiting the Declaration of Tokyo," *The Lancet,* vol. 373, no. 9660 (January 2009).

219 Roy Jenkins announced that hunger strikers: For a close examination of the dynamics that prompted this shift in policy, see Miller, *A History of Force Feeding,* chap. 7. Also see "Why H-Block Hunger Strikers Were Not Force Fed," *Irish Times*, July 5, 2016.

219 By triumphing in the particular manner: Dolours Price, "Post Traumatic Stress Syndrome," *The Blanket*, June 29, 2006.

CHAPTER 17

220 Ian Paisley... described: "Fury As IRA Terror Girl Goes Free," *Daily Express*, April 23, 1981; " 'She Should Be Left to Rot,' " *Daily Mail*, April 23, 1981.

220 "taken for a sucker": "Price Release Sparks Protest," *Irish Times*, April 23, 1981; "IRA 'Trick' Freed Bomb Girl," *Daily Star*, April 23, 1981.

220 Years later, Dolours would: Dolours Price, "Post Traumatic Stress Syndrome," *The Blanket*, June 29, 2006.

220 Technically, she was released "on license": M. W. Hopkins (Northern Ireland Office) to Michael Alexander (10 Downing Street), July 31, 1981 (National Archives, Kew).

220 But several months after her release: Clive Whitmore, principal private secretary, Downing Street, to M. W. Hopkins, Northern Ireland Office, August 3, 1981 (National Archives, Kew).

221 she published a story: Dolours Price, "Mind Over Matter Can Lead to Death," *Irish Press*, December 6, 1982.

221 Reports from this surveillance: Derek Hill (Northern Ireland Office) to William Rickett (Downing Street), February 2, 1983 (National Archives, Kew).

221 In fact, one intelligence report: "Dolours Price/Rea," memo marked "Secret," prepared by M. W. Hopkins, October 24, 1984 (National Archives, Kew).

221 working on a book about her experience in Brixton: "The Saturday Column," *Irish Times*, November 20, 1982.

222 But she managed to publish an excerpt: Interview with Eamonn McCann; Price, "Afraid of the Dark," *Krino* no. 3 (Spring 1987), p. 10.

222 Price reconnected with Stephen Rea: "The Trying Game," *Times* (London), June 5, 1993.

222 He would avert his eyes: "Wolf Wistful; Janet Watts Meets Stephen Rea," *Guardian*, February 3, 1977.

222 Rea had grown up: "Fame, Family & Field Day," *Belfast Telegraph*, December 6, 2006.

223 "I grew up in a mixed area": "Stephen Rea: 'I Never Wanted to Be a Polite Actor,' " *Telegraph*, March 25, 2016.

223 In a children's production: "Wolf Wistful; Janet Watts Meets Stephen Rea," *Guardian*, February 3, 1977.

223 He loved the city but felt: Ibid.

223 After half a century of repression: "The Trying Game," *Times* (London), June 5, 1993.

223 Rea ended up living in West Belfast: Ronan Bennett, "Don't Mention the War: Culture in Northern Ireland," in *Rethinking Northern Ireland*, ed. David Miller (New York: Addison Wesley Longman, 1998), p. 210.

223 "Ireland squanders talent": "Wolf Wistful; Janet Watts Meets Stephen Rea," *Guardian,* February 3, 1977.

223 Rea was becoming: "Stephen Rea: 'I Never Wanted to Be a Polite Actor,'" *Telegraph,* March 25, 2016.

223 During those years, Rea faced: Bennett, "Don't Mention the War: Culture in Northern Ireland," in *Rethinking Northern Ireland,* p. 210.

223 As a gifted mimic: "Fame, Family & Field Day," *Belfast Telegraph,* June 12, 2006.

224 "triumphant in terms of the language": "The Trying Game," *Times* (London), June 5, 1993.

224 For the ceremony, they chose St. Patrick's Cathedral: Interview with Raymond Murray.

224 Mindful, perhaps, of the spectacle: "Dolours Price Marries Actor," *Irish Times,* November 5, 1983; "Dolours Price Weds in Secret," *Belfast Telegraph,* November 4, 1983.

224 When an English tabloid: "Secret Wedding for Actor and Car Bomb Girl," *Daily Mail,* November 5, 1983.

224 Rea had also reconnected: Carole Zucker, *In the Company of Actors: Reflections on the Craft of Acting* (New York: Routledge, 2001), pp. 110–11.

224 On opening night, scaffolding: Marilynn J. Richtarik, *Acting between the Lines: The Field Day Theatre Company and Irish Cultural Politics 1980–1984* (Washington, D.C.: Catholic University of America Press, 2001), p. 23.

225 Friel and Rea decided: Brian Friel, *Brian Friel in Conversation,* ed. Paul Delaney (Ann Arbor: University of Michigan Press, 2000), p. 127; Zucker, *In the Company of Actors,* pp. 110–11.

225 The company came to include: Richtarik, *Acting between the Lines,* p. 65.

225 "cultural wing of the Provos": Bennett, "Don't Mention the War: Culture in Northern Ireland," in *Rethinking Northern Ireland,* p. 207.

225 "political action in the widest sense": "Stephen Rea's Tribute to Brian Friel: A Shy Man and a Showman," *Irish Times,* October 2, 2015.

225 Part of the idea for the company: "Working Both Ends of the Terrorist's Gun," *Newsweek,* February 7, 1993.

225 But there was not a unionist among them: Richtarik, *Acting between the Lines,* pp. 66, 74.

225 And, having joined the circus: "Two Vehicles Carry an Irish Actor to America," *New York Times,* November 22, 1992.

225 Price helped manage the books: Dolours Price to Julie (no last name specified), May 16, 1986 (Papers of the Field Day Theatre Company, National Library of Ireland).

225 They crisscrossed the island: Zucker, *In the Company of Actors,* p. 111.

225 In some rural areas: This is an anecdote that Rea related in *The Story of Field Day,* documentary, produced by Johnny Muir (BBC Northern Ireland, 2006).

225 In England, a rumor circulated: "How Can They Let Back the Girl Bomber Who Ruined My Husband's Life?" *Daily Express,* December 2, 1983.

226 The British tabloids sounded the alarm: Ibid.

226 Price did not make the trip, in the end: Jonathan Duke-Evans (Northern Ireland Office) to Tim Flesher (10 Downing Street), August 30, 1985 (National Archives, Kew).

226 She was careful to mail: Derek Hill (Northern Ireland Office) to Tim Flesher (10 Downing Street), March 17, 1983 (National Archives, Kew).

226 "I think we are just being played along here": She handwrote this on Derek Hill's March 17, 1983, letter to Tim Flesher; Thatcher's position is also summarized in a March 21, 1983, letter from Flesher to Hill (National Archives, Kew).

226 In May 1985, a police officer in Folkestone: Jonathan Duke-Evans (Northern Ireland Office) to Tim Flesher, August 30, 1985 (National Archives, Kew).

226 The couple had taken up residence: Dolours Price to Julie (no last name specified), May 16, 1986 (Papers of the Field Day Theatre Company, National Library of Ireland).

226 After the incident in Folkestone: Jonathan Duke-Evans to Tim Flesher, August 30, 1985 (National Archive, Kew).

226 In November, an aide wrote: Neil Ward to Margaret Thatcher, November 5, 1985 (National Archive, Kew).

227 A report by Special Branch: Jonathan Duke-Evans to Tim Flesher, August 30, 1985 (National Archive, Kew).

227 In fact, she would rather: Charles Powell (Downing Street) to Jim Daniell (Northern Ireland Office), November 6, 1985 (National Archive, Kew).

227 Some civil servants worried: Neil Ward to Charles Powell, December 16, 1985 (National Archive, Kew).

227 In a prim flourish of willful disassociation: Margaret Thatcher handwriting on letter from Jonathan Duke-Evans to Tim Flesher, August 30, 1985 (National Archive, Kew).

227 Gleeful write-ups described: "High Life for IRA Bomber," *Times* (London), August 28, 1988.

227 "It is a sensitive matter": "IRA Bomber Avoids Royal Theater Date," *Telegraph,* February 3, 1987.

227 Rea would later remark: "Price Husband's TV Role," *Evening Herald,* March 18, 1986.

227 "The people in my profession": "Stephen Rea: 'I Never Wanted to Be a Polite Actor,'" *Telegraph,* March 25, 2016.

228 Nevertheless, he was obliged: "The Trying Game," *Times* (London), June 5, 1993.

228 *Never, ever mention the missus*: "Even Better Than the Rea Thing," *Irish Independent,* February 18, 2000.

228 "What I bring is an understanding": "Patriot Games," *People,* February 8, 1993.

228 On the rare occasion: "The Trying Game," *Times* (London), June 5, 1993.

228 "I could never be a soldier": "History Boys on the Rampage," *Arena* (BBC, 1988).

229 She canvassed for a Sinn Féin candidate: Jonathan Duke-Evans to Tim Flesher, August 30, 1985 (National Archive, Kew).

229 Adams trimmed his hair: Moloney, *Secret History of the IRA,* p. 188.

229 "Vote Gerry Adams!": Dolours Price, "Get On with It," *The Blanket,* September 14, 2004.

CHAPTER 18

230 On March 6, Mairéad Farrell was shot: In 1995, the European Court of Human Rights ruled that the soldiers had not been operating under a "shoot to kill" policy, but that the three IRA members did not pose the sort of immediate risk that would have necessitated shooting them and that they could have been arrested instead. For more on Farrell's life and death, see "Death of a Terrorist," *Frontline* (PBS, 1989); "Priest, Writing Eulogy, Recalls Woman in IRA," *New York Times,* March 16, 1988; McKittrick et al., *Lost Lives,* pp. 1112–15.

230 But before they had a chance to carry out: See *McCann and Others v. The United Kingdom,* application no. 18984/91, European Court of Human Rights (1995).

230 He had grown up in Tipperary: Martin McKeever, *One Man, One God: The Peace Ministry of Fr Alec Reid C.Ss.R.* (Dublin: Redemptorist Communications, 2017), p. 1.

230 Reid moved to Belfast before: McKeever, *One Man, One God,* p. 17.

231 The founder of the monastery: John Conroy, *Belfast Diary: War As a Way of Life* (Boston: Beacon Press, 1995), pp. 1–2.

231 a priest "on the streets": "Priest Tried to Revive Dying British Soldier," *South China Morning Post,* March 22, 1988.

231 "In for a penny, in for a pound": McKeever, *One Man, One God,* p. 21.

231 Reid possessed an unerring faith: *14 Days,* documentary (BBC, 2013).

231 Adams, who lived near Clonard, had grown up: Adams, *Before the Dawn,* p. 33.

231 "Behind the Scenes": H-BC.

231 clutching a cigarette: *14 Days.*

231 He had no particular party: Ibid.

232 "You meet God in the midst of the Troubles": Ibid.

232 Evidently, the authorities: Archival footage of the funeral.

232 Having been elected to Westminster: "Belfast Candidate Wins Parliament Seat for IRA," Reuters, June 11, 1983.

232 Reaching into his jacket: "3 Killed by Grenades at IRA Funeral," *New York Times,* March 17, 1988.

232 Reid thought immediately: "Gunfire, Grenades Kill 3 at IRA Funeral," *Chicago Tribune,* March 17, 1988.

232 Reid heard the sharp crack: This account draws on, among other sources, McKittrick et al., *Lost Lives,* pp. 1117–20.

233 Adams seized a megaphone: Archival footage.

233 A slow-motion chase ensued: Archival footage; "3 Killed by Grenades at IRA Funeral," *New York Times,* March 17, 1988; "Gunfire, Grenades Kill 3 at IRA Funeral," *Chicago Tribune,* March 17, 1988.

233 Michael Stone, an East Belfast loyalist: Martin Dillon, *Stone Cold: The True Story of Michael Stone and the Milltown Massacre* (London: Random House, 1992), p. 151.

233 Stone did not succeed in hitting Adams: McKittrick et al., *Lost Lives,* p. 1117.

233 And so a second giant funeral was arranged: Much of this account is drawn from *14 Days*.

233 Adams had darkly suggested: Dillon, *Stone Cold*, p. 169.

233 The following Saturday, Father Reid: McKeever, *One Man, One God*, p. 33. (Brady's name is sometimes rendered in the Irish spelling: Caoimhín Mac Brádaigh.)

233 Brady had been a cabdriver: McKeever, *One Man, One God*, p. 34; McKittrick et al., *Lost Lives*, p. 1120.

233 The victims would be buried in the same ground: *14 Days*.

234 Father Reid walked out: McKeever, *One Man, One God*, p. 34.

234 But just as Reid was: Ibid., p. 34.

234 The vehicle accelerated out of nowhere: Archival footage; McKittrick et al., *Lost Lives*, p. 1121.

234 As hundreds of mourners swarmed: A photograph clearly captures one of the soldiers with a gun in his hand. *14 Days*.

234 "It's the peelers!": "From Irish Pulpit, Sense of Revulsion," *New York Times*, March 21, 1988.

234 One of the men had indeed: McKeever, *One Man, One God*, p. 34.

234 But even as the mob: Archival footage. It was Wood who fired into the air. McKittrick et al., *Lost Lives*, p. 1121.

234 They were soldiers: "Murdered Soldiers 'Defied Orders,'" *Guardian*, March 21, 1988. Rumors persist in Belfast that the soldiers may not have simply happened onto the funeral by mistake but had been engaged in some sort of covert surveillance.

234 they were hemmed: Ibid.

234 Somebody arrived with a lug wrench: McKeever, *One Man, One God*, p. 34.

234 Reid saw the men getting: *14 Days*; McKeever, *One Man, One God*, p. 34.

234 There was a madness in the air: *14 Days*.

235 Scrambling down onto the ground: "Father Alec Reid Reveals How He Tried to Save Two British Soldiers Killed in One of the Most Shocking Episodes of the Troubles," *Independent*, March 10, 2013.

235 "Would somebody get an ambulance!": McKeever, *One Man, One God*, p. 34.

235 But a voice above him growled: "Father Alec Reid Reveals How He Tried to Save Two British Soldiers Killed in One of the Most Shocking Episodes of the Troubles," *Independent*, March 10, 2013.

235 The soldiers were thrown: McKittrick et al., *Lost Lives*, p. 1121. McKeever, *One Man, One God*, p. 34.

235 Reid was running: McKeever, *One Man, One God*, p. 35.

235 David Howes was twenty-three: McKittrick et al., *Lost Lives*, p. 1124.

235 Derek Wood, who was twenty-four: Ibid., p. 1121; "Murdered Soldiers 'Defied Orders,'" *Guardian*, March 21, 1988.

235 The two men were left there: *14 Days*.

235 "Father, that man is dead": Ibid.

235 Reid looks directly at the camera: The photographer was David Cairns. "Father Alec Reid Reveals How He Tried to Save Two British Soldiers Killed in One of the Most Shocking Episodes of the Troubles," *Independent*, March 10, 2013.

236 "People have had enough": "Priest Tried to Revive Dying British Soldier," *South China Morning Post*, March 22, 1988.

236 "Physical force is a sign of the desperation of the poor": Ibid.

237 Before he left the requiem Mass: "Father Alec Reid Reveals How He Tried to Save Two British Soldiers Killed in One of the Most Shocking Episodes of the Troubles," *Independent*, March 10, 2013; "Fr Alec Reid Death," *Belfast Telegraph*, November 23, 2013.

237 For years, he had tried: McKeever, *One Man, One God*, pp. 21–23.

237 had come to believe that the surest: *14 Days*. Also see Moloney, *Secret History of the IRA*, pp. 232–33.

237 "pushing an open door": McKeever, *One Man, One God*, p. 31.

237 But to Brendan Hughes: H-BC.

237 Only the Church had the status: McKeever, *One Man, One God*, p. 28.

237 The one conceivable scenario: Ibid., p. 30.

237 "They bomb factories": Paul Routledge, *John Hume* (London: HarperCollins, 1997), p. 217.

238 "Sinn Féin will disappear up their own contradiction": Ibid., p. 211.

238 Six months after Hume made these remarks: McKeever, *One Man, One God*, pp. 31–32.

238 At the time Reid sent his letter: Ibid., p. 33. There had been discussions about the possibility of talks before this, but they had foundered. See Adams, *A Farther Shore*, pp. 44–45.

238 Hume had always said: Routledge, *John Hume*, p. 216.

238 In the fall of 1987, the IRA: "Bombing in Ulster Kills 11 in Crowd; IRA Is Suspected," *New York Times*, November 9, 1987.

238 Adams apologized for the attack: "Making the Words Flow Like Blood," *Times* (London), November 12, 1987.

238 "an act of sheer savagery": Routledge, *John Hume*, p. 216.

239 It could be hazardous: "Firebomb Attack on Home of John Hume," *Irish Times*, May 9, 1987.

239 Nevertheless, on January 11, 1988: George Drower, *John Hume: Man of Peace* (London: Victor Gollancz, 1996), p. 133.

239 They had spoken: According to Adams, the first meeting took place in 1986. Adams, *A Farther Shore*, p. 45.

239 It would be politically dangerous: Routledge, *John Hume*, p. 214.

239 Hume experienced the same dissonance: John Hume, *A New Ireland: Politics, Peace, and Reconciliation* (Boulder, Colo.: Roberts Rinehart, 1996), p. 115.

239 In claustrophobic Belfast: McKeever, *One Man, One God*, p. 33.

240 As Reid ministered to the men: Ibid., p. 35.

240 Reid returned to Clonard Monastery: *14 Days*.

240 Adams had no intention: "Belfast Candidate Wins Parliament Seat for IRA," Reuters, June 11, 1983.

240 "I am not a member of the IRA": "Making the Words Flow Like Blood," *Times* (London), November 12, 1987.

241 Mac Stíofáin growled, "All of them": *Behind the Mask.*

241 The media, dating back: See, for instance, "Gerry Adams Is Held by Troops," *Belfast Telegraph,* July 19, 1973; "Sinn Féin Leader to See Minister," *Times* (London), November 6, 1982; "In the Shadow of Violence," *Times* (London), May 28, 1983.

241 Adams defended the morality: "I Am an IRA Volunteer," *Republican News,* May 1, 1976.

241 A few years after writing: "Sinn Féin Boss Denies IRA Control," Reuters, December 14, 1982; "IRA Tries New Mix—Violence, Politics," *Los Angeles Times,* December 18, 1982.

241 Opponents joked: "Making the Words Flow Like Blood," *Times* (London), November 12, 1987.

242 Yet the walls outside the headquarters: "IRA Politicians Shift Tactics for Election," Associated Press, May 23, 1983.

242 Such contradictions may simply: "The Case Against Gerry Adams," *Irish People,* September 23, 1978.

242 But he fought the charges: "Sinn Féin Not the Same As IRA, Says Court," *Guardian,* September 7, 1978.

242 "an enigmatic role to play": "Sinn Féin Vice-President Gerry Adams," *Irish People,* November 27, 1982.

243 "The presence of the gun in Irish politics": Ibid.

243 "Brian'll phone them": "Junior Executive Types Canvass with Adams," *Irish Times,* June 7, 1983.

243 He published a book of gauzy: Gerry Adams, *Falls Memories: A Belfast Life.*

243 He appointed a press aide: "IRA Politicians Shift Tactics for Election," Associated Press, May 23, 1983.

243 Sinn Féin began to open: "A Gunman Cleans Up His Act," *Observer,* April 17, 1983.

244 Instead, McGuinness continued: Ibid.

244 Some nationalists from the SDLP: Ibid.

244 In his first address: "Terrorism Continues As Sinn Féin Heads for Wider Role in Politics," *Times* (London), November 14, 1983.

244 Just before Christmas in 1983: "Thatcher Moves to Silence Men Behind the IRA," *Times* (London), December 23, 1983.

244 "had not gone right": "Adams Denies Rift in Republican Ranks," *Times* (London), December 20, 1983.

244 The following October, a volunteer placed: "Bomb Ours, Says IRA," *Guardian,* October 13, 1984. For a fascinating fictional exploration of this event, see Jonathan Lee's novel *High Dive* (New York: Knopf, 2016).

245 "Today we were unlucky, but remember": McKittrick and McVea, *Making Sense of the Troubles,* p. 162.

245 "a blow *for* democracy": "Sinn Féin 'Fears Murder Plot,'" *Times* (London), November 5, 1984.

245 "I don't like to hand myself to them on a plate": "Thatcher and the IRA: Dealing with Terror."

245 After an arrest in 1983: "Adams Arrested," *Irish Times,* June 9, 1983.

245 The MP for West Belfast: "Gunmen Wound Sinn Féin Leader," *Boston Globe,* March 15, 1984; "Adams Shot Three Times after Court Appearance," *Irish Times,* March 15, 1984.

245 After years on the run, Adams tended: "Gerry Adams Is Shot 3 Times in Street Attack," *Times* (London), March 15, 1984.

245 He had grown so fearful: "Gunmen Wound Sinn Féin Leader," *Boston Globe,* March 15, 1984.

245 Adams had taken to predicting: "Gerry Adams Is Shot 3 Times in Street Attack," *Times* (London), March 15, 1984.

245 Two gunmen fired a dozen shots: "Gunmen Wound Sinn Féin Leader," *Boston Globe,* March 15, 1984; "Adams Shot Three Times after Court Appearance," *Irish Times,* March 15, 1984; "Public Statement by the Police Ombudsman Under Section 62 of the Police (Northern Ireland) Act 1998: Relating to the Complaints in Respect of the Attempted Murder of Mr. Gerry Adams on 14 March 1984," Police Ombudsman for Northern Ireland (2014).

246 "I have followed too many coffins": "Gunmen Wound Sinn Féin Leader," *Boston Globe,* March 15, 1984.

246 But from his bed at Royal Victoria Hospital: "Adams Says Army Knew of 'Loyalist' Attack Plan," *Times* (London), March 16, 1984.

246 They greeted the news: "An Everyday Story of Ulster Folk," *Times* (London), March 16, 1984.

CHAPTER 19

247 When Brendan Hughes was finally released: H-BC.

247 "I called her to the jail": "Decommissioned Provos Thrown on Scrap Heap," *Sunday Tribune,* April 16, 2006.

247 Sometimes Hughes would go for a walk: Ibid.

247 There were places: H-BC.

248 This way, Adams could keep repeating: "Hughes No Longer Toes the Provo Line," *Sunday Tribune,* December 17, 2000.

249 Hughes traveled to New York City: Interview with Martin Galvin.

249 "Shoot postmen?": H-BC.

249 "I don't want your fucking money!": Ibid.

250 When Twomey died: Ibid.

250 A few days after New Year's in 1989: Birth announcement for Fintan Daniel Sugar Rea, Papers of the Field Day Theatre Company, National Library of Ireland.

250 Just over a year later: "'Game' Player," *Entertainment Weekly,* December 11, 1992.

250 "Know any babysitters?": Dolours Price to Colette Nellis, May 30, 1990, Papers of the Field Day Theatre Company, National Library of Ireland; Oscar

Rea birth announcement, Papers of the Field Day Theatre Company, National Library of Ireland.

250 "cracked about them": "Patriot Games," *People,* February 8, 1993.

250 Seamus Heaney composed: "Seamus Heaney Loved Dirty Jokes? Tell Us Another One," *Irish Times,* February 23, 2017.

251 "I'd find it kind of phony": "Two Vehicles Carry an Irish Actor to America," *New York Times,* November 22, 1992.

251 "It's never the right time to publish": "The Trying Game," *Times* (London), June 5, 1993.

251 What this meant in practice: On the broadcasting ban in general, see Ed Moloney, "Closing Down the Airwaves: The Story of the Broadcasting Ban," in *The Media and Northern Ireland: Covering the Troubles,* ed. Jim Smith (London: Macmillan, 1991).

251 "There was nothing to stop us": "Fury Over TV Dirty Trick," *Daily Mail,* April 10, 1990.

252 "The problems will never be solved": "Why I Spoke for Gerry Adams," *Independent,* November 4, 1993.

252 One of the characters: "How We Made The Crying Game," *Guardian,* February 21, 2017.

253 "Redemption through suffering": "Two Vehicles Carry an Irish Actor to America," *New York Times,* November 22, 1992.

253 "You mustn't assume that my politics": "The Trying Game," *Times* (London), June 5, 1993.

253 "That's a political statement": "'Game' Player," *Entertainment Weekly,* December 11, 1992.

253 In December 1992, Rea and Price: "Patriot Games," *People,* February 8, 1993.

253 "She would have been ideally suited": Interview with Carrie Twomey.

253 To Rea, it was a story: "Patriot Games," *People,* February 8, 1993.

253 There were ordinary, decent people: Ibid.

253 "I've had enough": "A Man Who Laughs at His Demons," *Irish Times,* February 20, 1993.

254 In August 1994, the IRA: Dolours Price, "Rummaging," *The Blanket,* July 9, 2004.

254 "Whatever soul searchings": Padraic Pearse, "Why We Want Recruits," in *The Collected Works of Padraic H. Pearse: Political Writings and Speeches* (Dublin: Éire-Gael Society, 2013), p. 66.

254 The one major concession: Ibid., p. 173.

255 As one former IRA volunteer: McKearney, *The Provisional IRA,* p. 179.

255 "In return for ending the armed insurrection": Ibid., p. 176.

255 One day the following summer: "IRA Victims Campaign Stepped Up," *Irish Times,* June 27, 1995.

255 "Four women and eight men came into our home": Ibid.

255 Helen was thirty-seven: In 1998, Helen became a grandmother, at 40. "Family's Plea to IRA over Fate of Mother," *Guardian,* May 13, 1998.

255 At one point, an opportunity had emerged: "IRA Embarrassed by Family's 'Secret Burial' Campaign," *Guardian,* August 30, 1995.

255 If childhood had been difficult: Interview with Michael McConville.

255 served a prison sentence in England: "Woman Beaten As She Intervened in Loyalist Attack on Belfast Home," *The Irish Times,* June 19, 1995.

256 But Michael and Helen had clashed: Interview with Michael McConville.

256 In 1992, Jean McConville's oldest child: Death certificate for Anne McConville. She was born November 28, 1952, and died September 29, 1992.

256 Helen peered into the coffin: "Jean McConville's Daughter: 'If I Give Up Fighting, They've Won,'" *Observer,* July 6, 2014.

256 An old fellow slipped McKendry a bookie's docket: "An IRA Death Squad Took Our Mother. There'll Be No Peace for Us until We Find Her Body," *Daily Express,* July 23, 1998.

256 He was twenty-two: "Secret Graves of the Missing Ones," *Sunday Tribune,* July 5, 1998.

256 Over the years, there were rumors: Ibid.

256 McKinney was left with a nagging: "IRA Victims Campaign Stepped Up," *Irish Times,* June 27, 1995.

256 After years of frightened silence: "Secret Graves of the Missing Ones," *Sunday Tribune,* July 5, 1998.

256 "I could accept now": "Five Men Quizzed on 'Disappeared,'" *Belfast Telegraph,* January 24, 1996.

256 For years, she had refused: "Secret Graves of the Missing Ones," *Sunday Tribune,* July 5, 1998.

257 Had he suffered: "Kevin and the Pain That Has Never Disappeared," *Belfast Telegraph,* August 30, 2013.

257 Reid would hear things sometimes: "Grim Reunion for Family As Dig for Body Begins," *Telegraph,* May 31, 1999.

257 At one point, a rumor: "Kin of Missing Appeal to IRA," *Boston Globe,* August 28, 1995.

257 In hopes of raising awareness: "Clinton and Mandela Get Grief Symbol," *Belfast Telegraph,* June 26, 1995.

257 When the McConvilles and other families: "The Disappeared: And That's Not in Latin America We're Discussing, It's Mainland Britain," *Daily Mail,* May 11, 1995.

257 mothers of the disappeared: "Ireland Calling: The Disappeared Reappear," *Irish Voice,* June 15, 1999.

258 "We have a simple message": "Families of Vanished Victims Open Campaign," *Belfast News Letter,* June 26, 1995.

258 McKendry had visited the Sinn Féin: "IRA Embarrassed by Family's 'Secret Burial' Campaign," *Guardian,* August 30, 1995.

258 "Gerry, are you trying to make an idiot of my wife?": Ibid.

258 At the end of the summer in 1995: "Adams Called On to Pressurize IRA over Graves of 'Disappeared,'" *Irish Times,* August 16, 1995.

CHAPTER 20

263 He had granted a visa to Gerry Adams: "U.S. Shifts, Grants Visa to President of IRA's Political Wing," *Washington Post,* January 31, 1994.

263 Clinton took to the podium: this account is drawn from a video of the event.

263 a passage from a poem: Seamus Heaney, *The Cure at Troy: A Version of Sophocles'* Philoctetes (New York: Farrar, Straus & Giroux, 1991), p. 77.

264 The cease-fire would eventually end: "IRA Smash Ceasefire," *Guardian,* February 10, 1996.

264 For a week in April 1998, negotiators holed up: "The Long Good Friday," *Observer,* April 11, 1998.

264 The chief negotiator was an American: See George Mitchell, *Making Peace* (Los Angeles: University of California Press, 2000).

264 "the tenacity of a fanatic": The observer was the novelist Colum McCann. "Ireland's Troubled Peace," *New York Times,* May 15, 2014.

264 Outside, as flurries of sleet battered: "The Long Good Friday," *Observer,* April 11, 1998.

265 "I don't know what the real deal is": Memorandum of a telephone conversation between Bill Clinton and Tony Blair, June 10, 1999, Clinton Digital Library.

265 But the fiction that Adams had never been a paramilitary: One of the British negotiators, Jonathan Powell, pointed out, "The IRA was a proscribed organisation and we could not talk to its leaders as such. Of course we knew the people we were talking to as Sinn Féin leaders were also leaders of the IRA." Jonathan Powell, *Great Hatred, Little Room: Making Peace in Northern Ireland* (London: Vintage, 2009), p. 24.

265 "An Ireland in which the guns are silent": "Hope and History Rhyme Once More," *An Phoblacht,* June 25, 1998.

266 Paul Bew was enjoying: Interview with Paul Bew. Documenting the Troubles before the participants started dying appears to have been Paul Bew's idea. When Bew consulted with Ed Moloney, it was Moloney who proposed the specific notion of compiling an oral history. Interview with Ed Moloney; Moloney Massachusetts affidavit.

266 He had been a student: Interview with Ed Moloney.

267 the government used a court order: "Journalist Wins Right to Keep Notes from Police," *Independent,* October 28, 1999.

267 Moloney had grown convinced: Interview with Ed Moloney.

268 proposed something more specific: Ibid.

268 Anyone who violated the credo of silence: "Secrets from Belfast," *Chronicle of Higher Education,* January 26, 2014.

268 He talked about "laying down the tapes": Interview with Paul Bew.

269 At sixteen, he lied about his age: Interview with Anthony McIntyre.

269 After writing a dissertation: "Decommissioned Provos Thrown on Scrap Heap of History," *Sunday Tribune,* April 16, 2006.

269 In 2000, he met a young American woman: Interview with Anthony McIntyre.

270 Bew endorsed the idea of enlisting his former advisee: Interview with Paul Bew.

270 Boston College received a grant of $200,000: "Secrets from Belfast," *Chronicle of Higher Education,* January 26, 2014.

270 (Originally, Moloney had wanted): Interview with Ed Moloney.

270 For the loyalist interviews: Interview with Wilson McArthur.

270 Before they finished dinner at Deanes: "Secrets from Belfast," *Chronicle of Higher Education,* January 26, 2014.

271 After apartheid ended: There is a vast literature on the truth and reconciliation process in South Africa, but I would recommend in particular Antjie Krog, *Country of My Skull: Guilt, Sorrow, and the Limits of Forgiveness in the New South Africa* (New York: Three Rivers Press, 2000).

271 In 2001, Martin McGuinness: "McGuinness Confirms IRA Role," BBC, May 2, 2001.

272 Then he leaned into the microphone: "Adams Warns Ministers IRA Has Not Gone Away," *Independent,* August 14, 1995.

272 "the phenomenology of sectarian violence": "Secrets from Belfast," *Chronicle of Higher Education,* January 26, 2014.

273 Even if the authorities did somehow learn: Interview with Ed Moloney.

273 The author of some notorious crime: Ibid.

273 "the man who in the name of Ireland": Padraic Pearse, "Ghosts," in *The Collected Works of Padraic H. Pearse,* p. 123.

273 This kind of absolutism formed: Interview with Anthony McIntyre.

274 No Sinn Féin official ever: McKearney, *The Provisional IRA,* p. 185.

274 "monopoly over the memory": Ian McBride, "The Truth About the Troubles," in *Remembering the Troubles: Contesting the Recent Past in Northern Ireland,* ed. Jim Smyth (Notre Dame, Ind.: University of Notre Dame Press, 2017), p. 11.

274 He used encrypted email: O'Neill affidavit.

275 O'Neill was an expert on "archival security": Robert K. O'Neill, ed., *Management of Library and Archival Security: From the Outside Looking In* (Binghamton, N.Y.: Haworth Press, 1998), p. 1.

275 It was only in a separate set of documents: Interview with Anthony McIntyre.

CHAPTER 21

276 In 1993, the apartment block: Roy, "Divis Flats," *Iowa Historical Review,* vol. 1, no. 1 (2007).

276 During the 1980s, a so-called demolition committee: "Wrecking Ball Brings Hope to Slum," Associated Press, October 31, 1993.

276 The British Army continued to occupy the roof: The British Army began to move out only in 2005, as part of a "demilitarization" process.

277 "Welcome to my cell": "Hughes No Longer Toes the Provo Line," *Sunday Tribune,* December 17, 2000.

277 "You never really leave prison": "Decommissioned Provos Thrown on Scrap Heap of History," *Sunday Tribune,* April 16, 2006.

277 The apartment was decorated: Ibid.

278 to remind him: Ibid.

278 Lately he had taken to joking, darkly: Ibid.

278 He liked Divis Tower: "Hunger Striker Fights for Eyesight," *Irish Republican News,* October 20, 2006.

278 His doctor told him to stop drinking: "Decommissioned Provos Thrown on Scrap Heap of History," *Sunday Tribune,* April 16, 2006.

278 Mackers still remembered: Interview with Anthony McIntyre.

279 But once they started: Ibid.

279 At one point Hughes joked: H-BC.

279 But above all, Hughes talked: Interview with Anthony McIntyre.

279 He joked that GFA: Brendan Hughes, "The Real Meaning of G.F.A.," *The Blanket,* October 8, 2000.

280 In prison, when the Provos conducted: "Interview with Brendan Hughes," *Fourthwrite* no. 1, Spring 2000.

280 By denying that he had ever played: H-BC.

281 "the Armani suit brigade": Interview with Anthony McIntyre.

281 "Painting murals": "Hunger Striker Fights for Eyesight," *Irish Republican News,* October 20, 2006.

282 "into bad company": "Hughes No Longer Toes the Provo Line," *Sunday Tribune,* December 17, 2000.

282 Hughes felt that this overture: Interview with Anthony McIntyre.

283 His IRA masters punished him by shooting: Interviews with Richard O'Rawe and Anthony McIntyre.

283 According to O'Rawe, the prisoners received: Richard O'Rawe, *Blanketmen: The Untold Story of the H-Block Hunger Strike* (Dublin: New Island, 2005), pp. 176–80.

283 O'Rawe and another negotiator smuggled a message: Ibid., p. 181.

283 But word came back from the outside: Ibid., p. 184.

283 Six more men died before: Ibid., prologue.

284 In terms of republican policy: O'Rawe, *Blanketmen,* p. 253.

284 In prolonging the strike: Interview with Richard O'Rawe.

284 "Guys died here for fucking nothing!": Ibid.

284 "The hunger strike made Sinn Féin's successful": Ed Moloney, introduction to *Afterlives: The Hunger Strike and the Secret Offer That Changed Irish History,* by Richard O'Rawe (Dublin: Lilliput Press, 2010), p. xii.

285 To O'Rawe it seemed: Interview with Richard O'Rawe. For a thorough and nuanced discussion of the merits of O'Rawe's claims and the assertions and counter-assertions of various other figures who were associated with the strike, see O'Doherty, *Gerry Adams,* chapter 14.

285 McKenna had brain damage: "Hughes No Longer Toes the Provo Line," *Sunday Tribune,* December 17, 2000; H-BC.

285 Like McKenna, he bore: "Hunger Striker Fights for Eyesight," *Irish Republican News,* October 20, 2006.

286 "He couldn't commit to either jump": Interview with Carrie Twomey.

286 Hughes recalled Dr. Ross: H-BC.

286 Later, he learned: H-BC. Ed Moloney's book based on the Hughes oral history was the first time that the tragic story of Dr. Ross was publicly reported (see Moloney, *Voices from the Grave,* p. 242), but few other details of this episode are known. I was able to confirm the basic facts with David Nicholl, an English doctor whose father, also a doctor, attended medical school with Ross and with Dr. Hernán Reyes, who visited the prison with the International Committee of the Red Cross in 1986 and spoke with medical staff about the strike.

286 "And to hear people who I would have died for": H-BC.

287 If it was McClure who had day-to-day command: Ibid.; Interview with Anthony McIntyre.

CHAPTER 22

288 Gypo identifies a Dublin: Liam O'Flaherty, *The Informer* (New York: Harcourt, 1980), p. 22.

288 The tout occupies: See Ron Dudai, "Informers and the Transition in Northern Ireland," *British Journal of Criminology,* vol. 52, no. 1 (January 2012).

288 Gerry Adams once remarked: "Adams Offers 'Regret' As Digging Resumes," BBC, May 31, 1999.

288 the English have employed spies: Ed Moloney and Anthony McIntyre, "The Security Department: IRA Defensive Counterintelligence in a 30-Year War Against the British" (unpublished paper, April 2006).

288 Campbell's specialty: Unless otherwise noted, material relating to Trevor Campbell is derived from two interviews with Campbell.

290 rough questioning and torture: "Inside Castlereagh: 'We Got Confessions by Torture,'" *Guardian,* October 11, 2010.

293 (Roy McShane, who served): "The Leader, His Driver, and the Driver's Handler: Chauffeur Revealed As MI5 Agent," *Guardian,* February 9, 2008.

294 This cadre of inquisitors: Interview with Gerard Hodgins; "The Hunter and His Prey," *Spotlight* (BBC Northern Ireland, 2015).

294 For decades, the most fearsome: "How, and Why, Did Scappaticci Survive the IRA's Wrath?" *Irish Times,* April 15, 2017.

294 Along with a man named John: Eamon Collins, *Killing Rage* (London: Granta, 1997), chapter 18.

294 His method seldom varied: "Double Blind," *The Atlantic,* April 2006.

294 "Every army attracts psychopaths": H-BC.

294 The signs of Scap's handiwork: "Accused IRA Man Denies Being Agent for Security Services," *Independent,* May 14, 2003.

294 After the bodies surfaced: "The Hunter and His Prey," *Spotlight.*

295 Martin McGuinness had been coming: "A Path Paved with Blood: The Family of IRA Victim Frank Hegarty Insist That Martin McGuinness Lured Him to His Death," *Daily Mail,* September 25, 2011.

295 (In 2011, McGuinness): "McGuinness Denies Involvement in 1986 Killing," *Irish Times,* September 30, 2011.

295 ("Death, certainly"): The original interview was in "The Long War," from the BBC series *Panorama* (1988). Subsequently declassified files from the Republic of Ireland lend support to the suggestion that McGuinness was involved. See "Martin McGuinness Set Up Meeting Where Suspected IRA Informer Frank Hegarty Was Killed, Bishop Claimed," *Irish News,* December 29, 2017.

295 "If you confess, you're dead": Interview with Trevor Campbell.

296 "the disappearance of people": Interview with Anthony McIntyre.

297 Bell was a hard-liner: Moloney, *Secret History of the IRA*, pp. 113–15.

297 "There was only one man": H-BC.

298 They had found each other: Interview with Anthony McIntyre.

298 She was living in Dublin: "Cast in the Middle of the Long Conflict in Northern Ireland," *New York Times*, February 15, 1998.

298 their Belfast accents: Father Raymond Murray, funeral oration for Dolours Price.

298 Her marriage: "Stephen Rea Breaks Up with Bomber," *Irish Independent*, July 13, 2003.

298 There, she surrounded herself: Interview with Anthony McIntyre; contemporary photos of Price.

298 She would invite a guest: Interview with Tara Keenan-Thomson.

298 a law course at Trinity: Dolours Price, "Don't Be Afraid, Do Not Be Fooled," *The Blanket*, January 16, 2007.

298 "You'd know you had never been to prison!": "Woman in the Technicolor Coat Became the Talk of Our Class," *Belfast Telegraph*, January 25, 2013.

299 She felt as though: Dolours Price, "Rummaging," *The Blanket*, July 9, 2004.

299 She was troubled: Interview with Carrie Twomey.

299 Many of her old comrades: Interview with Francie McGuigan.

299 Joe Lynskey staring back at her: Interview with Patrick Farrelly.

299 She never came back: "Woman in the Technicolor Coat Became the Talk of Our Class," *Belfast Telegraph*, January 25, 2013.

299 "The settlement betrayed": Interview with Eamonn McCann.

299 "For what Sinn Féin has achieved": RTÉ interview with Dolours Price, excerpted in *I, Dolours*.

299 a concept in psychology called "moral injury": See Jonathan Shay, *Achilles in Vietnam: Combat Trauma and the Undoing of Character* (New York: Scribner, 2003), p. 20; Robert Emmet Meagher, *Killing from the Inside Out: Moral Injury and Just War* (Eugene, Ore.: Cascade Books, 2014), pp. 3–5; Brett T. Litz et al., "Moral Injury and Moral Repair in War Veterans: A Preliminary Model and Intervention Strategy," *Clinical Psychology Review* 29 (2009).

300 At a republican commemoration: "Gerry Adams Was My Commander, Says IRA Bomber," *Telegraph*, March 16, 2001.

300 This sort of outspokenness: "Jilted Lady," *Times* (London), March 24, 1999.

300 Price occasionally attended: "'Misled' SF Members Urged to Join Former Colleagues," *Irish Times*, November 10, 1997.

300 but she was not a joiner: Dolours Price, "Bun Fights & Good Salaries," *The Blanket*, March 27, 2007.

300 "What are you going to get": Interview with Ed Moloney.

300 Her boys: Dolours Price, "Money… Money… Money," *The Blanket*, January 17, 2005.

300 After a series of sectarian: "Cast in the Middle of the Long Conflict in Northern Ireland," *New York Times*, February 15, 1998.

300 "the guns will be sealed in concrete": Dolours Price, "Get On with It," *The Blanket*, September 14, 2004.

301 "Bobby, he told us": Dolours Price, "UnHung Hero," *The Blanket*, August 3, 2004.

301 (Sands's own family): "Hunger Striker Bobby Sands Is Just a Money-Spinner for Sinn Féin," *Belfast Telegraph*, March 1, 2016.

301 her sainted aunt Bridie: P-TKT.

301 *Is this what we killed for?*: Dolours Price, "Bun Fights & Good Salaries," *The Blanket*, March 27, 2007.

301 *What was it really all about?*: Dolours Price, "I Once Knew a Boy," *The Blanket*, July 17, 2004.

301 Occasionally, she saw: P-TKT.

301 "It's like a woman who can lift cars": Ibid.

302 "your children will bear the mark of Cain": Interview with Anthony McIntyre.

CHAPTER 23

303 For three decades: Interview with Geoff Knupfer.

303 But Knupfer took her hand: "Fourth 'Moors Murders' Victim Found, Fifth Sought," United Press International, July 2, 1987.

304 "she began to deteriorate before our eyes": Interview with Geoff Knupfer.

304 "You cannot mourn someone": "Speaking for the Dead," *Guardian*, June 14, 2003.

304 In Chile, more than three thousand: "Chile Sentences 33 for Pinochet's Disappeared," *Financial Times*, March 23, 2017.

304 In Argentina, the number: "Children of Argentina's 'Disappeared' Reclaim Past, with Help," *New York Times*, October 11, 2015.

304 The commission ultimately: "The Disappeared," a list retrieved from the website of the Independent Commission for the Location of Victims' Remains.

304 you could list the victims: Ibid.

305 Under a rhododendron bush: "Police Recover Remains of 'Disappeared' IRA Victim," *Guardian*, May 28, 1999; "A Touch of Irony As IRA Delivers Victim's Remains," *Irish Independent*, May 29, 1999.

305 It held the remains: For further detail on Molloy's role in the IRA and the mechanics of his informing, see Moloney, *Secret History of the IRA*, pp. 133–40.

305 in a remote area of County Louth: Unless otherwise noted, details of this episode are drawn from "A Prayer Before Dying: IRA Took Priest to Disappeared Victim Before Murder," BBC News, November 3, 2013.

305 This wasn't true: Moloney, *Secret History of the IRA*, p. 134.

306 Nor did he ever report the incident to the police: "A Prayer Before Dying: IRA Took Priest to Disappeared Victim Before Murder," BBC News, November 3, 2013. The priest subsequently left the priesthood, and died more than a decade ago.

306 They had been killed for stealing a gun: Margaret McKinney, "The Disappearance of Brian McKinney," in *The Disappeared of Northern Ireland's Troubles,* p. 52; "Their Sons Were Best Friends. In 1978 They Were Disappeared by the IRA," *Belfast Telegraph,* February 4, 2017.

306 Massive backhoes lumbered: "Combing the Sands Where a Mother's Bones Are Said to Lie," *Independent,* June 2, 1999.

306 some of them worried: "Ireland Calling: Digging for the Disappeared," *Irish Voice,* June 15, 1999.

307 When they spoke of Jean: *Disappeared,* documentary, directed by Joanna Head (October Films, 1999).

307 Jim McConville, who was six: Anonymous source; "Woman Beaten As She Intervened in Loyalist Attack on Belfast House," *Irish Times,* June 19, 1995.

307 had struggled with alcohol, and with his temper: "Sons Recall 30 Years of Painful Memories," *Irish News,* October 24, 2003.

307 IRA representatives had acknowledged: "Woman Says IRA Confirms Murder of Mother," *Irish Times,* December 5, 1998; "IRA Admits Killing Widow Who 'Disappeared' 26 Years Ago," *Guardian,* December 5, 1998.

307 "admitted being a British army informer": "Ahern and Blair Join Talks, But Trimble, Adams Hold to Positions," *Irish Times,* March 30, 1999.

307 The children were gratified: Interview with Michael, Susan, and Archie McConville.

308 "People wouldn't look at us": "The Bitter Tears of Jean's Children," *Guardian,* December 7, 1999.

308 Archie wondered: "Sons Recall 30 Years of Painful Memories," *Irish News,* October 24, 2003.

308 She was an overworked: Interview with Michael McConville.

308 "While they were torturing her": *Disappeared.*

308 the skeleton of a dog: "Combing the Sands Where a Mother's Bones Are Said to Lie," *Independent,* June 2, 1999.

308 Sympathetic locals: "Digging for the Disappeared," *Irish Voice,* June 15, 1999.

309 "Where are we going to bury her?": This whole exchange was captured on video, in *Disappeared.*

309 Helen wanted to bury: "Give Me My Mam," *Observer,* May 30, 1999. Michael McConville also recounted this in an interview.

309 "Them boys who done it": *Disappeared.*

309 "But it's tearing us": "The Bitter Tears of Jean's Children," *Guardian,* December 7, 1999.

309 Inside the IRA, the disappeared: Confidential interview.

309 "It is time to allow families": "IRA Victims Campaign Stepped Up," *Irish Times,* June 27, 1995.

309 In 1998, a longtime IRA man: Interview with Anthony McIntyre. In an apparent reference to Storey, the IRA announced at the time that one of its "most senior officers" was working to find the hidden graves ("'Disappeared' Phone Bid," *Belfast Telegraph,* September 7, 1998). Also see "Police Forced to Free Ex-IRA Boss Bobby Storey after Learning of Immunity," *Sunday Life,* December 1, 2014.

310 She advised Storey: Interview with Ed Moloney.

310 But Helen noticed: "Jean McConville's Daughter: 'If I Give Up Fighting, They've Won,'" *Observer,* July 6, 2014.

310 During a meeting: Interview with Michael McConville.

310 "During war, horrible things": "Adams Is Accused of Justifying Deaths," *Irish News,* June 1, 1999.

310 "Thank God I was in prison": Moloney, *Secret History of the IRA,* p. 125.

310 ("I got confused about the dates"): "Gerry Adams: Unrepentant Irishman," *Independent,* September 8, 2009.

310 "He went to this family's house": H-BC.

311 "They should get down here": "The Agony Goes On," *Belfast Telegraph,* May 31, 1999.

311 Also, the topography: "IRA Panic Over Lost Bodies," *Guardian,* June 1, 1999.

311 Some nights, she would: *Disappeared.*

311 "Where's my son?": "Kevin and the Pain That Has Never Disappeared," *Belfast Telegraph,* August 30, 2013. Also see McKee, "The Disappearance of Kevin McKee."

311 "Put that in the hot press": Ibid.

312 She allowed Dolours Price: Anonymous source.

312 When Eamon Molloy's body: "The IRA and the Disappeared: Tell Us Where Kevin Is Buried and I'll Shake Hands," *Irish Times,* October 5, 2013.

312 Whenever a baby boy: Ibid.

312 Peat cutters sometimes: "The Dark Secrets of the Bog Bodies," *Minerva,* March/April 2015.

312 Seamus Heaney became fixated: Seamus Heaney, *Preoccupations: Selected Prose, 1968–1978* (London: Faber, 1980), pp. 57–58.

312 The photographs of these gnarled bodies: Ibid., pp. 57–58.

312 "barbered / and stripped": Seamus Heaney, "Bog Queen," in *North: Poems* (London: Faber, 1975), p. 25.

312 Heaney grew up harvesting peat: Anthony Bailey, *Acts of Union: Reports on Ireland 1973–1979* (New York: Random House, 1980), p. 128.

313 Reviled though the practice: The British Army disappeared people as well. See Pádraig Óg Ó Ruairc, *Truce: Murder, Myth, and the Last Days of the Irish War of Independence* (Cork: Mercier Press, 2016), pp. 80–81. See also Lauren Dempster, "The Republican Movement, 'Disappearing' and Framing the Past in Northern Ireland," *International Journal of Transitional Justice,* vol. 10 (2016).

313 Nobody knows precisely how many people: To take one recent example: "Body Exhumed in Clare of British Soldier Killed and Secretly Buried in 1921," *Irish Examiner,* May 14, 2018.

313 Some nights, the children: "Combing the Sands Where a Mother's Bones Are Said to Lie," *Independent,* June 2, 1999.

313 "They made a laughingstock of us": *Disappeared.*

313 This was a cruel twist: Ibid. Asked which of his siblings most resembled his mother, Michael McConville responded, "I can't really answer that. I couldn't really tell you, to be honest, because I really forget which way my mother looks like."

313 Once, Helen took her children: "Give Me My Mam," *Observer,* May 30, 1999.

314 The car pulled away: Interview with Michael McConville.

CHAPTER 24

315 Only twenty or so people: "How Three Sharply Dressed Robbers Walked into Belfast's Intelligence Hub," *Guardian,* March 22, 2002.

315 After decades: Interview with Trevor Campbell.

315 In fact, four months earlier: " 'New Era' As NI Police Change Name," BBC News, November 4, 2001.

315 Even so, Castlereagh: "Who Stole the Secrets of Room 2/20?" *Observer,* March 23, 2002.

315 At the gate: Unless otherwise noted, these details are drawn from "How Three Sharply Dressed Robbers Walked into Belfast's Intelligence Hub," *Guardian,* March 22, 2002.

316 Then they placed a pair of headphones: "Raid on Anti-Terror Hub Puts Informers at Risk," *Telegraph,* March 20, 2002.

317 They left behind only one clue: "Who Stole the Secrets of Room 2/20?" *Observer,* March 23, 2002.

317 The police immediately: "Police Helped IRA Steal Special Branch Secrets," *Telegraph,* September 28, 2002.

317 "an act of war": "Analysis: Story Behind the Break-In," BBC News, April 19, 2002.

317 A man who worked: "Castlereagh Break-In Row: Chef 'Relieved but Angry,' " *Belfast Telegraph,* July 4, 2009.

317 "mythological status": "Castlereagh Break-In: The Same Old (Bobby) Storey?" *Irish Echo,* April 16, 2002.

318 But the visual implication: "The British Spy at Heart of IRA," *Times* (London), August 8, 1999; "Focus: Scappaticci's Past Is Secret No More," *Times* (London), May 18, 2003.

318 "the crown jewel": "The British Spy at Heart of IRA," *Times* (London), August 8, 1999.

318 "You know this Stakeknife": P-TKT.

318 During the Cold War: See David C. Martin, *Wilderness of Mirrors: Intrigue, Deception, and the Secrets That Destroyed Two of the Cold War's Most Important Agents* (Guilford, Conn.: Lyons Press, 2003).

318 Between 1980 and 1994: "The Hunter and His Prey," *Spotlight.*

318 But not all of them: Martin Ingram and Greg Harkin, *Stakeknife: Britain's Secret Agents in Ireland* (Madison: University of Wisconsin Press, 2004), p. 33. See, for instance, "Anthony Braniff—IRA Statement," *An Phoblacht,* September 25, 1003.

319 When Brendan Hughes got out of prison: H-BC.

319 He also secretly worked: Ibid.

319 The TVs were bugged: Interview with Joe Clarke and Gerry Brannigan.

319 Before he could be executed: "Informant 'Killed by IRA Despite Warning from British Spy,' " *Telegraph,* April 11, 2017; "Exposed: The Murky World of Spying During the Troubles," *Irish Times,* April 11, 2017.

319 Hughes found that he was increasingly uneasy: H-BC.

319 At the most senior levels: "Half of All Top IRA Men 'Worked for Security Services,'" *Belfast Telegraph,* December 21, 2011.

319 But just over a year: "How Stakeknife Was Unmasked," *Guardian,* May 12, 2003.

320 "a golden egg": "Freddie Scappaticci Was Our Most Valuable Spy in IRA During Troubles: British Army Chief," *Belfast Telegraph,* April 20, 2012.

320 Stakeknife wasn't Gerry Adams: "How Stakeknife Was Unmasked," *Guardian,* May 12, 2003.

320 "I am not guilty": "Wearing Short Sleeves and Tan, Scappaticci Steps from the Shadows to Say: I'm No Informer," *Independent,* May 15, 2003.

320 He had been a double agent: Ingram and Harkin, *Stakeknife,* p. 61.

320 It has been suggested: Ibid., p. 66.

321 But as an army-wide internal affairs: This observation is from Tommy McKearney's remarks in "The Hunter and His Prey," *Spotlight.*

321 In fact, when Scappaticci: "Wearing Short Sleeves and Tan, Scappaticci Steps from the Shadows to Say: I'm No Informer," *Independent,* May 15, 2003.

321 "I still can't believe it": "Double Blind," *The Atlantic,* April 2006.

321 But then, Donaldson was a spy: "Adams Says 'Securocrats' Out to Create New Crisis," *Irish Times,* December 17, 2005.

321 "blackmailed, bullied, coerced": "Donaldson Admits to Being British Agent Since 1980s," *Irish Times,* December 16, 2005.

321 Like a portal into: "Dennis Donaldson: Squalid Living after a Life of Lies," *Sunday Tribune,* March 26, 2006.

321 But a lucky horseshoe: "Dead Man Walking," *Times* (London), April 9, 2006.

321 Donaldson grew a penitential beard: "'Spy' Donaldson Living in Donegal," *Derry Journal,* March 21, 2006.

322 someone arrived at the cottage and killed him: "Spy and Former SF Official Donaldson Shot Dead," *Irish Times,* April 4, 2006.

322 (It has never been ascertained): "Denis Donaldson Murder: The Unanswered Questions That Bedevil Gerry Adams," *Belfast Telegraph,* September 22, 2016.

322 "The one preconception": "Double Blind," *The Atlantic,* April 2006.

322 But they allowed that this number: "Exposed: The Murky World of Spying During the Troubles," *Irish Times,* April 11, 2017. On conjectural mathematics, behold the airtight logic in an account by one former Special Branch official: "Agents in illegal republican terrorist organisations saved at least 16,500 lives in the Troubles. A former [Special Branch] detective chief superintendent assesses that 15 well-placed agents were active at any one time in the IRA (1:33 ratio when based on an IRA of 500). On a yearly basis, considering a well-placed agent on average saved 37 lives per year, this equates to 555, which over 30 years is 16,650 lives." William Matchett, *Secret Victory: The Intelligence War That Beat the IRA* (Belfast: self-published, 2016), pp. 100–101.

322 Scappaticci would ultimately: "Top Spy 'Stakeknife' Allegedly Linked to 50 Killings 'Unlikely to Ever Face Prosecution,'" *Irish Independent,* April 27, 2016.

323 As early as 1975: Colin Wallace to Tony Staughton, the chief information officer at the Army Information Service at Lisburn, August 1975. Cited in "Death Squad Dossier," *Irish Mail on Sunday*, December 10, 2006. For more on Wallace, a fascinating figure, see *Interim Report on the Report of the Independent Commission of Inquiry into the Dublin and Monaghan Bombings*, Houses of the Oireachtas (Ireland), December 2003, and Paul Foot, *Who Framed Colin Wallace?* (London: Macmillan, 1989).

323 "deliberately stirring up conflict": Letter from Colin Wallace, September 30, 1975, also cited in "Death Squad Dossier," *Irish Mail on Sunday*, December 10, 2006.

323 Loyalist gangs, often operating: See Anne Cadwallader, *Lethal Allies: British Collusion in Ireland* (Cork: Mercier Press, 2013).

323 "We were there to act like a terror group": "Britain's Secret Terror Force," *Panorama*.

324 White's remit: Interview with Raymond White.

324 "But don't tell us the details": Ian Cobain, *The History Thieves: Secrets, Lies and the Shaping of a Modern Nation* (London: Portobello, 2016), p. 186.

324 After a stint in prison: Ingram and Harkin, *Stakeknife*, p. 25.

324 Nelson was every bit: "'Nelson Files' Link Authorities to UDA Death Squads," *Irish Independent*, November 14, 2015.

324 but in fact the government *did*: According to an unpublished autobiographical account written by Nelson before he died, which I obtained, the army did not want Adams to be killed. That would be "totally counterproductive," his handlers told him, because Adams had emerged, even by 1984, as someone who might steer the republican movement away from violence. Nelson maintains that the army knew in advance of the plan to kill Adams and allowed it to proceed—but not before they had tampered with the ammunition, in order to prevent the assassination from succeeding. In 2014, the police ombudsman of Northern Ireland investigated these claims and asserted that the authorities had not known in advance about the attack, and that the bullets had not been tampered with. See "Public Statement by the Police Ombudsman Under Section 62 of the Police (Northern Ireland) Act 1998 Relating to the Complaints in Respect of the Attempted Murder of Mr. Gerry Adams on 14 March 1984," Police Ombudsman for Northern Ireland (2014). But the late journalist Liam Clarke, who was well sourced and highly reliable, maintained, in a 2011 article, that the story about military intelligence doctoring the bullets used to shoot Adams had in fact been "confirmed by the Defense Advisory Committee." See "Half of All Top IRA Men 'Worked for Security Services,'" *Belfast Telegraph*, December 21, 2011.

325 One night in February 1989: Kevin Toolis, *Rebel Hearts: Journeys within the IRA's Soul* (New York: St. Martin's Press, 1995), pp. 84–85.

325 Members of the RUC: De Silva Report, p. 15.

325 It was Nelson who: Ingram and Harkin, *Stakeknife*, p. 197; Peter Cory, *Cory Collusion Inquiry Report: Patrick Finucane* (London: Stationery Office, 2004), pp. 53–54.

325 A subsequent inquiry stopped short of concluding: De Silva Report, p. 23.

325 (Finucane's family, convinced): "Pat Finucane's Widow Calls de Silva Report 'a Whitewash,'" *Guardian*, December 12, 2012.

326 So the FRU devised: "Was an IRA Informer So Valuable That Murder Was Committed to Protect Him?" *Guardian*, September 25, 2000.

326 A Belfast Italian: Notarantonio had apparently been involved in the IRA as a younger man but was no longer. See "Come Spy with Me," *Irish Times,* May 17, 2003.

326 One morning, Notarantonio: "Innocent Victim of Ulster's Dirty War," *Guardian,* January 12, 2001.

326 One of them was Freddie Scappaticci: Ingram and Harkin, *Stakeknife,* p. 218.

326 "In almost thirty years": "Shadowy Group Linked to Collusion and Murder," *Times* (London), September 13, 2005.

326 In 1990, a fire: "Stevens Enquiry 3: Overview & Recommendations," report by Sir John Stevens, April 17, 2003, p. 13; John Stevens, *Not for the Faint-Hearted: My Life Fighting Crime* (London: Orion, 2006), p. 185.

326 In 2012, the British prime minister: "Prime Minister David Cameron Statement on Patrick Finucane," December 12, 2012.

326 There was a provision: See the Belfast Agreement (1998), section 10: "Prisoners." The implementing legislation was the Northern Ireland (Sentences) Act of 1998.

327 There was one notable: See Kieran McEvoy, Louise Mallinder, Gordon Anthony, and Luke Moffett, "Dealing with the Past in Northern Ireland: Amnesties, Prosecutions and the Public Interest," paper (2013), p. 15.

327 But it wouldn't budge: Deposition of John Garland, Inquest on the Body of Jean McConville, Coroner's District of County Louth, April 5, 2004.

328 "There was a single gunshot": Report of Postmortem Examination on Jean McConville, by pathologist M. Cassidy, September 1, 2003.

328 A flattened lead bullet: Report of Postmortem Examination on Remains Believed to Be Jean McConville, by pathologist R. T. Shepherd, August 28, 2003.

328 Four years after: "Beach Body 'Is Mother Killed by IRA 30 Years Ago,' " *Telegraph,* August 28, 2003.

328 The skeleton's: Postmortem Examination, September 1, 2003.

329 Tights, underwear: Postmortem Examination, August 28, 2003.

329 "Is there a nappy pin?": Interviews with Michael McConville and Archie McConville.

329 "All of our lives": Archie McConville deposition.

329 Father Alec Reid...attended the funeral: "Waiting Comes to an End As Mother Is Laid to Rest," *Irish News,* November 3, 2003.

329 But some others: Interview with Nuala O'Loan.

329 When the remains: "Daughter Demands Justice for IRA Victim," *Irish News,* April 7, 2004.

329 "The criminal case": "Forensics May Trap McConville Killers," *Irish News,* February 24, 2004.

CHAPTER 25

330 The process had unfolded: "IRA Destroys All Its Arms," *New York Times,* September 27, 2005.

330 The gun was on display: "Insults Fly at Decommissioning Priest's Meeting," *Irish Examiner,* October 12, 2005.

330 The destruction proceeded: This catalog of weapons is drawn from "IRA Destroys All Its Arms," *New York Times,* September 27, 2005.

330 The man seemed very aware: "Insults Fly at Decommissioning Priest's Meeting," *Irish Examiner,* October 12, 2005.

330 With his brother Terry: Interviews with Anthony McIntyre and Terry Hughes.

331 When he got back to Belfast: Interview with Terry Hughes.

331 But the family chose not to intervene: Ibid.

331 For the Sinn Féin leader: Interview with Tommy Gorman.

331 In the symbolic calculus: Interview with Terry Hughes.

332 He looked lonely: Dolours Price, "Gerry, Come Clean, You'll Feel Better," *The Blanket,* February 26, 2009.

332 Then he shouldered: The suggestion that it took some doing for Adams to get to the coffin has been widely made. It was confirmed for me by witnesses such as Anthony McIntyre and Tommy Gorman. In an account, the journalist Liam Clarke wrote, "In order to be filmed with the coffin, Adams had to push his way past Real IRA supporters who wanted to hijack Hughes's legacy. Martin McGuinness was more coy." "A Coffin Adams Had to Carry," *Times* (London), February 24, 2008.

332 "We were there in grief": Dolours Price, "Irish News Report of the Funeral of Brendan Hughes," *The Blanket,* February 24, 2008.

332 "He was my friend": "Death of Brendan Hughes," *An Phoblacht,* February 21, 2008.

332 But O'Rawe found: Interview with Richard O'Rawe.

333 "If you publish this": Interview with Ed Moloney.

333 "If I die before this comes out": Interview with Richard O'Rawe.

333 "No matter how history": O'Rawe, *Blanketmen,* p. 251.

333 Bik McFarlane, who had: "Former Comrades' War of Words over Hunger Strike," *Irish News,* March 11, 2005.

333 (McFarlane changed his story): "British 'Had No Intention of Resolving the Hunger Strike,'" *Belfast Telegraph,* June 4, 2009.

333 He never missed: Interview with Richard O'Rawe. The book is *Afterlives.*

334 "access to this vital piece": Dolours Price, "A Salute to Comrades," *The Blanket,* May 18, 2005.

334 "I am a former prisoner": "Brendan Hughes: O'Rawe Told Me His Concerns," *Irish News,* May 19, 2006.

334 "I've made tapes": Interview with Richard O'Rawe.

334 "take things from shops": "Former IRA Bomber Price Acquitted of Alcohol Theft," *Irish News,* August 24, 2010.

334 Price had been struggling: Ibid. On PTSD: Interview with Carrie Twomey.

334 In 2001, she was caught: "Her Name Is Dolours, the IRA Bomber Who Married a Hollywood Star. Now She Has Become an Alcoholic," *Daily Mirror,* March 30, 2001.

334 she was thrown out of Maghaberry Prison: "Murky Maghaberry," *Republican News,* January 31, 2006.

335 "I don't want to know": Interview with Eamonn McCann.

335 "free-loading": Gerry Bradley and Brian Feeney, *Insider: Gerry Bradley's Life in the IRA* (Dublin: O'Brien Press, 2009), p. 16.

335 "The only thing I know": Ibid., p. 7.

335 "I'm just telling my story": "Death of 'Whitey' Bradley," *Irish Republican News,* October 28, 2010.

335 Bradley was forced to flee: "IRA Chief Suicide Horror," *Daily Mirror,* October 28, 2010.

335 Ostracized and in poor health: "Former IRA Man Gerry 'Whitey' Bradley Found Dead in Car," BBC News, October 28, 2010.

335 "Is history never to be recorded properly?": "IRA Gunman Turned Author Found Dead," UTV, October 28, 2010.

335 Using the Boston College transcript: Ed Moloney, *Voices from the Grave,* p. 1.

335 The secret of the archive: "Brendan Hughes Revelations—Book Tells IRA Secrets," *Irish News,* March 29, 2010.

336 "make it impossible for certain forms": Faber & Faber catalog, January–June 2010.

336 "He wasn't well": "Adams Linked to IRA Actions," *Irish Republican News,* March 29, 2010.

336 "a malign agenda": Ibid.

336 One night, someone smeared: "SF Deny Journalist in Danger," *Sunday World,* April 11, 2010. On Collins, see Toby Harnden, *Bandit Country: The IRA & South Armagh* (London: Hodder & Stoughton, 1999), pp. 446–47.

337 When the college forwarded: "A Preliminary Note on Embargoes," Ed Moloney, background document provided to the author.

337 "He is not an academic": Anthony McIntyre, email message to Tom Hachey (undated, late June 2010). McIntyre was not alone in this perception of Morrison, who, according to the writer Toby Harnden, "was known within the IRA as the 'Lord Chief Justice' because he was the man who held the power of life or death over an informer." Harnden, *Bandit Country,* p. 284.

337 He was caught off guard: Interview with Wilson McArthur.

338 One history professor: The graduate student was Megan Myers, and she ended up citing the archive in her dissertation, *Moving Terrorists from the Streets to a Diamond-Shaped Table: The International History of the Northern Ireland Conflict, 1969–1999* (Department of History, Boston College, December 2011). Tom Hachey, email message to Ed Moloney, June 4, 2010.

338 "I would strongly urge": Ed Moloney, email message to Tom Hachey, June 4, 2010.

338 There should be a strict protocol: Ed Moloney, email message to Tom Hachey, June 7, 2010.

338 "to the entire scholarly": Tom Hachey, email message to Anthony McIntyre, June 21, 2010.

339 Lynskey was not on the list: Maria Lynskey interview, *Marian Finucane Show,* RTÉ Radio, April 4, 2015.

339 "I knew him and he disappeared": "Gerry Adams Interview: No Parade Unless the Residents Support One," *Irish News,* February 11, 2010.

339 Dolours Price read the interview: Interview with Allison Morris.
339 "the flattery of the Americans": Dolours Price, "An Open Letter to Gerry Adams," *The Blanket,* July 31, 2005.
340 "This is the only freedom": Ibid.
340 "a great rage": Interview with Eamonn McCann.
340 When she read the Adams interview: Interview with Allison Morris.
340 The next morning: Ibid.
341 Morris was struck: Ibid.
341 Price seemed to her: "Death of Dolours Price," *Irish News,* January 25, 2013.
341 Lynskey was "a gentleman": Ibid.
341 "The man's a liar": Interview with Allison Morris.
341 "My aunt Marian": Ibid.
341 "She is not well": Carrie Twomey, email message to Ed Moloney, October 14, 2011, in which Twomey relays a conversation with Marian Price about Marian's version of events.
341 "Your sister's a grown woman": Interview with Allison Morris.
342 Price had "vital information": "Dolours Price's Trauma over IRA Disappeared," *Irish News,* February 18, 2010.
342 "the final days of mother-of-10": Ibid.
342 Before the article ran: Interview with Allison Morris.
342 Price lied: Ibid.; interview with Dennis Godfrey.
342 Price fingered Adams directly: "Gerry Adams and the Disappeared," *Sunday Life,* February 21, 2010.
342 "has made taped confessions": Ibid.
343 Morris must have shared: Interview with Allison Morris; Ciarán Barnes, email message to author.
343 "a long-standing opponent": "Dolours Price's Trauma over IRA Disappeared," *Irish News,* February 18, 2010.
344 "There obviously are issues": "I Didn't Order Jean's Killing," *Sunday Life,* February 21, 2010.
344 It was the same criticism: "Gerry Adams: 'I'm Happy with Who I Am … It's Very Important to Be a Subversive," *Guardian,* January 24, 2011.
344 "Brendan said what Brendan said": Ibid.

CHAPTER 26
345 In 2006, the police ombudsman: Interview with Nuala O'Loan.
345 But she located intelligence files: Police Ombudsman's Report.
345 "She is not recorded": Ibid.
346 "We knew throughout all the years": "McConville Family Relieved Their Mother's Name Is Finally Cleared," *Irish News,* July 8, 2006.
346 "The IRA accepts he rejects": IRA Statement on the Abduction and Killing of Mrs. Jean McConville in December 1972 (July 8, 2006), available on the CAIN website.
346 She refused to specify: Transcript of an interview conducted with Nuala O'Loan for *Voices from the Grave.*

346 If she had been a tout: Interview with Anthony McIntyre.

347 There was also a mystery relating: Interview with Trevor Campbell.

347 dug through old British files: The researcher was James Kinchin-White. The radio, which was made by a Norwegian company, was a handheld transmitter/receiver called a Stornophone. James Kinchin-White, email message to author. There is a reference in the report of the Bloody Sunday Inquiry to the use of Stornophone radios ("nicknamed Stornos") by the army in 1972. See *Report of the Bloody Sunday Inquiry,* British House of Commons (2010), vol. IX, chapter 181.

347 They even managed to track down: The image, dated 1972, is in the collection of the Soldiers of Gloucestershire Museum, England.

348 Michael also wrote off as ludicrous: Interview with Michael McConville.

349 But in a few significant particulars: Police Ombudsman's Report.

349 seven nights earlier, on November 29: Ibid.

349 Helen remembers: Interview with Michael McConville; McKendry, *Disappeared,* p. 17.

350 no evidence of a British soldier: Police Ombudsman's Report.

350 But it was tempting: One interesting fragment of circumstantial evidence to consider: in a recollection published in 2011, another former resident of Divis Flats, Mary Kennedy, recalls an uncannily similar incident from her own childhood: "There was a Brit injured outside the door of the flat. He wasn't shot. A kid threw a brick and hit him on the side of the head. Mammy was in bed, not well, and it was Carol went down and got her. Mammy trailed him off the balcony. The Sticks were coming up the balcony to shoot him and she said, 'Not in front of my children. You're not doing it,' and she took him into the hall. She got shouted at. We got up the next morning and there were things written on the walls outside: Touts; Brit Lovers; Touts out. The whole thing affected me in that I hated my mammy going out because I imagined she wasn't coming back. The only place she was allowed to go on her own was the bathroom. Even when she was going to the shop, it was, 'I'm going with you.' You were afraid of going to school and coming home and her not being there." This independent account captures the degree of social sanction associated with being perceived to have brought comfort to a British soldier, though Mary Kennedy's mother (also named Mary Kennedy) was not taken away and shot. Bill Rolston, *Children of the Revolution: The Lives of Sons and Daughters of Activists in Northern Ireland* (Derry: Guildhall Press, 2011), pp. 139–40.

351 Ravenous for more information: Interview with Michael McConville.

351 "pulled the trigger": "Arrest Adams Now," *Sunday Life,* February 21, 2010.

351 "regarding an alleged violation": BC Motion to Quash.

CHAPTER 27

352 "Total confidentiality": May 16, 2011, conference call.

352 "We are not going to allow our interviewers": Ibid.

352 The very idea seemed ludicrous: "N. Ireland Papers on Disarmament Archived at BC," *Boston Globe,* March 27, 2011.

353 "hung out to dry": May 16, 2011, conference call.

353 insurance against any quiet, dead-of-night handover: "Secret Archive of Ulster Troubles Faces Subpoena," *New York Times,* May 13, 2011.

353 He also spoke to *The Boston Globe*: "BC Ordered to Give Up Oral History Tapes on IRA," *Boston Globe,* May 14, 2011.

353 the more likely Boston College: Interview with Ed Moloney.

353 But Hachey scolded: Tom Hachey, email message to Ed Moloney, May 15, 2011.

353 but while the cops: For a provocative exploration of this theme, see Eamonn McCann, "Norman Baxter's Long Crusade," *Counterpunch,* February 13, 2012. Moloney fastened on an incident in which detectives from the PSNI visited Jim McConville in January 2011 at Magilligan prison, where he was being held, and suggested that he fill out a legal complaint indicating that he believed the interviews at Boston College might shed light on the circumstances of his mother's death. This would empower the police to subpoena the archive, Moloney contended. The PSNI's suggestion that the McConville family might be able to use the contents of the archive to launch a civil suit against those responsible for their mother's death amounted, he believed, to a "bribe." Ed Moloney Complaint to the Police Ombudsman of Northern Ireland, October 6, 2015. See Ed Moloney, "Boston College Case: PSNI Detectives Offered 'Bribe' to McConville Family Member to Enable Invasion of Archive," *The Broken Elbow* blog, September 30, 2015.

353 For decades, the men of the RUC: "Mothers Angry at 'Betrayal' of RUC's Dead," *Guardian,* September 10, 1999.

354 "This is a vendetta": May 16, 2011, conference call.

354 Moloney thought that he detected: Interview with Ed Moloney.

354 When he encountered skittish participants: May 16, 2011, conference call; interview with Wilson McArthur.

354 "You may want to refer this to your legal people": Ed Moloney, email message to Bob O'Neill, January 30, 2001.

354 The following day, O'Neill: Bob O'Neill, email message to Ed Moloney, January 31, 2001.

355 But in the end, it appears: Interviews with Ed Moloney and Anthony McIntyre; "Secrets from Belfast," *Chronicle of Higher Education,* January 26, 2014. O'Neill declined to be interviewed for this book.

355 The contract that each participant signed: "BC Reflects on Missteps in Northern Ireland Project," *Boston Globe,* May 18, 2014.

355 that was the last time that Hachey: Interviews with Ed Moloney and Anthony McIntyre.

355 Before the end of May: Government's Opposition to Motion to Quash.

355 Hughes transcripts and recordings were unredacted: Interview with Ed Moloney.

355 "I would bet the mortgage": Ed Moloney, email message to Tom Hachey, May 31, 2011.

355 "happily go to jail": Ibid.

356 the least Boston College could do: Interview with Anthony McIntyre.

356 Now that the authorities: Ed Moloney, email message to Tom Hachey, June 2, 2011.

356 In a line that would: Tom Hachey, email message to Ed Moloney, June 2, 2011.

356 The university agreed to fight the Price subpoena: BC Motion to Quash.

356 "'omerta' in the Mafia": Ibid.

356 "it is an offense punishable by death": Moloney Massachusetts affidavit.

356 The Belfast Project was not a work of journalism: For a comprehensive discussion of the ethical and legal issues surrounding this case, see Ted Palys and John Lowman, "Defending Research Confidentiality 'to the Extent the Law Allows': Lessons from the Boston College Subpoenas," *Journal of Academic Ethics,* vol. 10, no. 4 (2012).

357 Nobody had assassinated: Government's Opposition to Motion to Quash.

357 The government also suggested: Ibid.

357 U.S. officials had clearly been duped: Memorandum of Trustees of Boston College in Reply to Government's Opposition to Motion to Quash Subpoenas and in Opposition to Government's Motion to Compel, July 15, 2011 (U.S. District Court of Massachusetts, M.B.D. no. 11-MC-91078).

357 But by August, Moloney's dire prediction: Motion of Trustees of Boston College to Quash New Subpoenas, August 17, 2011 (U.S. District Court of Massachusetts, M.B.D. no. 11-MC-91078).

357 Kerry wrote to the secretary of state: John Kerry to Hillary Clinton, January 23, 2012.

358 The Massachusetts branch: "In Re: Request from the United Kingdom Pursuant to the Treaty Between the Government of the United States of America and the Government of the United Kingdom on Mutual Assistance in Criminal Matters," Amicus Curiae Brief of American Civil Liberties Union of Massachusetts in Support of Appellants, February 27, 2012.

358 But by the time the subpoenas: Interview with James Cronin.

358 When it was originally conceived: "Secrets from Belfast," *Chronicle of Higher Education,* January 26, 2014.

358 When the details: Interviews with current and former members of the Boston College history faculty.

358 He was an old friend: Ibid.

358 "no visible support": Thomas Hachey, email message to Ed Moloney, May 15, 2011.

358 endeavoring to bar access by graduate students: Interview with James Cronin.

359 "is not and never was": "'Belfast Project' Is Not and Never Was a Boston College History Department Project," statement by the Department of History, Boston College, May 5, 2014.

359 "Nobody trusted the integrity": Interview with James Cronin.

359 Moloney and Mackers brought their case: "In Re: Request from the United Kingdom Pursuant to the Treaty Between the Government of the United States

of America and the Government of the United Kingdom on Mutual Assistance in Criminal Matters in the Matter of Dolours Price," Opinion, First Circuit Court of Appeals, May 31, 2013.

359 But in the spring of 2013: *Moloney v. United States* Petition Denied, Supreme Court of the United States, Order List: 569 U.S., April 15, 2013.

359 In determining which of the interviews: Jeffrey Swope, email message to Anthony McIntyre, December 20, 2011.

359 "lead me across the boundary": Anthony McIntyre, email message to Jeffrey Swope, December 20, 2011.

359 Judge Young asked Bob O'Neill: Transcript of a judicial conference held by Judge William Young, December 22, 2011.

359 So over several days one Christmas: Ibid. Also: Findings and Order, Judge William Young, United States District Court, District of Massachusetts, January 20, 2012.

359 He found that six of the participants: Lawyer's notes of a hearing before Judge William Young, December 22, 2011.

359 "Dolours Price did not mention Jean McConville": "Adams Says Bombing Claims False," *Irish Times*, September 27, 2012.

360 "The subject of that unfortunate": Moloney Belfast affidavit.

360 "The truth is that the interviews that Anthony McIntyre": Ibid.

360 Technically, this was true: Interview with Anthony McIntyre.

360 But there was another set of recordings in the archive: Interview with Ed Moloney.

360 What he proposed: Interview with Ed Moloney.

361 It was Bridie's suffering: Price interview in *I, Dolours*.

361 She talked about getting beaten at Burntollet: Unless otherwise noted, the material in this section is drawn from *I, Dolours* and from P-EM.

361 Like the Mau Mau cloaked in sheets: There were other instances in which this technique is known to have been used to identify IRA suspects in Belfast. In a 2000 interview, the former IRA volunteer Tommy Gorman recounted being arrested in December 1971: "In the cellar there were these blankets with eyeholes cut out of them, and we heard voices behind the eyeholes saying, 'Yeah, that's him.'" "Tommy Gorman: Recalling the Maidstone," *Andersonstown News*, September 9, 2000.

362 Along with Wee Pat McClure: P-EM.

362 Price bought McConville fish and chips: "Old Bailey Bomber Dolours Price Accused Gerry Adams of Being Behind the Abductions of 'The Disappeared,'" *Telegraph*, May 2, 2014.

364 she deliberately missed: Moloney would not tell me whether Price told him that she missed, and he redacted the transcript of this conversation in such a way that it is unclear whether she said so in the context of this interview. But Price also confided in Anthony McIntyre about the circumstances of the shooting, and told him that she deliberately missed.

365 "These people do come into my mind": P-EM.

366 They were still there three years later: "Row over Interviewee Identities," UTV News, July 28, 2013.

366 Moloney pleaded with Bob O'Neill: Interview with Ed Moloney.

CHAPTER 28

367 At Massereene Barracks on Saturday nights: "Antrim Soldier Shooting: Dead Soldiers Just Minutes from Leaving for Afghanistan," *Telegraph*, March 9, 2009.

367 Dressed in desert camouflage: Ibid.

367 Then a third car: "Army Attack 'Brutal and Cowardly,'" BBC News, March 9, 2009.

367 After a sustained initial volley: "Chilling Video at Trial Opening," *Irish Echo*, November 9, 2011.

367 more than sixty rounds in half a minute: "Terrorists Murder Ulster Policeman," *Scotsman*, March 10, 2009.

367 Two other soldiers were wounded: "Tributes Paid to Murdered Northern Ireland Soldiers," *Guardian*, March 9, 2009.

368 Twelve years had passed: "Shootings Were Attempt at Mass Murder, Says PSNI," BBC News, March 8, 2009.

368 Even the deliverymen: "Real IRA Claims Responsibility for Antrim Barracks Murder," *Telegraph*, March 8, 2009.

368 "This was an act": "Antrim Soldier Shooting: Dead Soldiers Just Minutes from Leaving for Afghanistan," *Telegraph*, March 9, 2009.

368 Then, eight months: "Old Bailey Bomber Held over Murder of Soldiers," *Independent*, November 18, 2009.

368 As she stood at the checkout: The authorities released the CCTV video, including this image. See "Marian Price Sentenced for Massereene Attack Phone Link," *Irish Times*, January 7, 2014.

368 It was Marian Price: "Old Bailey Bomber 'Bought Phone Real IRA Used to Claim Murder of Soldiers,'" *Guardian*, November 19, 2013.

368 "Armed struggle *does* have a place": "Republicans' Defiant Dame Warns of War," *Observer*, February 4, 2001.

368 Marian was ultimately charged: "Old Bailey Bomber Marian Price on New Charge," *Guardian*, July 22, 2011.

369 There was another charge: "Old Bailey Bomber Charged over Dissident Threats to Police," *Irish Times*, May 16, 2011.

369 While he recited: "Marian Price and the Lost Document," *Irish Times*, February 18, 2012.

369 For the next two years: "Republican Marian Price Reveals Horror of Seven Months' Solitary Confinement in Prison," *Sunday World*, December 18, 2011.

369 Dolours was distraught: "Jailed Republican Price in Legal Limbo Despite Her Illness," *Irish Times*, July 21, 2012.

369 "victim of psychological torture": Ibid.

369 The very month: "Irish Eyes Are Smiling: Show of Respect Turns Queen into Runaway Favourite," *Guardian*, May 19, 2011.

369 A former schoolmate of Dolours's: P-EM.

369 She welcomed the historic: "Major Terror Alert As Queen Visits Ireland," *Daily Express,* May 17, 2011.

369 Marian was still in prison: "'Historic Handshake' for Queen and Ex-IRA Leader Martin McGuinness," *Independent,* June 26, 2012.

370 "They must make a verdict": "Paisley and McGuinness Mark New Era," *Guardian,* May 8, 2007.

370 "It never has been": "Republican Marian Price Reveals Horror of Seven Months' Solitary Confinement in Prison," *Sunday World,* December 18, 2011.

370 "another generation": "Republicans' Defiant Dame Warns of War," *Observer,* February 4, 2001.

370 a poster girl of the truly dire years: Interview with Eamonn McCann.

371 At the hearing: "Marian Price Sentenced for Massereene Attack Phone Link," *Irish Times,* January 7, 2014.

371 And she spent hours: Interview with Eamonn McCann; "Republican Marian Price Reveals Horror of Seven Months' Solitary Confinement in Prison," *Sunday World,* December 18, 2011.

371 Armed with the Boston College interviews: "Corporals' Killer Arrested over McConville Murder," *Irish News,* April 3, 2014; "MLA's Sister Released in McConville Investigation," *Irish News,* April 11, 2014; "Sinn Féin Candidate Quizzed About Jean McConville Murder," *Irish News,* April 19, 2014.

371 Only one person had actually been charged: "Republican Charged in Connection with 1972 McConville Murder," *Irish News,* March 22, 2014.

372 emeritus professor of political optics: "The Jean McConville Killing: I'm Completely Innocent. But What Are My Accusers' Motives?" *Guardian,* May 7, 2014.

372 Adams glided into the station: Ibid.

372 "for a kind of score settling reason": "IRA Bomber Says Gerry Adams Sanctioned Mainland Bombing Campaign," *Telegraph,* September 23, 2012.

373 "what they'd been driven to do": "Disillusioned Republicans Breached IRA's Code of Secrecy," *Irish Times,* November 7, 2013.

373 "I wanted very much": "IRA Bomber Says Gerry Adams Sanctioned Mainland Bombing Campaign," *Telegraph,* September 23, 2012.

373 "numerous rumors": "Gerry Adams Interview: No Parade Unless the Residents Support One," *Irish News,* February 11, 2010.

373 But in his own memoir: This exchange is taken from *The Disappeared.*

373 "if you don't ask, you can't tell": Ibid.

373 In 2009, a woman named Áine Tyrrell: "Adams' Brother Sought over Alleged Abuse," RTÉ News, December 19, 2009.

373 In an interview on the program: Ibid.

374 In fact, Liam Adams: "Adams Said RUC Should Not Be Used over Abuse," *Irish Times,* December 22, 2009.

374 Gerry would subsequently claim: "Adams' Paedophile Brother Was Youth Worker in Dundalk," *Sunday Tribune,* December 20, 2009.

374 But by the time he did so: "Adams Is a Liability with Much to Explain," *Times* (London), December 27, 2009.

374 "culture of concealment": "Gerry Adams Reveals Family's Abuse by Father," *Guardian,* December 20, 2009.

374 Áine Tyrrell would later allege: "Gerry Adams' Niece Reveals: 'The Beard Tried to Get Me to Gag Press over Abuse,'" *Belfast Telegraph,* October 7, 2013.

375 "would provide a follow-up": "Adams Is a Liability with Much to Explain," *Times* (London), December 27, 2009.

375 even in the antic, bloody days of late 1972: Confidential interview.

375 The brigade staff "would have had to sit and thrash it out": P-EM.

375 In the police station at Antrim: "The Jean McConville Killing: I'm Completely Innocent. But What Are My Accusers' Motives?" *Guardian,* May 7, 2014.

375 "a crutch to withstand their inquisition": Adams, *Before the Dawn,* p. 191.

376 When it emerged that Adams had effectively covered: "Adams' Family Values Strip Him of All Moral Authority," *Sunday Tribune,* December 27, 2009.

376 "an embittered rump of the old RUC": "Gerry Adams Arrested: Martin McGuinness Speaks at Falls Road Rally Demanding Sinn Féin Leader's Release," *Belfast Telegraph,* May 3, 2014.

377 With Divis Tower visible: Footage of the May 3, 2014, rally, *An Phoblacht* video news.

377 It was Bobby Storey: Footage of May 3, 2014, rally, Sky News. On his being the enforcer: "IRA Calls in Peace 'Fixer,'" *Times* (London), January 8, 1995.

377 He had joined the IRA: "'Big Bobby': Arrests, Interrogations, Imprisonment, and Struggle—the 'Storey' of His Life," *An Phoblacht,* December 18, 2008.

377 In fact, he was reputed: "'Key Spymaster' a Crucial Adams Ally," *Irish News,* November 1, 2007; "We Will Defend the Integrity of the Republican Struggle: Interview with Bobby Storey," *Hot Press,* June 12, 2009. Storey's home was raided after the break-in. See "Bobby Storey: 'Enforcer' Is Key Ally of Gerry Adams," *Belfast Telegraph,* May 6, 2014.

377 Storey was also widely: "We Will Defend the Integrity of the Republican Struggle: Interview with Bobby Storey," *Hot Press,* June 12, 2009; "Bobby Storey: 'Enforcer' Is Key Ally of Gerry Adams," *Belfast Telegraph,* May 6, 2014.

377 It was the largest bank robbery: "10 Facts About the IRA's £26.5m raid on Northern Bank," *Belfast Telegraph,* December 19, 2014.

377 "Call me old fashioned": Dolours Price, "Money ... Money ... Money," *The Blanket,* January 17, 2005.

377 But he had the mien of a thug: For a vivid illustration of this side of Storey's personality, see Malachi O'Doherty, *The Trouble with Guns: Republican Strategy and the Provisional IRA* (Belfast: Blackstaff Press, 1998), pp. 1–3.

378 "dare touch our party leader": Footage of the May 3, 2014, rally, BBC News.

378 "We ain't gone away, you know": Ibid.

378 Storey was quoting: "Sinn Féin Hints at Possible Renewal of IRA Violence," Associated Press, August 14, 1995.

378 The McConville children: Detective Inspector Peter Montgomery to Joe Mulholland & Co Solicitors, October 21, 2013.

378 an unambiguous threat: Interview with Michael McConville.

378 Mackers, too, saw pure menace: Interview with Anthony McIntyre.

379 With rhetoric like Storey's: Interview with Richard O'Rawe.

379 A new epithet: Interview with Anthony McIntyre; interview with Richard O'Rawe.

379 good people into touts: "The Boston Time Bomb," *Sunday Life,* May 11–13, 2014.

379 Mackers had instructed: Interview with Anthony McIntyre and Carrie Twomey; "Ex-Provo's Life Is at Risk over IRA Tapes Row, Court to Be Told," *Belfast Telegraph,* July 5, 2012.

379 "There was a sustained": "The Jean McConville Killing: I'm Completely Innocent. But What Are My Accusers' Motives?" *Guardian,* May 7, 2014.

379 "which formed the mainstay": "Boston College Says It Will Return Interviews about the North," *Irish Times,* May 7, 2014.

379 "It's finished": "Gerry Adams Freed in Jean McConville Murder Inquiry," BBC News, May 4, 2014.

380 the PSNI forwarded a file on him: Ibid.

380 "I will not lose a night's sleep over it": "Jailed Republican Price in Legal Limbo Despite Her Illness," *Irish Times,* July 21, 2012.

380 On the day she died: "Dolours Price-Rea Died from Prescription Drugs Mix," *Irish Times,* April 15, 2014.

380 When he came back that evening: Ibid.

380 A postmortem: Ibid.

380 She was sixty-two: The many obituaries asserting that Price died at sixty-one are based on an erroneous date of birth. She was born on December 16, 1950.

380 In 1975, when the Price sisters: "IRA Leaders at Price Funeral," *Irish Press,* February 19, 1975.

380 the authorities allowed Marian: "Marian Price Released to Attend Sister's Wake," *Irish Times,* January 28, 2013. In a gesture ripe with irony, lawyers for Marian, in seeking her release, summoned a doctor to testify about the emotional trauma that can arise when one is denied the opportunity to properly grieve following the death of a loved one. Interview with Darragh Mackin.

380 The following day, black flags: "Old Bailey Bomber Dolours Price Buried in Belfast," *Irish Times,* January 29, 2013.

381 "A baptismal name": Angela Nelson, "L'Addio a Dolours Price," *The Five Demands* blog, January 29, 2013.

381 He recalled her early years: "Dolours Price-Rea Died from Prescription Drugs Mix," *Irish Times,* April 15, 2014.

381 He pointed out that forty years earlier: Angela Nelson, "L'Addio a Dolours Price," *The Five Demands* blog, January 29, 2013.

381 "It broke our hearts and it broke our bodies": "Crying Pain for Stephen; Actor's Farewell to Dolours," *Daily Mirror,* January 29, 2013.

381 "If Dolours had a big fault": "Old Bailey Bomber Price Buried," *Belfast Telegraph,* January 29, 2013.

382 "we are imprisoned within ideals": "Crying Pain for Stephen; Actor's Farewell to Dolours," *Daily Mirror,* January 29, 2013.

382 "the self-destructive nature of her condition": "Dolours Price-Rea Died from Prescription Drugs Mix," *Irish Times,* April 15, 2014.

382 "They committed suicide for years": Interview with Carrie Twomey.

382 "death by misadventure": "Dolours Price-Rea Died from Prescription Drugs Mix," *Irish Times,* April 15, 2014.

382 When the graveside orations: "Crying Pain for Stephen; Actor's Farewell to Dolours," *Daily Mirror,* January 29, 2013; "Hundreds of Mourners Crowd Church As Actor Stephen Rea and Sons Carry Coffin of Dolours Price," *Irish Independent,* January 28, 2013.

CHAPTER 29

383 "much reduced form": "Paramilitary Groups in Northern Ireland," assessment commissioned by the Secretary of State for Northern Ireland (October 19, 2015).

383 Gerry Adams dismissed the report as "nonsense": "Gerry Adams Rejects Reports on IRA Existence," *Irish Examiner,* October 22, 2015.

383 "men and women in balaclavas": "Gerry Moriarty: Robinson Gambles That Adams and McGuinness Can Finally Make the IRA Go Away," *Irish Times,* October 21, 2015.

384 But the truth was that most residents: *Segregated Lives: Social Division, Sectarianism and Everyday Life in Northern Ireland,* Institute for Conflict Research, 2008; "Liam Neeson in Call for More Integrated Schools," BBC News, February 8, 2017.

384 But the talks foundered: Interview with Richard Haass.

385 When the Belfast City Council voted: "Flag Protesters Storm Belfast City Hall," *Irish Examiner,* December 3, 2012; "Union Flag Dispute: Riot Breaks Out in East Belfast," BBC News, January 15, 2013.

386 "A decision has now been taken": "Ivor Bell to Be Prosecuted over Jean McConville Murder," *Irish Times,* June 4, 2015.

386 He had trouble climbing: "Ivor Bell Remanded over Jean McConville Murder," RTÉ, March 24, 2014.

386 They worked intimately together: Moloney, *Secret History of the IRA,* p. 242.

386 Bell was a great proponent of physical force: Ibid., p. 14.

386 Bell grew concerned: Ibid., pp. 242–43.

387 So Bell retreated from the movement: Ibid., pp. 244–45.

387 "Go and ask Gerry": H-BC.

387 In court, a prosecutor suggested: "Forms to Identify Interview Tapes 'Lost,'" *Irish News,* May 8, 2014.

387 (The charges against Bell): "Ex-IRA Chief Granted Extended Bail from Jean McConville Trial," *Guardian,* October 14, 2016.

387 "totally inadmissible": "Voice Analyst Enlisted in Jean McConville Murder Case," *Irish Times,* October 30, 2014.

387 "unreliable and subjective": "Bell Lawyer Claims Boston Tapes Are Unreliable and Inaccurate," *Irish News,* June 7, 2014.

387 his client hadn't even been in Belfast: Ibid.

388 Anthony McIntyre knew exactly who Z was: "Forms to Identify Interview Tapes 'Lost,'" *Irish News,* May 8, 2014.

388 "Is the person on the tape Ivor Bell?": "Ivor Bell to Be Prosecuted over Jean McConville Murder," *Irish Times,* June 4, 2015.

388 the prosecutors announced: "Voice Analyst Enlisted in Jean McConville Murder Case," *Irish Times,* October 30, 2014.

388 Experts in "forensic phonetics": This is a decidedly imperfect science. See "Voice Analysis Should Be Used with Caution in Court," *Scientific American,* January 25, 2017.

388 Besides, the context: "Jean McConville Murder: Veteran Republican Ivor Bell to Stand Trial," *Belfast Telegraph,* July 7, 2016.

388 If you listen to the recording: "Ivor Bell Remanded over Jean McConville Murder," RTÉ, March 24, 2014.

388 A PSNI detective who had also: Ibid.

389 But the director of public prosecutions: "Revolutionary Appointment Reflects 'Transformation' in Northern Society," *Irish Times,* December 3, 2011.

389 The PSNI official who signed off: "Profile: Drew Harris of the PSNI," *Belfast Telegraph,* September 20, 2014. In June 2018, Harris was appointed commissioner of the Garda, the police force in the Republic of Ireland.

389 After prosecutors listened: "Adams Won't Be Charged over Jean McConville Murder," *Irish News,* July 10, 2015.

389 Would the British soldiers who shot unarmed civilians: "McConville Accused Calls in Voice Analyst," *Irish News,* October 31, 2014.

390 The PSNI had a "legacy" unit: Interview with Mark Hamilton; "Figures Dismiss Army 'Witch Hunt' Allegations," *Irish News,* January 27, 2017.

391 "When this crime happened, I was a *baby*": Interview with Mark Hamilton.

391 "With both the passage of time": "'No Stone to Be Left Unturned' in Stakeknife Probe," RTÉ, June 11, 2016.

391 Scappaticci was still in hiding: "Top Spy 'Stakeknife' Allegedly Linked to 50 Killings 'Unlikely to Ever Face Prosecution,'" *Irish Independent,* April 27, 2016.

391 "He is currently in custody at an undisclosed location": "'IRA Informer' Fred Scappaticci Arrested over Dozens of Murders," *Independent,* January 30, 2018.

391 Scappaticci was released without charges: "Man Believed to Have Been IRA Double Agent 'Stakeknife' Released on Bail," *Guardian,* February 2, 2018.

391 Perhaps he had a cache of secret evidence: "How, and Why, Did Scappaticci Survive the IRA's Wrath?" *Irish Times,* April 15, 2017.

392 When his father died, in the spring of 2017: Interview with Henry McDonald.

392 led by the family ice cream truck: "Freddie Scappaticci's Father Laid to Rest in Belfast," *Irish News,* April 13, 2017.

392 In the vacuum of accountability: Interview with Kevin Winters.

392 The families of numerous victims: "Stakeknife: Alleged One-Time Top British Agent Inside IRA Facing at Least 9 Separate Lawsuits," *Belfast Telegraph,* December 13, 2016.

392 a "jolly good" unit: "Soldiers Who Shot 13 Dead 'Not Thugs,'" *Guardian,* September 24, 2002.

392 Lately, he had been assisting his wife: "Lady Elizabeth Kitson OBE of Yelverton Writes a Book About Her Famous Show Pony Legend," *Tavistock Times Gazette*, August 22, 2016.

392 A woman named Mary Heenan sued: "Widow Seeks Damages Relating to Claims against British General Frank Kitson," *Irish Times*, April 30, 2015.

392 "reckless as to whether state agents would be involved": Statement of Claim, *Mary Heenan v. Ministry of Defence and Chief Constable of Police Service of Northern Ireland and General Sir Frank Edward Kitson*, High Court of Justice in Northern Ireland, Queen's Bench Division (2015).

392 "a year younger than me": "Widow Seeks Damages Relating to Claims against British General Frank Kitson," *Irish Times*, April 30, 2015.

392 a mere commander of troops: Defence of Third Defendant, *Mary Heenan v. Ministry of Defence and Chief Constable of Police Service of Northern Ireland and General Sir Frank Edward Kitson*, High Court of Justice in Northern Ireland, Queen's Bench Division (December 24, 2017).

393 "We never instigated": "Army General Sued over 1973 Loyalist Murder," *Telegraph*, April 27, 2015.

393 When police and prosecutors pursued cases: "Northern Ireland Troubles Army Veterans Slam 'Witch Hunt,'" *Belfast Telegraph*, December 12, 2017.

393 no "imbalance of approach": "Cases against Terrorist Suspects Far Outweigh Ones Involving Ex-Army and Police, PPS Insists," *Belfast Telegraph*, January 31, 2017.

393 "hierarchy of victims": See Susan McKay, *Bear in Mind These Dead* (London: Faber, 2008), part II, chapter 3.

393 the "ideal victim": Bill Rolston, *Unfinished Business: State Killings and the Quest for Truth* (Belfast: Beyond the Pale, 2000), p. xi.

394 "The designation stops at the border of each tribe": Cited in Alain Finkielkraut, *In the Name of Humanity: Reflections on the Twentieth Century* (New York: Columbia University Press, 2000), pp. 5–6.

394 "ignoring the tapes of the UVF members": "Boston College Tapes Request 'Politically Motivated,'" BBC News, August 25, 2011.

394 The police obtained a new subpoena: "Winston 'Winkie' Rea to Be Charged over 1991 Murder of Two Catholic Workmen," *Belfast Telegraph*, November 28, 2016.

394 When he showed up in court to deny the charges: "Loyalist Winston Rea Denies Conspiracy to Murder Catholic Men and Paramilitary Activity," *Irish News*, October 24, 2017.

395 "the token Prod": "Ulster Loyalist's Murder Case 'a Cynical Attempt to Protect Police," *Guardian*, June 6, 2016.

395 "I would describe the PSNI stance": Anthony McIntyre interview on the podcast *Off the Record*, February 27, 2015.

395 "I won't go into any detail": Detective Chief Inspector Peter Montgomery, PSNI, to the Public Prosecution Service, February 9, 2015.

395 "not only did he discuss his own terrorist activities": Ibid.

395 One day in April 2016: Jeffrey Swope, email message to Anthony McIntyre, April 23, 2016.

395 The authorities were alleging: Detective Chief Inspector Peter Montgomery, PSNI, to the Public Prosecution Service, February 9, 2015.

396 then the state could fish happily: Interview with Anthony McIntyre.

396 Had the police actually checked: Fourth Affidavit of Anthony McIntyre, in the Matter of an Application by Anthony McIntyre for Judicial Review, High Court of Northern Ireland, Queens Bench Division, August 2016.

396 In 2010, the body of Peter Wilson: *Walking the Line,* radio documentary, produced by Ciaran Cassidy (RTÉ Radio, 2014); "Peter Wilson: 'Disappeared' by the IRA, Found at the Beach His Family Treasured," *Belfast Telegraph,* November 3, 2010.

397 The scandal of the Boston tapes: Interview with Geoff Knupfer and Dennis Godfrey.

397 "complete confidence": "Forms to Identify Interview Tapes 'Lost,'" *Irish News,* May 8, 2014.

397 They brought in a cadaver dog: "'Preliminary Work' Begins to Recover Remains of Joe Lynskey," *Irish News,* November 7, 2014.

397 In December, Lynskey's niece: "Disappeared Victim's Family 'Hopeful' As Dog Aids Search," *Irish News,* December 2, 2014.

397 "Something's here!": Interview with Geoff Knupfer.

397 Someone alerted Maria Lynskey: "Emotional Scenes As Families of Two IRA 'Disappeared' Visit Site," *Irish Independent,* June 26, 2015.

397 Investigators had discovered: Interview with Geoff Knupfer.

397 But they had discovered: Ibid.; "Courage and Resilience of Family Praised As Disappeared Man Finally Gets Proper Burial," *Irish News,* September 16, 2015.

398 "aging philosopher king": David Ireland, *Cyprus Avenue* (London: Bloomsbury, 2016), p. 16.

398 "I think that Gerry Adams has disguised himself": Ibid., p. 16.

399 "No, this is the *now*": Ibid., p. 43.

399 "Because I was so institutionalized": HIA transcript.

399 As he was succumbing to cancer: "Billy McConville Brought His Family Back Together, Mourners Told," *Irish News,* July 26, 2017.

399 "You were so strong and unbelievably brave": "Son of Murdered Jean McConville Brought His Family Back Together, Funeral Told," *Irish Examiner,* July 26, 2017.

399 "plunged Billy and his brothers and sisters": "Billy McConville Brought His Family Back Together, Mourners Told," *Irish News,* July 26, 2017.

400 "properly follow the course of proceedings": "Republican Charged over Jean McConville Murder 'Has Dementia,'" *Irish Times,* December 5, 2006.

400 wanted to inspect Bell's medical record: Ibid.

400 The firm announced: Matthew Jury, email message to author; "McConville Daughter to Seek Civil Case," *Irish News,* October 1, 2015.

400 "We have already been fighting for justice for 40-odd years": "Jean McConville's Family Will 'Fight to the Bitter End for Justice,'" *Independent,* May 4, 2014.

CHAPTER 30

402 I interviewed a man who had seen McClure: Interview with Joe Clarke.

403 Then, one day, I learned: The friend was Adam Goldman, now of *The New York Times.*

403 McClure died in 1986: According to an obituary, McClure died after "a brief illness." He was forty-six. "Patrick F. McClure, Obituary," *Record-Journal* (Meriden, Conn.), December 5, 1986.

403 For five years before his death: Ibid.

403 he was a parishioner at his local Catholic church: "Patrick F. McClure— Obituary," *Observer* (Southington, Conn.), December 11, 1986.

404 And he gave me one further clue: I contacted two representatives for Gerry Adams seeking a reaction to this claim, but neither responded to confirm or deny.

405 "he wanted my sister to be his driver": P-EM.

405 A representative for Adams: Richard McAuley, email message to author.

407 "something that the sisters had done together": Anonymous source.

407 He never wrote back: The lawyer, whom I wrote to several times, by email and post, was Peter Corrigan, of KRW Law, who also represented Ivor Bell.

407 Some observers wondered: "Gerry Adams: 'I Won't Be a Puppet Master,'" *Belfast Telegraph,* January 4, 2018.

408 "Martin McGuinness was a freedom fighter": "Gerry Adams: 'Martin McGuinness Was Not a Terrorist,'" BBC News, March 23, 2017.

408 "the whiff of cordite" about him: "Adams 'Relaxed' over Poll Doubting His Denial of IRA Membership," *Irish Times,* May 20, 2014. Many voters also believed Adams played a role in the disappearance of Jean McConville: "Half of Voters Believe Adams Was Involved in McConville Murder," *Irish Independent,* May 17, 2014.

408 surreal culmination on Twitter: In 2016, Adams released a slim compendium, *My Little Book of Tweets* (Cork: Mercier Press, 2016).

408 ("I do love teddy bears"): "Gerry Adams Tweets: Ducks, Teddy Bears and a Dog Called Snowie," BBC News, February 14, 2014.

408 "Charles Manson showing you his collection": Damien Owens (@Owens Damien), "Gerry Adams tries too hard to be cute and whimsical on Twitter. It's like Charles Manson showing you his collection of tea cosies," Twitter, January 2, 2014, 1:11 p.m.

408 "propagandizing for his own humanity": O'Doherty, *Gerry Adams,* p. 68.

409 democratic action: Alvin Jackson, *Home Rule: An Irish History, 1800–2000* (New York: Oxford University Press, 2003), p. 287.

409 "getting a hundred people to push this boat out": H-BC.

409 the war may be won by demography: "'Catholic Majority Possible' in NI by 2021," BBC News, April 19, 2018.

409 After the 2008 fiscal crisis and the subsequent recession: "Survey Deals Blow to Sinn Féin Hopes of United Ireland," *Guardian,* June 17, 2011.

410 "Outbreeding Unionists may be an enjoyable pastime": "The Survivor," *Guardian,* April 30, 2001.

410 inevitably, complicates that split identity: For a meditation on the border in the age of Brexit, see Susan McKay, "Diary," *London Review of Books,* March 30, 2017.

410 "But I just think the notion of Irish unity": "Gerry Adams Takes Parting Shot at UK—Brexit Has BOOSTED United Ireland Campaign," *Daily Express,* February 9, 2018.

410 he would like to see a new referendum: "Gerry Adams Tells Irish America of Party's Aim for a Unity Referendum Within Five Years," *Irish News,* November 10, 2017.

410 "only if I achieve the situation where my people": Gerry Adams (as Brownie), "I Am an IRA Volunteer," *Republican News,* May 1, 1976.

411 "I am perfectly at peace": "I Don't Have Any Blood on My Hands," *Sunday Life,* February 21, 2010.

411 "Through the whole Troubles, there was never any hassle": Interview with Michael McConville.

411 Pigeons were one of the first animals: Andrew Blechman, *Pigeons: The Fascinating Saga of the World's Most Revered and Reviled Bird* (New York: Grove Press, 2006), p. 11.

411 Sometimes, when they get home after a long race: Kevin C. Kearns, *Dublin Street Life & Lore: An Oral History* (Dublin/Glendale, N.Y.: Glendale, 1991), pp. 195–98.

SELECTED BIBLIOGRAPHY

Adams, Gerry. *Before the Dawn: An Autobiography.* Dingle, Ireland: Brandon, 2001.
————. *Cage Eleven.* New York: Sheridan Square Press, 1993.
————. *Falls Memories: A Belfast Life.* Niwot, Colo.: Roberts Rinehart, 1994.
————. *A Farther Shore: Ireland's Long Road to Peace.* New York: Random House, 2005.
Alexander, Yonah, and Alan O'Day, eds. *The Irish Terrorism Experience.* Brookfield, Vt.: Dartmouth, 1991.
Bailey, Anthony. *Acts of Union: Reports on Ireland, 1973–1979.* New York: Random House, 1980.
Bell, J. Boyer. *The Secret Army: The IRA.* New Brunswick, N.J.: Transaction, 1997.
Beresford, David. *Ten Men Dead: The Story of the 1981 Irish Hunger Strike.* New York: Atlantic Monthly Press, 1987.
Bishop, Patrick, and Eamonn Mallie. *The Provisional IRA.* London: Heinemann, 1987.
Blechman, Andrew. *Pigeons: The Fascinating Saga of the World's Most Revered and Reviled Bird.* New York: Grove Press, 2006.
Bloom, Mia. *Bombshell: Women and Terrorism.* Philadelphia: University of Pennsylvania Press, 2011.
Boulton, David. *The UVF: An Anatomy of Loyalist Rebellion.* Dublin: Torc Books, 1973.
Boyd, Andrew. *Holy War in Belfast.* Belfast: Pretani Press, 1987.
Bradley, Gerry, and Brian Feeney. *Insider: Gerry Bradley's Life in the IRA.* Dublin: O'Brien Press, 2009.
Brady, Evelyn, Eva Patterson, Kate McKinney, Rosie Hamill, and Pauline Jackson. *In the Footsteps of Anne: Stories of Republican Women Ex-Prisoners.* Belfast: Shanway Press, 2011.
Cadwallader, Anne. *Lethal Allies: British Collusion in Ireland.* Cork: Mercier Press, 2013.
Carson, Ciarán. *Belfast Confetti.* Winston-Salem, N.C.: Wake Forest University Press, 1989.
Clark, Wallace. *Guns in Ulster.* Belfast: Constabulary Gazette, 1967.

Clarke, George. *Border Crossing: True Stories of the RUC Special Branch, the Garda Special Branch and the IRA Moles.* Dublin: Gill & Macmillan, 2009.

Cobain, Ian. *Cruel Britannia: A Secret History of Torture.* London: Portobello, 2013.

———. *The History Thieves: Secrets, Lies and the Shaping of a Modern Nation.* London: Portobello, 2016.

Collins, Eamon. *Killing Rage.* London: Granta, 1997.

Conroy, John. *Belfast Diary: War As a Way of Life.* Boston: Beacon Press, 1995.

———. *Unspeakable Acts, Ordinary People: The Dynamics of Torture.* Berkeley: University of California Press, 2000.

Coogan, Tim Pat. *The Famine Plot: England's Role in Ireland's Greatest Tragedy.* New York: Palgrave, 2012.

———. *The IRA.* New York: St. Martin's Press, 2002.

———. *On the Blanket: The Inside Story of the IRA Prisoners' "Dirty" Protest.* New York: Palgrave, 2002.

———. *The Troubles.* New York: Palgrave, 2002.

Darby, John, ed. *Northern Ireland: The Background to the Conflict.* Syracuse, N.Y.: Syracuse University Press, 1987.

D'Arcy, Margaretta. *Tell Them Everything.* London: Pluto Press, 1981.

Deane, Seamus. *Strange Country: Modernity and Nationhood in Irish Writing Since 1790.* New York: Oxford University Press, 1997.

de Rosa, Peter. *Rebels: The Irish Rising of 1916.* New York: Random House, 1990.

Devlin, Bernadette. *The Price of My Soul.* New York: Vintage, 1970.

Dillon, Martin. *The Dirty War: Covert Strategies and Tactics Used in Political Conflicts.* New York: Routledge, 1999.

———. *Stone Cold: The True Story of Michael Stone and the Milltown Massacre.* London: Random House, 1992.

———. *The Trigger Men.* Edinburgh: Mainstream, 2003.

Drower, George. *John Hume: Man of Peace.* London: Victor Gollancz, 1996.

Edwards, Ruth Dudley. *Patrick Pearse: The Triumph of Failure.* Dublin: Poolbeg Press, 1990.

Egan, Bowes, and Vincent McCormack. *Burntollet.* London: LRS, 1969.

Elkins, Caroline. *Imperial Reckoning: The Untold Story of Britain's Gulag in Kenya.* New York: Henry Holt, 2005.

Ellis, Walter. *The Beginning of the End: The Crippling Disadvantage of a Happy Irish Childhood.* Edinburgh: Mainstream, 2006.

English, Richard. *Armed Struggle: The History of the IRA.* New York: Oxford University Press, 2003.

Fairweather, Eileen, Roisín McDonough, and Melanie McFadyean. *Only the Rivers Run Free: Northern Ireland; The Women's War.* London: Pluto Press, 1984.

Farrell, Michael. *Northern Ireland: The Orange State.* London: Pluto Press, 1987.

———, ed. *Twenty Years On.* Dingle, Ireland: Brandon, 1988.

Faul, Dennis, and Raymond Murray. *The Hooded Men: British Torture in Ireland, August, October 1971.* Dublin: Wordwell Books, 2016.

Feeney, Brian. *Sinn Féin: A Hundred Turbulent Years.* Madison: University of Wisconsin Press, 2003.

Fiacc, Padraic. *The Wearing of the Black: An Anthology of Contemporary Ulster Poetry.* Belfast: Blackstaff Press, 1974.

Fiske, Alan Page, and Tage Shakti Rai. *Virtuous Violence: Hurting and Killing to Create, Sustain, End, and Honor Social Relationships.* Cambridge: Cambridge University Press, 2015.

Foot, Paul. *Who Framed Colin Wallace?* London: Macmillan, 1989.

Foster, R. F. *Modern Ireland, 1600–1972.* New York: Penguin, 1989.

Friel, Brian. *Brian Friel: Plays 1.* London: Faber, 1996.

Friel, Brian, and Paul Delaney. *Brian Friel in Conversation.* Ann Arbor: University of Michigan Press, 2000.

Geraghty, Tony. *The Irish War: The Military History of a Domestic Conflict.* London: HarperCollins, 2000.

Gurney, Peter. *Braver Men Walk Away.* London: HarperCollins, 1993.

Hamill, Heather. *The Hoods: Crime and Punishment in Belfast.* Princeton, N.J.: Princeton University Press, 2011.

Hamill, Pete. *Piecework: Writings on Men and Women, Fools and Heroes, Lost Cities, Vanished Calamities and How the Weather Was.* New York: Little, Brown, 1996.

Harnden, Toby. *Bandit Country: The IRA & South Armagh.* London: Hodder & Stoughton, 1999.

Hastings, Max. *Barricades in Belfast: The Fight for Civil Rights in Northern Ireland.* London: Taplinger, 1970.

Heaney, Seamus. *The Cure at Troy: A Version of Sophocles'* Philoctetes. New York: Farrar, Straus and Giroux, 1991.

———. *North: Poems.* London: Faber, 1975.

———. *Preoccupations: Selected Prose, 1968–1978.* London: Faber, 1980.

Hume, John. *A New Ireland: Politics, Peace, and Reconciliation.* Boulder, Colo.: Roberts Rinehart, 1996.

Huntley, Bob. *Bomb Squad: My War Against the Terrorists.* London: W. H. Allen, 1977.

Ingram, Martin, and Greg Harkin. *Stakeknife: Britain's Secret Agents in Ireland.* Madison: University of Wisconsin Press, 2004.

Ireland, David. *Cyprus Avenue.* London: Bloomsbury, 2016.

Jackson, Alvin. *Home Rule: An Irish History, 1800–2000.* New York: Oxford University Press, 2003.

Jackson, Mike. *Soldier: The Autobiography.* London: Bantam Press, 2007.

Jenkins, Roy. *A Life at the Centre.* London: Macmillan, 1991.

Kearns, Kevin. *Dublin Street Life and Lore: An Oral History.* Dublin: Glendale, 1991.

Keenan-Thomson, Tara. *Irish Women and Street Politics, 1956–1973.* Dublin: Irish Academic Press, 2010.

Kelly, Gerry. *Words from a Cell.* Dublin: Sinn Féin Publicity Department, 1989.

Kiely, Benedict. *Proxopera.* Belfast: Turnpike Books, 2015.

Kipling, Rudyard. *Collected Poems of Rudyard Kipling.* London: Wordsworth Editions, 1994.

Kitson, Frank. *Bunch of Five.* London: Faber, 2010.

———. *Gangs and Counter-Gangs.* London: Barrie Books, 1960.

————. *Low Intensity Operations: Subversion, Insurgency, Peace-Keeping.* London: Faber, 1991.

Krog, Antjie. *Country of My Skull: Guilt, Sorrow, and the Limits of Forgiveness in the New South Africa.* New York: Three Rivers Press, 2000.

Lee, Jonathan. *High Dive.* New York: Knopf, 2016.

MacAirt, Ciarán. *The McGurk's Bar Bombing: Collusion, Cover-Up and a Campaign for Truth.* Edinburgh: Frontline Noir, 2012.

MacEoin, Uinseann Ó Rathaille. *The IRA in the Twilight Years: 1923–1948.* Dublin: Argenta, 1997.

Mac Stíofáin, Seán. *Revolutionary in Ireland.* Edinburgh: R. & R. Clark, 1975.

Mansfield, Michael. *Memoirs of a Radical Lawyer.* London: Bloomsbury, 2009.

Martin, David C. *Wilderness of Mirrors: Intrigue, Deception, and the Secrets That Destroyed Two of the Cold War's Most Important Agents.* Guilford, Conn.: Lyons Press, 2003.

Matchett, William. *Secret Victory: The Intelligence War That Beat the IRA.* Belfast: self-published, 2016.

McCann, Colum. *TransAtlantic.* New York: Random House, 2013.

McCann, Eamonn. *War and an Irish Town.* London: Pluto Press, 1993.

McGuffin, John. *The Guinea Pigs.* London: Penguin, 1974.

McIntyre, Anthony. *Good Friday: The Death of Irish Republicanism.* New York: Ausubo Press, 2008.

McKay, Susan. *Bear in Mind These Dead.* London: Faber, 2008.

McKearney, Tommy. *The Provisional IRA: From Insurrection to Parliament.* London: Pluto Press, 2011.

McKeever, Martin. *One Man, One God: The Peace Ministry of Fr Alec Reid C.Ss.R.* Dublin: Redemptorist Communications, 2017.

McKendry, Séamus. *Disappeared: The Search for Jean McConville.* Dublin: Blackwater Press, 2000.

McKittrick, David, Seamus Kelters, Brian Feeney, and Chris Thornton. *Lost Lives: The Stories of the Men, Women, and Children Who Died As a Result of the Northern Ireland Troubles.* 2nd ed. Edinburgh: Mainstream, 2004.

McKittrick, David, and David McVea. *Making Sense of the Troubles: The Story of the Conflict in Northern Ireland.* Chicago: New Amsterdam Books, 2002.

Meagher, Robert Emmet. *Killing from the Inside Out: Moral Injury and Just War.* Eugene, Ore.: Cascade Books, 2014.

Miller, David, ed. *Rethinking Northern Ireland.* New York: Addison Wesley Longman, 1998.

Miller, Ian. *A History of Force Feeding: Hunger Strikes, Prisons and Medical Ethics, 1909–1974.* Basingstoke, U.K.: Palgrave Macmillan, 2016. (PDF).

Mitchel, John. *The Last Conquest of Ireland (Perhaps).* Glasgow: R. & T. Washbourne, 1882.

Mitchell, George. *Making Peace.* Los Angeles: University of California Press, 2000.

Moloney, Ed. *A Secret History of the IRA.* New York: Norton, 2002.

————. *Voices from the Grave: Two Men's War in Ireland.* New York: PublicAffairs, 2010.

Moloney, Ed, and Andy Pollak. *Paisley.* Dublin: Poolbeg Press, 1986.

Morrison, Danny. *Rebel Columns.* Belfast: Beyond the Pale, 2004.

Morrison, John F. *The Origins and Rise of Dissident Irish Republicanism.* London: Bloomsbury, 2013.

Mulholland, Marc. *Northern Ireland at the Crossroads: Ulster Unionism in the O'Neill Years.* London: Palgrave, 2000.

———. *Northern Ireland: A Very Short Introduction.* Oxford: Oxford University Press, 2002.

Murphy, Dervla. *A Place Apart: Northern Ireland in the 1970s.* London: Eland, 2014.

Murray, Raymond. *Hard Time: Armagh Gaol, 1971–1986.* Dublin: Mercier Press, 1998.

Myers, Kevin. *Watching the Door: Drinking Up, Getting Down, and Cheating Death in 1970s Belfast.* Brooklyn, N.Y.: Soft Skull Press, 2009.

O'Brien, Brendan. *The Long War: The IRA and Sinn Féin.* Syracuse, N.Y.: Syracuse University Press, 1999.

Ó Dochartaigh, Niall. *From Civil Rights to Armalites: Derry and the Birth of the Irish Troubles.* Cork: Cork University Press, 1997.

O'Doherty, Malachi. *Gerry Adams: An Unauthorised Life.* London: Faber, 2017.

———. *The Telling Year: Belfast 1972.* Dublin: Gill & Macmillan, 2007.

———. *The Trouble with Guns: Republican Strategy and the Provisional IRA.* Belfast: Blackstaff Press, 1998.

O'Donnell, Ruán. *16 Lives: Patrick Pearse.* Dublin: O'Brien Press, 2016.

———. *Special Category: The IRA in English Prisons,* vol. 1: *1968–1978.* Sallins, Ireland: Irish Academic Press, 2012.

———. *Special Category: The IRA in English Prisons,* vol. 2: *1978–1985.* Sallins, Ireland: Irish Academic Press, 2015.

O'Flaherty, Liam. *The Informer.* New York: Harcourt, 1980.

O'Malley, Padraig. *Biting at the Grave: The Irish Hunger Strikes and the Politics of Despair.* Boston: Beacon Press, 1990.

O'Neill, Robert K., ed. *Management of Library and Archival Security: From the Outside Looking In.* Binghamton, N.Y.: Haworth Press, 1998.

O'Rawe, Richard. *Afterlives: The Hunger Strike and the Secret Offer That Changed Irish History.* Dublin: Lilliput Press, 2010.

———. *Blanketmen: The Untold Story of the H-Block Hunger Strike.* Dublin: New Island, 2005.

Ó Ruairc, Pádraig Óg. *Truce: Murder, Myth, and the Last Days of the Irish War of Independence.* Cork: Mercier Press, 2016.

Patterson, Henry. *The Politics of Illusion: A Political History of the IRA.* London: Serif, 1997.

Pearse, Padraic. *The Collected Works of Padraic H. Pearse: Political Writings and Speeches.* Dublin: Éire-Gael Society, 2013.

Powell, Jonathan. *Great Hatred, Little Room: Making Peace in Northern Ireland.* London: Vintage, 2009.

Prisoners Aid Committee. *Irish Voices from English Jails: Writings of Irish Political Prisoners in English Prisons.* London: Prisoners Aid Committee, 1979.

Purdie, Bob. *Politics in the Streets: The Origins of the Civil Rights Movement in Northern Ireland*. Belfast: Blackstaff Press, 1990.

Rawlinson, Peter. *A Price Too High: An Autobiography*. London: Weidenfeld and Nicolson, 1989.

Richtarik, Marilynn J. *Acting Between the Lines: The Field Day Theatre Company and Irish Cultural Politics, 1980–1984*. Washington, D.C.: Catholic University of America Press, 2001.

Rolston, Bill. *Children of the Revolution: The Lives of Sons and Daughters of Activists in Northern Ireland*. Derry: Guildhall Press, 2011.

————. *Unfinished Business: State Killings and the Quest for Truth*. Belfast: Beyond the Pale, 2000.

Routledge, Paul. *John Hume*. London: HarperCollins, 1997.

Sanders, Andrew. *Inside the IRA: Dissident Republicans and the War for Legitimacy*. Edinburgh: Edinburgh University Press, 2012.

Shannon, Elizabeth. *I Am of Ireland: Women of the North Speak Out*. Boston: Little, Brown, 1989.

Shay, Jonathan. *Achilles in Vietnam: Combat Trauma and the Undoing of Character*. New York: Scribner, 2003.

Sluka, Jeffrey. *Hearts and Minds, Water and Fish: Support for the IRA and INLA in a Northern Ireland Ghetto*. Greenwich, Conn.: JAI Press, 1989.

Smyth, Jim, ed. *Remembering the Troubles: Contesting the Recent Past in Northern Ireland*. Notre Dame, Ind.: University of Notre Dame Press, 2017.

Stetler, Russell. *The Battle of Bogside: The Politics of Violence in Northern Ireland*. London: Sheed and Ward, 1970.

Stevens, John. *Not for the Faint-Hearted: My Life Fighting Crime*. London: Orion, 2006.

Stevenson, Jonathan. *We Wrecked the Place: Contemplating an End to the Northern Irish Troubles*. New York: Free Press, 1996.

Stringer, Peter, and Gillian Robinson. *Social Attitudes in Northern Ireland: The First Report*. Belfast: Blackstaff Press, 1991.

Taylor, Peter. *Behind the Mask: The IRA and Sinn Fein*. New York: TV Books, 1999.

————. *Brits: The War Against the IRA*. London: Bloomsbury, 2001.

————. *Provos: The IRA and Sinn Fein*. London: Bloomsbury, 1998.

Thatcher, Margaret. *The Path to Power*. New York: HarperCollins, 1995.

Tóibín, Colm. *Bad Blood: A Walk Along the Irish Border*. London: Picador, 2001.

Tóibín, Colm, and Diarmaid Ferriter. *The Irish Famine: A Documentary*. New York: St. Martin's Press, 2001.

Toolis, Kevin. *Rebel Hearts: Journeys within the IRA's Soul*. New York: St. Martin's Press, 1995.

Urban, Mark. *Big Boys' Rules: The SAS and the Secret Struggle Against the IRA*. London: Faber, 1992.

Wave Trauma Centre. *The Disappeared of Northern Ireland's Troubles*. Belfast: Wave Trauma Centre, 2012.

Winchester, Simon. *In Holy Terror*. London: Faber, 1975.

Wood, Ian S. *Britain, Ireland and the Second World War.* Edinburgh: Edinburgh University Press, 2010.

Woodham-Smith, Cecil. *The Great Hunger: Ireland, 1845–1849.* New York: Penguin, 1991.

Zucker, Carole. *In the Company of Actors: Reflections on the Craft of Acting.* New York: Routledge, 2001.

INDEX

Page numbers in *italics* refer to illustrations.

ILLUSTRATION CREDITS

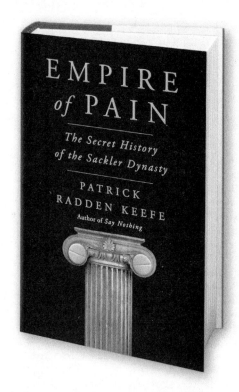